The
New International
Lesson Annual

2006–2007

September–August

Abingdon Press
Nashville

THE NEW INTERNATIONAL LESSON ANNUAL 2006–2007

Copyright © 2006 by Abingdon Press

This book is printed on acid-free paper.

Scripture quotations, unless otherwise noted, are from the *New Revised Standard Version of the Bible,* copyright 1989, Division of Christian Education of the National Council of the Churches of Christ in the United States of America. Used by permission. All rights reserved.

Scripture quotations marked (NIV) are taken from the HOLY BIBLE, NEW INTERNATIONAL VERSION®. NIV®. Copyright © 1973, 1978, 1984 by International Bible Society. Used by permission of Zondervan Publishing House. All rights reserved.

Scripture quotations marked KJV are from the King James or Authorized Version of the Bible.

ISBN 0-687-06284-5

ISSN 1084-872X

06 07 08 09 10 11 12 13 14 15 —10 9 8 7 6 5 4 3 2 1

MANUFACTURED IN THE UNITED STATES OF AMERICA

PREFACE

Thank you for joining the millions of people worldwide who use the International Sunday School Lessons as the basis for their Bible study each week. During 2006–2007 we will explore the Old Testament in a course focused on God's covenant; consider the ways in which the Gospel of John and several New Testament letters see in Jesus a portrait of God; examine 1 John and Revelation to discern God's current and future community; and look at several prophets, as well as 2 Kings and 2 Chronicles, to understand the commitment God expects from us.

Although adult learners often use *The New International Lesson Annual*, it is mainly designed for teachers of adults who want a solid biblical basis for each session and a teaching plan that will help them lead their classes. The following features are especially valuable for busy teachers who want to provide in-depth Bible study experiences for their students. Each lesson includes the following sections:

Previewing the Lesson highlights the background and lesson Scripture, focus of the lesson, three goals for the learners, a pronunciation guide in lessons where you may find unfamiliar words or names, and supplies you will need to teach.

Reading the Scripture includes the Scripture lesson printed in both the *New Revised Standard Version* and the *New International Version*. By printing these two highly respected translations in parallel columns, you can easily compare them for in-depth study. If your own Bible is another version, you will then have three translations to explore as you prepare each lesson.

Understanding the Scripture closely analyzes the background Scripture by looking at each verse. Here you will find help in understanding concepts, ideas, places, and persons pertinent to each week's lesson. You may also find explanations for Greek or Hebrew words that are essential for understanding the text.

Interpreting the Scripture looks at the lesson Scripture, delves into its meaning, and relates it to contemporary life.

Sharing the Scripture provides you with a detailed teaching plan. It is divided into two major sections: *Preparing to Teach* and *Leading the Class*.

In the *Preparing to Teach* section you will find a devotional reading related to the lesson for your own spiritual enrichment and a "to do list" to prepare your mind and classroom for the session.

The *Leading the Class* portion begins with "Gather to Learn" activities to welcome the students and draw them into the lesson. Here, the students' stories and experiences are highlighted as preparation for the Bible story. The next three headings of *Leading the Class* are the three main "Goals for the Learners." The first goal always focuses on the Bible story itself. The second goal relates the Bible story to the lives of the adults in your class. The third goal prompts the students to take action on what they have learned. You will find a variety of activities under each of these goals to help the learners fulfill them. The activities are diverse in nature and may include: listening, reading, writing, speaking, singing, drawing, interacting with others, and meditating. The lesson ends

---

with "Continue the Journey," where you will find closing activities, preparation for the following week, and ideas for students to commit themselves to action during the week, based on what they have learned.

In addition to these weekly features, you will find:

- **List of Background Scriptures,** which is offered especially for those of you who keep back copies of *The New International Lesson Annual*. This feature, located after the Contents, will enable you to locate Scripture passages used in the current year. At some future date you may want to refer back to these Scriptures.
- **Teacher enrichment article,** which in this volume is entitled "Walking the Walk." Readers familiar with *The New International Lesson Annual* will note that this feature has been moved to the front of the book. Material in the enrichment article is intended to be useful throughout the year, so we hope you will read it immediately and refer to it often. This particular article will help you to encourage the class members to live out the Scriptures they have studied.
- **Introduction to each quarter,** which provides you a quick survey of each lesson to be studied in the quarter. You will find the title, background Scripture, date, and a brief summary of each week's basic thrust. This feature is the first page of each quarter.
- **Meet Our Writer,** which follows each quarterly introduction, provides biographical information about each writer, including education, pastoral and/or academic teaching experience, previous publications, and family information.
- **The Big Picture,** written by the same writer who authored the lessons, and designed to give you a broader scope of the materials to be covered than is possible in each weekly lesson. You will find this background article immediately following the writer's biography in each quarter.
- **Close-up,** a new feature for 2006–2007. In this section you will find ideas related to the broad sweep of the quarter that the students can use individually or as a class to act on what they have been studying. These ideas are intended for use beyond the classroom.
- **Faith in Action,** also a new feature for 2006–2007. In this section you will find ideas related to the broad sweep of the quarter that the students can use individually or as a class to act on what they have been studying. These ideas are intended for use beyond the classroom.

I love to hear from our readers! If you ever have any questions or comments, please write to me and include your e-mail address and/or phone number. I will respond as soon as your message reaches my home office in Maryland.

Dr. Nan Duerling
Abingdon Press
PO Box 801
Nashville, TN 37202

We thank you for choosing *The New International Lesson Annual* and pray that God will work through this material, as you are guided by the Holy Spirit, to lead your students to the life-changing discipleship that Jesus yearns for in each of us. God's grace and peace be with you!

Nan Duerling, Ph.D.
Editor, *The New International Lesson Annual*

CONTENTS

FIRST QUARTER

God's Living Covenant
September 3–November 26, 2006

UNIT 1: IN COVENANT WITH GOD
(September 3-24)

UNIT 2: GOD'S COVENANT WITH JUDGES AND KINGS
(October 1-29)

UNIT 3: LIVING AS GOD'S COVENANTED PEOPLE
(November 5-26)

SECOND QUARTER

Jesus Christ: A Portrait of God
December 3, 2006–February 25, 2007

UNIT 1: CHRIST, THE IMAGE OF GOD
(December 3-31)

UNIT 2: CHRIST SUSTAINS AND SUPPORTS
(January 7-28)

UNIT 3: CHRIST GUIDES AND PROTECTS
(February 4-25)

THIRD QUARTER

Our Community Now and in God's Future
March 4–May 27, 2007

UNIT 1: KNOWN BY OUR LOVE
(March 4-25)

UNIT 2: A NEW COMMUNITY IN CHRIST
(April 1-29)

UNIT 3: LIVING IN GOD'S NEW WORLD
(May 6-27)

FOURTH QUARTER

Committed to Doing Right
June 3–August 26, 2007

UNIT 1: LIFE AS GOD'S PEOPLE
(June 3-24)

UNIT 2: WHAT DOES GOD REQUIRE?
(July 1-31)

UNIT 3: HOW SHALL WE RESPOND?
(August 5-26)

LIST OF BACKGROUND SCRIPTURES, 2006–2007

Old Testament

Genesis 9:1-17 ....September 3	Isaiah 1:10-20 ....June 17
Genesis 17 ....September 10	Isaiah 55:1-11 ....June 24
Exodus 19:1-6 ....September 17	Jeremiah 7:11-15 ....July 22
Exodus 24:3-8 ....September 17	Jeremiah 29:1-14 ....July 29
Joshua 24 ....September 24	Lamentations 3:25-33, 55-58 ....August 5
Judges 2:11-23 ....October 1	Ezekiel 18 ....August 12
Judges 4 ....October 8	Hosea 4:1-4 ....June 10
1 Samuel 7:3-13 ....October 15	Hosea 7:1-2 ....June 10
2 Samuel 7 ....October 22	Hosea 12:7-9 ....June 10
1 Kings 3 ....October 29	Hosea 14:1-3 ....June 10
1 Kings 18:20-39 ....November 5	Amos 5:10-15, 21-24 ....June 3
2 Kings 13:23-25 ....June 3	Amos 8:4-12 ....June 3
2 Kings 15:8-10 ....June 10	Micah 2:1-4 ....July 1
2 Kings 15:32-35 ....June 17	Micah 3:1-5, 8-12 ....July 1
2 Kings 22:1-20 ....November 12	Micah 6:6-8 ....July 1
2 Kings 23:1-37 ....November 12	Habakkuk 2:1-20 ....July 15
2 Kings 23:35-37 ....July 15	Zephaniah 3:1-13 ....July 8
2 Kings 23:36-37 ....July 22	Zechariah 1:1-6 ....August 19
2 Kings 25:1-2, 5-7 ....August 5	Zechariah 7:8-14 ....August 19
2 Chronicles 34:1-3 ....July 8	Zechariah 8:16-17, 20-21, 23 ....August 19
2 Chronicles 36:15-21 ....November 19	Malachi 2:17 ....August 26
2 Chronicles 36:22-23 ....November 26	Malachi 3:1-18 ....August 26
Ezra 1:5-7 ....November 26	Malachi 4:1-3 ....August 26
Psalm 137 ....November 19	

New Testament

Luke 19:28-40 ....April 1	1 John 1:1-10 ....December 17
John 1:1-34 ....December 24	1 John 2:1-6 ....December 17
John 5:19-29 ....January 14	1 John 2:7-17 ....March 4
John 6:25-59 ....January 21	1 John 3 ....March 11
John 7:37-39 ....January 21	1 John 4:7-21 ....March 18
John 8:12-20 ....January 28	1 John 5:1-12 ....March 25
John 8:31-59 ....January 7	Revelation 1:1-8 ....April 1
John 10:1-18 ....February 4	Revelation 1:9-20 ....April 8
John 11:1-44 ....February 11	Revelation 4 ....April 15
John 12:44-46 ....January 28	Revelation 5 ....April 22
John 14:1-14 ....February 18	Revelation 7 ....April 29
John 15:1-17 ....February 25	Revelation 19 ....May 6
John 20:1-18, 30-31 ....April 8	Revelation 21:1-8 ....May 13
Philippians 2:1-11 ....December 31	Revelation 21:9-15 ....May 20
Colossians 1 ....December 3	Revelation 22:1-5 ....May 20
Hebrews 1 ....December 10	Revelation 22:6-21 ....May 27

TEACHER ENRICHMENT ARTICLE: WALKING THE WALK

Weekly Bible study is an excellent way to "talk the talk." We gather to listen, learn, pray, question, doubt, support, affirm, and fellowship with our spiritual traveling companions. We delve into the Scriptures as we try to discern what they could have meant for their original audience, and what they might mean for our time and place. As the leader of the group, you have invested much time in thoughtful and prayerful preparation. Many students have also studied the lesson carefully. Yet, nothing seems to change. The Scriptures have been intellectually apprehended, perhaps even appreciated for their literary qualities. But people's lives remain the same. It's so easy for people to "learn" the Bible without letting it impact the way they live—how they think and act at work, play, within the family, and among the congregation. What can you do to further motivate the students you are privileged to teach to make the Scriptures, and more particularly, their relationship with Jesus Christ, the core of their lives? In some respects, the answer to this question is "nothing," for motivation is the work of the Holy Spirit, who speaks to each person in that still, small voice. In other respects, however, there is much you can do to "set the stage" so that adults will want to act on what they have learned. Let's take a look at some ways you can encourage people to "walk the walk" and consider the benefits of doing so.

Where Do We Find Ideas?

Ideas for living out our faith abound. "Faith in Action," a new quarterly feature in *The New International Lesson Annual* this year, provides suggestions specifically related to the Scriptures the class has been studying each quarter. Use these ideas however and whenever they are appropriate throughout the quarter. Since each class is different, you will need to help the class shape these broad suggestions to meet the needs and circumstances of the students, church, and community.

Another place to find ideas is the "Continue the Journey" section at the end of each lesson. Here you will find three ideas related to the Scriptures studied that week. These suggestions tend to be useful for individuals. They may involve contemplation, art, music, journaling, or sharing the faith with someone else. Unless each student has a copy of *The New International Lesson Annual,* be sure to copy the ideas onto newsprint each week as suggested.

A third way is to brainstorm with the class ideas related to the Scriptures under discussion that specifically pertain to your situation. For example, if your church is near a prison, could you arrange to engage in ministry with those who are incarcerated or their families? Or, if your congregation houses a child care center or preschool, would some of the class members be willing to act as "adopted" grandparents or "special friends" to those children who do not have or seldom see their extended families? If you are located near a hospice or nursing home, could you arrange for a team of volunteers to make regular visits with patients who would like to receive guests?

Ideas for action are limitless. Whatever you do, the question is this: *"How can the activities that we are planning enable us to live out the Scriptures in ways that glorify God, care for our global and local neighbors, and empower us to grow spiritually?"* Recognize that some activities will be better suited to some individual class members than to others. Find ways to include everyone. For example, if the group agrees to repair a home for an elderly widow, some of the class members will have the skills and/or physical prowess necessary to participate in this activity, but others may not. Likely, though, each person can find some way to support this valuable project. Several folks may be able to make lunch; some others could provide transportation to and from the job site; still others could clean the area when the work is finished; others may take the person whose home is being renovated out for a day trip while the work is in progress. In this way everyone has a stake in the project and can experience the faith community working together, while recognizing the great diversity and equal importance of gifts that exist within the body of Christ. As you and the class select one or more projects each quarter, different people's gifts and talents will be accented in a variety of ways.

How Do We Plan Our Project?

Planning is key to the success of any project. Once the group decides what its project will be, class members need to address the following issues. As you address each item, be sure to keep written notes so that dates, ideas, and names of people who have agreed to participate are not lost or forgotten. Have these notes photocopied and posted or distributed so that the adults can continue to check on the progress of the project. Written notes also help to jog participants' memories so that they recall any tasks they agreed to do.

- ❖ **Who is this project expected to benefit?** Seek out people who have genuine needs and try to meet them. Make sure that the group(s) or individual(s) involved want to accept your services. Sometimes you may have to work through a third party, such as a social worker or church agency that needs volunteers to meet the needs you are trying to address. Work with the appropriate parties to plan other aspects of the project.
- ❖ **Who among our group will participate?** Try to build immediate ownership in this project by enlisting volunteers for the various duties the class has discerned. Remember, different people have different gifts, but all are equally important. You may have to "think out of the box" to create jobs for some folks who feel reluctant about participating. Keep in mind that much of the work is accomplished prior to the actual event, so the fact that someone cannot be present on the day of the project does not mean that he or she cannot participate.
- ❖ **How much will this project cost?** Some projects, of course, require little financial investment. Others, however, will depend on money. You will need to estimate the cost and add some extra in case of overruns. Determine how these costs will be covered. Will the students each contribute? Will they do a fund-raiser? If so, who will be involved in the planning and execution of the event(s)? Will one or more class representatives go to a board or committee within the church to see if funds are available? If so, be sure that the class spokesperson who presents the need to the board is fully informed about the project and able to answer questions.
- ❖ **How will we inform the congregation?** Letting the whole church know that your class is undertaking a project is important. Your actions may motivate another class or small group to take action too. Or, they may ask to join with you. Also, if you need some specialized help, such as an electrician, a licensed tradesperson may step forward if the need is announced. Another reason to publicize the project is to bolster fund-raising efforts. Raising money is usually easier to do when the congregation understands what you plan to do, why, when, with whom, and how.

❖ **What resources do we need to undertake this project?** As previously mentioned, you may need someone who is highly skilled in a particular area to assist you. Money, of course, is also a resource. But so are books, DVDs or videos that may help to make the situation more real to the class members, or a guest speaker who can discuss, for example, the needs of a certain mission field that your class wants to visit. If you plan to do a project that will alter church property, one or more class representatives will likely need to attend at least one meeting to get permission from the board of trustees or other decision-making group. Again, depending on the nature of your project, insurance and liability issues may need to be taken into account.

❖ **When are we going to do this project?** Some projects can be done at any time, but others must meet deadlines. If, for example, your class wants to sponsor a church-wide drive to provide food and Christmas gifts for three families, you need to have the food collected and bagged and the gifts purchased and wrapped for delivery prior to December 25. To be sure you hit your deadlines, create a calendar, starting with the deadline. Move backward in time to determine when each of the steps has to be completed. If you find that you are too late in starting, postpone this activity and try another one now. If the project does not have to be completed by a specific date, push your original date back so that the group will have time to meet its goals. Especially if your class has never done a group project, you will want to do everything possible to ensure that the first experience is a good one.

❖ **How will we evaluate the success of our project?** God does not call us to be successful, only faithful. But, having said that, to be good stewards of the resources you have, you want to ensure that they are used wisely. Some results are quantifiable. For example, we set a goal of providing Christmas baskets and gifts to three families, and we exceeded that goal by collecting enough for five families. Some other goals cannot be measured but are equally important. For example, we all agreed to fast one day per week concerning escalating crime in our community. As a result of this fasting, class members pledge to take a variety of actions within the community to scale back the crime. We cannot easily quantify these results, but if taking action was a goal, then this project was certainly successful.

How Do We Get Started?

A crucial key for moving a class from "hearers" to "doers" is to start small. Encourage them to do some small service projects around the church to grow accustomed to working together, to see that they can be successful, and to begin to recognize the diversity of talents within the group. Choose "one time" events that do not require a lot of planning or advertising but do require the class members work together. Serving lunch after a summer church service, for example, involves cooks, servers, people who can set up and take down tables and chairs, and dishwashers.

Build on your experience to do activities such as missions trips to a local site or further away. Some members will be able to go, whereas others cannot, but many folks may be able to make a financial contribution to show their support. Mounting a letter writing campaign to elected officials is also something that most groups can do. Some class members also may be willing to appear before a legislative body to let the views of the class be known. Just be careful about speaking for the entire congregation unless you get permission from an appropriate board first.

At some point your group may want to move to a major project that requires long-range planning, fund-raising, recruiting volunteers, and possibly even visiting other churches to enlist cooperation. My own class reached this level after studying material from Habitat for Humanity and deciding that we wanted to be the catalyst for a build that included our church and two other ecumenical bodies. Much time and patience was needed to take all of the necessary steps, but we worked together, expanded our circle, kept reminding ourselves of prophetic biblical mandates concerning the poor, and were delighted when the day came to turn over the keys to a family we had gotten to know as we worked together to make their dream of home ownership a reality. Other house builds have followed, but none seemed as special as that first one when we were "learning the ropes" and constantly encouraging one another.

What Are the Benefits of Class Projects?

You may already have a class that does a great job of caring for one another: concerns and joys are lifted up, cards are sent, meals are shared, and people are recognized. In truth, you can say that your class acts as a community of faith. But in Acts 1:8 Jesus promises that we will receive the Holy Spirit and when we do we are to be his witnesses locally, regionally, and around the world. So, being the community of faith within our group, while commendable, is clearly not enough. We must move beyond the walls of our classroom and church building into the wider world as witnesses for Christ. Class projects are a way of doing just that. People not only hear us "talk the talk" but also see us "walk the walk" as we work with those who for whatever reason need to experience the love of God. People who are directly affected by what we do are changed, people who observe what we do are changed, and we ourselves are changed as we put our faith into action.

The bonds among the class members can grow stronger as the group struggles together to accomplish a shared goal. People can learn to be more patient and forgiving as mistakes are made, schedules run amuck, and the project veers off course. They grow to appreciate the gifts and talents that each one has to offer and can affirm the importance of each member of the body of Christ. Moreover, some people who want to see the church in action may be drawn to your class because it does live out what it professes to believe.

The class can also provide leadership within the church. Many things within a congregation can be accomplished because a Sunday school member has a "bright idea," shares it with the class, and the class becomes a catalyst for change. If one class can do this, so can others. Over time, new ministries develop because a Sunday school class took its mandate to be the people of God seriously. Naturally, the class does not want to become a maverick within the church, so care has to be taken to ensure that the group has gone before the necessary elected bodies within the church for approval, if necessary. The idea and energy of one class can also spark the elected leadership to rise to new heights as well.

Most importantly, the class members are becoming transformed into the image of God that we know so well in Jesus Christ. As we take on his roles of healer, teacher, advocate, shepherd, and faithful witness, we are acting as Jesus has called and taught us to act. His love is flowing through us as we reach out to other people, indeed to all creation, to make a difference. Those actions move all of us closer to the reign of God where we will find the shalom—the wholeness, righteousness, healing, and peace—that God longs for all of us to experience.

First Quarter
God's Living Covenant

SEPTEMBER 3, 2006—NOVEMBER 26, 2006

This new Sunday school year begins with a survey of the Old Testament that looks at the theme of covenant. Entitled "God's Living Covenant," this quarter covers events from the flood in Noah's day until after the Israelites returned from exile in Babylon.

Unit 1, "In Covenant with God," includes four sessions that explore God's covenants with Noah, Abram, the Israelites at Mount Sinai, and with the people who renewed the covenant at the edge of the promised land. In "Finding Security" on September 3 we consider God's covenant with Noah, as recorded in Genesis 9:1-15. "Trusting Promises," the lesson for September 10 on Genesis 17, looks at God's covenant with Abram. On September 17 we turn to Exodus 19:1-6 and 24:3-8 to learn about the people's acceptance of God's covenant in "Being Mutually Responsible." The unit ends on September 24 with "Making Life's Choices," a study of Joshua 24 that delves into the covenant renewal made as the people stood poised to enter the promised land.

In Unit 2, "God's Covenant with Judges and Kings," we will spend five weeks examining God's relationship to the people through the judges, especially Deborah, and with Samuel, David, and Solomon. "Seeking Deliverance," based on Judges 2:16-23, begins this unit on October 1. In this lesson we learn about how God sent judges to deliver the people after they had disobeyed and despaired. On October 8 in "Leadership Counts!" we encounter a specific judge, Deborah, whose story of leadership is told in Judges 4. We turn on October 15 to 1 Samuel 7:3-13 to study how "Prayer Makes the Difference" in the life of Samuel. "A Promise You Can Trust," the lesson for October 22, considers 2 Samuel 7 to learn how God will establish a covenant relationship with David. Unit 2 ends on October 29 with "God Answers Prayer," a lesson on 1 Kings 3, where we see God respond to Solomon's request for wisdom.

Unit 3, "Living as God's Covenanted People," includes four sessions that highlight the challenges Elijah and Josiah faced to keep the people faithful; exile as a consequence of breaking the covenant; and the restored relationship with those who returned from exile. "Depending on God's Power," the lesson for November 5, is rooted in 1 Kings 18:20-39. Here we see Elijah depending on God to overcome the people's belief in the power of Baal. On November 12 we turn in the lesson "Seeking Renewal" to 2 Kings 22–23 to study how King Josiah brought reforms and a renewal of the covenant with God. "Making Wrong Choices," the lesson for November 19, looks at 2 Chronicles 36:15-21 and Psalm 137 to see the bitter consequence of exile that resulted from continued disobedience of God's covenant. The quarter ends on November 26 with "Experiencing Forgiveness," a lesson based on 2 Chronicles 36:22-23 and Ezra 1:5-7, which shows how God offers the exiles forgiveness, restoration, and an opportunity to return home.

MEET OUR WRITER

DR. GAYLE CARLTON FELTON

Gayle Carlton Felton is an elder in the North Carolina Annual Conference. She has a B.A. degree from North Carolina Wesleyan College (1964), where she majored in American history. Her M. Div. is from Duke Divinity School (1982) and her Ph.D., with concentration in the history of Christianity, from Duke University (1987). She has served on the faculties of Meredith College and Duke Divinity School.

Gayle, who was a member of the denomination's Committee to Study Baptism (1989–1996), wrote the final version of "By Water and the Spirit: A United Methodist Understanding of Baptism," and presented the document to the 1992 and 1996 General Conferences. She continued as a member of an advisory team of the General Board of Discipleship that worked to reconcile the provisions of the *Discipline* with this document and with the ritual. She is the principal writer for "This Holy Mystery: A United Methodist Understanding of Holy Communion," which is an exposition of that sacrament comparable to the earlier work on baptism. "This Holy Mystery" was presented to the 2004 General Conference and approved. These documents now comprise the denomination's official interpretive positions on the sacraments.

Gayle is the author of *This Gift of Water: The Practice and Theology of Baptism Among Methodists in America* (1992), *By Water and the Spirit: Making Connections for Identity and Ministry* (1997, 1998), *The Coming of Jesus* (2000), and a variety of articles on Methodism, sacraments, and the teaching ministry of the church. She is the editor of *How United Methodists Study Scripture* (1999) and has previously contributed to *The New International Lesson Annual.* Currently, she is writing the commentary and study guide for "This Holy Mystery."

Gayle serves as a speaker, teacher, preacher, and consultant, working from the local to the general church level.

THE BIG PICTURE:
THE CONCEPT OF COVENANT

The concept of covenant is foundational to the Hebrew people's self-understanding and to our comprehension of the message of the Old Testament for both Judaism and Christianity. Archaeologists have contributed greatly to our insights about covenants as they have discovered thousands of examples in ancient cultures, especially that of the Hittite Empire of the Late Bronze Age (circa 1400–1200 B.C.). Outside of kinship, the most common basis of relationships between human beings in the ancient world was that of covenants. In general, a covenant can be defined as an agreement between two parties, with promises and responsibilities on both sides. A covenant establishes, delineates, and regulates a relationship. Examples in our experience include legal contracts and marriage vows. Even among human beings there are diverse covenants—between persons of equal rank and power, between vassal and lord, or granted by a king to his people. Covenants between human beings and God can, of course, never be agreements of parity, but they too are not always of the same type. As we analyze the most significant Old Testament covenants, we will observe some of this diversity.

There are nine common components of covenants, although not every covenant contains every component. 1) Covenants often begin with a preamble in which the parties involved are identified. This identification may include names, titles, and some indications of the status of those involved. 2) A historical prologue, of varying length and detail, may follow. In this preamble is a description of previous actions of at least one of the parties. This section provides the basis for the covenant in terms of past events relevant to it. 3) Covenants almost always have a list or description of the stipulations involved. Here the obligations of the parties to each other are articulated. The length of this section varies greatly, from an overall statement of responsibilities to a detailed delineation. 4) There may be specifications as to if and how the covenant will be publicly announced and where the treaty documents are to be deposited. 5) Frequency and procedure for renewal of the covenant may be included. 6) Many covenants are sealed with an oath, which may be either a verbal statement or a symbolic action, or both. 7) A symbolic action or object may be designated as the sign of the covenant. 8) A list of witnesses to the oath may follow. In ancient treaties, this was often a naming of various gods who would be the divine guarantors or enforcers of the covenant. 9) Covenants often conclude with a section of blessings and curses. These include blessings to be anticipated if the covenant is faithfully kept and calamities to be feared if the terms are violated.

Because the Hebrew people considered themselves to be in perpetual covenant relationship with God, the Old Testament is replete with stories of covenant-making and covenant-breaking. The most important Old Testament covenants are discussed in the lessons of this quarter. All of these covenants are between God and human beings. Certainly there would have been other kinds of covenants in Hebrew culture, but it is those with the deity which define them as a people. As you study, recall the covenant components described in the last paragraph and apply them to the specific covenant being considered. As previously indicated, not every component will be found in every covenant. There are also other Old Testament covenants that are not covered in the quarter's lessons; a few of these will be mentioned here.

If we look at biblical covenants in chronological order, the simple covenant between God and Adam and Eve is first. The beautiful myth of God's creation of the universe and of humankind climaxes with God providing of all human needs, but warning that there was one tree of whose fruits they were not to eat. The covenant stipulated that they were to obey this prohibition or suffer dire consequences. Adam and Eve violated the covenant and severely damaged their relationship with God, with each other, and with the natural world. The covenant relationship that God had established with them would have preserved harmony and intimacy, but when they were unfaithful to it, sin was allowed to spread its poison to all humanity. Later God tried to wipe out the effects of sin through the flood and the destruction of all human beings except one faithful man and his family. In the lesson for September 3, we see that, after the flood, God bound the divine self in an unconditional covenant with Noah and all living creatures on the earth. The sign or seal of the covenant was the rainbow. In this covenant only God was bound; there was no obligation placed upon humanity. These two covenants—the Adamic and the Noahic—were universal; they applied to the divine relationship with all human beings.

The covenant between God and Abraham was the prototype of all biblical covenants. In Genesis 15, God unconditionally promised Abraham that the land to which God had brought him would belong to Abraham and his descendants in perpetuity. In the lesson for September 10 we look at another aspect of this covenant—the divine promise of a special relationship with Abraham's people and the requirement that they symbolize their obedience by the rite of circumcision.

It is in the covenant between God and the Hebrew people, represented by Moses, at Mount Sinai, that we find the most comprehensive expression of the components of covenant. On September 17, we observe the formation of Israel as a religious community in special relationship with God. There is a brief preamble and historical prologue followed by stipulations based on exclusive loyalty to Yahweh (Exodus 20:2-3)—the divine name revealed to Moses. The ethical responsibilities of the people are encapsulated in the Ten Commandments and expanded in the remainder of the Law. They pledge their obedience to the divine demands through which they will live out their identity as the covenant people. Provision for deposit into the ark of the tablets bearing the Law was made in Exodus 40:20 and Deuteronomy 10:5. Public reading was specified in Deuteronomy 31:10-11. In Deuteronomy 32, elements of the natural world are called upon as witnesses. Blessings and curses are graphically described in Deuteronomy 27 and 28. The symbolic action of an oath is recounted in Exodus 24:5-8.

Ceremonies of covenant renewal apparently became a feature of Hebrew religious life, although certainly this recommitment was honored more faithfully at some times than others. In the lesson for September 24 we study the covenant renewal ceremony in Joshua 24. The leadership of the judge and prophet Samuel drew Israel back to the covenant, as seen in the session for October 15. God's prophet Elijah engaged in a dramatic contest with the priests of Baal, as we will explore on November 5, in order to demonstrate to the people who was their real God to whom they must be loyal. The lesson for November 12 recounts the efforts of a king centuries later to call the people back to covenant loyalty.

During the period after their slavery in Egypt, their rescue by God and guidance in the wilderness, and their reentry to the promised land, the people of Israel were led by judges called forth by God. In the sessions on October 1 and 8, we learn how God continued to defend the covenant people, even when their wars were the result of their own unfaithfulness.

The session for October 22 explains the very important covenant made between God and King David. God promised that David's dynasty would rule Israel forever and that God would provide a righteous and just king under whose reign there would be a glorious time of deliverance and power. David's son Solomon continued his lineage and built the temple for God in Jerusalem, as we will study on October 29.

The story of the people of Israel in the Old Testament is one of repeatedly falling away from the covenant relationship, disobeying God, and being unfaithful. On November 19, we look at the disastrous defeat of the nation by the Babylonian Empire. The people were taken into captivity in an alien land where they struggled to figure out what it meant to be covenant people in those circumstances. Our final session examines the period of the Jews' return to Judah and their attempts to reestablish themselves in the land that God had given them so many centuries earlier. In the books of Ezra and Nehemiah, we have accounts of the people pledging themselves anew to the covenant relationship as they rebuild Jerusalem, the temple, their religion, and their identity.

In Jeremiah 31:31-34, the prophet voices God's promise of the coming of a new covenant. The Hebrew people had proven, through centuries of effort, temporary faithfulness, and repeated failure, that covenant relationship based on the keeping of the law was simply beyond the capability of human beings. The new coming will not depend upon obedience to an external legal code. The new covenant will be based upon a transformation of human beings so that they will know God personally. The will of God will be internalized; it will be written in their minds and hearts. This passage, in Hebrews 8:8-12, is the longest sequential quotation from the Old Testament to appear in the New. In all four narratives of the Last Supper—in Matthew 26, Mark 14, Luke 22, and 1 Corinthians 11—Jesus speaks of the cup from which he bids the disciples drink as holding his blood of the covenant or new covenant. As we will see, blood was often a sign of covenant-making. Jesus is saying that the new relationship between God and human beings, prophesied by Jeremiah, was coming to fruition in his blood—his death on the cross. Through his blood shed in his execution, humankind would be able to enjoy a renewed intimacy with God, be forgiven, and enabled to live as transformed beings whose wills reflect the divine will. A major theme in the New Testament is the relationship between Christ and the Christian community—a community held together and held to Christ in covenant. New persons entered into this community through the sacrament of baptism, just as they entered into the Jewish covenant with God by circumcision. These relationships were personal and intimate. They did not require defining through law; they were rooted in love. The commandment to love in John 13:34 defined the nature of the community and of their relationship to God in Christ. It was in the Eucharist (Holy Communion, Lord's Supper) that this love was most deeply formed and most fully expressed. The Christian church is a community bound in love and faithfulness to each other and to God in covenant relationship.

When we are studying the Old Testament, and especially in a survey such as the lessons of this quarter, there is sometimes a problem of confusion due to the different names used for God, for the land, and for the people. There is a diversity of names and metaphors applied to God in the Bible. Some of these terms are based on the generic Semitic word for "god," which is "El." Examples are "El Shaddai" (Exodus 19 and 1 Kings 19 contain this usage), "El Bethel" as in Genesis 31:13, and "Elohim" as Genesis 1:26. These names are translated simply as "God" by both the *New Revised Standard Version of the Bible* and the HOLY BIBLE, NEW INTERNATIONAL VERSION®, and so are not troublesome for readers. Much more important for us, is the term "Yahweh" which is understood as the personal name for God. This is the divine name revealed to Moses at the burning bush (Exodus 3). The Exodus event showed Israel who God is in relationship to them. The divine name probably means "I Am Who I Am" and, because the Hebrew language used no vowels, was rendered as YHWH and probably pronounced as "Yahweh." Yahweh is the God of the covenant, the God who bound the divine self in special relationship to Israel. In later Hebrew history, the term "Adonai" meaning "Lord" was substituted for Yahweh. This happened because deep reverence for the covenant name of God resulted in its being considered too sacred to voice aloud. Most English translations have followed this synagogue practice. In both the NRSV and NIV the name is rendered with small capital letters as LORD.

Names for the land that God gave to Israel vary also. For our usage, it is sufficient to recognize several terms as often referring to the same general area at the eastern end of the Mediterranean Sea (ignoring historical changes in its boundaries)—Canaan, the promised land, Israel, Judah, Palestine, and others.

There is similar diversity in terms used to refer to the people. In general, in the earlier period of Old Testament history, they are called the descendants of Abraham, descendants of Jacob, children of Israel (Jacob's God-given name), people of Israel, Israelites, Hebrews. The people understood themselves to have descended from the twelve sons of Jacob and were divided into tribes identified by those names. Some thousand years before the time of Christ, King David united the people under his rule as the nation of Israel with its capital at Jerusalem. After David's successor Solomon died, there was civil conflict and the nation was divided into two. Israel was retained as the name of the northern kingdom with its capital at Samaria. This northern kingdom comprised most of ten of the tribes; it was ruled by different lines of kings. Israel came to an end when it was conquered by the Assyrian Empire in 721 B.C. and its people scattered. The southern kingdom was called Judah and retained its capital in Jerusalem, which was also the location of the temple. It comprised largely the tribes of Judah and Benjamin and was ruled by the Davidic dynasty. Judah held off its various enemies until 587 B.C. when it was finally conquered by the Babylonian Empire and many of the people taken into captivity. The name "Jews" was derived from "Judah" during this time. Later some of the exiles returned to their land, rebuilt Jerusalem and the temple, and continued as Judah. The name Israel did not cease to be used when the nation by that name fell—it often referred to the entire remaining people and land. (Of course, the modern nation Israel was constituted in 1948 and is part of the same territory.) In addition, sometimes the biblical writers use a more specific tribal or clan name when actually meaning the whole people of the time; an example is the use of "Ephraim" in Hosea 11:3.

For purposes of our study during this quarter, a certain amount of looseness will be valuable when we and our material utilize these various terms. The crucial point is that God chose to come to this people and enter into a special covenant relationship with them as God worked through their history to redeem all of humankind.

Close-up: Timeline of Events
From Noah to King Cyrus' Proclamation

Lesson	Background Scripture	Major Character(s)	Approximate Time*
(1) Finding Security	Genesis 9:1-17	Noah	Pre-history
(2) Trusting Promises	Genesis 17	Abraham and Sarah	Around 2000 BC
(3) Being Mutually Responsible	Exodus 19:1-6; 24:3-8	Moses and the Hebrew people	Scholars differ widely on this date, from about 1440 BC (early date) to about 1280 BC (late date).
(4) Making Life's Choices	Joshua 24	Joshua and the Hebrew people	About 1240–1200 BC, if we use the late date for the exodus
(5) Seeking Deliverance	Judges 2:11-23	Various judges leading the Hebrew people	1200–1020 BC
(6) Leadership Counts!	Judges 4	Deborah, Barak	Sometime between 1200–1020 BC (Deborah was the fourth of twelve judges.)
(7) Prayer Makes the Difference	1 Samuel 7:3-13	Samuel, the Israelites, and the Philistines	Around 1050 BC
(8) A Promise You Can Trust	2 Samuel 7	Nathan and David	David reigned from 1000 until 960 BC .
(9) God Answers Prayer	1 Kings 3	Solomon	Solomon reigned from 960 until 930 BC.
(10) Depending on God's Power	1 Kings 18:20-39	Elijah, 450 prophets of Baal, all the Israelites	Elijah was first mentioned about 864 BC , during the reign of King Ahab in the northern kingdom, 869–850 BC.
(11) Seeking Renewal	2 Kings 22–23	King Josiah and the Israelites	Josiah reigned from 640–609 BC.
(12) Making Wrong Choices	2 Chronicles 36:15-21; Psalm 137	Israelites in exile in Babylon	In 587 BC Jerusalem fell to King Nebuchadnezzar.
(13) Experiencing Forgiveness	2 Chronicles 36:22-23; Ezra 1:5-7	Cyrus, King of Persia	Cyrus, who had conquered Nebuchadnezzar, issued his edict allowing the Israelites to return home from Babylon and rebuild the temple in 538–539 BC.

*The dates for the reigns of David, Solomon, Ahab, and Josiah are generally agreed upon, as are the dates for the fall of Jerusalem and King Cyrus' edict. As to the other dates, different sources use different dates. The purpose of this timeline is to give you a relative chronology, rather than an absolute date, for the events that we are studying in September, October, and November.

FAITH IN ACTION: LIVING OUT OUR COVENANT WITH GOD

During this quarter we will survey the Old Testament from the days of Noah through the conquest of Judah by the Babylonians and the edict of Cyrus in 538/539 BC, which allowed the exiled Israelites to return home. Each of our lessons will be broadly based on the theme of covenant. We will see how the people of God lived faithfully—and often unfaithfully—in light of God's covenants with them.

As Christians we are living under what Jeremiah (31:31-34) and Jesus (Luke 22:20) call the "new covenant." How, though, do you live that covenant out, both individually and corporately? Here are some ideas for the class to act on.

❖ God's covenant with Noah includes "every living creature of all flesh" (Genesis 9:15).

(1) Promote recycling in your community and do all in your power to reduce, reuse, and recycle whatever is entrusted to you so as to be a faithful steward of God's creation.

(2) Create a "backyard habitat" at your home or on the church grounds that will attract wildlife, birds, and butterflies. Be sure to include places for shelter and water. Use plants indigenous to your area that require little maintenance.

❖ Through Abraham, God promised that "all the families of the earth shall be blessed" (Genesis 12:3).

(3) Create class or church projects that will enable your congregation to be a blessing to others. These projects should serve those whom Jesus was most concerned about— the poor, vulnerable women and children, the sick, the imprisoned, the "Samaritan," and other marginalized members of society. Consider working ecumenically with one or more other churches in your area. Meet real needs in the community that you have identified by opening a soup kitchen, food pantry, Mothers Day Out program, preschool, school age daycare, homeless shelter (even on a limited basis, such as the winter months), repairing homes for those unable to do so, visiting persons in a nursing home, hospice, prison, or other facility.

❖ Moses gave God's covenantal law that all the people agree to abide by and which is later renewed through Joshua and Josiah.

(4) Choose an area of public policy that concerns the class, such as health care, care for older adults, care for the poor, housing, the environment, capital punishment, war and peace, justice for workers, issues surrounding the beginning and end of life, or immigration. Study local and national laws affecting the area(s) you have selected. Determine how these laws reflect biblical teachings and how they are in conflict. Mount a letter-writing campaign to elected officials to change public policy where you believe it is in conflict with biblical teachings. Consider going to elected officials in person to lobby for your position. Do whatever you can to build a coalition of support within the community. Stand your ground, but do so in all humility, remembering first that many issues that face us today have no biblical precedent and second, that people of faith differ on how to best approach these issues.

UNIT 1: IN COVENANT WITH GOD
FINDING SECURITY

PREVIEWING THE LESSON

Lesson Scripture: Genesis 9:1-15
Background Scripture: Genesis 9:1-17
Key Verse: Genesis 9:15

Focus of the Lesson:
We all long for some sense of security. What can we trust as being sound and secure? God promised all creation never to send another flood, and the rainbow serves as a reminder that God is keeping this promise.

Goals for the Learners:
(1) to learn about the covenant God made with Noah after the flood.
(2) to remember what God has done for them.
(3) to identify and affirm security that God provides for them.

Pronunciation Guide:
anthropomorphic (an thre pe mor' fik)
Ararat (air' uh rat)

Supplies:
Bibles, newsprint and marker, paper and pencils, hymnals, strips of construction paper, candles in different rainbow colors, matches, optional small blanket, straight pins

---

READING THE SCRIPTURE

NRSV

Genesis 9:1-15

¹God blessed Noah and his sons, and said to them, "Be fruitful and multiply, and fill the earth. ²The fear and dread of you shall rest on every animal of the earth, and on every bird of the air, on everything that creeps on the ground, and on all the fish of the sea; into your hand they are delivered.

NIV

Genesis 9:1-15

¹Then God blessed Noah and his sons, saying to them, "Be fruitful and increase in number and fill the earth. ²The fear and dread of you will fall upon all the beasts of the earth and all the birds of the air, upon every creature that moves along the ground, and upon all the fish of the sea; they are

3Every moving thing that lives shall be food for you; and just as I gave you the green plants, I give you everything. 4Only, you shall not eat flesh with its life, that is, its blood. 5For your own lifeblood I will surely require a reckoning: from every animal I will require it and from human beings, each one for the blood of another, I will require a reckoning for human life.

6 Whoever sheds the blood of a human,
    by a human shall that person's
      blood be shed;
  for in his own image
    God made humankind.

7And you, be fruitful and multiply, abound on the earth and multiply in it."

8Then God said to Noah and to his sons with him, 9"As for me, I am establishing my covenant with you and your descendants after you, 10and with every living creature that is with you, the birds, the domestic animals, and every animal of the earth with you, as many as came out of the ark. 11I establish my covenant with you, that never again shall all flesh be cut off by the waters of a flood, and never again shall there be a flood to destroy the earth." 12God said, "This is the sign of the covenant that I make between me and you and every living creature that is with you, for all future generations: 13I have set my bow in the clouds, and it shall be a sign of the covenant between me and the earth. 14When I bring clouds over the earth and the bow is seen in the clouds, **15I will remember my covenant that is between me and you and every living creature of all flesh; and the waters shall never again become a flood to destroy all flesh."**

given into your hands. 3Everything that lives and moves will be food for you. Just as I gave you the green plants, I now give you everything.

4"But you must not eat meat that has its lifeblood still in it. 5And for your lifeblood I will surely demand an accounting. I will demand an accounting from every animal. And from each man, too, I will demand an accounting for the life of his fellow man.

6"Whoever sheds the blood of man,
    by man shall his blood be shed;
  for in the image of God
    has God made man.

7As for you, be fruitful and increase in number; multiply on the earth and increase upon it."

8Then God said to Noah and to his sons with him: 9"I now establish my covenant with you and with your descendants after you 10and with every living creature that was with you—the birds, the livestock and all the wild animals, all those that came out of the ark with you—every living creature on earth. 11I establish my covenant with you: Never again will all life be cut off by the waters of a flood; never again will there be a flood to destroy the earth."

12And God said, "This is the sign of the covenant I am making between me and you and every living creature with you, a covenant for all generations to come: 13I have set my rainbow in the clouds, and it will be the sign of the covenant between me and the earth. 14Whenever I bring clouds over the earth and the rainbow appears in the clouds, **15I will remember my covenant between me and you and all living creatures of every kind. Never again will the waters become a flood to destroy all life."**

UNDERSTANDING THE SCRIPTURE

Genesis 9:1. The preceding chapter of Genesis ends with Noah, his family, and all the animals finally disembarking from the ark after more than a year aboard. Immediately, Noah builds an altar and sacrifices to God in gratitude for their delivery.

God, who these biblical writers thought of in very anthropomorphic (human) terms, is pleased and begins covenant making. God expresses good will and purpose for Noah's family. As the story has been told in chapters 6 through 8, all other human life had been obliterated by the flood. There must be a new beginning. Using the same words that had been addressed to Adam and Eve earlier (1:28), the family of Noah is charged to reproduce and, through their many offspring, repopulate the earth. Noah is here imaged as the new man, source of a new beginning for humankind. Because of this, Noah has often been portrayed as a prototype for Christ—the new Adam (Romans 5) and also the new Noah.

Genesis 9:2-3. The descendants of Noah are given authority over all other living creatures, just as the first humans had been (1:26, 28). But, the relationship between humans and the animals will now be one of alienation and fear, rather than harmony and peace. Prior to the flood, human beings had eaten only plants and their fruits (1:29). Now God approves their consumption of animals as well, although we are not told why. This changes the way that animal life relates to humans. We are now dangerous threats rather than co-creatures. Perhaps this is one of the results of human sin distorting the original goodness of creation.

Genesis 9:4. Blood was considered sacred and treated with utmost respect. Animals that are killed for food must be cleansed of their blood before being eaten. Blood was believed by the Hebrews to contain the vital life force of a creature and was not to be consumed. This teaching is in contrast to the practice of some other ancient societies in which the blood of an animal was drunk in the hope to infusing the animal's strength into the one consuming its blood. Leviticus 17:10-14 explains this Hebrew prohibition more fully. The association of blood with sacrifice (an animal killed for sacrifice) and atonement undergirds the New Testament understanding of the crucifixion of Jesus.

Genesis 9:5. Humanity is made responsible for life on the earth—both the life of animals and the life of human beings. Life is a gift of God and God requires that it be valued, accounted for, and protected. Covenants involve both promises and responsibilities. Here God stipulates that (1) the people must not consume the blood of a slaughtered animal, and (2) they must not shed the blood of their fellow humans.

Genesis 9:6. The lives of all human beings have immense worth to God because they are created in the image of God (1:26). Humans are to respect and care for all life as God's stewards. For a person to take the life of another is to violate the relationship with God as well as the relationship with the one killed. The seriousness of the offense is made clear by imposition of the penalty of death on a murderer. Enforcement of this law of God will require the development of institutions of human governance.

Genesis 9:7. The command to produce many offspring is reiterated. In order for humans to govern the earth as God's representatives, their numbers must increase rapidly. In Hebrew society a man's true wealth was seen to be in his children—mostly his sons. They would carry on his heritage and by doing so give him life beyond his physical death. Large families were valued and honored.

Genesis 9:8-9. God enters into a covenant with Noah and his descendants—all humankind. The covenant is initiated by God; it is God's plan for working out the divine purpose in the world. This covenant is more than a contract or agreement; it establishes a relationship. The covenant reveals something of the nature of God and of the divine expectations for us.

Genesis 9:10. This covenant will also include the rest of the created order. "Every living creature" is to be in relationship with God. While humanity is clearly the part of creation that extends to all that God has created. Humans are to exercise their authority over creation in ways that express this divine caring.

Genesis 9:11. As a part of the divine

covenant promise, God pledges that all life on earth will never again be destroyed by flood. Hebrews saw the sea as a place of chaos, mystery, and danger. Perhaps this is why this story associates destruction with water particularly.

Genesis 9:12-13. The sign of this enduring covenant between God and God's created order will be the rainbow. This is an appropriate sign, since it is associated with rainfall and is, thus, a potent reminder of God's promise to never again destroy the earth by water. Some commentators interpret these verses as meaning that the earth had not had rain and rainbows before the flood, but it is not clear that the story is saying that. Like the English language, Hebrew uses the same

word for a bow as a weapon and as a refraction of light after rain. Perhaps this signifies that God's "warfare" against human beings is at an end. God's bow is "hung up" and at rest. That which had been an instrument of war becomes a sign of peace. Although human sin remains a reality, God is going to be engaged in the work of redemption rather than of destruction.

Genesis 9:14-17. The covenant promise and its sign are repeated for greater emphasis. The rainbow is not only a sign to human beings of the covenant; it is a reminder to God. When God sees the rainbow in the sky, God remembers the divine promise and relationship with humans and other creatures of the earth.

INTERPRETING THE SCRIPTURE

The Rainbow Follows the Flood

Noah and his family emerge from a terrifying experience into a different and frightening world. For months their ship had floated directionless on the floodwaters that covered the earth. Then during the months grounded on Mount Ararat they must have wondered what lay ahead. Finally the surface of the earth was dry enough for them to disembark. They must have found a world almost devoid of life. Perhaps vegetation was beginning to grow in the soggy soil to nourish the animals that were also disembarking. Human and animal life had been preserved by God on the ark, but all else had been destroyed. A new start had to be made.

God acts to restore order to life on earth by establishing a covenant between God and Noah's family. This covenant was a precursor of the relationship that God would establish and reestablish with God's people throughout the rest of the Bible. How wonderful it must have been for these storm-battered human beings to be met by God. The terror of an unknown future was soothed by the real-

ization that God was continuing to work in their history—and even more, that God wanted to be in relationship with them.

God took the initiative and promised never again to destroy the earth in the way that they had experienced. To reassure and remind the people of this divine promise, God designated the rainbow as a recurring sign of the covenant relationship. The significance was not simply that God would not flood the earth. The deeper meaning was that God was, by God's own will and action, in enduring relationship with them. The covenant promise and its sign were given not only to Noah's family, but to "every living creature" (9:15) who would follow them on the earth through the centuries to come.

The Covenant-Making God

The ancient Hebrew people grew in their understanding of God through the events of their history. The God who is portrayed in Genesis 9 is different from God before the flood. In Genesis 6, God "saw that the wickedness of humankind was great in the earth" and "was sorry that he had made humankind" (6:5, 6). God decided to "blot out from the earth the human beings" God had created (6:7). After the flood, God is described as having changed. It is as if God has changed the divine mind and decided to relate to human beings in a different way. Evil, death, and destruction will not come from God. Divine punishment is replaced by divine grace. Divine judgment and punishment give way to reassurance and firm promise. A new intimacy is established between God and humankind. God is committed to relationship with human beings; we are God's covenant partners.

Frequently in the Old Testament, God's people cry out in times of suffering and ask whether God has forgotten them. The story of the covenant with the rainbow sign is assurance that God has not forgotten and will not forget. This is a God who remembers and who reminds. The covenant is our assurance that the world and our lives in it rest on a foundation of ultimate love, forgiveness, and graciousness.

It may be helpful to note that this story of the covenant with Noah was written during a bleak time in the history of the Jewish people. They had been conquered by the Babylonian Empire. The city of Jerusalem and the temple had been destroyed and most of the people slaughtered or carried into exile. Those living in exile in Babylonia were rather like Noah's family after the flood. They had experienced the annihilation of the world they had known. They were uncertain about the future. They questioned the actions of God. This story offered comfort and hope. God had made new beginnings after destruction before. God had promised to remember them. The present could be lived in confidence that God had not deserted them, that God was still committed to them in covenant relationship.

Just a Myth?

The stories of Noah, the flood, and the covenant that followed come from the period of Hebrew life known as the prehistory. Little factual or historical is known about this early period. The stories in Genesis are largely legends, which seek to tie Israel's present—specifically, the times in which they were actually written—to its distant past. The biblical writers probably did not intend that their stories be read as history; that was not their purpose. They aimed, instead, to explain important aspects of Israel's life as a people by recounting episodes in the past as origins and explanations.

Stories of great, destructive floods are common in the ancient histories of most of the peoples of the Middle East. Whether they preserve some memory of an early catastrophic event is unknown. Surely such a flood did not cover the whole earth, although it could have inundated the whole world that these peoples knew about. Probably these stories from different cultures have a similar purpose of illustrating God's wrath against human sinfulness and the new beginnings that had to take place afterward.

Another name for these ancient stories is myths. In biblical studies the term myth does not mean a fanciful, imaginary story. A biblical myth is a story that tells the truth about something at a level deeper than that which facts alone could convey. While myths are not historical or factual, they are true. They communicate ideas and realities that are of great importance and which can be better communicated in stories than any other way. An example from American history is the famous myth of George Washington as a boy cutting down a cherry tree and then telling the truth about it to his father. While the story is probably not factual, it is deeply true because it communicates the truth about the character of our first president. Biblical myths function in the same way. In them, a people seek to communicate deep truths about who they are and how they came to be.

"With Every Living Creature"

A theme in the opening chapters of Genesis is God's commitment to the whole created order. This is evident in the creation accounts in which God creates heavenly bodies, waters, vegetation, animals and birds, as well as human beings, and speaks approvingly of each. In the flood account, God makes covenant with "every living creature" (9:15), not with humans alone. Humans are designated as caretakers and stewards of the created order, exercising their authority over it as God's representatives. In a time when environmental pollution and degradation are rampant, we need to assume anew this responsibility. The earth is not ours to exploit and ravage; it is ours to love and enjoy as God does.

God values highly the lives of animals and, while allowing them to be food for human beings, insists that animals be respected and well-treated. Today the production methods of most large operations raising animals for food are clearly disrespectful of their intrinsic worth, and often downright cruel. Our society should be called to account for its misuse of this part of God's created order. Perhaps there is no clearer example of how we have distorted the appropriate relationship between ourselves and animals than our very vocabulary. We speak of actions as "humane," although humans often act in ways quite contrary to the meaning of that word. We use "bestial" to describe behavior that is often much more characteristic of humans than of animals. We need to remember that God's covenant includes the whole created order, and behave accordingly.

SHARING THE SCRIPTURE

PREPARING TO TEACH

Preparing Our Hearts

This week's devotional reading is found in Psalm 36:5-9. Note in verse 6 that the psalmist declares that God "save(s) humans and animals, alike." God is surely good! Divine care for humanity and all other creatures is very clearly seen in the covenant that God makes with Noah in Genesis 9. How have you, and perhaps your animal companions, experienced God's saving love? Do you feel secure in God's love? If not, what barriers prevent you from feeling this security?

Pray that you and the adult learners will rest secure in God's saving love.

Preparing Our Minds

Study the background Scripture, Genesis 9:1-17 and lesson Scripture, Genesis 9:1-15. As you prepare, think about what you can trust as being sound and secure.

Write on newsprint:
❑ information for next week's lesson, found under "Continue the Journey."
❑ activities for further spiritual growth in "Continue the Journey."

Option: Set up a worship table with a Bible and different colored candles that will symbolize a rainbow.

Option: Spread out a blanket on a table prior to class. Have straight pins available.

Review the introduction to the quarter, the article entitled "The Concept of Covenant," "Timeline of Events," and "Living Out Our Covenant with God," all of which directly precede this lesson. Decide how you will use each of these helps for this lesson and/or subsequent ones. Also read "Walking the Walk," which pertains to each of the four quarters.

LEADING THE CLASS

(1) Gather to Learn

❖ Welcome the class members and introduce any guests.

❖ Pray that all who have come today will experience God's presence and care.

❖ Distribute quarter sheets of paper and pencils. Ask the students to write something that would give them a sense of real security. For example, someone might write "$2 million, " while another writes "a family that will never forsake me." Ask everyone to place their unsigned papers on a bulletin board, table, or, if possible, a blanket that has been arranged on a table to symbolize a "security blanket."

❖ Encourage the adults to talk about why specific things or people provide security for them. Some students may wish to comment on how certain things provide only the illusion of security.

❖ Read aloud today's focus statement: **We all long for some sense of security. What can we trust as being sound and secure? God promised all creation never to send another flood, and the rainbow serves as a reminder that God is keeping this promise.**

(2) Learn about the Covenant God Made with Noah after the Flood

❖ Begin by giving an overview of this quarter's lessons. The quarterly introduction, found prior to this lesson, will help you to do that.

❖ **Option:** Retell the story of Noah's encounter with God and the flood if there are participants who may not know this story.

❖ Choose a volunteer to read aloud Genesis 9:1-15. If you have placed candles in rainbow colors on the worship table, light them as the Scripture is read.

❖ Select several students to role-play a conversation between Noah and his sons after God had finished speaking to them. Encourage the actors to raise questions, affirm reliance on God, or say whatever they think they would say under such extraordinary circumstances.

❖ Ask the class to look specifically at verses 1-7 and identify how creation is being reordered after the flood. Use information for these verses from Understanding the Scripture as needed.

❖ Invite the adults to examine God's covenant with Noah in verses 8-15 (or 17). Write on newsprint what God is covenanting and who is covered under the terms of this covenant.

❖ Use information for Genesis 9:12-13 in Understanding the Scripture to discuss the sign of this covenant, which is the rainbow.

❖ Give the students an opportunity to state what they know about contemporary and biblical covenants.

❖ Delve deeper into "covenant," which is this quarter's theme, by highlighting excerpts from "The Concept of Covenant," the background article found prior to this session.

❖ **Option:** Talk about some of the binding contracts that we routinely enter into today, such as a mortgage or other loan, marriage, pledges to organizations, and so on.

(1) **Why do we enter into these contracts?**

(2) **What do we hope to gain?**

(3) **What are we willing to give?**

(4) **How are these covenants similar to and different from a covenant with God?**

(3) Remember What God Has Done for the Learners

❖ Point out that the rainbow serves as a sign—a reminder—of the covenant between God and the earth. God was, in effect, promising to be in a relationship not only with Noah's family but also with all creation and the generations that would follow Noah. The rainbow also reminds us of the blessing and security that God's covenant provides for us.

❖ Invite the students to tell stories of times when God provided for them, perhaps in very unexpected ways. What sense of security did they find in God?

❖ **Option:** Here is a discussion starter or story you can read instead of asking the adults to tell their own stories. **The Williams family had been devastated by medical bills related to their father's critical illness and subsequent death. Creditors were hounding them, and there was barely enough money for necessities. God worked through a neighbor, who recognized their desperate circumstances, to rally her church to provide food and money for them. Instead of feeling abandoned and hopeless, Mrs. Williams and her children experienced God's love and care in a powerful new way.**

(4) Identify and Affirm the Security God Provides for the Learners

❖ Distribute strips of different colored construction paper and pencils or markers. Invite the students to write one sentence expressing reliance on God as the source of their security. Here are two examples: *(1) I trust God to care for me in all situations. (2) I know that I can depend upon God to provide all that I need.*

❖ Invite the students to create a rainbow effect by placing their strips of paper on a table or bulletin board.

❖ Read in unison Genesis 9:15, which is today's key verse, as a reminder of God's affirmation to us.

(5) Continue the Journey

❖ Pray that the adults will seek the true security that only God can provide.

❖ Read aloud this preparation for next week's lesson. You may also want to post it on newsprint for the students to copy. **Prepare for next week's session entitled "Trusting Promises" by reading Genesis 17, particularly verses 1-8 and 15-22. Keep this focus in mind as you study: It is difficult to trust a promise that runs counter to our experience and logic. What promises can we trust? God promised to give Abraham descendants and land, and these promises came true despite Abraham's doubts.**

❖ Read aloud the following three ideas. Challenge the students to commit themselves to use these activities as a springboard to spiritual growth.

(1) **Recall that Genesis 9:3 allows humans to eat "every moving thing," which is a change from the vegetarian lifestyle commanded in Genesis 1:29. Think about what you eat. How might a vegetarian diet benefit you—and the animals?**

(2) **Pay careful attention to any contracts you are asked to sign. How are they similar to and different from a covenant with God?**

(3) **Examine records of your material resources. Do you have enough to feel secure? If not, how much would it take to make you feel secure? Will "things" alone ever really make you secure?**

❖ Sing or read aloud "O Worship the King," a hymn that claims our trust in God.

❖ Ask the students to join you in repeating the familiar Mizpah Benediction from Genesis 31:49 to conclude the session: **The LORD watch between you and me, when we are absent one from the other.**

UNIT 1: IN COVENANT WITH GOD
TRUSTING PROMISES

PREVIEWING THE LESSON

Lesson Scripture: Genesis 17:1-8, 15-22
Background Scripture: Genesis 17
Key Verse: Genesis 17:5

Focus of the Lesson:
It is difficult to trust a promise that runs counter to our experience and logic. What promises can we trust? God promised to give Abraham descendants and land, and these promises came true despite Abraham's doubts.

Goals for the Learners:
(1) to study God's covenant with Abraham, who would be the ancestor of a multitude of nations.
(2) to explore their personal experiences of the reality of God's promises.
(3) to affirm trust in God's promises.

Pronunciation Guide:
Abram (ay' bruhm)   El Shaddai (el shad' i)
Ishmael (ish' may uhl)   Sarai (sair' i)

Supplies:
Bibles, newsprint and marker, paper and pencils, hymnals, concordance

---

READING THE SCRIPTURE

NRSV
Genesis 17:1-8, 15-22

¹When Abram was ninety-nine years old, the LORD appeared to Abram, and said to him, "I am God Almighty; walk before me, and be blameless. ²And I will make my covenant between me and you, and will make you exceedingly numerous." ³Then Abram fell on his face; and God said to him, ⁴"As for me, this is my covenant with you:

NIV
Genesis 17:1-8, 15-22

¹When Abram was ninety-nine years old, the LORD appeared to him and said, "I am God Almighty; walk before me and be blameless. ²I will confirm my covenant between me and you and will greatly increase your numbers."

³Abram fell facedown, and God said to him, ⁴"As for me, this is my covenant with

You shall be the ancestor of a multitude of nations. **⁵No longer shall your name be Abram, but your name shall be Abraham; for I have made you the ancestor of a multitude of nations.** ⁶I will make you exceedingly fruitful; and I will make nations of you, and kings shall come from you. ⁷I will establish my covenant between me and you, and your offspring after you throughout their generations, for an everlasting covenant, to be God to you and to your offspring after you. ⁸And I will give to you, and to your offspring after you, the land where you are now an alien, all the land of Canaan, for a perpetual holding; and I will be their God."

¹⁵God said to Abraham, "As for Sarai your wife, you shall not call her Sarai, but Sarah shall be her name. ¹⁶I will bless her, and moreover I will give you a son by her. I will bless her, and she shall give rise to nations; kings of peoples shall come from her." ¹⁷Then Abraham fell on his face and laughed, and said to himself, "Can a child be born to a man who is a hundred years old? Can Sarah, who is ninety years old, bear a child?" ¹⁸And Abraham said to God, "O that Ishmael might live in your sight!" ¹⁹God said, "No, but your wife Sarah shall bear you a son, and you shall name him Isaac. I will establish my covenant with him as an everlasting covenant for his offspring after him. ²⁰As for Ishmael, I have heard you; I will bless him and make him fruitful and exceedingly numerous; he shall be the father of twelve princes, and I will make him a great nation. ²¹But my covenant I will establish with Isaac, whom Sarah shall bear to you at this season next year." ²²And when he had finished talking with him, God went up from Abraham.

you: You will be the father of many nations. **⁵No longer will you be called Abram; your name will be Abraham, for I have made you a father of many nations.** ⁶I will make you very fruitful; I will make nations of you, and kings will come from you. ⁷I will establish my covenant as an everlasting covenant between me and you and your descendants after you for the generations to come, to be your God and the God of your descendants after you. ⁸The whole land of Canaan, where you are now an alien, I will give as an everlasting possession to you and your descendants after you; and I will be their God."

¹⁵God also said to Abraham, "As for Sarai your wife, you are no longer to call her Sarai; her name will be Sarah. ¹⁶I will bless her and will surely give you a son by her. I will bless her so that she will be the mother of nations; kings of peoples will come from her."

¹⁷Abraham fell facedown; he laughed and said to himself, "Will a son be born to a man a hundred years old? Will Sarah bear a child at the age of ninety?" ¹⁸And Abraham said to God, "If only Ishmael might live under your blessing!"

¹⁹Then God said, "Yes, but your wife Sarah will bear you a son, and you will call him Isaac. I will establish my covenant with him as an everlasting covenant for his descendants after him. ²⁰And as for Ishmael, I have heard you: I will surely bless him; I will make him fruitful and will greatly increase his numbers. He will be the father of twelve rulers, and I will make him into a great nation. ²¹But my covenant I will establish with Isaac, whom Sarah will bear to you by this time next year." ²²When he had finished speaking with Abraham, God went up from him.

UNDERSTANDING THE SCRIPTURE

Genesis 17:1. This account is parallel to Genesis 15 which is an earlier writer's version (known by scholars as J or Yahwist) of the making of a covenant between God and

Abraham. Chapter 17 was written by the Priestly authors (known by scholars as P) who worked around the time of the exile. Abram is said to be ninety-nine years old when he experiences this life-changing encounter with God. It is God who initiates the action, who appears to Abram unbidden. God identifies the divine self by a different name than that used in the Bible up to this point. "God Almighty" is the English rendering of *El Shaddai;* it is the name commonly used in accounts of the ancestral period of Hebrew history—the time of Abraham, Isaac, Jacob, and Joseph. *El Shaddai* occurs most often in the book of Job, which may have originated as an oral story in this period. The name probably means "God of the Mountains," referring either to divine power or to the place where God was thought to dwell. Some contemporary scholars think that it is most accurately translated as "God with Breasts" and emphasizes the feminine creative, nurturing aspects of God.

God immediately calls upon Abram to respond with acceptable behavior. He is to live justly and rightly, even as perfectly as possible, because he has been chosen for a very special role in the divine plan. There is no indication that Abram had been especially righteous prior to God's appearance to him, but clearly he is expected to be so as a consequence of it.

Genesis 17:2-4. God's message to Abram is that God intends to enter into a covenant relationship with him and to give him numerous descendants. Indeed, Abram will be the progenitor of many nations of people. Abram can only respond by humbling himself in a posture of utter submission and reverence. It is God who is establishing the covenant, nothing is said here about Abram's part. Nine times in the chapter, God calls it "my covenant." This covenant, unlike the earlier one with Noah, is with a chosen group of persons, rather than with all of humankind and creation.

Genesis 17:5. The name *Abram* meant "exalted father"—an ironic name for one who was not a father at all until late in life and whose fathering becomes such a huge part of Hebrew history. *Abraham* is a variation of the name; it is similar to the Hebrew for "ancestor of a multitude." The changing of Abram's name signifies that he is entering into a new phase of life, that he is in a new relationship.

Genesis 17:6. God tells Abraham that he will not only have many descendants, but that some of them will be royalty. The reference is probably to the later period of Hebrew history when their nation was ruled by great kings such as David and Solomon, as well as their less-illustrious successors.

Genesis 17:7. Here God reveals to Abraham that the covenant relationship will not only be with him, but will also be inherited by his descendants through the generations. It is an everlasting covenant because it expresses the nature and will of the eternal God.

Genesis 17:8. As one who had left his home and family in Mesopotamia to follow the call of God (Genesis 12:1-5), Abraham is a homeless foreigner, a displaced person. Now God tells him that the covenant includes the gift of a homeland. God promises to give Abraham and his heirs possession of the land of Canaan—territory east of the Mediterranean Sea, later called Palestine.

Genesis 17:9-14. Keeping the covenant—Abraham and his descendants' part of the covenant—includes circumcision. This ancient rite involves cutting off the foreskin of the male sexual organ. All males in the household are to be circumcised on the eighth day after birth. This requirement includes slaves as well; if they are acquired when they are older, they are to be circumcised before becoming part of the household. Circumcision is both an act of obedience in response to God's act of covenant making and a physical mark which is the sign of the covenant. Refusal or failure to be circumcised meant that one had violated the covenant, and such a man was to be expelled from the covenant community.

Genesis 17:15-16. The name of Abraham's wife *Sarai* is also to be changed as an indication of her role in this new relationship with God. *Sarah* means "princess" and was a variant of *Sarai.*

Genesis 17:17. The ludicrousness of what God is promising overcomes Abraham's awe and he falls on his face as in verse 3, but this time he is trying to cover his laughter. Not only is he himself almost a century old, but Sarah is decades beyond the time of childbearing.

Genesis 17:18-22. Abraham is already the father of one son—Ishmael, the son of the slave woman Hagar—who is thirteen years old according to Genesis 17:25. He asks that the covenant might be extended through this boy, but God refuses, insisting, despite all the evidence against it, that Abraham and

Sarah will have a son. Ishmael too will be blessed and be the progenitor of a great nation through his twelve sons. (This promise is fulfilled, as recorded in Genesis 25:16.) It will be the child not yet conceived who will inherit the covenant relationship. This son, to be born in a year, is to be named Isaac, meaning "he laughs," as a reminder to his parents of their expression of skepticism. This laughter motif recurs in Genesis 18:12-15 when Sarah laughs at the promise and in Genesis 21:6 when, after Isaac's birth, she says that everyone will join her in the laughter of joy. As Paul affirms in Romans 9:6-13, God is sovereign and has the prerogative to make choices that we do not understand.

Genesis 17:23-27. In these closing verses of the chapter we learn that Abraham acted promptly to fulfill his side of the covenant. He, Ishmael, and all other males in the household are circumcised as sign of the covenant relationship.

INTERPRETING THE SCRIPTURE

The Third Act

God's covenant with Abraham, recounted in Genesis 15 and 17, is a new act of God in the history of salvation that unfolds in the biblical story. This Abrahamic covenant may be thought of as the third stage of the journey. First, there was the covenant with the first human beings, symbolized by Adam and Eve, in Genesis 2:1-3, 15-17. This covenant was broken by human sin. The second covenant was with Noah as discussed last week. The covenant with Abraham is even more significant because it functions as the model by which all biblical covenants are understood. God is the initiator in establishing the covenant relationship and the covenant is everlasting on God's side. In the Abrahamic covenant it is God who swears an oath of fidelity. God is always faithful to the divine

promises and does not withdraw from or nullify the covenant. Human beings, however, can and do break the covenant through disobedience, self-centeredness, and grasping for power. The first humans violated the prohibition that God had established as their side of the relationship. Noah and his descendants fell quickly back into sinfulness. Abraham and his descendants are often disobedient to God. God is ever steadfast; humans are repeatedly unfaithful.

Circumcision and Baptism

Circumcision was a rite widely practiced in the ancient world, as well as the modern. The Hebrews, however, invested it with great religious significance. It was understood as an act of initiation into a community of people who were in special relationship with God. Circumcision symbolized the removal of impurity; it was an act of consecration. It signified entrance into the covenant relationship and served as a guarantee and identifying mark of that identity. Even today the word *tyrb* meaning literally "covenant" is commonly used in Judaism for the circumcision ceremony. It is a joyous occasion, celebrating the bestowal of the covenant sign.

In both Old and New Testaments, circumcision is also spoken of figuratively as well as physically. An example is Deuteronomy 30:6: "The LORD your God will circumcise your heart and the heart of your descendants, so that you will love the LORD your God with all your heart and with all your soul, in order that you may live." Paul uses the same figure in Romans 2:28-29: "For a person is not a Jew who is one outwardly, nor is true circumcision something external and physical. Rather, a person is a Jew who is one inwardly, and real circumcision is a matter of the heart—it is spiritual and not literal."

With few exceptions, physical circumcision has never been a Christian ritual. It is, however, very helpful to us as an analogy when we consider the meaning of Christian baptism. Colossians 2:11-12 makes the relationship clear: "In him also you were circumcised with a spiritual circumcision, by putting off the body of the flesh in the circumcision of Christ; when you were buried with him in baptism, you were also raised with him through faith in the power of God, who raised him from the dead." Baptism is "the circumcision of Christ." It functions for Christians in the same way that circumcision does for Jews—as a ritual of entrance into the covenant community and as a sign of the new covenant in Christ. The community of the new covenant is the Christian church and a person is initiated into it by baptism. Baptism is not something that a person does him or herself. It is something that a person receives. It bestows an identity, a hope, and a mission. It marks us as belonging to Christ and to Christ's church.

Just as infants only eight days old are initiated into the covenant community of Judaism, so we, even as infants, are to receive the sign of the covenant and become a part of the Christian community.

Radical Faithfulness

Covenant with God rests on the radical faithfulness of God. God desires to be in covenant relationship with us and acts to initiate it. Unlike human covenants, divine ones are always valid. The partners in a human marriage can destroy their covenant by living in defiance of it. While we can stray from our covenant with God, live in defiance of it, and reject the identity that it grants, the covenant still stands firm because God is ever faithful. Sinners that we are, we can never be so sinful that God expels us from the covenant community. Instead, God waits for us to repent, return, and reaffirm our allegiance. This is why the sacrament of baptism never needs to be repeated—indeed, cannot be repeated. It is an act of God, establishing God's side of the covenant with us. God's radical faithfulness means that the covenant relationship can never be destroyed. This does not mean that "once saved, always saved." Our salvation is dependent upon our acceptance of divine covenant grace and our living in accord with it. This does mean that "once baptized, always baptized"; once initiated and marked by God, always belonging to God— even if we repudiate that relationship. Think of a child born or adopted into a human family. That child belongs to that family—that is her identity, those are her relationships. She can reject that identity and violate those relationships, but she remains a part of the family, her parents' child, her siblings' sister. So it is in our covenant with God. Our God-given identity and relationship are permanent and we can always choose to accept or to reject them.

Living as persons in covenant relationship with God demands our radical faithfulness. Like Abraham, many times we believe that we have a better idea than God about how our lives should be lived. Abraham wanted God to accept Ishmael as the child of promise. It would be so much easier, so much more reasonable, so much more certain. But God makes a more difficult claim on Abraham and Sarah's lives; God requires them to believe and wait for that which they had not seen and did not think possible. They were like Jesus' disciples who could see no possible way by which the multitude might be fed, once the practical option of collecting food from them to share had yielded far too little. They were like the women at the foot of the cross who thought that all their hopes had been shattered when Christ died. They could not imagine the marvelous thing that God had in store. Radical faithfulness means believing in things that are as yet unseen, trusting God known to us in Jesus Christ even when all the evidence in our practical minds appears to be to the contrary.

God cannot be manipulated. Abraham had taken upon himself the duty of fulfilling God's word by using a way that God had not chosen. He had a child with the slave woman Hagar, a child who could legally be considered as his and Sarah's. He was acting in defiance of God's plan, rather than trusting God to be faithful to the divine promise. We too experience crises of faith when we fail to discern that God has a new and better way, when we fail to trust that God is creating new life. Discontinuity between the experience of our lives and what God has promised may cause us doubt and fear. God's radical faithfulness is our assurance. Our radical faithfulness is our response.

SHARING THE SCRIPTURE

PREPARING TO TEACH

Preparing Our Hearts

This week's devotional reading is found in Hebrews 6:13-20. Here the writer affirms the certainty of God's promise. Moreover, Genesis 22:17, which is quoted in Hebrews 6:14, has clearly been fulfilled. God has indeed kept the covenantal promise with Abraham. Of course, Abraham had "patiently endured" (6:15) for many years until the promise of offspring was ultimately fulfilled in the birth of Isaac. What do you believe about the reliability of God's promises? Do you trust them and expect them to be realized? Write in your spiritual journal about at least one promise you are waiting to have fulfilled.

Pray that you and the adult learners will trust God to be faithful to promises.

Preparing Our Minds

Study the background from Genesis 17 and lesson Scripture, found in verses 1-8, 15-22. As you contemplate these passages, consider whether or not you are willing to trust a promise that runs counter to your experience and to logic.

Write on newsprint:
❑ information for next week's lesson, found under "Continue the Journey."
❑ activities for further spiritual growth in "Continue the Journey."

Option for "Study God's Covenant with Abraham": Prepare a brief lecture on circumcision as a sign of the covenant, based on information in Understanding the Scripture for verses 9-14.

Option for "Explore the Learners' Personal Experiences of the Reality of God's Promises": Create a list of biblical promises, citing book, chapter, and verse, that you can use during the session.

LEADING THE CLASS

(1) Gather to Learn

❖ Welcome the class members and introduce any guests.

❖ Pray that the students will be open to the leading of the Holy Spirit as they study together this day.

❖ Read this quote from Colin Urquhart (1940—): **God is the God of promise. He keeps his word, even when that seems impossible; even when the circumstances seem to point to the opposite.**

❖ Invite the students to recount stories of divine promises that they claimed and hung on to even in the midst of uncertainty.

❖ Read aloud today's focus statement: **It is difficult to trust a promise that runs counter to our experience and logic. What promises can we trust? God promised to give Abraham descendants and land, and these promises came true despite Abraham's doubts.**

(2) Study God's Covenant with Abraham

❖ Choose a volunteer to read Genesis 17:1-8.

■ List on newsprint the terms of the covenant.

■ Compare this covenant with the one we studied last week that God made with Noah. (Note that unlike the covenant with Noah that set no stipulations on him, Abraham is called to "walk before [God], and be blameless" (17:1).)

■ Discuss these questions.

(1) Why would God choose Abram? (Point out that we really have no indication that he was particularly righteous prior to God's appearance before him.)

(2) How did Abram respond to God?

(3) Suppose God had called you to enter into this covenant. How might you have responded?

■ **Option:** Discuss circumcision as a sign of this covenant by using information from Understanding the Scripture for background verses 9-14.

❖ Select someone to read Genesis 17:15-22.

■ Identify the promises God makes to Abraham regarding Sarah and Ishmael. Consider the likelihood of these promises coming true if one simply looks at the situations of Sarah and Ishmael.

■ **Option:** Some students may questions why Abraham's son Isaac is seen as the child of the covenant promise, as stated in Genesis 17:21. Invite the class to express their opinions on the apparent exclusiveness of this relationship and the effect it might have on contemporary politics, especially in the Middle East.

(3) Explore the Learners' Personal Experiences of the Reality of God's Promises

❖ Suggest that the learners look through their Bibles to spot promises that they find especially meaningful. Have a concordance handy to help those who remember a few words but do not know where to locate the promise in the Scriptures. Distribute paper and pencils for the adults to write down the book, chapter, and verse of a few promises that they rely on.

❖ **Option:** If some of your class members are not well-versed in the Bible, make a list of promises yourself prior to class. Read several of them aloud and invite the participants to comment on how a particular promise has been fulfilled in their lives.

❖ Call on students who are willing to

share stories of divine promises they claimed in their own lives that were fulfilled, possibly despite overwhelming odds. You may wish to do this activity in pairs or small groups.

❖ Open the floor for the "flip side" of this discussion. Perhaps some participants will feel that a divine promise was not kept. Hear these concerns in love. If possible, help the adults to see that God does fulfill promises, even if not always in the way that we would hope. Be especially sensitive to persons who feel that the church has not always kept its word. Also be sensitive to members of the class who, like Sarah and Abraham, had (and may continue to have) issues with infertility.

❖ End this portion on a positive note by pointing out that God does bless us with fulfilled promises.

(4) Affirm Trust in God's Promises

❖ Read the second and third paragraphs of "Radical Faithfulness" in Interpreting the Scripture.

❖ Read this affirmation: **Lord, we know that with you all things are possible. We place before you these seemingly impossible situations that are so important to us. We trust, O God, that you will act in accordance with your plan for our lives and the lives of those we love to bring about resolution, for we know your promises are sure. And all the people of God said, AMEN and AMEN.**

(5) Continue the Journey

❖ Pray that all who have participated in today's session will recognize that God's promises are completely trustworthy and will be fulfilled in God's own time.

❖ Read aloud this preparation for next week's lesson. You may also want to post it on newsprint for the students to copy. **Prepare for next week's session entitled "Being Mutually Responsible" by reading background and lesson Scripture from Exodus 19:1-6 and 24:3-8. Ponder these ideas as you study the lesson: Healthy, successful relationships depend on mutual commitment and responsibility. What does it mean to bear mutual responsibility for one another? God's promise in this text called for commitment and respect on both sides: If the people would honor God through obedience, God would treasure the people and set them apart.**

❖ Read aloud the following three ideas. Challenge the students to commit themselves to use these activities as a springboard to spiritual growth.

> **(1) Research Ishmael and his importance to Islam. Consider writing a report to present to the rest of the class.**
>
> **(2) Review promises you have made to people in recent months. Have you kept them? Are you working on them? If not, what changes do you need to make?**
>
> **(3) Keep a log of promises you believe God has made to you. Note the date and way in which each promise is fulfilled.**

❖ Sing or read aloud "The God of Abraham Praise."

❖ Ask the students to join you in repeating the familiar Mizpah Benediction from Genesis 31:49 to conclude the session: **The LORD watch between you and me, when we are absent one from the other.**

UNIT 1: IN COVENANT WITH GOD
BEING MUTUALLY RESPONSIBLE

PREVIEWING THE LESSON

Lesson Scripture: Exodus 19:1-6; 24:3-8
Background Scripture: Exodus 19:1-6; 24:3-8
Key Verse: Exodus 24:3

Focus of the Lesson:

Healthy, successful relationships depend on mutual commitment and responsibility. What does it mean to bear mutual responsibility for one another? God's promise in this text called for commitment and respect on both sides: If the people would honor God through obedience, God would treasure the people and set them apart.

Goals for the Learners:

(1) to place the understanding of God's law, represented by the Ten Commandments, in the context of God's covenant.
(2) to appreciate the need for mutual commitment and respect in covenant relationships.
(3) to re-enact a covenant ceremony.

Pronunciation Guide:

Decalogue (dek' uh log)   Horeb (hor' eb)
Jebel Musa (jeb' el moo' sa)   Rephidim (ref' i dim)
theophany (thee of' uh nee)

Supplies:

Bibles, newsprint and marker, paper and pencils, hymnals, map of the exodus, small token, such as a bookmark, optional photos of Sinai region

READING THE SCRIPTURE

NRSV
Exodus 19:1-6

¹On the third new moon after the Israelites had gone out of the land of Egypt, on that very day, they came into the wilderness of Sinai. ²They had journeyed from

NIV
Exodus 19:1-6

¹In the third month after the Israelites left Egypt—on the very day—they came to the Desert of Sinai. ²After they set out from Rephidim, they entered the Desert of Sinai,

Rephidim, entered the wilderness of Sinai, and camped in the wilderness; Israel camped there in front of the mountain. [3]Then Moses went up to God; the LORD called to him from the mountain, saying, "Thus you shall say to the house of Jacob, and tell the Israelites: [4]You have seen what I did to the Egyptians, and how I bore you on eagles' wings and brought you to myself. [5]Now therefore, if you obey my voice and keep my covenant, you shall be my treasured possession out of all the peoples. Indeed, the whole earth is mine, [6]but you shall be for me a priestly kingdom and a holy nation. These are the words that you shall speak to the Israelites."

and Israel camped there in the desert in front of the mountain.

[3]Then Moses went up to God, and the LORD called to him from the mountain and said, "This is what you are to say to the house of Jacob and what you are to tell the people of Israel: [4]'You yourselves have seen what I did to Egypt, and how I carried you on eagles' wings and brought you to myself. [5]Now if you obey me fully and keep my covenant, then out of all nations you will be my treasured possession. Although the whole earth is mine, [6]you will be for me a kingdom of priests and a holy nation.' These are the words you are to speak to the Israelites."

Exodus 24:3-8

[3]**Moses came and told the people all the words of the LORD and all the ordinances; and all the people answered with one voice, and said, "All the words that the LORD has spoken we will do."** [4]And Moses wrote down all the words of the LORD. He rose early in the morning, and built an altar at the foot of the mountain, and set up twelve pillars, corresponding to the twelve tribes of Israel. [5]He sent young men of the people of Israel, who offered burnt offerings and sacrificed oxen as offerings of well-being to the LORD. [6]Moses took half of the blood and put it in basins, and half of the blood he dashed against the altar. [7]Then he took the book of the covenant, and read it in the hearing of the people; and they said, "All that the LORD has spoken we will do, and we will be obedient." [8]Moses took the blood and dashed it on the people, and said, "See the blood of the covenant that the LORD has made with you in accordance with all these words."

Exodus 24:3-8

[3]**When Moses went and told the people all the LORD's words and laws, they responded with one voice, "Everything the LORD has said we will do."** [4]Moses then wrote down everything the LORD had said.

He got up early the next morning and built an altar at the foot of the mountain and set up twelve stone pillars representing the twelve tribes of Israel. [5]Then he sent young Israelite men, and they offered burnt offerings and sacrificed young bulls as fellowship offerings to the LORD. [6]Moses took half of the blood and put it in bowls, and the other half he sprinkled on the altar. [7]Then he took the Book of the Covenant and read it to the people. They responded, "We will do everything the LORD has said; we will obey."

[8]Moses then took the blood, sprinkled it on the people and said, "This is the blood of the covenant that the LORD has made with you in accordance with all these words."

UNDERSTANDING THE SCRIPTURE

Introduction. In the last lesson, we focused on Abraham and learned about the covenant that God established with him and

would continue through his and Sarah's son, Isaac. God promised that Abraham's descendants would create many nations (or tribes) and gave them ownership of the land of Canaan. Decades later, Abraham's grandson Jacob was the one through whom the covenant relationship would be continued and passed on to his twelve sons. During this period, the Hebrew people left Canaan to escape famine conditions and moved to Egypt where one of the twelve brothers was already living. Joseph had been sold into slavery in Egypt by his jealous brothers, but through his God-given talents had become a very high official in pharaoh's government. During Joseph's lifetime his family and their descendants were well-cared for in Egypt, but later a different dynasty of rulers forced them into slavery. After more than four centuries of bondage, the Hebrews escaped under the leadership of Moses. God enabled them to pass through the sea and go into the desert wilderness. For forty years the Hebrew people lived in the desert; some of the most formative events of their history occurred there.

Exodus 19:1-2. The events recounted in this chapter took place three months after the Hebrews had left Egypt. They had traveled to the eastern part of the Arabian peninsula to the foot of a mountain called Sinai or Horeb. Most scholars believe that this was the approximately 7400 foot tall mountain known today as Jebel Musa. The Hebrew people camped at this place for eleven months. The events recorded in the rest of Exodus, all of Leviticus, and almost all of the first ten chapters of Numbers happened during that time.

Exodus 19:3. Sinai was a sacred location chosen by God as a place of meeting. Later in this chapter there is a dramatic theophany—a direct encounter with God. The mountain is described in terms that evoke the image of a volcano, but, since there is no sign of volcanic activity in the area, was probably imagery of a violent thunderstorm. Moses is the representative of the people and he alone climbs the mountain to hear God's voice and carry back the message. The Hebrews are often referred to as

Israelites because Jacob had been given the name Israel (Genesis 32:28).

Exodus 19:4. God reminds the Israelites of their deliverance from Egypt. They have escaped pharaoh and been brought to meet God. The metaphor of God as an eagle is a strong mother image that evokes the idea that God has carried them safely through danger and cared for them. (See Deuteronomy 32:10-12 for an expansion on this image.) As in the covenant with Abraham, God is the initiator, and it is God's gracious action that makes the covenant possible.

Exodus 19:5-6. God tells the Israelites that all peoples on earth are God's, but that they alone have the opportunity for a special relationship with God. If they will obey the covenant laws which he is giving them through Moses, they will be commissioned as God's instrument on behalf of the rest of the world. These words are very similar to 1 Peter 2:5, 9 which is part of a baptismal sermon based on this Old Testament passage. Israel is to be "holy"—consecrated or set apart for service to God. Israel is to be "priestly"—to function as mediator between God and the people of other nations.

Exodus 24:3. Moses, acting as mediator between God and the people, announces to them God's unconditional laws (the Decalogue or Ten Commandments), as well as case laws for particular situations (the book of the covenant found in Exodus 21:1–23:19). These are the legal expression of the covenant—the regulations and responsibilities of the Hebrews' side of the covenant. The people affirm that they accept and will obey.

Exodus 24:4-5. Moses recorded the laws in writing and then built an altar and set up twelve stone pillars. The altar represented God and the pillars, the twelve tribes into which Israel was organized—each tracing its ancestry back to one of the sons of Jacob/Israel. These events preceded the establishment of the priesthood and any man could offer sacrifices on behalf of the whole people. Slaying and burning animals was a common way of thanking, praising, and petitioning God. Leviticus 1 and 3 describe in detail the sacrificial system in its fully developed pattern.

Exodus 24:6. Because the Hebrews believed that blood was the very essence and vehicle of life, it had great religious significance. In Genesis 9, as a part of the covenant with Noah, God had allowed human beings to use animals for food, with this stipulation: "Only, you shall not eat flesh with its life, that is, its blood" (9:4). Covenants were ratified in blood as a sign of utter commitment and dedication. A part of the significance of circumcision as a sign of the covenant between God and Abraham was the shedding of blood that the act required. The concept of the importance of blood is foundational to the New Testament understanding of the death of Jesus Christ.

In Matthew 26:28, Jesus said to his disciples the night before he was to be crucified: "Drink from it [the cup], all of you; for this is my blood of the covenant, which is poured out for many for the forgiveness of sins." Here Moses collects the blood that was drained from the sacrificed animals and throws half of it on the altar, representing the divine side of the covenant.

Exodus 24:7-8. Moses reads to the gathered people all of the covenant laws that God had communicated to him on the mountain. The people promise that they will be obedient to these commands. In response to their pledge of fidelity, Moses throws the other half of the blood on the crowd, symbolizing the relationship with God that they had ratified. The two sides of the covenant relationship were established, with promises and responsibilities on both.

INTERPRETING THE SCRIPTURE

What Does It Mean to Be
God's Chosen People?

This lesson and the one last Sunday are clear in their statements that God chose the Hebrews—the people of Israel—out of all the peoples of the earth. God's reasons are not revealed; indeed, they are not even mentioned. For the Hebrews what was important was to understand what it was that they had been chosen for, not why they had been chosen. God's choice or election of them was a foundational part of their self-understanding as a people. They knew that they had not been selected because of any particular piety or power. They were no better than any other people. And yet, God had come to Abraham, sent him on a journey, and promised him a multitude of descendants and a homeland. Even more important, God promised to be with Abraham and his descendants in a special way. God bound the divine self in relationship with

Israel by making promises and assuming responsibilities. These covenant promises were passed on from one generation to another of Abraham's heirs. In this lesson, we see God spelling out the demands of the covenant relationship, the laws that Israel was to obey. To be God's chosen people meant being expected to live in accord with God's nature and will.

Many Christians struggle with the idea of God's choice of the people later called Jews. Perhaps it seems strange to us that God would "play favorites." Perhaps the sufferings of the Jews through the centuries make any idea of them as especially chosen very hard to accept. But, the Old Testament is abundantly clear on the point and the teachings of both Jesus and Paul confirm this special relationship. If we are to understand the Bible, we must understand the concept of the chosen people.

The beginning point is a realization that all the earth and all its peoples belong to

God. God elects one nation of people to serve as an instrument for the divine purpose in the world. Israel is chosen not for its own benefit and blessing, but in order to bring the benefit and blessing of salvation to all people. The God of the Bible is a God who works in and through human history. God's choice of Israel meant that in their history—in their relationship with God and with other peoples—the divine nature and purpose would be most clearly communicated. In the history of God's work of salvation, Israel would have a special role.

But, what does this election mean for Israel? In Exodus 19:5, the nation is called God's "treasured possession." The relationship will be not only one of utility—God's using the Hebrews for God's purpose—but also one of loving intimacy. The nation is described as "a priestly kingdom" in the next verse. The ancient service of priests in many cultures was that of a mediator between humans and God. Even today, this idea shapes some of our interpretation of the role of ordained clergy. Through Israel God would reach out to all humankind. Israel would be a bridge, a crossover, a point of connection. In the same verse, Israel is called "a holy nation." To be holy is to be consecrated for service to God, to be set apart for divine purposes. Much would be required of Israel and much would be afflicted upon it as a result of this role.

An obvious question is whether or not the Jewish people are still God's chosen today. Christians differ sharply in their answers. I believe that God's election was for all time and that the Jews still play a unique part in God's work in the world. I believe that God still is in a special relationship with the Jews as God's chosen people. Certainly though, the role of instrument or mediator of salvation now belongs also to the Christian church. We are the community of the new covenant—a covenant sealed by the blood of Christ rather than the blood of circumcision or of sacrificial animals. In 1 Peter 2:9, the language of Exodus 19 is repeated as descriptive of Gentiles—non-Jews—who had come into saving relationship with God and who, along with converted Jews, composed the New Testament Christian church. A major theme of the Old Testament is that God is in covenant relationship with and works for our salvation through the history of his chosen community of Israel. A major theme of the New Testament is that there is another community in covenant relationship with God and through whose history God works for salvation. This community is the body of Christ, established through his life, death, and resurrection.

The Place of Law

Christians sometimes speak of law as the opposite of grace, and we are sometimes taught that the gospel frees us from the demands of law. This idea needs careful examination, because it is only partially true. In the Exodus account, law is the product of divine grace; law is granted not imposed; it is a gift not a burden. When, at Mount Sinai, God gave the Decalogue and the book of the covenant to Israel through Moses, it was in order to be certain that the people understood what it meant to live in covenant relationship with God. Law was not a way of entering into the covenant; the covenant was already established. Law was the spelling out of the content of the life of faith to which the community was called. Covenants are always two-sided; they involve promises and responsibilities for both parties. God had told Israel what God would do for them; now God tells Israel what is expected from them. The people promise to obey the law. Divine action and human response are paired.

Many of the specific laws that are recorded in Exodus, Leviticus, Numbers, and Deuteronomy are shaped by the culture of ancient Israel. They were not intended to express God's eternal commands for every time and place. Even within these books, ordinances are placed at various points in the story, differing as history moves on. As the poet James Russell Lowell expressed it: "New occasions teach new duties; time makes ancient good uncouth; They must upward still and onward, Who would keep abreast of truth." It is the concept or principle of law that binds Christians as well as Jews. Our God who has entered into covenant with us expects, even demands, right behavior from us. This behavior is usually defined in terms of what will make life best for the most people. God desires that the order and justice intended in cre-

ation might be made manifest in human lives. Obeying God's law is a way of communicating the nature of God and witnessing to what God has done. Israel is to treat other people as God has treated them. The law is a collection of practical ordinances that specify what this means in the actual situations of life. Israel is given the task of advancing righteousness and conforming the social order to God's will. The covenant people are to shape their lives around the eternal values of compassion and justice.

SHARING THE SCRIPTURE

PREPARING TO TEACH

Preparing Our Hearts

This week's devotional reading is found in Psalm 119:33-40. In this section of a psalm extolling the glories of God's law, the writer asks God to teach the divine law so that he may faithfully keep it throughout his life. In contrast to the idea that some Christians have that the law is an onerous burden, the psalmist proclaims that he delights in God's commandments. Spend time this week reading from the Torah, the teachings of God, found in the first five books of the Bible.

Pray that you and the adult learners will seek to know and fulfill God's expectations for you.

Preparing Our Minds

Study the background and lesson Scripture, Exodus 19:1-6 and 24:3-8. Think about what it means to say that relationships are dependent upon mutual commitment and responsibility.

Write on newsprint:

❑ information for next week's lesson, found under "Continue the Journey."

❑ activities for further spiritual growth in "Continue the Journey."

Locate a map showing the exodus.

Plan comments on the Understanding the Scripture portions you will use in "Place the Understanding of God's Law in the Context of God's Covenant."

Select bookmarks to give to the class.

LEADING THE CLASS

(1) Gather to Learn

❖ Welcome the class members and introduce any guests.

❖ Pray that those who have come today will appreciate the relationship God offers to us through the covenant in Christ.

❖ Invite the students to imagine that they have a contract to write a book entitled *How to Build and Maintain Successful Relationships.* Help them to list on newsprint the main points they would want to include in such a book. Some adults may want to suggest chapter headings.

❖ Read aloud today's focus statement: **Healthy, successful relationships depend on mutual commitment and responsibility. What does it mean to bear mutual responsibility for one another? God's promise in** this text called for commitment and respect on both sides: If the people would honor God through obedience, God would treasure the people and set them apart.

(2) Place the Understanding of God's Law in the Context of God's Covenant

Covenants

❖ Review with the class the covenants you have studied to date between God and Noah and God, and Sarah and Abraham. Recall the features of these covenants, as well as their signs (the rainbow and circumcision, respectively).

❖ Choose one person to read Exodus 19:1-2.

■ Use the information for these two verses in Understanding the Scripture to set the scene for today's story.

■ Locate Rephidim, the wilderness of Sinai, and Mount Horeb/Sinai on a map. If you have any photos of these areas, they would help the students to better understand the terrain and conditions there.

❖ Select a volunteer to read Exodus 19:3-6.

■ Note how God recalls the divine care and protection already afforded to the people.

■ Identify the mutual responsibilities inherent in this covenantal relationship by analyzing what God offers to the people and what God expects of them. You may want to list these ideas on newsprint. Point out that this section comes just prior to God's giving of the Decalogue.

❖ Read Exodus 24:3-8. Ask the class to read the people's response in verses 3b and 7b.

■ Use the information from these verses in Understanding the Scripture to explain any symbolism of this covenant ratification ceremony. Be sure to note the significance of the use of blood.

■ Note that in verse 3 when Moses

refers to "all the words of the LORD and all the ordinances" he is speaking about the Ten Commandments and the book of the covenant.

■ Invite the students to page through Exodus 20, 21, 22, and 23:1-19, which include the Ten Commandments and the book of the covenant. Identify the promises God makes to the people and what God expects of the people.

■ Discuss these questions with the students.

(1) What impact do you think these laws would have on the people individually and as a society?

(2) Which of these laws seem particularly appropriate for us today—even if they are laws that we do not currently observe?

(3) Point out that in verses 3 and 7 the people promise to be obedient unto God. Suppose you had been among the crowd. Could you have honestly promised to do all that God had commanded? Why or why not?

(3) Appreciate the Need for Mutual Commitment and Respect in Covenant Relationships

❖ Divide the class into three groups, or multiples of three if the class is large. Distribute newsprint and a marker to each group. Assign groups to identify characteristics of:

Group 1: a relationship between two people who are mutually committed to one another.

Group 2: a relationship between a person and Christ who are mutually committed to one another.

Group 3: a relationship among church members who are mutually committed to one another.

❖ Provide time for the groups to report back to the entire class. Post the newsprint, if possible.

❖ **Option:** If time permits, compare what the students have written for this activity with the ideas they suggested for the "Gather to Learn" activity. Note any similarities and differences.

❖ Encourage the students to comment on any insights they have gained about how their relationships with Christ and with other people could be better if all parties involved were mutually responsible to one another.

(4) Reenact a Covenant Ceremony

❖ Invite the students to look at the ideas they have previously generated concerning mutually responsible relationships.

❖ Select several of these ideas/behaviors that would be appropriate for relationships among class members. Write them on a sheet of newsprint. If time permits, reword the ideas so that they are in a form such as "We covenant together to . . ."

❖ Talk about these ideas until you have built a consensus. Note that while we are looking for everyone's input here, God simply presented the laws to the people and their only option was the choice to obey them or not.

❖ Encourage the students to read aloud what they have written, pledging that they will uphold this covenant.

❖ Distribute whatever small token you have been able to obtain, such as bookmark with the Ten Commandments, and tell the class to consider this as a sign of the covenant you have made and ratified together.

(5) Continue the Journey

❖ Pray that the participants will go forth with renewed commitment to be responsi-

ble for the people with whom they are in relationships.

❖ Read aloud this preparation for next week's lesson. You may also want to post it on newsprint for the students to copy. **Prepare for next week's session entitled "Making Life's Choices" by reading Joshua 24, especially verses 1, 14-24. Keep these ideas in mind as you prepare the lesson: Life is full of choices. What choices matter most? Joshua told the people that the most important choice they could make was to serve God.**

❖ Read aloud the following three ideas. Challenge the students to commit themselves to use these activities as a springboard to spiritual growth.

   (1) Research the meaning of a blood covenant. What is involved in making such a covenant? What is at stake when parties enter into this kind of relationship?

   (2) Reread Exodus 19:3-6 and compare it to 1 Peter 2:9. Write in your spiritual journal about how you see yourself in relation to these verses. In what ways do you envision yourself as "chosen," part of the "priesthood" and part of the "holy nation" that is God's own people?

   (3) Make a special effort this week to bear responsibility for a person with whom you are in some kind of relationship.

❖ Sing or read aloud "On Eagle's Wings," which is based on Exodus 19:4.

❖ Ask the students to join you in repeating the familiar Mizpah Benediction from Genesis 31:49 to conclude the session: **The LORD watch between you and me, when we are absent one from the other.**

UNIT 1: IN COVENANT WITH GOD
MAKING LIFE'S CHOICES

PREVIEWING THE LESSON

Lesson Scripture: Joshua 24:1, 14-24
Background Scripture: Joshua 24
Key Verse: Joshua 24:15

Focus of the Lesson:
Life is full of choices. What choices matter most? Joshua told the people that the most important choice they could make was to serve God.

Goals for the Learners:
(1) to hear Joshua's final words to the tribes of Israel at Shechem.
(2) to relate the covenant renewal ceremony to their own lives.
(3) to choose to serve God.

Pronunciation Guide:
Mesopotamia (mes uh puh tay' mee uh)
Shechem (shek' uhm)

Supplies:
Bibles, newsprint and marker, paper and pencils, hymnals, map showing Shechem

---

READING THE SCRIPTURE

NRSV
Joshua 24:1, 14-24

¹Then Joshua gathered all the tribes of Israel to Shechem, and summoned the elders, the heads, the judges, and the officers of Israel; and they presented themselves before God.

¹⁴"Now therefore revere the LORD, and serve him in sincerity and in faithfulness; put away the gods that your ancestors served beyond the River and in Egypt, and serve the LORD. **¹⁵Now if you are unwilling to serve the LORD, choose this day whom you will serve,**

NIV
Joshua 24:1, 14-24

¹Then Joshua assembled all the tribes of Israel at Shechem. He summoned the elders, leaders, judges and officials of Israel, and they presented themselves before God.

¹⁴"Now fear the LORD and serve him with all faithfulness. Throw away the gods your forefathers worshiped beyond the River and in Egypt, and serve the LORD. **¹⁵But if serving the LORD seems undesirable to you, then choose for yourselves this day whom you will serve,**

whether the gods your ancestors served in the region beyond the River or the gods of the Amorites in whose land you are living; **but as for me and my household, we will serve the LORD."**

[16]Then the people answered, "Far be it from us that we should forsake the LORD to serve other gods; [17]for it is the LORD our God who brought us and our ancestors up from the land of Egypt, out of the house of slavery, and who did those great signs in our sight. He protected us along all the way that we went, and among all the peoples through whom we passed; [18]and the LORD drove out before us all the peoples, the Amorites who lived in the land. Therefore we also will serve the LORD, for he is our God."

[19]But Joshua said to the people, "You cannot serve the LORD, for he is a holy God. He is a jealous God; he will not forgive your transgressions or your sins. [20]If you forsake the LORD and serve foreign gods, then he will turn and do you harm, and consume you, after having done you good." [21]And the people said to Joshua, "No, we will serve the LORD!" [22]Then Joshua said to the people, "You are witnesses against yourselves that you have chosen the LORD, to serve him." And they said, "We are witnesses." [23]He said, "Then put away the foreign gods that are among you, and incline your hearts to the LORD, the God of Israel." [24]The people said to Joshua, "The LORD our God we will serve, and him we will obey."

whether the gods your forefathers served beyond the River, or the gods of the Amorites, in whose land you are living. **But as for me and my household, we will serve the LORD."**

[16]Then the people answered, "Far be it from us to forsake the LORD to serve other gods! [17]It was the LORD our God himself who brought us and our fathers up out of Egypt, from that land of slavery, and performed those great signs before our eyes. He protected us on our entire journey and among all the nations through which we traveled. [18]And the LORD drove out before us all the nations, including the Amorites, who lived in the land. We too will serve the LORD, because he is our God."

[19]Joshua said to the people, "You are not able to serve the LORD. He is a holy God; he is a jealous God. He will not forgive your rebellion and your sins. [20]If you forsake the LORD and serve foreign gods, he will turn and bring disaster on you and make an end of you, after he has been good to you."

[21]But the people said to Joshua, "No! We will serve the LORD."

[22]Then Joshua said, "You are witnesses against yourselves that you have chosen to serve the LORD."

"Yes, we are witnesses," they replied.

[23]"Now then," said Joshua, "throw away the foreign gods that are among you and yield your hearts to the LORD, the God of Israel."

[24]And the people said to Joshua, "We will serve the LORD our God and obey him."

UNDERSTANDING THE SCRIPTURE

Introduction to the book of Joshua. After the dramatic experience of covenant-making with God at Mount Sinai, which we considered last Sunday, the Hebrew people remained in the desert wilderness for several decades. Moses led them in this convoluted sojourn during which they received miraculous help from God in order to survive. God had told Moses that they must stay in the wilderness until the generation that left Egypt had died. At the end of Deuteronomy, Moses himself died—within sight of the promised land, but not allowed to enter it. Leadership of the Israelites passed to Joshua. At the beginning of the book of Joshua, the people were encamped east of the Jordan River. God commanded them to go into the land and held back the waters of the Jordan for them to cross over. The rest of the book recounts a series of military victories as the Israelites defeated the various Canaanite powers. The conquered land was divided and assigned to the tribes as their territories. The final chapter, which is our subject today, is Joshua's farewell address as he prepares to die. In this address, he calls upon the people to renew their covenant with God.

Joshua 24:1. Shechem had developed into an important religious and political center for Israel and may even have been the site where the ark of the covenant was kept. As the mediator of the covenant—the role he had been given after the death of Moses, Joshua assembles the community for a ceremony of covenant renewal. The gathered people were made up of the tribal confederation of Israel, plus people from Shechem and other Canaanite areas who wanted to join them peacefully.

Joshua 24:2. Joshua uses the standard prophetic formula to introduce his words as being from God. A summary of God's actions in Hebrew history begins here and continues through verse 13. The account of ancestral history begins in Mesopotamia with mention of Abraham's father Terah and the acknowledgment that he served other gods.

Joshua 24:3. God had brought Abraham out of that environment, across the Euphrates River, and into Canaan, where he fathered Isaac.

Joshua 24:4. Isaac fathered twin sons, Esau and Jacob. Esau was not the chosen one through whom the covenant would be continued, but he is given land as a possession. The moving of Jacob and his sons to Egypt is not explained in this sharply abbreviated summary of the stories in Genesis 11-50.

Joshua 24:5-7. Beginning in verse 5 and continuing through verse 13, God speaks through Joshua with both second and third person pronouns to refer to the Hebrews. This makes vivid the continuity of the Hebrews' present with their past. God's actions in the lives of the ancestors are applied to new generations. The exodus—the great event through which Israel was constituted—is told. The emphasis is on God's marvelous acts of sending plagues on Egypt, enabling the Hebrews to cross the Sea of Reeds, and destroying their Egyptian pursuers. (Sea of Reeds is the accurate translation of what is often rendered as the Red Sea.) These dramatic events of liberation are followed by the wilderness years. These verses refer to the events in the book of Exodus. Note that there is no reference to the covenant at Sinai.

Joshua 24:8. The small Amorite kingdom on the eastern side of the Jordan River was destroyed by the Israelites because its king would not allow them to pass through his territory. (See Numbers 21:21-32.)

Joshua 24:9-10. The kingdom of Moab was located just south of the Amorites. Its king tried to enlist a Mesopotamian soothsayer to curse Israel. The soothsayer Balaam was a worshiper of the God of Israel and blessed Israel instead. (See Numbers 22–23.)

Joshua 24:11. This verse lists some of the kingdoms and people that God enabled the Hebrews to conquer as they fought their way through the land. Note that the city of Jericho is only mentioned, in contrast to the dramatic story of its fall in Joshua 6.

Joshua 24:12-13. These verses expand on God's words at the end of verse 11: "I handed them over to you." It was the power of God on their behalf and not the strength of the Israelites that allowed them to win these victories. "The hornet" may be a reference to Egypt, part of which used the hornet as its symbol. More likely, it could be translated as "panic." Elsewhere we are told that the fear of the Israelites preceded them and demoralized their enemies. Israel is the beneficiary of God's actions for them and the present generation has inherited the blessings of land, towns, and fruits.

Joshua 24:14-15. Joshua calls on the people to make a choice between the God who has blessed them so richly throughout their history and the false gods of Mesopotamia and Canaan.

Joshua 24:16-18. The gathered people answer Joshua by affirming their understanding of God's actions and promising to serve God faithfully.

Joshua 24:19-24. Joshua challenges the people by questioning their willingness to obey and serve God alone, rejecting the false gods that tempt them. The gathered crowd are vehement in their profession of loyalty.

Joshua 24:25-28. In response to their profession, Joshua reminds the people of the laws that they are promising to obey. He writes these ordinances in a law book so that they will be available to guide Israel. It is implied that the oak tree is the same one that Abraham traveled to when he left Mesopotamia and where he first received the promise of the land (Genesis 12:6). The stone pillar that he erects is a tangible reminder of this renewal of covenant loyalty.

Joshua 24:29-33. The chapter and book close with the death and burial of Joshua, praise for the obedience of the people, the reburial of Joseph's remains which had been brought from Egypt, and the death and burial of a priest associated with Joshua. Joshua and Joseph are said to have died at the same age. This is a way of establishing a parallel between the one who took Israel into Egypt and the one who brought them back to the land.

INTERPRETING THE SCRIPTURE

"Not by Your Sword or by Your Bow. . . ."

At numerous places in the Old Testament, we find recitals of the major events in Israel's salvation history—accounts of the mighty acts of God on their behalf. These accounts vary significantly depending upon the interest and emphasis of the particular writer. (Deuteronomy 25:4-9, Psalms 78, 105, 106, 135, and 136 are good examples.) All of these summaries are completely clear that it is God who has played the leading role in the drama of salvation. Israel well understood that God took the initiative for God's own reasons to determine the outcome of historical events. If they were in danger of forgetting, God reminded them. This was essential because if Israel failed to recognize the role of God, it could not comprehend and live out its role as covenant people.

To put it in New Testament terms: God is a God of grace, not simply a God of law. In fact, law is itself grace, because it reveals God's will so that the covenant people can live in accord with it. Israel could not and did not do anything for themselves, except react to what God did. As far back in Christian history as Augustine in the fourth century, this divine grace has been called *prevenient.* (This is, of course, the English translation.) The word *prevenient* is one of the many English words whose meaning is not immediately clear due to changes in usage over the years. *Prevenient* means to precede or to come before. John Wesley, the founder of Methodism, grounded his entire theological understanding on this concept. Grace always comes first. Human response can only take place in response to grace. At every step of our salvation journey, God's initiative, God's loving outreach, is necessary in order to enable us to choose to accept or to reject.

"A Jealous God"

It may seem strange to attribute jealousy to God, since jealousy is not usually thought of as an admirable quality in human beings. But, this is terminology with which God describes the divine self so we need to comprehend its meaning. God's jealousy is paired with the grace discussed above. It is because God is jealous that God makes radical demands upon the Israelites and upon us. This quality of jealousy is one of the attributes that sets the God of Judaism and Christianity apart from other deities. In many religions of both the ancient and modern worlds, a multiplicity of gods are recognized and worshiped. There may be gods and goddesses for the various aspects of nature and for diverse situations in human life. The gods may specialize in particular kinds of functions in relation to people. In the Canaanite culture into which the Israelites were entering, there was belief in numerous gods, including idols of wood and stone. The God who enters into covenant with Israel is adamant that God will not be simply one of a pantheon. This has been stated in the Ten Commandments (Exodus 20:1-3) and is reiterated in the covenant renewal at Shechem. Israel's God demands an exclusive relationship and radical obedience. There are to be no divided loyalties, no "hedging of bets," no other deities "on the side."

The covenant between God and Israel, as well as between Christ and the church, is relational. To be in covenant with God is to define oneself as God's, to pledge total allegiance to God's will. It is not a covenant that once entered into can be set aside from the daily realities of life or made abstract and impersonal. To be in covenant relationship is to be continually focused on God, constantly in communication with God, always obedient to God's commands. Covenant people are to live in ways that unfailingly reflect God's holiness. The keeping of law is the outward expression of complete devotion to God. The jealousy of God warns us away from any attempts to please God by partial commitment and superficial obedience. Of course, such perfection is impossible for us; we depend always on divine grace to compensate and to forgive our shortfalls.

In chapter 9, Book IV, of his classic book *Mere Christianity,* C. S. Lewis tells a parable borrowed from George MacDonald about a house in order to illustrate God's will for our lives. He says that often when people come to Christ they are seeking to improve their lives, to be reformed, made better people. They ask God to do some repairs of the house—fix the roof, repair the steps, replace broken windows, put on a new coat of paint. But, when God goes to work they are amazed, even frightened. God is not stopping with repairs; God is completely remodeling—building new wings, running up towers, expanding and beautifying until the former house can scarcely be recognized. God is doing this, Lewis says, because while the person might have wanted only repairs on their little house, God is building a mansion and God intends to come and live there. Being in covenant relationship with God demands surrender and transformation.

Choosing God

As Joshua spoke to the assembled people, his emphasis was on what God had done in the past among their ancestors in the faith and the necessity of choice for the present generation. It was not and is not enough to inherit the covenant; conscious decision is required. In most denominations, infants and children can be baptized into the covenant community long before they are capable of making choices. This is analogous to the initiation of Hebrew boys by circumcision, the act which marked them as members of the covenant community. But as Christians we insist that there comes a point in an individual's life when he or she is mature enough to make moral decisions and undertake responsibilities. This does not mean that the person understands all that is involved in living in covenant with God. There is no age at which that is really true. The person having reached an age of moral accountability can and must choose whether or not he or she wants to affirm a desire to be in relationship with God and live as God commands. Many denominations use the name confirmation for the ritual in which that choice is professed. Joshua 24 points out to us that such decisions and professions are not necessarily permanent in the lives of inconstant human beings. Therefore, there is the need for periodic reaffirmations in which persons can proclaim again their choice of God and commit themselves anew to the relationship and responsibility of the covenant.

God has given us the gift of free will and endowed us with the ability to choose who we will serve. As Christians, we have a huge advantage over the people of Joshua's day. They knew God through the divine action in their history and through the laws and ordinances that stipulated how they were to live. We know God that way as well. We also have the fullness of divine revelation in Jesus Christ who showed us God's nature and will, and showed us who we are to be and how we are to live. We can choose God in the light of Jesus Christ.

SHARING THE SCRIPTURE

PREPARING TO TEACH

Preparing Our Hearts

This week's devotional reading is found in Psalm 51:1-12, which is a penitential psalm, ascribed to David after the prophet Nathan had called him to account for his adulterous relationship with Bathsheba. As you contemplate this psalm, think about how it speaks to God on your behalf regarding sin and guilt. When you do today's background reading, consider this psalm in light of Joshua 24:19, where Joshua states that God "will not forgive your transgressions or your sins." Would the psalmist agree with this assessment? Why or why not? Call upon God to create in you a clean heart this day and then make choices that will enable you to live with purity.

Pray that you and the adult learners will recognize sin and make a conscious choice to avoid it.

Preparing Our Minds

Study the background Scripture, which is Joshua 24, and lesson Scripture, Joshua 24:1, 14-24. As you work with this material think about all the choices you are required to make and which ones matter most.

Write on newsprint:
❑ information for next week's lesson, found under "Continue the Journey."
❑ activities for further spiritual growth in "Continue the Journey."

LEADING THE CLASS

(1) Gather to Learn

❖ Welcome the class members and introduce any guests.
❖ Pray that all who have gathered will be ready and willing to serve God.
❖ Read aloud this list of choices. Tell the class they can only vote for one choice per pair. Have those who are in favor of the choice signify by standing, if able, or raising

their hands. Tell the class there are no right or wrong answers here.

- a really gooey dessert OR a low-fat, low-calorie snack.
- an extra day a week off OR a bigger paycheck.
- a vehicle that was very affordable that you didn't like OR one that stretched your budget but that you really enjoyed driving.
- a family that loved you OR a public that adored you.
- an exciting night out OR a quiet night at home.
- a job you dislike that pays well OR a job that is right up your alley but does not pay well.

❖ Read aloud today's focus statement: **Life is full of choices. What choices matter most? Joshua told the people that the most important choice they could make was to serve God.**

(2) Hear Joshua's Final Words to the Tribes of Israel at Shechem

❖ Locate Shechem on a map.
- Choose a narrator and someone to read Joshua's words in Joshua 24:1, 14-24. Ask students who use the same translation to read in unison 24:16b-18, 21, 22c, 24. Point out that just as the heads of households would agree with Joshua's request, so, too, these readers are representatives who are agreeing on behalf of the entire class.
- Use information under "A Jealous God" to talk about Joshua's seemingly strange reply that the people cannot serve God because God is holy and jealous.
- Identify with the students some of the "radical demands" that they believe God is making upon their lives. In other words, in what ways must they live differently from their non-Christian neighbors in order to be loyal to God?

❖ Talk with the class about their understanding of what it means to choose God. What does that entail? How does one's choice of God show forth in the way one lives?

❖ Invite the students to give some concrete examples to illustrate how one's choice to serve God affects their lives.

(3) Relate the Covenant Renewal Ceremony to the Learners' Lives

❖ Point out that to participate in a covenant renewal ceremony, one must be related to God, not on one's own terms but as the transformed person God intends those who live in a covenant relationship to be.

❖ Distribute paper and pencils. Read aloud this parable told by C. S. Lewis in *Mere Christianity,* and referenced in "A Jealous God" in Interpreting the Scripture.

"Imagine yourself living in a house. God comes to rebuild that house. At first, perhaps, you can understand what He is doing. He is getting the drains right and stopping the leaks in the roof and so on: you knew that those jobs needed doing and so you are not surprised. But presently He starts knocking the house about in a way that hurts abominably and does not seem to make any sense. What on earth is He up to? The explanation is that He is building quite a different house from the one you thought of—throwing out a new wing here, putting an extra floor there, running up towers, making courtyards. You thought you were going to be made into a decent little cottage: but He is building a palace. He intends to come and live in it Himself."

❖ Ask the students to write confidentially about the changes God needs to make in their lives so that they can live more fully in covenant relationship with God.

❖ Provide an opportunity for volunteers to comment on what they imagine being "rebuilt" for covenant living entails and whether or not they are willing to undergo such extensive "renovations."

(4) Choose to Serve God

❖ Ask the students to stand in a circle, if possible. If the class is large, form several circles. Read aloud today's key verse, Joshua 24:15.

❖ Go around each circle and ask participants who are willing, to say, **"As for me, I will serve the Lord."** (Be sure not to pressure anyone who is not ready to make such a commitment.)

❖ Go around each circle again, this time asking each participant who is willing to state one action he or she will take this week to enact some kind of service for God.

(5) Continue the Journey

❖ Pray that the adults will go forth, cognizant that the choices they make may have far-reaching consequences.

❖ Read aloud this preparation for next week's lesson. You may also want to post it on newsprint for the students to copy. **Prepare for next week's session entitled "Seeking Deliverance" by reading the background Scripture from Judges 2:11-23 and lesson Scripture from verses 16-23. Let these ideas guide your study: We all long to be delivered from desperate situations, even those of our own making. Where can** we look for help? Whenever the Hebrew people cried to God, God raised someone (a judge) to save them.

❖ Read aloud the following three ideas. Challenge the students to commit themselves to use these activities as a springboard to spiritual growth.

(1) **Make a mental note of all the choices you make on a specific day. What are the options? Why did you make each of the selections you chose? If you could redo any of these choices, would you make a different selection? If so, why?**

(2) **Try to look at yourself objectively for several hours. How do the choices you make indicate that you are serving God? If you are making poor choices, what changes do you need to make?**

(3) **Look at some of the choices your government is making. Do you agree that a particular choice is in keeping with God's will? How will you let elected officials know what you think?**

❖ Sing or read aloud "I Have Decided to Follow Jesus," found on page 2129 in *The Faith We Sing*.

❖ Ask the students to join you in repeating the familiar Mizpah Benediction from Genesis 31:49 to conclude the session: **The LORD watch between you and me, when we are absent one from the other.**

UNIT 2: GOD'S COVENANT WITH JUDGES AND KINGS
SEEKING DELIVERANCE

PREVIEWING THE LESSON

Lesson Scripture: Judges 2:16-23
Background Scripture: Judges 2:11-23
Key Verse: Judges 2:16

Focus of the Lesson:
We all long to be delivered from desperate situations, even those of our own making. Where can we look for help? Whenever the Hebrew people cried to God, God raised someone (a judge) to save them.

Goals for the Learners:
(1) to identify the cycle of disobedience, despair, and deliverance in Judges.
(2) to become sensitive to examples of this cycle in the world and church today.
(3) to practice asking God for help in times of trouble.

Pronunciation Guide:
Ashtoreth (ash' tuh reth)　　　　　　Astarte (as tahr' tee)
Baal (bay' uhl OR bah' ahl)　　　　　Canaanite (kay' nuh nite)

Supplies:
Bibles, newsprint and marker, paper and pencils, hymnals

READING THE SCRIPTURE

NRSV
Judges 2:16-23

[16]Then the LORD raised up judges, who delivered them out of the power of those who plundered them. [17]Yet they did not listen even to their judges; for they lusted after other gods and bowed down to them. They soon turned aside from the way in which their ancestors had walked, who had obeyed the commandments of the LORD; they did not follow their example. [18]Whenever the

NIV
Judges 2:16-23

[16]Then the LORD raised up judges, who saved them out of the hands of these raiders. [17]Yet they would not listen to their judges but prostituted themselves to other gods and worshiped them. Unlike their fathers, they quickly turned from the way in which their fathers had walked, the way of obedience to the LORD's commands. [18]Whenever the LORD raised up a judge for

Lord raised up judges for them, the Lord was with the judge, and he delivered them from the hand of their enemies all the days of the judge; for the Lord would be moved to pity by their groaning because of those who persecuted and oppressed them. [19]But whenever the judge died, they would relapse and behave worse than their ancestors, following other gods, worshiping them and bowing down to them. They would not drop any of their practices or their stubborn ways. [20]So the anger of the Lord was kindled against Israel; and he said, "Because this people have transgressed my covenant that I commanded their ancestors, and have not obeyed my voice, [21]I will no longer drive out before them any of the nations that Joshua left when he died." [22]In order to test Israel, whether or not they would take care to walk in the way of the Lord as their ancestors did, [23]the Lord had left those nations, not driving them out at once, and had not handed them over to Joshua.

them, he was with the judge and saved them out of the hands of their enemies as long as the judge lived; for the Lord had compassion on them as they groaned under those who oppressed and afflicted them. [19]But when the judge died, the people returned to ways even more corrupt than those of their fathers, following other gods and serving and worshiping them. They refused to give up their evil practices and stubborn ways.

[20]Therefore the Lord was very angry with Israel and said, "Because this nation has violated the covenant that I laid down for their forefathers and has not listened to me, [21]I will no longer drive out before them any of the nations Joshua left when he died. [22]I will use them to test Israel and see whether they will keep the way of the Lord and walk in it as their forefathers did." [23]The Lord had allowed those nations to remain; he did not drive them out at once by giving them into the hands of Joshua.

UNDERSTANDING THE SCRIPTURE

Introduction to Judges 2. Chapter 2 of Judges picks up the story of the Israelite people just after the ceremony of covenant renewal at Shechem, which we studied in the last lesson. It may be helpful to know that this book contains more than one version of Hebrew history. Later editors did not think it necessary to resolve all the contradictions, but let the various accounts stand together. At the very beginning of Judges, Joshua had died and the tribes were in battle with their enemies. Unlike the book of Joshua, Judges makes it clear that the Israelites did not win all the conflicts nor wipe out all of their Canaanite foes. Their victories allowed them to establish toeholds in the hill country of Palestine and around the perimeters of the land. Strong Canaanite city-states retained their power and their

territory. Thus, the Israelites were forced to live among their enemies and work out their lives in the midst of Canaanite culture. At the beginning of Judges 2, the angel of the Lord delivered the message that because Israel had not been faithful to the covenant, the Canaanites "shall become adversaries to you, and their gods shall be a snare to you"(2:3).

Then abruptly in verse 6 of chapter 2, the story returns to Joshua at the end of the covenant renewal ceremony. Joshua's death and burial are retold, as at the end of the book of Joshua. The writer sets the stage for upcoming events by saying that "the people worshiped the Lord all the days of Joshua, and all the days of the elders who outlived Joshua . . ." (2:7). But when everyone of that generation died, "another generation grew up after them, who did not know the LORD or the work that he had done for Israel" (2:10). This is the background against which the events of today's lesson occur.

Judges 2:11. Israel was experiencing what must have been a difficult time of transition. No longer was there leadership of the caliber of Moses and Joshua. In fact, any central authority seems to have disappeared. At the same time, the people were making a radical transition in economy and society. They were changing from a nomadic, animal-herding style of life to a settled agricultural culture. Their former loyalty to their covenant with God changed also. They began to do evil and to worship false gods. Such actions are the first part of the pattern or cycle that will continue throughout the book.

Joshua 2:12. God is identified repeatedly in terms of the mighty acts that God had done for Israel, especially the exodus. The people chose to reverence other gods—false gods—and the Lord was provoked to anger. It should not be surprising to us that God gets mad; anger is not always a bad thing. One of the basic affirmations of Judaism and Christianity is the personal nature of God. God's emotions are an aspect of the divine personality.

Joshua 2:13. The Baals and the Astartes or Ashtoreths (NIV) were Canaanite deities, referred to here in the plural because of the many local cults that worshiped them. Baal means "lord" or "master." Baal was the god of weather and fertility; his powers were believed to bring life-giving rain to the earth and fruitfulness to the wombs of women and animals. The Canaanites believed that the storm clouds were Baal's chariot; the thunder was his voice; the lightening, his weapons. Baal was pictured standing on a bull—symbol of virility and strength. The worship of Baal involved sacred prostitution. The female consort of Baal was Astarte or Ashtoreth, goddess of war and of fertility. She was pictured as a beautiful woman and symbolized by the evening star. The

worship of Baal and Astarte was exceedingly tempting to the Israelites who were just making the transition to an agricultural economy. Could they be sure that their God (Yahweh) could influence the forces of nature essential to productive crops? Was Yahweh perhaps just a God of the mountains and the desert?

Joshua 2:14-15. God's anger is the second aspect of the cyclical pattern that was developing. God allows the Israelites to be raided and looted by their enemies. We are not told precisely who these plunderers were. They may have been enemy powers or simply roving gangs of bandits. Regardless, although the people of Israel tried to protect themselves, they were too weak. They believed that they were experiencing the suffering that God had warned them of if they forsook the covenant.

Joshua 2:16. God's act of raising up judges to deliver Israel is the third part of the pattern. The book of Judges tells us about twelve judges who, over the period of time from Joshua's death to the rise of the monarchy, served as leaders of the people. Probably these judges were military leaders, perhaps in tribal militias. As they were successful in leading in battle, they became respected and may have taken roles in the governing structure of Israel. Most importantly, they were charismatic leaders who were elevated by the power of God to deliver Israel from the oppression of its enemies.

Joshua 2:17. Even the saving work of the judges did not cause Israel to reform and return to their covenant responsibilities. The temptation of the false gods was too great; they could not resist. This behavior is contrasted unfavorably with the example set by their faithful, obedient ancestors.

Joshua 2:18-19. Here is the fourth and last aspect of the cyclical pattern that characterizes much of the book of Judges: After a brief period of improvement, Israel relapses into unfaithfulness when the judge dies. The spiral is one of progressive deterioration, as each time of apostasy is worse than the previous one.

Joshua 2:20-21. Out of anger at their unfaithfulness and disobedience, God declares that the enemy states that were not conquered at the time of Joshua's death will be allowed to remain intact. Israel will be unable to rid itself of the oppressions of its enemies.

Joshua 2:22-23. There is some disparity between these verses and the two preceding ones. Here, for the first time, Israel's foes are said to be left in their existing status of power in order to test the faithfulness of Israel. This concept of testing is presented also in Deuteronomy 13:1-5. Whatever God's motive, the pattern is clear. Throughout the remainder of the Old Testament, Israel will live through cycles of unfaithfulness, suffering, deliverance, and relapse.

INTERPRETING THE SCRIPTURE

The Cycle of Covenant Relationship

When the people of Israel entered the land of Canaan, God's marvelous promises to them had almost been fulfilled. Through the centuries they had been blessed, cared for, rescued, and guided. They had received the divine promise of covenant faithfulness, had it reaffirmed to succeeding generations, received the laws to direct their lives according to God's will, and been brought to the land that God had given them. God's plan to bless them and to bless all nations of the earth through them appeared close to fruition. But unfortunately, the people of ancient Israel were entirely too much like the people of modern North America. They had a major problem with constancy. In times of peril and trouble, they turned to the Lord and sought help. In safe and easy times, they were inclined to assert themselves and make their own rules for living. They became attentive to the voice of God only under the pressure of crisis. When conditions improved, they strayed again.

The book of Judges is a warning of what happens when God's covenant people cease to live in right relationship with God. Israel literally forgot who it was—a people called out by God to live in intimacy with God. When they no longer lived as covenant people, their very identity was being denied. When they refused to live as people of God, the mission for which God had raised them up was being neglected and jeopardized. The covenant of salvation always has two sides. God is steadfast and faithful, no matter what. Israel repeatedly abandoned its covenant responsibility by refusing loyalty and obedience. Relationship with God goes two ways. God does not force us into loving relationship—as if there were any such possibility. Love is the opposite of force. God's gifts, no matter how abundant and how gracious, must be accepted by us willingly. The challenge of living in covenant loyalty is ongoing. There is always the temptation to follow other gods and reject divine values. This challenge confronts each of us as individuals; it confronts the church and the larger society. It is easy to name the false gods that tempt us as individuals. Certainly they include wealth, control, image, and entertainment. The church may be tempted to pursue wealth in the form of real estate, power through secular politics, and popularity through superficial worship and capitalistic values. In the larger society of the United States today, we see a succumbing to the lures of global dominance, disproportionate wealth, and pervasive violence. God is always faithful; we are often faithless. As individual Christians and as the church, we risk losing our identity as people in covenant with God and our mission of serving as channels of God's grace in a needy, suffering world.

The Faithfulness of Our Covenant God

God's plan for peace and plenty for Israel was shattered by Israel's stubborn unwillingness to maintain their side of the relationship. But, God does not throw up the divine hands and withdraw. God neither destroys rebellious Israel nor replaces them with another people. God moves to pick up the pieces of the divine purpose and continues to work with Israel. God tries again, and again, and again. . . . What strange behavior from a sovereign, omnipotent God! God would seem to have a whole range of better options for the plan of salvation than to keep on trying with these uncooperative people—picking them up, brushing them off, and watching them fall again. In the deepest sense, though, God has no other option, not if God is to be faithful to the divine nature. Can God act contrary to that nature and still remain God? The sovereignty of God is not based in force or coercion. It is based in the essential unchanging nature of God. The creator and sovereign of the universe will not and cannot be unfaithful; the divine nature is steadfast love. God cannot help being gracious and merciful; that is who God is.

This does not mean that there is no price to be paid for sin. Divine grace is not cheap. The guilty are not cleared and protected from the consequences of their wrongdoing. Israel suffered terribly as the result of its transgressions. People suffer debilitating, destructive consequences of their wrong choices and actions. But while the guilty are not spared, they are not abandoned either. Just as loving faithfulness is the essence of God's nature, life-restoring forgiveness is the essence of God's will. God demands obedience and promises forgiveness. Throughout the Bible, divine grace relentlessly pursues unfaithful people. The ultimate divine act of grace is the cross of Jesus Christ.

Retribution or Restoration

The cyclical pattern described in the book of Judges and really through the rest of Old Testament history is frequently understood to be one of sin, punishment, repentance, and reinstatement. But is this pattern consistent with the nature and will of God as we have examined them in the last section? Note that in Joshua 2:18, the Israelites are said to be "groaning" in their suffering. The Hebrew word translated as "groaning" means lamenting or wailing, not repenting. There is nothing said in the passage about repentance. When God heard their groaning, God's heart was moved to pity and compassion, and God responded even without their repentance. Perhaps what appears to be divine punishment is actually the inherent consequences of the choices people have made. God allows God's covenant partners freedom of action. The results of those actions may be suffering for both humans and for God. We experience no pain that God does not share. In the person of Jesus Christ, God entered our human condition and took upon the divine self the suffering that sin creates.

What has happened in the nation of South Africa in recent years is a powerful illustration. The end of apartheid had been widely expected to set off a violent civil war fueled by desire for vengeance and retribution. Such a conflict seemed inevitable in light of the oppression, discrimination, and violence that non-white South Africans had endured for so long. Archbishop Desmond Tutu describes what actually happened in his book *No Future Without Forgiveness.* The new leaders of the nation became convinced that acts of revenge would only kindle an endless cycle of violence in which everyone would suffer. But trying to move into the future by simply ignoring the horrors of the past was impossible, even wrong. The pain of the victims needed to be recognized and respected. A process was devised through which the oppressors were given opportunities to confess their wrongs, make reparations to the victims if possible, and receive forgiveness rather than punishment. Only through forgiveness could South African society be healed. Here is a contemporary example of restorative, rather than retributive, justice.

God's justice is always restorative. Punishment has no value in itself; revenge motivates further evil. Israel's hope for the future and ours rests in the God who forgives the past and by so doing creates the future.

SHARING THE SCRIPTURE

PREPARING TO TEACH

Preparing Our Hearts

This week's devotional reading is found in Deuteronomy 6:4-9. This passage opens with the *Shema,* a historic confession of faith that Israel's God is the one God. These words invite people to commit themselves unreservedly to God. Furthermore, the people are admonished to be ever mindful of God's commandments to teach them to their children. What happens when we truly live with single-minded devotion to God? What happens when we forget or ignore that God is God and begin to worship other gods? Are you truly loving God with all of your being this day?

Pray that you and the adult learners will live in faithful obedience and loyalty to God.

Preparing Our Minds

Study the background Scripture from Judges 2:11-23 and lesson Scripture, verses 16-23. As you delve into the Scripture think about where you look for help in a desperate situation.

Write on newsprint:

❑ chart for "Identify the Cycle of Disobedience, Despair, and Deliverance in Judges."

❑ information for next week's lesson, found under "Continue the Journey."

❑ activities for further spiritual growth in "Continue the Journey."

LEADING THE CLASS

(1) Gather to Learn

❖ Welcome the class members and introduce any guests.

❖ Pray that the participants will be open to God's grace as mediated through the word that you will be studying today.

❖ Read the following scenario and discuss the accompanying questions.

The Talbert family had endured tremendous stress because their oldest child, Tim, flaunted the Christian teachings and values of his family and experimented with drugs. His attempts to support his addiction led to theft within the family and then to crimes in the community. He was not a "Lone Ranger," but had fallen in with the wrong crowd. Pleadings from his family were useless. One day, in the midst of a break-in, Tim struck a homeowner who had surprised him. Tim shoved this man hard, causing him to fall and hit his head. As this man's life was hanging in the balance, Tim began to realize what he was doing and his role in this man's critical medical state and, possibly, death.

• **Suppose you were Tim's pastor. What would you say when you visited him in jail just after he was apprehended?**

- **Suppose you were Tim. How would you respond to your situation? What would you expect God to do?**
- **How do you think God might respond in such a situation?**

❖ Read aloud today's focus statement: **We all long to be delivered from desperate situations, even those of our own making. Where can we look for help? Whenever the Hebrew people cried to God, God raised someone (a judge) to save them.**

(2) Identify the Cycle of Disobedience, Despair, and Deliverance in Judges

❖ Bridge the gap between last week's lesson and this one by reading or retelling information from "Introduction to Judges 2," found in Understanding the Scripture.

❖ Ask a volunteer to read the story of Israel's unfaithfulness as told in Judges 2:11-23.

❖ Post this chart on newsprint. Work with the class to fill in the right column, or fill it in yourself as you present a lecture on this information. Post this newsprint where everyone can see it throughout the rest of the session.

Cycle Stage	Example from Judges
Disobedience/ Unfaithfulness	Did evil in God's sight by worshiping Baal
Despair	Abandoned God who became angry with them and allowed them to be plundered
Deliverance	God raised up Judges (military leaders) who overcame the plunderers
Relapse into Disobedience	People did not listen but lusted after other gods

(3) Become Sensitive to Examples of This Cycle in the World and Church Today

❖ Read or retell "The Cycle of Covenant Relationship" in Interpreting the Scripture.

❖ Divide the class into groups and distribute markers and newsprint, which they are to label "Current Example." Encourage each group to look again at the cycles and suggest a specific disobedience that they believe is occurring within the church. How is the church falling into despair? What signs of hope for deliverance do you see? How has (or might) the church relapse into disobedience?

❖ Invite a spokesperson for each group to discuss how they see this ancient cycle repeating itself in the church today. Post their newsprint if space is available.

❖ Open the floor for other ideas about how the church as a body and its individual members may be unfaithful to God. Invite the students to discuss how they might intervene to bring about positive change.

(4) Practice Asking God for Help in Times of Trouble

❖ Distribute paper and pencils for this confidential assignment. Ask the students to consider the cycle they have just explored in light of their individual lives. In what ways are they currently being unfaithful to God? How has this disobedience caused them to feel despair—or has it? What remedies do they hope to receive from God? Under what circumstances might they relapse into old habits so as to start the cycle all over again?

❖ Distribute another sheet of paper to each student and ask them to complete one of these two options.

   ■ **Option 1:** Write a prayer in which you confess your unfaithfulness to God and describe your despair. Ask God for deliverance from this situation, which may be one of your own making.

■ **Option 2:** Sketch a visual representation of your disobedience, despair, and deliverance. Perhaps you will choose a circle, square, or other geometric shape.

❖ Use Psalm 121 as words of assurance to help the class members recognize that their help comes from God. If you have a hymnal with a Psalter, read this psalm responsively. If not, read this short psalm aloud yourself.

(5) Continue the Journey

❖ Pray that the participants will be sensitive to times when they are not living in covenant with Christ and seek God's deliverance so that they may begin anew.

❖ Read aloud this preparation for next week's lesson. You may also want to post it on newsprint for the students to copy. **Prepare for next week's session entitled "Leadership Counts!" by reading the background Scripture from Judges 4 and focusing your attention on verses 4-10 and 12-16. Keep in mind these ideas as you prepare this lesson: Strong leaders may get results when no one else can. What characterizes a strong leader? Deborah modeled strong leadership by** obeying God and supporting Barak with her presence.

❖ Read aloud the following three ideas. Challenge the students to commit themselves to use these activities as a springboard to spiritual growth.

(1) **Write a prayer asking God to deliver your nation from one or two specific idols that it serves. Pray this prayer daily.**

(2) **Be aware of someone who may be seeking help. Sometimes people are able to articulate their needs, but often it is difficult for those in crisis to ask for assistance. Do whatever you are able to do.**

(3) **Think of ways that you believe God has used to test you. Why were you in need of testing? What kind of "grade" do you think you "earned" on this test? What changes did you make as a result of this testing?**

❖ Sing or read aloud "I Want a Principle Within."

❖ Ask the students to join you in repeating the familiar Mizpah Benediction from Genesis 31:49 to conclude the session: **The LORD watch between you and me, when we are absent one from the other.**

UNIT 2: GOD'S COVENANT WITH JUDGES AND KINGS
LEADERSHIP COUNTS!

PREVIEWING THE LESSON

Lesson Scripture: Judges 4:4-10, 12-16
Background Scripture: Judges 4
Key Verses: Judges 4:8-9

Focus of the Lesson:
Strong leaders may get results when no one else can. What characterizes a strong leader? Deborah modeled strong leadership by obeying God and supporting Barak with her presence.

Goals for the Learners:
(1) to analyze the story of how Deborah helped Barak defeat Sisera's army.
(2) to reflect on leadership qualities they may possess, in light of Deborah's qualities as a strong leader of God's people.
(3) to commit themselves to support women and men leaders in the church.

Pronunciation Guide:
Abinoam (uh bin' oh uhm)	Barak (bair' ak)
Ephraim (ee' fray im)	Jabin (jay' bin)
Jael (jay' uhl)	Kedesh (kee' dish)
Lappidoth (lap' i doth)	Naphtali (naf' tuh li)
Ramah (ray' muh)	Sisera (sis' uh ruh)
Wadi Kishon (wah' dee kish' ee uhn)	Zebulun (zeb' yuh luhn)
Harosheth-ha-goiim (*NIV:* Haggoyim) (huh roh' shith hu goi' im)	

Supplies:
Bibles, newsprint and markers, paper and pencils, hymnals, map, craft paper, tape or tacks

---

READING THE SCRIPTURE

NRSV
Judges 4:4-10, 12-16

⁴At that time Deborah, a prophetess, wife of Lappidoth, was judging Israel. ⁵She used

NIV
Judges 4:4-10, 12-16

⁴Deborah, a prophetess, the wife of Lappidoth, was leading Israel at that time.

to sit under the palm of Deborah between Ramah and Bethel in the hill country of Ephraim; and the Israelites came up to her for judgment. [6]She sent and summoned Barak son of Abinoam from Kedesh in Naphtali, and said to him, "The LORD, the God of Israel, commands you, 'Go, take position at Mount Tabor, bringing ten thousand from the tribe of Naphtali and the tribe of Zebulun. [7]I will draw out Sisera, the general of Jabin's army, to meet you by the Wadi Kishon with his chariots and his troops; and I will give him into your hand.'" [8]Barak said to her, **"If you will go with me, I will go; but if you will not go with me, I will not go." [9]And she said, "I will surely go with you;** nevertheless, the road on which you are going will not lead to your glory, for the LORD will sell Sisera into the hand of a woman." Then Deborah got up and went with Barak to Kedesh. [10]Barak summoned Zebulun and Naphtali to Kedesh; and ten thousand warriors went up behind him; and Deborah went up with him.

[12]When Sisera was told that Barak son of Abinoam had gone up to Mount Tabor, [13]Sisera called out all his chariots, nine hundred chariots of iron, and all the troops who were with him, from Harosheth-ha-goiim to the Wadi Kishon. [14]Then Deborah said to Barak, "Up! For this is the day on which the LORD has given Sisera into your hand. The LORD is indeed going out before you." So Barak went down from Mount Tabor with ten thousand warriors following him. [15]And the LORD threw Sisera and all his chariots and all his army into a panic before Barak; Sisera got down from his chariot and fled away on foot, [16]while Barak pursued the chariots and the army to Harosheth-ha-goiim. All the army of Sisera fell by the sword; no one was left.

[5]She held court under the Palm of Deborah between Ramah and Bethel in the hill country of Ephraim, and the Israelites came to her to have their disputes decided. [6]She sent for Barak son of Abinoam from Kedesh in Naphtali and said to him, "The LORD, the God of Israel, commands you: 'Go, take with you ten thousand men of Naphtali and Zebulun and lead the way to Mount Tabor. [7]I will lure Sisera, the commander of Jabin's army, with his chariots and his troops to the Kishon River and give him into your hands.'"

[8]Barak said to her, **"If you go with me, I will go; but if you don't go with me, I won't go."** [9]**"Very well," Deborah said, "I will go with you.** But because of the way you are going about this, the honor will not be yours, for the LORD will hand Sisera over to a woman." So Deborah went with Barak to Kedesh, [10]where he summoned Zebulun and Naphtali. Ten thousand men followed him, and Deborah also went with him.

[12]When they told Sisera that Barak son of Abinoam had gone up to Mount Tabor, [13]Sisera gathered together his nine hundred iron chariots and all the men with him, from Harosheth Haggoyim to the Kishon River.

[14]Then Deborah said to Barak, "Go! This is the day the LORD has given Sisera into your hands. Has not the LORD gone ahead of you?" So Barak went down Mount Tabor, followed by ten thousand men. [15]At Barak's advance, the LORD routed Sisera and all his chariots and army by the sword, and Sisera abandoned his chariot and fled on foot. [16]But Barak pursued the chariots and army as far as Harosheth Haggoyim. All the troops of Sisera fell by the sword; not a man was left.

UNDERSTANDING THE SCRIPTURE

Judges 4:1. Today's Scripture passage continues the story of the Israelite people

after they had entered the land of Canaan, the land that God had promised to give to them. There was continual conflict between them and the groups of people who already lived in the land. Sadly, Israel was repeatedly unfaithful to its covenant relationship with God and failed to obey God's law. Their history became a cycle of sinfulness, suffering, and restoration as God, who remained faithful, delivered them again and again from their oppressors. God raised up a series of leaders called judges whose task was to rally the people to fight their enemies and to be faithful to God. After the death of the judge Ehud (Judges 3:15-30), the nation had again fallen into sinfulness. Ehud was a hero of the tribe of Benjamin who was empowered by God to lead Israelite rebellion against the Moabite king Eglon who had oppressed them for eighteen years. Ehud assassinated the enemy king and led Israel in defeating Moab.

Judges 4:2. As a result of their evil-doing, God allowed Israel to be overcome by the forces of Jabin the king of the Canaanite city of Hazor. Hazor was located about nine miles north of the Sea of Galilee. It was particularly important because of its location near major trade routes. Sisera was the commander of the armies of Hazor. Sisera is not a Semitic name; he was probably a Philistine—a seafaring people who lived along the eastern coast of the Mediterranean Sea.

Judges 4:3. Significant technological shifts were taking place during this period of human history. At least some of the Canaanites had advanced into the early Iron Age; they used the strong metal iron to fashion implements of war. The Israelites were not as technologically advanced; they did not have chariots, but fought on foot. After two decades of dominance by Hazor, the situation of the Israelites appeared hopeless and as usual they cried to God in their despair.

Judges 4:4-5. Deborah, whose name means "bee," is introduced as a prophetess. This designation is used of only three women in the entire Old Testament. None of the male judges are called prophets. Apparently she was greatly respected and

considered to be a spokesperson for God. The people of Israel came to her to arbitrate their disputes. In fact, Deborah is the only judge who is explicitly said to function in a legal capacity. The Hebrew words which are translated "wife of Lappidoth" are thought by some scholars to be more correctly rendered "woman of torches." The enemies of Israel at this point included not only the Canaanites of Hazor in the northern part of the land, but also the Philistines in the south and central areas.

Judges 4:6. Deborah began the effort to free her people by selecting and summoning a strong military commander. His name "Barak" means "thunderbolt" or "lightning." His fame in Hebrew history was enduring; he is mentioned in Hebrews 11:32 as one of the heroes of faith. Deborah made it clear to Barak that it was not her, but God who was commanding him. Barak was told to take troops from two of the tribes and go to Mount Tabor—an isolated peak located to the north of the Jezreel Valley. Because Mount Tabor is taller (about 1850 feet) than any of the surrounding land and, at that time, heavily wooded, it provided a strong vantage point from which to launch the battle.

Judges 4:7. Through Deborah, God told Barak that the enemy general Sisera would meet his forces at a stream that flowed through the Jezreel Valley. This would have been considered a strong position for Sisera's army because his chariots would have plenty of maneuvering room.

Judges 4:8-10. When Barak insisted that Deborah go with him, he may have been testing her confidence in his success. In effect, he treated her as a symbol of the presence and power of God. Deborah did not hesitate in agreeing, but warned Barak that he will not reap glory, but rather that a woman will. This is naturally thought at the time to be a reference to Deborah herself, but was probably her anticipation of Jael's role.

Judges 4:11. The Kenites, called Midianites elsewhere, were descendants of Moses' father-in-law. They were a tribe of traveling metalsmiths who had probably worked on the Canaanite chariots. The clan of Heber lived apart from the other Kenites; this explains why Sisera would later seek shelter there.

Judges 4:12-16. The battle began, with Deborah functioning like a king at the head of the Israelite troops. By the action of God, the Canaanite charioteers panicked and tried to flee the battlefield, but were killed by the Israelite warriors.

Judges 4:17-20. General Sisera fled from the battle on foot and went to the tent of Heber, a Kenite who was an ally of Hazor. Heber was not home, so Sisera was met by Heber's wife Jael. Jael probably realized that she had to defend herself, so she feigned welcome to Sisera. His entering her tent with her husband absent violated the rules of hospitality and may have further con-

vinced Jael that she was in danger, probably, of being raped. When Sisera asked her for water, she gave him goat's milk, perhaps hoping that it would make him sleepy. He commanded her to guard the entrance of the tent and even to lie to protect him.

Judges 4:21-24. It is not possible to be sure of Jael's motives. Perhaps she was simply frightened; perhaps she was a secret worshiper of God; perhaps she realized that Israel had won the battle and wanted to ingratiate herself with the victorious side. After Sisera fell asleep, she hammered a tent peg through his head. Nomadic women erected the tents when their families moved, so she would have been handy with the hammer. When Barak arrived at her tent in pursuit of Sisera, she invited him in and showed him the body of his executed enemy.

INTERPRETING THE SCRIPTURE

A Mother in Israel

Chapter 5 of Judges is a poetic account of the Israelites' victory over the Canaanites, which was recounted in prose in chapter 4. The Song of Deborah in chapter 5 may be the very oldest part of the Old Testament. It was surely sung through the centuries and taught by one generation to another long before it was recorded in writing. In verse 7, Deborah is called "a mother in Israel"—a term of great honor. Certainly her role in these events marks her as an unusual figure in the biblical story. Deborah is the only female judge and one of only four prophetesses named in the Old Testament. (Three other women are named as prophetesses in the Old Testament: Miriam in Exodus 15:20, Huldah in Second Kings 22:14, and Noadiah in Nehemiah 6:14. In Luke 2:36, Anna is called a prophetess.) Her role as a military leader is unique in Israel's history. She is the strongest example of female leadership in the entire Bible. The role of Jael, called in Judges 5:24 "most

blessed of women," shatters the stereotypes of women of the time as forcefully as her hammer and peg shattered Sisera's head. She is a woman of courage, decisiveness, and action—even violent action. Jael is one of the few women whose words in conversation are recorded in Scripture.

Deborah and Jael are exceptional. Even better known female characters such as Ruth and Esther are not so remarkable. The book of Judges mentions nineteen different women who played various parts in Israel's history during this period. This is more than are found in any other book of the Bible. The women portrayed in the earlier portion of Judges are much stronger figures. Later in the book the role of women becomes that of victims of the actions of men.

Unfortunately, gender has not ceased to be an issue in the twenty-first century church. The church has tended to be quite conservative in its view of women—far behind secular society. For example, women in the United States received the right to vote in 1920, as a result of the ratification of the nineteenth amendment to the Constitution; women did not receive full clergy rights in what is now The United Methodist Church until thirty-six years later, when the General Conference of 1956 voted to grant those rights. Opportunities for both lay and clergy women have certainly expanded in the mainline Protestant churches, but many Christians still do not fully grasp and practice the idea of full gender equality. In the Roman Catholic Church, the Southern Baptist Convention, and many smaller denominations, the place of women continues to be severely restricted. This is a challenge for those who understand Christ's message of equality and inclusion—a challenge to work actively for change.

The Problem of Violence

Much of the leadership we see in Judges is exercised by men celebrated as heroes whose actions are violent—Gideon who slaughtered the Midianites (chapter 7), and Samson who brought down the house on thousands of Philistines (chapter 16). In today's lesson from Judges 4, we see a bloody battle in which "all the army of Sisera fell by the sword" (4:16), and witness the death of the Canaanite army commander Sisera at the hand of a woman, Jael, who drove a tent peg through his skull (4:21). The image of God as a warrior who orders people to annihilate their enemies—men, women, children, even sometimes animals, cannot be reconciled with our image of Christ as the Prince of Peace, the Suffering Servant, the Crucified Lord. We have to remember, though, that Israel saw itself as God's chosen people, as a holy nation set apart to serve God's purpose of salvation for the whole world. Anything that threatened the fulfillment of that role had to be destroyed utterly. When enemies contested the Israelites for possession of the land of promise, those enemies endangered that which belonged to Israel as a divine gift. So, while we may find the violence that runs rampant through Judges, as well as other parts of the Old Testament, to be very disconcerting, we have to remember that most of the Hebrew writers of Scripture firmly believed that God who had entered into covenant relationship with Israel approved and utilized unspeakable violence to defend God's people.

Being a Leader

What are the qualities of leadership that are exemplified by Deborah? She was highly respected in the Israelite community, so much so that the people were willing to submit their disputes to her for settlement. We are not told how she came into this position, but she must have manifested caring, ability to listen, and honesty. Deborah was recognized by her community as a woman of wisdom—one who was capable of understanding situations and people, as well as rendering insightful and fair decisions. Deborah must have been a woman who was close to God and open to hearing and heeding God's voice. Probably her strengths as a judge were the outgrowth of her communion with God. She was uncompromising in her words to Barak. Her communication with the divine made her confident of God's will in that time and place. She must also have been assertive and proactive—able to comprehend circumstances and act decisively. Note that it was she who sent for the military leader Barak and called him into the role that God intended. She did not simply assign him a task, but gave specific instructions as to how it was to be accomplished. Perhaps most impressive, Deborah was courageous. She did not hesitate when Barak insisted that she accompany him into battle. Deborah's leadership called forth the best efforts of others. She exhorted and encouraged Barak, assuring him that God was in control of the battle.

What can we learn about leadership for Christians today from examining the qualities of Deborah? Christians are called to lead in both churches and communities. To deny possessing any gifts for leadership is to refuse to recognize what God has gifted us with. As individuals, none of us may possess the combination of qualities that we see in Deborah, but we can work together and pool our gifts. One may be endowed with wisdom; another, deeply respected; another, willing to act; still another, courageous. All of us can have compassion and concern for the needs of others; we can be fair and honest; we can encourage and praise the efforts of others. All Christians are called to live in close fellowship with God through which we can receive guidance and sometimes answers to just what it is that God desires of us. Finally, leadership requires followers. It has been said that all who see themselves as leaders need to look behind them continually to be certain they have followers. The old joke line, "I'm their leader, which way did they go?" does not describe Christian leadership. Granted there may be times when a leader must stand alone, against the opinions and desires of others. But, effective leadership over a period of time must be supported by the efforts of those who follow. All of us can follow—not blindly or dully, but with enthusiasm and willingness to participate. Only then can the church and the world be moved toward the redeemed order in Jesus Christ.

SHARING THE SCRIPTURE

PREPARING TO TEACH

Preparing Our Hearts

This week's devotional reading is found in Psalm 91. The psalmist firmly believes that God can be trusted to provide protection for the righteous even in the midst of the most horrific situations. What does your own experience reveal about God's ability to protect and deliver you? What does the image of God covering you, nestling you as a bird would (91:4), suggest to you about God? The psalmist writes in verse 5, "You will not fear the terror of the night." Perhaps this describes you, but if it does not, what has to happen for you to place your full trust and confidence in God?

Pray that you and the adult learners will trust God to keep and care for you.

Preparing Our Minds

Study the background from Judges 4 and lesson Scripture, verses 4-10, 12-16. As you study think about the traits of a strong leader who can get results.

Write on newsprint:
❑ commitment for "Make a Commitment to Support Women and Men Leaders in the Church."
❑ information for next week's lesson, found under "Continue the Journey."
❑ activities for further spiritual growth in "Continue the Journey."

Plan a lecture to set the stage for "Analyze the Story of How Deborah Helped Barak Defeat Sisera's Army." Also plan any other lectures that you wish to use for this portion of the lesson.

LEADING THE CLASS

(1) Gather to Learn

❖ Welcome the class members and introduce any guests.

❖ Pray that today's participants will be open to the leading of the Holy Spirit.

❖ Brainstorm answers to these questions, one at a time, with the class and record their answers on newsprint.

(1) **Who are strong leaders on the world and national scene today?**

(2) **What are the characteristics of these leaders who are able to attract followers and get results?**

❖ Read aloud today's focus statement: **Strong leaders may get results when no one else can. What characterizes a strong leader? Deborah modeled strong leadership by obeying God and supporting Barak with her presence.**

(2) Analyze the Story of How Deborah Helped Barak Defeat Sisera's Army

❖ Set the stage for today's lesson by giving a brief lecture on Judges 4:1-3. The Understanding the Scripture section will be useful to you.

❖ Use a detailed map from the time period of the Israelite's settlement in Canaan to show the locations of Ramah, Bethel, Kedesh, Mount Tabor, Haroshethhagoiim, and River Kishon. (The battleground is between Megiddo and Taanach where there is a pass opening into the Jezreel Valley near where streams flow together forming Wadi Kishon, which can be dry during dry season). Also locate the areas of the tribes of Zebulun and Naphtali.

❖ Select three volunteers to read the parts of the narrator, Deborah, and Barak. Read Judges 4:4-10, 12-16.

❖ Consider Deborah first. Ask the students to comment on what the text says about her. Be prepared to augment the discussion with information from Understanding the Scripture. If you prefer, state this information in a brief lecture.

❖ Look at the characteristics of an effective leader that you brainstormed during the "Gather to Learn" portion. Encourage the students to determine which of these traits applies to Deborah and put a check by the appropriate traits. Invite the adults to add other leadership traits that may be evident in Deborah that were not included on their list.

❖ Look next at Barak's leadership traits. Put an asterisk beside these. Add any others that have not yet been identified on the class list.

❖ Compare and contrast the traits that Deborah and Barak exhibit. How do these two leaders complement each other?

❖ Compare and contrast these traits with those characteristics that we value in modern church leaders by discussing these questions.

(1) **Which of the leadership traits evident in Barak and/or Deborah do we often see in modern church leaders?**

(2) **Which of the leadership traits evident in Barak and/or Deborah seem to be in short supply in the modern church?**

(3) **How might your congregation be different if you had more people with Deborah's leadership qualities?**

(3) Reflect on Leadership Qualities the Learners May Possess in Light of Deborah's Qualities As a Strong Leader of God's People

❖ Distribute paper and pencils. Ask the students to look at the list they have brainstormed together and confidentially write any leadership traits that they possess. They may have traits to add to their own list that were not on the class list.

❖ Encourage them to identify and list on their sheets any ways that they are using these traits to build up the kingdom of God. Their activities may be carried out within the walls of the church, but will likely also reach out into the community and world.

❖ Hold a frank discussion about the leadership traits that this particular congregation needs at this point in its history. Perhaps an age group, such as youth or older adults, needs leaders. Perhaps a specific kind of ministry needs leaders, such as the educational ministry or mission projects. What difference would it make to the church if such leaders could be identified and placed in positions for service?

(4) Make a Commitment to Support Women and Men Leaders in the Church

❖ Post a sheet of craft paper on a wall or bulletin board. Have markers available. Ask the students to write the names of leaders in the church who have been an inspiration to them and/or have helped the congregation grow or thrive because of their dedication. If the class is large, consider using several sheets of paper.

❖ Call out the posted names, one at a time. Invite the students to comment on what they remember about a particular leader. (Recognize that you may not have time to discuss each name listed. Also remember that one or more class member's name may appear on the list.)

❖ Conclude this discussion by asking the adults to read in unison this commitment, which you will post on newsprint: **We give thanks to you, O God, for these servants who, like Deborah and Barak, have put the needs of your people ahead of their own. We commit ourselves to support these leaders in prayer and with whatever service we are gifted to offer, so that your kingdom may come.**

(5) Continue the Journey

❖ Pray that the adults will go forth with a new appreciation for the important role that leaders play among God's covenant people.

❖ Read aloud this preparation for next week's lesson. You may also want to post it on newsprint for the students to copy. **Prepare for next week's session entitled "Prayer Makes the Difference" by reading 1 Samuel 7:3-13, which is both our lesson** and background Scripture. Pay particular attention to these ideas: Praying for others shows our concern for them and, at some level, engages us with their plight. What are the effects of praying for others? Samuel prayed for the Israelites when they were threatened by the Philistines, and God saved them.

❖ Read aloud the following three ideas. Challenge the students to commit themselves to use these activities as a springboard to spiritual growth.

(1) Look around at the leadership in your own church. How many people have stepped forward to offer their gifts and talents? Who else could you talk to about assuming a leadership role? Take some action this week.

(2) Consider how you and your congregation view female leadership. Have attitudes changed over the years? If so, how? What particular gifts have women, including clergywomen, brought to your congregation and/or denomination?

(3) Evaluate your own leadership style. Do you work well with people? Are they pleased to follow you? Do you communicate needs clearly and delegate authority? Consider reading a book on church leadership. What new ideas can you glean to make your own style more effective?

❖ Sing or read aloud "¡Canta, Débora, Canta!" which is based on the story of Deborah as told in Judges 5.

Ask the students to join you in repeating the familiar Mizpah Benediction from Genesis 31:49 to conclude the session: **The LORD watch between you and me, when we are absent one from the other.**

UNIT 2: GOD'S COVENANT WITH JUDGES AND KINGS

PRAYER MAKES THE DIFFERENCE

PREVIEWING THE LESSON

Lesson Scripture: 1 Samuel 7:3-13
Background Scripture: 1 Samuel 7:3-13
Key Verse: 1 Samuel 7:9

Focus of the Lesson:
Praying for others shows our concern for them and, at some level, engages us in their plight. What are the effects of praying for others? Samuel prayed for the Israelites when they were threatened by the Philistines, and God saved them.

Goals for the Learners:
(1) to explore how Samuel, who served as judge and priest, interceded by asking God to save the Israelites from the Philistines.
(2) to consider the effects of praying for others.
(3) to make a commitment to pray daily for an individual or group in need.

Pronunciation Guide:
Ashtoreth (ash' tuh roth)   Astarte (as tahr' tee)
Baal (bay' uhl, bah ahl')   Beth-car (beth kahr')
Deuteronomic (dyoo tuh roh nom' ik)   Ebenezer (eb' uh nee' zuhr)
Jeshanah (jesh' uh nuh)   Mizpah (miz' puh)
Philistine (fi lis' teen)

Supplies:
Bibles, newsprint and marker, paper and pencils, hymnals, map showing Mizpah

---

READING THE SCRIPTURE

NRSV
1 Samuel 7:3-13

³Then Samuel said to all the house of Israel, "If you are returning to the LORD with all your heart, then put away the foreign gods and the Astartes from among you. Direct your heart to the LORD, and serve him

NIV
1 Samuel 7:3-13

³And Samuel said to the whole house of Israel, "If you are returning to the LORD with all your hearts, then rid yourselves of the foreign gods and the Ashtoreths and commit yourselves to the LORD and serve him only,

only, and he will deliver you out of the hand of the Philistines." 4So Israel put away the Baals and the Astartes, and they served the LORD only.

5Then Samuel said, "Gather all Israel at Mizpah, and I will pray to the LORD for you." 6So they gathered at Mizpah, and drew water and poured it out before the LORD. They fasted that day, and said, "We have sinned against the LORD." And Samuel judged the people of Israel at Mizpah.

7When the Philistines heard that the people of Israel had gathered at Mizpah, the lords of the Philistines went up against Israel. And when the people of Israel heard of it they were afraid of the Philistines. 8The people of Israel said to Samuel, "Do not cease to cry out to the LORD our God for us, and pray that he may save us from the hand of the Philistines." 9So Samuel took a sucking lamb and offered it as a whole burnt offering to the LORD; **Samuel cried out to the LORD for Israel, and the LORD answered him.** 10As Samuel was offering up the burnt offering, the Philistines drew near to attack Israel; but the LORD thundered with a mighty voice that day against the Philistines and threw them into confusion; and they were routed before Israel. 11And the men of Israel went out of Mizpah and pursued the Philistines, and struck them down as far as beyond Beth-car.

12Then Samuel took a stone and set it up between Mizpah and Jeshanah, and named it Ebenezer; for he said, "Thus far the LORD has helped us." 13So the Philistines were subdued and did not again enter the territory of Israel; the hand of the LORD was against the Philistines all the days of Samuel.

and he will deliver you out of the hand of the Philistines." 4So the Israelites put away their Baals and Ashtoreths, and served the LORD only.

5Then Samuel said, "Assemble all Israel at Mizpah and I will intercede with the LORD for you." 6When they had assembled at Mizpah, they drew water and poured it out before the LORD. On that day they fasted and there they confessed, "We have sinned against the LORD." And Samuel was leader of Israel at Mizpah.

7When the Philistines heard that Israel had assembled at Mizpah, the rulers of Philistines came up to attack them. And when the Israelites heard of it, they were afraid because of the Philistines. 8They said to Samuel, "Do not stop crying out to the LORD our God for us, that he may rescue us from the hand of the Philistines." 9Then Samuel took a suckling lamb and offered it up as a whole burnt offering to the LORD. **He cried out to the LORD on Israel's behalf, and the LORD answered him.**

10While Samuel was sacrificing the burnt offering, the Philistines drew near to engage Israel in battle. But that day the LORD thundered with loud thunder against the Philistines and threw them into such a panic that they were routed before the Israelites. 11The men of Israel rushed out of Mizpah and pursued the Philistines, slaughtering them along the way to a point below Beth Car.

12Then Samuel took a stone and set it up between Mizpah and Shen. He named it Ebenezer, saying, "Thus far has the LORD helped us." 13So the Philistines were subdued and did not invade Israelite territory again.

UNDERSTANDING THE SCRIPTURE

1 Samuel 7:3. The book of Judges ends with this assessment of the plight of Hebrew society at the time: "In those days there was no king in Israel; all the people did what was right in their own eyes" (21:25). This is the background against which the book of 1 Samuel begins. Israel had again fallen into disobedience and disloyalty to God and needed God to deliver them. First Samuel 7:3 expresses the Deuteronomic interpretation of history that characterizes the books of Joshua, Judges, 1 and 2 Samuel, and 1 and 2 Kings. The Deuteronomic editors of these books saw much of Hebrew history as a recurring cycle of sin, suffering, and deliverance. A new enemy had emerged—one that will plague the Israelites for decades—the Philistines. These people had probably entered Canaaan soon after the Israelites and were their major rivals for the land.

In the opening chapters of 1 Samuel we learn something about the birth and child-hood of Samuel. His mother Hannah was a woman of faith who appealed to God to enable her to bear a son. Samuel was the fruit of that prayer (1 Samuel 1 and 2). When he was a young boy, Samuel went to live at the shrine of Shiloh with Eli, the high priest. There he experienced God's call upon his life in the voice and the vision in the night (1 Samuel 3:10-14). In chapter 7, Samuel called upon the people to return to their God, Yahweh, alone and renounce the foreign gods that tempted them into disobedience.

1 Samuel 7:4. The worship of these Canaanite gods and goddesses must have been widespread. Archaeologists have dis-covered numerous statues of them, espe-cially of Astarte—the goddess of fertility. These deities were believed to control nature and to determine the fate of crops, livestock, and even human reproduction. They were particularly attractive to the Israelites who were then settling down into an agricultural economy. Despite the appeal of the Canaanite deities, the people of Israel, in response to Samuel's words, renounced them, and promised to serve Yahweh faithfully.

1 Samuel 7:5. Mizpah was located about eight miles north of Jerusalem in the terri-tory of the Benjamite tribe. Samuel's role was like that of Moses earlier; he was medi-ator between the Hebrew people and God.

In Psalm 99:6 and Jeremiah 15:1, he is explic-itly linked with Moses. The verb that is translated "pray" in the NRSV is more accu-rately rendered by the NIV as "intercede."

1 Samuel 7:6. The pouring out of a liquid as sacrifice to God is called a libation. These were usually done with wine; in fact this is the only place in the Old Testament that records the use of water. Perhaps the scarcity of water in a desert culture meant that it was precious enough to be used as a sacrifice. The people came together in an expression of repentance and humility. Pouring out of water and fasting were parts of the cleansing ritual. In the Christian sacrament of baptism, water is used as a representation of cleansing from sin (and other meanings as well).

1 Samuel 7:7. The Philistines may have thought that this gathering of the Israelites was in preparation for rebellion, and so decided to strike first. Or perhaps they sim-ply saw it as an opportune time for an attack.

1 Samuel 7:8-9. Just as their ancestors had cried to Moses at Mount Sinai, these Israelites call to Samuel to be their mediator. He was serving in a priestly role of speaking and sacrificing to God on behalf of the peo-ple. The sacrifice is of a lamb that had not yet been weaned. An animal had to be at least eight days old before it could be sacri-ficed, according to Leviticus 22:27. A "whole burnt offering" was one that was completely consumed by the fire.

1 Samuel 7:10-11. Israel undertook no military action, either offensively or defen-sively in the face of the Philistine assault. They depended upon and trusted God; everything was left to divine intervention. It cannot be determined precisely what is meant by God's "thunder[ing] with a mighty voice." It may have been thunder-bolts or earthquake. But whatever way God chose to express divine power on Israel's behalf, it was effective in making the Philistines panic and run, being pursued and killed by Israel's forces.

1 Samuel 7:12. Like Joshua in the earlier

conquest of the land, Samuel set up a commemorative stone to mark the victory. Ebenezer means "stone of help." In 1 Samuel 4:1, Israel had been defeated by the Philistines at a place called Ebenezer. While it is unlikely that this was the same location, the use of the name is a meaningful way of expressing the change in Israel's situation.

A well-known Christian hymn is "Come, Thou Fount of Every Blessing." Its second stanza begins: "Here I raise mine Ebenezer;/ hither by thy help I'm come;/ and I hope, by thy good pleasure,/ safely to arrive at home." Many who sing it do not know this Scripture that explains that an Ebenezer is a reminder of the necessity of depending upon God for help.

1 Samuel 7:13. This verse might be taken to mean that conflict with the Philistines was over, but that was not the case. As the books of Samuel continue, we are told of Saul and David's wars against these enemies. It simply indicates that the Philistines did not return to attack Israel immediately. What matters here is not the exact history but the theological understanding that "the hand of the LORD" can be trusted. Samuel also can be trusted to lead the people. Perhaps if the people had truly trusted the power of God's hand, the idealized "history" described here would have become a reality. Instead, as chapter 8 reports, the people demand a king rather than totally trusting in the Lord.

INTERPRETING THE SCRIPTURE

Renewing the Covenant, Yet Again

Covenant renewal is a theme that runs through Old Testament history from the time of Abraham. Sometimes it is God who is doing the renewing. God's promises to Abraham are repeated and passed on to Abraham's descendants—first Isaac, then Jacob, then the twelve sons of Jacob and their descendants, and ultimately the Christian church. The church has not supplanted or replaced the Jews as a people in covenant with God, but through the work of Christ we too enter into covenant relationship with God.

God's covenant promises are renewed when God graciously reminds us and reaffirms the relationship. God's promises do not, like those on the human side, need to be renewed because they have been broken or forgotten. God is always faithful to the covenant relationship. But it is much different for us. We fall away, pursue other gods, cease to be obedient. When we realize our sin and return to God, our side of the covenant needs renewal. This happened at Shechem in the time of Joshua (Joshua 24) and again in 1 Samuel 7 under the leadership of Samuel. Especially as Israel entered into new situations and faced new challenges, they tended to stray from God. Samuel called the people back, demonstrated that they can depend on God, and strengthened their faith.

The crucial conflict in 1 Samuel 7 is not the military and political one between Israel and the Philistines. It is a theological crisis. Samuel calls upon Israel to put away idolatrous gods and to "direct [their] heart[s] to the LORD." The people are to serve Yahweh alone—to be loyal and obedient. This is the perennial struggle of God's covenant people of every age. How hard it is to give up the enticing gods of secularism! Every person has an individual list of what these gods are, but every person has them. To serve only God is a lifelong struggle. Sometimes we almost succeed; mostly we fail miserably. But our failures are never the end; they are rather calls to renewal—to remembering that we are bound in covenant relationship with God, to take up again the responsibilities of that relationship, to rest anew on the never-failing mercies of our divine covenant partner.

Cry and Answer

A basic pattern of interaction between God and God's people is that of cry and answer. Samuel "cried out to the LORD for Israel and the LORD answered him"(7:9). Joseph cried out to God from an Egyptian prison; Moses, from the shore of the sea; Habakkuk, from his watchtower; Job, from the deepest despair; Daniel, from a den of lions. And God answered. The book of 1 Samuel may have been written during the Babylonian Captivity; it assured the Jews of that day that they could cry to God from exile and be answered.

As human beings who stand before God, we are to recognize and express our inability to cope with life and to attain salvation. We confess our weakness and our neediness. God responds to cries of human need. God changes situations. God offers new possibilities for life even within circumstances of darkness and distress. Our hope for salvation rests in the divine answer to our human cries. I have long remembered and often used a brief anonymous prayer that I once read in the student newspaper at a college where I was teaching:

God, I am at the end of all my resources.

Child, you are only at the beginning of mine.

Pray, That the Lord Our God May Save Us

In the face of the Philistine threat, the people of Israel called upon Samuel to pray to God for them. Intercessory prayer—our prayers for God to do something for someone else—is the most difficult kind of prayer for most of us to understand. In truth, we cannot possibly understand it, even if we practice it regularly. All prayer is a mystery. Why would God do something because we ask for it that God would not have done anyway? Can we persuade God to act in a certain way? Why does God want us to pray? Apparently God does desire our prayers; Jesus prayed and taught the disciples to do so. Prayer is irrational; it makes no sense in our scientifically and technologically sophisticated world. And yet, we pray. Pollsters report that more than eighty percent of Americans say that they pray, at least sporadically. And we pray not only for ourselves, but also for others. Why? What good does it do?

One significant aspect of prayer is its effect upon the person who prays. When we pray we learn to look more honestly at our situations, our motives, and our actions. In prayer we come to know ourselves more intimately and to acknowledge our neediness. Our petty complaints and trivial problems shrink to their proper size. Our superficial gratitude and facile presumptions are revealed to us. We begin to see ourselves through God's eyes.

But is this all that is going on? Is prayer a form of auto-suggestion? Is it purely subjective? If so, we can accomplish the same things by meditation or talk therapy. I believe that there is an external, objective reality involved. Our prayers are conversations with God; they include communication on both sides. If we will stop telling God so busily what we desire, we may hear God telling us God's will and plans. I believe that prayers have effects that go beyond us. Jesus prayed for the disciples in the Garden of Gethsemane; Paul wrote to the churches assuring them of his prayers for them; in James we are exhorted to pray for the sick. These examples indicate that prayer can cause things to change. How this works is beyond our comprehension. There are numerous references in the Old Testament to God changing the divine mind. A salient instance is Abraham's negotiation with God over how many right-eous men must be found to spare Sodom from destruction (Genesis 18). In some inex-plicable way, our prayers do sometimes influence God's actions in relation to other people and to ourselves.

Even more mysterious than our prayers for ourselves are our prayers for others. Subjectively, when we pray for other people our sensitivity to their needs may be increased. Our caring about them may be deepened; our insights, enhanced. There is also much evidence that intercessory prayer has real effects upon those who are prayed for. Recent medical studies have shown that persons for whom we pray are helped, even if they do not know that they are being

prayed for. Obviously there is nothing auto-matic or magical here. Prayer certainly does not always accomplish the ends to which it is directed and we do not know why. When Moses and later Samuel prayed for the Hebrew people, they were acting in a priestly role. One of the emphases in the Protestant Reformation of the sixteenth cen-tury was the priesthood of all believers. This means not only that we can approach God without any mediator except Christ, but also that we can be priests to other people by approaching God on their behalf. Intercessory prayer is the duty as well as the privilege of Christian people. Prayer does make a difference!

SHARING THE SCRIPTURE

PREPARING TO TEACH

Preparing Our Hearts

This week's devotional reading is found in Psalm 31:14-24. Here the psalmist affirms trust in God, who delivers him from enemies. The writer urges readers to love God and wait for God, confident that divine help will come. Note in verse 22 that the psalmist is certain that God hears when he calls out for help. Take stock of your own life. Do you trust that God will act on your behalf? Do you wait for God to act on the divine timetable, or do you take things into your own hands when answers to prayer seem to be slow in coming? Pray that you and the adult learners will trust God to answer prayers and meet your needs.

Preparing Our Minds

Study the background and lesson Scripture, both of which are found in 1 Samuel 7:3-13. As you study, consider

how prayer engages you in the plight of others as you pray for them. Also think about how your intercessory prayers affect the people for whom you are praying.

Write on newsprint:
❏ information for next week's lesson, found under "Continue the Journey."
❏ activities for further spiritual growth in "Continue the Journey."

Plan a brief lecture based on 1 Samuel 5 and 6 to help the students understand the context of the Philistine threat. Since this is not part of the background Scripture, you will need to do some research on these chapters.

Option: Identify the events in today's Scripture passage by listing them on newsprint or giving a brief lecture.

LEADING THE CLASS

(1) Gather to Learn

❖ Welcome the class members and introduce any guests.

❖ Pray that all who have come will encounter God today in a new and fresh way.

❖ Select volunteers to tell stories of times when prayers that other people prayed for them gave them strength, wisdom, healing, or something else that they needed at that moment.

❖ Read aloud today's focus statement: **Praying for others shows our concern for them and, at some level, engages us in their plight. What are the effects of praying for others? Samuel prayed for the Israelites when they were threatened by the Philistines, and God saved them**.

(2) Explore How Samuel, Who Served As Judge and Priest, Interceded, Asking God to Save the Israelites from the Philistines

❖ Give a brief lecture on 1 Samuel 5 and 6 to set the stage for today's story and help the students recognize why the Israelites "were afraid of the Philistines" (7:7).

❖ Point out Mizpah on a map. Note that this city was in the area of the tribe of Benjamin.

❖ Choose one person to read 1 Samuel 7:3-6, a second volunteer to read 7-11, and a third to read 12-13.

❖ List on newsprint the events recorded in this story. You may want to have the students identify the events, or you may choose to do this yourself as a lecture.

■ Samuel challenged the people to turn away from the gods of their neighbors and repent.
■ The people obeyed Samuel and served only God.
■ Samuel had the people gather at Mizpah so that he could intercede for them.
■ They offered a sacrifice, fasted, prayed, repented, and Samuel judged the people.

■ Sensing an opportunity, the Philistines rose up against Israel.
■ The Israelites asked Samuel to intercede for them, so he made a whole burnt offering and cried out to the Lord, who answered him.
■ God "thundered with a mighty voice" (7:10) as the Philistines drew near, which threw them into a state of confusion, allowing the Israelites to pursue them as far as Beth-car.
■ Samuel set up Ebenezer, "Stone of Help," for God had helped the people win the victory over the Philistines.
■ The Philistines were subdued for a time.

Talk with the class about any patterns they see here. Be sure they recognize the Deuteronomistic Historian's theology, which affirms that repentance and faithfulness bring help from God and victory.

Discuss the role that intercessory prayer played in this story.

(3) Consider the Effects of Praying for Others

❖ Invite the class members to give the first name of someone who they believe is in need of prayer, or a situation in the world, nation, or community that stands in need of prayer. List these names and situations on newsprint.

❖ Read this quote from Richard Foster (1942–), a contemporary Quaker writer whose books on spirituality and prayer have already become classics: **Perhaps the most astonishing characteristic of Jesus' praying is that when he prayed for others, he never concluded by saying, "If it be thy will." Nor did the apostles or prophets when they were praying for others. They obviously believed that they knew what the will of God was before they prayed the prayer of faith. They were so immersed in the milieu of the Holy Spirit that when they encountered a specific situation, they knew what should be done. Their praying was so positive that it often**

took the form of a direct, authoritative command.

❖ Spend time now in prayer. Encourage any student who wishes to say a sentence prayer for one of the identified people or situations. Ask the "pray-ers" to end their sentences with, **"Lord, in your mercy,"** and have the class respond, **"hear our prayer."**

❖ Suggest that the students discuss how they believe intercessory prayers affect not only the persons who are prayed for but also the ones who are doing the praying. Perhaps some students will be able to cite specific examples from their own experiences.

(4) Make a Commitment to Pray Daily for an Individual or Group in Need

❖ Distribute paper and pencils. Ask the students to write these words at the top of the page: **Believing that God hears and answers prayers, I commit myself to pray daily for . . .** Encourage each participant to select at least one name or situation from the list made earlier to complete the sentence.

❖ **Option:** Help the students to be accountable to one another by choosing a prayer partner. Both partners may pray for the same situations and people. Suggest that they check in with each other at least once during the week to talk about how their intercessory prayer time is going.

(5) Continue the Journey

❖ Pray that the students will honor their commitments to pray and in doing so will feel moved to compassion for these people and situations.

❖ Read aloud this preparation for next week's lesson. You may also want to post it on newsprint for the students to copy. **Prepare for next week's session entitled "A Promise You Can Trust" by reading 2 Samuel 7, which is our background Scripture and our lesson Scripture, verses 8-17. Keep these ideas in front of you as you study the lesson: Trustworthy promises mean more to us than ones easily broken. What is an example of a promise we can trust? God promised to secure David's lineage and throne, and Christians celebrate the eternal nature of this promise as fulfilled in Jesus Christ.**

❖ Read aloud the following three ideas. Challenge the students to commit themselves to use these activities as a springboard to spiritual growth.

(1) **Pray for at least one person or situation each day during the coming week.**

(2) **Use a concordance to find words related to the root "pray." If you use a computerized concordance, type in pray*. How many uses did you find? Look up some of these references to prayer. Jot down any insights that bubble up as you study.**

(3) **Recall a time when prayer made a real difference in your life. Tell someone about this experience.**

❖ Sing or read aloud "Come, Thou Fount of Every Blessing," based in part on 1 Samuel 7:12.

❖ Ask the students to join you in repeating the familiar Mizpah Benediction from Genesis 31:49 to conclude the session: **The LORD watch between you and me, when we are absent one from the other.**

UNIT 2: GOD'S COVENANT WITH JUDGES AND KINGS
A PROMISE YOU CAN TRUST

PREVIEWING THE LESSON

Lesson Scripture: 2 Samuel 7:8-17
Background Scripture: 2 Samuel 7
Key Verse: 2 Samuel 7:16

Focus of the Lesson:
Trustworthy promises mean more to us than ones easily broken. What is an example of a promise we can trust? God promised to secure David's lineage and throne, and Christians celebrate the eternal nature of this promise as fulfilled in Jesus Christ.

Goals for the Learners:
(1) to examine God's covenant with David, as revealed by the prophet Nathan.
(2) to reflect on how God's promise to David impacts their lives as Christians.
(3) to thank God for keeping promises.

Pronunciation Guide:
theocratic (thee uh krat' ik)

Supplies:
Bibles, newsprint and marker, paper and pencils, hymnals

READING THE SCRIPTURE

NRSV
2 Samuel 7:8-17

⁸Now therefore thus you shall say to my servant David: Thus says the LORD of hosts: I took you from the pasture, from following the sheep to be prince over my people Israel; ⁹and I have been with you wherever you went, and have cut off all your enemies from before you; and I will make for you a great name, like the name of the great ones of the earth. ¹⁰And I will appoint a place for my people Israel and will plant them, so that

NIV
2 Samuel 7:8-17

⁸"Now then, tell my servant David, 'This is what the LORD Almighty says: I took you from the pasture and from following the flock to be ruler over my people Israel. ⁹I have been with you wherever you have gone, and I have cut off all your enemies from before you. Now I will make your name great, like the names of the greatest men of the earth. ¹⁰And I will provide a place for my people Israel and will plant

they may live in their own place, and be disturbed no more; and evildoers shall afflict them no more, as formerly, [11]from the time that I appointed judges over my people Israel; and I will give you rest from all your enemies. Moreover the LORD declares to you that the LORD will make you a house. [12]When your days are fulfilled and you lie down with your ancestors, I will raise up your offspring after you, who shall come forth from your body, and I will establish his kingdom. [13]He shall build a house for my name, and I will establish the throne of his kingdom forever. [14]I will be a father to him, and he shall be a son to me. When he commits iniquity, I will punish him with a rod such as mortals use, with blows inflicted by human beings. [15]But I will not take my steadfast love from him, as I took it from Saul, whom I put away from before you. [16]**Your house and your kingdom shall be made sure forever before me; your throne shall be established forever.** [17]In accordance with all these words and with all this vision, Nathan spoke to David.

them so that they can have a home of their own and no longer be disturbed. Wicked people will not oppress them anymore, as they did at the beginning [11]and have done ever since the time I appointed leaders over my people Israel. I will also give you rest from all your enemies.

"'The LORD declares to you that the LORD himself will establish a house for you: [12]When your days are over and you rest with your fathers, I will raise up your offspring to succeed you, who will come from your own body, and I will establish his kingdom. [13]He is the one who will build a house for my Name, and I will establish the throne of his kingdom forever. [14]I will be his father, and he will be my son. When he does wrong, I will punish him with the rod of men, with floggings inflicted by men. [15]But my love will never be taken away from him, as I took it away from Saul, whom I removed from before you. [16]**Your house and your kingdom will endure forever before me; your throne will be established forever.'"**

[17]Nathan reported to David all the words of this entire revelation.

UNDERSTANDING THE SCRIPTURE

Introduction. Several decades of Hebrew history have passed between our last lesson and this chapter. The era of the judges ended with the people's insistence on having a king to rule them. At the Lord's sign, Samuel anointed Saul as the first king. Later, God was not pleased with how Saul reigned and sent Samuel to find and anoint the shepherd boy David, although he would not come to the throne until after Saul's death.

2 Samuel 7:1. At the time when the Scripture for today's lesson picks up the story, David had gained prominence and power. He had conquered the Philistines who had fought Israel for so long. He had conquered the city of Jerusalem and estab-

lished his government there. He had been acclaimed as king by all of the Hebrew people and had brought the ark of the covenant—the symbol of God's presence—to Jerusalem. There was peace in the land and King David had built himself a palace. This is the first use in the chapter of the word translated "house." Here it means "palace"; other meanings will emerge later.

2 Samuel 7:2. Nathan is introduced into the account here for the first time. He must have been a court prophet and, as such, an important adviser of the king. In chapter 12, he will confront David about the king's acts of adultery and murder. Cedar was an expensive wood that had to be imported from Phoenicia or Lebanon. The origin of the ark is recorded in Exodus 25. It was a wooden chest (about 45x27x27 inches) that was carried with the Israelites during their time in the desert wilderness after the exodus. The ark contained the tablets of stone upon which the law was written and other holy objects. The ark represented God's presence. It was apparently still housed in the tent of meeting (Exodus 29:41-45), as it had been in the wilderness.

2 Samuel 7:3. Nathan gives his approval to the project of building a temple.

2 Samuel 7:4-6. Nathan had spoken too quickly and without consulting God. During the night God instructed him to tell David that the Lord did not want the king to build a temple. God had always lived in a place that was mobile—the tent of meeting and the more elaborate tent called the tabernacle. A fixed place of dwelling might limit the divine freedom. In this verse as in the next and in verse 13, "house" means "temple."

2 Samuel 7:7. God had not asked any of the judges to build a temple. David had been wrong about the divine priorities. Or perhaps God knew that David's motives for the project had more to do with enhancing himself than reverencing God.

2 Samuel 7:8-9. In these verses, God through Nathan reminded David of all that God had done for him since he was a simple shepherd boy. God promised to do even more to make David great.

2 Samuel 7:10. God also promised to enable Israel to settle down in peace in their own territory.

2 Samuel 7:11. God is playing on the word "house." In this verse and in verses 16, 19, 25-27, and 29, the word means "dynasty"—a line of rulers from the same family. This divine promise was unconditional; it was not predicated on anything that David did.

2 Samuel 7:12-13. After David's death his son will build a temple for God. No reason is given here, but in 1 Chronicles 22:7-10 God tells David that he cannot build the temple because of the blood that he has shed in warfare. The promise is repeated; the kingship of this son and his descendants will be perpetual.

2 Samuel 7:14-15. These verses describe God's future relationship with David's son and successor, Solomon. The language is familial, denoting a special relationship. God will discipline Solomon, but the covenant promise will endure. The word "but" in verse 15 means "nevertheless."

2 Samuel 7:16-17. Nathan ended his message from God to David by repeating twice more that the covenant with the house of David will be everlasting.

2 Samuel 7:18-20. David's prayer in response to God's words begins here and continues through the remainder of the chapter. He went into the tent where the ark was and "sat before the LORD." David first praised God in an attitude of astonishment and wonder. He was deferential in expressing his gratitude for this covenant with him and his family. David addressed God seven times in this prayer as "LORD God"—a title that appears only one other time (1 Samuel 14:41) in the two books of Samuel. He referred to himself as "servant" ten times. Note that in verse 19, the king expressed his hope that God would make clear to the people the status given to David and his family.

2 Samuel 7:21-24. David's acclaim of God continued with expressions of gratitude not only for what God would do for David and his descendants, but also what God had done for the nation of Israel throughout its history. His words were a recapitulation of other descriptions of the role of Israel. Deuteronomy 7:6-8 is an example: "For you are a people holy to the LORD your God; the LORD your God has chosen you out of all the peoples on earth to be his people, his treasured possession. It was not because you were more numerous than any other people ... for you were the fewest of all peoples. It was because the LORD loved you and kept the oath that he swore to your ancestors...."

2 Samuel 7:25-26. At this point in his

prayer, David shifted from an attitude of amazed deference to one of insistence. "Do as you have promised," he asked, almost seeming to demand that God keep the divine word.

2 Samuel 7:27-29. David continued to lay claim to God's promise and ask God to confirm and keep it, so that his family might enjoy the blessings of this covenant forever. Perhaps the king's tone here was not really so much one of demand as of pleading. Surely it must have been exceedingly difficult for David to accept the reality of this everlasting covenant that God was granting.

INTERPRETING THE SCRIPTURE

The Unconditional Covenant

One of the striking aspects of the Davidic covenant is that God sets no conditions for it. Decades earlier Saul had been anointed as the first king of the Hebrew nation. But during the years of his reign he committed a series of acts that displeased God and "the LORD was sorry that he had made Saul king over Israel" (1 Samuel 15:35c). God then sent Samuel to Bethlehem to anoint one of the sons of Jesse to be the next king. This was, of course, David who at the time of his anointing was only a boy. Years later when Saul died on the battlefield, by deliberately falling on his own sword, the way was open for David to ascend to the throne. Significantly, the ethical requirements that God had enforced for Saul were not imposed upon David. God's covenant with David was unconditional. Here we see again in the Old Testament what will become one of the major themes of the New—unconditional grace, the free promise of the good news of salvation available to all. We should not understand this as meaning that the moral demands of the covenant God made with the people at Sinai had been completely removed. Even David and his descendants on the throne will be punished for their transgressions of divine law. David suffered the death of his and Bathsheba's first son because of the way he had taken her from her husband. The king committed other sins that caused tragic results in his family. Still, God's commitment endured in spite of sin. Half a millennium later in their history, the Hebrew people were defeated by their enemies and both of the nations into which David's kingdom had divided were conquered. The people were taken off into exile in foreign lands. In times when all hope seemed to be lost, the retelling of the story of God's unconditional covenant with David's dynasty offered promise for the future. God's covenant promises endured; God was not finished working with and through the Davidic line for the salvation of God's people.

God's Promises to David

Through the words of the prophet Nathan, God reminded David of the special relationship they had shared since David was a boy. Obviously God had "had his eye on David" throughout David's life. Probably he was only a young teenager when God chose him to be the second king of Israel and sent the prophet Samuel to anoint him. God had protected him from the enmity of Saul who had sought to kill him. God had given him victory over the various enemies who opposed his kingship and over the territories that became parts of the kingdom. God had enabled him to triumph over Israel's longtime foe, the Philistines. In our Scripture passage for today, God promised David rest from this constant struggling with enemies. God also promised to establish the people of Israel in a place of their own. David would not only be a king, but he would also originate a dynasty—a line of kings who would rule the nation after him. David's successor on the throne would build the house for God, the temple, that David had wanted to build. God would establish the Davidic line of kingship forever.

Not all of these promises came true in the literal sense that the people of Israel over the years expected. The Davidic line of rulers apparently ended with the Babylonian defeat of the nation some four centuries later. But faithful Jews looked for God to intervene in their history and reestablish the promised Davidic kingdom.

The Hope for a Messiah

The seventh chapter of 2 Samuel is one of the most important in the Old Testament because it provides one of the major foundations for the messianic hopes of both Judaism and Christianity. Historically, the dynasty founded by David came to an end in 587–586 B.C. when Jerusalem was conquered, the temple destroyed, and the people of Judah taken away from their land and into exile in Babylonia. But because of the unconditional nature of the divine promise, the prophets encouraged the people to expect that God would again intervene in their history and restore them through a descendant of David. Examples are found in Isaiah 9:6-7, 11:1-16; Jeremiah 23:5-6, 30:8-9, 33:14-16; Ezekiel 34:23-24, 37:24-25. The messianic hope among the Jewish people took a variety of forms in Old Testament times and throughout their history even to today. At least one prominent form of it was the expectation of a human agent of Davidic descent who would be God's Messiah or Anointed One. The coming of this messiah would not represent the end of the world, but be a messiah who would save God's people within the process of human history.

This Davidic descendant would inherit the kingship of David and be the ideal king in a restored theocratic nation.

The early Christians saw the fulfillment of the divine promise in Jesus who was called Christ—the Greek form of the term messiah. Jesus announced the coming of the kingdom of God, which would bring about a transformation in human history. New Testament writers presented Jesus as the son of David in order to identify him as the inheritor and fulfillment of the messianic promise. See Matthew 1:1, Romans 1:3 and Revelation 3:7 as examples. Today the Revised Common Lectionary used in many denominations has 2 Samuel 7:1-11, 16 as the Old Testament lesson for the fourth Sunday of Advent, Year B. During the Advent season we look forward to the coming of Christ as God's promised deliverer. This reading is paired with the Gospel lesson from Luke 1:26-38, which is the account of the annunciation of the angel Gabriel to Mary and stipulates the direct connection between David and Jesus: "And now, you will conceive in your womb and bear a son, and you will name him Jesus. He will be great, and will be called the Son of the Most High, and the Lord God will give to him the throne of his ancestor David. He will reign over the house of Jacob forever, and of his kingdom there will be no end" (1:31-33).

Mary's response to the announcement of the son to be born to her was to sing the beautiful canticle that we call the *Magnificat* (Luke 1:46-55). By comparing the two it is easy to see that Mary's song was based on the song of Hannah when she learned that she was to become the mother of Samuel (1 Samuel 2:1-10). Both songs celebrate the coming reversals of political and economic power in human history that will result from the coming of God's anointed king. In Hannah's song the anticipated king was David; in Mary's, it was Jesus. Through every age, God is working to establish the conditions of justice, power, and peace that will characterize the divine kingdom. This is a crucial word to the church today to remind us that we must understand our own faith to be always concerned about these same realities. God's word is sure and we can trust that divine promises will come to pass in God's own time and way.

SHARING THE SCRIPTURE

PREPARING TO TEACH

Preparing Our Hearts

This week's devotional reading is found in Psalm 5, which is attributed to David. In this psalm David not only prays to be delivered from his enemies but he trusts that God will do just that. Read and meditate on this psalm. Are there ways in which you see yourself as someone who is like David? Try writing a psalm or prayer expressing both your needs and your trust that God will provide for you.

Pray that you and the adult learners will feel free to petition God to meet your needs, whatever those needs may be.

Preparing Our Minds

Study the background Scripture, 2 Samuel 7, and lesson Scripture, verses 8-17. As you read, think about experiences you have had with promises: When are they likely to be broken, and when are they likely to be kept?

Write on newsprint:
❑ questions for "Reflect on How God's Promise to David Impacts the Learners Lives As Christians."
❑ information for next week's lesson, found under "Continue the Journey."
❑ activities for further spiritual growth in "Continue the Journey."

Plan any lectures that you will use.

LEADING THE CLASS

(1) Gather to Learn

❖ Welcome the class members and introduce any guests.

❖ Pray that the adults will be open to new ideas found in familiar passages of Scripture.

❖ Discuss this question with the class: **How do you know that you can trust someone?** Here are some possible answers, which you may prefer to use as the basis for a brief lecture. You may want to list ideas on newsprint.

■ You get to know the person well before you are willing to trust him or her.

■ Through this knowing you form a positive attachment.

■ The person's past actions have been reliable and trustworthy; therefore, if he or she makes a promise, you can rely on it.

■ If you have been betrayed in the past, you have learned strategies for rebuilding relationships and building new relationships.

■ You have learned to trust yourself.

❖ Point out that God is always trustworthy and will keep divine promises, even when there seems to be no way that is possible.

❖ Read aloud today's focus statement: **Trustworthy promises mean more to us than ones easily broken. What is an example of a promise we can trust? God promised to secure David's lineage and throne, and Christians celebrate the eternal nature of this promise as fulfilled in Jesus Christ.**

(2) Examine God's Covenant with David, As Revealed by the Prophet Nathan

❖ Use information from verses 1-7 in Understanding the Scripture to set the scene for today's lesson. Be sure to note that in verse 8 God is speaking to Nathan, who is the "you" at the beginning of this verse.

❖ Choose a volunteer to read 2 Samuel 7:8-17.

❖ Look at verses 8-9a and talk about David's history with God. Consider what God has done for David, and how those actions would prompt David to rely on God's promise.

❖ Ask the participants to read silently 2 Samuel 7:9b-17. Prompt the students to identify what God is promising to David and to Israel. List these promises on newsprint. (See information in Understanding the Scripture for ideas.) Be sure to note that God's promise of a "house" refers to a dynasty.

❖ Read or retell "The Unconditional Covenant" in Interpreting the Scripture to help the class recognize that the promises God made to David had "no strings attached."

❖ Look again at the list made for 2 Samuel 7:9b-17 and consider how many of these promises have already become reality.

■ David did become a "great name," considered the most important king in Israel's history (7:9).
■ There was a time of relative peace for the Israelites in their own land (7:10).
■ God did raise up a dynasty from David (7:11-12), which began with his son Solomon.
■ David's son Solomon did build a house (here meaning a temple) for God (7:13).
■ God and Solomon did have an intimate relationship, as described in 1 Kings 3:3-15. God may punish Solomon but will neither take away divine love nor give the throne to someone else as God did with King Saul (7:14-15).
■ David's throne will be established forever (7:16).

❖ Note that if we look at Israel's history, the kingdom split after Solomon's death. The northern kingdom (Israel) ended in 721 B.C. when the Assyrians overran it. The southern kingdom (Judah) was destroyed in 587 B.C. by the Babylonians under King Nebuchadnezzar. Hence, it appears that David's line ended.

❖ Point out that because God made an unconditional promise to David, the prophets continued to look for a messiah from the line of David. Ask volunteers to look up and read these examples.

■ Isaiah 9:6-7
■ Isaiah 11:1-16
■ Jeremiah 23:5-6
■ Jeremiah 30:8-9
■ Jeremiah 33:14-16
■ Ezekiel 34:23-24
■ Ezekiel 37:24-25

❖ Read or retell the second and third paragraph of "The Hope for a Messiah" to demonstrate how the Christian church believes that God's unconditional promise to David was fulfilled in Jesus.

(3) Reflect on How God's Promise to David Influences the Learners' Lives As Christians

❖ Divide the class into pairs or small groups. Ask them to discuss these two questions, which you may want to write on newsprint.

(1) Do you believe with the early Christians that God's promise to David was fulfilled in Jesus? Why or why not?

(2) What difference does it make in your life if you believe that God's promise to David was ultimately fulfilled in Jesus?

❖ Ask the groups to report back. Note common themes that run through these reports.

(4) Thank God for Keeping Promises

❖ Distribute paper and pencils. Invite the students to meditate on David's words of thanksgiving to God, which you will read (below), and then to pray silently their own prayers, thanking God for keeping promises and bringing them to the point that they are today. Some students may wish to record their prayer on paper.

❖ Read aloud the following selected verses from David's Prayer in 2 Samuel 7:18-29, which is part of today's background Scripture: [18]Then King David went in and sat before the LORD, and said, "Who am I, O Lord GOD, and what is my house, that you have brought me thus far? ... [21]Because of your promise, and according to your own heart, you have wrought all this greatness, so that your servant may know it. [22]Therefore you are great, O LORD God; for there is no one like you, and there is no God besides you."

Allow time for the students to meditate, pray, and write if they choose.

(5) Continue the Journey

❖ Break the silence by praying that all who have studied together this day may trust in God's promises, believing that God is indeed a promise-keeper.

❖ Read aloud this preparation for next week's lesson. You may also want to post it on newsprint for the students to copy. **Prepare for next week's session entitled "God Answers Prayer" by reading 1 Kings 3, noting particularly verses 3-14. Keep this focus in mind as you prepare the lesson: Most people want to understand the world** around them and learn to make wise choices in it. What is the source of such wisdom? Solomon gained tremendous wisdom by asking God for it, and God granted his prayers.

❖ Read aloud the following three ideas. Challenge the students to commit themselves to use these activities as a springboard to spiritual growth.

(1) Search your Bible this week for examples of promises that God has made. How have these been fulfilled, or are we still awaiting their fulfillment? What emotions come to mind when you realize that God keeps promises?

(2) Compare Jesus' genealogy in Matthew 1:1-17, which begins with Abraham and ends with Jesus, and Luke 3:23-38, which traces Jesus' lineage back through Joseph to Adam. Although you will note some differences, focus on similarities, especially in regard to David. Which names are familiar to you?

(3) Make and keep a promise to a significant person in your life.

❖ Sing or read aloud "Standing on the Promises."

❖ Ask the students to join you in repeating the familiar Mizpah Benediction from Genesis 31:49 to conclude the session: **The LORD watch between you and me, when we are absent one from the other.**

UNIT 2: GOD'S COVENANT WITH JUDGES AND KINGS
GOD ANSWERS PRAYER

PREVIEWING THE LESSON

Lesson Scripture: 1 Kings 3:3-14
Background Scripture: 1 Kings 3
Key Verse: 1 Kings 3:12

Focus of the Lesson:
Most people want to understand the world around them and learn to make wise choices in it. What is the source of such wisdom? Solomon gained tremendous wisdom by asking God for it, and God granted his prayers.

Goals for the Learners:
(1) to learn about Solomon's prayer for wisdom in 1 Kings.
(2) to identify characteristics of biblical wisdom and discern where they are embodied in people today.
(3) to pray for a "hearing heart."

Pronunciation Guide:
Gezer (gee'zuhr)
Gibeon (gib' ee uhn)

Supplies:
Bibles, newsprint and marker, paper and pencils, hymnals, optional meditative music on CD or tape and appropriate player

OCTOBER 29

READING THE SCRIPTURE

NRSV
1 Kings 3:3-14

³Solomon loved the LORD, walking in the statutes of his father David; only, he sacrificed and offered incense at the high places. ⁴The king went to Gibeon to sacrifice there, for that was the principal high place; Solomon used to offer a thousand burnt offerings on that altar. ⁵At Gibeon the LORD

NIV
1 Kings 3:3-14

³Solomon showed his love for the LORD by walking according to the statutes of his father David, except that he offered sacrifices and burned incense on the high places.

⁴The king went to Gibeon to offer sacrifices, for that was the most important high place, and Solomon offered a thousand

appeared to Solomon in a dream by night; and God said, "Ask what I should give you." [6]And Solomon said, "You have shown great and steadfast love to your servant my father David, because he walked before you in faithfulness, in righteousness, and in uprightness of heart toward you; and you have kept for him this great and steadfast love, and have given him a son to sit on his throne today. [7]And now, O LORD my God, you have made your servant king in place of my father David, although I am only a little child; I do not know how to go out or come in. [8]And your servant is in the midst of the people whom you have chosen, a great people, so numerous they cannot be numbered or counted. [9]Give your servant therefore an understanding mind to govern your people, able to discern between good and evil; for who can govern this your great people?"

[10]It pleased the Lord that Solomon had asked this. [11]God said to him, "Because you have asked this, and have not asked for yourself long life or riches, or for the life of your enemies, but have asked for yourself understanding to discern what is right, [12]I now do according to your word. **Indeed I give you a wise and discerning mind; no one like you has been before you and no one like you shall arise after you.** [13]I give you also what you have not asked, both riches and honor all your life; no other king shall compare with you. [14]If you will walk in my ways, keeping my statutes and my commandments, as your father David walked, then I will lengthen your life."

burnt offerings on that altar. [5]At Gibeon the LORD appeared to Solomon during the night in a dream, and God said, "Ask for whatever you want me to give you."

[6]Solomon answered, "You have shown great kindness to your servant, my father David, because he was faithful to you and righteous and upright in heart. You have continued this great kindness to him and have given him a son to sit on his throne this very day.

[7]"Now, O LORD my God, you have made your servant king in place of my father David. But I am only a little child and do not know how to carry out my duties. [8]Your servant is here among the people you have chosen, a great people, too numerous to count or number. [9]So give your servant a discerning heart to govern your people and to distinguish between right and wrong. For who is able to govern this great people of yours?"

[10]The Lord was pleased that Solomon had asked for this. [11]So God said to him, "Since you have asked for this and not for long life or wealth for yourself, nor have asked for the death of your enemies but for discernment in administering justice, [12]I will do what you have asked. **I will give you a wise and discerning heart, so that there will never have been anyone like you, nor will there ever be.** [13]Moreover, I will give you what you have not asked for—both riches and honor—so that in your lifetime you will have no equal among kings. [14]And if you walk in my ways and obey my statutes and commands as David your father did, I will give you a long life."

UNDERSTANDING THE SCRIPTURE

1 Kings 3:1. This opening verse sets the story in the time after Solomon had succeeded his father David on the throne and before the building of the temple. The old fortress area within Jerusalem was called the City of David; this name continued to be

used for the city as it expanded. The granting of pharaoh's daughter to Solomon in marriage was very significant. Egyptian rulers rarely agreed to such alliances, preferring to have the daughters of other monarchs given to Egyptian princes. This marriage indicated the strong position of power and prestige that the Hebrew nation of Judah was gaining in the region. As a dowry, pharaoh gave his daughter the Canaanite town of Gezer, which Egypt had earlier captured. Gezer would prove important to Solomon because it was located at a crossroad of two major trade routes. One went northward to Egypt and the other to the Mediterranean Sea at Joppa. Possession of this strategic location enabled Solomon to profit richly from trade, as well as to import materials for the building of the temple. This Egyptian princess was the most important and probably Solomon's favorite of his many wives. She resided in the old fortress area until a separate palace was constructed for her years later.

1 Kings 3:2. High places were hilltop shrines where Canaanites and others practiced the sacrifices and other rituals of their religion. Apparently, the Hebrew people constructed their own shrines in these same areas, in some cases literally on top of the earlier ones. Worship at these hilltop shrines was problematic for the people of Judah—and their king—although it was not actually outlawed until later. According to Numbers 33:52, pagan worship sites were to be destroyed. In Deuteronomy 12:1-14 worship of God outside of the city of Jerusalem was prohibited because of the fear that the Hebrew faith would be contaminated by pagan influence. The writer or editor of 1 Kings 3:2 was justifying Solomon's practice of worshiping at the high places by pointing out that the temple had not yet been built in Jerusalem.

1 Kings 3:3. Solomon's conduct in the early years of his kingship was judged to be exemplary. His only major mistake was his worship of God at the high places.

1 Kings 3:4. Gibeon was located about seven miles from Jerusalem. After the destruction of the shrine at Shiloh by the Philistines (1 Samuel 4:1-18), Gibeon apparently became the most important place for the Hebrew people's worship. According to

the Chronicles, the tabernacle and the ancient bronze altar for burnt offerings were there (1 Chronicles 16:39-40; 21:29; 2 Chronicles 1:3, 6, 13.) The figure of one thousand may be literally accurate—huge numbers of animals were sacrificed by the kings on occasion—or it could simply be indicative of a very large number.

1 Kings 3:5. Divine revelations through dreams appear in both the Old and New Testaments. Examples are Jacob's dream at Bethel of a ladder to heaven (Genesis 28:10-17) and Joseph's dream in which he was told that Mary was pregnant with a child of the Holy Spirit (Matthew 1:20-21). Solomon may have intentionally sought to receive a dream revelation and prepared for it by sacrificing and by sleeping at Gibeon.

1 Kings 3:6. Solomon thanked God for the divine faithfulness to his father David. He praised the righteousness of his father. The language here is that of the covenant; Solomon was bringing the covenant relationship before God.

1 Kings 3:7. Solomon's language here is figurative; he had been born about halfway through David's reign. He must have been about twenty years of age at the time. The reference to "a little child" was an expression of humility. "How to go out or come in" was an expression covering the responsibilities of leadership in general.

1 Kings 3:8-10. The large number of Hebrew people was fulfillment of God's covenant promise to Abraham (Genesis 13:16, 22:17-18). Solomon prayed for knowledge and discernment to be capable of ruling wisely. In verse 10 there is a glimpse into the mind of God.

1 Kings 3:11-13. Prayers for longevity, wealth, and revenge were typical for kings, but Solomon asked for none of these. God granted to him what he had asked for—the wisdom and ability to discern right and wrong. God also generously gave the king the riches and prestige that he had not requested. Solomon's wisdom and wealth were to exceed that of all others. Christians are reminded of Jesus' promise that all things would be given to those who first seek the kingdom of God (Luke 12:31).

1 Kings 3:14. God did not grant Solomon long life unconditionally. That would depend upon how faithfully he obeyed the covenant. Sadly, the king did not turn out to be faithful and probably lived to be only about sixty years old.

1 Kings 3:15. The ark of the covenant—the symbol of divine presence—had been brought to Jerusalem by David. When Solomon returned from Gibeon, he thanked God through sacrifices and generous food for his servants.

1 Kings 3:16. The remainder of the chapter relates the famous story of Solomon's decision in the case of two women who claimed the same baby—the best-known example of his wisdom. This traditional folktale can also be found in the literature of other peoples in the area. Hebrew society was organized in such a way that even those of low class could approach the king directly to seek justice.

1 Kings 3:17-28. The women undoubtedly lived in the same brothel; such places were common in ancient, as well as modern, cities. Note that Solomon does not attempt to "get to the bottom" of the case. He asked no questions, sought no witnesses. His decision was an echo of Hebrew law that called for the division of disputed property if the dispute could not be resolved. He depended completely upon being able to interpret the women's reactions well enough to identify the real mother. When news of the decision spread among the people, they recognized the king's God-given ability to dispense justice with insight and prudence.

INTERPRETING THE SCRIPTURE

Ruling Wisely

The conversation between God and Solomon in the king's dream delineates two competing patterns of kingship, and of all types of government. In the time of Samuel, the people of Israel had asked, almost demanded, that God give them a king to rule in place of the line of judges. There are two traditions reflected in the Old Testament about this. One indicates that God granted this request freely and worked through the kings as God had worked through the judges and Moses and Joshua before them. The other tradition presents the people's desire for a king as an expression of unfaithfulness. God grants a monarchy reluctantly and through Samuel warns the people about the abuses that monarchy might bring (1 Samuel 8:10-22). Solomon chose to be the kind of king who is described in Deuteronomy 17:14-20—he would revere God and obey the law. Solomon speaks of himself as God's servant four times in verses 6-9. He is portrayed as a loyal vassal in covenant relationship with his Lord in verses 6 and 14. In verses 8 and 9, he states that his goal is to provide for the welfare of God's people. This is the language of royal ideology—an understanding of the king as "God's son," acting for God and in intimate covenant relationship with God. Read Psalm 89:19-37 for a fulsome description. In only a little less extreme language, monarchs in European nations long claimed what was called "the divine right of kings."

It must, unfortunately, be said that Solomon proved unable to maintain the ideals that he articulated in 1 Kings 3. If he retained the divine gift of wisdom, he chose not to use it. He married numerous foreign women who brought competing religious beliefs and practices into the heart of the kingdom. He devoted himself enthusiastically to the accumulation and display of wealth. He abused the people over whom he ruled by oppressive taxes and forced labor. By the time of his death, the nation was close to revolt. In the early part of the reign of his son who refused to renounce his policies, the nation split into a northern kingdom of Israel with a new line of rulers and the southern kingdom of Judah, which continued to be ruled by David's dynasty.

Both the Old and New Testaments make clear that God is concerned about the governments under which people live. The United States is not equivalent to ancient Israel, and we do not believe that our governing authorities are always chosen by God. While we are confident that God ultimately works out the divine will in human history, we know that God allows it to be violated and repudiated in the course of events. What does Solomon's story have to say to us as twenty-first century American citizens? Those who are in positions to execute power can share Solomon's prayer for wisdom and discernment to govern justly and well. Those outside positions of power can be courageous critics and faithful prophets who point out abuses and work for change in leadership and policies. For Christians, the only ideal governing authority is Jesus Christ. The Revised Common Lectionary pairs 1 Kings 3 with Matthew 13:44-52, which reflects the priorities of the divine kingdom. God's will for human authority structures is made clear in Jesus' words: "whoever wishes to be great among you must be your servant" (Matthew 20:26).

A Discerning Heart and Mind

The New International Version uses the phrase "discerning heart" (3:9) where the New Revised Standard uses "understanding mind." There is no substantive distinction in meaning, but there is a difference in nuance and connotation. To speak of the mind is to enter into the realm of the intellect, the

rational, the logical. To speak of the heart implies emotion, affection, and compassion. Christians need both a discerning mind and a discerning heart. God is the creator and giver of our minds; it is God's intent that we be rational beings and that we apply our logic to our Christians beliefs and principles. I am puzzled by people who seem to believe that faith and reason are in opposition and that one must choose between them. Faith is not irrational; it is supra-rational. Fortunately, our faith is not limited to that which we can understand intellectually. Faith is not counter to reason, but reason can take us only so far. Faith transcends reason and enables us to believe and to follow even when we do not understand. To have a discerning mind is to use all one's intellectual powers in the pursuit of truth, to be willing to recognize the limits of reason, and to be open to God's leading which we perceive but cannot understand.

A discerning heart involves the inner core of a human being. It has to do with the direction toward which one is oriented and to whom or what one is open. A part of being in right relationship with God is to intentionally position one's inner being toward God—to be constantly aware of God's presence, ever open to God's leading. When King Solomon asked for a discerning heart, he was petitioning God to empower him to discriminate wisely between those things that were in accord with the covenant relationship and those that were not. Solomon knew that as a king who was the religious as well as the political leader of his people, he must be able to judge right from wrong. He needed from God both the ability to perceive the right courses of action for himself, but also to make right decisions for his people. The story of the two women who claimed the living child illustrates the power of the discerning heart. Solomon decided this case not so much by logical reasoning as by the judgment of the heart. His insight was on a psychological level. He knew instinctively what the reactions of the two women meant; he knew in his heart.

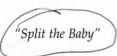
"Split the Baby"

The most famous instance of King Solomon's God-given wisdom is this episode of domestic conflict between two mothers. "Split the baby" is a popular cliché in legal circles today. It is, for example, the principle upon which legal decisions are made when irrevocable disagreements exist between a couple who are divorcing. Dividing everything down the middle may not be the truly fair solution, but it is at least clear and legally justifiable. It is, of course, not so simple when a child is the focus of dispute. Because Solomon's prayer was answered and he has received wisdom from God, he was able to "see into the hearts" of these mothers and know what the final outcome of his seemingly dreadful order would be.

God had not granted Solomon simply understanding of the divine will, but also deep insight into the motivations and desires of human beings. Solomon understood human nature and used that understanding to make decisions as king. The unnamed mother whose baby was alive was prepared to surrender her son; she would lose him for herself in order to save his life. This mother was willing to experience the agony of losing a child in order to achieve higher purposes than her own desires. We catch here a glimpse into the nature of our parent God whose love for us exceeds even the deepest of human loves. God is willing to surrender the divine self for us—even to the cross.

SHARING THE SCRIPTURE

PREPARING TO TEACH

Preparing Our Hearts

This week's devotional reading is found in Psalm 119:97-104. Psalm 119, which includes 176 verses, celebrates God's law. In today's reading, the psalmist describes his constant dedication to the Torah and exclaims that God's law has made him wiser than his enemies, his elders, and even his teachers. If you were asked to rate your devotion to God's word on a scale of one to ten, where would you rate? How does the amount of time that you spend studying and devotionally reading the Bible support or challenge your rating? What changes might you need to make in your daily routine to have more time to concentrate on God's word? Write a commitment to action in your spiritual journal.

Pray that you and the adult learners will seek God's wisdom continually.

Preparing Our Minds

Study the background Scripture, 1 Kings 3 and lesson Scripture, verses 3-14. As you encounter these passages, consider the source of wisdom that enables you to understand the world and make wise choices.

Write on newsprint:
- ❑ questions for "Identify Characteristics of Biblical Wisdom and Discern Where They Are Embodied in People Today."
- ❑ information for next week's lesson, found under "Continue the Journey."
- ❑ activities for further spiritual growth in "Continue the Journey."

Plan a lecture if you choose Option 1 for "Learn about Solomon's Prayer for Wisdom in 1 Kings."

LEADING THE CLASS

(1) Gather to Learn

❖ Welcome the class members and introduce any guests.

❖ Pray that each learner who has come today will be aware of the powerful effect that prayer has on their lives and the lives of others.

❖ Write these words on newsprint: *If I could just understand…* Invite the students to call out endings to this sentence. They may wish to think especially about "understanding why" and "understanding how."

❖ Engage the students in conversation as to why it would be important to them to understand "why" or "how" something was the way it was. Help them to recognize that they are seeking to be wise in some specific area.

❖ Read aloud today's focus statement: **Most people want to understand the world around them and learn to make wise choices in it. What is the source of such wisdom? Solomon gained tremendous wisdom by asking God for it, and God granted his prayers.**

(2) Learn about Solomon's Prayer for Wisdom in 1 Kings

❖ Present information about Solomon in one of these ways.

Option 1: Research the life of Solomon by using information from the lesson and other resources. Do a brief lecture on your findings.

Option 2: Invite the students to state information they know about Solomon and list these ideas on newsprint. If you choose this option, be sure you have some solid knowledge in order to correct misperceptions and/or expand ideas.

❖ Choose three volunteers to read 1 Kings 3:3-14 as a drama. One reader is the narrator, another will speak the words of God, and the third will read Solomon's part.

❖ Continue the prior discussion about Solomon by adding any new insights gained from this passage. List them on newsprint, if you chose that option.

❖ Identify exactly what Solomon prayed for (see 3:9).

❖ Encourage the students to talk about ways in which Solomon's prayer perhaps surprised them.

❖ Discuss how God's response to this prayer either challenged some of the students' understandings of how God works or strengthened those understandings. Think especially about the fact that God gave Solomon what he asked for—and much more.

❖ Encourage the adults to talk about how this godly wisdom affected Solomon as a king.

(3) Identify Characteristics of Biblical Wisdom and Discern Where They Are Embodied in People Today

❖ Ask the following questions. (Be sure to note that the wisdom tradition, which is filled with ideas on "practical wisdom" is only one strand of biblical wisdom. We see biblical wisdom in many places other than Wisdom literature.)

(1) **How do you define "wisdom"?**
(2) **Which biblical characters do you believe embody wisdom?**
(3) **What are some of the traits of these people?**
(4) **In whom do you see some of these traits today?**
(5) **How does biblical wisdom challenge some of the currently accepted political, social, or economic "wisdom"?**

❖ Divide the class into small groups to discuss these questions, which you will post on newsprint.

(1) **How would our nation be different if we truly lived according to God's wisdom?**
(2) **What am I willing to do to make this vision a reality?**

❖ Invite the groups to report back to the class. Affirm the students' ideas for making the vision a reality. Perhaps some of these ideas can be shaped into viable action.

(4) Pray for a "Discerning Heart"

❖ Read or retell "A Discerning Heart and Mind" in Interpreting the Scripture.

❖ Use "Split the Baby" in Interpreting the Scripture, taken from 1 Kings 3:16-28, which is part of today's background Scripture, to illustrate how Solomon used the wisdom God gave him to settle an important dispute.

❖ Ask the students to comment on how a "discerning heart" enables one to act wisely.

❖ Provide an opportunity for the learners to pray for a "discerning heart" so that they might have whatever wisdom they need in their lives to do their jobs well, to interact wisely with their families, or to give wise leadership to the church. Suggest that they ask God for a "discerning heart" that is sensitive and open to divine leading.

❖ **Option:** Play some meditative instrumental music in the background as the adults silently lift their prayers.

❖ **Option:** Distribute paper and pencils so that students who prefer to write their prayers may do so.

(5) Continue the Journey

❖ Pray that the learners will recognize that God does answer prayers that are offered in accordance with the divine will.

❖ Read aloud this preparation for next week's lesson. You may also want to post it on newsprint for the students to copy.

Prepare for next week's session entitled "Depending on God's Power" by reading the background Scripture from 1 Kings 18:20-39. Our lesson will focus on 1 Kings 18:20-24, 30-35, 38-39. As you read the lesson, concentrate on these ideas: Sometimes we need to depend on a power greater than ourselves. What power can we depend on? At a very critical moment, Elijah depended on God's power, and he was not disappointed.

❖ Read aloud the following three ideas. Challenge the students to commit themselves to use these activities as a springboard to spiritual growth.

(1) **Think about a situation that is challenging or perplexing you. Pray that God will give you the wisdom needed to deal with this problem.**

(2) **Recall that Solomon connected wisdom with living well. Write in your spiritual journal about your understanding of how wisdom enables us to live well. As you think about this connection, what new discoveries do you make?**

(3) **Pray for the leaders of the world, nation, community, and church. Ask God to endow them with the wisdom they need to lead effectively.**

❖ Sing or read aloud "Sweet Hour of Prayer."

❖ Ask the students to join you in repeating the familiar Mizpah Benediction from Genesis 31:49 to conclude the session: **The LORD watch between you and me, when we are absent one from the other.**

UNIT 3: LIVING AS GOD'S COVENANTED PEOPLE
DEPENDING ON GOD'S POWER

PREVIEWING THE LESSON

Lesson Scripture: 1 Kings 18:20-24, 30-35, 38-39
Background Scripture: 1 Kings 18:20-39
Key Verse: 1 Kings 18:39

Focus of the Lesson:
Sometimes we need to depend on a power greater than ourselves. What power can we depend on? At a very critical moment, Elijah depended on God's power, and he was not disappointed.

Goals for the Learners:
(1) to delve into the story of Elijah's triumph over the priests of Baal at Mount Carmel.
(2) to relate the contest to modern examples of God's power.
(3) to act in ways that demonstrate trust in and dependence on God's power.

Pronunciation Guide:
seah (see' uh)

Supplies:
Bibles, newsprint and marker, paper and pencils, hymnals, optional reference books for research on Baal worship

READING THE SCRIPTURE

NRSV
1 Kings 18:20-24, 30-35, 38-39

[20]So Ahab sent to all the Israelites, and assembled the prophets at Mount Carmel. [21]Elijah then came near to all the people, and said, "How long will you go limping with two different opinions? If the LORD is God, follow him; but if Baal, then follow him." The people did not answer him a word. [22]Then Elijah said to the people, "I, even I only, am left a prophet of the LORD; but

NIV
1 Kings 18:20-24, 30-35, 38-39

[20]So Ahab sent word throughout all Israel and assembled the prophets on Mount Carmel. [21]Elijah went before the people and said, "How long will you waver between two opinions? If the LORD is God, follow him; but if Baal is God, follow him."

But the people said nothing.

[22]Then Elijah said to them, "I am the only one of the LORD's prophets left, but Baal has

Baal's prophets number four hundred fifty. [23]Let two bulls be given to us; let them choose one bull for themselves, cut it in pieces, and lay it on the wood, but put no fire to it; I will prepare the other bull and lay it on the wood, but put no fire to it. [24]Then you call on the name of your god and I will call on the name of the LORD; the god who answers by fire is indeed God." All the people answered, "Well spoken!"

[30]Then Elijah said to all the people, "Come closer to me"; and all the people came closer to him. First he repaired the altar of the LORD that had been thrown down; [31]Elijah took twelve stones, according to the number of the tribes of the sons of Jacob, to whom the word of the LORD came, saying, "Israel shall be your name"; [32]with the stones he built an altar in the name of the LORD. Then he made a trench around the altar, large enough to contain two measures of seed. [33]Next he put the wood in order, cut the bull in pieces, and laid it on the wood. He said, "Fill four jars with water and pour it on the burnt offering and on the wood." [34]Then he said, "Do it a second time"; and they did it a second time. Again he said, "Do it a third time"; and they did it a third time, [35]so that the water ran all around the altar, and filled the trench also with water.

[38]Then the fire of the LORD fell and consumed the burnt offering, the wood, the stones, and the dust, and even licked up the water that was in the trench. [39]**When all the people saw it, they fell on their faces and said, "The LORD indeed is God; the LORD indeed is God."**

four hundred and fifty prophets. [23]Get two bulls for us. Let them choose one for themselves, and let them cut it into pieces and put it on the wood but not set fire to it. I will prepare the other bull and put it on the wood but not set fire to it. [24]Then you call on the name of your god, and I will call on the name of the LORD. The god who answers by fire—he is God."

Then all the people said, "What you say is good."

[30]Then Elijah said to all the people, "Come here to me." They came to him, and he repaired the altar of the LORD, which was in ruins. [31]Elijah took twelve stones, one for each of the tribes descended from Jacob, to whom the word of the LORD had come, saying, "Your name shall be Israel." [32]With the stones he built an altar in the name of the LORD, and he dug a trench around it large enough to hold two seahs of seed. [33]He arranged the wood, cut the bull into pieces and laid it on the wood. Then he said to them, "Fill four large jars with water and pour it on the offering and on the wood."

[34]"Do it again," he said, and they did it again.

"Do it a third time," he ordered, and they did it the third time. [35]The water ran down around the altar and even filled the trench.

[38]Then the fire of the LORD fell and burned up the sacrifice, the wood, the stones and the soil, and also licked up the water in the trench.

[39]**When all the people saw this, they fell prostrate and cried, "The LORD—he is God! The LORD—he is God!"**

UNDERSTANDING THE SCRIPTURE

1 Kings 18:20. After the death of King Solomon in 931 B.C., the Hebrew nation had split into the northern kingdom of Israel and the southern kingdom of Judah. Ahab was a northern monarch who reigned from 874–853 B.C. He was judged by later histori-

ans as one of the worst of the kings because of his unfaithfulness to the covenant with God. Elijah was God's prophet, called to speak the word of God to Ahab and the people of Israel. In the earlier verses of chapter 18, we learn that the nation had been suffering a severe drought for three years. The king had been hunting for Elijah who had managed to elude him, but at this point the prophet himself initiated a meeting with Ahab. Elijah directed the king to call the people together, along with hundreds of prophets of the pagan Canaanite religions. The assembly was to be at Mount Carmel, a high ridge located close to the Mediterranean Sea, which was an old place of worship. It is possible that Elijah chose this location because it would have suffered less from the drought and the prophets of Baal may have claimed that this was due to the power of the god.

1 Kings 18:21. Elijah first addressed the assembled people of Israel, indicting them for their lack of faithfulness and commitment. The Hebrew word that the NRSV translates as "limping" and the NIV, as "waver," literally referred to birds hopping back and forth from one branch to another, settling nowhere. We would express this as "straddling the fence." By their silence, the people chose Baal by default since Yahweh required absolute fidelity.

1 Kings 18:22. Elijah was not the only living prophet of God, but he was the only one willing to stand up in public.

1 Kings 18:23. The implication is that both religious traditions practiced animal sacrifice.

1 Kings 18:24. Both Yahweh and Baal were said by their followers to ride thunderstorms as their chariots and to speak in the thunder (see Psalm 29 and 104).

1 Kings 18:25. Elijah wanted the prophets of Baal to have every apparent advantage. This, of course, adds to the drama of the account.

1 Kings 18:26. For three hours, the prophets of Baal entreated their god to answer with the sign of fire. They danced ecstatically around the altar in a ritual familiar in many religions.

1 Kings 18:27. Elijah mocked the prophets with sharp satire, ridiculing Baal. He suggested that the god might be other-

wise engaged and so unable to respond. The phrase translated "wandered away" in the NRSV and as "traveling" in the NIV is a Hebrew euphemism for relieving himself.

1 Kings 18:28. In desperation, the prophets of Baal ritualistically gashed themselves in an act of self-sacrifice still seen in some religions today. This practice is forbidden for God's people in Deuteronomy 14:1 and Leviticus 19:28.

1 Kings 18:29. The time for the afternoon sacrifice was 3:00 P.M., so Baal's prophets had been calling upon him for six hours with no response.

1 Kings 18:30. The altar may have been destroyed at the order of Ahab's wife Jezebel, a Phoenician princess who ardently opposed the worship of Yahweh and promoted Baalism.

1 Kings 18:31-32. The symbolism of something built with twelve stones denoting the original twelve tribes recurs in the Old Testament. Elijah may have been symbolizing unity under the covenant despite the political separation of the two nations. The trench around the altar is described in terms of measures for seed; it would have held many gallons.

1 Kings 18:33-35. To make the task more difficult and, therefore, more dramatic, Elijah had twelve jars of water poured over the sacrifice and the altar so that all was thoroughly soaked.

1 Kings 18:36-37. Elijah's approach to God was in sharp contrast to that of the prophets of Baal. He spoke to Yahweh as the God of the ancestors of the nation and the faith, asking God to answer him and demonstrate the divine reality and power. His appeal was also a reminder to the gathered people of God's mighty acts in their history and God's intention to reclaim them.

1 Kings 18:38. While the description of what happened sounds like that of a lightning bolt, it was clearly understood by all present to be a miraculous occurrence. The power of the fire from heaven annihilated the altar, animal, fuel, and even the dust and water. Yahweh sent a clear and powerful message that Yahweh alone was God and that Elijah was his chosen prophet.

1 Kings 18:39. The Israelite people were awed and prostrated themselves in worship. They acclaimed Yahweh with an often-used formula which avowed that the true deity was Yahweh, the God of their ancestors. Once again, as so many times in their history, God had come to them to draw them back from unfaithfulness and into the covenant relationship.

It is unpleasant and troubling to continue our reading into verse 40, which is the actual end of the passage. With the help of the Israelites in capturing them, Elijah took the prophets of Baal down to a streambed and killed all 450 of them. Despite our reservations about its morality, this radical act was intended to demonstrate that the choice between Yahweh and false gods was one of life and death significance. No compromise was possible when covenant loyalty to God was at stake.

INTERPRETING THE SCRIPTURE

Contest on the Mountaintop

First Kings 18 is one of the most dramatic stories in the entire Bible. Its writer was a genius at constructing a story of escalating tension and theatrical climax. We can visualize the scene in our minds: the king in royal apparel, the prophet hardened and rough, the gathered people full of curiosity, the prophets of Baal haughty and condescending. They are together in response to the king's orders, on a mountaintop from which they can see the Mediterranean. King Ahab does not address the assembly at all; center stage belongs to the man who had initiated the gathering—Elijah, Yahweh's prophet. In a style reminiscent of Joshua's appeal in Joshua 24, Elijah challenges the Israelites to make a decisive choice. Very unlike the response to Joshua, these people do not answer at all. They are neither repentant nor defiant; they are cowed, or bored, into silence. The prophet must do something dramatic in order to reach these passive, lukewarm, vacillating people. Are there similar moments in our own lives today? Times when we are either nonchalant or timid in the face of decisions that must be made about our loyalties to Jesus Christ? In an increasingly secular culture, we Christians find ourselves confronted

with hard choices about our allegiance to God and our willingness to take bold stands for the faith.

The people approve of the contest the prophet has devised. What do they expect? What are they hoping for? Who are they "pulling for"? Is this indeed a real competition for the loyalties of those who were supposed to be God's covenant people? Elijah directs the preparation of two identical altars and sacrificial animals. The drama intensifies as the prophets of Baal make their appeals. Humor is introduced when Elijah ridicules their efforts and their god. When finally the Baal worshipers must acknowledge their failure, Elijah builds the suspense of the occasion to a crescendo by beckoning the crowd to draw closer. Somewhat in the style of a magician, he magnifies the difficulty in order to make his "trick" even more impressive. Then, without flourish or bravado, Elijah asks God to send fire and God responds spectacularly.

What fun the Israelites through the years must have had with this account! Skillful storytellers around campfires and kneading bowls must have related it with mesmerizing intensity and breath-holding suspense. Children surely asked their parents repeatedly, "Tell us the story of Elijah and the prophets of Baal!" Whenever Israel needed to be reassured of their God's power, this story was celebrated. Are there occasions in your personal life that function this way for you? What historical incidents in the 2000 years of Christianity might be similarly told and celebrated? How could we in our witnessing to Christ develop and use the tactics of Elijah?

How Many Gods?

There are places in some of the books of the Old Testament where the existence of other gods in addition to Yahweh appears to have been assumed. These are usually in very ancient portions of Scripture from periods when the faith of Israel was evolving. Even the First Commandment of the Decalogue (Exodus 20:2), "You shall have no other gods before me," acknowledges that other gods are rivals of Yahweh for the allegiance of Israel. God repeatedly reminds the people that Yahweh is a jealous God who will not accept divided loyalties. To worship Yahweh and to be in covenant relationship with Yahweh demand the rejection of other deities.

Polytheism is an attractive theological option. It is even a reasonable one. For humans, it seems natural to think of each nation having its own gods and of the larger world being ruled by a variety of deities—a god of the sun, the moon, the rain, the trees, the crops, the home, and so on. Polytheism allows one to "hedge one's bets": to seek to please more than one god rather than to put "all of our eggs into one basket." Polytheism also allows to some degree the ability to choose the gods with whom we are most comfortable and give only lip service to the rest.

Are we in comparable situations in our own day? It is very difficult for many dwellers in the twentieth-first century to believe that the God of the Bible is still relevant to the astonishingly different culture in which we live. Somehow the Christian church must find ways to confront the larger culture with a vision of God that has meaning in contemporary life. Frankly, I fear that we are failing abysmally. We are often presenting a narrow, intolerant caricature of God who is the projection of our own fears and prejudices. We proclaim a god whose concern for Americans is far greater than for other nationalities. We assert that God's will is identical with the platform of one political party and the program of one group of political leaders. This is polytheism; indeed, it is blasphemy. We are guilty of creating a god who represents our values rather than shaping ourselves to reflect the values of God.

American Christianity is currently so divided about the nature and will of God that our conflicting teachings must be a source of both confusion and derision to those outside the church (and to many within). Especially over the issue of homosexuality we have deep divisions. Christians need to ask ourselves what kind of message is being sent to the world when we are so conflicted over an issue of social justice. Surely the society about us must be asking who Christians are and what our churches really stand for when Christ's message of love and inclusion is replaced by prejudice and exclusion.

How many gods do we seek to please? Are we "limping" between loyalties like birds hopping about in the trees? The biblical God is one who demands exclusive and ultimate loyalty. We know God much better than did the people of Elijah's day because we have been given the experience of God in human flesh in Jesus Christ. Only in Christ do we find the model for our values and the paradigm for our actions. The prophet speaks to us: "If the LORD is God, follow him" (18:21).

We Depend on God

John Wesley, the founder of Methodism, taught that the meaning of faith could be conveyed in one word—trust. To be in right relationship with God is to recognize our dependence on the deity and to trust that divine power will guide us in our journeys of faith. Probably few of us would be so audacious as Elijah who put God to a very dramatic public test. We must assume that the prophet had been assured by God that this demonstration of divine power was God's plan.

Too often we trust in God only after we have exhausted all other options. There is a story of a rock climber who had fallen and was hanging precariously from a steep rock

wall. Desperate for help, he cried to heaven, "Is there anybody up there?" God answered immediately: "Yes, my son, I am here and will take care of you. Just turn loose the rope and I will catch you as you fall." The climber did not trust these words and cried again, "Is there anybody ELSE up there?" The truth is that there is no one else—no one we can rely on, no one we can truly trust except God. Whether we are able to acknowledge it or not, we are dependent upon God.

SHARING THE SCRIPTURE

PREPARING TO TEACH

Preparing Our Hearts

This week's devotional reading is found in Psalm 86:8-13. Here the psalmist extols the uniqueness of God and gives thanks. In verse 11 the writer asks for an "undivided heart," which is one whose sole loyalty is to God. As you read today's lesson, think about the importance of an undivided heart. Can you honestly say that you are focused solely on God, or do you have other priorities that are higher than your relationship with God? Meditate on this psalm and consider how you believe God might view your heart.

Pray that you and the adult learners will live with undivided loyalty toward God.

Preparing Our Minds

Study the background Scripture, 1 Kings 18:20-39, and lesson Scripture, verses 20-24, 30-35, 38-39. As you prepare this session, think about the power(s) that you depend on.
Write on newsprint:
❏ information for next week's lesson, found under "Continue the Journey."
❏ activities for further spiritual growth in "Continue the Journey."

Option: Plan a brief lecture on Baal worship for "Delve into the Story of Elijah's Triumph Over the Priests of Baal at Mount Carmel."

LEADING THE CLASS

(1) Gather to Learn

❖ Welcome the class members and introduce any guests.
❖ Pray that everyone who has come will be open to the leading of the Spirit and test the ideas they hear and read this day.
❖ Ask the students to call out as many sources of power as they can think of. List these ideas on newsprint. Examples may include: *steam, oil, gas, diesel, wind, generator, solar,* or *battery.*
❖ Talk with the class about which sources they have listed that seem most dependable. Are there any sources that are always available?
❖ Read aloud today's focus statement: **Sometimes we need to depend on a power greater than ourselves. What power can we depend on? At a very critical moment, Elijah depended on God's power, and he was not disappointed.**

(2) Delve into the Story of Elijah's Triumph Over the Priests of Baal at Mount Carmel

❖ Choose volunteers to read the parts of Elijah, a narrator, and the priests of Baal (at least two persons for part of verse 26). Ask the rest of the class to respond as the Israelites in verses 24 and 39. Read 1 Kings 18:20-39 as a drama.

❖ Point out that this story was originally told around campfires and other gatherings. Ask the class to envision this scene as a movie. Invite them to talk for a few moments about:
- the actor they would choose for the role of Elijah.
- the kind of music (perhaps specific pieces) that would play in the background to intensify the scene.
- the special effects they would use to bring this scene to life. Be sure to consider the sights, sounds, and smells that need to be evoked.

❖ Provide reference books, such as Bible dictionaries, and ask several class members to prepare a brief report on Baal and worship practices associated with this Canaanite deity. Or, do the research yourself and present a brief lecture.

❖ Note that the Israelites apparently believed that they could worship God and Baal, despite God's strict injunctions against such divided loyalties. Encourage the students to talk about how we, too, may be guilty of worshipping more than one God. (See "How Many Gods?" in Interpreting the Scripture.)

❖ Ask the students to talk with a partner or small group about the kind of faith that Elijah must have had to take such public action, believing that God would respond.

❖ Suggest that the students meditate briefly on how they experience and depend upon God's power in their own lives.

❖ End this portion by inviting volunteers to comment on their reliance on the power of God.

(3) Relate the Contest to Modern Examples of God's Power

❖ Read aloud this account of God mightily at work in the twentieth century.

The Lutheran Church in East Germany was instrumental in bringing about the fall of the Berlin Wall and the transition from Communism to a unified Germany. Monday afternoon prayer vigils, which began in 1983 at Saint Nikolai Church in Leipzig, were set in place as a way to respond to the threat of nuclear power from both Soviet and American missiles. Other churches also started prayer vigils. The church had played a leading role by protecting people of faith—and those with no faith at all—who wanted to emigrate from East Germany. Many faithful people remained in East Germany to work for change. The "New Forum" movement, a coalition of Christians and environmentalists, was founded on September 9, 1989 to debate ideas previously considered taboo. Large, peaceful demonstrations were held weekly. On October 18, Eric Honecker, who had overseen the building of the Berlin Wall in 1961 to prevent the mass exodus of people from Soviet-controlled East Germany, was forced to resigned. The Berlin Wall fell on November 9, 1989, and Germany was reunified October 3, 1990.

❖ Invite the class members to comment on how they see (perhaps witnessed first-hand), God at work in this peace movement that changed the course of history. Consider how the people of God "stepped up to the plate" to bring about this change. Help the class members to imagine the kind of faith and dependence on God that allowed this momentous event to occur.

❖ Discuss these questions, adding your own questions and examples as you choose.
(1) Where else have you seen God working to bring about changes that did not seem possible?
(2) What current situations need to be surrounded by prayer and peaceful protest to bring about change?

(3) **What connections can you see between God acting in Elijah's day and God acting in Berlin or other current situations?**

(4) Act in Ways That Demonstrate Trust in and Dependence on God's Power

❖ Distribute paper and pencils. Ask the students to make a confidential list of the "Baals" in their lives, those "gods" such as money and power that keep them from putting their whole trust and dependence on God.

❖ Suggest that the adults write about any changes they will make to demonstrate their complete trust in and dependence on God. Perhaps this writing will take the form of a prayer.

❖ Conclude this section by asking the students to put this paper in their Bibles so that they can review it and act on it this week.

(5) Continue the Journey

❖ Pray that all who have participated today will go forth with a renewed confidence in God's power.

❖ Read aloud this preparation for next week's lesson. You may also want to post it on newsprint for the students to copy. **Prepare for next week's session entitled "Seeking Renewal" by reading 2 Kings 22–23. From this lengthy background passage, we will focus on 2 Kings 22:8-10 and 23:1-3, 21-23. As you study, keep these ideas in mind: Life provides us with many opportunities for second chances and** other forms of renewal. What spurs us to seek renewal? Reading the book of the covenant drove Josiah to lead the people in a magnificent ceremony of covenant renewal.

❖ Read aloud the following three ideas. Challenge the students to commit themselves to use these activities as a springboard to spiritual growth.

(1) **Talk with someone this week who has not chosen to follow Christ. Listen to his or her reasons for following another faith—or no faith. Discuss why Christ is so important as a source of dependable, higher power in all aspects of your life.**

(2) **Recall that this week's passage uses sacrifice as an important motif. When Micah asks what one should bring to the Lord, the answer is not animal sacrifice, but justice, kindness, and a humble walk with God (Micah 6:6-8). What kinds of sacrifices are you making to bring about justice, show kindness to others, and walk humbly with God? Record your answers in a spiritual journal.**

(3) **Write a prayer in which you ask God for help in making a life decision.**

❖ Sing or read aloud "A Mighty Fortress Is Our God."

❖ Ask the students to join you in repeating the familiar Mizpah Benediction from Genesis 31:49 to conclude the session: **The LORD watch between you and me, when we are absent one from the other.**

UNIT 3: LIVING AS GOD'S COVENANTED PEOPLE
SEEKING RENEWAL

PREVIEWING THE LESSON

Lesson Scripture: 2 Kings 22:8-10; 23:1-3, 21-23
Background Scripture: 2 Kings 22–23
Key Verse: 2 Kings 23:3

Focus of the Lesson:
Life provides us with many opportunities for second chances and other forms of renewal. What spurs us to seek renewal? Reading the book of the covenant drove Josiah to lead the people in a magnificent ceremony of covenant renewal.

Goals for the Learners:
(1) to explore the events that led to the covenant renewal during Josiah's reign.
(2) to recognize the need for spiritual renewal in their lives.
(3) to engage in activities that promote spiritual renewal.

Pronunciation Guide:
Amon (am' uhn)   Hilkiah (hil ki' ah)
Jehoiakim (ji hoi' uh kim)   Josiah (joh si' uh)
Manasseh (muh nas' uh)   Shaphan (shay' fuhn)

Supplies:
Bibles, newsprint and marker, paper and pencils, hymnals

READING THE SCRIPTURE

NRSV
2 Kings 22:8-10

⁸The high priest Hilkiah said to Shaphan the secretary, "I have found the book of the law in the house of the LORD." When Hilkiah gave the book to Shaphan, he read it. ⁹Then Shaphan the secretary came to the king, and reported to the king, "Your servants have emptied out the money that was found in the house, and have delivered it into the

NIV
2 Kings 22:8-10

⁸Hilkiah the high priest said to Shaphan the secretary, "I have found the Book of the Law in the temple of the LORD." He gave it to Shaphan, who read it. ⁹Then Shaphan the secretary went to the king and reported to him: "Your officials have paid out the money that was in the temple of the LORD and have entrusted it to the workers and

hand of the workers who have oversight of the house of the LORD." [10]Shaphan the secretary informed the king, "The priest Hilkiah has given me a book." Shaphan then read it aloud to the king.

2 Kings 23:1-3, 21-23

[1]Then the king directed that all the elders of Judah and Jerusalem should be gathered to him. [2]The king went up to the house of the LORD, and with him went all the people of Judah, all the inhabitants of Jerusalem, the priests, the prophets, and all the people, both small and great; he read in their hearing all the words of the book of the covenant that had been found in the house of the LORD. [3]**The king stood by the pillar and made a covenant before the LORD,** to follow the LORD, keeping his commandments, his decrees, and his statutes, with all his heart and all his soul, **to perform the words of this covenant that were written in this book. All the people joined in the covenant.**

[21]The king commanded all the people, "Keep the passover to the LORD your God as prescribed in this book of the covenant." [22]No such passover had been kept since the days of the judges who judged Israel, even during all the days of the kings of Israel and of the kings of Judah; [23]but in the eighteenth year of King Josiah this passover was kept to the LORD in Jerusalem.

supervisors at the temple." [10]Then Shaphan the secretary informed the king, "Hilkiah the priest has given me a book." And Shaphan read from it in the presence of the king.

2 Kings 23:1-3, 21-23

[1]Then the king called together all the elders of Judah and Jerusalem. [2]He went up to the temple of the LORD with the men of Judah, the people of Jerusalem, the priests and the prophets—all the people from the least to the greatest. He read in their hearing all the words of the Book of the Covenant, which had been found in the temple of the LORD. [3]**The king stood by the pillar and renewed the covenant in the presence of the LORD**—to follow the LORD and keep his commands, regulations and decrees with all his heart and all his soul, **thus confirming the words of the covenant written in this book. Then all the people pledged themselves to the covenant.**

[21]The king gave this order to all the people: "Celebrate the Passover to the LORD your God, as it is written in this Book of the Covenant." [22]Not since the days of the judges who led Israel, nor throughout the days of the kings of Israel and the kings of Judah, had any such Passover been observed. [23]But in the eighteenth year of King Josiah, this Passover was celebrated to the LORD in Jerusalem.

UNDERSTANDING THE SCRIPTURE

2 Kings 22:1-2. Josiah's reign lasted from 640 until 609 B.C. Josiah was a good king, unfailingly faithful to God following the example of his royal ancestor, the great King David. Josiah was the last righteous king of Judah in the time before the nation was conquered by the Babylonians and the people taken into exile. The prophets Jeremiah, Zephaniah,

and Nahum were active during Josiah's reign.

2 Kings 22:3-7. These events occurred when Josiah was twenty-six years old. Shaphan served as secretary of state for the king. Collection of money for repairs to the temple had been going on since the reign of Jehoash (also known as Joash), more than a century and a half earlier, but the work of repair had apparently moved very slowly. Josiah ordered the high priest to turn these funds over directly to the construction workers and to trust them to utilize the money honestly and appropriately. Probably the king was attempting to speed up the repair work by putting resources to buy materials into the hands of the workers themselves.

2 Kings 22:8-10. The high priest reported to the king's secretary his discovery of a scroll, either in the collection box or in the rubbish created by the construction work. Hilkiah may have already known of the existence of the scroll and chosen this opportunity to bring it to the attention of the king. Or, the scroll may have been hidden in the collection box or elsewhere in the temple. When Shaphan returned to Josiah, he told the king about the discovery of the scroll and read its contents to him. This scroll most likely contained some portions of the book of Deuteronomy. If it was a version of Deuteronomy, it had likely been written during the reign of Hezekiah several decades earlier and suppressed during the rule of unfaithful monarchs.

2 Kings 22:11-13. The king's reaction was that of sorrow and repentance. He sent a delegation of officials to inquire of God as to what actions should be taken. This response indicated that the scroll contained such words as Deuteronomy 6:13-15 and 28:15-68. Prophets were frequently consulted in times of emergency in order to hear from God.

2 Kings 22:14. There is no explanation as to why the king's officers consulted with Huldah rather than seeking out the better known prophets such as Jeremiah or Zephaniah. The episode indicates that female prophets were known in Judah and that they shared equal status with those who were male. Huldah lived in a newer section of Jerusalem located between the inner and outer walls of the city.

2 Kings 22:15-17. Using the traditional prophetic formula, "Thus says the LORD,"

Huldah instructed the officers to tell Josiah that the words of the scroll were true. Jerusalem would be destroyed because of God's anger against the people for their unrighteousness. In violation of the law, they had ignored Yahweh and worshiped other gods. Destruction was inescapable.

2 Kings 22:18-20. Huldah sent a special message to the king: Because he had sorrowed and repented when the words of the scroll were read to him, God would allow him to die peacefully before the coming disaster fell upon the land. This prophecy of a peaceful death may seem confusing in view of the fact that Josiah actually died in battle. According to verse 20, the king's death would be peaceful compared to the catastrophe that would befall the nation—a disaster Josiah would not live to witness.

2 Kings 23:1-2. Josiah assembled all the people, their leaders, and the priests and prophets at the temple. There he read to them the scroll—called at this point the "book of the covenant" rather than "the book of the law" as it had been earlier (22:8, 11). This term indicates that the king made clear that the reading presented their responsibilities as God's covenant people.

2 Kings 23:3. Standing by the pillar in front of the temple, Josiah acted as covenant mediator, as had Moses, Joshua, and Samuel before him. Monarch and people rededicated themselves to living in obedience to the laws of the covenant.

2 Kings 23:4-5. The degree of apostasy in Judah is indicated by the fact that objects for worship of false gods were in the temple itself. At the order of Josiah, the priests brought them out and destroyed them. Priests of the pagan religions and priests who had led sacrifices in the high places outside of Jerusalem were thrown out of their positions.

2 Kings 23:6-15. An idol of the female fertility goddess was brought out, burned, and pulverized. Its ashes were strewn over graves of the poor to completely defile the goddess. Male prostitutes at the pagan shrines were ejected. Agents of the king tried to stamp out all sacrifices outside the temple and throughout the country. Geba was on the northern border of Judah and Beer-sheba on the southern. Josiah tried, although unsuccessfully, to get all priests to join the temple staff. The goal of all of this action was centralization of worship in the temple so that pagan elements might be purged and guarded against. Also destroyed were Canaanite altars for child sacrifice to the god Molech, located in the Valley of Hinnom south of Jerusalem. Horses dedicated to the sun god may have included both live horses and images. Statues of such horses were said to stand in front of the temple and live ones pulled the chariots carrying images of the sun god in processions. Altars and sacred sites built by previous kings for worship of heavenly bodies and other pagan gods were destroyed and defiled.

2 Kings 23:16-18. Josiah left standing the tomb of a prophet who had earlier come from Judah to warn the people (see 1 Kings 13).

2 Kings 23:19-20. Josiah's actions reached even into the northern kingdom of Israel. In brief, he did everything possible to destroy totally the worship of false gods.

2 Kings 23:21-23. This Passover was the climax of the reforms. It was celebrated at the temple rather than in homes and villages.

2 Kings 23:24-27. The writer judges Josiah to be the best of all the kings, yet God's coming destruction was not averted.

2 Kings 23:25-37. Josiah died in battle with the Egyptians and was succeeded, according to the will of the people, by his youngest son Jehoahaz. The Egyptian pharaoh Neco soon imprisoned and deported the new king, replacing him with Josiah's oldest son Eliakim. Judah became a vassal state of Egypt, paying heavy tribute to its masters, and suffering again from unfaithful monarchs.

INTERPRETING THE SCRIPTURE

Historical Events and Divine Purpose

We have emphasized repeatedly that the God of the Bible is a God who works out the divine purpose in and through the events of human history. Believing this, however, does not mean that it is always easy to discern God at work or to know what is in accordance with and what is in defiance of God's will. Most of the events of Hebrew history in the Old Testament have already been interpreted for us by the biblical writers. But even there, mystery sometimes prevails when God does not seem to act in ways consistent with what we understand divine purpose to be.

Our Scripture passage for today needs to be set in historical context. The writer of Kings rated each monarch according to his faithfulness to the requirements of the covenant with God. Josiah, whose reign we focus on today, came to the throne of the southern kingdom of Judah as a child. He followed two kings—Manesseh and Amon—who had restored worship in the high places, built altars for pagan gods, participated in occult practices, and used violence against the innocent. The judgment of the writer is that they "did what was evil in the sight of the LORD" (2 Kings 21:2, 20) Josiah was made king as the result of civil conflict in which the people of Judah supported him against the forces of Amon's servants who had assassinated the king. The story of Josiah's reign is also related in Second Chronicles 34–35.

The northern kingdom of Israel had already been conquered by the Assyrians in 721 B.C. and its people taken into exile, from which they never returned as a group. Judah had managed to hold off total defeat, but lived in the threatening shadow of Assyrian power. Josiah's sad death will occur when, in a revolt against Assyria, he leads his army to halt the advance of Egypt, an Assyrian ally. By this time, the capital city of Assyria had already fallen to the next great power in the area—the Medes and Chaldeans, called the Babylonians in the Bible. Josiah must have seen the possibility of overthrowing the domination of the declining empire. Instead, his forces were defeated by the Egyptians and Josiah was killed. Judah fell under the control of the Egyptians for a period. Josiah's eventual successor was his son who was given the name Jehoiakim by the Egyptians as an indication of their control. Jehoiakim was judged to be an evil king because he returned to the ways of Manasseh and Amon. He reinstated idolatrous worship in the temple, oppressed the people, was dishonest and unjust. In Jeremiah 36, we read of Jehoiakim's reaction to the reading of Jeremiah's scroll warning against unfaithfulness and the coming disaster which would result from it. In contrast to the earlier response of Josiah to such a reading, Jehoiakim cut up the scroll piece by piece as it was read to him and burned the pieces in his brazier.

Josiah was the last king of Judah who was faithful to the covenant. He went to great lengths to utterly destroy everything in Judah that violated the law of God and to return the nation to covenant loyalty. For his efforts, God apparently postponed the conquest of Judah for two decades, but did not rescind the punishment of which the nation had been warned. Why not? Throughout the Deuteronomic history of the Hebrews (the books of Deuteronomy through Kings), the repeated pattern had been unfaithfulness, suffering, repentance, and restoration. The events around Josiah's reign did not conform to that pattern. Repentance and reform were not answered by reconciliation and restoration. Instead the best king since David was killed and the nation moved ever closer to desolation. The book of Kings was possibly edited during the time of the exile—when the nation had been conquered and many of the people carried into captivity. This story reminded them and reminds us that God's ways are complex, mysterious, and uncontrollable. We must be careful in assessing God's work in human history, for the divine hand is working in situations in which we do not perceive it. Often God is working in ways that seem strange and contrary to our expectations. As people of biblical faith, we remember that the divine purposes will be fulfilled, even when it seems that the flow of events is moving in the opposite direction.

Theological Lessons from Josiah

One of the lessons we can learn from Josiah's story is that the faith of one person, even a very important one, cannot provide salvation for others. The king himself was rewarded for his efforts to turn Judah back to the Lord and restore covenant faithfulness. The nation was not spared as reward for the king's efforts. I am reminded of the saying that "God has no grandchildren." Believing, trusting faith in God can neither be vicarious nor inherited. No one can accept Christ on behalf of another; each of us must do it for ourselves. Similarly, no matter how faithful our family, friends, or leaders might be, their faith is not sufficient for us. Certainly we are influenced, even shaped, by the faith of others, but belief and acceptance must be decisions that we make for ourselves.

I find it intriguing that Josiah did not ask God to deliver the nation from destruction. Immediately after the scroll was read to him, he hoped that it was not too late and sent officials to consult the prophetess. How did he react when Huldah affirmed that the coming desolation was inevitable? He carried forward the work of reform vigorously, rooting out every vestige of apostasy and returning Judah to the Lord. Josiah's labors were not intended either to win favor with God or to cause a change in the divine intention. Because Josiah obeyed the covenant with God, he acted faithfully, without promise of favor for his actions. Christians behave as those who are following Christ, not for rewards, but because that is the way that Christ's disciples are called

to live. How we live is an expression of who we authentically are.

The career of Josiah also shows us that salvation is not a result of our pious actions. If works were enough, Josiah should have been able to save his people by working hard. Works are not enough; salvation is not the result of what we do. Romans 1:1-3, 16-17 makes clear that salvation is always a gift, never a reward. It is only through grace—God's free and unmerited favor toward us—that we have the possibility of saving relationship in covenant with God.

SHARING THE SCRIPTURE

PREPARING TO TEACH

Preparing Our Hearts

This week's devotional reading is found in Psalm 103:1-18, which focuses on God's goodness and willingness to forgive. As in other biblical passages, here we are reminded that God "is merciful and gracious, slow to anger and abounding in steadfast love" (103:8). Notice in verse 18 the reference to keeping the covenant, which has been the focal point of this quarter's lessons. How are you keeping covenant with God? What experiences have you had with God's mercy, goodness, and love? Write a short essay expressing your understanding of the nature of God. Or, write a psalm giving thanks for the mercy and love with which God blesses you.

Pray that you and the adult learners will experience anew each day the blessings God so freely offers to you.

Preparing Our Minds

Study the background Scripture, which includes both chapters 22 and 23 of 2 Kings. The lesson Scripture delves into 2 Kings 22:8-10 and 23:1-3, 21-23. Identify situations that prompt you to seek renewal.

Write on newsprint:
❑ information for next week's lesson, found under "Continue the Journey."
❑ activities for further spiritual growth in "Continue the Journey."
Plan a lecture or another method for giving historical background for "Explore the Events That Led to the Covenant Renewal During Josiah's Reign."

Option: Contact one or two students early in the week and ask them to prepare brief reports of Manasseh and Amon, the grandfather and father, respectively, of Josiah. Their stories are told in 2 Kings 21.

LEADING THE CLASS

(1) Gather to Learn

❖ Welcome the class members and introduce any guests.
❖ Pray that all who have come today will be open to renewing their commitments to God.
❖ Ask the students to indicate first, how many have been on a spiritual retreat, and second, how many would like to participate in one. (If you have a group that would like to go on a spiritual retreat, consider doing

one with the help of your pastor and/or another resource person.)

❖ Invite those who have been on a retreat to summarize what they hoped to gain from the retreat, what they did while they were on retreat, and how they might have been transformed.

❖ Talk with the class about how they know from experience, or can imagine, that a retreat affords an opportunity to renew one's commitment to Christ.

❖ Read aloud today's focus statement: **Life provides us with many opportunities for second chances and other forms of renewal. What spurs us to seek renewal? Reading the book of the covenant drove Josiah to lead the people in a magnificent ceremony of covenant renewal.**

(2) Explore the Events That Led to the Covenant Renewal During Josiah's Reign

❖ Note that today's lesson has some important historical background. Use Understanding the Scripture and "Historical Events and Divine Purpose" to create an introductory lecture. Or, read aloud "Historical Events and Divine Purpose" to set the stage.

❖ **Option:** Invite the students who agreed prior to class to present reports on King Manasseh and King Amon.

❖ Choose three volunteers to read 2 Kings 22:8-10, 23:1-3, 23:21-23, respectively.

❖ Talk with the class about a pattern of unfaithfulness, repentance, and renewal that is evident in this story.

❖ Discuss these questions.

(1) **How does Josiah's response to the discovery of the law book (likely a portion of Deuteronomy) lay the groundwork for a renewal of the covenant?**

(2) **What role does this special Passover play?** (Note that it underscores the importance of the covenant renewal.)

(3) **What has to happen or be recognized in order for your congregation as a body to renew its covenant with God?**

(4) **How might you celebrate such a renewal?**

(3) Recognize the Need for Spiritual Renewal in the Learners' Lives

❖ Read aloud the following information and guided imagery activity.

Thanksgiving is almost upon us and the season of Advent will begin in a few weeks on December 3. This is supposed to be a season of reflection and renewal as we await the second coming of Christ and recall with joy his coming in the flesh as a babe in Bethlehem. Yet, just as the scroll in the temple of Josiah's day revealed how far the people had strayed from God, so too, our holiday preparations may gauge our commitment to God.

Close your eyes and imagine yourself getting ready for Christmas. See yourself preparing your home. What will you do? How much time will this take? How much money will you spend? (Pause)

Think now about the people on your gift list. Why are you buying them gifts? How much will you spend? How will these gifts enrich their lives? (Pause)

Consider the kinds of celebrations you will attend and/or host. What needs to be done to prepare for these? How much will they cost? Who will be invited? (Pause)

As you think of your preparations, gifts, and celebrations, imagine what Jesus would say about all of this. Would he commend you for your time, effort, and expense? Or would he point out that your resources could be used more wisely? Would he feel comfortable at your celebrations? (Pause)

Think about how you will prepare yourself spiritually during Advent to celebrate Christmas. What would Jesus say about these plans? (Pause)

Finally, what changes do you need to make to recommit yourself to Christ? How will you do that? What first steps will you take? (Pause)

❖ Invite volunteers to comment on ways that they intend to renew and recommit themselves with God's help.

(4) Engage in Activities That Promote Spiritual Renewal

❖ Ask the students to identify ways that they experience spiritual renewal. List their ideas on newsprint. Here are some ideas to add: *worship, prayer, Bible study, Holy Communion, singing hymns, devotional Bible reading, spiritual retreats, and engaging in service for others.*

❖ Distribute hymnals, paper, and pencils. Divide the class into small groups. Encourage each group to find hymns, prayers, or other acts of worship that emphasize renewing one's commitment to God. Suggest that they focus on one choice and be prepared to present that to the class.

❖ Invite each group to lead the class in one of the hymns, prayers, or acts of worship they have selected. They may, for example, offer a prayer, sing or say a hymn, read a Scripture passage, or recite a creed. While you will not have a carefully crafted worship service using this method, each group will have had an opportunity to present some aspect of worship that is meaningful to them.

❖ Close this portion of the lesson by suggesting that the adults each write on their papers one activity they will do this week to promote their own spiritual renewal.

(5) Continue the Journey

❖ Pray that the learners will go forth committed to seeking a renewed relationship with God through Jesus Christ.

❖ Read aloud this preparation for next week's lesson. You may also want to post it on newsprint for the students to copy. **Prepare for next week's session entitled "Making Wrong Choices" by reading background Scripture from 2 Chronicles 36:15-21 and Psalm 137. Our session will explore in depth 2 Chronicles 36:15-21 and Psalm 137:1-6. Concentrate on these ideas as you study: Stubborn and prideful behavior often leads to painful consequences. What price is paid for such foolish choices? After Israel and Judah consistently rebelled against God, the people went into exile, where they longed for the relationship they had had with God.**

❖ Read aloud the following three ideas. Challenge the students to commit themselves to use these activities as a springboard to spiritual growth.

(1) Make arrangements to go on a personal retreat with the goal of committing yourself anew to Christ. Check with your pastor and/or the Internet for help in locating retreat centers.

(2) Search for books and articles on simplifying Christmas celebrations to help you plan an alternative to high-stress, costly preparations so as to focus more on your commitment to Christ.

(3) Write in your spiritual journal about evidence that you are committed to Christ. Think about who you are, what you do, and how you use whatever has been entrusted to you. Pledge yourself anew to Christ.

❖ Sing or read aloud "Breathe on Me, Breath of God."

❖ Ask the students to join you in repeating the familiar Mizpah Benediction from Genesis 31:49 to conclude the session: **The LORD watch between you and me, when we are absent one from the other.**

UNIT 3: LIVING AS GOD'S COVENANTED PEOPLE
MAKING WRONG CHOICES

PREVIEWING THE LESSON

Lesson Scripture: 2 Chronicles 36:15-21; Psalm 137:1-6
Background Scripture: 2 Chronicles 36:15-21; Psalm 137
Key Verse: Psalm 137:1

Focus of the Lesson:
Stubborn and prideful behavior often leads to painful consequences. What price is paid for such foolish choices? After Israel and Judah consistently rebelled against God, the people went into exile, where they longed for the relationship they had had with God.

Goals for the Learners:
(1) to summarize the account of the fall of Jerusalem as described in 2 Chronicles.
(2) to relate to the depth of loss felt by the Judeans over the loss of Jerusalem and Judah.
(3) to share their own stories of loss and ways God helped them through it so as to
    encourage others.

Pronunciation Guide:
Chaldean (kal dee' uhn)   Eliakim (i li' uh kim)
Jehoahaz (ji hoh' uh haz)   Jehoiachin (ji hoi' uh kin)
Jehoiakim (ji hoi' uh kim)   Nebuchadnezzar (neb' uh kuhd nez' uhr)
Zedekiah (zed uh ki' uh)

Supplies:
Bibles, newsprint and marker, paper and pencils, hymnals, somber music and appropriate player, colored pencils

---

READING THE SCRIPTURE

NRSV

2 Chronicles 36:15-21

¹⁵The LORD, the God of their ancestors, sent persistently to them by his messengers, because he had compassion on his people and on his dwelling place; ¹⁶but they kept mocking the messengers of God, despising

NIV

2 Chronicles 36:15-21

¹⁵The LORD, the God of their fathers, sent word to them through his messengers again and again, because he had pity on his people and on his dwelling place. ¹⁶But they mocked God's messengers, despised his

his words, and scoffing at his prophets, until the wrath of the LORD against his people became so great that there was no remedy. ¹⁷Therefore he brought up against them the king of the Chaldeans, who killed their youths with the sword in the house of their sanctuary, and had no compassion on young man or young woman, the aged or the feeble; he gave them all into his hand. ¹⁸All the vessels of the house of God, large and small, and the treasures of the house of the LORD, and the treasures of the king and of his officials, all these he brought to Babylon. ¹⁹They burned the house of God, broke down the wall of Jerusalem, burned all its palaces with fire, and destroyed all its precious vessels. ²⁰He took into exile in Babylon those who had escaped from the sword, and they became servants to him and to his sons until the establishment of the kingdom of Persia, ²¹to fulfill the word of the LORD by the mouth of Jeremiah, until the land had made up for its sabbaths. All the days that it lay desolate it kept sabbath, to fulfill seventy years.

words and scoffed at his prophets until the wrath of the LORD was aroused against his people and there was no remedy. ¹⁷He brought up against them the king of the Babylonians, who killed their young men with the sword in the sanctuary, and spared neither young man nor young woman, old man or aged. God handed all of them over to Nebuchadnezzar. ¹⁸He carried to Babylon all the articles from the temple of God, both large and small, and the treasures of the LORD's temple and the treasures of the king and his officials. ¹⁹They set fire to God's temple and broke down the wall of Jerusalem; they burned all the palaces and destroyed everything of value there.

²⁰He carried into exile to Babylon the remnant, who escaped from the sword, and they became servants to him and his sons until the kingdom of Persia came to power. ²¹The land enjoyed its sabbath rests; all the time of its desolation it rested, until the seventy years were completed in fulfillment of the word of the LORD spoken by Jeremiah.

Psalm 137:1-6

¹ **By the rivers of Babylon—**
　there we sat down and there we wept
　when we remembered Zion.
² On the willows there
　we hung up our harps.
³ For there our captors
　asked us for songs,
　and our tormentors asked for mirth,
　　saying,
　"Sing us one of the songs of Zion!"
⁴ How could we sing the LORD's song
　in a foreign land?
⁵ If I forget you, O Jerusalem,
　let my right hand wither!
⁶ Let my tongue cling to the roof of my
　　mouth,
　if I do not remember you,
　if I do not set Jerusalem
　above my highest joy.

Psalm 137:1-6

¹ **By the rivers of Babylon we sat and wept**
　when we remembered Zion.
² There on the poplars
　we hung our harps,
³ for there our captors asked us for songs,
　our tormentors demanded songs of joy;
　they said, "Sing us one of the songs of
　　Zion!"
⁴ How can we sing the songs of the LORD
　while in a foreign land?
⁵ If I forget you, O Jerusalem,
　may my right hand forget its skill.
⁶ May my tongue cling to the roof of my
　　mouth
　if I do not remember you,
　if I do not consider Jerusalem
　my highest joy.

UNDERSTANDING THE SCRIPTURE

Introduction. Second Chronicles 36 resumes the story of Hebrew history after the death of Josiah. One of his sons, Jehoahaz, was proclaimed king by the people, but his reign lasted just three months until Pharaoh Neco of Egypt deposed and deported him. Neco installed Jehoahaz's brother, Eliakim, whose name was changed to Jehoiakim. His evil reign lasted for eleven years before King Nebuchadnezzar carted him off to Babylonia. At the same time, Nebuchadnezzar looted the temple and carried some of the sacred vessels to his own palace. A young son of Jehoiakim named Jehoiachin ruled briefly, but met the same fate as his father. The Babylonians placed his brother Zedekiah on the throne. Zedekiah was the last king of Judah before the exile. He was described by the writer of Chronicles in verse 13 as having "stiffened his neck and hardened his heart against turning to the LORD, the God of Israel." Further, "All the leading priests and the people also were exceedingly unfaithful, . . . and they polluted the house of the LORD . . . " (36:14). Even the capture of their king and the looting of the sacred temple vessels had not convinced the people of Judah of their plight.

2 Chronicles 36:15-16. In verses 15 and 16, God is presented as having compassion on the people and repeatedly reaching out to them. God is identified as the God of their ancestors as a reminder of the covenant relationship. But all the divine efforts were without effect as the people persisted in their sinfulness and refused to heed God's word as conveyed through the prophets. God's messengers were not only ignored, but even ridiculed. Jeremiah 7 and 37 are examples of this interaction between the people and the prophet of God. Finally, divine anger replaced compassion and "there was no remedy."

2 Chronicles 36:17-18. The next verses summarize the account found in 2 Kings 25:1-21. The king of the Chaldeans was Nebuchadnezzar; his empire centered in Babylon was a product of the combined forces of the Chaldeans and the Medes. These verses have a strong emotional tone, more apparent in Hebrew than in English. The writer poetically piles up descriptive terms and uses parallelism to emphasize the horror of the events. The Judean people were killed indiscriminately. The temple was thoroughly plundered; all the religious treasures, as well as those belonging to the king and other government officials, were taken off to Babylon.

2 Chronicles 36:19. In the same emotional tone, the writer related the totality of the destruction. The temple and all the palaces of the city were burned. The protective walls of Jerusalem were not only breached, but razed. Anything of value that was not taken to Babylon was destroyed.

2 Chronicles 36:20. The inhabitants who were not killed were taken to Babylon to serve as slaves. This verse introduces the first faint note of hope when it declares that this servitude would last until the kingdom of Persia established itself in the place of the Babylonians.

2 Chronicles 36:21. The reference is to Jeremiah 25:11-12: "This whole land shall become a ruin and a waste, and these nations shall serve the king of Babylon seventy years. Then after seventy years are completed, I will punish the king of Babylon and that nation, the land of the Chaldeans, for their iniquity, says the LORD." In this verse (36:21) the sin for which Judah was being punished was that of having neglected the observance of sabbatical years for the land. Exodus 23:10-11 established this law: "For six years you shall sow your land and gather in its yield; but the seventh year you shall let it rest and lie fallow, so that the poor of your people may eat; and what they leave the wild animals may eat." Leviticus 25:4 declares that the seventh year shall be a year of complete rest for the land. Some of the purposes served by this law were practical—to allow the land to recover some of its productivity by lying unused. Probably the most significant point, though, was that this Sabbath year emphasized divine ownership of the land—it was to be used with responsible stewardship and its fruit shared among the people and with the animals. Certainly this was not the only sin of which the nation was guilty; it is used here as a symbol for their violation of the covenant responsibilities. The law of the sabbatical year allowed the writer to calculate the length of the exile as seventy years.

Psalm 137:1-3. This painful psalm is a lament over the sufferings of the Jews in exile in Babylonia. The intensity of its language reflects the powerful emotions the people felt. The psalm is divided into three stanzas. The first three verses express the sorrow and suffering that the people experienced. The rivers are the network of irrigation canals from the Tigris and Euphrates rivers in Babylonia. Zion is Jerusalem, the holy city—God's dwelling place on earth. Psalms such as 76, 84, and 87 were songs in praise of Zion.

Psalm 137:4-6. These verses express, in emotional language and powerful hyperbole, the writer's solemn oath of loyalty to Jerusalem.

Psalm 137:7-9. The final stanza is a call for revenge against Judah's enemies. The Edomites, descendants of Jacob's brother Esau, had participated in the Babylonian sacking of Jerusalem in 587 B.C. As is powerfully expressed in Obadiah 10–14, there was historic animosity between the peoples of Israel and Edom: "For the slaughter and violence done to your brother Jacob, shame shall cover you, and you shall be cut off forever.... The house of Jacob shall be a fire, the house of Joseph a flame, and the house of Esau stubble..." (Obadiah 10, 18). The Babylonians are personified as a woman—common usage for ancient cities. The shocking words of the last line refer to a common practice in ancient warfare and are probably a cliché for all the horrors of war. In the New Testament book of Revelation 18, the utter destruction of the hated city of Babylon is described in vindictive, poetic language. Also the actual city in the mind of the writer here was Rome; it is the memory of oppression by Babylon that provides the energy and the images of this account.

INTERPRETING THE SCRIPTURE

A Shocking Psalm

The captive Jewish community in Babylonia may have been forced to sing for the entertainment of their conquerors, but their "songs of Zion" were double-edged. The psalms were lyrical and beautiful, but laced with bitterness. We are reminded of many of the African-American spirituals from the time of slavery. These haunting songs often expressed the hope for freedom and the desire for revenge, couched in music that the white owners enjoyed without comprehending its message.

Psalm 137 is rather shocking to Christian readers of our day. The bitter outcry of hatred and vengeance disturbs us; it contradicts our sense of appropriate attitudes and emotions. Certainly it was such a psalm that John Wesley had in mind when he wrote in *Sunday Service for the Methodists in North America* (1784) that he had edited the psalter to remove some of the material that was not fit for the mouths of Christian people.

There is a disconcerting chasm between the sentiments of Psalm 137 and the teachings of Jesus about loving one's enemies, as well as his words of forgiveness for his executioners, uttered from the cross. How can this psalm be understood and used in our time?

Psalm 137 was composed by a person who had just recently returned to Judah from captivity in Babylonia or was still there in exile. As the author recalled his experiences, he was overwhelmed by bitter memories of oppression and brutality. His anger could not be contained, and it was given expression in this violent outburst. Perhaps the best that can be said about the psalm is that it is an authentic statement of unbridled anger, directed to God rather than put into action against the enemy. Probably the author had no opportunity to enact the violence that he felt and would have done so if he could have. The psalm is a venting of this powerful emotion in startlingly honest prayer. This is one of the reasons that the psalms have such enduring significance through Christian history. In them, the whole gamut of human emotions find expression. The psalms assure us that there is nothing that we ever think or feel that cannot be taken to God. We do not need to clean up our language or repress our feelings. God can handle our authentic human sorrow, pain, anger, complaint, and vengeance.

The Chronicler's Theology: Sin

The books of First and Second Samuel and First and Second Kings tell the story of Jewish history up to the time of the conquest by the Babylonian Empire and deportation into captivity. First and Second Chronicles tell much of the same story, but from a different perspective and with different emphasis. Chronicles is written after the exile. God's judgment on Judah's sinfulness had brought destruction and conquest, but there was still hope. The exile had allowed the land itself to rest and revive. A purified remnant of people would be restored to a purified land.

The books of Kings tend to blame Judah's unfaithful kings for the sinful condition of the nation. In Chronicles, the role of the kings is not overlooked, but emphasis is placed on the apostasy of the people. This sinfulness of the people is twofold—first, they reject God's will and rebel against the covenant relationship; second, they reject the divine call to repentance. Ultimately, the exile was caused not just by sin, but by the people's stubborn unwillingness to respond to the message of the prophets and repent. In 2 Chronicles 7:14, God made this very clear: "If my people who are called by my name humble themselves, pray, and seek my face, and turn from their wicked ways, then I will hear from heaven, and will forgive their sin and heal their land." Sin could be forgiven and brokenness healed, but those who consistently turn away from God and refuse to receive the divine forgiveness condemn themselves.

The Chronicler's Theology: Human Responsibility

The story of Judah's defeat and destruction by the Babylonians is clearly presented as the result of wrong choices by the human beings involved. Beginning with the kings and continuing through all ranks of the people, Judah had turned its back upon God and refused to listen to the divine offers of forgiveness brought to them by the prophets. That generation condemned itself and suffered the consequences of its own behavior.

The beauty in the midst of this desolation was that God had not and would not desert the Jewish people. The ancient covenant, so often violated and renewed, was still in force. While the generation whose unfaithfulness had resulted in destruction was lost, God would not invoke the warning of Deuteronomy 9:14 that God might "destroy them and blot out their name from under heaven." The divine purposes for which God had entered into covenant with them endured.

As announced through the prophet, God affirmed: "Know that all lives are mine; the life of the parent as well as the life of the child is mine: it is only the person who sins that will die"(Ezekiel 18:4). Every generation and every individual has free will and moral accountability. We are not punished or held responsible for the misdeeds of others; it is our own actions that determine our fates. This does not mean, unfortunately, that we may not sometimes experience the consequences of the sins of others. It does mean that God gives to each of us sufficient grace that we can make decisions about our relationships with God and with other people. It is those decisions and the actions which result from them that God holds us responsible for.

The Chronicler's Theology: Hope

The destruction suffered by Jerusalem and the temple is more extensive than in Kings and the elimination of the people from the land, by death and captivity, is much more complete. Even in the face of these dire descriptions, however, Chronicles concludes on a note of hope. The writer used texts from Jeremiah and Leviticus and wove them into a message of hope for the future. The exile would not be forever; it would last for only seventy years. This meant that few of the deportees would themselves return to the land, but opened the possibility that their children would be able to do so. The people are assured of the reality of divine presence with them still—the God who had brought them out of bondage in Egypt and into the land promised to Abraham, will again raise them up and dwell with them.

Verse 20 hints that the exile will only last until "the establishment of the kingdom of Persia." The Chronicler's account ends with 36:22-23, which tells of the rise of Cyrus, king of the Persians. This king was used by God as an instrument of the divine will as surely as the Babylonian king Nebuchadnezzar had been. Nebuchadnezzar had brought destruction; Cyrus offered release: "Thus says King Cyrus of Persia: The LORD, the God of heaven, has given me all the kingdoms of the earth, and he has charged me to build him a house at Jerusalem, which is in Judah. Whoever is among you of all his people, may the LORD his God be with him! Let him go up" (36:23). Thus begins the period of restoration as the Jews return home from exile.

SHARING THE SCRIPTURE

PREPARING TO TEACH

Preparing Our Hearts

This week's devotional reading is found in Proverbs 1:20-33. Here we see Wisdom personified as a woman. She "cries out in the streets" (1:20), warning those who refuse to listen to her. Under what circumstances have you made wrong choices that could have been avoided had you heeded God's wisdom? What consequences have you had to face as a result of these poor choices? Read the selection from Proverbs 1 several times and ponder what difference it would make in your life if you heeded Wisdom's call.

Pray that you and the adult learners will be mindful of the consequences of any choices you make.

Preparing Our Minds

Study the background from 2 Chronicles 36:15-21 and Psalm 137. Today's lesson Scripture is 2 Chronicles 36:15-21 and Psalm 137:1-6. Think about the price that one pays for making foolish choices.

Write on newsprint:
❏ information for next week's lesson, found under "Continue the Journey."

❑ activities for further spiritual growth in "Continue the Journey."

Option: Prepare a lecture for "Summarize the Account of the Fall of Jerusalem As Described in 2 Chronicles."

Determine how you will present the Chronicler's theology of sin, human responsibility, and hope for "Summarize the Account of the Fall of Jerusalem As Described in 2 Chronicles."

Select the music you will use for "Relate to the Depth of Loss Felt by the Judeans Over the Loss of Jerusalem and Judah." Have the appropriate player at hand.

LEADING THE CLASS

(1) Gather to Learn

❖ Welcome the class members and introduce any guests.

❖ Pray that those who have gathered today will pledge themselves to live daily in covenant with God.

❖ Brainstorm with the class answers to this question: **What examples can you name of the modern Christian church engaging in behavior that may lead to painful consequences?** List ideas on newsprint.

❖ Talk about what the church needs to do to repent and turn around its actions and/or attitudes to live faithfully in covenant with God.

❖ Read aloud today's focus statement: **Stubborn and prideful behavior often leads to painful consequences. What price is paid for such foolish choices? After Israel and Judah consistently rebelled against God, the people went into exile, where they longed for the relationship they had had with God.**

(2) Summarize the Account of the Fall of Jerusalem As Described in 2 Chronicles

❖ Choose a volunteer to read 2 Chronicles 36:15-21.

❖ Discuss these questions with the class,

or answer them yourself in a brief lecture. You will find ideas in Understanding the Scripture.

(1) **What does this passage say to you about God?**
(2) **What does this passage say regarding the people of God?**

❖ Present the Chronicler's theology of sin, human responsibility, and hope. You will find these three issues in the Interpreting the Scripture portion.

❖ Invite the students to respond to the Chronicler's theology by discussing how this theology relates to their own understandings of sin, human responsibility, and hope.

❖ Conclude this portion of the session by referring back to the "Gather to Learn" activity. Prod the students to note similarities and differences between the Judeans and us modern church members. Encourage them to state their beliefs about God's possible dealings with us.

(3) Relate to the Depth of Loss Felt by the Judeans Over the Loss of Jerusalem and Judah

❖ Read Psalm 137:1-6 responsively, if you have access to a Psalter, such as found in *The United Methodist Hymnal* (# 852-853). Otherwise, choose a volunteer to read Psalm 137:1-6.

❖ Ask the students to imagine themselves with the Israelites in Babylon. What emotions well up within them as they consider the devastation to their homeland and their exile? Play some somber music, such as a requiem by Mozart or another composer, as the students meditate. You may be able to borrow a CD of this music at your local library.

❖ Distribute paper, pencils, and colored pencils or markers. Give the adults these two options.

Option 1: Encourage the students to write words, sentences, or a brief poem about how they feel in this strange land.
Option 2: Encourage the students to draw a picture or just use colors to

illustrate how they feel in this strange land.

❖ Invite volunteers to share their words or art. The important thing here is not writing or artistic ability. Rather, the work is to express empathy with the plight of the Israelites who lost everything due to their poor choices and unwillingness to repent.

(4) Share the Learners' Stories of Loss and Ways God Helped Them through It So As to Encourage Others

❖ Divide the class into small groups. Ask the groups to talk about losses they have experienced and how God empowered them to deal with this loss and move on. Here are some losses for the groups to consider: *death of a loved one; limitations due to a physical illness or injury; spouse, due to divorce; job; home; friends; pets; homeland, perhaps due to war or other upheaval; community, perhaps due to a natural catastrophe.*

❖ Distribute newsprint and a marker to each group. Ask them to identify common themes that they heard as they listened to each other's stories. One theme, for example, may be that God was present with them in their suffering; even though the situation did not change, God was upholding them. Also ask each group to talk about what difference, if any, there is between a loss that happens to us and one that our poor choices bring upon us.

❖ Invite a spokesperson for each group to report on major themes.

❖ Post the newsprint that each group prepared. See if any themes common to the entire class emerge.

❖ Encourage the students to comment on any surprises, affirmations, or new insights they had as a result of discussing their losses.

(5) Continue the Journey

❖ Pray that the participants will recognize that poor choices lead to consequences that were probably avoidable.

❖ Read aloud this preparation for next week's lesson. You may also want to post it on newsprint for the students to copy. **Prepare for next week's session entitled "Experiencing Forgiveness" by reading 2 Chronicles 36:22-23 and Ezra 1:5-7, which is both the background and Scripture passage for this session. Focus on these ideas as you read: Many people experience forgiveness after they have done something wrong. How do we experience God's forgiveness? The Israelites knew God had forgiven them when they were allowed to return home and rebuild.**

❖ Read aloud the following three ideas. Challenge the students to commit themselves to use these activities as a springboard to spiritual growth.

(1) Research the Chaldeans (Babylonians). Who were these people? How did their civilization affect the Israelites? What do we know about King Nebuchadnezzar?

(2) Spend time in prayer repenting for a wrong choice that you have made. In what ways do you experience a renewed relationship with God as a result of this repentance?

(3) Identify some prophets in the modern church. What evidence do you have to demonstrate that we are or are not heeding their words? What consequences do you expect the church to have to pay if we are not listening to our prophets?

❖ Sing or read aloud "By the Babylonian Rivers," based on Psalm 137:1-4, and found in *The Faith We Sing.*

❖ Ask the students to join you in repeating the familiar Mizpah Benediction from Genesis 31:49 to conclude the session: **The LORD watch between you and me, when we are absent one from the other.**

UNIT 3: LIVING AS GOD'S COVENANTED PEOPLE

EXPERIENCING FORGIVENESS

PREVIEWING THE LESSON

Lesson Scripture: 2 Chronicles 36:22-23; Ezra 1:5-7
Background Scripture: 2 Chronicles 36:22-23; Ezra 1:5-7
Key Verse: 2 Chronicles 36:23

Focus of the Lesson:
Many people experience forgiveness after they have done something wrong. How do we experience God's forgiveness? The Israelites knew God had forgiven them when they were allowed to return home and rebuild.

Goals for the Learners:
(1) to unpack Cyrus' proclamation of return for the exiles and his response to their request to rebuild a house of God in Jerusalem.
(2) to relate to the emotions associated with exile, forgiveness, and return.
(3) to forgive and restore a relationship with someone from whom they have been estranged.

Pronunciation Guide:
Cyrus (sy' ruhs)   Ephiphanes (i pif' uh neez)
Hasmonean (haz muh nee' uhn)   Levite (lee' vyt)
Marduk (mahr' dyook)

Supplies:
Bibles, newsprint and marker, paper and pencils, hymnals, map of Jerusalem and Babylon

---

READING THE SCRIPTURE

NRSV
2 Chronicles 36:22-23

²²In the first year of King Cyrus of Persia, in fulfillment of the word of the LORD spoken by Jeremiah, the LORD stirred up the spirit of King Cyrus of Persia so that he sent a herald throughout all his kingdom and also declared in a written edict: ²³"Thus says

NIV
2 Chronicles 36:22-23

²²In the first year of Cyrus king of Persia, in order to fulfill the word of the LORD spoken by Jeremiah, the LORD moved the heart of Cyrus king of Persia to make a proclamation throughout his realm and to put it in writing:

King Cyrus of Persia: **The LORD, the God of heaven, has given me all the kingdoms of the earth, and he has charged me to build him a house at Jerusalem, which is in Judah. Whoever is among you of all his people, may the LORD his God be with him! Let him go up."**

[23]"This is what Cyrus king of Persia says: **" 'The LORD, the God of heaven, has given me all the kingdoms of the earth and he has appointed me to build a temple for him at Jerusalem in Judah. Anyone of his people among you—may the LORD his God be with him, and let him go up.' "**

Ezra 1:5-7
[5]The heads of the families of Judah and Benjamin, and the priests and the Levites—everyone whose spirit God had stirred—got ready to go up and rebuild the house of the LORD in Jerusalem. [6]All their neighbors aided them with silver vessels, with gold, with goods, with animals, and with valuable gifts, besides all that was freely offered. [7]King Cyrus himself brought out the vessels of the house of the LORD that Nebuchadnezzar had carried away from Jerusalem and placed in the house of his gods.

Ezra 1:5-7
[5]Then the family heads of Judah and Benjamin, and the priests and Levites—everyone whose heart God had moved—prepared to go up and build the house of the LORD in Jerusalem. [6]All their neighbors assisted them with articles of silver and gold, with goods and livestock, and with valuable gifts, in addition to all the freewill offerings. [7]Moreover, King Cyrus brought out the articles belonging to the temple of the LORD, which Nebuchadnezzar had carried away from Jerusalem and had placed in the temple of his god.

UNDERSTANDING THE SCRIPTURE

2 Chronicles 36:22. Verses 22 and 23 of 2 Chronicles 36 are almost identical to Ezra 1:1-3. Some scholars have suggested that Chronicles, Ezra, and Nehemiah were originally written or edited as a single book. More likely, the writer of Ezra simply used this repeated material to indicate the continuity of the story being told. Verse 22 was cited at the end of the previous lesson. It indicated that the period of exile in Babylon was about to come to an end and that the Jews would be given opportunity for a new start. It was a change in the power dynamics of international politics that allowed this to happen. The Babylonian Empire (also called the Chaldean or Neo-Babylonian) that had defeated the people of Judah, destroyed Jerusalem and the temple, and taken many inhabitants of the land into captivity, was falling. A new power was arising—the Persian Empire. In 549 B.C., Cyrus, the Persian leader, had conquered Media and shaped an empire out of these and other smaller territories. The "first year" cited was the first year after Cyrus' conquest of Babylonia. In the prophecies of Isaiah, Cyrus is called by name as the Lord's instrument: God "says of Cyrus, 'He is my shepherd, and he shall carry out all my purpose.'" As for Jerusalem, "'It shall be rebuilt,' and of the temple, 'your foundation shall be laid' " (Isaiah 44:28). In the next chapter, Cyrus is called the Lord's "anointed" or messiah (45:1). This is the only place in the Old Testament where this term is used to refer to someone who was not an Israelite. God says, "I have aroused Cyrus in righteousness, and I will make all his paths straight; he shall build my city and set my exiles free . . ." (45:13).

Jeremiah was also one of the prophets of the exilic period; his prophecy is mentioned here as having foretold the events that were taking place: "Then after seventy years are completed, I will punish the king of Babylon and that nation, the land of the Chaldeans, for their iniquity, says the LORD, making the land an everlasting waste" (Jeremiah 25:12). In Jeremiah 29:10-11, the effects on the Jews of the fall of Babylon are specified: "For thus says the LORD: Only when Babylon's seventy years are completed will I visit you, and I will fulfill to you my promise and bring you back to this place [Judah]. For surely I know the plans I have for you, says the LORD, plans for your welfare and not for harm, to give you a future with hope." The exilic period did not really last for seventy years. If one counts from the fall of Jerusalem and the temple and the final deportation of people into Babylon, the time is closer to fifty years. Perhaps Jeremiah was counting from the first deportation of any of the people in 605 B.C. to the time of the first return in 538 B.C. It is also quite possible that the seventy-year figure was not intended to be literal, but to signify a long, but limited, time period.

2 Chronicles 36:23. This verse contains the words of the official edict which King Cyrus had recorded and announced throughout his empire—the largest in the world at the time. As presented here, the edict implied that either God had spoken directly to Cyrus or that the king was aware of the Jewish prophecies about him. Some scholars of an earlier era taught that Cyrus had been influenced by Daniel, who served in his court. This is very unlikely and not mentioned in the story of Daniel, presented in the biblical book of that name. The benevolence of Cyrus' edict is in accord with what is known of his policies outside of biblical material. Cyrus understood that tolerance

toward the religions of conquered peoples was beneficial to his empire. People who had received such respect were much easier to rule and less likely to rebel. There is historical evidence of similar treatment of the Babylonians conquered by Cyrus.

Ezra 1:5. In response to the edict allowing them to return to their homeland, some groups of Jews prepared for the journey. Not all would choose to return. Some had settled comfortably in Babylon; others feared the arduous travel and the hardships of rebuilding. The Jews were organized in extended family groups—tribes or clans headed by patriarchs.

Ezra 1:6. This return to Judah has significant overtones of a new exodus. The Gentile neighbors of the Jews provided them with resources for the journey and rebuilding, much as the Egyptians had aided their ancestors centuries earlier (Exodus 11:2; 12:35-36).

Ezra 1:7. It was common practice for the images of gods and goddesses of a defeated nation to be taken as an act of humiliation and sign that the gods of the conqueror were superior. The Jews made no images of Yahweh. But, when the Babylonian king Nebuchadnezzar conquered Judah in 587 B.C., he had the Temple sacked and its equipment made of bronze, silver, and gold carried off as booty (2 Kings 25:13-17). There it had been placed in temples of Marduk and other Babylonian deities. Apparently, Cyrus had captured these vessels when he conquered Babylon. In accord with his policy of returning the images of gods to their people, Cyrus returned the temple vessels to the Jews so that they might carry them back to Jerusalem. The return of this equipment is important because it signified continuity between the first temple—that of Solomon—and the second, which would be rebuilt by these returning exiles.

INTERPRETING THE SCRIPTURE

Forgiveness and Restoration

In the beautiful poetry of Second Isaiah (chapters 40–55), God assures the Hebrew people that the sufferings of the exile are over: "Comfort, O comfort my people, says your God. Speak tenderly to Jerusalem, and cry to her that she has served her term, that her penalty is paid, that she has received from the LORD's hand double for all her sins" (Isaiah 40:1-2). God's covenant people had sinned terribly and had paid the consequences. Now they had been forgiven: "I am He who blots out your transgressions for my own sake, and I will not remember your sins" (Isaiah 43:25). The covenant relationship was intact; they were still God's chosen people, still God's instrument for the redemption of all peoples.

Perhaps the first emotion experienced in response to forgiveness is simply that of relief. Like the ancient Jews, we feel relief that the conflict is over, the suffering ended, and the relationship restored. Such experience may serve as a reminder in the future and help us to avoid the actions that threaten our relationships with God and with other people. This is resolve—determination to behave properly and to honor the relationship.

Sometimes the emotional responses to forgiveness may include resentment. It is not easy to be forgiven. We dislike being in the position of needing it. To be forgiven is to receive from another something that one has the power to give or to withhold. We may resent the very generosity of spirit that makes forgiveness possible. Perhaps it is because we then can see so clearly in another that which we lack. We might hope that such an experience might motivate us to develop within ourselves the gift of forgiving others.

Forgiveness is often followed by opportunities for restitution. This is, of course, a basic principle of most of the multiple-step help programs, such as Alcoholics Anonymous. Forgiveness has its concrete expression in actions to repair or repay. This is not always possible, but at the very least, we can apologize to those we have offended. Simply acknowledging that our transgressions were real and that we are authentically sorry for them, is a form of restitution.

People of the Covenant, People of the Book

The period of Hebrew history initiated by the edict of Cyrus is called the restoration. It was a time when almost everything had to be reclaimed and rebuilt. The land, the city, the temple were all in ruins. Even more basically, their faith and their identity as a people required restoration. In spite of the repeated warnings of the prophets, many in Judah before the conquest had refused to believe that God would give them up to their enemies. The covenant promises had sometimes been interpreted as guarantees of divine protection. Especially, many had relied on God's covenant with David's dynasty, believing that the kings from that lineage would never be overthrown. During the exilic period, much reconsideration had taken place in the light of the events of history. As the Jews returned to Judah, they brought back a chastened and changed religion. After the destruction of the temple and the impossibility of maintaining the sacrificial system, a new institution had been developed during the exile. The synagogue was both a place of worship and of study. It enabled the people to hold on to some of their traditions and to continue their study of Scripture. Another change was their sense of relationship with the promised land. While the land always remained important, the Jews had to learn that their faith could exist even in a foreign land. The God who was giver of the land transcended the land; God was universal, not local. Their self-understanding of themselves as a people in covenant relationship to God endured, but was modified in the face of a changed historical situation. Separated during the exile from many of the sources of their self-identity, the Jews began developing a new sense of themselves. They shaped an understanding of covenant as it was to be lived out in Diaspora—the scattering of the people from their homeland into the various nations of the earth. This new understanding has been essential to the survival of Judaism through the centuries. Finally, the Jewish people increasingly became the people of the book. Rather than anticipating new revelations of God in history or more prophetic communication, they turned to intense study of the sacred word as recorded in Scriptures (many of which were written during the period).

End of the Hebrew Bible, But Not of Hebrew History

The arrangement of books in the Hebrew Bible differs from that in our Christian versions. In the Hebrew Bible, the book of Chronicles is placed last. This means that the account of Hebrew history ends with the period of exile and the hope of restoration implied by the edict of Cyrus. From the books of Ezra and Nehemiah, as well as the prophetic books of Haggai and Zechariah, we learn more about the developments that followed. Not all of the Jews returned to Judah. Apparently, at least during the latter years of exile, they had been treated well in the Babylonian Empire and some of them chose to remain there. Those who did return home came in several different groups over a period of time. They faced arduous tasks of survival and restoration. Jerusalem and the temple lay in utter ruins. The economy had been decimated. Portions of the land had been inhabited by foreigners and there were neighboring peoples who opposed Jewish restoration. A modest new temple was built. It was such a disappointing replacement that the elderly who remembered the grandeur of Solomon's temple wept at its sight. For more than two centuries, Judah remained a poor, powerless province on the fringes of the Persian Empire.

Eventually the Persians were defeated and Judah became a part of the huge empire of Alexander the Great. The Bible tells nothing about that period except for veiled allusions to Alexander in the apocalyptic part of the book of Daniel. After Alexander's death, his empire was divided between his three most powerful generals. After some struggle for supremacy, Judah became part of the Seleucid Empire. This was a time of bitter suffering for the Jews as the Seleucid king Antiochus Epiphanes attempted to obliterate their religion. There was no period of comparable persecution until World War II and the holocaust under the Nazis. The noncanonical books of Maccabees relate some of the horrors of the time. As a result of the Maccabean revolt, Judah entered a period of independence and rule by its own Hasmonean dynasty for about a century. This promising era was ended when the Romans conquered the land and became its masters through the rest of the intertestamental and New Testament periods.

SHARING THE SCRIPTURE

PREPARING TO TEACH

Preparing Our Hearts

This week's devotional reading is found in Jeremiah 29:10-14. Jeremiah's words must have been both chilling and comforting to the Israelites. Exile in Babylon would come and would last for seventy years (though it actually lasted fifty years). But, God was not abandoning the people and would eventually restore them to their own land. When have you had to go through a difficult time before you could be restored to your former home or status? Consider how sin and subsequent forgiveness affect your life.

Pray that you and the adult learners will recognize their sins and seek forgiveness.

Preparing Our Minds

Study the background and lesson Scripture, both found in 2 Chronicles 36:22-23 and Ezra 1:5-7. As you read, think about how you experience God's forgiveness.

Write on newsprint:
❑ information for next week's lesson, found under "Continue the Journey."
❑ activities for further spiritual growth in "Continue the Journey."

Plan a lecture to provide background for "Unpack Cyrus' Proclamation of Return for the Exiles and His Response to Their Request to Rebuild a House of God in Jerusalem."

Do some research on Cyrus II, also known as Cyrus the Great, and be prepared to report to the class about this Persian king.

LEADING THE CLASS

(1) Gather to Learn

❖ Welcome the class members and introduce any guests.

❖ Pray that those who have gathered will be open to God's word and ready to experience God's love and forgiveness.

❖ Read this synopsis of an amazing story of forgiveness, reported on March 24, 2005 by United Methodist News Service.

Scott Everett, the oldest of the Reverend Walt Everett's three sons, was shot to death by Mike Carlucci, a drug seller and addict who described himself as the "troublemaker of the neighborhood." Scott, age 24, was at home when the shooting occurred. Shortly after the first anniversary of Scott's death, his father wrote a three-page letter to Carlucci, detailing the "extremely difficult" year he had had since his son's death. At the sentencing, Carlucci had expressed remorse, and in this letter Reverend Everett wrote, "I do accept your apology and, as hard as these words are to write, I add: I forgive you."

Carlucci tried to overcome his drug and alcohol addictions while in prison. A counselor suggested that he pray for forgiveness. Mike recalled saying, "God, please forgive me for what I have done." He reported, "I honestly can say that from that moment on, my life began to get better."

As a result of the initial letter, which Reverend Everett wrote mainly for himself, other letters were exchanged and eventually a meeting between the two men was arranged. Instead of shaking hands, the two embraced, beginning a series of monthly visits that lasted for two years. Then, Reverend Everett supported Mike as he petitioned for an early release, which the parole board agreed to after Mike had served only three years.

Reverend Everett stated, "I told them I didn't think he was same guy who had gone to prison, that he could be a productive member of society and that God had made tremendous changes in Mike's life."

Speaking about his experience, Reverend Everett said, "God prodded me, prodded me, until I was able to forgive. And I'm thankful for that. I feel sorry for people who can't because they live with that pain for the rest of their lives."

❖ Invite the students to comment on:
■ how God's forgiveness and the forgiveness of Reverend Everett affected Mike Carlucci.
■ how forgiveness transformed Reverend Everett.
■ how they might have acted under similar circumstances.

❖ Read aloud today's focus statement: **Many people experience forgiveness after they have done something wrong. How do we experience God's forgiveness? The Israelites knew God had forgiven them when they were allowed to return home and rebuild.**

(2) Unpack Cyrus' Proclamation of Return for the Exiles and His Response to Their Request to Rebuild a House of God in Jerusalem

❖ Choose a volunteer to read 2 Chronicles 36:22-23.
■ Use information from these two verses in Understanding the Scripture to help the students understand the historical background.
■ Locate Babylon and Jerusalem on a map. Choose volunteers to use the scale of miles to determine how many miles the Israelites had to travel to get home.
❖ Select someone to read Ezra 1:5-7.
❖ Discuss these questions, using Understanding the Scripture as needed for background.
(1) **What does Cyrus' declaration tell you about him as a human being and as a ruler?**
Option: Report briefly on any information you have found regarding Cyrus. Much data is available on the Internet. Cyrus

and the Persians had defeated Nebuchadnezzar of Babylon.
(2) **How do you see Cyrus as God's chosen agent?**
(3) **Does it surprise you that God uses people who are not Israelites to achieve divine purposes? Why or why not do you find yourself surprised?**
(4) **Why do you suppose that not all the Israelites returned home to Palestine when King Cyrus gave them an opportunity to go home and rebuild the temple?**
■ Note in verse 7 that Cyrus will return to the temple objects that King Nebuchadnezzar looted from it.

❖ Encourage the students to speak about what this story says to them about the nature of God and the people whom God chooses to carry out the divine will.

(3) Relate to the Emotions Associated with Exile, Forgiveness, and Return

❖ Brainstorm with the class examples of groups of people who live in exile. List ideas on newsprint. Try to include obvious and not so obvious groups, such as: *refugees; victims of natural disasters who are displaced; widowed/divorced people who may no longer fit into their previous social network; children of divorce who often travel from parent to parent; ill people who feel excluded because of the limitations of their illness; poor people who do not have access to the food and shelter that most of the society takes for granted.*

❖ Divide into teams and assign one or more of the groups of exiles you have brainstormed about to each team. (Be aware that some members of the team may also fit into the identified group.) Ask each team to list on paper any emotions that they can imagine the identified group members feeling. Also ask them to list any emotions associated with restoration and return to "normal" living, if such a return was possible.

❖ Invite the teams to report to the whole class.

❖ **Option:** Solicit volunteers who have had experiences of exile and return to tell their stories briefly.

(4) Forgive and Restore a Relationship

❖ Distribute paper and pencils. Challenge the students to think of someone who at some time in their life had betrayed them or acted in a way that caused this relationship to rupture. Perhaps they will think of a family member or close friend with whom they have been feuding. Ask the adults to write:
- ■ what happened.
- ■ how it affected the relationship.
- ■ steps they took to try to restore the relationship.
- ■ how they had hoped that God would treat this person.

❖ Provide time for silent meditation.

❖ Encourage the students to write a prayer of forgiveness.

❖ Suggest that the students write a plan of action as to how they will approach this person and offer forgiveness. (Be sure to note that forgiving an action does not mean that we need to put ourselves in harm's way again, especially if the person who needs forgiveness was abusive.)

❖ Close this portion of the session by challenging the students to execute their plan, both for the sake of the other person and to help heal themselves.

(5) Continue the Journey

❖ Pray that the students will go forth knowing that they are forgiven and reconciled unto God and as forgiven people they are called to forgive others.

❖ Read aloud this preparation for next week's lesson. You may also want to post it

on newsprint for the students to copy. **Prepare for next week's session entitled "Seeking Reconciliation" by reading Colossians 1, noting especially verses 15-23. This lesson is the first in the winter quarter, which is entitled "Jesus Christ: A Portrait of God." Keep this focus in mind as you study: People sometimes struggle with understanding who God is. Is there a means by which we can obtain this understanding? The Colossians passage affirms that Jesus, the Son of the Most High God, is both human and divine, and that he thus reveals God to us.**

❖ Read aloud the following three ideas. Challenge the students to commit themselves to use these activities as a springboard to spiritual growth.

(1) **Offer forgiveness to someone who has wronged you. Be aware that this person may not even know that he or she has done anything for which forgiveness is warranted.**

(2) **Make a list in your spiritual journal of sins for which you need to be forgiven. Review this list each day and pray not only for forgiveness but also for guidance as to how to avoid these sins in the future.**

(3) **Lend support and a helping hand to someone who has recently relocated to your area. Do whatever you can to help this individual or family find their way and become acclimated to their new environment.**

❖ Sing or read aloud "Forgive Our Sins as We Forgive."

❖ Ask the students to join you in repeating the familiar Mizpah Benediction from Genesis 31:49 to conclude the session: **The LORD watch between you and me, when we are absent one from the other.**

SECOND QUARTER
Jesus Christ: A Portrait of God

DECEMBER 3, 2006–FEBRUARY 25, 2007

The three units of this winter study help us to know who Jesus is. One way we learn about him is through his work and teachings. Together, the thirteen lessons provide a framework for understanding where Jesus came from and what he came to do. To create this portrait of Jesus, we will study the books of John, Philippians, Colossians, Hebrews, and 1 John.

Unit 1, "Christ, the Image of God," is a five-session study appropriate for Advent/ Christmas reflection. "Seeking Reconciliation," the lesson for December 3, explores Colossians 1 as it asks the question, "who is Jesus?" The session for December 10, "Learning about God," examines Hebrews 1 to discover how God would answer the question posed last week. The answer, according to Hebrews, is that God "has spoken to us by a Son." On December 17 we investigate 1 John 1:1–2:6 in "Walking in the Light" to discern how Jesus is the light. The Christmas Eve lesson, "Receiving the Word," based on the familiar passage in John 1:1-34, considers Jesus as the Word who became flesh and dwelled among us. This unit ends on December 31 with a study of Philippians 2:1-11, "Keeping the Balance," which reflects on how humiliation and exaltation converged in Jesus.

The four sessions in Unit 2, "Christ Sustains and Supports," focus on the source of Jesus' authority and several of his "I am" sayings in the Gospel of John. The unit begins on January 7 with "Be Free!," a session rooted in John 8:31-59 in which Jesus tells his disciples to continue in his word so that they will know the truth, and that truth will make them free. "Ultimate Fairness," the session for January 14, explores Jesus' teachings in John 5:19-29 concerning Jesus' authority to judge. On January 21 in the session "Lasting Results" we encounter Jesus as "the bread of life." This unit ends on January 28 with a study of Jesus' "I am the light of the world" teaching in a lesson entitled "Overcoming Darkness" from John 8:12-20 and 12:44-46.

Unit 3, "Christ Guides and Protects," is a four-session study that continues the focus on Jesus' "I am" sayings, found in the Gospel of John. These lessons look especially at Jesus' relationship with Christians from a corporate perspective. As the unit opens on February 4, we hear Jesus declare in John 10:1-18 that he is "the good shepherd" who offers "Protection from Evil" by laying down his life for the sheep. "Life after Death," the session for February 11, explores Jesus' saying in John 11:1-44 that he is "the resurrection and the life." On February 18 we meet Jesus in John 14:1-14 as "the way, the truth, and the life." The winter quarter closes on February 25 with a lesson entitled "Secure Connections." These connections refer to Jesus' teachings in John 15:1-17 that he is the vine and we are the branches who must abide in him if we are to be fruitful.

MEET OUR WRITER

DR. KAY HUGGINS

Someone recently asked me, "Why do you write curriculum for adult Christians?" I discovered I could not answer that question briefly. Instead, I began where I began, in Northern California. There I learned humility naturally; I spent many days and nights in the Redwood forest. There also I learned caution. Floods, forest fires, and earthquakes inspired a sense of awe before God's power and terror. From my earliest years, I humbly desired to know God, even as I wondered if such knowledge were possible. The geography in which I grew up raised insistent spiritual questions in my young soul. Perhaps I write curriculum for adult Christians because those questions still stir my soul.

But geography—even spiritually powerful geography—is not a sufficient response to the question, "Why do you write curriculum for adult Christians?" I would be dishonest if I didn't credit all the teachers and preachers who took this teenage questioner seriously. In the small Methodist church of my childhood, the youth were challenged to sort through Scripture, to struggle through prayer, and to persevere in loving one another. We were given a full dose of Christian education. I credit my desire to study Scripture and to encourage others to do likewise to the faithful teachers, pastors, youth advisors, and camp counselors of my teenage years. Their commitment to Jesus produced in me a thirst for Scripture. During those teenage years my faith was propositional and slightly judgmental; still, I developed an almost magnetic attraction to God's word. Perhaps I write curriculum for adult Christians because I was such a Scripture-thirsty teenager.

Geography and education set my soul on a search, but I was restless until through the blessing of Christian community I experienced the love of Christ. I've been privileged to be a part of several types of communities: wealthy and poor, educated and prosaic, quietist and charismatic, socially engaged and intentionally withdrawn. A particular slice of gospel prompted each community's rhythm. Through this rich mosaic of faith, I met Jesus again and again and again. The encounters continue in congregation after congregation. Surely, one reason I write curriculum materials for adult Christians is the cloud of witnesses I've been blessed to know.

There's one final way to answer my friend's question: I am called to a ministry of words! Although writing was a ministry "in addition to" my pastoral ministry during my first quarter century, I strongly anticipate that Christian writing will be at the center of my ministry for the second quarter century. Why? I believe God called me through all my senses while a child in northern California, inspired my mind to search the Scriptures through the youth ministry of a Methodist congregation, surrounded me with a magnificent, international and intercultural community of saints, and sat me down at a computer to do what I am called to do: minister through words on a printed page. At this point in my life, this challenging, creative, and deadline-persistent ministry is a blessing I'm glad to extend to you.

THE BIG PICTURE: IMAGES OF JESUS

A Portrait?

One fall, the Georgia O'Keefe Museum in Santa Fe aired an engaging radio advertisement. The gallery had assembled a collection of photographs from northern New Mexico of the various places painted by Georgia O'Keefe in her many landscapes of the region. The ad invited the audience to study the photographs and then the painting. "In the paintings," the ad announced, "you'll see what the photographs missed." It is a clever play on our assumptions about the two artistic mediums. Generally, photographs are assumed to be accurate presentations of the world as it really is. Yet, we also know that every photograph is shot from a particular angle, uses a specific shutter speed, and is printed after a series of decisions on cropping, color intensity, paper type, and size of print. Photographs tell us what the photographer saw and wanted us to see. On the other hand, we know portraits tell us more. Portraits reveal the inner content of a person. Portraits emphasize some features and ignore other attributes. Portraits evoke emotions. Portraits make us wonder and return for a second, third or fortieth look. "Jesus Christ: Portrait of God" is the title for this quarter's study. The very title poses questions. If Jesus is a portrait of God,

- who is the artist?
- what medium and style is used?
- was there a commission to paint?
- is this a realistic or an abstract portrait?

Even as such questions bubble up, a greater concern confounds us. Since God is, after all, invisible, how can a human reveal the invisible? Suddenly, our reasoning has taken us back to the predicament of the first-century witnesses to Jesus Christ. How is it possible to see God through Jesus?

I suggest that we use the same technique implied by the O'Keefe Museum advertisement. Look at the portrait to see what was missed by the photograph. In other words, during this quarter we will be sensitive to the actual lines and shades drawn by Gospel editors, Letter writers, teachers, and preachers of the first-century Christian community. Although, after nearly two thousand years of looking at Jesus, we think we know more than they—just wander through a Christian bookstore or visit a seminary library—their portrait of Jesus Christ still may reveal more than we know. In order to honor their portrait, we will honor the particularities of setting, cultural context, and life experience of first-century Christians. What we receive may not be as fully developed as a photograph, but it may be even more meaningful. The lessons for this quarter invite us into the earliest responses to the question: Who is Jesus Christ? The early church, with many brush strokes and colors, responds: Jesus Christ is a portrait of God.

The Questions We Bring

Christology (kris tol' uh jee) is the study of the nature and identity of Jesus. The primary question of Christology is: Who is Jesus? and the secondary questions, nettlesome and necessary, are:

- who is authorized to answer?
- what evidence is available?
- how is the answer presented?
- why is this important?

Let's consider each secondary question before addressing the primary christological question. First, *Who is authorized to answer?* From the perspective of the twenty-first century, this is a difficult question. The truth of Jesus Christ has always been considered to be a "possession" of the church. Given the diversity among and within the Christian community, it is difficult to find one authoritative voice. However, there is a formula of faith that guides as we listen for authoritative statements: what is and has been believed by Christians in all places and times. The authoritative voice of the church speaks through a historical voice that has a contemporary relevance. Who gets to answer the christological questions? The believers do! As a community and as individuals, this is a question whose answer comes from within the church, regardless of its diversity or temporal setting.

The church, everywhere and always, is authorized to explain Jesus to the world, What evidence is available? The church reaches out to three genres of evidence: the revelation of God's word in Scripture, the treasury of wisdom in the institutional church, and the testimony of individual believers. This evidence is received with certain conditions. Scripture is, refined by scholarship, able to sort out fact from fiction, cultural adaptation from universal truth, and authentic word within the linguistic puzzles of living and dead languages. Without scholarship, the evidence provided by Scripture would be confusing at best. With scholarship the possibility of providing credible evidence increases. The wisdom of the institutional church is tested by continuity and self-critique. As an institution, the church has a central mission: to be Jesus Christ in the world. Whenever the institution deviates from this mission its witness is devaluated; whenever the institution critiques itself and returns to its central mission, it offers useful evidence. Finally, there are the millions of faithful believers who by their words, deeds, and lives witness to the identity of Jesus Christ. Their testimony is refined in the caldron of everyday life; indeed, the witness of ordinary saints (believers who have lived and died in Christ) is among the most powerful evidence for the truth of Jesus. In this quarter, we use Scriptures from the New Testament to expand our understanding of church history and the lives of early Christians. In this way, we test the evidence for ourselves, even as we use the three sources of Scripture, church history and tradition, and individual experience.

Although the church and individuals have, in every generation, answered the christological question through art, literature, ethical behavior, worship, and devotion, the primary resource remains the written testimony of Scripture. Yet, every age struggles not only to understand the Bible's meaning but also to understand the form of the Bible. Such struggles address the secondary question: How is the answer presented? In this quarter we study passages from five different sources: an uncontested and a contested letter of Paul (Philippians and Colossians, respectively), a first-century sermon disguised as a letter (Hebrews), a pastoral letter (First Letter of John), and the Gospel of John. For each source, more information may be inferred about the audience than known about the author. Nonetheless, we will strive to recognize the distinctive characteristics of style in order to understand how these shape and focus the message. Knowing the forms of presentation helps the contemporary student understand the original audience, author, and message.

Finally: Why is this important? This is a question that demands a soulful response. Intellectually, there can be no ultimately satisfying answer to the identity of Jesus. He was and is and always will be a mystery. Yet in a spiritual sense, his identity is of utmost importance in Christianity. Struggling to comprehend Jesus ensures a vitality to faith that refreshes and nourishes belief. If one has not wrestled with this question, as a mature Christian, conversion is stunted and faith becomes inadequate to the challenges of contemporary life. The christological question, who is Jesus? is a matter of life and death for Christians.

The Frame of Culture

The frame of a portrait has consequences. For example, a scholar is painted with the backdrop of her books; although her degrees and awards are not included, her love of learning is introduced. There is more to her world than books on shelves, yet the books suggest the woman. In the same way, the New Testament documents do not tell everything that could be told about Jesus. Rather, important hints are recorded and arranged. It is up to the reader(s) to follow these hints. In the early Christian churches many hints were easy to follow because believers shared several common experiences, including:

- apostolic preaching with its particular pattern of apologetic witness (that is, a witness that presents, explains, and defends Christian faith and doctrines);
- orally presented stories and words of Jesus—both memorized for witnessing to others and for personal edification;
- active recollection of the Hebrew Scriptures (among Jewish converts);
- education in rhetoric and logic (among the Gentile converts);
- spiritual intuition that in Jesus Christ God was doing a new thing.

As contemporary Christians we have other common resources and experiences. Although there no longer exists a standard for formula preaching, contemporary sermons succeed by a lively connection between the Bible and everyday life. We want application rather than apologetics. Additionally, we are literate Christians; although there is a strong oral tradition, especially through hymnody and lessons for children, we prefer written resources to study, learn, and communicate our faith. The implications are significant: Early congregations knew, with an immediacy, the trigger words that linked the witness to Jesus with God's covenant with Israel. Since contemporary audiences do not carry the words of the Hebrew Scriptures in hearts and memory, we rely on pastors, teachers, and students of Scripture to provide these links for us. Likewise, contemporary education does not emphasize rhetoric and logic; we stress science, technology, and historical/global awareness.

These cultural differences provide the backdrop for the first-century portrait of Jesus. The actual portrait is framed by the circumstances of the developing Christian communities. The passages selected for this study are drawn from written documents addressed to five communities by five authors aware of the specific challenges of each. There are, however, general circumstances that unite these particular communities:

(1) the integration of Jewish and Gentile converts into a single community of faith;
(2) the growing hostilities toward Christians (as a new sect distinct from Judaism) and the real possibility of physical, social, or economic persecution;
(3) the discontinuity experienced between Christian ethics and secular social norms.

Let's consider these general "frames" for the portrait of Jesus Christ according to our experience and by that of the first-century churches.

Integration. Ordinarily integration means that one (new) group is invited to join another (established) group. Integration in the contemporary church, thereby, includes the challenge to educate the new members into the culture of the established group and the possibility that the faith of the established group will be reshaped by the spiritual contribution of the newer members. In the early church, however, everyone was a convert. Established power systems and points of personal privilege were only modestly present. Jewish converts and Gentile converts, alike, were learning to live in a new way. The newness heightened the spiritual insight of both groups; yet, both groups had prejudices. For the early church, regardless of actual composition, the theological understanding that Jesus unifies creation was essential. Being one in Christ was not a membership recruitment strategy; it was a life or death reality within a community composed of former enemies.

Hostilities toward Christians. Be honest: Where do you face hostility because of your Christian faith? Many Christians have lost touch with the experience of religious persecution because the contemporary church has become so insular. On the whole, most North American Christians lead lives free from social, political, economic, or physical harassment. We are out of touch with this dynamic of early Christian experience. But the New Testament documents recognize this reality. They are keenly aware that one's faith will impact social standing in the community, business and economic opportunities, political rights and protections, personal and family security.

As the wave of Christianity swelled in Jerusalem, Palestine, and finally throughout the Roman Empire, tensions multiplied. In the Jewish religious leadership the first signs of dangers were countered by an official distancing from those who followed Jesus. Gradually, this distancing became official policy, and the Roman authorities were convinced that the followers of Jesus were beginning a dangerous religion. Persecutions followed swiftly. The theological truth that Jesus (and his way) triumphed over all forces of evil was a truth early Christians needed. Again, this doctrine was essential; the theology of the New Testament documents was honed by persecution and expulsion, by trial and temptation, and by life and death.

Christian Ethics. In our contemporary experience, Christian ethics are integrated into a holistic Christian lifestyle. Rare is the individual who considers each and every decision, commitment, or financial arrangement as an individual ethical choice. Rather, modern Christians strive to live Christian lives formed by spiritual values and characterized by consistency with those values. Within a closed system, such a holistic approach works well; however, when contemporary Christians step beyond their safety zones, ethical reflection surges. The snug systems and comfortable conclusions of America do not fit a Third World crisis or an unprecedented natural calamity. In the early church, the dynamic and disruptive surrounding culture pushed Christian communities to reflect on ethical behavior within the congregation and community. Most of the documents in the New Testament emphasize ethical behavior within the community. Mutuality, common concern, and service distinguished the Christians' relationships with one another. Although there is less material devoted to the ethics of Christian living in the society, the implications are clear. From the training camp of the congregation to the village square or marketplace, Christians witnessed to their Lord by their generous love.

What More Do You See?

As you study the three units of this quarter, be prepared to see more than expected. You will see several portraits of Jesus, and each portrait presents a slice of the truth about him. There is no need to harmonize these portraits; it is best to allow them the grace of resting, side by side, in your heart. Use your intellect to examine each portrait; use your spiritual sensitivity to receive from these portraits a fresh perception of Jesus; use your natural inquisitiveness to consider the question, What more do you see? If you allow your mind, spirit, and imagination to work together, I guarantee you will be blessed by this quarter's study, "Jesus Christ: a Portrait of God."

Close-up: Biblical Images and Names of Jesus
Selected from the *New Revised Standard Version*

Advocate 1 John 2:1
Almighty Revelation 1:8
Alpha and Omega Revelation 1:8; 22:13
Amen Revelation 3:14
Apostle and high priest of our confession Hebrews 3:1
Atoning sacrifice for our sins 1 John 2:2
Author of life Acts 3:15
Beginning and end Revelation 22:13
Blessed and only sovereign 1 Timothy 6:15
Bread of God John 6:33
Bread of life John 6:35; 6:48
Chief shepherd 1 Peter 5:4
Christ 1 John 2:22
Cornerstone Acts 4:11; Ephesians 2:20; 1 Peter 2:6
Deliverer Romans 11:26
Descendant of David Revelation 22:16
Eternal life 1 John 1:2; 5:20
Everlasting Father Isaiah 9:6
Gate John 10:9
Faithful and True Revelation 19:11
Faithful and true witness Revelation 3:14
Faithful witness Revelation 1:5
First and last Revelation 1:17; 2:8; 22:13
Firstborn of the dead Revelation 1:5
God John 1:1; 20:28; Hebrews 1:8; 2 Peter 1:1; 1 John 5:20
Good shepherd John 10:11, 14
Great shepherd Hebrews 13:20
Head of the church Ephesians 1:22; 4:15; 5:23
Heir of all things Hebrews 1:2
High Priest Hebrews 2:17; 4:14
Holy and Righteous One Acts 3:14
Hope 1 Timothy 1:1
Hope of glory Colossians 1:27
Husband 2 Corinthians 11:2
I am John 8:58
Image of God 2 Corinthians 4:4
King Eternal 1 Timothy 1:17
King of Israel John 1:49
King of the Jews Matthew 27:11
King of kings 1 Timothy 6:15; Revelation 19:16
King of the nations Revelation 15:3
Lamb Revelation 13:8
Lamb of God John 1:29
Last Adam 1 Corinthians 15:45
Life John 11:25; 14:6

Light of the world John 8:12
Lion of the tribe of Judah Revelation 5:5
Living one Revelation 1:18
Living stone 1 Peter 2:4
Lord 2 Peter 2:20
Lord of all Acts 10:36
Lord of glory 1 Corinthians 2:8
Lord of lords Revelation 19:16
Lord is our righteousness Jeremiah 23:6
Man of heaven 1 Corinthians 15:48
Mediator 1 Timothy 2:5
Mediator of a new covenant Hebrews 9:15
Mighty God Isaiah 9:6
Mighty savior Luke 1:69
Morning star Revelation 22:16
Origin of God's creation Revelation 3:14
Our great God and Savior Titus 2:13
Paschal lamb 1 Corinthians 5:7
Pioneer and perfecter of our faith Hebrews 12:2
Pioneer of salvation Hebrews 2:10
Power of God 1 Corinthians 1:24
Prince of Peace Isaiah 9:6
Prophet Acts 3:22
Resurrection John 11:25
Righteous Branch Jeremiah 23:5
Righteous One Acts 7:52
Rock 1 Corinthians 10:4
Root of David Revelation 5:5; 22:16
Ruler of the kings of the earth Revelation 1:5
Savior Ephesians 5:23; Titus 1:4; 3:6; 2 Peter 2:20
Son of David Luke 18:39
Son of God John 1:49; Hebrews 4:14
Son of Man Matthew 8:20
Son of the Most High Luke 1:32
Source of eternal salvation for all who obey him Hebrews 5:9
Stone the builders rejected Acts 4:11
True bread John 6:32
True light John 1:9
True vine John 15:1
Truth John 14:6
Way John 14:6
Wisdom of God 1 Corinthians 1:24
Wonderful Counselor Isaiah 9:6
Word John 1:1
Word of God Revelation 19:13

FAITH IN ACTION:
LIVING IN THE IMAGE OF JESUS

During this quarter we are studying how we see God revealed in Jesus. Our study examines many different images, some of which we can mirror and others of which are his alone as the Son of God. We will explore several of these images and discern what we can do to embody them. You may also want to lead the class in brainstorming how they could live out selected images from the "Close-up" page entitled "Biblical Names and Images of Jesus."

❖ Jesus said, "I am the light of the world" (John 8:12), and the Gospel writer referred to him as "the light of all people" (John 1:4). Jesus told us to "let your light shine before others, so that they may see your good works and give glory to your Father in heaven" (Matthew 5:16).

(1) Enlist class members who will volunteer to work at a local shelter or halfway house where recovering addicts or abused women and children live. Remind the students that whatever tasks they undertake will offer a beacon of light to people who have been living in darkness and fear.

(2) Encourage class members to serve as advocates for those who are blind. Check the phone book and Internet for agencies in your area, perhaps including a school for visually impaired children.

(3) With a class team survey your church facility. Is it "user friendly" for a visually impaired person? What changes need to be made, based on recommendations from agencies that serve the visually impaired? Work together to make these changes.

❖ Jesus said, "I am the bread of life" (John 6:35). We, of course, cannot make that claim, but we are expected to feed the hungry (Matthew 25:35) and share spiritual food with brothers and sisters in need.

(4) Start a soup kitchen at your church, or regularly go to an established kitchen that serves those who are homeless and/or food insecure. Many people do not have enough money to feed their children and themselves throughout the month. They need to know that the church not only says it cares about them but is willing to meet their needs.

(5) Work ecumenically in the community to establish a food pantry where people in financial need can go to get groceries that will last several days.

(6) Establish a food co-op that enables community members to purchase high quality fruits, vegetables, and herbs from local farmers.

❖ Jesus said, "I am the good shepherd" (John 10:11). We acknowledge that we are not *the* good shepherd, but we can be good shepherds to people who need guidance.

(7) Pull together a team of experienced young parents who will mentor new parents, perhaps holding regular meetings and/or simply being available to talk. Consider a similar team for new grandparents.

(8) Form a shepherds' group to visit homebound church members or nursing home residents or hospice patients. Focus on listening to concerns and helping with small tasks. As appropriate, class members may act as advocates for the people they visit.

UNIT 1: CHRIST, THE IMAGE OF GOD
SEEKING RECONCILIATION

PREVIEWING THE LESSON

Lesson Scripture: Colossians 1:15-23
Background Scripture: Colossians 1
Key Verses: Colossians 1:15-16

Focus of the Lesson:
People sometimes struggle with understanding who God is. Is there a means by which we can obtain this understanding? The Colossians passage affirms that Jesus, the Son of the Most High God, is both human and divine, and that he thus reveals God to us.

Goals for the Learners:
(1) to study Colossians' view of Jesus Christ as the creator and ruler of the universe.
(2) to discern how the revelation of God in Jesus Christ impacts their faith.
(3) to pray focusing on the relationship between God and Jesus described in Colossians 1 and what this means to them.

Pronunciation Guide:
christological (krist uh loj' i kuhl)

Supplies:
Bibles, newsprint and marker, paper and pencils, hymnals

READING THE SCRIPTURE

NRSV
Colossians 1:15-23

¹⁵He is the image of the invisible God, the firstborn of all creation; ¹⁶for in him all things in heaven and on earth were created, things visible and invisible, whether thrones or dominions or rulers or powers— all things have been created through him and for him. ¹⁷He himself is before all things, and in him all things hold together. ¹⁸He is

NIV
Colossians 1:15-23

¹⁵He is the image of the invisible God, the firstborn over all creation. ¹⁶For by him all things were created: things in heaven and on earth, visible and invisible, whether thrones or powers or rulers or authorities; all things were created by him and for him. ¹⁷He is before all things, and in him all things hold together. ¹⁸And he is the

the head of the body, the church; he is the beginning, the firstborn from the dead, so that he might come to have first place in everything. [19]For in him all the fullness of God was pleased to dwell, [20]and through him God was pleased to reconcile to himself all things, whether on earth or in heaven, by making peace through the blood of his cross.

[21]And you who were once estranged and hostile in mind, doing evil deeds, [22]he has now reconciled in his fleshly body through death, so as to present you holy and blameless and irreproachable before him—[23]provided that you continue securely established and steadfast in the faith, without shifting from the hope promised by the gospel that you heard, which has been proclaimed to every creature under heaven. I, Paul, became a servant of this gospel.

head of the body, the church; he is the beginning and the firstborn from among the dead, so that in everything he might have the supremacy. [19]For God was pleased to have all his fullness dwell in him, [20]and through him to reconcile to himself all things, whether things on earth or things in heaven, by making peace through his blood, shed on the cross.

[21]Once you were alienated from God and were enemies in your minds because of your evil behavior. [22]But now he has reconciled you by Christ's physical body through death to present you holy in his sight, without blemish and free from accusation—[23]if you continue in your faith, established and firm, not moved from the hope held out in the gospel. This is the gospel that you heard and that has been proclaimed to every creature under heaven, and of which I, Paul, have become a servant.

UNDERSTANDING THE SCRIPTURE

Introduction. The letters of the New Testament provide a vital link between the preachers and teachers that formed new communities of faith and those who matured in faith within those communities. Although there were many, many letters written by various gospel missionaries addressing a diversity of congregations, only twenty-one letters are preserved in the New Testament as apostolic documents. These few, however, disclose the foundations of faith, the imaginative methods of teaching and the process of Christian formation among the early generations of Christians. The majority of these letters carry the authority of the Apostle Paul (thirteen are directly attributed to Paul and/or a colleague in ministry, while Hebrews is traditionally attributed to him). However, the careful reader notices variations of style, theological content and teachings among the New Testament letters. Even the casual

reader wonders if these come from a single source. The scholarly debate on Paul's authorship is, seemingly, endless; the Letter to the Colossians is one of the contested letters. Arguments in support of Paul's authorship of Colossians are as numerous as those in favor of a pseudonymous author. Be assured that in the first century the audience received the letter as a blessing.

Colossians 1:1-2. The first verse offered names and a relationship—both reasons to rejoice; therefore, with the original audience, we note Paul's name, the relationship among Timothy, Paul, the congregation in Colossae and the "will of God." The second verse foreshadows the letter's central theological issue. Notice that "the faithful" are addressed as residing in two locations: they are *in* Christ and *in* Colossae. This letter concerns the challenge—both ancient and contemporary—of Christian living in a particular place at a particular time. The letter's salutation concluded with the characteristic Christian blessing of grace and peace and a final affirmation of the Christian kinship uniting author and audience.

Colossians 1:3-14. A letter requires more than a signature to substantiate authenticity; every author must earn credibility. In this case, after the salutation comes a testimony of the author's prayer life. Paul's prayers of gratitude are poured out to God in remembrance of the congregation's faith, love, and hope. Evidently, Paul also received reports about the growing maturity of the congregation and this information summoned his prayers of intercession. Two graces formed Paul's prayers: growth in spiritual understanding and maturity in Christian living. Again, foreshadowing the central theological issue (living in Christ and in Colossae), the prayer poignantly appealed that the congregation be strengthened and able to endure "everything with patience" and with gratitude. This prayer powerfully united author and audience. Paul's keen focus was directed on the key challenge before the community; therefore, the community would have heard, with gratitude, his spiritual advice as it addressed their actual circumstances. The relevancy of the message was critical; in early Christian communities, faith was not an abstraction—faith was a way of life. The Colossians desired to live lives consistent with their confession of faith in Jesus, and the author addressed this desire. With words that recalled God as the deliverer of Israel, the author affirmed God's deeds of rescue, redemption, and forgiveness of sins through Jesus Christ. His words simultaneously affirmed the solid foundation of the faith, love and, particularly, hope (1:4-5) that distinguished the Colossian community of faith. With careful attention to spiritual matters, ethical challenges, and faith's firm foundation, the author established authenticity, credibility, and relationship. Upon this base the letter develops.

Colossians 1:15-20. The next few verses sing! Indeed biblical scholars detect, beneath the text, an ancient hymn of praise to Christ. The theme, Christ is the image of the invisible God, was appropriate to the congregation's worship and to life. As a doctrine of faith, this statement was the touchstone of Christian belief; as a motivation for ethical living, it provided necessary guidance. Yet, it is significant that these words are poetic phrases to be sung or chanted by the whole community in worship. Unpacking the text without honoring the context of worship robs the words of their original power. This is a passage best approached as a collection of images of Christ rather than sorted into a first-century christological argument. (To assist in collecting these images, they are set in italics.) The first image is of Christ as the *firstborn of all creation.* This phrase presented two ancient doctrines of Israel: God alone is the creator of all and every "firstborn" belongs to God. Beside this firstborn image is placed the image of the unity of creation: *in Christ all things hold together.* The process for achieving this unity was *the church*—the new creation *headed by Christ* through which the *redemption of everything* was coming to be. These images made sense because of the special relationship between God and Christ: Their full and complete relationship reconciled heaven and earth. Thus the early Christian community sang praises to Christ who was:

- the first-born of all creation,
- the pattern of reconciliation, and
- the only human completely related to God, "for in him all the fullness of God was pleased to dwell" (1:19).

In this hymn of praise, the congregation understood the source of their faith, love, and hope. As they sang, so they believed: In Christ they knew about, belonged to, and worked with the invisible God of all creation.

Colossians 1:21-29. The text ends as personally as it began. However, at the ending the congregation's faithfulness received a broader context: Jesus Christ has reconciled and prepared the congregation as a holy offering to God. All the "work" of reconciliation was accredited to Christ, but the "maintenance" of faith was charged to the congregation. Paul, as a servant of the gospel, also knew a great deal about the effort and necessity of maintaining faith. His own life of successes and sufferings modeled the course of Christian faith: Miraculously, Christ was in the midst of his life's joys and sorrows and, miraculously, Christ was also in the midst of the Christian community in Colossae. Christ's presence,

in Paul's life and among the Colossians, was recognized through spiritual insight, testimonies of gospel ministers, and the physical creation of new communities of faith, hope, and love. Paul, emboldened by the mystery of Christ's abiding presence, challenged the Colossians to continue in Jesus' way. He recognized the process included both toil and struggle, but ultimately, for all Christians the course that Jesus provided satisfies every human hope and longing. By his words and his life, Paul affirmed Christ's way as worthy because Jesus was not a spiritual abstraction, but an ever-present image of the invisible God.

INTERPRETING THE SCRIPTURE

Bound Together by a Letter

It is the season of letter writing! Soon cards and notes, family epistles, and end of the year reviews will fill mailboxes. The wonderful experience of reaching out to one another through letters and cards is a persistent and well-appreciated aspect of our Christmas preparation. Think about the letters you receive; do some stir memories even before they are opened, while others set hands to trembling with apprehension? The mixture of emotions provoked by the receipt of Christmas cards and letters is similar to the circumstances of the early Christian communities as they received letters from former missionaries, traveling teachers, and renowned apostles of the church. The letters carried news of individuals, answers to theological questions, commendations or corrections regarding Christian living, and most of all hope. Each letter was read to the whole community as they gathered for worship; it is likely that many of these letters were treasured and reread to the community time after time. Yet, then as now, the challenge of letter writing was to bring together a letter writer with an audience. Words must

be selected to remind the reader of the past relationship, to acknowledge that despite changes in circumstances the relationship persists, and to cultivate the relationship's endurance into the future. Whenever we read a New Testament letter, it is wise to listen for the relational tone of the first few verses. In the Letter to the Colossians this relationship is particularly rich and full: Paul acknowledged his apostolic authority, mentioned a beloved brother in the faith (Timothy), and stressed the kinship in Christ among the one who wrote and those who received the letter. These believers were bound together, literally, by a letter. Regardless of our academic questions and our critical judgments, the relationship through which the letter communicates is palpable. Receiving a letter from a friend in Christ is a holy moment; as those letters and cards begin to fill your mailbox, remember some letters are Christian blessings to be treasured and savored.

The Hymn within the Message

Many types of religious Christmas cards include the words of a familiar carol.

Phrases like *Silent Night, Joy to the World, Away in a Manger,* and *O Little Town of Bethlehem* are meant to capture a particular emotional tone. These words make us sing (or at least hum), and their melodies transport us to Christmas Eve services when all was still and holy. The power of carols to invoke memories of worship intensifies the message of Christmas cards. In verses 15-18 of our passage a similar power is at work. Most scholars suggest that these words are actually the words of a hymn of praise to Christ used by the early Christian communities in worship. No copy of this hymn exists, and perhaps the versions sung in different communities included local adaptations; nonetheless, the poetic feel of the words and the way images are strung together suggest that these words are well-worn worship words. The impact of hearing a hymn quoted within a letter from a beloved apostle is obvious: The whole congregation remembered other services when bread was broken, prayers recited, and members enjoyed moments of spiritual refreshment in Christ. The hymn did not teach something new; rather it gathered together, emotionally and spiritually, the core belief of the community. In this hymn Christ is praised as the image of God, the one who reveals God's purpose of reconciliation, the one who abides with the church and leads the community to live in ways that please God. There is neither theological argument nor doctrinal teaching; there is only praise within this hymn. Yet, as Christ is praised, so he is known. The community sings and comprehends the gospel message: Christ is the image of God.

A Pleasing Relationship

The passage we are studying describes the relationship that existed between Jesus and God in several ways. Each piece of the description provides an insight into the spiritual life and challenge of the early Christian community. Christ is described as the firstborn of all creation; this phrase assures the community that Jesus' teaching is not an afterthought or something tacked onto God's original intentions in creation. The truth that Jesus taught was, is, and always will be God's original truth: Creation is to be united, full of peace, and sharing a glad communion with God. As there is perfect congruity between God and Jesus, creation is also whole (the New Testament Greek word may also be translated as completeness or perfection). The Christians are directed to recognize this wholeness within their community. In their life together, as each individual confesses Christ and strives to follow Christ's leadership, the whole community experiences peace, grace, and joy. The final blessing on their experience of Christian community is divine pleasure. This pleasure is first identified as the delight of God in and through Christ, but is gently stretched to cover each and every believer. According to Colossians 1:19-20, God's pleasure begins in the fullness of the relationship with Jesus and flows from that relationship to reconcile all things "whether on earth or in heaven." This reconciliation happened through Jesus' death on the cross. Paul combined two ideas to express Christ's reconciliation: *Blood* signifies the violent manner in which Jesus was crucified, while the *cross* recalls the ignominy of his death. These two words mark the boundary between hope and despair; yet God raised up Jesus from a violent, ignoble death to a glorious, eternal life. Thereby, Jesus has obtained a peace that cannot be disrupted by any condition or overcome by any power. By his death and resurrection, peace now flows from Christ to those who trust in him. Jesus has gone to the boundary between hope and despair in order to reconcile all creation. By his death, peace abounds in heaven and on earth. Creation rejoices as God's pleasure spreads over all.

An Image of Hope

The passage, however, is more than a hymn and more than an affirmation of God's great deed of reconciliation in Jesus. This passage has a purpose: to encourage and inspire a community of Christians facing hardships. The central issue for the community was neither a lack of understanding of Christian beliefs nor a shortage of faith; rather, this was a community that must mature in order to survive. Their faith in Jesus was a pure and generous gift of God. However, this gift must be nurtured and cultivated. To encourage their growth, Paul recalled the amazing transformation that faith has initiated among the members of the congregation: They were spiritual strangers to God, hostile thoughts filled their minds, and they acted upon these thoughts with sinful deeds. Nevertheless,

these who were far, far from God were reconciled through Christ's life, death, and resurrection. Their rescue, however, was only the first step of faith. A faithful Christian life was (and is!) composed of many, many steps. Paul charged the Colossians to continue in faith by holding onto the hope of the gospel. In order to emphasize this teaching, Paul offered the image of his own ministry as "a servant of this gospel" (1:23). Because he had faced trials and temptations, he identified with the anxieties of the congregation. Although Paul did not know what awaited him, he offered his ministry as an image of faithful conduct. The Colossians drew assurance from his example. Paul's hope rested on Jesus; therefore, he was able to move forward in faith. Observing him, the Colossians understood more profoundly the impact of Jesus, the image of God.

SHARING THE SCRIPTURE

PREPARING TO TEACH

Preparing Our Hearts

This week's devotional reading is found in Isaiah 9:2-7. Here we see an image of the child who will be named "Wonderful Counselor, Mighty God, Everlasting Father, Prince of Peace" (9:6). This One will sit on the throne of David. For Christians, this One is Jesus, God's Messiah, who will govern with "justice and with righteousness" (9:7). How does Isaiah's description square with your image of Christ? Why do you think the early Christian church believed that the One whom Isaiah described could be seen in Jesus? Ponder this familiar messianic prophecy as you begin to consider this quarter how Christ is the image of God.

Pray that you and the adult learners will grow in your understanding of the person and nature of Jesus Christ.

Preparing Our Minds

Study the background Scripture in Colossians 1 and lesson Scripture, verses 15-23. Think about the means by which we can obtain an understanding of who God is.

Write on newsprint:
- ❑ list of questions for "Discern How the Revelation of God in Jesus Christ Impacts the Learners' Faith."
- ❑ information for next week's lesson, found under "Continue the Journey."
- ❑ activities for further spiritual growth in "Continue the Journey."

Plan an optional lecture on images of Christ for "Study Colossians' View of Jesus Christ as the Creator and Ruler of the Universe."

Review the introduction to the quarter, the article entitled "Images of Jesus," "Biblical Images and Names of Jesus," and "Living in the Image of Jesus," all of which directly precede this lesson. Decide how you will use each of these helps either for this lesson or in subsequent sessions.

LEADING THE CLASS

(1) Gather to Learn

❖ Welcome the class members and introduce any guests.

❖ Pray that those who have come will approach today's lesson with fresh eyes of faith so as to better understand who Jesus is.

❖ Invite the class members to call out as many descriptive words and phrases as they can to describe Jesus. Since we really do not know much about his appearance, most of the descriptions will have to focus on his character and ministry. List these ideas on newsprint. You may wish to add other descriptive words from the list entitled "Biblical Images and Names of Jesus." Or, if you use a lecture format, read selected images from this list.

❖ Discuss with the students how these images of Jesus help them to know God.

❖ Read aloud today's focus statement: **People sometimes struggle with understanding who God is. Is there a means by which we can obtain this understanding? The Colossians passage affirms that Jesus, the Son of the Most High God, is both human and divine, and that he thus reveals God to us.**

(2) Study Colossians' View of Jesus Christ as the Creator and Ruler of the Universe

❖ Begin by giving an overview of this quarter's lessons. The quarterly introduction, found prior to this lesson, will help you do that.

❖ Introduce this quarter's material by highlighting excerpts from "Images of Jesus," the "Big Picture" article found prior to this session.

❖ Choose a volunteer to read Colossians 1:15-23.

❖ List on newsprint all of the words and

phrases that you find here that describe who Jesus is. Encourage the use of multiple translations of the Bible so as to discern the richness of these descriptions. Either have the class members call out ideas, or do this yourself as a lecture.

❖ Discuss with the class what these descriptions reveal to them about Christ. Encourage the adults to comment on any new insights they have gleaned about who Jesus Christ is.

(3) Discern How the Revelation of God in Jesus Christ Impacts the Learners' Faith

❖ Distribute paper and pencils. Invite the students to look again at the list of descriptive words and phrases they made earlier in the session, or that you read, plus the list they made based on Colossians 1:15-23. Challenge them to choose one or two descriptors that particularly grab their attention. Ask them to write in prose or poetry how this description informs and/or impacts their own faith.

❖ Divide into small groups or pairs and ask the students to read what they have written and discuss their ideas with others. Post these questions for them to consider.

    (1) **How does the descriptive word or phrase you have selected help you to know Christ better?**

    (2) **What difference does this image make in your relationship with Christ?**

    (3) **How might your relationship with Christ be different if this image of him had not been included in the Bible?**

    (4) **How is your faith deepened or broadened because you can envision Christ in this way?**

(4) Pray Focusing on the Relationship between God and Jesus Described in Colossians 1

❖ **Option 1:** Read the "Affirmation from 1 Corinthians 15:1-6 and Colossians 1:15-20" found on page 888 of *The United Methodist Hymnal.*

❖ **Option 2:** Recite the historic "Nicene Creed," which is found in most hymnals. If time permits, discuss how the early Christians who wrote this creed apparently perceived Jesus.

❖ **Option 3:** Work with the class to create a prayer or litany that praises Jesus as both human and divine. Offer this prayer or litany together.

(5) Continue the Journey

❖ Pray that all who have come today will experience the reconciliation with God that Christ offers to them.

❖ Read aloud this preparation for next week's lesson. You may also want to post it on newsprint for the students to copy. **Prepare for next week's session entitled "Learning about God" by reading Hebrews 1 and focusing on verses 1-9. As you study this passage, keep these thoughts in mind: People have varying ideas about Jesus Christ, where he came from, how he is related to God, and how he is able to reveal God to us. Is there a definitive concept about Jesus? The writer of Hebrews tells us that Jesus Christ came from God and is superior to the angels.**

❖ Read aloud the following three ideas. Challenge the students to commit themselves to use these activities as a springboard to spiritual growth.

(1) **Create art, perhaps a picture or clay sculpture, illustrating your concept of the phrase "in him [Jesus Christ] all things hold together."**

(2) **Talk with another Christian about how you envision Christ and what impact these images have on your faith. Ask this person to tell you about an image of Christ that is especially meaningful for him or her.**

(3) **Think about your favorite hymns. Sing or hum them as you think about what they say to you about who Christ is. Consider whether or not the hymns you have selected accurately reflect the images of Christ recorded in the Bible.**

❖ Sing or read aloud "Jesus Shall Reign."

❖ Say this benediction from Jude 24–25 to conclude the session. Include the students by asking them to echo it as you read: **Now to him who is able to keep you from falling, and to make you stand without blemish in the presence of his glory with rejoicing, to the only God our Savior, through Jesus Christ our Lord, be glory, majesty, power, and authority, before all time and now and forever. Amen.**

UNIT 1: CHRIST, THE IMAGE OF GOD

LEARNING ABOUT GOD

PREVIEWING THE LESSON

Lesson Scripture: Hebrews 1:1-9
Background Scripture: Hebrews 1
Key Verses: Hebrews 1:1-2

Focus of the Lesson:
People have varying ideas about Jesus Christ, where he came from, how he is related to God, and how he is able to reveal God to us. Is there a definitive concept about Jesus? The writer of Hebrews tells us that Jesus Christ came from God and is superior to the angels.

Goals for the Learners:
(1) to explore the view in Hebrews that Jesus Christ came from God, is God's exact counterpart, and is superior to the angels.
(2) to express their views of the relationship between Jesus and God, and Jesus and the angels.
(3) to discern what it means to say that God spoke to humanity through the Beloved Son, Jesus, and share this view with others.

Pronunciation Guide:
Magnificat (mag nif' uh kat)

Supplies:
Bibles, newsprint and marker, paper and pencils, hymnals, pictures of Jesus

---

READING THE SCRIPTURE

NRSV
Hebrews 1:1-9

¹Long ago God spoke to our ancestors in many and various ways by the prophets, ²but in these last days he has spoken to us by a Son, whom he appointed heir of all things, through whom he also created the worlds. ³He is the reflection of God's glory and the exact imprint of God's very being,

NIV
Hebrews 1:1-9

¹In the past God spoke to our forefathers through the prophets at many times and in various ways, ²but in these last days he has spoken to us by his Son, whom he appointed heir of all things, and through whom he made the universe. ³The Son is the

and he sustains all things by his powerful word. When he had made purification for sins, he sat down at the right hand of the Majesty on high, [4]having become as much superior to angels as the name he has inherited is more excellent than theirs.

[5]For to which of the angels did God ever say,

"You are my Son;
   today I have begotten you"?
Or again,
"I will be his Father,
   and he will be my Son"?
[6]And again, when he brings the firstborn into the world, he says,
"Let all God's angels worship him."
[7]Of the angels he says,
"He makes his angels winds,
   and his servants flames of fire."
[8]But of the Son he says,
"Your throne, O God, is forever and ever,
   and the righteous scepter is the scepter
     of your kingdom.
[9]You have loved righteousness and hated wickedness;
   therefore God, your God, has anointed
     you
   with the oil of gladness beyond your
     companions."

radiance of God's glory and the exact representation of his being, sustaining all things by his powerful word. After he had provided purification for sins, he sat down at the right hand of the Majesty in heaven. [4]So he became as much superior to the angels as the name he has inherited is superior to theirs.

[5]For to which of the angels did God ever say,

"You are my Son;
   today I have become your Father" ?

Or again,

"I will be his Father,
   and he will be my Son" ?

[6]And again, when God brings his firstborn into the world, he says,

"Let all God's angels worship him."

[7]In speaking of the angels he says,

"He makes his angels winds,
   his servants flames of fire."

[8]But about the Son he says,

"Your throne, O God, will last for ever
   and ever,
   and righteousness will be the scepter of
     your kingdom.
[9]You have loved righteousness and hated
   wickedness;
   therefore God, your God, has set you
     above your companions
   by anointing you with the oil of joy."

UNDERSTANDING THE SCRIPTURE

Hebrews 1:1-4. Although this book in the Bible is titled "The Letter to the Hebrews," for purposes of interpretation, it is best to understand the text as a sermon. Quite likely an actual correspondence was attached and the whole piece was read to Christian communities gathered for worship. The document, however, is in the rhetorical style of first-century preaching: repetitions of exposition and exhortation. As with all New Testament texts, the exposition of Christian faith leads directly to applications for Christian living. In the Letter to the Hebrews, the first exposition section (Chapter 1) began with an uncontested belief, using a lengthy sentence that includes verses 1-4, that throughout Israel's history God communicated through the prophets. From this one belief, the author circles around various revelations before the advent of Jesus. The first two verses deal with God's method of proclamation. Notice the careful parallel between Israel's past and the Christian present:

- God spoke/God has spoken;
- long ago/in these last days;
- to our ancestors/to us;
- by the prophets/by a Son.

The affirmations from the past are not debated. These are common truths accepted by all Israelites. The affirmation from the Christian present, however, required explanation:

- The "last days" was an eschatological phrase implying the time of God's complete redemption;
- "us" indicated the Christian community;
- "a Son" is a title-in-formation for God's self-revelation in Jesus' life, death, and resurrection.

This exposition rested on three roles attributed to Jesus. First, as God's son he bore an exact likeness to God; second, as a priest he made a perfect sacrifice for sin; third, as a reigning king he shared God's glory. The introduction concludes with an idea unfamiliar to a contemporary audience, but certainly known by the original audience: the affirmation of Jesus as superior to angels.

Hebrews 1:5-9. Hebrews is designed to build from easy-to-understand concepts to more complex and challenging ideas. Although the contemporary reader may be interested in angels, for the early Christians angels were an integral part of the received tradition. In the Hebrew and Greek languages the words translated as "angel" carried two meanings. First and generally, an angel was a messenger from God. Second and specifically, an angel was a spiritual being. The contrast is crucial. The author of the Letter to the Hebrews acknowledged

the various ways God has spoken to the people through the prophets. Prophecy brought God's word to the people in comprehensible human words and deeds. The prophets were the communicative link between God and humanity. The angels however were spiritual beings. Their "job description" was also that of messenger for divine truth and direction. Angels, however, were not human; they were heavenly beings who beheld God's glory, worshiped God alone, and ministered according to God's bidding. Their appearance was unpredictable, yet their impact on human history was decisive. According to the Letter to the Hebrews, the revelation received by the Christian community was delivered by one who was greater than all angels. To prove this statement, the author turned to Scripture. Interestingly, the passages were introduced as a form of God's speech, rather than by the familiar New Testament introduction "as it is written" or by Jesus' own construction "you have heard it said." The point is clear—the people of Israel recognized the divine word within the written words of Scripture. In this section, most of the proof-texts come from the Book of Psalms, the worship book of Israel; two quotes come from the historical writings. The passages selected are

- Hebrews 1:5: Psalm 2:7 and 2 Samuel 7:14;
- Hebrews 1:6: Deuteronomy 32:43;
- Hebrews 1:7: Psalm 104:4;
- Hebrews 1:8-9: Psalm 45:6-7.

If you read these passages in your Bible do not be confused; the author of the Letter to the Hebrews is quoting, perhaps from memory, from the Septuagint, the Greek translation of the Hebrew Scriptures. There is no word for word agreement with your English Bible. The proof-text argument began with an assertion commonly understood: God called Jesus "son," but this title was never applied to angels. Moreover, God promised that a son of David would become God's beloved own son. The allusion is to Deuteronomy 32, the poetic last song of Moses. This song concludes with an imperative of praise for God's complete victory. Those who knew this story and song knew that when God's reign over creation was complete both heaven and earth would praise God. At this point, the author has written only well known "facts of faith," but now these facts are applied to Jesus. Using a lengthy quote from Psalm 45, a royal wedding song, Jesus is extolled as sharing God's everlasting throne (the symbol of God's authority and power), and God's righteous scepter (the symbol of God's justice and mercy). Jesus lived a life characterized by powerful love of all things righteous and an authoritative rejection of all things wicked; by these two qualities he revealed his true relationship to God. Jesus was God's son on earth; following Jesus' death, God elevated and anointed him as the one to share in God's eternal reign.

Hebrews 1:10-14. The series of proof texts continues with quotes from the Psalms. In verses 10-12 the quote is from Psalm 102:25-27, a prayer for restoration that contrasted the ups and downs of human history with the imperishable, unchanging nature of God. With this quote the author stated the obvious: what God does endures forever. Implicit in this statement was the concept that since God granted Jesus the status of son, priest, and king, this status was genuine and eternal. The quote from Psalm 110:1 provides the final answer to the rhetorical question from verse 5, "to which of the angels did God ever say . . ." Indeed, God never elevated an angel to reigning authority (to God's throne). However, God did raise Jesus, the son, to this unique status. One final proof text assured the audience that their past belief in prophecy and in angels was not misplaced. Chapter 1 concludes with the believers being reminded that angels continued to offer spiritual service at God's initiation. There was no contest among the spiritual beings; Jesus shared God's divinity fully and eternally, while the angels received God's instructions to act in particular historical moments.

INTERPRETING THE SCRIPTURE

Please, Don't Touch the Angels

In our home Christmas decorating is a family activity. Since everyone helps, the ornaments on the tree cluster according to children's heights, stockings hang in a mismatched array and, frequently, decorations unexpectedly break. One Christmas our teenage daughter, noticing the broken wings and less-than-stately condition of many of our angels, announced she'd be arranging the angels. She hung, posted, and posed every angel around the nativity scene and then finally added a warning, "Please, don't touch the angels." I've kept that note and display it each year; I enjoy telling the story of a teenager's concern for the preservation of our angels. The incident, however, discloses more than a sweet family memory. Many Christians are raised with a taboo about angels. With the miracles and healings from the New Testament, angels are pushed to the sidelines of our contemporary theological reflection. They are confined to the "first-century world," a world sadly lacking the sophistication of our modern times. However, every year as Christmas approaches, out come the angels. They are prominent in carols, featured on greeting cards, and essential to the Christmas stories from Matthew and Luke. Indeed, it is hard to imagine a Christmas season devoid of angels. Yet, for the most part, my daughter's little sign still applies. We don't touch the angels; we've been conditioned to keep our distance from such. Yet, as with many other leaps over the cultural and temporal divide between New Testament and contemporary times, this leap to understand the place, purpose, and power of angels also strengthens contemporary faith. So for this lesson, let's ignore the "Please, don't touch the angels" sign and reach into the world of those who received the Letter to the Hebrews—a world of powers and beings, seen and unseen.

Jesus Is God's Excellent Word

This letter opens with a bold and beloved proclamation: God spoke in the past and God speaks in the present. How often do we hear the lament, "Oh, if we could hear God speak today as in Bible times…" and silently nod in agreement. When we do so, we fail to notice the various ways God spoke in those biblical days. The author of Hebrews knows that variety as well as his audience. Both were well aware that throughout the history of Israel, God employed an amazing range of communication techniques. Consider:

- Moses encountered God in a burning bush;
- Miriam drew close to God as she danced with her tambourine;
- Saul knew ecstatic moments;
- Joseph heard divine messages in his dreams;
- Elijah received God's assurance in a still, small voice;
- Job was confronted by God's voice booming out of a whirlwind;
- Jeremiah received a prophetic commission that came as an audible call.

The list increases with every biblical character mentioned. Moreover, these unique and individual encounters with God were remembered and recorded in the Torah, the histories, the writings, and the prophetic books of the Hebrew Scriptures. Thus, these written documents were believed to contain God's word. Whenever faithful Israelites yearned to hear God's word, there was a reliable source available in Scripture. While reading, meditating upon, and discussing Scripture the people actually heard God's word. Yet even then, the people longed for a new word from God. Finally, when the time was right, God spoke the new and longed-for word: Jesus. Jesus, as God's Word, was related to all the previous ways and words of God's communication, yet Jesus was God's most excellent Word. While not discrediting the past deeds of God, the author of Hebrews carefully crafted the explanation of Jesus' superiority over all previous communications. The first affirmation concerned Jesus' nature. Jesus reflected God exactly because Jesus was God's own son; their kinship was timeless and complete. The second affirmation concerned Jesus' ministry; throughout his life, Jesus ministered in absolute obedience to God's will. The third affirmation focused on the effect of Jesus' ministry; as a compassionate priest Jesus' life announced God's grace toward Israel and through Israel to the whole creation. The final affirmation concerned Jesus' current status; the author held that by his resurrection and ascension, Jesus shared fully in God's reigning glory. By these affirmations, the author assured the whole community that Jesus came from God, lived his human life in complete relationship with God, and was raised up to dwell with God. Thus, Jesus was God's most excellent Word.

God's Words to Angels

The excellence of Jesus did not eliminate the significance of God's former methods of communication. The prophetic words of Scripture were still powerful and true. Indeed, as the early Christian community sought to understand Jesus they turned first to the sacred stories, laws, and prophecies of the Hebrew Scriptures. As for the common belief in angels as God's messengers, any author who wanted his message taken seriously must affirm the importance of angelic messengers. Our author was careful; the readers were invited to remember what God had and had not said concerning angels. The argument began with a rhetorical question lifted from Psalms 2:7, a royal psalm of God's son. The implied answer demonstrated that the audience understood that angels were not related to God as children to parent. Angels were, rather, spiritual beings who worshiped God—God as creator, redeemer, and sustainer of all creation. Moreover, as spiritual beings, angels were also attentive to God's will, took particular delight in the spiritual duty to worship God, and served God's purposes through interventions on earth. Everyone in the audience believed in angels; therefore, the author did not challenge that belief but shifted the belief from primary to lesser importance. Using a string of related ideas drawn from Scripture, the excellence of Jesus' word was distinguished from the divine word and work of angels. All this supports the core affirmation: Jesus is God's most excellent word.

Jesus Is Greater Than . . .

The final proof text came from Psalm 45:6-7, a royal wedding psalm. Although the context suggested the dignity and drama of a palace wedding, the use of the psalm, in this case, was literal. In these words, the early

Christian community discovered Jesus' unique identity. The words of the psalm describe a king who reigned forever, yet has "earned" his title by righteousness and just deeds. These words matched, with precision, the early church's concept of Jesus. By his unique life, Jesus differed from both angels and humans. Since Jesus was, after all, thoroughly human, his obedience surpassed that of all spiritual beings. Since Jesus' connection to God was deeper and more intimate than any human connection, he was distinguished from all humans. Although it was centuries before the church formulated a doctrine of Jesus' nature (A.D. 325, the Nicene Creed's formulation—Jesus "of one Being with the Father"), the Letter to the Hebrews prepared the way for this doctrine. Jesus as the image of God offered humanity the chance to see God. By listening to his teachings, meditating on his life and death, and following in his faithful footsteps, the early church received this most excellent communication from God. As they received him, they accepted the many and various words of the prophets, as well as the ancient and contemporary intervention of angels. Still Jesus, as greater than these, became the first and the last word the believers needed.

SHARING THE SCRIPTURE

PREPARING TO TEACH

Preparing Our Hearts

This week's devotional reading is found in Luke 1:46-55. This beloved passage, known as the "Magnificat," reveals Mary's understanding of who the child she is carrying will be. What does this passage say to you about Jesus? How did his life fulfill Mary's expectations? Write in your spiritual journal thoughts on your concept of Jesus' identity.

Pray that you and the adult learners will seek to know Jesus more intimately.

Preparing Our Minds

Study the background, Hebrews 1, and lesson Scripture, found in Hebrews 1:1-9. Think about where Jesus came from, how he is related to God, and how he is able to reveal God to us.

Write on newsprint:
❏ questions for "Discern What It Means to Say That God Spoke to Humanity

through the Beloved Son, Jesus, and Share This View with Others."
❑ information for next week's lesson, found under "Continue the Journey."
❑ activities for further spiritual growth in "Continue the Journey."

Locate pictures of Jesus. You may find individual paintings around the church that you can borrow. You can also find such pictures in art books at your local library, or available for download from the Internet.

Prepare a brief lecture for the portion entitled "Explore the View in Hebrews That Jesus Christ Came from God, Is God's Exact Counterpart, and Is Superior to the Angels."

LEADING THE CLASS

(1) Gather to Learn

❖ Welcome the class members and introduce any guests.

❖ Pray that as the students delve into today's lesson they will choose to become more intimately acquainted with Christ.

❖ Show several pictures of Jesus that you have selected. If you are using books and the class is large, divide into groups so that everyone can see the details of the pictures. Invite the students to talk about how the artist has envisioned Jesus. Is he, for example, strong, compassionate, depicted as a member of the ethnic group of the artist, accessible to people? How do the colors, light, other figures, and perspective affect the image of Christ that comes through in this picture? If you worked in groups, encourage brief reports from each one.

❖ Read aloud today's focus statement: **People have varying ideas about Jesus Christ, where he came from, how he is related to God, and how he is able to reveal God to us. Is there a definitive concept about Jesus? The writer of Hebrews tells us that Jesus Christ came from God and is superior to the angels.**

(2) Explore the View in Hebrews That Jesus Christ Came from God, Is God's Exact Counterpart, and Is Superior to the Angels

❖ Choose a volunteer to read Hebrews 1:1-9.

❖ Use the information for Hebrews 1:1-4 in Understanding the Scripture to draw parallels between Israel's past and the Christian present. Also explain the use of "last days," "us," and "a son."

❖ Talk with the class about the roles that Jesus plays, according to verses 1-4. Ask the students to state the significance for Christians in general, and for them in particular, of Jesus assuming these roles.

❖ Point out that Jesus' superiority to the angels is attested to by several quotations from the Old Testament used in Hebrews. Assign students to look up and read aloud each of these passages. (Use information from Understanding the Scripture for verses 5-9 to explain why the quotes from our Old Testament may not be exactly like what they find in Hebrews. Note also that Psalm 102:25-27 is quoted in verses 10-12 and Psalm 110:1 is quoted in verse 13, but these verses in Hebrews are beyond the scope of today's lesson.)
■ Hebrews 1:5: Psalm 2:7
■ Hebrews 1:5: 2 Samuel 7:14
■ Hebrews 1:6: Deuteronomy 32:43
■ Hebrews 1:7: Psalm 104:4
■ Hebrews 1:8-9: Psalm 45:6-7

❖ Compare and contrast the images of Christ found in Hebrews 1 with those we studied last week in Colossians 1. On one sheet of newsprint list any similarities. Talk about how these likenesses, found in two different biblical books, affirm who Jesus is. On another sheet write the differences. Discuss how these differences broaden our understanding of Jesus.

(3) Express the Learners' Views of the Relationship between Jesus and God, and Jesus and the Angels

❖ Read or retell "Please, Don't Touch the Angels" from Interpreting the Scripture.

❖ Invite the students to respond to this section by stating their own views about angels.

❖ Encourage the students to comment on ways they believe Jesus is "the exact imprint of God's very being" (1:3). Discuss why this idea is so important to the Christian faith.

❖ Use "Jesus Is Greater Than . . ." from Interpreting the Scripture as a catalyst for discussing the adults' interpretation of Jesus' identity.

❖ Prompt the class to voice their understandings and questions concerning the relationship between Jesus and God and Jesus and the angels.

(4) Discern What It Means to Say That God Spoke to Humanity through the Beloved Son, Jesus, and Share This View with Others

❖ Distribute paper and pencils. Ask the adults to jot down ways that they believe God speaks to them through Jesus. Post these questions for them to consider.
 (1) **What is Jesus' message?**
 (2) **How is who he is part of that message?**
 (3) **What does Jesus disclose about God?**

❖ Invite the students to talk with the class or a small group concerning their beliefs about how God speaks through Jesus. Note common themes. If the adults work in groups, ask them to report on the common themes they have discerned.

(5) Continue the Journey

❖ Pray that those who have participated in today's session will recognize and give thanks for the long-awaited appearance of God, enfleshed in Jesus the Christ.

❖ Read aloud this preparation for next week's lesson. You may also want to post it on newsprint for the students to copy. **Prepare for next week's session entitled "Walking in the Light" by reading 1 John**

1:1–2:6. Our lesson Scripture is 1 John 1:1–2:5. As you ponder this message, keep these ideas in mind: People seek meaningful relationships that add to their self-esteem and self-worth. Where can we cultivate such a relationship that is always affirming and esteem-enhancing? John tells us that in God there is found the type of relationship that not only reveals the need for a life-changing encounter with God but also provides the benefits of a relationship that contributes to our spiritual maturity.

❖ Read aloud the following three ideas. Challenge the students to commit themselves to use these activities as a springboard to spiritual growth.
 (1) **Look up information on the topic of angels. Read some accounts of people who believe that they have encountered angels. Think about what you believe about the existence and work of angels. How have angels affected your life?**
 (2) **Page through a hymnal or book of Christmas carols. Note the number of songs that refer to angels. What attitudes do these carols convey concerning angels?**
 (3) **Select and read one of the biblical books of prophesy, perhaps Amos, Micah, or Hosea. What message is God conveying through this prophet? What effect does this message have on your life?**

❖ Sing or read aloud "Majesty, Worship His Majesty."

❖ Say this benediction from Jude 24–25 to conclude the session. Include the students by asking them to echo it as you read: **Now to him who is able to keep you from falling, and to make you stand without blemish in the presence of his glory with rejoicing, to the only God our Savior, through Jesus Christ our Lord, be glory, majesty, power, and authority, before all time and now and forever. Amen.**

UNIT 1: CHRIST, THE IMAGE OF GOD
WALKING IN THE LIGHT

PREVIEWING THE LESSON

Lesson Scripture: 1 John 1:1–2:5
Background Scripture: 1 John 1:1–2:6
Key Verse: 1 John 1:5

Focus of the Lesson:
People seek meaningful relationships that add to their self-esteem and self-worth. Where can we cultivate such a relationship that is always affirming and esteem-enhancing? John tells us that in God there is found the type of relationship that not only reveals the need for a life-changing encounter with God but also provides the benefits of a relationship that contributes to our spiritual maturity.

Goals for the Learners:
(1) to explore the characteristics of Jesus Christ as described in 1 John 1:1–2:5.
(2) to identify ways that they are "walking in the light."
(3) to make a commitment to pursue spiritual growth.

Supplies:
Bibles, newsprint and marker, paper and pencils, hymnals

READING THE SCRIPTURE

NRSV
1 John 1:1-10

¹We declare to you what was from the beginning, what we have heard, what we have seen with our eyes, what we have looked at and touched with our hands, concerning the word of life—²this life was revealed, and we have seen it and testify to it, and declare to you the eternal life that was with the Father and was revealed to us—³we declare to you what we have seen and heard so that you also may have fellowship with us; and truly our fellowship is with the

NIV
1 John 1:1-10

¹That which was from the beginning, which we have heard, which we have seen with our eyes, which we have looked at and our hands have touched—this we proclaim concerning the Word of life. ²The life appeared; we have seen it and testify to it, and we proclaim to you the eternal life, which was with the Father and has appeared to us. ³We proclaim to you what we have seen and heard, so that you also may have fellowship with us. And our fellowship is

Father and with his Son Jesus Christ. ⁴We are writing these things so that our joy may be complete.

⁵**This is the message we have heard from him and proclaim to you, that God is light and in him there is no darkness at all.** ⁶If we say that we have fellowship with him while we are walking in darkness, we lie and do not do what is true; ⁷but if we walk in the light as he himself is in the light, we have fellowship with one another, and the blood of Jesus his Son cleanses us from all sin. ⁸If we say that we have no sin, we deceive ourselves, and the truth is not in us. ⁹If we confess our sins, he who is faithful and just will forgive us our sins and cleanse us from all unrighteousness. ¹⁰If we say that we have not sinned, we make him a liar, and his word is not in us.

1 John 2:1-5

¹My little children, I am writing these things to you so that you may not sin. But if anyone does sin, we have an advocate with the Father, Jesus Christ the righteous; ²and he is the atoning sacrifice for our sins, and not for ours only but also for the sins of the whole world.

³Now by this we may be sure that we know him, if we obey his commandments. ⁴Whoever says, "I have come to know him," but does not obey his commandments, is a liar, and in such a person the truth does not exist; ⁵but whoever obeys his word, truly in this person the love of God has reached perfection.

with the Father and with his Son, Jesus Christ. ⁴We write this to make our joy complete.

⁵**This is the message we have heard from him and declare to you: God is light; in him there is no darkness at all.** ⁶If we claim to have fellowship with him yet walk in the darkness, we lie and do not live by the truth. ⁷But if we walk in the light, as he is in the light, we have fellowship with one another, and the blood of Jesus, his Son, purifies us from all sin.

⁸If we claim to be without sin, we deceive ourselves and the truth is not in us. ⁹If we confess our sins, he is faithful and just and will forgive us our sins and purify us from all unrighteousness. ¹⁰If we claim we have not sinned, we make him out to be a liar and his word has no place in our lives.

1 John 2:1-5

¹My dear children, I write this to you so that you will not sin. But if anybody does sin, we have one who speaks to the Father in our defense—Jesus Christ, the Righteous One. ²He is the atoning sacrifice for our sins, and not only for ours but also for the sins of the whole world.

³We know that we have come to know him if we obey his commands. ⁴The man who says, "I know him," but does not do what he commands is a liar, and the truth is not in him. ⁵But if anyone obeys his word, God's love is truly made complete in him.

UNDERSTANDING THE SCRIPTURE

1 John 1:1-4. Unlike most New Testament letters, the First Letter of John opens abruptly. The opening sentence is a testimony of authenticity through experience. Evidently this approach was effective. The early Christian communities cherished this letter, together with its stylistic companions 2 and 3 John, as personal and practical guides to Christian faith. All three letters have intrigued biblical scholars from then to the present day. Traditionally, the author was considered to be John, the son of Zebedee. It is impossible, however, to discover any hard evidence to support this claim. Many scholars support the theory that the author was the same individual, or at least from the same theological school of thought as the author of the Gospel of John. For our purposes, it is sufficient to assume that this document, while not in a traditional form of a letter, is an authentic communication sent by a pastor or teacher to proclaim the gospel, to exhort a Christian community, and to encourage individuals in their Christian living. The author's authority, based on what "we" have heard and seen, is expressed by verbs in the past perfect tense, implying a continuous experience radiating out from a single past event. The effect is much like the ripples from a stone tossed into a still pond. The truth of the gospel initiated by Jesus has a historical dimension *and* it continues to impact the world through those who hear, see, testify, and declare this truth. Thus, Jesus' authority activates the church as his followers share their witness. The author writes with this purpose in mind. The goal of the First Letter of John is to increase the influence, fellowship, and joy of the community's testimony to Christ.

1 John 1:5-10. The content of this letter is morality, but the rhetorical style is metaphorical: God is light and in God's light there is no darkness at all. The light of God exposed the two ways humans live in the world: Either one walked in the light or one stumbled in darkness. The potential for stumbling (that is, sin) was rooted in a desire to hold onto the pre-conversion relationships, patterns, and behaviors of life. Without a conscious effort to place Christ's way at the center of one's existence, one continued to walk in darkness. First-century Christianity was not only a belief about God as the one true light to be worshipped; it was also an enlightened lifestyle to be lived. The point of this lifestyle, however, was not moral perfection, but the orientation to live in fellowship with Christ. One of the most significant aspects of such fellowship was the opportunity to be renewed, cleansed, and forgiven by Christ. Those who failed to notice their tendency toward sin or their actual sins also failed to appreciate and appropriate Christ's grace

and power. Thus darkened in thought, those who claimed to be sinless arrogantly judged God to be inconsequential—or worse, a liar.

1 John 2:1-2. The first chapter emphasized God's light, Jesus' forgiveness, and the community's access to both in words that could be read as harsh and critical. In the second chapter, however, the tone shifts to tenderness. The First Letter of John was not written to chastise the failings of the community, but to christen the faithful intentions of the community. The congregation was addressed as "my little children"; these words suggested tenderness rather than submission. Those who heard this letter assumed the role of student or learner; they listened because the voice they heard sang with a sweet authority. They wanted to know more about their faith, to mature as Christians, and to live together as a faithful community. The author matched their desire with words full of mercy and love. The previous discussion of sin, 1:5-10, was the prelude to a deeper lesson on a mature response to sin. In 2:1-4, the good news of the gospel was declared to be a forgiven life, not a sin-free life. The First Letter of John expressed the quality of the forgiven life through the relationship possible—even to the sinner—with Jesus Christ. First, Jesus was presented as an advocate, one called upon to stand beside the sinner. The role of the advocate drew upon a legal metaphor admired by Gentile Christians who appreciated the Roman legal system. In the next verse, Jesus was presented as a priest who offered a sacrifice for sin. This worship image was easily accessed and understood by Christians from a Jewish background. The two images combined to teach each segment of the congregation directly and indirectly. Because they understood a metaphor drawn from their particular vocabulary, each group was affirmed. Because each group heard a less familiar metaphor applied to Jesus, both groups were challenged to consider the breadth of Jesus' saving grace. Indeed, by his grace of advocacy and sacrifice, Jesus saved both the Jew and the Gentile.

1 John 2:3-6. The tender note of the second chapter continued with encouragement. Certainty in matters of faith is always an issue within a young congregation. In order to address this issue, a simple formula was offered: Knowledge of Christ results in lives of obedience. Again, an interesting emphasis was placed on the morality of the community. There may be many commandments from the law, the community, and even the teachings of Jesus, but there was only one Word to be obeyed. The Word was Jesus, God's full expression of love. Those who obeyed Jesus, the Word, discovered that God's love was continually being perfected in them. But woe to the one(s) who claimed to know the Lord, but failed to lead lives characterized by his love. They found themselves on that slippery slope of self-deception and darkened understanding. If such persons actually existed within the community, they were neither named nor condemned. The Letter was careful to keep the responsibility for discernment and judgment where it belonged: within the membership of the community. The community was encouraged to test their own faith by the question: Are we walking in the light? Moreover, this same test applied to any who claimed knowledge of God through understanding of Jesus. Thus, the knowledge of Christian faith was perfectly wedded to abiding in the deeds of justice, mercy, and love that characterized Jesus' own walk with God.

INTERPRETING THE SCRIPTURE

A Worthy Testimony

During the weeks before Christmas, the news media publishes good news! There is reprieve from the usual horror of war, domestic violence, greed, and deception. Instead, homeless shelters, food kitchens, and ordinary acts of charity are featured. Indeed, many television and radio stations become involved in the seasonal donation drives or fund-raising efforts. In the midst of their reporting, however, an occasional voice breaks the seasonal option for charity with an authority honed by years of commitment to victims of violence, injustice, and poverty. These rare voices come from individuals who "not only talk the talk, but also walk the walk." Their testimony is stunning. In a similar way, the author of the letters of John spoke with such a stunning voice. While not honed on the front lines of contemporary social ills, this voice was tested through the challenges facing the formation of a new religious community. These challenges included the oversight of teaching and preaching, the ordering of community life, and the formation of a morality based not on laws but on love. The only authority by which the author wrote was an intimate and profound relationship with Jesus. The relationship was genuine: The author claimed to be one of the circle of followers who had seen, heard, and touched Jesus. Moreover, the author's experience with Jesus had increased as his engagement with Christian communities increased. As Jesus' way, purpose, and meaning were taught, preached, and practiced, the author's commitment and joy increased. Because deep engagement in the community deepened the author's faith, the epistle rings with an attractive authenticity. As the voice of an individual who has served on the frontlines of contemporary social issues offers a casual audience insight into the depth of life, so the voice of the author of the First Letter of John presents a striking faith. The authority is attractive.

Knowing and Doing

True authority often speaks simply. In this letter the words and concepts are easy to grasp—yet their richness invites pondering and deep reflection. Using the image of God as light, the author brings together two realities that belong together, yet frequently are dissociated: what is known and what is done. In the light of God all creation makes sense: There is beauty, order, justice, truth, goodness, and wholeness. The ancient flavor of Ecclesiastes seasons this section: "I know that whatever God does endures forever; nothing can be added to it, nor anything taken from it; God has done this, so that all should stand in awe before him." (Ecclesiastes 3:14) But, whereas the wisdom of Ecclesiastes devolves into a fatalistic acceptance of life's fleeting pleasures, the First Letter of John soars with inspiration for moral living. The great, good light of God shines in the community of those who trust in Jesus. There is no sad sigh, rather as a cheerleader rallies enthusiasm in a crowd this author inspires ordinary individuals to walk with confidence. This confidence begins in the understanding of God as light, intensifies as Jesus shares this light with the world, and continues as the community lives within his light. The metaphor works. Those who know God through Jesus' revelation live that knowledge with actual deeds of love. This is the simple truth of the gospel as presented in 1 John. Yet, it is also a truth ignored, tested, and avoided by Christians lacking maturity of faith. Evidently, this lack of maturity occasionally showed up among "teachers." Whether within the family or church, the early church knew the temptation common to teachers: knowing the subject, but failing to live the subject. All who know God validated their knowledge through their lives.

Help for Sinners

This announcement, of the gospel's unity of knowing God and living according to Jesus' teaching, immediately sparked concerns. Evidently, the author was well aware of the various responses to his simple state-

ment of the gospel. Therefore, without hesitation two very different responses were considered. First, some Christians became so engrossed in their knowledge about God that they failed to discipline their personal conduct. Whenever knowledge was valued over morality, self-examination ceased to be a daily practice. Soon, these thinkers of great thoughts slipped into an ethereal state of imagined perfection—essentially sinlessness. The author directed those within the audience holding this view to examine themselves. The teaching point is clear: All claims to sinless living were based upon self-deceit. The second response, more likely to be encountered in an ordinary congregation, came from Christians distraught by the enormity of their sins. Focusing on their failures, errors, and ugly deeds in everyday life, some Christians felt completely beyond God's grace. To these distraught believers, the author offered a sure antidote: Jesus is the way back to God. Using two images, a legal advocate and a priestly sacrifice, the author encouraged the community to look to Jesus for the help that he is willing to give. These two directions had the potential to humble the arrogant and console the depressed. Those who focused too intently on knowledge as their spiritual food were encouraged to consider their actions. Those who focused too intently on their moral failures were encouraged to consider the grace of Jesus. The good news of the gospel, as presented in the First Letter of John, brought both thoughts and deeds to God's light. The light resplendent in Jesus and in the community was sufficient to restore individuals, communities, and, indeed, the whole world to God.

A Worthy Standard

Let's return to that one stunning, authentic voice that sounds above the secular promotion of Christmas charities. What qualities make such a voice unique? Surely, authority is communicated by personal charisma. Frequently, authority is perfected by experience and tenure. Occasionally, however, authority surprises us: The speaker's voice is halting, the dress and posture unbecoming, the dialect too thick. Moreover, we recognize something more than the congruity of words and deeds. There is an undefined "something" that attracts our attention and confirms our hunch; this is a voice worthy of our attention. In the First Letter of John, the undefined "something" emerges in the unity of right knowledge of God and faithful walking in Jesus' way. The "something" extra is expressed in 2:5, "but whoever obeys his [Jesus'] word, truly in this person the love of God has reached perfection." There are so many words of Jesus that his teachings fill four Gospels. The injunctions and cautions (sometimes bent to form rules and regula-

tions) derived from Jesus' teachings are legion. Yet, the word of Jesus is singular. Jesus, God's Word to our world, offers only one word to his disciples: love. On the last night that Jesus was with his disciples, according to the Gospel of John, Jesus reviewed his teachings with those who shared his table. He instructed them to abide in his word, to trust the Holy Spirit to guide them, and to become obedient to one new commandment. The disciples were to love each other as Jesus loved them. This form of love, dramatically remembered as a servant washing the feet of his friends, is the path into God's perfect love. Indeed, by loving one another Christians uncover a worthy standard. This standard is marked by God's own love; it is both perfect (2:5 NRSV) and complete (2:5 NIV).

SHARING THE SCRIPTURE

PREPARING TO TEACH

Preparing Our Hearts

This week's devotional reading is found in Ephesians 5:8-14. Here the author of this letter reminds the church at Ephesus that although they were once enveloped in darkness they are now to "live as children of light" (5:8). The writer goes on to warn the believers that they are to steer clear of works of darkness. As you meditate on this passage, think about what it means to you to walk in the light of Christ. What kinds of beliefs, actions, and attitudes characterize those who walk in the light? How would you evaluate your own walk—Are you in light, darkness, or perhaps shadows? What changes do you need to pray about making?

Pray that you and the adult learners will be aware of what it means to walk in the light and faithfully follow that path.

Preparing Our Minds

Study the background Scripture found in 1 John 1:1–2:6, and lesson Scripture, 1 John 1:1–2:5. As you study, think about how you can cultivate relationships that are affirming and esteem-enhancing.

Write on newsprint:
❏ information for next week's lesson, found under "Continue the Journey."
❏ activities for further spiritual growth in "Continue the Journey."

Plan how you will present information from Understanding the Scripture, as suggested for "Explore the Characteristics of Jesus Christ as Described in 1 John 1:1–2:5."

LEADING THE CLASS

(1) Gather to Learn

❖ Welcome the class members and introduce any guests.

❖ Pray that the students will focus their attention on characteristics of Jesus that they are called to emulate.

❖ Distribute paper (preferably unlined) and pencils. Ask the students to draw a circle in the center and write their name in it. Then tell them to draw lines from the circle, as spokes on a wheel, and write the names of other persons with whom they are often in contact. These may include family members, co-workers, neighbors, church members, and members of other organizations to which they belong. There is no minimum or maximum number of spokes. Next, ask the class to look at their "wheels" and place a + by the names of those people with whom they are in a relationship where they feel affirmed and respected.

❖ Invite the students to comment on the characteristics of relationships that they find affirming. They need not mention names, but rather focus on traits that make this relationship so positive. List these traits on newsprint.

❖ Read aloud today's focus statement: **People seek meaningful relationships that add to their self-esteem and self-worth. Where can we cultivate such a relationship that is always affirming and esteem-enhancing? John tells us that in God there is found the type of relationship that not only reveals the need for a life-changing encounter with God but also provides the benefits of a relationship that contributes to our spiritual maturity.**

(2) Explore the Characteristics of Jesus Christ as Described in 1 John 1:1–2:5

❖ Choose a volunteer to read 1 John 1:1-4.
■ Ask the students to imagine that they had known Jesus, as the author of this letter claims.
(1) **What is the basis for your authority to speak about Jesus?**
(2) **What would your testimony have been?** (See "A Worthy Testimony" in Interpreting the Scripture for additional ideas.)

(3) **What do you know firsthand about Jesus?**
(4) **Why are you writing this letter?**
■ Use information from Understanding the Scripture, verses 1-4, to add to the discussion.
❖ Select someone to read 1 John 1:5-10.
■ Turn off lights and pull down shades to make the room as dark as possible. Encourage the students to talk about the difficulties one may encounter when walking or working in darkness. (Be sure to be sensitive to those who may be visually impaired.)
■ Make the room as light as possible. Invite the class to note differences between walking and working in the light and in the darkness.
■ Discuss these questions.
(1) **How do we come into the light of Christ?**
(2) **What are the benefits of walking in the light of Christ?**
■ Use information from Understanding the Scripture, verses 5-10, and "Help for Sinners" in Interpreting the Scripture to augment the discussion.
❖ Enlist a class member to read 1 John 2:1-5.
■ Note that Jesus is presented as "an advocate with the Father" (2:1). Discuss what that means. Use information from Understanding the Scripture to help you.
■ Point out that in 2:2 Jesus is presented as a priest. Consider what that means.
■ Talk about how obeying Christ is the opposite side of the same coin as knowing Christ. Invite the students to comment on why obedience is so important.

(3) Identify Ways the Learners Are "Walking in the Light"

❖ Look again at the list of affirming traits generated during the "Gather to Learn" portion.

❖ Solicit additional ideas as to characteristics of people who are walking in the light of Christ.

❖ Provide quiet time for the adults to ponder these questions, which you will need to read aloud.

    (1) What evidence supports my claim that I am walking in the light of Christ?

    (2) What else can I do to meet the standard of the light of Christ?

❖ Break the silence by asking volunteers to give testimony to the impact that the light of Christ has on their lives.

(4) Make a Commitment to Pursue Spiritual Growth

❖ Read aloud this hymn penned by Bernard Barton in 1826.

Walk in the light! so shalt thou know
That fellowship of love
His Spirit only can bestow,
Who reigns in light above.

Walk in the light! and thou shalt find
Thy heart made truly His,
Who dwells in cloudless light enshrined
In whom no darkness is.

Walk in the light! and thine shall be
A path, though thorny, bright:
For God, by grace, shall dwell in thee,
And God himself is light.

❖ Encourage the adults to comment on how this hymn depicts walking in the light as a means of spiritual growth.

❖ Invite all who wish to do so to make a silent commitment to pursue spiritual growth by walking in the light of Christ.

(5) Continue the Journey

❖ Break the silence by praying that each student will, with God's help, be faithful to whatever commitment he or she has made.

❖ Read aloud this preparation for next week's lesson. You may also want to post it on newsprint for the students to copy. **Prepare for next week's session entitled "Receiving the Word" by reading the lesson Scripture from John 1:1-18 and background Scripture from John 1:1-34. As you read the familiar Prologue to John's Gospel, concentrate on these directional markers: People need to feel that God is with them. What does it mean for God to enter our world? John suggests that in Jesus Christ, God entered into human experience as a human in order to bring humanity back into relationship with divinity.**

❖ Read aloud the following three ideas. Challenge the students to commit themselves to use these activities as a springboard to spiritual growth.

    (1) Think about how this passage from 1 John presents Jesus as the image of God. What actions can you take this week so as to embody that image as you walk in the light of Christ?

    (2) Be aware of how the media portrays the good news of Jesus' birth. Evaluate what you see and hear for biblical accuracy.

    (3) Write a prayer of confession, recognizing that Jesus is the atoning sacrifice for our sins.

❖ Sing or read aloud "I Want to Walk as a Child of the Light."

❖ Say this benediction from Jude 24–25 to conclude the session. Include the students by asking them to echo it as you read: **Now to him who is able to keep you from falling, and to make you stand without blemish in the presence of his glory with rejoicing, to the only God our Savior, through Jesus Christ our Lord, be glory, majesty, power, and authority, before all time and now and forever. Amen.**

UNIT 1: CHRIST, THE IMAGE OF GOD
RECEIVING THE WORD

PREVIEWING THE LESSON

Lesson Scripture: John 1:1-18
Background Scripture: John 1:1-34
Key Verse: John 1:14

Focus of the Lesson:
People need to feel that God is with them. What does it mean for God to enter our world? John suggests that in Jesus Christ, God entered into human experience as a human in order to bring humanity back into relationship with divinity.

Goals for the Learners:
(1) to focus on the images John used to describe Jesus Christ.
(2) to reflect on the continuing incarnation of the gospel in their lives.
(3) to celebrate the incarnation of Jesus Christ.

Supplies:
Bibles, newsprint and marker, paper and pencils, hymnals

READING THE SCRIPTURE

NRSV
John 1:1-18

¹In the beginning was the Word, and the Word was with God, and the Word was God. ²He was in the beginning with God. ³All things came into being through him, and without him not one thing came into being. What has come into being ⁴in him was life, and the life was the light of all people. ⁵The light shines in the darkness, and the darkness did not overcome it.

⁶There was a man sent from God, whose name was John. ⁷He came as a witness to testify to the light, so that all might believe through him. ⁸He himself was not the light,

NIV
John 1:1-18

¹In the beginning was the Word, and the Word was with God, and the Word was God. ²He was with God in the beginning. ³Through him all things were made; without him nothing was made that has been made. ⁴In him was life, and that life was the light of men. ⁵The light shines in the darkness, but the darkness has not understood it.

⁶There came a man who was sent from God; his name was John. ⁷He came as a witness to testify concerning that light, so that through him all men might believe. ⁸He himself was not the light; he came only as a

but he came to testify to the light. [9]The true light, which enlightens everyone, was coming into the world.

[10]He was in the world, and the world came into being through him; yet the world did not know him. [11]He came to what was his own, and his own people did not accept him. [12]But to all who received him, who believed in his name, he gave power to become children of God, [13]who were born, not of blood or of the will of the flesh or of the will of man, but of God.

[14]And the Word became flesh and lived among us, and we have seen his glory, the glory as of a father's only son, full of grace and truth. [15](John testified to him and cried out, "This was he of whom I said, 'He who comes after me ranks ahead of me because he was before me.'") [16]From his fullness we have all received, grace upon grace. [17]The law indeed was given through Moses; grace and truth came through Jesus Christ. [18]No one has ever seen God. It is God the only Son, who is close to the Father's heart, who has made him known.

witness to the light. [9]The true light that gives light to every man was coming into the world.

[10]He was in the world, and though the world was made through him, the world did not recognize him. [11]He came to that which was his own, but his own did not receive him. [12]Yet to all who received him, to those who believed in his name, he gave the right to become children of God—[13]children born not of natural descent, nor of human decision or a husband's will, but born of God.

[14]The Word became flesh and made his dwelling among us. We have seen his glory, the glory of the One and Only, who came from the Father, full of grace and truth. [15]John testifies concerning him. He cries out, saying, "This was he of whom I said, 'He who comes after me has surpassed me because he was before me.'" [16]From the fullness of his grace we have all received one blessing after another. [17]For the law was given through Moses; grace and truth came through Jesus Christ. [18]No one has ever seen God, but God the One and Only, who is at the Father's side, has made him known.

UNDERSTANDING THE SCRIPTURE

John 1:1-5. The Gospel of John opens with poetry. Even in translation the words and rhythm alert our ears that this is not "ordinary prose." As a beloved passage, our text for today also comes wrapped in sentiment and appreciation. Poetry, sentiment, and appreciation make exegesis difficult on any day, but on Christmas Eve, it may be impossible to do challenging analytical work. Therefore, with this day in mind, this background section takes a gentler approach. Let's begin with the question: why poetry? Consider the four beginnings from the Gospels:

- Matthew begins with genealogy and moves to a birth narrative;

- Luke opens with birth, then moves to a genealogy;
- Mark skips the early days and genealogy, to begin with the mature Jesus' baptism and beginning of ministry; and
- the Gospel of John opens, oddly, with a poem.

Most people want to know the "facts" of a birth; believers want to be able to trace the family tree; future generations deserve to know how the ministry began. A poem neither pretends to offer facts, although facts frequently hold the images together, nor does a poem define reality, although a strong sense of what's "real" emerges through images and allusions. So why poetry? The answer lies in the culture of first-century Palestine. In that culture, poetry was not only appreciated, it formed the highest standard of respect. In a preliterate culture, the wisest and most respected members of the community were expected to be masters of poetry. Mastering poetry meant, first, that the speaker be steeped in the traditions of the community. The Gospel of John demonstrates such familiarity as the first line, "In the beginning" connected this poem with the first poem of Scripture, Genesis 1. Second, the speaker was expected to enhance the received tradition in such a way that it became more accessible, more interesting, or more compelling. Notice how boldly this Gospel referred to "the Word" before God actually speaks—giving to the Word a place within God prior to God's creative activity. Third, in the actual recitation of poetry, honor and authority was conferred on the speaker. Perhaps this is the best answer to our "why poetry?" question: A poetic opening granted authority to the author. In summary, the first five verses establish 1) the Word was always with God, 2) God created all light and life by the Word, and 3) the divine light will never be squelched by darkness. The poet spoke, the audience understood; a creation story was before them.

John 1:6-13. This poet, however, did not follow the usual pattern of retelling the tradition. Instead, a new element was introduced: a man sent from God named John. The shift was shocking—from the eternal word to a well-known religious character. Yet the poet's purpose was to fold the tradition of Israel into the story of Jesus. John the Baptist forged the link between the old story and the new story. In the Gospel of John, John the Baptist has one role to play: He is the first witness to Jesus, specifically the first witness to Jesus' metaphorical role as light. John the Baptist was a supporting character in this poem; he set the stage. In

the next section, verses 10-13, the true light is described by relationship and function—but not by name. The audience, appreciative of poetic devices and wise in the tradition of Jesus, knew immediately that Jesus was the person behind the pronoun "he." These are the initial claims made about Jesus:

- he is, was, and always will be related to God's created world;
- this relationship is intimate;
- not all of Jesus' people acknowledge or accept him;
- by accepting a relationship with Jesus humans received a new status as children of God;
- this status is not achieved by bloodline or earned by human activity;
- only Jesus can give the status of child of God and the empowerment of light and life.

John 1:14-18. This section deals with the mystery of the incarnation. The simple phrase, "the Word became flesh and lived among us," was the bold claim that Jesus not only came from God, but also shared God's identity in his human life on earth. The unique status of Jesus was designated, again poetically, as the "father's only son." Jesus was unique, however, not only due to his eternal relationship with God, but also due to his capacity to reveal God to humans. In Jesus, ordinary men and women saw God's grace and truth. Again, the significance of a witness giving testimony moves the poem forward. John the Baptist is mentioned for the second time as a witness. His function, a link between the first creation and the new creation, is poetically explained. John was of the present age; Jesus came from the eternal God and his status, although perceived at a particular point in time, was eternal. The testimony to Jesus as God's incarnate Word was not abstract (and impractical) theology; rather, Jesus was an actual person who offered particular gifts to humanity. Foremost among those gifts was "grace upon grace," the abundance of God's love for all creation and for each individual within creation. Returning to the ancient tradition, the poet now clarifies a troubling issue. Since Jesus' grace was so abundant, did the law have any further use? The response was logical: The law came through a man, Moses, but the revelation of Jesus is full of God's grace because of Jesus' unique relationship to God. Only Jesus, the child "close to the Father's heart," saw and was able to make God known. The mystery of the incarnation is presented as a poem to introduce a detailed presentation of Jesus. In the beginning, however, all one needed to know was Jesus' unique, eternal, and loving relationship with God.

John 1:19-34. The final section focuses, again, on the testimony of John. Priests and Levites from Jerusalem (the institutional side of Israel) questioned him about his identity and purpose. John replied, quoting the prophet Isaiah to explain that he was God's appointed witness. The Pharisees, representing the conservative-yet-faithful spectrum of the religion, questioned him about his activities. John stated his purpose was testimony not prophecy. Finally, in verse 29, Jesus arrived! John fulfilled his role in God's history: He testified to Jesus. John the Baptist is the first in a long line of witnesses upon which the Gospel of John rests.

INTERPRETING THE SCRIPTURE

Light Shining in Darkness

Do you cherish one particularly memorable Christmas Eve service? Was it in a grand cathedral or a small country church? Were you worshiping as a stranger, but welcomed as a dear friend, or was your whole family filling a pew? As a pastor, I've marked my ministry by the services for Christmas Eve. My memories are rich, but one service stands out. It was in a small village in Western Pennsylvania; I was "filling in" for a congregation whose pastor had recently retired. As I met with the worship committee before the service, I asked for any last minute instructions. One young man succinctly said: "Remember to raise your candle." A slightly older woman corrected him, "Everyone knows that; besides, if she can't catch on, what good is she?" As a gentle chuckle grew, I pondered the meaning of this exchange. With the service underway, I focused my attention on the story, the carols, the prayers and, of course, the sermon. The service was to end with candlelighting. We'd agreed that I would recite John 1:1-15 as the ushers spread the light throughout the sanc-

tuary. The organist played "Silent Night" softly as I spoke these beautiful words from the Gospel of John; then, as all the candles were shining against the darkness that surrounded, the congregation began to sing "Silent Night." It took me one stanza to understand the young man's caution, "Remember to raise your candle." This congregation followed a tradition of raising their candles with each word related to light. The impact was dramatic; whenever they sang a "light" word, everyone raised candles to shoulder height. The sanctuary was transformed from soft to bright light. On the last stanza everyone held their candles high above their heads. The room glowed so brilliantly, I saw Jesus' own light radiating over the small congregation. This simple, liturgical act perfectly demonstrated the power and purpose of the light that shines in the darkness. Christ's light intensifies and spreads as believers lift up their individual lights.

Pointing to the Light

The beauty of John 1:1-15 comes both from the poetic words and from the gentle arrangement of ideas. The passage opens with three strong concepts: word, life, and light. These three, each sustained by God's own self, weave a memorable pattern. God's preferred mode of creation is by "the Word" (*logos* in Greek). In Genesis 1, God speaks creation into order: separating light from darkness, dividing the waters from above from the waters from below, and causing the waters below to be gathered together and the dry land to appear. All living plants and animals are "spoken" into existence; even human beings spring from a verbal declaration (Genesis 1:26). The speech of God is powerful, but before each utterance changed the world (literally!), a Word already existed. This Word-prior-to-speech contained the truth, beauty, and love of God's intention. In the Gospel of John, the Word is the metaphor that describes Jesus' unique relationship to God.

- Jesus, as the Word, was always with God;
- Jesus, as the Word, participated in all God's creative acts;
- Jesus, as the Word, shared all God's intentions;
- Jesus, as the Word, spoken at a particular historical moment, gave light to all people.

Word, life, and light belonged together in God and in Jesus. Yet, these three, though intimately related, were not always recognized. It took an individual of spiritual insight and patient prayer to grasp the connection. Such an individual was John the Baptist; according to the opening of the Gospel of John, he was the man sent from God to testify to Jesus. He was to point to Jesus and compel others to see what he saw: that the true light that enlightens everyone was entering the world.

Welcoming Jesus

The Gospel of John is rich in imagery; it is also starkly honest. The reality of Jesus' rejection by "the world" and by "his own"

is always present in this Gospel. It is faced directly and with honesty. There are few verses more poignant than John 1:10-11. Imagine, creation failing to recognize the creator's plan. Imagine, God's chosen people failing to welcome God's own son. Human words can barely hold such sorrow. Yet, there it is in the opening poem of Jesus. Word, light, and life met ignorance, resistance, and rejection. The shadow of the cross darkens this page. Yet, in the face of such sorrow, some "believed in his name." At this point in the Gospel Jesus' name has not been mentioned; clearly, the author is addressing the audience at the level of individual belief. Each Christian must speak the name Jesus Christ (or, more likely, use the phrase, "Jesus is Lord!") to confirm belief. Those who received this gospel knew Jesus' name; the author was speaking to them. Because they knew and believed in Jesus, he gave them power to live in a whole new relationship to God and with one another. No longer were they strangers, aliens, or children of God by the law of Moses. In Jesus all were united as brothers and sisters, children of one Creator, one Father. The new status as children of God was God's intended purpose . . . the reason God spoke the word Jesus. Therefore, by the very act of welcoming Jesus, something new began. The something new sparked change, whether spontaneously, as in a conversion of dramatic consequences, or gradually, as in a child's growth toward Christian maturity. Nonetheless, as the believer welcomes Jesus, the empowerment to live as God's child started things changing.

Jesus among Us

Imagine Jesus coming to your home. How would you welcome him? What food would you serve? How would you introduce him to the family and the neighbors? What would you want to ask him? The fantasy of being in the physical presence of Jesus is captivating. Indeed, many

Christians assume that faith would be easier if only they had the disciples' advantage. The first followers knew Jesus; they saw and touched him. But those of us who believe centuries after his life can only imagine him. There are guides, however, to our imagination: beautiful and strong words such as "And the Word became flesh and lived among us, and we have seen his glory, the glory as of a father's only son" (1:14). In these words, packed with theological content and faithful testimony, we hear and receive the glory of Jesus. The glory that we hear is as hidden and as obvious as the glory that the disciples saw. Remember, not everyone saw Jesus' glory as he walked among the crowds; the disciples, however, recognized Jesus' inner spiritual glory. In the same way, not everyone who saw Jesus was attracted to him; some, particularly the poor, felt so because in his presence they experienced the justice, righteousness, and love of God. Finally, Jesus' glory was not a substance that clung to his physical body; Jesus looked, walked, ate, and slept just as every other human creature. No, those disciples who saw Jesus' glory saw with spiritual eyes; the vast majority of Christians have heard Jesus' glory with spiritual ears. The passage for this Christmas Eve day rings with glory: God's glory shared with Jesus, Jesus' glory enlightening his believers, and the glory testified to by faithful witnesses. We believe because we have heard such glory in the Word of Scripture.

SHARING THE SCRIPTURE

PREPARING TO TEACH

Preparing Our Hearts

This week's devotional reading is found in Isaiah 53:1-6. This is part the fourth of Isaiah's "Servant Songs" (52:13–53:12). This song is filled with descriptions of a servant who suffers for others. Since the earliest days of the church, Christians have applied this passage to Jesus. How do you see Jesus in this passage? What connections can you make between this passage and the one we are reading today on Christmas Eve in which John speaks of God's Word becoming flesh? As you think of the tiny babe whose birth we celebrate, meditate also on the sacrifices that the work God sent him to do required.

Pray that you and the adult learners will be prepared to receive not only a newborn in a manger but also the Savior of the world.

Preparing Our Minds

Study the background Scripture from John 1:1-34 and lesson Scripture, John 1:1-18. Since this is a very familiar passage, do your best to read as if you are approaching it for the first time in order to glean new insights. Ponder what it means for God to enter our world.

Write on newsprint:
❑ information for the introductory chart in "Focus on the Images John Used to Describe Jesus Christ."
❑ information for next week's lesson, found under "Continue the Journey."
❑ activities for further spiritual growth in "Continue the Journey."

LEADING THE CLASS

(1) Gather to Learn

❖ Welcome the class members and introduce any guests.
❖ Pray that the adults will celebrate the coming of Jesus, God's Word, into the world.
❖ Read "Light Shining in Darkness" in Interpreting the Scripture to set the tone for

today's lesson. Note especially that this pastor "saw Jesus' own light radiating over the small congregation."

❖ Invite the students to tell stories of memorable Christmas Eve services in which they, too, experienced the light of Christ.

❖ Read aloud today's focus statement: **People need to feel that God is with them. What does it mean for God to enter our world? John suggests that in Jesus Christ, God entered into human experience as a human in order to bring humanity back into relationship with divinity.**

(2) Focus on the Images John Used to Describe Jesus Christ

❖ Introduce the background Scripture for today's lesson by pointing out the following information. As an option, write this data on newsprint.

■ Verses 1-18, traditionally known as the Prologue to John's Gospel, read like a hymn that is celebrating the coming of the Word into the world.
■ Verses 1-5 depict the eternal Word as light and life.
■ Verses 6-8 portray John the Baptist as a witness to the light.
■ Verses 9-13 describe the light, or Word, coming into the world.
■ Verses 14-18 announce that the Word has become flesh and lives among us.
■ Verses 19-34 tell the story of John the Baptist's witness on behalf of Jesus.

❖ Select one volunteer to read John 1:1-5, 10-18, and another to read verses 6-9.

❖ Ask the class to state what this passage tells them about Jesus. Be sure to include the images that John names, such as *Word, life,* and *light*. Write their ideas on newsprint.

❖ Talk about what each of the listed images evokes for the students and how they perceive that Christ embodies each of these images. Use information from "Pointing to the Light" in Interpreting the Scripture to broaden the discussion.

(3) Reflect on the Continuing Incarnation of the Gospel in the Learners' Lives

❖ Note that in John 1:12 we learn that Jesus gave those who believed in him the "power to become children of God." Discuss the meaning of this phrase with the learners.

❖ Consider how being a child of God affects the class members' lives by discussing these questions.

(1) How does your status as a child of God affect your faith and your relationship with others?
(2) How do you see yourself as living in the way Jesus taught and modeled for us?
(3) People clearly saw God enfleshed in Jesus. In what ways might they see God in you?

(4) Celebrate the Incarnation of Jesus Christ

❖ Distribute paper and pencils. Direct the students to write the letters **I-N-C-A-R-N-A-T-I-O-N** vertically on the page, one letter per line. Then ask them to write an acrostic poem that conveys an image of the incarnate Christ. One need not be a poet to do this activity; one word per letter would be sufficient. Here is an example for those who wish to write a more developed poem.

In the stillness of the
Night, under Bethlehem's starlit sky,
Christ the Savior was born.
"Alleluia," sang the angels,
"Rejoice, for the Messiah has come."
Nestled in Mary's arms, the newborn slept
As shepherds who heard amazing news hurried
To see what God had done.
In a feeding trough, on a bed of hay, the
Only begotten Son, the Creator of all that is,
Now has taken on flesh to become like us.

❖ Divide into pairs or groups and encourage the students to read their poems to one another as an act celebrating the incarnation of Christ.

(5) Continue the Journey

❖ Pray that all who have participated today will go forth having received God's Word, incarnate in Christ.

❖ Read aloud this preparation for next week's lesson. You may also want to post it on newsprint for the students to copy. **Prepare for next week's session entitled "Keeping the Balance" by reading Philippians 2:1-11, which is both our background and lesson Scripture. Mull over these ideas as you study: Some people avoid humility as a sign of weakness, while others embrace it to the point that they become proud of their humility! Is it possible to balance a sense of humility with an appropriate level of self-esteem? Pointing out that Jesus Christ achieved the perfect balance between humility and exaltation, Paul urges Christians to take on the mind of Christ.**

❖ Read aloud the following three ideas. Challenge the students to commit themselves to use these activities as a springboard to spiritual growth.

(1) **Sing Christmas carols. As you do, consider the image of Christ that each one conveys to you. Are there images that you find more meaningful than others? Why do you think these particular images touch you?**

(2) **Do some research on John the Baptist. Use books and/or the Internet. Who was he? What group did he belong to? What was his relationship with the prophet Elijah? What was the purpose of his message?**

(3) **Tell someone else about Jesus this week. Perhaps you can use an anecdote to explain how he is the light of your life.**

❖ Sing or read aloud "Hark! the Herald Angels Sing."

❖ Say this benediction from Jude 24–25 to conclude the session. Include the students by asking them to echo it as you read: **Now to him who is able to keep you from falling, and to make you stand without blemish in the presence of his glory with rejoicing, to the only God our Savior, through Jesus Christ our Lord, be glory, majesty, power, and authority, before all time and now and forever. Amen.**

UNIT 1: CHRIST, THE IMAGE OF GOD

KEEPING THE BALANCE

PREVIEWING THE LESSON

Lesson Scripture: Philippians 2:1-11
Background Scripture: Philippians 2:1-11
Key Verse: Philippians 2:3

Focus of the Lesson:
Some people avoid humility as a sign of weakness, while others embrace it to the point that they become proud of their humility! Is it possible to balance a sense of humility with an appropriate level of self-esteem? Pointing out that Jesus Christ achieved the perfect balance between humility and exaltation, Paul urges Christians to take on the mind of Christ.

Goals for the Learners:
(1) to explore Christ's humility and exaltation as presented in Philippians 2.
(2) to identify and affirm a balanced practice of humility in their own lives.
(3) to act with the mind of Christ.

Supplies:
Bibles, newsprint and marker, paper and pencils, hymnals

READING THE SCRIPTURE

NRSV
Philippians 2:1-11

¹If then there is any encouragement in Christ, any consolation from love, any sharing in the Spirit, any compassion and sympathy, ²make my joy complete: be of the same mind, having the same love, being in full accord and of one mind. **³Do nothing from selfish ambition or conceit, but in humility regard others as better than yourselves.** ⁴Let each of you look not to your own interests, but to the interests of others. ⁵Let

NIV
Philippians 2:1-11

¹If you have any encouragement from being united with Christ, if any comfort from his love, if any fellowship with the Spirit, if any tenderness and compassion, ²then make my joy complete by being likeminded, having the same love, being one in spirit and purpose. **³Do nothing out of selfish ambition or vain conceit, but in humility consider others better than yourselves.** ⁴Each of you should look not only to your

the same mind be in you that was in Christ
Jesus,

    6 who, though he was in the form of God,
      did not regard equality with God
      as something to be exploited,
    7 but emptied himself,
      taking the form of a slave,
      being born in human likeness.
      And being found in human form,
    8 he humbled himself
      and became obedient to the point of
        death—
      even death on a cross.
    9 Therefore God also highly exalted him
      and gave him the name
      that is above every name,
    10 so that at the name of Jesus
      every knee should bend,
      in heaven and on earth and under the
      earth,
    11 and every tongue should confess
      that Jesus Christ is Lord,
      to the glory of God the Father.

own interests, but also to the interests of
others.

    5Your attitude should be the same as that
of Christ Jesus:
    6Who, being in very nature God,
      did not consider equality with God
      something to be grasped,
    7but made himself nothing,
      taking the very nature of a servant,
      being made in human likeness.
    8And being found in appearance as a man,
      he humbled himself
      and became obedient to death—
      even death on a cross!
    9Therefore God exalted him to the highest
      place
      and gave him the name that is above
      every name,
    10that at the name of Jesus every knee
      should bow,
      in heaven and on earth and under the
      earth,
    11and every tongue confess that Jesus
      Christ is Lord,
      to the glory of God the Father.

UNDERSTANDING THE SCRIPTURE

Philippians 2:1-2. The Letter to the
Philippians, authored by the Apostle Paul,
addressed a small congregation that he had
organized and nurtured as a fellowship of
believers. Clearly, a warm, personal tie
existed between Paul and the congregation
in Philippi; the warmth is demonstrated in
this letter by Paul's frequent use of the word
"joy." Although written while a prisoner,
whether under house arrest awaiting transport to Rome or from his cell in Rome, this
epistle literally sings. For the congregation in
Philippi, this letter was a beloved document
of encouragement, hope, and blessing; it continues to inspire Christian witness in contemporary congregations. In the opening two
verses of our passage, Paul reminds the
Philippians of their intimate relationship:

They are encouraged in Christ, consoled by
God's love, and united in the Spirit. In addition to these spiritual truths, as brothers and
sisters in Christ, the author and the congregation shared a mutual compassion and
sympathy. Indeed, Paul called to mind their
previous relationship in order to make a specific request. Paul asked them to complete
his joy. Joy will fully abound, in the congregation and with Paul, through the harmony
achieved by Christian love radiating from a
common mind within the congregation.

Philippians 2:3-4. This common mind
was explained by descriptions of two sets of
contrasting behaviors. In each set, Paul
described the negative behavior first and
then offered a positive behavior. The first
set concerned believers' ambitions—or to

use contemporary terminology, "motivation." A negative behavior began in conceit and selfish ambitions and led to a false sense of one's importance. Rarely has Paul anything good to say about personal boasting; he taught, rather, that any boasting done by Christians should be boasting in the Lord. This concept was undoubtedly part of his preaching and teaching with the Philippian congregation. Reminding them to put aside selfish ambition and conceit, therefore, was not a new spiritual direction; it originated with the first preaching of the gospel and continued throughout the early years of congregational spiritual formation. Likewise, the congregation was trained in humility. Such training did not result in the false modesty or lack of self-esteem, so detrimental to Christ-like joy and obedience. Rather, humility began with the recognition of the rights and needs of others while acknowledging the various ways in which God's grace flowed through others. Indeed, since all believers were incorporated into Christ, they no longer claimed individuality and personal ambition. In the Christian community mutuality fostered positive evaluation of others and extended to the interests, needs, and contributions of each and every member of the community. Essentially, Paul reminded the Philippians that their Christian faith included a unique perspective toward themselves and their brothers and sisters in Christ. Continuing in a teaching mode, Paul's second set of behaviors contrasted those who "looked out for number one" with those who attended to the well-being of others. Notice that Paul was not attacking any particular individual; he addressed the whole congregation by the second person plural, "you," designating not one, but all the members.

Philippians 2:5-8. Paul wrote with confidence; in all likelihood, he trusted, completely, the congregation's understanding of the spiritual values of humility and service to one another. However, he was writing to inspire more than intellectual assent. Paul aimed his words at a soul level; his goal was to impact both the mind and the spirit of the congregation. Therefore, his language shifted from prose to poetry. In 2:5, a simple statement filled the congregation with a renewed vision of themselves. Notice the use of the passive tense: The congregation was encouraged to allow the mind of Christ full sway within the community. The mind of Christ established the distinctive Christian perspective on God, on creation, on community, and on individuals. If the mind of Christ had full sway within the community, then the community would live together in the joy and peace of Christ. This uplifting idea was elaborated by a hymn. Chapter 2:6-11 is ordinarily printed as poetry. The origins of this poem or hymn are unknown. Consider:

- it does not conform to the standard of Greek poetry;
- it contains many parallelisms reminiscent of Hebrew poetry;
- some scholars detect an Aramaic rhythm beneath the lines;
- other scholars suggest that Paul is embellishing a well-known and beloved early hymn of faith;
- some scholars even claim that Paul has "Christianized" a gnostic hymn.

Whatever the source, these few stanzas are written across the soul of Christianity. They beautifully describe the mind of Christ as humble, self-emptying, and obedient. The humility of Christ was (and is) unique; only Jesus, the Son of God, set aside divinity to live within the human community. His self-emptying took the form of a slave. The image of Jesus kneeling to wash the disciples' feet was a significant impression on the minds of believers. As he fulfilled his mission—to serve, not to be served—Jesus grew in the human virtue of obedience. He, therefore, willingly walked to his death. Obedience taught Jesus that self-emptying was God's particular path for redemption. His death on the cross signified the fulfillment of all humility, self-emptying, and obedience.

Philippians 2:9-11. The first stanza of the hymn testified to Jesus' mindset; the second stanza offered God's confirmation. After the shocking ending, an abhorrent death on a cross, a great "therefore" sounded. Because of all that was written in the first stanza—the humility, the self-emptying and the obedience—God acted. Jesus received a name above all other names; this was the symbolic evidence of the divine status and power that belonged to the risen Lord. The name of Jesus was wonderfully attractive; people from every nation and every time joined together in the worship of Christ. Using an image from the prophet Isaiah (45:23), Paul presented the scene of universal worship. The worship of Christ, however, does not glorify Christ. Rather, true Christian worship glorifies God. Just as Jesus was humble, self-emptying, and obedient during his earthly life, so the risen Christ is humble, self-emptying and obedient as he shares God's glory. The glory Christ had and shared was the glory of the only son of the Father; as the hymn concluded, a universal chorus praised Christ and glorified God the Father of all.

INTERPRETING THE SCRIPTURE

Taking Stock

As one year ends and another begins, self-evaluation increases. January brings greater numbers at gyms, boosts in sales of diet aids, and even a wider participation in Sunday morning worship. It seems that there is always something worthy of correction: sagging muscles, tight clothes, or spiritual slackness. The old year ends, the self-reflection adjusts previous directions, and millions head into the new year with new or renewed commitments. We do not know the time of year that the Philippian congregation received this letter from their former pastor. But, the end of one year and beginning of a new year would be a prime time. Consider the letter's flow, in Chapter 1 Paul created a rich emotional tone by the opening words of the letter. He shared his constant remembrance and his steadfast prayers for the congregation. He stated his heartfelt goal for their maturity in Christ. Indeed, he explained that he wanted Christ's love to "overflow more and more" (1:9) in the congregation. With this as the backdrop, Paul's subsequent words were filled with encouragement, consolation, and compassion. Each word was actually an invitation to the congregation to take stock of their corporate life. The phrases "encouragement in Christ" (2:1) and "consolation from love" (2:1) suggested the social dynamic of mutual caring within the community. His phrase, "sharing in the Spirit" (2:1), directed the congregation to take stock of their worship of God. As the congregation evaluated their common life, their worship and their witness, Paul knew that they would resolve to be diligent and thoughtful in their Christian living. Paul trusted this outcome because he knew and loved those to whom he wrote.

A Common Mind

Paul offers an unusual reason for the Philippians to take stock of their Christian faith and witness. He connects their activity to his personal joy. A prisoner's appeal for joy is precious and poignant. Surely, such an appeal was not easily dismissed. However, the fulfilling of Paul's request may have given the Philippians pause. Consider how you might feel if someone suggested that your community should strive to "be of the same mind, having the same love, being in full accord and of one mind" (2:2). The initial response might be resistance; after all, in our contemporary society individuality is valued over uniformity. We expect to exercise our freedom of thought, action, and belief; the mere suggestion of sameness violates this value. Paul, however, was not suggesting that the Philippians walk in matched steps. Rather, he wanted their common life to be guided by the principles of love, mutual service, and trust in God that characterized Jesus' life. A comparison with our notion of democracy demonstrates Paul's point. For democracy to flourish, we expect:

- a respect for the voice of each and every member of society;
- the participation of all in the decision-making process;
- the willingness from all to allow the majority to set the course;
- the freedom of the minority to call the majority to accountability.

According to Paul, the Philippian community was to be guided by principles that must be commonly accepted. There can be no democracy when portions of the society are silenced. There can be no Christian witness without the recognition that Christ died for the sins of the world. There can be no democracy without the tension between majority and minority. There is no Christian faith without the humility that places the needs of the other before self-interests. The principles that Paul wanted the congregation in Philippi to cultivate were ancient and modest: the golden rule and care of neighbor. These two elements established the foundation for Christ's mind to develop within the community.

Jesus' Humility

Pause for a moment to remember your favorite stories of Jesus. What attracts you to this man? How do you describe his core values? Is there a hymn that expresses your esteem of Jesus? The Apostle Paul turned to a hymn to remind the congregation in Philippi of Jesus' core value. The power of quoting a hymn is intense: Emotions related to deep spiritual experiences are called up by the music of worship. While these verses printed in our New Testament are beautiful and moving, imagine their impact when joined to a familiar hymn tune such as "Amazing Grace" or "Jesus Loves Me." Paul addressed both the spirit and the mind of the congregation as he described Jesus' mind. The first characteristic of Jesus is overwhelming respect for God; though Jesus shared intimately in God's very being, Jesus did not strive to make himself "equal" to God. Instead, Jesus "emptied himself" of all claims on divinity in order to fully live within the human community. Respect for God allowed Jesus to live within the human community as an equal, but even within the human community he did not demand equality! As a human, Jesus knew his purpose was to serve. Thus, he patterned his life on the humble image of a slave. He served God with an obedient spirit and his neighbors with love. The consequence of his mind-set, however, was a violent and sad death on a cross. This summary of Jesus' life, even as accompanied by the sweet music of worship, startles. It is impossible to hear the meekness of Jesus and his life's end on the cross without wondering, "Was he really right?" Humility leads one into ruthless hands; ruthless hands are full of violence and death. This is not an attractive advertisement for a humble life.

God's Response

But, thanks be to God, the Letter to the Philippians sings on. Jesus' humility is not judged by his death, but by his resurrection and exaltation. Because he was respectful of God, because he lived a full (and perfect) human life, and because his obedience persisted through an ignoble death, Jesus was raised up by God. God conferred upon Jesus a glorious name signifying his worth. Moreover, Jesus' status as God's beloved Son transcended all the sin, evil, and ugliness besetting humans. Jesus was the means by which all humanity would come to know and praise God. He did not give in to these very human propositions. He chose community with the weak and outcast over power. He prayed for courage, wisdom, and strength rather than sought material security or wealth. He trusted God rather than call on the assistance of angels. His life ended painfully, but his death was only one part in God's redemption. There was more to come: resurrection, ascension, return, and complete reconciliation were glimpsed beyond the experience of crucifixion. This glimpse of God's reconciled world re-evaluated Jesus' mindset and lifestyle; no

longer was he a meek minister maligned by the masses. The man, his teachings, and his life were confirmed as worthy of God's ultimate approval. His steadfast reverence for God, humility, and service to others were divinely blessed. This, then, was Paul's encouragement for the Philippians. Just as Jesus patiently bore his role, so Paul commended a patient practice of Christian principles. Just as the Philippians understood the perfectly balanced life of Jesus, so contemporary Christians continue to practice humility, mutual encouragement, and Christian care of the neighbor.

SHARING THE SCRIPTURE

PREPARING TO TEACH

Preparing Our Hearts

This week's devotional reading is found in 1 Peter 3:8-12. The author writes in verse 8 that we are to have "unity of spirit, sympathy, love for one another, a tender heart, and a humble mind." Furthermore, we are to steer clear of evil and do good. These are helpful words, but what do they really mean to us in the twenty-first century? What does "unity of spirit" look like when the Christian church includes all kinds of people with very diverse theological views and biblical interpretations? How can we be humble in mind when we think we have a great idea and want to get our point across? Think about how you apply Peter's teaching to your own life.

Pray that you and the adult learners will live as those who have been schooled in the teachings and example of Christ.

Preparing Our Minds

Study the background and lesson Scripture, both of which are found in Philippians 2:1-11. As you prepare for this

session think about how one can balance Christ-like humility with an appropriate level of self-esteem.

Write on newsprint:
❏ information for next week's lesson, found under "Continue the Journey."
❏ activities for further spiritual growth in "Continue the Journey."

LEADING THE CLASS

(1) Gather to Learn

❖ Welcome the class members and introduce any guests.
❖ Pray that all who participate in today's session will be open to the Spirit's leading.
❖ Read aloud these excerpts from an article entitled "On Humility" by Rabbi Dr. Jonathan Sacks.

Humility is the orphaned virtue of our age. . . . This is a shame. Humility—true humility—is one of the most expansive and life-enhancing of all virtues. It does not mean undervaluing yourself. It means valuing other people. It signals a certain openness to life's grandeur and the will-

ingness to be surprised, uplifted, by good-ness wherever one finds it. . . . [T]he capacity to admire. That, I think, is what the greater part of humility is, the capacity to be open to something greater than oneself. False humility is the pretence that one is small. True humility is the consciousness of standing in the presence of greatness, which is why it is the virtue of prophets, those who feel most vividly the nearness of G-d.

❖ Invite the students to respond by agreeing or disagreeing with Rabbi Sacks' comments or by modifying them to express their own understanding of humility.

❖ Read aloud today's focus statement: **Some people avoid humility as a sign of weakness, while others embrace it to the point that they become proud of their humility! Is it possible to balance a sense of humility with an appropriate level of self-esteem? Pointing out that Jesus Christ achieved the perfect balance between humility and exaltation, Paul urges Christians to take on the mind of Christ.**

(2) Explore Christ's Humility and Exaltation as Presented in Philippians 2

❖ Choose someone to read Philippians 2:1-4.
◾ Look carefully at the points Paul is making here. You may want to ask the students to turn in their Bibles to the additional references in Philippians.
  • Unity of the mind: 2:5; 3:15; 4:2
  • Actions motivated by humility: 2:8; 3:21; 4:12
  • Priority of needs of others: 1:23-26; 2:20, 25-26
◾ Encourage the students to talk briefly about what each of the three emphases would look like if the modern church took them seriously.
❖ Select a volunteer to read Philippians 2:5-11.
❖ **Option:** If you have access to *The*

United Methodist Hymnal, read "Canticle of Christ's Obedience," number 167, responsively.
◾ Use the bulleted information under Philippians 2:5-8 in Understanding the Scripture to help the students discover what is known about this poetry.
◾ Ask half the class (perhaps subdivided into smaller groups) to look at verses 5-8 to discern how Jesus' humility manifested itself.
◾ Ask the other half of the class to look at God's response to Jesus' humility in verses 9-11.
◾ Invite the groups to report back. Use, as needed, information from "Jesus' Humility" and "God's Response" in Interpreting the Scripture.
◾ Wrap up this section by asking the students to discuss what these verses tell them about Jesus and about God.

(3) Identify and Affirm a Balanced Practice of Humility in the Learners' Lives

❖ Post a sheet of newsprint. Invite the students to complete this sentence: *"Humility is . . ."*.
❖ Talk about these definitions in light of what we have learned about humility this morning. Are all of the definitions appropriate for Christian living? Do some need the counterbalance of healthy self-esteem? If so, what changes need to be made in the definitions?
❖ Provide time for the adults to talk about the challenges of living with humility in our day. You may wish to read this anecdote from Rabbi Sacks' article as a humorous introduction to the discussion: **How virtues change! Moses, the greatest hero of Jewish tradition, is described by the Bible as "a very humble man, more humble than anyone else on the face of the earth." By today's standards he was clearly wrongly**

advised. He should have hired an agent, sharpened up his image, let slip some calculated indiscretions about his conversations with the Almighty and sold his story to the press for a six-figure sum. With any luck, he might have landed up with his own television chat show, dispensing wisdom to those willing to bare their soul to the watching millions. He would have had his fifteen minutes of fame. Instead he had to settle for the lesser consolation of three thousand years of moral influence.

(4) Act with the Mind of Christ

❖ Brainstorm with the class answers to this question: **What are some concrete actions we can take to demonstrate that we have the same mind as Christ by living with Christ-like humility?** List ideas on newsprint.

❖ Distribute paper and pencils. Challenge the students to select at least two ideas from the list and write several sentences explaining what they intend to do.

❖ Give each person an opportunity to say one action he or she intends to take and affirm their plans.

(5) Continue the Journey

❖ Pray that the students will strive to live with the balanced sense of humility that Jesus modeled for us.

❖ Read aloud this preparation for next week's lesson. You may also want to post it on newsprint for the students to copy. **Prepare for next week's session entitled "Be Free!" by reading background Scripture from John 8:31-59. The lesson** will spotlight John 8:31-38, 48-56, 58-59. Consider these ideas as you work with this lesson: Human beings often seek help when trying to free themselves from destructive behavioral patterns. What source of help is available to us when we seek freedom from sin? John says that we are made free in Jesus, who is from above.

❖ Read aloud the following three ideas. Challenge the students to commit themselves to use these activities as a springboard to spiritual growth.

   (1) **Memorize Philippians 2:5-11. Focus on one verse each day, mining its meaning and remembering its words. By the end of the week you should know the entire passage.**

   (2) **Be alert for opportunities to look to the interests of others and respond accordingly.**

   (3) **Get in the habit of pausing before you speak or act and ask yourself this question, "Will my words or actions reflect the mind of Christ?"**

❖ Sing or read aloud "He Is Lord," which is based on Philippians 2:9-11.

❖ Say this benediction from Jude 24–25 to conclude the session. Include the students by asking them to echo it as you read: **Now to him who is able to keep you from falling, and to make you stand without blemish in the presence of his glory with rejoicing, to the only God our Savior, through Jesus Christ our Lord, be glory, majesty, power, and authority, before all time and now and forever. Amen.**

UNIT 2: CHRIST SUSTAINS AND SUPPORTS
BE FREE!

PREVIEWING THE LESSON

Lesson Scripture: John 8:31-38, 48-56, 58-59
Background Scripture: John 8:31-59
Key Verses: John 8:31-32

Focus of the Lesson:
Human beings often seek help when trying to free themselves from destructive behavioral patterns. What source of help is available to us when we seek freedom from sin? John says that we are made free in Jesus, who is from above.

Goals for the Learners:
(1) to examine John's account of Jesus' encounter with the crowd.
(2) to reflect on how the freedom Christ brings affects their lives.
(3) to apply the promise of God's freedom to their lives and tell others what a difference it makes.

Supplies:
Bibles, newsprint and marker, paper and pencils, hymnals

READING THE SCRIPTURE

NRSV
John 8:31-38, 48-56, 58-59

[31]Then Jesus said to the Jews who had believed in him, **"If you continue in my word, you are truly my disciples; [32]and you will know the truth, and the truth will make you free."** [33]They answered him, "We are descendants of Abraham and have never been slaves to anyone. What do you mean by saying, 'You will be made free'?"

[34]Jesus answered them, "Very truly, I tell you, everyone who commits sin is a slave to sin. [35]The slave does not have a permanent place in the household; the son has a place

NIV
John 8:31-38, 48-56, 58-59

[31]To the Jews who had believed him, Jesus said, **"If you hold to my teaching, you are really my disciples. [32]Then you will know the truth, and the truth will set you free."**

[33]They answered him, "We are Abraham's descendants and have never been slaves of anyone. How can you say that we shall be set free?"

[34]Jesus replied, "I tell you the truth, everyone who sins is a slave to sin. [35]Now a slave has no permanent place in the family, but a

there forever. ³⁶So if the Son makes you free, you will be free indeed. ³⁷I know that you are descendants of Abraham; yet you look for an opportunity to kill me, because there is no place in you for my word. ³⁸I declare what I have seen in the Father's presence; as for you, you should do what you have heard from the Father."

⁴⁸The Jews answered him, "Are we not right in saying that you are a Samaritan and have a demon?" ⁴⁹Jesus answered, "I do not have a demon; but I honor my Father, and you dishonor me. ⁵⁰Yet I do not seek my own glory; there is one who seeks it and he is the judge. ⁵¹Very truly, I tell you, whoever keeps my word will never see death." ⁵²The Jews said to him, "Now we know that you have a demon. Abraham died, and so did the prophets; yet you say, 'Whoever keeps my word will never taste death.' ⁵³Are you greater than our father Abraham, who died? The prophets also died. Who do you claim to be?" ⁵⁴Jesus answered, "If I glorify myself, my glory is nothing. It is my Father who glorifies me, he of whom you say, 'He is our God,' ⁵⁵though you do not know him. But I know him; if I would say that I do not know him, I would be a liar like you. But I do know him and I keep his word. ⁵⁶Your ancestor Abraham rejoiced that he would see my day; he saw it and was glad." . . . ⁵⁸Jesus said to them, "Very truly, I tell you, before Abraham was, I am." ⁵⁹So they picked up stones to throw at him, but Jesus hid himself and went out of the temple.

son belongs to it forever. ³⁶So if the Son sets you free, you will be free indeed. ³⁷I know you are Abraham's descendants. Yet you are ready to kill me, because you have no room for my word. ³⁸I am telling you what I have seen in the Father's presence, and you do what you have heard from your father."

⁴⁸The Jews answered him, "Aren't we right in saying that you are a Samaritan and demon-possessed?"

⁴⁹"I am not possessed by a demon," said Jesus, "but I honor my Father and you dishonor me. ⁵⁰I am not seeking glory for myself; but there is one who seeks it, and he is the judge. ⁵¹I tell you the truth, if anyone keeps my word, he will never see death."

⁵²At this the Jews exclaimed, "Now we know that you are demon-possessed! Abraham died and so did the prophets, yet you say that if anyone keeps your word, he will never taste death. ⁵³Are you greater than our father Abraham? He died, and so did the prophets. Who do you think you are?"

⁵⁴Jesus replied, "If I glorify myself, my glory means nothing. My Father, whom you claim as your God, is the one who glorifies me. ⁵⁵Though you do not know him, I know him. If I said I did not, I would be a liar like you, but I do know him and keep his word. ⁵⁶Your father Abraham rejoiced at the thought of seeing my day; he saw it and was glad."

⁵⁸"I tell you the truth," Jesus answered, "before Abraham was born, I am!" ⁵⁹At this, they picked up stones to stone him, but Jesus hid himself, slipping away from the temple grounds.

UNDERSTANDING THE SCRIPTURE

John 8:31-33. Theological, rather than chronological, units determine the structure of John's Gospel. Moreover, the author loops these themes together in an interlocking pattern. Most individual texts relate back to a previous story or teaching and foreshadow another story or teaching yet to come. The wholeness of the Gospel is accomplished by an intricate weave that gradually reveals the true identity of Jesus as the Son of God and light of the world. The first section of our passage illustrates the Gospel writer's style. First comes the glance backward to John 8:12-30 where

Jesus testifies in truth on the Father's behalf. This testimony is received by the Pharisees with argumentation, misinterpretation, and finally, belief (8:30). In our passage, the author introduces a new element: The truth that Jesus brings results in freedom. Two distinct voices debate this theme. The voice of the early Christian community claimed allegiance to Jesus who came from God, taught God's word, died on a cross, rose from the dead, and remains with the community through the gift of his Spirit. This voice emphatically affirmed that Jesus' teachings brought freedom and an unending relationship with God. The second voice represented the first-century Jewish community opposing Jesus; this voice was fond of romanticizing their own religious past. In our passage, this voice affirmed, ". . . (we) have never been slaves to anyone" (8:33). In the first round of the debate, Jesus simply stated that freedom comes from truth. The implication was just as simple: Lies (including lies about history) cannot bring liberation. Using two finely tuned voices to present the perspectives of the Christian community and the Jewish community, this passage reveals the theological distinctions and growing separateness among first-century Palestinian religious groups.

John 8:34-38. Next, the debate moved forward as Jesus redefined the concept of slavery from historical oppression to sinful behavior. Throughout this section the audience (representing all of Israel) was addressed as a whole: Sin was not a private action, but a corporate rebellion against God. The goal of the nation, in these score-keeping days, was to amass a sufficiency of righteousness in order to tip God's judgment toward blessing rather than cursing the nation. Israel's freedom was God's supreme blessing. Therefore, as Jesus shifted the context of slavery from political slavery to the spiritual condition of sin, he also redefined freedom. According to Jesus, freedom was not dependent upon any physical or political reality; freedom was a spiritual gift available through God's truth. At this point the debate heated up. First, Jesus acknowledged his opponents' previous claim to be "descendants of Abraham"; then, he suggested that their own actions—even their supposedly secret plans to kill him—negated their status. A true relationship to God, according to the Gospel of John, comes only through believing the truth as revealed by the Son of God. With a vigor that must have sounded like blasphemy to the audience, Jesus declared that his teaching came from his privileged status with God. Since his audience encountered God in law, prophets, and worship, they should recognize the identity of Jesus with God's ancient covenant with Israel.

John 8:39-47. The second round of the debate opened with the Jews reasserting their status as descendants of Abraham. Jesus, again, challenged their status by comparing it with their actions. He subtly referred to their ancestor, Abraham, who was renowned for hospitality (see Genesis 18). Yet, the Jews who argued with Jesus refused him even the hospitality of listening to him and, further, they plotted his murder. Therefore, Jesus claimed they were not children of God, but of the devil. The offended Jews defended their legitimate status by appealing to God rather than to physical ancestry; by this claim they redirected the argument from a material to a spiritual content—the exact content Jesus used in his opening remarks about true, Son-given freedom (8:32). Jesus continued to move the argument along a spiritual course by introducing the concept of love. Love for God was the most pressing religious duty in Israel. The first lesson taught to a Jewish toddler was the Shema: "Hear, O Israel: The LORD is our God, the LORD alone. You shall love the LORD your God with all your heart, and with all your soul, and with all your might" (Deuteronomy 6:4-5). Nothing was more important than loving God. Jesus accused his audience of betraying their love of God by rejecting the one sent from God.

This failure to love was actually a choice to honor another parent, the devil. The assignation was dramatic, but it also illuminated the lying that was epidemic in the Jewish community. Not only was Jesus' teaching resisted and not only was a conspiracy growing against him, but the "reinterpretation of sacred history" ("we . . . have never been slaves to anyone," 8:33) turned faith into fable and demonstrated the family's identity with the devil. According to the argument's flow, those who rejected Jesus were not members of God's family. This was a harsh, harsh argument.

John 8:48-59. Jesus' harsh words were returned in kind. The opponents declared that he was either a Samaritan (a disdained, broken branch of the family tree of Israel) or a man possessed by a demonic spirit. The name-calling was a challenge of honor. Jesus accepted the challenge with another blanket declaration: Whoever dishonored him, dishonored God. Jesus' role as God's witness to the world was like that of an emissary. First-century cultural codes assumed that the respect paid to an emissary was equivalent to the respect due the sender. Likewise, mistreatment of an emissary was mistreatment of the sender. Finally, Jesus slipped back into his original role of spiritual teacher. As he offered truth and freedom to his audience, now he offered the end of death. Once again, the author of the Gospel demonstrated Jesus' fondness for metaphorical speech. Jesus' truth, freedom, and promise of no death metaphorically described an indissoluble relationship with God. As in previous encounters in the Gospel of John (Nicodemus in Chapter 3 and the Samaritan woman of Chapter 4), this story also included a failure to distinguish Jesus' metaphorical language from his direct speech. Confusion increased, and in this case there were two significant outcomes. First, Jesus declared his pre-existence with God using the religiously charged words "I am," the name of God as recorded in Exodus 3:14. Second, the Jews were so angered they began to pick up stones in order to execute Jesus on the spot.

INTERPRETING THE SCRIPTURE

A Way to Freedom

Isn't it great to be at the beginning of a new year? For a few precious days there is more resolve for righteous living, more dedication to significant relationships, an increased passion for justice, and even a bit more joy than despair. The simple act of turning the calendar to the new year seems to cancel disillusionment. Even as the second week begins, expectations continue high:

- This year we will be more loving, kind, and generous.
- This year we will not give into discouragement.
- This year we will see the world as God sees it.
- This year, we will cherish truth . . . regardless.

The flavor of a new year seasons Jesus' teaching from the Gospel of John, chapter 8. Our key verse makes a good beginning for a study and a new year: Knowing the truth makes us free. The truth within these words is the very heartbeat of Scripture. The truth that brings freedom is neither an abstract scrap of theology nor a critical analysis of the human condition. The truth that brings freedom is God's unique Word, Jesus. This truth is imprinted on creation, even though the divine imprint is smudged by reckless and thoughtless human activities. The same truth is discerned through numerous wisdom traditions, yet always somewhere beyond the limits of human intellect. The truth that humans seek, in reflection on the natural world and by intellectual or spiritual efforts, comes from God's revelations. In our Christian understanding, the truth of God was revealed in the covenant between God and Israel and perfected through the written accounts of history, law, wisdom, and prophecy. Finally, when the time was right, the truth of God lived within human culture as the Galilean peasant, Jesus of Nazareth. The truth he lived, taught, and inspired was God's truth—the only truth able to free humans to be what God intends. By living God's truth, Jesus initiated a path toward freedom that disciples from ancient to contemporary days have discovered to be as hopeful as the annual turn of the calendar. This year, we will see the world as God sees it: truthfully. This year, we will live in the world as God intends: freely. This year, we will know the truth and it will make us free.

Jesus' Power to Free

According to Jesus and to the witness of the first-century church, freedom came through recognizing, believing, knowing, doing, and continuing in Jesus' way. For contemporary believers, as well as the original communities of faith, each step in this freeing process posed unique problems. In our text, the Jews are reprimanded for their failure to recognize Jesus. Indeed, Jesus called them to accountability because he was disappointed by their inattention to their God-given gifts of guidance. The Jewish community had the benefit of God's guidance through Scripture, priests, and prophets. They should have recognized God's truth in the person and deeds of Jesus. Failure to know God's eternal truth, naturally, led to a lack of belief in Jesus' word. Jesus argued that disbelief was actually a subtle lie. Some Jews, however, both recognized and believed. For them, the next step was to live according to Jesus' way. This way, uniquely distinct from the then

current interpretation of obedience, had little to do with following rules and much to do with living a free and loving life. The lifestyle promoted by Jesus was not based on the categories of sin and disobedience. Rather, Jesus' way "streamed" from the Father. Jesus directed his disciples to stay in this stream by attending to his word.

The Gift of Freedom

The gift of freedom is never abstract. When one is released from an assignment at work, there is a sigh of relief. When years of sobriety reshape dependent people into ones who experience healthy relationships, there is joy. When a debt is satisfied (or canceled), a party demonstrates the change of sentiments. Freedom is more than a physical condition; it is a deeply personal and profoundly spiritual condition. Sadly, we forget the spiritual nature of freedom. In many ways our North American culture equates freedom with material resources. Common wisdom teaches that with enough money in the bank, Americans are free. But, precisely the opposite seems to happen and anxieties multiply:
- there is never enough money;
- there are always threats from the stock market's roller coaster;
- inflation is a crafty thief;
- the future is unpredictable.

Although frequently disillusioned, most Americans cling to the belief that money guarantees freedom. Few learn the lesson that money brings many worries. The culture of the first century, however, was not founded on the principle of money equals freedom. The first-century Jewish culture valued religious affiliation. Those who were in good standing in the religious community were free. Freedom, however, also had a physical or political reality. Freedom was the opposite of slavery: no master, military commander, foreign ruler, or culture of occupation oppressing everyday life. As Jesus taught he addressed freedom in a whole new way. His point of reference was neither the security that money supposedly purchased, the privilege of an inherited religious status, or a social/political liberation. Jesus spoke of freedom as a life of radical dependence on God. This was Jesus' teaching: Truth brings freedom; freedom brings life with God; life with God is not limited. The first aspect of his teaching was revelatory: Neither reason nor circumstances explained freedom. Instead, true freedom came from insight into God. The second aspect of freedom was known only as one "continues" in Jesus' way. Freedom was not a revelation given for intellectual delight, but rather was a revelation to be lived. Finally, Jesus taught that freedom could not be bound by any force in this material world—or by any force from the spiritual realm. The freedom Jesus offered was stronger than death (since it came from the very being of God) and triumphant over the devil (since it was constructed upon truth not fashioned from lies). According to Jesus, by the freedom he offers "you will be free indeed" (8:36).

Timeless Truth

Jesus' spiritual connection with God was so intimate that time was meaningless to him. He spoke of always being with God. He fearlessly faced humiliation, harm, or death—everyday. He expected to dwell eternally with God. He prayed all night, because prayer, not sleep, was necessary; he told his disciples that his nourishment came not from bread, but from God's word. His life was completely "God filled" and by his example others tasted new life. The new life, initiated through Jesus' life, ministry, and teaching, was energized by the gift of his Spirit and protected by the creation of the church. This God-filled life passed from Jesus, through his Spirit, to his believers; in the community of the church, everyday people began to live "God-filled" lives. As they did so, the truth they lived gave their lives a timeless quality. What happened in the first-century church continues to happen in contemporary congregations. As believers recognize, believe, know, do, and continue in Jesus' way, life becomes lighter, freer, and less bound to the daily march of minutes and the annual turn of the calendar. The "God-filled" life is extraordinarily rich right here, right now. But, the warning from John 8:59 is also right here, right now: The world does not cherish timeless truth. Indeed, many would rather pick up stones to fight than welcome the stranger, love the enemy, invite the sinner to dinner, or pray for those who plan some evil. Regardless of the world's response, those who follow Jesus choose his timeless truth. They are alive, freely and eternally.

SHARING THE SCRIPTURE

PREPARING TO TEACH

Preparing Our Hearts

This week's devotional reading is found in John 14:23-31. Imagine the scene: Jesus is with the disciples during his last Passover. He has washed their feet, foretold his betrayal and Peter's denial, and now is reassuring his friends that the Holy Spirit, the Advocate, will come. Jesus makes clear in verse 23 that those who love him will keep his word. In contrast, those who do not love Jesus fail to keep his word. Love, obedience, and discipleship are inseparable. Examine your own life. What would Jesus say about how your obedience reflects your love for him?

Pray that you and the adult learners will continue not only to study God's word but also to keep it, for in keeping it we are true disciples.

Preparing Our Minds

Study the background Scripture from John 8:31-59 and lesson Scripture, verses 31-38, 48-56, 58-59. Ponder the sources of help that are available to you when you want to seek freedom from destructive behavioral patterns and other sin.

Write on newsprint:

❏ information for next week's lesson, found under "Continue the Journey."

❏ activities for further spiritual growth in "Continue the Journey."

LEADING THE CLASS

(1) Gather to Learn

❖ Welcome the class members and introduce any guests.

❖ Pray that those who have come to class today will gain new understandings of how Christ sustains and supports them.

❖ Write the words *"Freedom is . . ."* on a sheet of newsprint. Ask the students to call out words or phrases to complete this thought and write their ideas on the newsprint.

❖ See if there are any unifying ideas. For example, students may think of freedom from a political or economic viewpoint. Or, they may think in personal terms, such as "free to do things my way." Note that Jesus speaks of freedom in a different context, which we will explore today.

❖ Read aloud today's focus statement: **Human beings often seek help when trying to free themselves from destructive behavioral patterns. What source of help is available to us when we seek freedom from sin? John says that we are made free in Jesus, who is from above.**

(2) Examine John's Account of Jesus' Encounter with the Crowd

❖ Select volunteers to read John 8:31-38, where Jesus explains that his true disciples are the ones who continue in his word, which leads them to truth, and in turn sets them free. You will need a narrator, someone to read the words of Jesus, and at least two people to respond as the Jews.

■ Look especially at today's key verses, John 8:31-32. As a class or in groups, paraphrase (state in one's own words) what Jesus is saying here.

■ Help the class understand Jesus' argument by reading or creating a brief lecture from the information for verses 31-33 and 34-38 in Understanding the Scripture. Be sure to note that Jesus is not talking about truth in some abstract form, but specifically about the truth of God as it is revealed through him.

■ Provide time for the students to raise questions or offer insights.

❖ Choose a narrator, someone to read the words of Jesus, and at least two people to respond as the Jews. Ask these volunteers to read John 8:48-56, 58-59.

■ A word of caution: Point out that John's words need to be read and understood in the context of their time when the synagogue was powerful and John's community was small and powerless. There is a "sibling rivalry" going on here, as those who followed Jesus were still Jews. Be sure the students recognize that, despite the harsh language, this intra-Jewish squabble cannot be used to justify anti-Semitism. Underlying this squabbling there is a timeless truth.

■ Focus on the core of Jesus' message: What is he saying to us today? Use "Timeless Truth" in Interpreting the Scripture to augment the discussion.

(3) Reflect on How the Freedom Christ Brings Affects the Learners' Lives

❖ Post a sheet of newsprint on which you have written, *"To say that I am free in Christ means . . ."*. Write students' responses. Compare these answers to the ones offered during the "Gather to Learn" portion when we spoke of freedom in general.

❖ Read "The Gift of Freedom" from Interpreting the Scripture. Encourage the students to talk about the relationship between freedom and money, freedom and one's physical being, and freedom and political reality.

(4) Apply the Promise of God's Freedom and Tell Others What a Difference It Makes

❖ Read again John 8:33-34. Invite the students to name sins or destructive behaviors that affect contemporary people. Jot down these ideas on newsprint.

❖ Distribute paper and pencils. Tell the adults that this activity will be confidential. They are to write one or more sins or destructive behaviors with which they have wrestled. Their choice does not necessarily need to be on the class' list. What is the problem? What might have to happen in order for them to be free? What resources are available to them in their relationship with Jesus, the Bible, and the church to help them?

❖ Challenge the students to take immediate steps to confront this problem. Suggest that they tell someone else what freedom in Christ means to them. Depending upon the circumstances, they may or may not want to speak about their own specific challenge(s).

(5) Continue the Journey

❖ Pray that the participants will seek and find freedom in Christ by listening to and obeying his word.

❖ Read aloud this preparation for next week's lesson. You may also want to post it on newsprint for the students to copy. **Prepare for next week's session entitled "Ultimate Fairness" by reading background and lesson Scripture from John 5:19-29. Focus your reading on these ideas:**

Many times we question the fairness or appropriateness of a particular judgment or decision. Is it possible for decisions to be unbiased and completely fair? John says Jesus has authority that comes directly from God; because God and Jesus are perfect, their decisions are perfect.

❖ Read aloud the following three ideas. Challenge the students to commit themselves to use these activities as a springboard to spiritual growth.

(1) Ponder this question: What enslaves you? Is there something in your life to which you are "addicted"? Talk with others who have overcome this problem. Join a support group. Pray for God's guidance.

(2) Search your heart to see if your relationship with someone is damaged because you have lied or misrepresented yourself. Consider carefully how you will set yourself—and the relationship—free by telling the truth. Choose an appropriate time and place to take whatever action you need to take.

(3) Consider the connection between knowing Jesus and keeping his word. How does your behavior reflect obedience to the Lord? What changes do you need to make in order to be more faithful? Take steps to make these changes.

❖ Sing or read aloud "Let My People Seek Their Freedom."

❖ Say this benediction from Jude 24–25 to conclude the session. Include the students by asking them to echo it as you read: **Now to him who is able to keep you from falling, and to make you stand without blemish in the presence of his glory with rejoicing, to the only God our Savior, through Jesus Christ our Lord, be glory, majesty, power, and authority, before all time and now and forever. Amen.**

UNIT 2: CHRIST SUSTAINS AND SUPPORTS
ULTIMATE FAIRNESS

PREVIEWING THE LESSON

Lesson Scripture: John 5:19-29
Background Scripture: John 5:19-29
Key Verse: John 5:24

Focus of the Lesson:
Many times we question the fairness or appropriateness of a particular judgment or decision. Is it possible for decisions to be unbiased and completely fair? John says Jesus has authority that comes directly from God; because God and Jesus are perfect, their decisions are perfect.

Goals for the Learners:
(1) to explore Jesus' words regarding his authority and his relation to God.
(2) to reflect on the significance of Jesus' relation to God and its impact on their faith.
(3) to tell others what it means to believe in Jesus.

Pronunciation Guide:
eschatological (es kat uh loj' i kuhl)   eschatology (es ku tol' uh jee)
Septuagint (sep' too uh jint)   synoptic (sin op' tik)

Supplies:
Bibles, newsprint and marker, paper and pencils, hymnals

READING THE SCRIPTURE

NRSV
John 5:19-29

[19]Jesus said to them, "Very truly, I tell you, the Son can do nothing on his own, but only what he sees the Father doing; for whatever the Father does, the Son does likewise. [20]The Father loves the Son and shows him all that he himself is doing; and he will show him greater works than these, so that you will be astonished. [21]Indeed, just as the Father raises

NIV
John 5:19-29

[19]Jesus gave them this answer: "I tell you the truth, the Son can do nothing by himself; he can do only what he sees his Father doing, because whatever the Father does the Son also does. [20]For the Father loves the Son and shows him all he does. Yes, to your amazement he will show him even greater things than these. [21]For just as the Father

the dead and gives them life, so also the Son gives life to whomever he wishes. [22]The Father judges no one but has given all judgment to the Son, [23]so that all may honor the Son just as they honor the Father. Anyone who does not honor the Son does not honor the Father who sent him. [24]**Very truly, I tell you, anyone who hears my word and believes him who sent me has eternal life, and does not come under judgment, but has passed from death to life.**

[25]"Very truly, I tell you, the hour is coming, and is now here, when the dead will hear the voice of the Son of God, and those who hear will live. [26]For just as the Father has life in himself, so he has granted the Son also to have life in himself; [27]and he has given him authority to execute judgment, because he is the Son of Man. [28]Do not be astonished at this; for the hour is coming when all who are in their graves will hear his voice [29]and will come out—those who have done good, to the resurrection of life, and those who have done evil, to the resurrection of condemnation."

raises the dead and gives them life, even so the Son gives life to whom he is pleased to give it. [22]Moreover, the Father judges no one, but has entrusted all judgment to the Son, [23]that all may honor the Son just as they honor the Father. He who does not honor the Son does not honor the Father, who sent him.

[24]"**I tell you the truth, whoever hears my word and believes him who sent me has eternal life and will not be condemned; he has crossed over from death to life.** [25]I tell you the truth, a time is coming and has now come when the dead will hear the voice of the Son of God and those who hear will live. [26]For as the Father has life in himself, so he has granted the Son to have life in himself. [27]And he has given him authority to judge because he is the Son of Man.

[28]"Do not be amazed at this, for a time is coming when all who are in their graves will hear his voice [29]and come out—those who have done good will rise to live, and those who have done evil will rise to be condemned."

UNDERSTANDING THE SCRIPTURE

John 5:19-23. The passage under consideration has three distinct styles: an explanation to a controversy, a teaching for disciples, and a general theological statement. In John 5:1-18, Jesus healed a man who waited by a healing pool in Jerusalem on the Sabbath. Afterward, some Jews interrogated the healed man. They were concerned that the healing took place on the Sabbath and was, therefore, an instance of breaking the law of Sabbath rest. Although the man did not know Jesus' name, he later met Jesus in the temple and learned his identity. After Jesus cautioned the man to resist sin, the healed man returned to the Jews and informed them that Jesus was the man who healed him. These Jews immediately found

and interrogated Jesus; he defended the healing by claiming that since his Father did not cease work on the Sabbath, he also worked. Accordingly, Jesus was considered to be dangerous: He not only broke the law, but outrageously made himself equal with God. The Gospel author concludes this story by explaining this healing was the impetus for Jesus' persecution. In the first section of our passage (5:19-23), Jesus defended himself by intensifying rather than qualifying his relationship to God. He explained that all his deeds were dependent upon God. Whenever Jesus saw God at work, he responded by co-operating. Moreover, Jesus participated *only* in God's reconciling, healing, and restorative deeds. According to the

Gospel of John, rather than following his "own" agenda Jesus acted strictly within the confines of God's agenda. The relationship between Jesus and God, however, was neither formal nor structured. It was based on love and guided by grace. As Jesus saw the mighty deeds of God increase, he was confident that even greater things were to come. These greater things were distinguished by two divine characteristics: They were life-giving and they executed judgment. According to Jewish legal understanding, these two activities were the only two types of divine work that continued at all times, even on the Sabbath. Jesus claimed these activities in his ministry. As Jesus healed the lame man, he gave life to him; as he instructed him to go and sin no more, he judged him. In other words, Jesus acted exactly as God would act toward a broken individual encountered on a Sabbath (or any other!) day. Jesus concluded his justification with a rhetorical sleight of hand. Insisting that God gave him exclusive permission to judge others, Jesus explained that whoever dishonored him also dishonored God. His opponents were backed into a difficult corner. On the one hand, they could not refute his logic regarding the legality of divine works (giving life and judging) on the Sabbath. On the other hand, they could not accept the implications of his logic because it made Jesus equal with God.

John 5:24-27. At this point in the Gospel of John, Jesus abruptly stopped his self-defense and turned to his disciples. The phrase, "Very truly, I tell you..." is a rhetorical device to indicate a teaching section; it is used twice, indicating two separate points (5:24, 25). The first point established a chain of events related to growth in faith: First came hearing; hearing produced believing; believing resulted in eternal life. The alternative to eternal life was judgment and death. In verse 24, the audience learned that by hearing and believing they escaped the fearsome reality of judgment and had (already) passed into eternal life. Since Jesus

was speaking to an actual audience, this verse applied to their current situation. Judgment and death were current realities—signified by the choice for darkness and the deadly decision to sin. The second teaching point, verse 25, moved to the eschatological edge of the present time. Jesus stated that "the hour is coming," a familiar phrase from the Gospel of John that usually referred to Jesus' betrayal/crucifixion/death. In this case, however, it indicated a vision. This vision relied upon two scenes from the Book of Daniel the audience knew and loved. The passages are:

- Daniel 7:13, a description of one like a son of man coming to reign over all creation;
- Daniel 12:1-3, a description of the awakening of the dead.

Jesus boldly declared that by his voice even the dead would be raised up to life (see John 11:43-44). After the teaching section (5:24, 25) came the theological discussion of Jesus' identity by examining the two divine attributes: to give life and to judge. Jesus gave life as he healed; Jesus exercised the authority to judge as he cautioned against sin. Finally, Jesus' identity was sealed by the phrase "Son of Man." This is the only instance in the Gospel of John of this phrase lacking the article "the" in the Greek; a literal translation of the Greek reads "he is Son of Man," the same construction used by the Septuagint in Daniel 7:13. The description of Jesus' identity was complete: He was the life-giving, judgment-making Son of Man whose power and authority belonged to God.

John 5:28-29. This presentation of Jesus' identity as the eschatological Son of Man caused "astonishment." This word, appearing in the Gospel of John six times, is usually employed to describe the result provoked by a specific deed or action of Jesus:

- 3:7, Jesus tells the disciples not to be astonished that they must be "born from above";

- 4:27, Jesus' disciples are astonished that he is speaking with a woman;
- 5:20, people will be astonished by the greater deeds that Jesus will do;
- 7:15, the Jews at the temple are astonished by the teaching ability of Jesus, an uneducated man;
- 7:21, Jesus chides the crowd because they are astonished by "one work."

In John 5:28, however, astonishment was linked to Jesus' identity. Whereas the previous statement in verse 25 combined the present and the future, "the hour is coming, and is now here," these concluding verses (5:28-29) describe the future. The hour is coming when the dead will hear and be raised; then, God's judgment will be completed. These two settings (5:25, 28) mirror one another perfectly: Whether the dead were lost in sin or sealed in the grave, it was the voice of Jesus that gave life and judged. In each case the decisive event was hearing the voice of Jesus. This double treatment presented a wonderful promise. As believers listened to and heard the voice of Jesus in the present, so would they listen for and hear the voice of Jesus in the future. The Gospel of John thus presented eschatology as a doctrine of comfort: Jesus' followers had, indeed, passed from death to life eternal. There was nothing to fear; the future judgment matched the present judgment.

INTERPRETING THE SCRIPTURE

Divine Insight

There is a lot of talk these days about spirituality. Everyone, it seems, is interested in the spiritual side of life. Books offer a myriad of spiritual approaches, conferences teach various ways to cultivate one's spiritual life, and even television programs feature "offstage" advice from God. As Christians who worship and study Scripture faithfully, all this interest in spirituality is somewhat amusing. After all, this has been the pursuit of Christianity for centuries. Interestingly, the Gospel of John is a textbook for developing spiritual insight and vision. This Gospel, as distinct from the Synoptic Gospels of Matthew, Mark and Luke, has a particularly spiritual viewpoint. The Synoptics (this Greek word means a unified or common way of seeing) present the reality of God's grace in Jesus by a careful description of his deeds, an accurate account of his teachings, and a scene-by-scene unfolding of his life, death, resurrection, and ascension. The Gospel of John, however, prefers what might be described as double vision. In this Gospel, every word, deed, and response to Jesus is charged with spiritual meaning. Our passage is an excellent illustration of this Gospel's double vision. Jesus defended his Sabbath healing by claiming that he does only what he "sees the Father doing" (5:19). Whereas the Jews saw an illegal activity, Jesus saw, with divine insight, a man bereft of spiritual resources and in need of God's amazing grace. Jesus acted on his divine insight and healed the man. The Jews reacted to his gracious deed and began to plot his death. The result was a clash between the practical, physical interpretation of the Sabbath healing and the spiritual, divinely inspired interpretation of the Sabbath healing. As a recounting of circumstances and regulation, the incident caused anger among the Jews; however, as a sign of God's redemptive love, the story became a symbol of God's grace to all.

Dependable Judgment

The law of Moses was the standard of judgment in Jesus' era. There were intricate interpretations and prudent pronouncements by the rabbis; yet, when all was said and done, the standard remained: God expected the chosen people to live in conformity with the law. Jesus was not a stranger to the law of Moses. As every other young Jewish male, he studied the law and became proficient in its application and argument. Although not a rabbi, Jesus was considered to be an inspired and authoritative teacher. His teaching, however, rarely focused on the minutia of the law (as was common among the rabbinical teachers). Instead, Jesus had an uncanny capacity for moving into the law's spiritual core. Jesus discusses God's judgment from the perspective of a loving relationship. The relationship between God, the loving Father, and Jesus is displayed:

(1) in the present time, the Father shows Jesus what he is doing;

(2) in the future, the Father will show Jesus even greater deeds;

(3) in God's work and Jesus' work, which defy the power of death;

(4) in the Father giving the responsibility of judgment to the Son, and

(5) in the Father willingly sharing all honor with Jesus.

Work, responsibility, authority, and honor are equally shared by God with Jesus. The reason for this "sharing" is simple: The Father loves the Son; Jesus loves God. Because love, not rigid or righteous application of rules, is at the heart of judgment, the feeling of judgment softens. As Jesus saw humanity with divine insight, so he judged with divine love.

Living Beyond Fear

The early Christian communities lived under the shadow of persecution—social, economic, and physical. This shadow created numerous fears. Yet throughout the New Testament, fear is downplayed. The Gospel of John reduced fear by emphasizing the words of Jesus. The Greek phrase translated "Very truly, I tell you" in the NRSV and "I tell you the truth" in the NIV, may be literally translated "I solemnly assure you." Whenever an extra dose of assurance is required, this phrase introduces a statement so true, so serious, and so essential that it literally is a matter of life and death. In our passage, the phrase is used three times; each time the audience is called to attend to a critical teaching. In John 5:19, the phrase signals the disclosure of the relationship between Jesus and God. His ministry, spiritual insight, and miraculous deeds have one source: God's love. His life is a sign to his disciples of the unbreakable bond possible between God and humanity. In 5:24, Jesus offered the assurance that hearing the gospel leads to believing in Jesus and believing in Jesus brings the blessing of eternal life, as well as the freedom from future judgment. This was a lesson designed to rid a community of fear—immediately and thoroughly. The second lesson was constructed upon the first. Remember, the size of the early Christian community was small, yet already some had died as martyrs and others were living as clandestine Christians. Persecution produced a double-edged fear. On the one side was the fear of a brutal death; on the other side was the consequences of denying Christ. Death ended earthly life, while denying Jesus made a believer's life death-like. Over both experiences, Jesus' voice continued to call believers. Confronting both sides of the fear, Jesus' words assured the early believers there was a spiritual continuity between present and future. This continuity was maintained by grace: the grace of forgiveness during life and the grace of eternal life with God following death. Therefore, Jesus assured all (from that distant time to this present day) that life, not death, was the inheritance of those who heard and believed (5:25).

An Astonishing Glimpse

Spiritual insight, dependable judgment, and a life free from fear are blessings within our lesson, but the Gospel of John has one more lesson. There must be a response! In this case, the response is astonishment. When humans glimpse God's amazing love and power, the proper response is awe. This is how our passage concludes—with an astonishing glimpse of God's final word on creation. Jesus announced that in the final hour, those who hear and believe, live; those that refuse to hear and believe are condemned. This statement is astonishing in its simplicity. Indeed, contemporary Christians often complicate the idea of a final judgment with hedges and scorecards similar to first century Jewish Pharisees. Yet, the matter is decided at a soulful level; the heart that hears and turns to Jesus guides the believer to live in a new way. Jesus' way begins, continues, and concludes with a radical trust in God. In Matthew 25, the Last Judgment scene is dramatized as the separation of the nations; in that setting surprise (rather than astonishment) flavors the scene. However, both glimpses of the final judgment function in a similar way: Those who trust in Jesus for this life discover their trust rightly placed in the final hour. Evil, arrogance, and all ungodly deeds are destroyed; goodness, humility, and deeds of justice and mercy are gathered into God's presence. There is nothing new in this astonishing glimpse. To this day, the vision continues to flash with confident hope. Jesus is headed toward God's unending glory; he invites his followers to travel with him.

SHARING THE SCRIPTURE

PREPARING TO TEACH

Preparing Our Hearts

This week's devotional reading is found in 2 Timothy 4:1-5. Notice what Paul is urging Timothy to do. How does this message relate to you and your ministry? This passage links with today's Scripture study as we think about Jesus, "who is to judge the living and the dead" (4:1). Do you think of Jesus as judge or only in one of his other roles, such as teacher or healer? What difference does it make in your spiritual life when you act as Paul teaches Timothy and realize that ultimately Jesus is our judge?

Pray that you and the adult learners will recognize that Jesus had authority to make eternal judgments and will do so on the basis of kingdom standards of fairness.

Preparing Our Minds

Study the background and lesson Scripture, both of which are found in John 5:19-29. As you prepare, recall times when you have questioned the fairness of a particular decision and wondered if unbiased judgments were possible.

Write on newsprint:
- ❑ list of categories for "Gather to Learn."
- ❑ questions under "Reflect on the Significance of Jesus' Relation to God and Its Impact on the Learners' Faith."
- ❑ information for next week's lesson, found under "Continue the Journey."
- ❑ activities for further spiritual growth in "Continue the Journey."

Plan an optional lecture for "Explore Jesus' Words Regarding His Authority and His Relation to God" if you choose to answer the questions yourself.

LEADING THE CLASS

(1) Gather to Learn

❖ Welcome the class members and introduce any guests.

❖ Pray that the participants will glean new insights from today's lessons that will enable them to experience a fuller relationship with Jesus.

❖ Challenge the students to think of at least one unfair decision made in each of the following areas. Suggest that they keep their descriptions of the incident brief so that more examples can be included. Write this list on newsprint and add the students' ideas.

- Criminal trials
- Sports
- Employment
- Housing (Think also of how community and condo association decisions affect homeowners.)
- Immigration
- Insurance
- Consumer affairs
- Business competition

❖ Read aloud today's focus statement: **Many times we question the fairness or appropriateness of a particular judgment or decision. Is it possible for decisions to be unbiased and completely fair? John says Jesus has authority that comes directly from God; because God and Jesus are perfect, their decisions are perfect.**

(2) Explore Jesus' Words Regarding His Authority and His Relation to God

❖ Select a volunteer to read John 5:19-29 as if he (or she) were Jesus speaking. Point out that this passage is part of an extended theological discussion in which Jesus talks about his relationship with God. Note that such extended discussions, often called discourses, are found only in John.

❖ Raise these theological questions for discussion, or answer them yourself in a short lecture.

(1) **What does this passage tell you about Jesus?**

(2) **What does it tell you about God?**

(3) **What does it say about the relationship between the Father and the Son?**

❖ Look again at verses 24-29, which speak about judgment. Talk with the class about these ideas:

- their understanding of the nature of God in relation to judgment. (Recognize that some students will see God only as loving and forgiving; judgment is not part of their theology.)
- their beliefs about eternal life in relation to judgment.

❖ Wrap up this portion of the lesson by asking volunteers to state what surprised them most about today's passage. Perhaps there were ideas that they had not considered or had set aside.

(3) Reflect on the Significance of Jesus' Relation to God and Its Impact on the Learners' Faith

❖ Note that Jesus claims that his relationship with God is one of total dependence. Distribute paper and pencils. Ask the students to write a paragraph in which they consider their own relationship with God. Read aloud these questions to stimulate the students' thinking and/or post them on newsprint.

(1) **Are you totally dependent upon God?**

(2) **If not, what areas of your life do you need to bring under God's authority?**

(3) **What barriers prevent you from doing this?**

(4) **How can the church help you?**

(5) **How can your faith in Christ help you?**

❖ Talk together about ways that the church can help class members to be in a relationship with Christ that recognizes both love and authority. (You might, for example, think of some expectations your congregation and/or denomination has of members, for we are not the independent "free agents" that some folks would prefer to be.)

(4) Tell Others What It Means to Believe in Jesus

❖ Divide the class into pairs or small teams. Encourage each person to give a brief testimony as to their relationship with Jesus and how his authority directs their life.

❖ Bring the class together and invite volunteers to comment on the impact someone's testimony had on them.

(5) Continue the Journey

❖ Pray that the students will go forth with a renewed commitment to live under the authority of Christ Jesus.

❖ Read aloud this preparation for next week's lesson. You may also want to post it on newsprint for the students to copy. **Prepare for next week's session entitled "Lasting Results" by reading background Scripture from John 6:25-59 and 7:37-39. The lesson will highlight John 6:34-40 and 7:37-39. Let these ideas help you focus your reading: People constantly search for those experiences or possessions that can provide satisfaction and a sense of fulfillment. Can we discover someone or something that can provide spiritual satisfaction? John suggests that Jesus portrays himself as the life-giver in whom there is complete satisfaction.**

❖ Read aloud the following three ideas. Challenge the students to commit themselves to use these activities as a springboard to spiritual growth.

(1) Think about a decision affecting your life or family that you felt was unfair. Write in your spiritual journal about this incident, why you feel it was unfair, and ways in which it has affected you. Pray for God's grace and wisdom as to how to handle this situation.

(2) Consider how parents act as authority figures within a family. Think about your own parent(s) and/or how you parent your children. Would you say these relationships are based on love and care, or something else, such as a desire to wield power? How can you make these relationships more like the one between the Father and Son?

(3) Write a prayer expressing submission to God's authority. Pray this prayer daily this week.

❖ Sing or read aloud "Only Trust Him."

❖ Say this benediction from Jude 24–25 to conclude the session. Include the students by asking them to echo it as you read: **Now to him who is able to keep you from falling, and to make you stand without blemish in the presence of his glory with rejoicing, to the only God our Savior, through Jesus Christ our Lord, be glory, majesty, power, and authority, before all time and now and forever. Amen.**

UNIT 2: CHRIST SUSTAINS AND SUPPORTS
LASTING RESULTS

PREVIEWING THE LESSON

Lesson Scripture: John 6:34-40; 7:37-39
Background Scripture: John 6:25-59; 7:37-39
Key Verse: John 6:35

Focus of the Lesson:
People constantly search for those experiences or possessions that can provide satisfaction and a sense of fulfillment. Can we discover someone or something that can provide spiritual satisfaction? John suggests that Jesus portrays himself as the life-giver in whom there is complete satisfaction.

Goals for the Learners:
(1) to unpack Jesus' statement that he is both the bread of life and living water.
(2) to reflect on the human search for meaning and purpose, especially in their own lives.
(3) to develop a plan to locate and utilize sources for spiritual nurture.

Supplies:
Bibles, newsprint and marker, paper and pencils, hymnals, variety of breads, pitcher, basin, water

---

READING THE SCRIPTURE

NRSV
John 6:34-40

[34]They said to him, "Sir, give us this bread always."

[35]Jesus said to them, **"I am the bread of life. Whoever comes to me will never be hungry, and whoever believes in me will never be thirsty.** [36]But I said to you that you have seen me and yet do not believe. [37]Everything that the Father gives me will come to me, and anyone who comes to me I will never drive away; [38]for I have come

NIV
John 6:34-40

[34]"Sir," they said, "from now on give us this bread."

[35]Then Jesus declared, **"I am the bread of life. He who comes to me will never go hungry, and he who believes in me will never be thirsty.** [36]But as I told you, you have seen me and still you do not believe. [37]All that the Father gives me will come to me, and whoever comes to me I will never drive away. [38]For I have come down from

down from heaven, not to do my own will, but the will of him who sent me. ³⁹And this is the will of him who sent me, that I should lose nothing of all that he has given me, but raise it up on the last day. ⁴⁰This is indeed the will of my Father, that all who see the Son and believe in him may have eternal life; and I will raise them up on the last day."

heaven not to do my will but to do the will of him who sent me. ³⁹And this is the will of him who sent me, that I shall lose none of all that he has given me, but raise them up at the last day. ⁴⁰For my Father's will is that everyone who looks to the Son and believes in him shall have eternal life, and I will raise him up at the last day."

John 7:37-39

³⁷On the last day of the festival, the great day, while Jesus was standing there, he cried out, "Let anyone who is thirsty come to me, ³⁸and let the one who believes in me drink. As the scripture has said, 'Out of the believer's heart shall flow rivers of living water.'" ³⁹Now he said this about the Spirit, which believers in him were to receive; for as yet there was no Spirit, because Jesus was not yet glorified.

John 7:37-39

³⁷On the last and greatest day of the Feast, Jesus stood and said in a loud voice, "If anyone is thirsty, let him come to me and drink. ³⁸Whoever believes in me, as the Scripture has said, streams of living water will flow from within him." ³⁹By this he meant the Spirit, whom those who believed in him were later to receive. Up to that time the Spirit had not been given, since Jesus had not yet been glorified.

UNDERSTANDING THE SCRIPTURE

John 6:25-34. Although the Gospel of John was circulated as a written document, most individuals "heard" the Gospel read in corporate worship. The culture was not particularly literate, but they were steeped in oral communication. Particular words reverberated with deep theological and practical significance; these words triggered insight into the teachings of Jesus, the practice of communal life and individual appropriation of Christianity. In today's texts some "trigger words" are *food, bread, works of God, eternal life, seeing, believing, water, hunger, thirst,* and *heaven.* The author of the Gospel was skilled in a poetic style employing a double (or multiple) meaning for individual words, descriptions of events and Jesus' teachings. We know from the Synoptic Gospels (Matthew, Mark, and Luke) that Jesus taught by the use of parables. The author of the Gospel of John expanded the parable style to present the whole gospel. The author's purpose is to

present the entire story of Jesus as a parable that challenges the reader/hearer to consider the meanings behind the story of Jesus' ministry. The importance of not rushing to a quick analysis is demonstrated by the opening comments of Jesus to the crowd in John 6:26-27. Jesus sensed that the crowd followed him because of his miracles. Using the metaphor of bread, he challenged them to "work . . . for the food that endures for eternal life" (6:27). He suspected those he fed the previous day (6:1-14) failed to understand that sign. His suspicion was confirmed as the crowd shifted from interest in bread to interest in the requirements for pleasing God. First, they failed to recognize God's grace in bread; then they desired to please God by doing something extraordinary. Jesus replied that the only "work" necessary was belief in Jesus. The crowd, however, demanded another sign, such as the bread Moses gave their ancestors. Using the poet's gift of metaphor, Jesus' words described God's grace as the true bread that comes down from heaven to nourish the world. The crowd requested their slice, hardly realizing the significance of their own words.

John 6:35-42. This section includes the first of many "I am" statements, some of which include a descriptive phrase following the "I am": "I am the bread of life" (6:35, 48); "the living bread" (6:51); "the light of the world" (8:12; 9:5); "the good shepherd" (10:11, 14); "the gate" (10:7, 9); "the resurrection and the life" (11:25); "the way, and the truth, and the life" (14:6); "the true vine" (15:1). There are also usages of "I am" without a reference (such as Jesus' response to the Samaritan woman, "I am he, the one who is speaking to you," John 4:26. See also 6:20; 8:24, 28, 58; 13:19; 18:5, 6, 8). The "I am" statements used with and without descriptions indicate a revelatory rather than a discursive style. This "I am" statement, therefore, was not a christological title defining Jesus, but an entry point into Jesus' divine identity ("I AM" is Israel's name for God). The metaphor of bread brought together the exodus history, prophetic teachings, and the audience's experience of the hunger. Jesus sealed the teaching succinctly: Those who saw and believed in Jesus have eternal life now and resurrection on the final day. Jesus' words provoked the crowd's complaint—reminiscent of Israel's wilderness complaining (Exodus 15:24, 16:2, 7, 12, and Numbers 11:1, 14:2, 27). Their complaints about Jesus, however, were not based on their physical needs of food for survival; rather, they complained because Jesus, a common Galilean peasant, assumed a standing far above them. They were unable to think of Jesus as one of them and from God. But, Jesus' mysterious identity was precisely that.

John 6:43-59. In the final section, Jesus stretched the "I am the bread of life" statement to cover not only his identity, but also the eternal destiny of his believers. Since he was primarily a teacher (rabbi), Jesus alluded to the prophetic hope of being taught directly by God (Isaiah 54:13 and Jeremiah 31:34). Using his own experience of God—an experience free from past, present, or future limitations—Jesus explained that he alone had seen God and now taught with divine directness. To emphasize the point, Jesus reiterated that those who knew God recognized him, but those who were ignorant of God, rejected him. This time, however, Jesus raised the stakes: Those who received his gifts (of divine teaching, revelation, and bread), received eternal life, while those who rejected his gifts suffered the consequences of rejecting God. Finally he stretched the metaphor fully: To believe in Jesus was to receive him completely. Moreover, what seemed impossible was simply God's designed path to life eternal: Those who, metaphorically, ate the heavenly bread (Jesus) lived forever with Jesus in the presence of God.

John 7:37-39. The theme of Jesus as bread for the hungry and drink for the thirsty continues with a new audience and a new context. This crowd came to Jerusalem to participate in the liturgical life of their nation. The Feast of Tabernacles, also known as the Festival of Booths, commemorated the time of wandering in the wilderness and the subsequent divine gift of the law. This festival was the last of the three pilgrim festivals; Passover and Pentecost occurred at the beginning of the agricultural cycle and the Festival of Booths came in the fall of the year, just before the celebration of the New Year. The festival included several unique liturgical activities and required that each family provide an outdoor simple structure in which to take their meals. Thus this festival was a corporate recollection of Israel's rebellion in the wilderness and in God's gracious gift of the law. This was not a hostile crowd; it was a reverent, religiously intent audience. Moreover, Jesus knew the impact of these liturgical events on the pilgrims. For example, Jesus knew that, at dawn, on seven consecutive days the pilgrims walked with the priests to the Pool of Siloam. There the high priest scooped water into a golden pitcher, carried the water and poured the water over the altar to remind them of water that came from the rock in the desert (see Numbers 20:2-13). Therefore, when Jesus invited all who were thirsty to come to him, his audience was primed to understand his invitation. Although Jesus' scriptural quote was an association of several snatches of Scripture (see Proverbs 18:4; Isaiah 12:3, 43:19-20, 44:3; Jeremiah 2:13, 17:13; Ezekiel 47, and Zechariah 14:8), the crowd recognized his words as a summary of the life-giving attribute of God. Jesus claimed that life-giving quality was his to give to them. Some in the crowd heard with belief, others listened with questions, and others responded with anger and fear. Verse 39 is not speaking about God's Spirit in general, but rather, refers to John's understanding that the gift of the Spirit is known in the church only after the crucifixion, resurrection, and ascension of Jesus.

INTERPRETING THE SCRIPTURE

An Easy Misunderstanding

"They just don't get it," is a common explanation of the insensitivity of one group or individual toward another group or individual. Although this misunderstanding comes easily, "getting" another's reality takes patient listening, practiced questioning, and a restraint before jumping to a judgment. Our passage for today opens with an easy misunderstanding; unfortunately, no one in the biblical crowd following Jesus seemed willing to listen, question, or restrain judgment. Instead, their failure to "get it" distanced them from Jesus. Not wanting that to be our position, we approach this text with a readiness to listen, question, and restrain our snap judgments. Let's consider the crowd's situation. Only the day before, Jesus had fed a very large crowd (about 5,000 according to John 6:10) with only one boy's five barley loaves and two fish. Many in the crowd interpreted the miracle as a sign that Jesus was a prophet. By the next day, however, when hunger was setting in again, the crowd's interest returned to their stomachs. With his eyes opened by his unique spiritual insight, Jesus perceived the crowd's agenda: They were not looking for signs of God's power and purpose; instead, they were interested in food. Nevertheless, Jesus taught them. He encouraged them to work for the food that endured. The crowd, however, could not listen. Moreover, their question missed the point of Jesus' brief lesson. The crowd demanded a definition of the type of work they should be doing; Jesus further explained his lesson by reinterpreting the word "work" to mean belief. Unfortunately, by the time he refined his teaching, the crowd was ready for entertainment. So Jesus tried another approach; he spoke of the bread of heaven not as a sign, but as the necessity for life. Without hesitation, and seemingly with one voice, the crowd cried, "Give us this bread always." They did not listen; they asked irrelevant questions; they jumped to a self-centered conclusion. They failed to "get it" and their failure disclosed their lack of interest in Jesus' revelation. The same concern could be raised within the contemporary world. Perhaps "listen, question, and restrain" are good contemporary caution signs from this text.

Life's Necessities

Recently, a colleague offered a helpful insight for this text. He was talking about the amazing number of choices available to his preschool children. From food to clothing, from educational video games to experiential learning environments, his children's lives were a steady diet of choices. Pondering the richness of their choice environment led this parent to introduce his children to a weekly outing to a secluded community pond. There was only one rule for the outing: take nothing, just go. Without the usual bundle of equipment, toys, food, flavored drinks, sweaters, sunglasses, outdoor gadgets and games for the car, dad loaded his little ones into the car once a week to enter the world of nature. And, to his delight, after a few months, the pond was no longer the most boring place imaginable. Rather, it teemed with tadpoles, tiger lilies, dragonflies, and diving ducks. Away from all the things his culture offered as necessities for a preschooler's life, one dad made a small course adjustment. The result of his experience and his reflection: Too many choices led to stress and discontent, but one good option led to joy.

His reflection could be written over the words of Jesus in John 6:35-40. In this passage, Jesus directed attention to life's true necessities. Jesus was not insensitive to human needs; rather, Jesus was more sensitive to the spiritual need and desire of humans. As a group, we are very needy. We humans need food, clothing, comfort, water, rest, work, community, and love. But Jesus knew our primary need—the need able to reorder all other needs—is our need of God. Knowing God does not eliminate the human need for food; rather, knowing God confronts our gluttony, inspires our generosity, and teaches us a lean and gentle approach to consumption. Knowing God does not eradicate all terrors in the world, but the individual whose life comes from God has a security that is courageous on behalf of others and joyful in the midst of personal crisis. Jesus offered the crowd this spiritual lesson: God first, always, and eternally. Unfortunately, the crowd's preoccupation

with their needs, interests, concerns, and crises stopped up their ears and blinded their eyes. They acted like cranky preschoolers with too many choices and too little joy.

Single Vision Versus Spiritual Insight

When my friend took his children to the pond, he was not only getting them away from what he described as "too many choices about too many things," but he was also teaching them the interconnections of all life. At the pond, his children observed mystery and miracle. The two year old asked "why?"; and the four year old asked "how?"; and dad frequently answered with words about "who." The world of nature opened both children and father to awe before the wonders of the pond. Indeed, that little space of land became as sacred as any sanctuary and those weekly walks as holy as any Palm Sunday processional. Father and children were developing, each in an appropriate and unique way, the skill of seeing God in the world. Indeed, they were moving away from a single vision able to observe, describe, define, and manipulate, toward the spiritual insight leading to awe, humility, blessing, and revelation. The crowd of Galileans following Jesus, evidently, never got that lesson. They named what they saw and lost interest. The mere naming of Jesus' parents ended the discussion of his identity. They knew all that was needed: Jesus was a Galilean, end of interest. Because they looked only upon the surface facts, they failed to see the richer reality of Jesus. True, he was the son of known members of the community, but Jesus was also the spiritual Son of God. Too bad they hadn't lingered pond-side to consider the holy mystery of the frog within the tadpole or the evening cool within the gathering clouds!

Come to Me

What does Jesus do with folks like that crowd or folks like us? How does Jesus respond to people who won't listen, who don't ask relevant questions, or who jump to snap judgments? And what about those who refuse to look any deeper than "just the facts"? The good news of today's lesson is this: Jesus kept offering invitations. When the crowd was dull and listless, Jesus shared his personal truth. If the audience became emotional or self-centered, Jesus offered God's grace. Even to those who arrogantly claimed wisdom greater than

God's, Jesus still said, "Come to me." Regardless of the condition of the crowd, audience, or worshiping communities (yours or mine), Jesus invites each and all into life abundant and eternal communion with God. Jesus did not do this because he was an exceptional human being; Jesus offered life because he was (and is) uniquely connected with God. Together they acted (and continue to act) that all may have life and have it abundantly.

SHARING THE SCRIPTURE

PREPARING TO TEACH

Preparing Our Hearts

This week's devotional reading is found in Ephesians 3:14-21. Paul prays that the Christians at Ephesus will be strengthened by the Holy Spirit and that the love of Christ might dwell in them. When you think about the "love of Christ," what does that mean to you? Write in your spiritual journal about one or two experiences in which you unmistakably experienced the love of Christ. How have you shared that love with others? What will you do this week to tell and show others that God loves them?

Pray that you and the adult learners will continue to seek a close, intimate relationship with Jesus Christ.

Preparing Our Minds

Study the background Scripture in John 6:25-59 and 7:37-39, and lesson Scripture, John 6:34-40 and 7:37-39. As you mull over these readings, think about the experiences, possessions, or people who provide us with a sense of fulfillment.

Write on newsprint:
- ❑ "I feel satisfied when..." for the "Gather to Learn" portion.
- ❑ information for next week's lesson, found under "Continue the Journey."

- ❑ activities for further spiritual growth in "Continue the Journey."

Fill a pitcher with water prior to the session. Place it and the basin you have brought on a worship table. As a visual reminder that Jesus is the bread of life, set out several different types of bread either in whole loaves or broken.

LEADING THE CLASS

(1) Gather to Learn

- ❑ Welcome the class members and introduce any guests.
- ❑ Pray that the love and peace of God will surround this group as they seek to grow closer to God and each other by studying the word.
- ❑ Post a sheet of newsprint that reads, "I feel satisfied when...". Go around the room and ask each person to finish the sentence. Their answers may range from "I finish a good book" to "I have a chance to be with my family" to "my favorite team wins the pennant."
- ❑ See if the class can find any common threads among their answers. Is satisfaction found most often in doing, being, having, or something else?
- ❑ Read aloud today's focus statement: **People constantly search for those**

experiences or possessions that can provide satisfaction and a sense of fulfillment. Can we discover someone or something that can provide spiritual satisfaction? John suggests that Jesus portrays himself as the life-giver in whom there is complete satisfaction.

(2) Unpack Jesus' Statement That He Is Both the Bread of Life and Living Water

❖ Ask a volunteer to read John 6:34-40.
■ Invite the students to name words that really stood out for them as they listened. Possibilities include: *bread, hungry, thirsty, will, see, believe, eternal life* (see John 6:25-34 in Understanding the Scripture. Note that additional words are included in verses 25-33.) List these ideas on newsprint.
■ Discuss why these words are so emotionally and theologically charged. What other biblical images and ideas do these words evoke? Point out the worship table with bread, water, and a basin. (Perhaps they will bring to mind the idea of manna in the wilderness or the bread of communion.)
■ Read or retell "Life's Necessities" from Interpreting the Scripture. Discuss insights that class members glean from this selection.
❖ Choose someone to read John 7:37-39.
■ Provide background information on the Festival of Booths (or Tabernacles) from John 7:37-39 in Understanding the Scripture.
■ Pour the water-filled pitcher into a basin. Be sure to lift the pitcher high enough for everyone to see.
■ Provide time for the students to meditate silently on how this water can become for them a river of "living water," which Jesus says is the Holy Spirit.

■ Encourage the students to talk with a partner about how they perceive a river of "living water" to be flowing freely in their own lives.

(3) Reflect on the Human Search for Meaning and Purpose, Especially in the Learners' Lives

❖ Ask the students to flash back to a period in their lives when they felt life had real meaning. Distribute paper and pencils and encourage them to write about what they were doing, who they were with, and why life seemed so meaningful at that particular time. Perhaps they were shaping the life of a child, or developing a relationship that would become extremely important, or serving others, or creating something that would enrich the lives of others.
❖ Suggest that they compare that period that seemed so meaningful to another time, perhaps now, when their lives do not seem to have as much meaning. What is different? How might Jesus, the source of life, be able to make life more meaningful?
❖ Invite volunteers to talk about discoveries they made from this exercise.

(4) Develop a Plan to Locate and Use Sources for Spiritual Nurture

❖ Encourage the class to name ways they experience spiritual nurture or formation in their own lives. Ideas, which you will list on newsprint may include: *prayer, Bible study, social action, retreat time, healing, fasting, journaling.*
❖ Ask the students to add to each item on the list a place where they may practice this means of nurture, or a book or other resource that will help them engage in it.
❖ Distribute paper and pencils if you have not already done so. Tell the students to copy the list and mark with an asterisk any ideas that they might find useful. Challenge them to begin to use these resources this week.

(5) Continue the Journey

❖ Pray that each one who has come today will be filled as they are nourished by the "bread of life."

❖ Read aloud this preparation for next week's lesson. You may also want to post it on newsprint for the students to copy. **Prepare for next week's session entitled "Overcoming Darkness" by reading John 8:12-20 and 12:44-46, both of which are our lesson and background Scripture. Keep these ideas in mind as you study the lesson: The fear or avoidance of darkness is a common experience for many people. Is there any light available that can dispel the spiritual darkness in which so many people find themselves? John says that the light Jesus provides reaches into areas that are out of bounds for physical light.**

❖ Read aloud the following three ideas. Challenge the students to commit themselves to use these activities as a springboard to spiritual growth.

(1) **Fast from food for one day this week, or part of a day if you must eat for health reasons. Write in** your spiritual journal about your experience of physical hunger. **Compare and contrast physical hunger and thirst with spiritual hunger and thirst.**

(2) **Offer the "bread of life" to someone else by bearing witness to what Christ has done in your life.**

(3) **Ponder the ways in which your life has meaning and purpose as a result of knowing the living God through Jesus Christ. Seek a more intimate relationship to find greater meaning.**

❖ Sing or read aloud "Become to Us the Living Bread."

❖ Say this benediction from Jude 24–25 to conclude the session. Include the students by asking them to echo it as you read: **Now to him who is able to keep you from falling, and to make you stand without blemish in the presence of his glory with rejoicing, to the only God our Savior, through Jesus Christ our Lord, be glory, majesty, power, and authority, before all time and now and forever. Amen.**

UNIT 2: CHRIST SUSTAINS AND SUPPORTS
OVERCOMING DARKNESS

PREVIEWING THE LESSON

Lesson Scripture: John 8:12-20; 12:44-46
Background Scripture: John 8:12-20; 12:44-46
Key Verse: John 8:12

Focus of the Lesson:
The fear or avoidance of darkness is a common experience for many people. Is there any light available that can dispel the spiritual darkness in which so many people find themselves? John says that the light Jesus provides reaches into areas that are out of bounds for physical light.

Goals for the Learners:
(1) to explore Jesus' statement that he is the light of the world.
(2) to reflect on the significance of this image for their faith.
(3) to make a commitment to reflect Christ's light in all aspects of living.

Supplies:
Bibles, newsprint and marker, paper and pencils, hymnals

READING THE SCRIPTURE

NRSV
John 8:12-20

¹²Again Jesus spoke to them, saying, **"I am the light of the world. Whoever follows me will never walk in darkness but will have the light of life."** ¹³Then the Pharisees said to him, "You are testifying on your own behalf; your testimony is not valid." ¹⁴Jesus answered, "Even if I testify on my own behalf, my testimony is valid because I know where I have come from and where I am going, but you do not know where I come from or where I am going. ¹⁵You judge by human standards; I judge no one. ¹⁶Yet even if I do judge, my judgment is valid; for

NIV
John 8:12-20

¹²When Jesus spoke again to the people, he said, **"I am the light of the world. Whoever follows me will never walk in darkness, but will have the light of life."**

¹³The Pharisees challenged him, "Here you are, appearing as your own witness; your testimony is not valid."

¹⁴Jesus answered, "Even if I testify on my own behalf, my testimony is valid, for I know where I came from and where I am going. But you have no idea where I come from or where I am going. ¹⁵You judge by

it is not I alone who judge, but I and the Father who sent me. [17]In your law it is written that the testimony of two witnesses is valid. [18]I testify on my own behalf, and the Father who sent me testifies on my behalf." [19]Then they said to him, "Where is your Father?" Jesus answered, "You know neither me nor my Father. If you knew me, you would know my Father also." [20]He spoke these words while he was teaching in the treasury of the temple, but no one arrested him, because his hour had not yet come.

John 12:44-46

[44]Then Jesus cried aloud: "Whoever believes in me believes not in me but in him who sent me. [45]And whoever sees me sees him who sent me. [46]I have come as light into the world, so that everyone who believes in me should not remain in the darkness."

human standards; I pass judgment on no one. [16]But if I do judge, my decisions are right, because I am not alone. I stand with the Father, who sent me. [17]In your own Law it is written that the testimony of two men is valid. [18]I am one who testifies for myself; my other witness is the Father, who sent me."

[19]Then they asked him, "Where is your father?"

"You do not know me or my Father," Jesus replied. "If you knew me, you would know my Father also." [20]He spoke these words while teaching in the temple area near the place where the offerings were put. Yet no one seized him, because his time had not yet come.

John 12:44-46

[44]Then Jesus cried out, "When a man believes in me, he does not believe in me only, but in the one who sent me. [45]When he looks at me, he sees the one who sent me. [46]I have come into the world as a light, so that no one who believes in me should stay in darkness."

UNDERSTANDING THE SCRIPTURE

John 8:12. In the teaching section of the Gospel of John, chapters 2–12, a pattern reoccurs frequently:
- a scene is set,
- a controversy suggested or described,
- a teaching offered and finally,
- the response to Jesus noted.

Since John's Gospel is composed thematically, it is easy to overlook the setting in examining the theological theme. However, the setting, characters, and context are more than props for a theological discussion. Rather, these add to the theme and develop, subtly, the theology. Chapter 8 is composed of two such scenes of conversation and controversy between Jesus and the religious community assembled in Jerusalem. Our

briefer section (8:12-20) and the longer debate (8:21-59) are both introduced by the word "again". This word gives the reader a clue that what will be discussed was not an isolated event, but a repeated interaction between Jesus and his religious community. In the Gospel of John, Jesus attended several of the Jerusalem festivals. He used the pilgrimage and the liturgical acts as symbols to explain his ministry. Our text is a good example of Jesus' use of a particular aspect of a religious festival as a teaching tool. During the week of the Festival of Tabernacles, as the sun descended and a new day began, priests set four great golden lamps in the Court of Women. The wicks for these lamps were made by twisting together the priests' ritual clothing from the previous year. Once the lamps were lighted, the dancing began and the courtyard was filled with infectious joy. It was an impressive celebration of light; indeed the light from these four lamps was so intense that it was described, poetically, as reflected in every courtyard throughout the city of Jerusalem. Jesus used the symbolism of this festive light as he claimed to be light to the world.

John 8:13-18. The response to Jesus' claim was swift and on-the-mark. The Pharisees objected to his testimony on legal grounds. They showed no interest in the content of his words, but were, rather, interested in the authority substantiating them. From the Pharisees' perspective, there was no validity without the testimony of a witness. A similar circumstance is recorded in John 5:31. In that instance, Jesus responded to those who demanded a witness by claiming John the Baptist as his witness. In our passage, no such accommodation was made to the Pharisees. The two passages show the growing distance between Jesus and his opponents. In this case Jesus validated himself with an assertion of divine authenticity: his relationship with God. Jesus was so thoroughly grounded in God that those who saw him saw not merely a man, but a man reflecting God's presence, purpose, and glory. To judge Jesus according to human standards, therefore, was a sad mistake. Jesus' standard was both human and divine. As a human, Jesus judged no one, but rather offered to all the gift of God's grace. As divine, Jesus judged all since his offer of light and life determined how individuals related to or rebelled from God.

John 8:19-20. When Jesus stated that "the Father who sent me testifies on my behalf," the Pharisees wrongly thought he meant his human father. Assuming that his father's testimony would settle the issue of validity, the Pharisees demanded to know the whereabouts of this man. The words clanged with irony—then and now. A profound lack of religious sensitivity resided within the Pharisees; they were men trained to know (and observe) the minutiae of law, ethical behavior, ritual purity, and propriety. However, as the Gospels make painfully clear, these men failed to love, know, and see God. Jesus stated their religious failure by these words: "You know neither me nor my Father. If you knew me, you would know my Father also" (8:19). This statement is the core truth for the Gospel of John's portrait of Jesus. Jesus' purpose is to make God known. God's purpose is self-revelation through Jesus. Jesus' mode of operation is to cooperate with God's redemptive activity already in process. God's activity is intensified by the obedience of Jesus. As perfectly matched partners, God and Jesus act as one spiritual force. Yet, the Pharisees (and all who approach life only as a material or physical reality) failed to recognize God in Jesus; that failure demonstrated their limited knowledge of God. In the end, however, they did nothing but walk away. Although Jesus was a controversial man, teaching a truth they could not validate, the Pharisees were powerless. They could neither intimidate nor arrest him, for his time/God's time was not yet come.

John 12:44-46. These verses, a prologue to the Last Supper, are a terse summary of Jesus' whole teaching ministry. Nothing new is presented; the dominant themes of belief, revelation of God in Jesus, and the presentation of salvation to the world are familiar themes. This final offer, however, was pitched in the voice of a prophet "crying in the wilderness" (Isaiah 40:3-5, 9-11). Previously in the Gospels, this passage was associated with John the Baptist, but here it reverberates into a summary of Jesus' ministry, identity, and invitation giving Isaiah's words new meaning. In Isaiah 40:3-5, the voice cried out in the wilderness alerting people that the glory of the Lord is about to be revealed. In Isaiah 40:9-11, the voice spoke within Jerusalem to declare God's presence and to describe God's compassion toward the people. The Gospel of John unites these images from Isaiah to introduce Jesus' final revelation of God's glory and compassion. In addition to the subtle inference from Isaiah, the actual words of Jesus reflect the poetic prologue to John's Gospel:

- Jesus was sent from God to bring light and life to the world.
- Jesus came in order that all might believe, and believing, might see God's glory.
- Jesus became the shining light that cannot be overcome in the darkness.

- He was not sent to judge the world, but to save the world.

Nevertheless, as his light shines all people are faced with a decision. Will they remain in the darkness or step into the marvelous light and life of God? This question radiates through the centuries; it continues to burn brightly to illumine hearts and minds of contemporary Christians; its light shines on generations of believers yet to come. No wonder Jesus chose this special image to teach his lesson: I am.

INTERPRETING THE SCRIPTURE

A Special Place, A Special Lesson

It's the end of January. The season of Christmas is far behind; most of the bills underwriting our gaiety are paid or due; the days are beginning to lengthen and the oppressive cold and darkness ease. The economic predictions of the new year are receiving a first test; seed catalogues for spring flowers and summer vegetables arrive; Christians are beginning to consider Lenten practices. Yet, before we rush into spring, let's recognize what has just transpired. Once again, by a series of reflections on light, the Christian calendar has led us from Advent to Christmas and from Christmas to Epiphany. During Advent we heard, "The people who walked in darkness have seen a great light" (Isaiah 9:2a). On Christmas Eve, the story of Jesus' birth was wrapped not only in music, but also in the light of millions of candles in the hands of worshipers. Christmas Day burst with joy— everything seemed lighter, brighter. Next, Epiphany brought the worshiping community into the light. After that brilliant celebration, we are prepared for the Lenten walk with Jesus toward Jerusalem and death. We Christians use the image of Christ's light shining in the darkness as we journey over the darkest days. In Jesus' time, earth's natural passage through darkness received a concentration of light before, rather than during, that journey. In first-century Palestine, the celebration of light was part of the Festival of Tabernacles (also known as Booths). This pilgrim festival occurred in the fall, while days were still long and light was abundant. Indeed, the festival began with the rising of a harvest moon shedding a luminous light throughout the night. In addition to the splendid moonlight, all the pilgrims gathered in the Court of Women to dance by the light of four huge golden lamps. Music, moonlight, and bright flames encouraged the soul of the people. Soon, the days would grow short and darkness surround. Before the darkness took hold, the people of Israel cheered themselves before their God, the Creator God who separated light from darkness and who ordained the moon to rule the night and the sun the day. No wonder Jesus chose this special image to teach his distinctive lesson: I am the light of the world!

A Measured Approach

How do you judge the validity of a teacher's lesson or a preacher's words? Some judge according to intellectual accountability and others by sincerity. Some judgments are based on the opinions of others and other judgments are visceral. In truth, most judgments rest on a complex arrangement of evidence, emotion, fact, and fiction. Not so for the Pharisees in Jesus' time. These men knew about validation. There were specific rules of testimony; when those rules were followed, validity naturally showed the truth. All it took was the agreement of two witnesses. Thus, when the Pharisees noticed that people were actually interested in the Galilean teacher, all they needed to dismiss him was the validation exercise. Without a second witness, there was no validity to his words and no truth in him. The procedure seems almost laughable until we are stung by Jesus' words, "You judge by human standards" (8:15). That statement collides with many of our everyday choices, decisions, and judgments—some of which are based strictly on human standards with minimal reference to God's standards. Indeed, we are hard pressed to know how else to judge; we are humans after all! Yet, Jesus chided the Pharisees for using human systems and excluding the possibility of spiritual revelation. He proclaimed himself as the brilliant light of God shining in the darkness. His teaching was controversial because it challenged the assumed distinction between God and humanity. Yet, those who observed Jesus closely and listened carefully to his words discovered something of God in this man. For them, Jesus' words rang true without the complement of another witness. The Pharisees, however, became more resolute in their determination to invalidate Jesus and his claims.

The Wrong Question

Based on their observation and their surface attention to Jesus' explanation, the Pharisees jumped upon Jesus' assertion that his Father testified on his behalf. Evidently, they failed to notice that Jesus consistently spoke in the spiritual language of metaphor. When Jesus said, "I am the light of the world," he did not mean he was a physical light encircling creation with radiance; he was offering a spiritual metaphor. Just as physical light reveals and makes visible all things material, so Jesus revealed and made visible all things spiritual. The darkest corner of a cave is penetrable by a small beam of flashlight or torch; the darkest fears of humanity are reordered once the spiritual light of God's love radiates through the soul. Jesus' metaphorical speech continued as he called God his Father. According to the Gospel of John, Jesus was always with God; yet this Father/son relationship can be seen as a metaphor to explain the unique relationship between Jesus and God. According to the metaphor:

- the Son shared a familial identity with Father; the Father shared his authority and purpose with the Son;
- the Son represented his Father before the world; the Father blessed the Son's mission and ministry;
- the Father loved the Son; the Son loved the Father.

The metaphor worked: It revealed the presence of God in the person of Jesus. The Pharisees, however, missed the metaphor and asked, literally, the wrong question, "Where is your Father?" Jesus, then, dropped the metaphor and said quite plainly: "You know neither me nor my Father" (8:19). Spiritual truth shined in Jesus' words, casting the darkness of the Pharisees in high relief. Their wrong question provoked judgment from Jesus, and Jesus' judgment was correct. The Pharisees rejected both Jesus and God; they chose, instead, a measured approach that led to the wrong question. They were, indeed, lost in their own dark, human standards.

The Light Shines in the Darkness

The dark, human standards that typified the Pharisees' approach to religion could not, however, extinguish God's gift of light. From the prologue to John's Gospel (1:1-18) through the conclusion of Jesus' public ministry, God's light breaks through. The poetic affirmation of John 1:5, "The light shines in the darkness, and the darkness did not overcome it," was dramatized by Jesus time and time again in the Gospel account of his ministry:

- Jesus healed physical blindness as a sign of the gift of spiritual insight God provides.
- Jesus challenged people to see the gift of God in him.
- Jesus employed the metaphor of light to explain his revelation of God.
- Jesus even concluded his ministry with a final teaching about light.

In John 12:44-46, Jesus reiterated three core lessons. First, he confirmed that belief in Jesus was really belief in God. Jesus had no interest in supplanting God; he merely revealed God. Second, Jesus acknowledged that whoever truly saw Jesus—with the eyes of the heart—truly saw God. Their glory was one, as was their intention, activity, and purpose. Finally, Jesus offered the critical assurance his audience desired. Jesus compared himself to light shining in the world; seeing, believing, and continuing in him ensured light throughout one's earthly life and glory, rather than darkness, forever. His summary was neither novel nor dramatic, but it did offer precisely what his listeners desired: an experience of God's brilliant light sufficient to overcome all darkness. The offer Jesus made then continues to shine from the pages of Scripture, in the witness of the church, and around the world wherever believers reflect to others the light of Christ.

SHARING THE SCRIPTURE

PREPARING TO TEACH

Preparing Our Hearts

This week's devotional reading is found in Isaiah 35:3-10. The prophet is writing to Israelites held captive in Babylon to help them prepare for and anticipate a return to their homeland, Zion. How would you have felt if you had been one of those exiles and had heard these prophetic words? What promises do you see in this passage? How does reading this passage make you feel? What connections, if any, do you see between this passage and Jesus? Talk with another Christian about your ideas.

Pray that you and the adult learners will rejoice in God's promises, even as they await their fulfillment.

Preparing Our Minds

Study the background and lesson Scripture, both of which are found in John 8:12-20 and 12:44-46. Think about where you can find light to dispel spiritual darkness.

Write on newsprint:
❏ information for next week's lesson, found under "Continue the Journey."
❏ activities for further spiritual growth in "Continue the Journey."

Plan how you will present the information from Understanding the Scripture and Interpreting the Scripture for "Explore Jesus' Statement That He Is the Light of the World."

LEADING THE CLASS

(1) Gather to Learn

❖ Welcome the class members and introduce any guests.
❖ Pray that the students will open their eyes, ears, and hearts to see, hear, and receive the love of God.

❖ Invite the students to complete this sentence: *When I think of myself in a situation where there is no light, I . . . .* Write their responses on newsprint. Encourage the students to talk about how they feel in such situations.

❖ Read aloud today's focus statement: **The fear or avoidance of darkness is a common experience for many people. Is there any light available that can dispel the spiritual darkness in which so many people find themselves? John says that the light Jesus provides reaches into areas that are out of bounds for physical light.**

(2) Explore Jesus' Statement That He Is the Light of the World

❖ Choose three readers to take the parts of Jesus, the Pharisees, and the narrator. Read John 8:12-20.

- Use information from John 8:12 in Understanding the Scripture and "A Special Place, A Special Lesson" in Interpreting the Scripture to explain symbolism related to the Feast of Tabernacles.
- Ask the class to identify Jesus' arguments concerning the validity of his witness about who he is and what he has come to do. List these points on newsprint. Contrast these with what the Pharisees believe constitutes a reliable witness. Also list these points.
- Help the class to draw conclusions about Jesus' witness by reading or retelling "A Measured Approach" and "The Wrong Question" in Interpreting the Scripture.

❖ Ask someone to read John 12:44-46, which summarizes Jesus' teaching.

(1) **What do these verses tell you about the relationship between Jesus and God?**

(2) **What is Jesus trying to tell us about himself when he says that he has "come as light into the world" (12:45)?**

(3) Reflect on the Significance of This Image for the Learners' Faith

❖ Enjoin the learners to close their eyes and imagine themselves in these scenarios. Be sure to pause long enough to give them time to reflect on each situation.

- **Imagine yourself home alone in the midst of a raging storm when all the lights go out. How do you feel as you grope in the darkness to find a flashlight or candles? How does your feeling change when your flashlight beams a bit of brightness into the dark? How do you feel when the power is restored and all the lights are on again?** (pause)
- **You are camping in the woods on a cloudy night. Neither the moon's light nor the stars can penetrate the shroud of darkness. You sit next to the campfire, seeing the faces of your fellow campers. How is this scene a metaphor for the way Christ is a light to the world?** (pause)

❖ Provide an opportunity for the students to comment on their reflections.

❖ Talk about the difference that the light of Christ makes in their lives.

(4) Make a Commitment to Reflect Christ's Light in All Aspects of Living

❖ Distribute hymnals, paper, and pencils. Ask the students to page through to find hymns that speak to them through the image of light. In the topical index in the back of the hymnal, readers may find a category for "light." Ask the students to focus on one or two hymns and mine them for an understanding of Jesus as the light. Also consider how this image of light can be applied to their lives. Suggest that they jot down the page number of the hymn and any ideas they became familiar with as a result of this study.

❖ Provide an opportunity for the students to talk with the class or a small group about their findings.

❖ Challenge the students to write their answers to this question, which you will read aloud: **Given the understanding that as a follower of Christ I walk in his light, what will I do in the coming week to reflect his light in my life?**

(5) Continue the Journey

❖ Pray that the participants will go forth to live in the light of Christ.

❖ Read aloud this preparation for next week's lesson. You may also want to post it on newsprint for the students to copy. **Prepare for next week's session entitled "Protection from Evil" by reading background Scripture from John 10:1-18 and lesson Scripture from John 10:1-5, 7-18. Focus on these ideas as you study: People seek protection from those elements that pose a threat to their well-being. Is it possible to find protection in our fearful world? Jesus uses the image of a shepherd to imply that he provides spiritual protection for people.**

❖ Read aloud the following three ideas. Challenge the students to commit themselves to use these activities as a springboard to spiritual growth.

(1) **Take note of how you feel when you are walking in an unlighted area. Are you fearful, worried that you may stumble, or concerned that you will not be able to find** your way? **How does your attitude change when you are walking in the light? How can you relate your physical responses to experiences of spiritual darkness and light?**

(2) **Listen to the news for examples of people acting as if they are in the midst of spiritual darkness. What kinds of attitudes and actions characterize their speech and behavior? Are there "aha" times when these people recognize their condition and move toward the light? If so, what prompted these "aha" experiences?**

(3) **Sing a hymn that for you captures the essence of what it means to live in the light of Jesus. Study the words. Are there any you would change to better fit your own theology?**

❖ Sing or read aloud "Shine, Jesus, Shine," which is found on page 2173 of *The Faith We Sing*.

❖ Say this benediction from Jude 24–25 to conclude the session. Include the students by asking them to echo it as you read: **Now to him who is able to keep you from falling, and to make you stand without blemish in the presence of his glory with rejoicing, to the only God our Savior, through Jesus Christ our Lord, be glory, majesty, power, and authority, before all time and now and forever. Amen.**

UNIT 3: CHRIST GUIDES AND PROTECTS
PROTECTION FROM EVIL

PREVIEWING THE LESSON

Lesson Scripture: John 10:1-5, 7-18
Background Scripture: John 10:1-18
Key Verse: John 10:11

Focus of the Lesson:
People seek protection from those elements that pose a threat to their well-being. Is it possible to find protection in our fearful world? Jesus uses the image of a shepherd to imply that he provides spiritual protection for people.

Goals for the Learners:
(1) to explore Jesus' statement that he is the good shepherd.
(2) to reflect on the significance of this image for their faith.
(3) to give thanks for times when Jesus acted as a shepherd in their lives.

Supplies:
Bibles, newsprint and marker, paper and pencils, hymnals, magazine pictures of objects of protection, tacks or tape

---

READING THE SCRIPTURE

NRSV
John 10:1-5, 7-18

¹"Very truly, I tell you, anyone who does not enter the sheepfold by the gate but climbs in by another way is a thief and a bandit. ²The one who enters by the gate is the shepherd of the sheep. ³The gatekeeper opens the gate for him, and the sheep hear his voice. He calls his own sheep by name and leads them out. ⁴When he has brought out all his own, he goes ahead of them, and the sheep follow him because they know his voice. ⁵They will not follow a stranger, but they will run from him because they do not know the voice of strangers."

NIV
John 10:1-5, 7-18

¹"I tell you the truth, the man who does not enter the sheep pen by the gate, but climbs in by some other way, is a thief and a robber. ²The man who enters by the gate is the shepherd of his sheep. ³The watchman opens the gate for him, and the sheep listen to his voice. He calls his own sheep by name and leads them out. ⁴When he has brought out all his own, he goes on ahead of them, and his sheep follow him because they know his voice. ⁵But they will never follow a stranger; in fact, they will run away from

[7]So again Jesus said to them, "Very truly, I tell you, I am the gate for the sheep. [8]All who came before me are thieves and bandits; but the sheep did not listen to them. [9]I am the gate. Whoever enters by me will be saved, and will come in and go out and find pasture. [10]The thief comes only to steal and kill and destroy. I came that they may have life, and have it abundantly. [11]"I am the good shepherd. The good shepherd lays down his life for the sheep. [12]The hired hand, who is not the shepherd and does not own the sheep, sees the wolf coming and leaves the sheep and runs away—and the wolf snatches them and scatters them. [13]The hired hand runs away because a hired hand does not care for the sheep. [14]I am the good shepherd. I know my own and my own know me, [15]just as the Father knows me and I know the Father. And I lay down my life for the sheep. [16]I have other sheep that do not belong to this fold. I must bring them also, and they will listen to my voice. So there will be one flock, one shepherd. [17]For this reason the Father loves me, because I lay down my life in order to take it up again. [18]No one takes it from me, but I lay it down of my own accord. I have power to lay it down, and I have power to take it up again. I have received this command from my Father."

him because they do not recognize a stranger's voice."

[7]Therefore Jesus said again, "I tell you the truth, I am the gate for the sheep. [8]All who ever came before me were thieves and robbers, but the sheep did not listen to them. [9]I am the gate; whoever enters through me will be saved. He will come in and go out, and find pasture. [10]The thief comes only to steal and kill and destroy; I have come that they may have life, and have it to the full. [11]"I am the good shepherd. The good shepherd lays down his life for the sheep. [12]The hired hand is not the shepherd who owns the sheep. So when he sees the wolf coming, he abandons the sheep and runs away. Then the wolf attacks the flock and scatters it. [13]The man runs away because he is a hired hand and cares nothing for the sheep.

[14]"I am the good shepherd; I know my sheep and my sheep know me—[15]just as the Father knows me and I know the Father—and I lay down my life for the sheep. [16]I have other sheep that are not of this sheep pen. I must bring them also. They too will listen to my voice, and there shall be one flock and one shepherd. [17]The reason my Father loves me is that I lay down my life—only to take it up again. [18]No one takes it from me, but I lay it down of my own accord. I have authority to lay it down and authority to take it up again. This command I received from my Father."

UNDERSTANDING THE SCRIPTURE

John 10:1-5. The context for our passage is the account of a Sabbath healing of a man born blind (John 9:1-12) and an extended dialogue conducted by the Pharisees (9:13-41). The healing disclosed the themes of spiritual blindness, the saving significance of Jesus' word, and Jesus' ability to use God's power in redemptive, restorative, and healing ways. The Pharisees' dialogue raised the issue of authority, the role of the

law, and the recognition of (and response to) God's grace in Jesus. The monologue of Chapter 10, while not addressing these themes directly, built upon them. The section opens with a formula phrase, "Very truly, I tell you" (NRSV) or "I tell you the truth" (NIV), that alerted the reader to a shift in style from dialogue to monologue. The first truth Jesus offered was framed as a mini-parable or extended metaphor. By this image he invited the audience to consider the characteristics of a "good" shepherd as:

- one with authority to enter by the gate,
- one who knows and is known by the sheep,
- one who goes ahead of the flock, and
- one whom the flock follows willingly.

In contrast to the good shepherd were thieves, bandits, strangers, and hired hands; these bad shepherds cared more for their personal security and needs than for those of the flock. The audience and Jesus were in agreement about this brief teaching; all recognized his true words about shepherds, sheep, and the flock.

John 10:6. At verse 6, the editor's voice interrupts to explain the type of figure of speech used by Jesus. His style was identified by a Greek word used in the Septuagint (a Greek translation of the Hebrew Scriptures) to translate "parable," "proverb," or "riddle." The unifying characteristic of these figures of speech was their open-ended quality. In other words, the editor flagged Jesus' words as a figure of speech and alerted the audience that Jesus' teaching was deeper than a description of the role of the shepherd. Next the editor informed the reader that the audience, an unspecified "they," did not understand Jesus. Looking back to the previous dialogue (9:13 and following), the Pharisees were the likely candidates to fill the role of "they." In that story, not only did the Pharisees reject Jesus, they "drove out" the healed man (9:34). This wording conveys a harsh fact: The Pharisees excommunicated the man from the religious community. Their interest was in maintaining the rules, not in celebrating God's grace in the healed man. The editor may be suggesting that the very same Pharisees, whose blind-spots were revealed in 9:35-41, once again failed to understand Jesus. The Pharisees heard the characteristics of the good shepherd described without a hint of self-reflection or examination. They failed to see themselves as poor shepherds unwilling to nurture, guide, and protect God's flock.

John 10:7-16. In verse 7, the text returned to the voice of Jesus. This monologue combined two metaphors ("I am the gate" and "I am the good shepherd") with Jesus' terse theological teachings. In a tightly packed text, we read illustrations relating to shepherds and sheep, note several inferences to Old Testament prophecies and promises, hear Jesus' occasional verbal jab at the audience, and understand Jesus' ministry and relationship with God ... all wrapped in two metaphors and designed to disclose Jesus' identity and mission. The first image Jesus explored was his identity as the gate of the sheepfold. In his metaphorical role as the gate, Jesus provided the point of contact between God and the flock. In distinction to Jesus, all others (a reference to the Pharisees within the audience, rather than Old Testament prophets and leaders) were thieves. The verbs—"steal," "kill," and "destroy"—illustrated the danger and death these thieves brought to the flock. Jesus, on the other hand, offered abundant life. The second teaching wove the image of the good shepherd with Jesus' conduct of ministry, his relationship to God, and a collection of Old Testament shepherd allusions (specifically, Psalm 23 and Ezekiel 34). From the passage, we glean these activities of the good shepherd:

- he lays down his life for the sheep.
- he knows the sheep of his flock.
- he will gather other sheep and enlarge his flock.

The allusions to Jesus' ministry are easily identified. Jesus' death was not defeat, but became the source of ultimate protection for his believers. Jesus' knowledge of those who turned to him was based within a relationship of intimacy; knowing his flock was not an abstract activity, but rather a relationship of love. Finally, during his ministry Jesus crossed the boundary lines between those the religious community assumed to be "acceptable" and those who were morally or ritually outcasts, as well as Samaritans or Gentiles. Ultimately, Jesus, the good shepherd, gave his life for his flock. By the conclusion of this section the distinctions were sharp: security and life offered by the good shepherd, or danger and death dealt by the hired hand.

John 10:17-18. Our passage concludes with direct speech from Jesus about his death and his relationship to God. Two verses summarize the theological perspective of the Gospel of John regarding Jesus' death. The key words are "love" and "power." In John's Gospel, Jesus used the word "love" infrequently during his public ministry. His teaching on love was concentrated in the farewell discourse, Chapters 13-17. In the farewell discourse, Jesus commanded his disciples to abide in his word and to love one another. In our passage, Jesus foreshadowed that teaching as he connected God's love and Jesus' obedience. Moreover, in the loving relationship between Jesus and God, God shared power with Jesus. He was able to face his death not as a victim, but as a man in complete control of himself. In the Gospel of John, the language of love and power explained how Jesus laid down his life and took it up again. This claim differs from the Synoptic Gospels' perspective on Jesus' death and resurrection. In Matthew, Mark, and Luke, Jesus' life ended at the hands of sinful men and it is God who raised him up. Yet the Synoptic Gospels and John agree on the context of Jesus' death and resurrection: Both events are understood only by the intense relationship that exists between God, Jesus, and the world.

INTERPRETING THE SCRIPTURE

Called by Name

In the church's collection of beloved images, those of Jesus as the good shepherd and his followers as his true flock are among the most beloved. Although few in contemporary society have an actual experience with sheep and shepherds, the imagery continues to impress itself on the Christian collective consciousness. Bolstered by Bible passages from both the Old Testament (notably, Psalm 23) and the New Testament (the parable of the lost sheep, Luke 15:3-7), the fascination with these two images passes from generation to generation through liturgy, art, and music. One aspect of the shepherd/sheep image that is not emphasized is the relationship between the shepherd and the sheep. This may be because adults don't like the suggestion that they are herded as docile creatures (or as obstinate ones!). Protective arms cradling a little lost lamb intrigues, but a herd of bleating sheep being driven into a pen repulses.

There is something so offensive about the "group think" of sheep-herding, that the image is dismissed before it is examined and applied. If we pause, however, to observe the dynamics between the sheep and the shepherd, something emerges that nurtures our faith. Let's begin with the sheep. They are notably more headstrong than intelligent. If a sheep (not a lamb but a full-grown, hefty sheep) sets a direction, there is little that restrains or redirects. Once, as a young woman visiting a small farm, I was sent to bring in two ewes from their feeding ground to the barn. I accepted the task because I thought it would be easy: unloose the tether, lead the ewes through the gate and into the barn. But the ewes were huge and I was a slightly nervous stranger. They bolted, rammed me into the fence and charged the barn door with me in tow. Slightly humiliated, I asked my host, "How does your ten-year old son manage those two ewes?" "Easily," came his reply, "The sheep know my son." The relationship between shepherd and sheep is crucial to the task of herding. The sheep must become familiar with the shepherd; the shepherd must earn the status of protector. A key to the relationship is the practice of naming and calling each sheep by name. Over time, the sheep learn the shepherd's voice and the distinct sound of each name. Contemporary Christians may not warm to all the associations between shepherd and sheep, but these two continue to inform our faith. First, Jesus, the good shepherd, protects the whole flock. Second, Jesus, the good shepherd, calls his believers by name. In Jesus' flock believers are named and protected.

Entering into Life

Our passage is well known, so well known that when it is read or heard more smiles than questions are provoked. We sink into the meanings and forget that the well known also has a particular context and place in a larger gospel message. The context for this passage is the growing tension between Jesus and some of the religious authorities of his faith. In Chapter 9, a controversy arose (once again) on a Sabbath day, after Jesus healed a man born blind . . . once again. The Pharisees heard about Jesus' action and branded him a lawbreaker. They were ready to bar from the religious life of the Jewish community the blind man, Jesus, and any who demonstrated interest or belief in him. These Pharisees are the shadows behind our passage; inadvertently, they highlight the difference between Jesus' approach and the approach of the current religious leaders. His estimation of their commitment to and concern for the flock was exceedingly low; indeed, Jesus stated that their lack of relationship with the flock made them dangerous. These "thieves" were only interested in stealing (enhancing their own status and standing), killing (purging the unfit from the community), or destroying (judging

individuals and scattering the flock). Jesus, on the other hand, was interested in life in all its fullness. Jesus did not steal his followers; rather, he offered invitations and awaited graceful responses. Jesus did not judge by legal, ritual, or financial considerations. He assumed the law, worship, and stewardship were results of, not thresholds to, discipleship. Finally, Jesus brought people into community; his ministry promoted abundant life for all. Jesus, as the gate and as the good shepherd, was the connection between humans and God. He was the precise point of entrance into life.

One Flock, One Shepherd

In our passage, Jesus spoke controversial words: "I have other sheep that do not belong to this fold. I must bring them also, and they will listen to my voice. So there will be one flock, one shepherd" (10:16). During his lifetime, the controversy related to the boundary lines that indicated God's chosen people. The "other sheep" in Jesus' day referred to the ritually unclean, the morally suspect, the Samaritans, and all inhabitants of the Gentile nations. It was a radical idea that the likes of these others would be welcomed among God's people. Jesus, however, was quite clear about the dimension of his ministry; God sent Jesus to the world in and with love. His commission was to love. The Gospels abound with incidents of Jesus loving the "outsiders." Jesus showed compassionate love:

- to the blind and the lame (ritually unclean);
- to the tax collectors and prostitutes (morally suspect);
- to the Samaritans (as the woman at the well and her whole community); and
- to various Gentiles (those whom he healed and welcomed to his table).

He acted out his mission before he stated it; nevertheless, when the statement came, it was controversial. The Pharisees bristled because they believed in their standards, judgments, and entrance requirements. Although we may find their response amusing, in the contemporary church we continue to think these same thoughts. Jesus' radical approach of opening the doors and loving all who enter made the Pharisees uncomfortable and, if we are honest, continues to be unsettling. Yet, Jesus' proclamation resounds over our fears. His goal is one flock, one shepherd; in other words, a unified world secured by a single protector.

The Only Command

The contrast between the Pharisees and Jesus is striking. The disciples of the Pharisees studied the law in order to know God's will; Jesus' disciples learned about God by living side by side with Jesus. The Pharisees prized intellectual agility and the ardent practice of disciplined living. Jesus cultivated an atmosphere of love and encouraged deeds based on joy and gratitude. The Pharisees assumed the law taught the correct way to relate to God; Jesus simply loved God, loved his neighbors, and taught his disciples through these relation-ships. The Pharisees' way to know God began in the head; Jesus' way sprang from the heart. The goal in each path was to unite head, heart, and will in the love of God. Sadly, however, Jesus observed that the Pharisees were stuck in their heads; Jesus accused them of knowing the details of the law, but forgetting the higher commands of justice and mercy (Luke 11:42). Therefore, he taught his disciples a different way:

- He shared with them his own delight in loving God, neighbor, and life itself.
- He invited them into the warmth of his relationship with God.
- He sent them out to offer compassion to strangers.
- He challenged their preoccupation with security.
- He taught a dynamic dependence on God.

Love was his method, practice, and outcome. Among Jesus' flock, knowledge, ethical behavior, and a right relationship with God came through loving. In the end, he had only one commandment for them (and for us): to love one another as he loved them.

SHARING THE SCRIPTURE

PREPARING TO TEACH

Preparing Our Hearts

This week's devotional reading is found in Isaiah 40:10-14. Note in verse 11 the beloved image of God as a shepherd feeding, carrying, and gently caring for a flock of lambs. Check the word "shepherd" in a concordance. You will find this word mentioned over one hundred times in the Bible. Look at as many citations as possible, especially those that relate to God or Jesus as the good shepherd. What do you learn about the nature and role of the good shepherd? Who are some familiar figures in the Bible who were shepherds before God called them to another vocation?

Pray that you and the adult learners will seek the loving care and protection of God the good shepherd.

Preparing Our Minds

Study the background Scripture, John 10:1-18, and lesson Scripture, John 10:1-5, 7-18. As you study, think about elements that pose a threat to your well-being and decide if it is possible to find protection from these threats.

Gather pictures of objects that people use to make themselves feel safe. Perhaps you will choose pictures of a car with airbags, a house with a fence and/or security system, a gun, knife, baseball bat, insurance policy, and so on. Be sure you have tape or tacks to affix these to a wall or bulletin board where everyone can see them.

Write on newsprint:

❑ information for next week's lesson, found under "Continue the Journey."

❑ activities for further spiritual growth in "Continue the Journey."

Prepare the optional lecture for "Explore Jesus' Statement That He Is the Good Shepherd."

LEADING THE CLASS

(1) Gather to Learn

❖ Welcome the class members and introduce any guests.

❖ Pray that all who have gathered today will experience God's love and protection.

❖ Pass around or mount on a wall or bulletin board the pictures you have selected of objects that make people feel safe. Talk about why we feel safe when we have these objects and vulnerable when we do not. Consider the advantages and disadvantages of relying on each of these objects.

❖ **Option:** Divide into groups, give each group a picture, and let the groups discuss why they feel safe with their object and the advantages and disadvantages they ascribe to it. Call the groups together to report back.

❖ Read aloud today's focus statement: **People seek protection from those elements that pose a threat to their well-being. Is it possible to find protection in our fearful world? Jesus uses the image of a shepherd to imply that he provides spiritual protection for people.**

(2) Explore Jesus' Statement That He Is the Good Shepherd

❖ Select a volunteer to read John 10:1-5, 7-18, in which Jesus describes himself as the good shepherd.

❖ Draw a vertical line on a sheet of newsprint. Label the left side "Good Shepherd" and the right side "Hired Hand." Encourage the students to call out characteristics, as described in the Bible passage, of each of these two persons. List their ideas. Compare and contrast these characteristics.

❖ Raise this question with the class: **What other biblical passages speak to you about God as the good shepherd?** (Students will likely mention Psalm 23 and perhaps Ezekiel 34. If time permits, turn to whichever references are named to see how the shepherd is described there. If you have checked references in a concordance, as suggested for "Preparing Our Minds," add whatever information you feel is appropriate here.)

❖ **Option:** Present a lecture based on the Understanding the Scripture portion. Your purpose is to help the class understand the major points of Jesus' discourse.

(3) Reflect on the Significance of This Image for the Learners' Faith

❖ Distribute paper and pencils. Encourage the students to think about Jesus' statement, "I am the good shepherd" (10:11). Ask them to write a short reflection in answer to this question: **In light of your understanding of what a good shepherd does, what does Jesus' statement mean for your life?**

❖ Provide time for students to discuss their answers. Be sure that they recognize that Jesus is able to protect them from threats. Students may point out threats from which they were not protected—a robber, drunk driver, and so on. If so, try to turn the discussion to help the students see that even though something bad happened to them, Jesus was present with them and guided them through this harrowing experience.

(4) Give Thanks for Times When Jesus Acted as a Shepherd in the Learners' Lives

❖ Ask the students to work with a partner or trio. Invite each student to tell a story about a time when they believe Jesus acted as the good shepherd to them. Encourage them to talk about why this experience was meaningful.

❖ Call the class together and write a litany of thanksgiving for times when Jesus has acted as a shepherd to them. To do this, begin by selecting a refrain and write that at the top of a sheet of newsprint. Then, ask the students to state one line that sums up their words of thanksgiving, such as "For your reassuring presence with me as my daughter was being treated for cancer." Number each entry.

❖ Read the litany, possibly by having the person who suggested a particular line say that and then the class will read the words of response.

(5) Continue the Journey

❖ Pray that the participants will recognize the caring, protective presence of God in their daily lives.

❖ Read aloud this preparation for next week's lesson. You may also want to post it on newsprint for the students to copy. **Prepare for next week's session entitled "Life after Death" by reading John 11:1-44 and focusing your attention on John 11:17-27. Consider these ideas as you study: Everyone eventually experiences the death of a family member or an acquaintance. What does Jesus teach about death? Jesus taught that death is not a permanent reality for those who have developed a personal relationship with him through faith,** because he has the power to overcome death.

❖ Read aloud the following three ideas. Challenge the students to commit themselves to use these activities as a springboard to spiritual growth.

(1) **Remember that "shepherd" was a familiar image for people who lived close to the land. Maybe you have never touched a sheep, much less known a shepherd by name. Brainstorm images representing God that are meaningful in your setting.**

(2) **Do some research on the characteristics of sheep. Now that you know more about them, what is your reaction to the idea of being compared to a sheep? Write in your journal about these traits and your response to them.**

(3) **Offer shepherd-like care to someone who needs it this week.**

❖ Sing or read aloud "Savior, Like a Shepherd Lead Us," which was inspired by John 10:1-29.

❖ Say this benediction from Jude 24–25 to conclude the session. Include the students by asking them to echo it as you read: **Now to him who is able to keep you from falling, and to make you stand without blemish in the presence of his glory with rejoicing, to the only God our Savior, through Jesus Christ our Lord, be glory, majesty, power, and authority, before all time and now and forever. Amen.**

UNIT 3: CHRIST GUIDES AND PROTECTS
LIFE AFTER DEATH

PREVIEWING THE LESSON

Lesson Scripture: John 11:17-27
Background Scripture: John 11:1-44
Key Verse: John 11:25

Focus of the Lesson:
Everyone eventually experiences the death of a family member or an acquaintance. What does Jesus teach about death? Jesus taught that death is not a permanent reality for those who have developed a personal relationship with him through faith, because he has the power to overcome death.

Goals for the Learners:
(1) to explore Jesus' statement that he is the resurrection and the life.
(2) to reflect on the significance of this image for their faith.
(3) to celebrate the life they have in Christ with others.

Pronunciation Guide:
Bethany (beth' uh nee)

Supplies:
Bibles, newsprint and marker, paper and pencils, hymnals, map, pictures of Christ's resurrection and/or people celebrating life, optional art supplies such as colored pencils

---

FEBRUARY 11

READING THE SCRIPTURE

NRSV
John 11:17-27

[17]When Jesus arrived, he found that Lazarus had already been in the tomb four days. [18]Now Bethany was near Jerusalem, some two miles away, [19]and many of the Jews had come to Martha and Mary to console them about their brother. [20]When Martha heard that Jesus was coming, she went and met him, while Mary stayed at

NIV
John 11:17-27

[17]On his arrival, Jesus found that Lazarus had already been in the tomb for four days. [18]Bethany was less than two miles from Jerusalem, [19]and many Jews had come to Martha and Mary to comfort them in the loss of their brother. [20]When Martha heard that Jesus was coming, she went out to meet him, but Mary stayed at home.

home. ²¹Martha said to Jesus, "Lord, if you had been here, my brother would not have died. ²²But even now I know that God will give you whatever you ask of him." ²³Jesus said to her, "Your brother will rise again." ²⁴Martha said to him, "I know that he will rise again in the resurrection on the last day." ²⁵Jesus said to her, **"I am the resurrection and the life. Those who believe in me, even though they die, will live,** ²⁶and everyone who lives and believes in me will never die. Do you believe this?" ²⁷She said to him, "Yes, Lord, I believe that you are the Messiah, the Son of God, the one coming into the world."

²¹"Lord," Martha said to Jesus, "if you had been here, my brother would not have died. ²²But I know that even now God will give you whatever you ask."

²³Jesus said to her, "Your brother will rise again."

²⁴Martha answered, "I know he will rise again in the resurrection at the last day."

²⁵Jesus said to her, **"I am the resurrection and the life. He who believes in me will live, even though he dies;** ²⁶and whoever lives and believes in me will never die. Do you believe this?"

²⁷"Yes, Lord," she told him, "I believe that you are the Christ, the Son of God, who was to come into the world."

UNDERSTANDING THE SCRIPTURE

John 11:1-16. Our passage is a richly nuanced narrative conveying powerful theological insights. There are two parts to the first scene: In verses 1-5 the details of the situation are presented, and in verses 6-16 Jesus offers interpretation on Lazarus' death and his own death. The shadow of the cross hangs over the tale of Lazarus by proximity to the Holy City, by the mention of Mary's anointing of Jesus (see John 12:3), and by Jesus' own words of interpretation (11:4). The irony present in the text is that the death of Lazarus and his restoration to life by Jesus provide the motivation for Jesus' execution. Jesus, however, is completely free from fear; he actively chooses his direction, time, and, ultimately, death. After three days, Jesus explained to his disciples that they were going to Bethany to restore Lazarus to life. Further, Jesus welcomed the opportunity because by it the disciples' faith would be strengthened. Thomas, who would later be dubbed "Doubting Thomas," spoke as the ideal disciple pledging his loyalty to Jesus and his willingness to die with him.

John 11:17-27. According to the folk wisdom of first-century Judaism, the soul of a dead individual hovered near the place of burial for three days. Thus the four days of Lazarus' entombment signified the finality of his death and set the stage for a remarkable miracle. When Jesus and his disciples arrived, the mourners included Mary, Martha, and a number of Jews from Jerusalem. Initially, Martha withdrew and spoke privately with Jesus. She complained of Jesus' failure to arrive earlier, yet still knew that "even now" God would respond to Jesus' prayers. Jesus began to comfort Martha with the standard consolation, "Your brother will rise again." Evidently, both Mary and Jesus believed, as did the Pharisees, in a general resurrection (see Daniel 12:2 and following). Martha accepted Jesus' comfort, yet her polite and affirming words provoked a profound response from Jesus. Referring to the moment of eschatological fulfillment, Jesus identified himself as both the resurrection and the life. He further explained that belief in him had two dimensions: Believers who died would live on, and believers who were alive would never die. In other words, Jesus boldly stated that by belief in him the living and the dead received a new kind of life—a life beyond the power and destruction of death. In response, Martha joined the chorus of those who rightly recognized Jesus:

- with Peter (6:68-69) she confessed that Jesus was the Messiah;
- with Thomas (20:28) she acknowledged him the Son of God;
- with the author of the Gospel she affirmed that Jesus was the one coming into the world (1:9-11) to grant life (20-31).

John 11:28-37. The scene with Martha was private; the scene with Mary was public. As Mary learned of Jesus' arrival, she got up quickly to go to him, accompanied by all the mourners. These Jews became the audience before whom and for whom the subsequent conversation and deeds are presented. They were witnesses—confused and questioning witnesses, but witnesses nonetheless. They provided the literal link between the events in Bethany and the events in Jerusalem. The scene was full of drama. The verbs used to describe Jesus' response connoted anger and agitation; these words are softened in translation to "greatly disturbed in spirit and deeply moved" (11:33b, NRSV) and "deeply moved in spirit and troubled" (11:33b, NIV). Such sentimentalized versions cast Jesus' response as an emotion (as the Jews explained it). In the raw words of the Greek language, however, it is clear that Jesus expressed a soulful agony that raged against all that limited life—whether such limitations came from lack of faith, fear of death, oppression, or sin. In his distress, Jesus asked the location of Lazarus' burial site; the scene concluded in confusion. There was a division among the Jews as to Jesus' relationship to Lazarus and Jesus' presumed power to heal. Jesus was agitated and angry. Mary slipped out of the scene. Something was about to happen, but Jesus' intentions were not stated.

John 11:38-44. This final section is masterfully told. The movement is stopped three times and although the miracle is briefly described, its significant points are obvious. Jesus' disciples, the Jews, Martha, and (presumably) Mary walked Jesus to the tomb. As his own tomb will be a cave sealed with a stone, so Jesus stands before Lazarus' tomb. He commanded that the stone be removed; Martha, however, interceded to stop the action. She explained, as if any explanation were needed, that after four days the smell of death would be intense. Jesus responded not only to Martha, but, by his choice of a plural pronoun, to all who could hear his voice. His rhetorical question prepared everyone for what was to come. Once the stone was rolled away, the action stopped again. This time, Jesus broke the "rush" to the miracle, by pausing to pray. This is the first instance in the Gospel of John of Jesus praying to God with the address, Father. Then with a loud shout, again displaying the decisiveness of Jesus' actions, Lazarus appeared. He came from the tomb bound by his burial cloth and with another cloth covering his face. The elements of Lazarus' burial and appearance were similar to and different from Jesus' own burial and appearance. Both were buried in a cave with a stone sealing the entrance. Both were wrapped in burial cloths. Unlike Jesus' hasty burial, there was time to rub Lazarus' body with perfumes and to tuck spices into the binding cloth. After Jesus' resurrection, the cloths and wrappings were left in the tomb; Lazarus emerged with the full display of death. Jesus was immediately free from the bounds of death. For Lazarus, there remained one more pause; Jesus spoke, "Unbind him, and let him go." Lazarus' return to life—to full, unbound life—perfectly matched Jesus' mission. Jesus came that the world would have life, abundantly, and eternally.

INTERPRETING THE SCRIPTURE

A Private Grief

In first-century Palestine, most cultural conventions of mourning were assigned to women. It was a sign of honor, to the deceased and the whole family, for a large number of mourners to gather at the time of death. The official period of corporate mourning followed the burial and lasted seven days; however, the period could be extended for up to a month. The immediate family mourned for a whole year. The women with Martha and Mary knew the conventions of public mourning: They cried, wailed, sang, and composed poems. With this intensity of emotion within the confines of their home, it was probably a relief for Martha to go out to greet Jesus. Perhaps with her friend she would be able to share her private experience of grief. Two aspects of the encounter stand out. First, Martha was free to speak her mind to Jesus. She shared her disappointment that he had not come earlier, her confidence that Jesus would have healed Lazarus, and her continued esteem of his spiritual relationship with God. Good friends are able to speak (and hear) both hard and loving words. The second noteworthy aspect of the encounter began with Jesus' words: "Your brother will rise again" (11:23b). This simple statement was an ordinary platitude exchanged among mourners. Even though Jesus knew his visit to Bethany would provoke something remarkable, Jesus began on the level of Martha's private grief. Often when contemporary mourners greet a bereaved friend the first words uttered are simple platitudes. A private grief is soothed by simple truths spoken by a true friend. In this case, the simple words of Jesus allowed Martha to see and affirm his true identity: the Messiah, the Son of God, the one coming into the world. Although her grief continued, her eyes were opened and she was prepared to behold the glory of God.

A Public Mourning

Although Martha had met Jesus alone, the mourners accompanied Mary as she went to Jesus. Private grief took on a public face as Jesus felt the full impact of Lazarus' death. Perhaps you have had a similar experience. Entering a full sanctuary for a funeral or memorial service sometimes feels like swimming in grief. There is a palpable sorrow that touches and intensifies with the addition of each mourner. In a corporate service, a shared sense of sorrow and loss creates the revelatory setting for God's grace. Before this group of mourners Jesus intended to act out the central claim of his belief: God gives life, and God's gift of life is both abundant and eternal. Such demonstrations, however, are not always immediately comprehended. Words spoken and deeds done during a funeral service are frequently "lost" on the audience. In our scene, the Jewish mourners were confused by what was happening. Some saw the demonstration of Jesus' friendship for the family of Lazarus, while others pondered his failure to prevent Lazarus' death. However confused or lost the religious witness to the community may be, spiritual truths corporately proclaimed are seeds full of faith's potential. Jesus' deeds may have initially provoked questions and concerns, but these Jews who mourned with Mary and Martha became the direct link to the events of Jesus' last week in Jerusalem. Perhaps:

- some were among those who cheered Jesus' entrance into the Holy City.
- some may have sat around him as he daily taught in the temple.
- some of those women may have been among the "daughters of Jerusalem" wailing as Jesus carried his cross through the city.
- some may have joined the other women in vigil at the foot of the cross.

One thing is certain: This group did not forget what they heard and saw. They took the story back to Jerusalem. What they observed hastened the hour when Jesus' revelation would be complete.

Slowing Down the Mourning

Our text is dotted with insights that are surprisingly contemporary. In the private conversation between Martha and Jesus, we learned that simple words exchanged among friends can open eyes and ears to unnoticed spiritual realities. As Jesus spoke and acted before the crowd of mourners, we learned that a public witness to God's grace is capable of planting seeds of faith. There are other lessons the text teaches. One is the technique of slowing down. When grief is present, whether held by an individual or by a group, the pace should be slow, allowing each word, deed, emotion, and spiritual insight time to reach its mark. In the scene at the tomb (11:38-44), the climax of Jesus' healing ministry, there are three "full stops." The first is initiated by Martha's objection to opening the tomb. This full stop provided the time required to acknowledge the reality of death. As the crowd wondered what would happen, Jesus redirected Martha's complaint from death to something undefined yet captured by the words, "glory of God." Once the tomb was unsealed, Jesus stopped the forward motion again. This time a prayer of thanksgiving restrained the mourners. Before all the mourners, Jesus prayed with the confidence of a son aware of his father's attention, constancy, and power. His prayer demonstrated his ministry's complete dependence on God; Jesus was not an independent miracle worker. Finally, Jesus yelled, "Lazarus, come out!" The once dead man stumbled forward, still bound by the wrappings of death. The miracle, however, was not complete. There was one more stop as the mourners unwrapped Lazarus. Up to this point in the story, the mourners heard Jesus' intentions, they saw Lazarus moving out from the tomb, they smelled life not death on him; finally, they touched his body as they unwrapped the funeral cloths. All their senses validated the miracle; the mourners were prepared to be Jesus' witnesses.

Life in the Face of Death

The story of the raising of Lazarus can be read as the enactment of the key verse for this lesson. Remember how Martha found comfort in the hope that her brother would one day rise again? As Jesus spoke the words, "I am the resurrection and the life" (11:25), he pulled God's future into the present. For three years, he witnessed to God's ultimate purpose through his ministry of healing, teaching, and spiritually powerful deeds. Yet, these signs were insufficient to break through the final barrier of death. The fullest demonstration of God's redemption would not be available to his followers until after his death and resurrection. Therefore, those who followed during his lifetime were beset by questions and doubts. Their concerns continue to beset contemporary believers:

- What is the point of believing?
- Can I really trust my life to Jesus? Why or why not?
- How is truth validated?
- Where is he going and where will I be if I follow him?

With these words, "I am the resurrection and the life," Jesus made his mission clear: Those who believed in him would have abundant and eternal life. His teaching was, of course, profoundly spiritual. It defied the physics of matter and the rationality of science. Rather, Jesus spoke of a life that was greater than the physically experienced life, a life beyond the clutches of death, and a life free from all fear. Those who physically died would live spiritually; those who lived would not die spiritually. Jesus was both resurrection and life . . . and we, with all his faithful followers, believe and receive these blessings from him.

SHARING THE SCRIPTURE

PREPARING TO TEACH

Preparing Our Hearts

This week's devotional reading is found in Jude 17–23. This short letter, which encourages its readers to stay strong in their faith and live virtuous lives, presents its final warnings in these verses. What does Jude say we are to do in order to prepare ourselves for eternal life? Write a response to Jude in your spiritual journal as if you were answering his letter. Let him know how you are acting on his words.

Pray that you and the adult learners will continually prepare yourselves to meet God.

Preparing Our Minds

Study the background Scripture from John 11:1-44, and lesson Scripture, verses 17-27. Ponder what Jesus teaches about death.

Write on newsprint:
❑ information for next week's lesson, found under "Continue the Journey."
❑ activities for further spiritual growth in "Continue the Journey."

Be prepared to retell the story of the death of Lazarus, recorded in John 11:1-16.

LEADING THE CLASS

(1) Gather to Learn

❖ Welcome the class members and introduce any guests.

❖ Pray that the Holy Spirit will guide all that is said and done as the group gathers for prayer, fellowship, and study.

❖ Read aloud the following quotations concerning death.

(1) All mankind is of one Author, and is one volume; when one man dies, one chapter is not torn out of the book, but translated into a better language; and every chapter must be so translated; God employs several translators; some pieces are translated by age, some by sickness, some by war, some by justice; but God's hand is in every translation, and his hand shall bind up all our scattered leaves again for that library where every book shall lie open to one another. (John Donne, 1572–1631)

(2) A funeral among men is a wedding feast among the angels. (Kahlil Gibran, 1883–1931)

(3) I cannot forgive my friends for dying; I do not find these vanishing acts of theirs at all amusing. (Logan Pearsall Smith, 1865–1946)

(4) Death is an awfully big adventure. (Sir James M. Barrie, 1860–1937)

(5) Death, the grisly terror. (John Milton, 1608–1674)

(6) I am ready to meet my Maker. Whether my Maker is prepared for the great ordeal of meeting me is another matter. (Winston Churchill on his 75th birthday)

(7) Death, the gate of life. (Bernard of Clairvaux, 1090–1153)

❖ Talk with the class about which one(s) of these statements express views they hold regarding death and why. Invite them to make additional observations concerning their attitudes or beliefs about death.

❖ Read aloud today's focus statement: **Everyone eventually experiences the death of a family member or an acquaintance. What does Jesus teach about death? Jesus taught that death is not a permanent reality for those who have developed a per-**

sonal relationship with him through faith, because he has the power to overcome death.

(2) Explore Jesus' Statement That He Is the Resurrection and the Life

❖ Set the context of today's lesson by retelling the story of the death of Lazarus, found in John 11:1-16. Add information from Understanding the Scripture and "A Private Grief" in Interpreting the Scripture to help the class members understand first-century Jewish mourning customs.

❖ Invite three volunteers to read the parts of the narrator, Jesus, and Martha as they appear in John 11:17-27.

❖ Study verses 17-27 to discern: the time, place, and people involved in this encounter between Jesus and Martha. Locate Jerusalem and Bethany on a map so the class members can see how close Jesus was to Lazarus' home.

❖ **Option:** Enlist several volunteers to play the role of the mourners. Ask someone else to interview them as a reporter might to discover how they view Jesus' visit.

❖ Discuss these questions with the class:
  (1) **What do you learn about Jesus?**
  (2) **What might you assume about Martha's relationship with Jesus and her grasp of his mission and ministry?**
  (3) **How are you similar to and different from Martha?**
  (4) **What kind of affirmation of faith are you willing to make regarding Jesus?**

(3) Reflect on the Significance of This Image for the Learners' Faith

❖ Read aloud "Life in the Face of Death" in Interpreting the Scripture.

❖ Go back to the four bulleted questions in "Life in the Face of Death" and encourage the students to answer them, perhaps in small groups.

❖ Note that both Mary and Martha (in the background Scripture) made pointed comments to Jesus. Distribute paper and pencils. Invite the students to think of questions or comments that they would like to make to Jesus regarding the death of a loved one. (Be sensitive to adults who have experienced a recent loss. Some may find this activity healing; for others it may be too painful to consider.)

❖ Encourage volunteers to read some of their questions and comments. The students may find that others share the same concerns.

(4) Celebrate with Others the Life the Learners Have in Christ

❖ Locate art books or prints illustrating the resurrection of Christ and/or people celebrating life. If you use the Internet, search for "pictures of resurrection of Christ." Post or pass around whatever pictures you have located. The resurrection image of the Isenheim Altarpiece by Matthias Grünewald (which you can find in books and online) is particularly exciting. Talk with the class about the emotions and questions these pictures evoke concerning eternal life. Also discuss how the artist's choice of subject, colors, and use of light helps to create a celebratory mood. Urge the adults to state how this picture for them embodies the idea that because Jesus is the resurrection and life we can celebrate new life.

❖ **Option:** Distribute art supplies, such as paper and colored pencils, and invite the students to express the feelings of celebration that they have concerning life in Christ. An easy way to do this for non-artists is simply to create random patterns with colors that express life and joy for them.

(5) Continue the Journey

❖ Pray that all who have participated in today's session will believe in the resurrection and life that Jesus offers to them.

❖ Read aloud this preparation for next week's lesson. You may also want to post it on newsprint for the students to copy. **Prepare for next week's session entitled "A Guide for Life" by reading John 14:1-14, which is both the background and lesson Scripture for this lesson. As you study, concentrate on these ideas: We all at some time have been lost or needed direction, either physically or spiritually. Where can we turn for guidance at those times? Jesus says he is the way and all other directions for life are to be found through him.**

❖ Read aloud the following three ideas. Challenge the students to commit themselves to use these activities as a springboard to spiritual growth.

(1) **Use the Internet and/or library to research Jewish mourning customs, both in the present day and the first century. If you have Jewish friends, talk with them about their traditions.**

(2) **Offer a listening ear to someone** who has recently lost a loved one. Avoid "pat" remedies for the pain of grief. Be especially sensitive if suicide, crime, or the death of a child is involved.

(3) **Spend time thinking about and looking at pictures of a deceased loved one. Recall this precious person's life and its impact on you. Envision this individual enjoying life with Christ.**

❖ Sing or read aloud "Christ the Victorious."

❖ Say this benediction from Jude 24–25 to conclude the session. Include the students by asking them to echo it as you read: **Now to him who is able to keep you from falling, and to make you stand without blemish in the presence of his glory with rejoicing, to the only God our Savior, through Jesus Christ our Lord, be glory, majesty, power, and authority, before all time and now and forever. Amen.**

UNIT 3: CHRIST GUIDES AND PROTECTS
A GUIDE FOR LIFE

PREVIEWING THE LESSON

Lesson Scripture: John 14:1-14
Background Scripture: John 14:1-14
Key Verse: John 14:6

Focus of the Lesson:
We all at some time have been lost or needed direction, either physically or spiritually. Where can we turn for guidance at those times? Jesus says he is the way and all other directions for life are to be found through him.

Goals for the Learners:
(1) to explore Jesus' statement that he is the way, the truth, and the life.
(2) to reflect on the significance of this image for their own faith.
(3) to pray for Jesus' guidance.

Supplies:
Bibles, newsprint and marker, paper and pencils, hymnals

READING THE SCRIPTURE

NRSV
John 14:1-14

[1]"Do not let your hearts be troubled. Believe in God, believe also in me. [2]In my Father's house there are many dwelling places. If it were not so, would I have told you that I go to prepare a place for you? [3]And if I go and prepare a place for you, I will come again and will take you to myself, so that where I am, there you may be also. [4]And you know the way to the place where I am going." [5]Thomas said to him, "Lord, we do not know where you are going. How can we know the way?" [6]Jesus

NIV
John 14:1-14

[1]"Do not let your hearts be troubled. Trust in God; trust also in me. [2]In my Father's house are many rooms; if it were not so, I would have told you. I am going there to prepare a place for you. [3]And if I go and prepare a place for you, I will come back and take you to be with me that you also may be where I am. [4]You know the way to the place where I am going."

[5]Thomas said to him, "Lord, we don't know where you are going, so how can we know the way?"

said to him, **"I am the way, and the truth, and the life. No one comes to the Father except through me.** [7]If you know me, you will know my Father also. From now on you do know him and have seen him."

[8]Philip said to him, "Lord, show us the Father, and we will be satisfied." [9]Jesus said to him, "Have I been with you all this time, Philip, and you still do not know me? Whoever has seen me has seen the Father. How can you say, 'Show us the Father'? [10]Do you not believe that I am in the Father and the Father is in me? The words that I say to you I do not speak on my own; but the Father who dwells in me does his works. [11]Believe me that I am in the Father and the Father is in me; but if you do not, then believe me because of the works themselves. [12]Very truly, I tell you, the one who believes in me will also do the works that I do and, in fact, will do greater works than these, because I am going to the Father. [13]I will do whatever you ask in my name, so that the Father may be glorified in the Son. [14]If in my name you ask me for anything, I will do it."

[6]Jesus answered, **"I am the way and the truth and the life. No one comes to the Father except through me.** [7]If you really knew me, you would know my Father as well. From now on, you do know him and have seen him."

[8]Philip said, "Lord, show us the Father and that will be enough for us."

[9]Jesus answered: "Don't you know me, Philip, even after I have been among you such a long time? Anyone who has seen me has seen the Father. How can you say, 'Show us the Father'? [10]Don't you believe that I am in the Father, and that the Father is in me? The words I say to you are not just my own. Rather, it is the Father, living in me, who is doing his work. [11]Believe me when I say that I am in the Father and the Father is in me; or at least believe on the evidence of the miracles themselves. [12]I tell you the truth, anyone who has faith in me will do what I have been doing. He will do even greater things than these, because I am going to the Father. [13]And I will do whatever you ask in my name, so that the Son may bring glory to the Father. [14]You may ask me for anything in my name, and I will do it."

UNDERSTANDING THE SCRIPTURE

John 14:1-3. The pattern (event, discussion, discourse, and response) used by the Gospel of John to explain individual teaching points expand to become the framework of Jesus' summary of his ministry (John 13-17):

- The event featured the portrayal of a loving relationship and of the betrayal of the same (John 13:1-30).
- The discussion flows into the discourse section by the question raised by Simon Peter, Thomas, and Philip.
- The disciples responded with a unanimous comment: "Yes, now you are speaking plainly, not in any figure of

speech! Now we know that you know all things, and do not need to have anyone question you; by this we believe that you came from God" (16:29-30).

- Jesus responded with a prayer for present disciples and those yet to believe (Chapter 17).

Thus the discourse at the Last Supper clarified Jesus' final teaching on maintaining, rather than betraying, a relationship in love. The question in our mind as we study is: What does it mean to be faithful in a relationship? The stakes are high in this discussion. In the opening verses of John 14, Jesus uses three imperatives: Do not be troubled!

Believe! Believe! The first verb connected the moment with three recent moments:

- Jesus' grief over the power of death over human hearts and hopes (John 11:33);
- Jesus' recognition that "his hour had come" (John 12:23-27);
- Jesus' personal response to washing the disciples' feet while knowing Judas' intentions (John 13:21).

In each of these moments, Jesus' heart was troubled by the power of evil and the lack of security humans felt when facing evil. Using the image of a house with numerous dwelling places or rooms, Jesus comforted his disciples with a physical image of closeness (his Father's house). Using the intimacy of their relationship he promised an eternal place of such closeness.

John 14:4-7. After introducing the image of the Father's house, Jesus selects the word "way" as the next metaphor to explore. The word has, of course, a surface and a symbolic meaning. On the surface, a way is a route or path to a particular destination; this is the meaning within Thomas' question. Jesus does not answer that question; rather, he applied the symbolic meaning of "way" to himself. The background of the symbol is discovered in the Old Testament wisdom tradition. In Proverbs, the "way" indicates the lifestyle of the wise and in Psalms, the "way" suggests a lifestyle in accord with the law and blessed by God. Both apply to the core values that direct living; neither suggest a direction to a particular place. Jesus used "the way" to reveal his relationship with God; his relationship determined his "way." To this image, Jesus added "truth and life." This combination was unique. Every Jew knew that all truth and all life came from God. Jesus, however, made the relational claim of identity with God and thereby claimed that God's truth and life were also in him. Moreover, Jesus offered that relationship to his disciples. The good news of the Gospel of John is this: Jesus is the person in whom his disciples meet, know, and live with God. They are invited into this unique relationship through their intimacy with Jesus.

John 14:8-11. Jesus' claim—that in him the disciples shared an everlasting, ever present relationship with God—was dramatic and daring. Philip's request, "Lord, show us the Father, and we will be satisfied" was just as dramatic and daring. However, as is so often the case in this Gospel, the question prompted a point of clarification. On the surface Philip asked that the transcendent nature of God be revealed and that the disciples' hunger for God be satisfied. However, his question revealed that he was still thinking literally. Once God was physically seen, reasoned Philip, there would be no more restlessness. Jesus, however, recognized the significance of both the spiritual unity and the physical separateness between God and humanity. Jesus did not come to earth to "be God in the world," but to reveal God to the world. Philip wanted to see God in order to believe; Jesus wanted Philip to look at the world in such a way that God's eternal purposes were obvious. Philip wanted a quick fix; Jesus responded by pointing, once again, to himself. Using the image of the mutuality between the Father and the Son, Jesus spoke clearly: "Whoever has seen me has seen the Father" (14:9). Jesus offered nothing more. He, the physical, real person with them at the table, was the only revelation of God necessary or provided. Jesus did, however, provide two ways to validate this revelation. The disciples were invited to believe him based on either his words or his deeds.

John 14:12-14. Finally, Jesus reminded the disciples of the amazing benefits of a faithful relationship to Jesus and, thereby, with God. Using a formula of introduction, "Very truly, I tell you" (NRSV) or "I tell you the truth" (NIV), Jesus explained to the disciples that if they remained in a close relationship with him, they would accomplish even greater works. All of Jesus' mighty deeds—whether individual healings, miracles defying nature, or prophetic preaching—revealed the reign of God within the world. By his word Jesus pointed to God's power, demonstrated God's new age, and declared God's presence. However, Jesus' heart was troubled. He knew that people, in general, and his disciples, in particular, lived in dread of death. Until he faced death, the doubting continued. Jesus knew that many people assumed (and some believed) that he was God's great prophet. He also knew that their assumption and belief ended at the point of death; once he died, all would condemn him to a silent and eternal rest with the prophets. Knowing there was another chapter in the story—beginning with his death—Jesus also knew that his disciples would offer the full testimony. They would be able to speak of Jesus as the dwelling place of God, as the way to stay in relationship with God, as the truth and life of God—and they would testify that death does not end life. The testimony of the disciples, therefore, was greater than all the revelatory works of Jesus. Their ministry would be greater because it testified to the whole story of Jesus' life and death, and because their relationship with Jesus was unending. In the disciples' ministry, Jesus saw the confirmation of his ministry and glimpsed greater deeds glorifying God.

INTERPRETING THE SCRIPTURE

Table Talks

As a young adult, I was privileged to live in Denmark and learn about the Danish tradition of table talks. At baptism, confirmation, marriage, important birthdays, and anniversaries the extended family and guests gather to celebrate the honored family member. Food is abundant and courses seem to be without number. Finally, as the evening draws to a conclusion, everyone remains at the table to listen to brothers and sisters, aunts and uncles, close kin and shirt-tail relations give short speeches to or about the honored individual. Some speeches are repetitions of prosaic wisdom, while others ring with profound insight and emotion. As a result of that exposure, when I read John 13–17, I see Jesus as a stately Dane formally addressing those closest to him. What's your image of a table talk? Is it a toast to the bride and groom or the final supper with dinner partners on a cruise? Perhaps, you, as hundreds of Christians, think of a beloved pastor behind a table reciting the words of institution before communion. In Jesus' culture, table talks were a common educational technique of the rabbis. After the lessons of the day and the blessing of a common meal, rabbis offered discourses on the day's themes. In many ways, Jesus was acting as an ordinary rabbi; however, by his awareness that his hour had come, this table talk was extraordinary. Jesus began with comfort and challenge; he wove resources and righteousness through it; he concluded with promises and a prayer. The theme throughout the table talk was Jesus' assurance that he would always be with his disciples and that they would always share in his relationship with God.

Way, Truth, and Life

Beloved passages take on their own life. This happens whenever the contemporary application overwhelms the original context. For example, the popular understanding of "the way, and the truth, and the life" (14:6) explains these three images as practical pieces of information for Christian living. Thus, "the way" becomes discipleship, "the truth" is discovered in the words of Jesus, and "the life" is the promise of life after death. Jesus, however, was talking to his disciples about *his identity*, ("I am"), not about the benefits of following him. The first question we should pose to the text is: How is Jesus the way, the truth, and the life? The second question is: What is the spiritual content of these words? When Jesus used "the way" to explain himself, he wasn't promising a room in heaven (as Thomas wrongly assumed); he was talking about the experience of knowing God right here and right now. Likewise, as Jesus applied the words "truth" and "life" to himself, he made other radical claims. First, he claimed God's truth resided within him. Since Jesus' words and deeds were exclusively dependent upon God, he did not hesitate to identify God's truth within his words. Next, the image of "life" connected with an aspect of Jesus' divinity previously enacted as Jesus gave life back to Lazarus. Finally, Jesus spoke about himself as way, truth, and life, in order that his disciples could hold onto him—on the very night that each disciple was tempted to betray or deny him. If they could keep their eyes fixed on Jesus as the way, the truth, and the life, then the relationship shared by Jesus and his disciples would expand to secure the disciples' relationship with God. By stringing together these three images, Jesus helped the disciples come to God, know God, and see God. This was a promise—not a set of life rules, a pattern of right words, or reservation in a heavenly abode—from Jesus to his disciples.

Show Me!

Philip was a man ready for a revelation. Perhaps he caught the urgency in Jesus' tone. Perhaps he remembered Jesus saying that his hour had come. Perhaps he felt reasonably certain of his comprehension of Jesus' teaching and confidently prepared to receive Jesus' fullest revelation. Still, given his culture, Philip made a shocking request: to see God (14:8). Throughout the history of the people of God, those who "saw" God were few:

- Jacob wrestled with a divine opponent until he was blessed with the name Israel (Genesis 32:28);
- Moses saw the "back of God" (Exodus 33:23);
- Isaiah saw the Lord high and lifted up in the temple (Isaiah 6:1).

However, ordinary people did not see God nor did exceptional people make images or sketches of the God they saw. Yet, Philip asked Jesus to show God to the disciples. There is something both absurd and dear in his request. It is absurd to think that Jesus can display the full reality of God in a material, visible manner. It is dear that his disciples imagine Jesus is able to do so. There is only one response Jesus can make. It is the heartbeat of the Gospel of John: If you want to see God, look at Jesus. The only way to see the spiritual in the material is to look at Jesus through the eyes of faith. Poignantly, Jesus states again what he has previously said:

- to the Jews who demanded a witness to validate Jesus' words and deeds (John 5:37-38);
- to those who listened to his teachings in the temple, but demanded to know his identity (John 8:25-27);
- to the Jews who wondered if he were the promised Messiah (John 10:25-30).

In each case, Jesus offered no new evidence or produced any new witnesses; he simply pointed to his relationship with God. Those with eyes and ears attuned to God recognized God's presence through him. Those whose way, truth, and life depended strictly on physical realities could neither recognize Jesus nor see God in him.

Greater Works

Even as the questions from Peter, Thomas, and Philip "miss the point," Jesus continued to bless and encourage his company of disciples. Specifically, he blessed the ministries by which they would glorify God. The conditions for the development of their ministries were serious. Jesus was going away. Throughout his absence, the disciples were to hold fast to their belief in Jesus and pray. Imagine how these words felt to the small group attending Jesus' table talk: separation, steadfast prayer, and belief regardless of humiliation or defeat. It is almost possible to hear the fearful pounding of the disciples' hearts. Yet, even as Jesus acknowledged the difficulties about to come, he did so with complete confidence in his disciples. Jesus plainly said the disciples will glorify God by their greater works. To all who "missed the point," Jesus promised their ministry a yield of greater works. How could he make such a promise? Did his exceptional spiritual insight allow him to see the true potential of these men? Was he confident that

the Spirit would teach them the lessons they failed to learn by his side? Was he building up the whole group, while secretly counting only on his inner circle? Such questions spring from a logical evaluation of Jesus' success as a teacher. However, the truth of Jesus' ministry—as the truth of your ministry and that of your congregation—is not based on logical signs of success. At the core of ministry is love: love for Jesus, love for one another, love for the stranger and the enemy, love for God. Jesus blessed his disciples and promised to fulfill their prayers because he loved them and knew they loved him. In the height and depth of emotions, in the present moment and eternal presence, in simple gesture and the profound sacrifice, among the wise and the simple only one condition mattered: the love between Jesus and his disciples. Whenever this condition is confirmed, greater works of ministry, compassion, and glorification of God abound.

SHARING THE SCRIPTURE

PREPARING TO TEACH

Preparing Our Hearts

This week's devotional reading is found in Ephesians 4:17-24. Here Paul reminds the people of Ephesus that "truth is in Jesus" (4:21). What do you mean when you affirm that Jesus is truth? How is your spiritual life affected by your belief that Jesus is truth? Check out verses 22-24 to see what Paul has to say about how we change when we accept the truth of Christ.

Pray that you and the adult learners will continually seek the truth of Christ and live according to that truth.

Preparing Our Minds

Study the background and lesson Scripture, both of which are found in John

14:1-14. As you study, think about where you can turn for guidance when you feel physically or spiritually lost and need direction.

Write on newsprint:
- ❏ information for next week's lesson, found under "Continue the Journey."
- ❏ activities for further spiritual growth in "Continue the Journey."

LEADING THE CLASS

(1) Gather to Learn

❖ Welcome the class members and introduce any guests.

❖ Pray that those who have come today will find God's truth in their lives and continue to walk in that way.

❖ Read the first question of this quiz aloud once. Read the answers again, this time asking students to choose A or B and signify their choice by either raising their hand or standing at their place. Repeat the process. State that this "quiz" has no right or wrong answers, but rather is intended to see how different people approach different types of situations.

(1) **If you are lost in a strange place, are you more likely to (A) ask directions or (B) try to find your own way?**

(2) **If you ask directions, are you more likely to (A) write them down or (B) try to remember them?**

(3) **If you try to find your own way, are you more likely to (A) use a map or (B) let your sense of direction guide you?**

(4) **If you have a spiritual problem, are you more likely to (A) pray and study Scripture or (B) talk with someone who you believe can lead you?**

(5) **If you are seeking a marriage partner, different career, or other new direction in your life, are you more likely to (A) meditate about your plans and their options or (B) find a group of like-minded Christians and discuss your dilemma with them?**

❖ Read aloud today's focus statement: **We all at some time have been lost or needed direction, either physically or spiritually. Where can we turn for guidance at those times? Jesus says he is the way and all other directions for life are to be found through him.**

(2) Explore Jesus' Statement That He Is the Way, the Truth, and the Life

❖ Choose volunteers to read the parts of Jesus, Thomas, and Philip in John 14:1-14.

❖ Use "Way, Truth, and Life" in Interpreting the Scripture to discern what Jesus really meant by these three descrip-

tions of himself. Consider how Thomas' question relates to these three words, but misunderstands Jesus' point. See verses 1-3 and 4-7 in Understanding the Scripture to clarify Jesus' points.

❖ Discuss the request that Philip raises, and Jesus' response. "Show Me" in Interpreting the Scripture and verses 8-11 in Understanding the Scripture will aid in this discussion.

❖ Begin a discussion of verses 12-14 by encouraging the students to explain what they think Jesus means by these verses. Add information from "Greater Works" in Interpreting the Scripture. Invite the adults to describe how the disciples might have felt when they heard Jesus say that they would do "greater works" than those that he had done.

❖ Talk with the students about any "greater works" that they currently see.

(3) Reflect on the Significance of This Image for the Learner's Faith

❖ Lead the class in reading today's key verse, John 14:6, in unison.

❖ Discuss these questions concerning the major points.

(1) **How do you know that you are following in the way of Jesus? What "road signs" are you looking for to point you in the right direction?**

(2) **When you say that something is true, what do you mean by that?** (Push the students a bit on this question. In the modern Western world, grounded as it is in rational thinking, many people assume that truth is empirically verifiable. In their view, if one cannot measure, quantify, or somehow "prove" an idea, it is not true. Faith does not enter into this way of thinking.)

(3) **What to you are the marks of real life? What relationship exists between your ideas of life and**

living as one who is created in the image of God?

❖ Raise these issues concerning the end of verse 6, "No one comes to the Father except through me." John wants us to understand that Jesus is the enfleshed presence of God in the world. As we come into relationship with Jesus, we can have new experiences with God. Furthermore, according to *The New Interpreter's Study Bible*, verse 6 tells us "how Jesus reveals God for those in a particular faith community." This is an identity issue related to who we are as Christians, not any indictment on other religions. Too often we have interpreted verse 6 to mean that Christianity is exclusive, but we should not understand this verse as "a statement about the relative worth of the world's religions." Encourage the class to consider how this interpretation could enable Christians to be more fully in dialogue with other religions, without compromising its own claims.

(4) Pray for Jesus' Guidance

❖ Invite the students to pray together, preferably holding hands in a circle. Ask the class members to go around the circle and in a sentence or two lift up a prayer asking God to guide themselves or someone else in whatever way such guidance is needed. Suggest that the students not go into any detail so as not to compromise the privacy of people for whom the class is lifting prayer.

❖ Offer the last sentence prayer yourself.

❖ Conclude the prayer time by leading the students in the Lord's Prayer.

(5) Continue the Journey

❖ Read aloud this preparation for next week's lesson. You may also want to post it on newsprint for the students to copy. **Prepare for next week's session entitled "Secure Connections" by reading both the background and Scripture lesson from John 15:1-17. Focus on these ideas as you read: We are all born to be in relationship with others, and we need them to be productive. Is there a relationship that can serve as a model for others? John says that being connected to Jesus is essential if we are to be productive in our lives.**

❖ Read aloud the following three ideas. Challenge the students to commit themselves to use these activities as a springboard to spiritual growth.

    (1) Use a Bible concordance to find references to "way," "truth," and "life." What insights do you gain from these words?

    (2) Make a list of your personal prayer requests. Which ones would seem to be in keeping with God's plan for your life? Which ones are simply wishes for material goods that you do not really need? Pray now for any items that you can truly say you are asking for in Jesus' name, that is, according to God's will.

    (3) Be alert and give thanks for ways in which God is leading you.

❖ Sing or read aloud "Come, My Way, My Truth, My Life," which is based on today's key verse, John 14:6.

❖ Say this benediction from Jude 24–25 to conclude the session. Include the students by asking them to echo it as you read: **Now to him who is able to keep you from falling, and to make you stand without blemish in the presence of his glory with rejoicing, to the only God our Savior, through Jesus Christ our Lord, be glory, majesty, power, and authority, before all time and now and forever. Amen.**

UNIT 3: CHRIST GUIDES AND PROTECTS
SECURE CONNECTIONS

PREVIEWING THE LESSON

Lesson Scripture: John 15:1-17
Background Scripture: John 15:1-17
Key Verse: John 15:5

Focus of the Lesson:
We are all born to be in relationship with others, and we need them to be productive. Is there a relationship that can serve as a model for others? John says that being connected to Jesus is essential if we are to be productive in our lives.

Goals for the Learners:
(1) to explore Jesus' statement that he is the true vine.
(2) to reflect on the significance of this image for their faith.
(3) to pray for a closer spiritual union with Christ.

Supplies:
Bibles, newsprint and marker, paper and pencils, hymnals, live potted plant

---

READING THE SCRIPTURE

NRSV
John 15:1-17

[1]"I am the true vine, and my Father is the vinegrower. [2]He removes every branch in me that bears no fruit. Every branch that bears fruit he prunes to make it bear more fruit. [3]You have already been cleansed by the word that I have spoken to you. [4]Abide in me as I abide in you. Just as the branch cannot bear fruit by itself unless it abides in the vine, neither can you unless you abide in me. **[5]I am the vine, you are the branches. Those who abide in me and I in them bear much fruit, because apart from me you can do nothing.** [6]Whoever does not abide in me

NIV
John 15:1-17

[1]"I am the true vine, and my Father is the gardener. [2]He cuts off every branch in me that bears no fruit, while every branch that does bear fruit he prunes so that it will be even more fruitful. [3]You are already clean because of the word I have spoken to you. [4]Remain in me, and I will remain in you. No branch can bear fruit by itself; it must remain in the vine. Neither can you bear fruit unless you remain in me.

[5]"I am the vine; you are the branches. If a man remains in me and I in him, he will bear much fruit; apart from me you can do nothing.

is thrown away like a branch and withers; such branches are gathered, thrown into the fire, and burned. [7]If you abide in me, and my words abide in you, ask for whatever you wish, and it will be done for you. [8]My Father is glorified by this, that you bear much fruit and become my disciples. [9]As the Father has loved me, so I have loved you; abide in my love. [10]If you keep my commandments, you will abide in my love, just as I have kept my Father's commandments and abide in his love. [11]I have said these things to you so that my joy may be in you, and that your joy may be complete.

[12]"This is my commandment, that you love one another as I have loved you. [13]No one has greater love than this, to lay down one's life for one's friends. [14]You are my friends if you do what I command you. [15]I do not call you servants any longer, because the servant does not know what the master is doing; but I have called you friends, because I have made known to you everything that I have heard from my Father. [16]You did not choose me but I chose you. And I appointed you to go and bear fruit, fruit that will last, so that the Father will give you whatever you ask him in my name. [17]I am giving you these commands so that you may love one another."

[6]If anyone does not remain in me, he is like a branch that is thrown away and withers; such branches are picked up, thrown into the fire and burned. [7]If you remain in me and my words remain in you, ask whatever you wish, and it will be given you. [8]This is to my Father's glory, that you bear much fruit, showing yourselves to be my disciples.

[9]"As the Father has loved me, so have I loved you. Now remain in my love. [10]If you obey my commands, you will remain in my love, just as I have obeyed my Father's commands and remain in his love. [11]I have told you this so that my joy may be in you and that your joy may be complete. [12]My command is this: Love each other as I have loved you. [13]Greater love has no one than this, that he lay down his life for his friends. [14]You are my friends if you do what I command. [15]I no longer call you servants, because a servant does not know his master's business. Instead, I have called you friends, for everything that I learned from my Father I have made known to you. [16]You did not choose me, but I chose you and appointed you to go and bear fruit—fruit that will last. Then the Father will give you whatever you ask in my name. [17]This is my command: Love each other."

UNDERSTANDING THE SCRIPTURE

John 15:1-4. Ordinarily in the Gospel of John, "I am" statements expand the understanding of Jesus' identity. In this passage the statement, "I am the vine" is used in a pastoral manner. The only other "I am" statements with a pastoral function are in Chapter 10: the images of the good shepherd and the gate for the sheep. The pastoral quality derives from the combination of two elements. First, a traditional biblical image of God's judgment is balanced with God's grace, and second, relationships are emphasized. The traditional image is found in Isaiah 5:1-7:

- God is the gardener who owns and cares for the vineyard;
- the people of God are the choice vines that receive the gardener's care and protection;
- good grapes are the expected yield from the people;
- the actual yield of wild grapes provokes the gardener's judgment.

In the Synoptic Gospels this imagery lies

behind the parable of the vineyard and tenants (Matthew 21:33-46, Mark 12:1-12; Luke 20:9-16). These emphasize the rebelliousness of Israel with a poignant addition of the murder of the owner's son. In the Gospel of John, the same images are used to suggest a complexity of relationships. For example, God prunes the disciples so they will bear more fruit; the pruning happens within the community whenever Jesus' disciples fail to emulate his lifestyle. God also cleanses the disciples (the Greek word may be translated "clean-cut," thus continuing the reference to gardening). The cleansing happens through Jesus' verbal teachings. Only as the disciples abide in Jesus are they able to produce the fruit pleasing to God.

John 15:5-7. The first reflection on this image cluster focuses on the relationship between Jesus as the vine and God as the vine grower. In the second reflection, the relationship between the disciples and Jesus is addressed. The verb "abide" unites the two reflections. A mutual abiding ensures the production of good grapes. The disciples, for their part, follow Jesus' example and words; Jesus, for his part, fulfills his God-given mission through his disciples' fidelity and deeds. However, the possibility of pruning continues to exist. Those disciples who fail to abide in Jesus and produce his works will wither; the result is a kind of spiritual death. However, the disciples that continue to model Jesus' behavior and keep his words have the assurance that their prayers will be answered. The blessings and risks of discipleship are balanced. Jesus offered both options based on the relationship that exists between a vine (ministry in the way of Jesus) that grows from the care and attention of the vine-grower (God). Throughout the Gospel of John the mutuality between God and Jesus is used to illustrate Jesus' ministry and identity. Here, at the conclusion of Jesus' teaching ministry, this relationship has a pastoral dimension. As two circles joined by a single weld, Jesus brings two relationships together to form a new unity. The God/Jesus relationship and the disciples/Jesus relationship have one sure, fast, and enduring point of connection: Jesus. Because he is faithful in both spheres, Jesus encouraged his disciples by affirming that their prayers—formed from his way and his words—would be granted.

John 15:8-11. The transition to teaching begins with the eighth verse; Jesus affirms that God will be glorified through the disciples. Their ministry is to be grounded in a relationship to Jesus (discipleship) and exhibited through their worthy deeds (fruit). The metaphor is beginning to stretch beyond its capacity; a new element must be added if Jesus' final message is to be clear. The phrases, "my Father" (15:1) and "bear fruit" (15:2, 4, 5), are united in verse 9 to introduce the new element of love. Jesus once again traced the circles of relationship: God loves Jesus and Jesus loves the disciples. The disciples are to stay within these circles of love. Moreover, Jesus uses his own faithfulness as a model for the disciples' faithfulness. Jesus' ministry was dependent on God's direction, power, and purpose; the disciples' ministry must be dependent on Jesus' teaching, promises, and gospel. However, such fidelity to Jesus is not generated by a sense of duty. Rather, as Jesus was obedient to God in a loving relationship, so the disciples are to abide in Jesus' love. The source of their ministry is, as was the case with Jesus' ministry, a faithful relationship founded on love. The outcome of such a loving relationship is joy. Rewards are not mentioned—only a complete joy. The progression of ideas is noteworthy: first comes the disciples' ministry that glorifies God, then comes the love that sustains relationships, and finally comes the fulfillment of joy.

John 15:12-17. The text circles back to the earlier commandment, to love one another, presented in 13:34. Here is a precise restatement, with neither additions nor deletions, yet, it is used to introduce the ultimate example of love: to lay down one's life for one's friends. The statement is richer in the Greek language as the verb "to love," *phileo,* and the noun "friend," *philos,* come from the same root. Indeed, one cannot be a friend without loving and one cannot love without being a friend. The ultimate gift of friendship, one which Jesus is about to offer on behalf of the whole world, is the gift of his life. Once again, there are expectations placed upon the disciples. As they love one another they are to keep their eyes focused on Jesus' manner of loving and their ears attuned to the truth Jesus has taught. No longer, however, does a discussion of failure intrude. Rather the disciples are "called" friends. This "call" from Jesus offers a whole new context for the disciples' obedience. Jesus invited the disciples into his full knowledge, experience, and rela-

tionship with God. Because of this, the disciples are wiser than they might realize. Moreover, there is nothing accidental about Jesus' expectations of their future. These followers did not choose Jesus. Jesus chose them and commissioned their ministry. The context for all ministry offered by the disciples was (and is) Jesus' choice and commission. Their ministry, as a continuation of Jesus' ministry, will be characterized by a relationship based on abundance (bearing fruit) and endurance (fruit that will last). The final verse summarizes all that Jesus has presented through the metaphor of the vine and prepares the disciples for a "plain speech"; the transition rests on the one command Jesus' disciples must fulfill: Love one another.

INTERPRETING THE SCRIPTURE

Metaphorically Speaking

The title for this quarter's study, "Jesus Christ: A Portrait of God," initially alerted us to the content of our study. This was to be a quarter to study Christology, the strand of Christian theology devoted to answering the question "Who is Jesus?" However, as we reviewed a collection of images of Jesus drawn from various New Testament sources and, especially, as we focused on John's "I am" statements, it became clear that the method of presentation is as important as the content presented. As ordinary citizens of North America, we are intellectually curious to name functions, to define purposes, and to master complexities. Most of our intellectual curiosity has a practical application. We want to be informed and competent members of our society. Our intellectual interests and our driven practicality at times hurry us to conclusions. We become impatient when the important facts

are not presented clearly. Indeed, this quarter's study may have triggered some impatient responses among your study partners. The reason is in plain sight: Scripture is, surprisingly, impractical when it comes to providing facts directly and succinctly. Scripture prefers stories, riddles, parables, poetry, unfinished thoughts, and implied mysteries. This preference is neither superficial nor inconsequential. Our Scriptures come from times and cultures that lived at a slow pace. Lives were brief, but days and seasons long. There was time to watch the miracles of a vineyard's growth and nights to star-gaze and contemplate. Many things were valued for their spiritual, rather than practical, aspect; embellished stories were loved as truer than true. Indeed, as our passages for this quarter revealed, the biblical culture was adept at speaking metaphorically. Unlike our desire to get the facts, the ancient cultures that gave us God's truth in Scriptures enjoyed pondering the parable or marveling through the metaphor. Metaphorical speech is invitational rather than informational speech. It is Scripture's preferred mode of talking about God.

The Necessary Relationship

You are studying these lessons throughout the winter, but I wrote them during the summer. Last winter the vines on my neighbor's fence looked like dead wood. This summer she anticipates a yield of about 100 pounds of grapes. The annual transformation from dead-looking winter vines to abundant branches lush with leaves and fruit is my personal illustration of Jesus' statement, "I am the true vine" (15:1). I watched my neighbor's son prune the gnarled branches and thought of the decisions made with every snip of the pruning shears. I noticed the hint of green beneath the brown and applauded the shoots that followed the late rains. There were insect and fungus inspections. New ties trained the new growth. And there was patience until a good and full harvest. Divine attributes are revealed in the gardener's work; as a gardener God is watchful and patient. Moreover, the vine itself changed from season to season:

- the winter was of a period of resting and waiting;
- during spring the vine drew water from the earth;
- early summer brought the energy of new growth;
- late summer is harvest time.

As the vine, Jesus' role in the lives of believers also changes. There are quiet times in the relationship as well as times of rapid growth and productivity. The branches, however, must stay in a healthy relationship with the vine if fruit is to be produced. Finally, comes the harvest. It is, as Jesus says, a time of joy. The metaphor worked as I watched my neighbor's grapevine. I am called to ponder the mysterious interrelationships of gardener, vine, branches, fruit, and harvest. I am able to ponder the graciousness of God, the sustaining nature of Jesus, my personal commitments, the service I offer, and the joy I experience through faith. The relationships are necessary: God to Jesus, Jesus to his followers, his followers to the world, and the world back to God in joyful reconciliation.

Keep on Loving

The words from this final passage, although rich in metaphor and religious imagery, are best interpreted through the setting of Jesus' last meal and teaching time with his disciples. In the Gospel of John, this meal opens as Jesus washes his disciples' feet and questions their understanding of his deed (Chapter 13). Although there is no mention of remembering Jesus through the sharing of bread and cup, there is an extended table talk. The meal is concluded with a prayer (Chapter 17). The emotions of that last meal must have been complex. Jesus' table talk included metaphorical and direct speech. He was pastoral; he was prophetic; he was prayerful. One word dominates this section: love. In the Gospel of John, the Greek words for love are grouped symmetrically: love is mentioned twelve times in the section describing Jesus' public ministry (Chapters 1–12) and eleven times in chapters devoted to his arrest, crucifixion, and resurrection (Chapters 18–21). Between these two sections comes the Last Supper (Chapters 13–17); in this section, the Greek words for "love" occur thirty-four times. The pattern makes sense. Much of life is spent caring for, responding to, and enjoying those we love; frequently we fail to speak the words of love, assuming that our actions are eloquent. After a loved one dies, thoughts of love continue, but often encased in silent daydreams. Those individuals who have the opportunity to be near a beloved friend or family member at the time of death discover the word "love" frequently in conversations. The last meal with Jesus was such a time to talk about loving. Indeed, Jesus revealed that love was the cause, promise, and fulfillment of his time with the disciples. He was sent from the Father's love and they were drawn to him by the Father's choice; he promised them his love would be sufficient in life and death; he explained that by love their ministries would glorify God and expand joy throughout the world. Jesus even gave his disciples a new title: friends. He only commanded that they keep on loving one another as he loved them. One word said it all: love.

Just One More Reminder

And then, Jesus said it one more time, "I am giving you these commands so that you may love one another" (15:17). While there was only one new commandment, to love, there were supports for that commandment. The first support is a relationship with Jesus. The essential quality of this relationship is abiding. Jesus' disciples are instructed to abide in Jesus' manner of living, to allow his word to abide in them, and

to abide within the spiritual security of Jesus' loving relationship with God. The second support is service to God. The disciples serve God by continuing Jesus' ministry. Such ministry has three (measurable!) outcomes:

- it produces enduring justice, wholeness and peace in the world;
- it glorifies God;
- it completes Jesus' joy among the disciples.

As the disciples abide in Jesus and serve God, they are able to freely, fully, and joyfully love one another. Jesus' new commandment turns out to be an invitation rather than a duty. While loving is rarely composed of easy deeds and simple emotions, loving is its own reward. The disciples of Jesus were to learn the significance of loving one another over and over again. Each new convert was a new person to give, receive, and share the disciples' relationship with Jesus and service to God. As the circles of believers expanded, complexities increased; yet at the heart of every Christian community one commandment continues to be sufficient: Christians, love one another as Jesus loves.

SHARING THE SCRIPTURE

PREPARING TO TEACH

Preparing Our Hearts

This week's devotional reading is found in Psalm 1. In this psalm, the writer encourages us to avoid the way of the wicked and choose the way of the righteous. Note that the righteous are said to "yield their fruit in its season" (1:3). In today's Bible lesson Jesus also talks about the importance of bearing fruit. You may be reading this lesson in a location where snow and cold weather abound, when trees are bare and fruit is definitely not in season. Study a tree or vine. What do you see now? What would

you expect to see during the growing season? What lessons can you take from this comparison concerning how Christians are to relate to Christ?

Pray that you and the adult learners will yield a bountiful crop of spiritual fruit.

Preparing Our Minds

Study the background and lesson Scripture, both of which are taken from John 15:1-17. Think about relationships and ask yourself if there is one that can serve as a model for all others.

Write on newsprint:

❑ questions for "Gather to Learn."

❑ information for next week's lesson, found under "Continue the Journey."

❑ activities for further spiritual growth in "Continue the Journey."

Bring a live potted plant or ask a student to do so.

LEADING THE CLASS

(1) Gather to Learn

❖ Welcome the class members and introduce any guests.

❖ Pray that all of today's participants will be aware of many ways in which Christ guides and protects them.

❖ Invite the students to talk with the class or small group about people who were role models for them as children or teens. Suggest that they consider these questions, which you may want to post on newsprint.

(1) What relationship did these role models have with you? Were they family members, teachers, coaches, neighbors?

(2) What behaviors and/or attitudes did these people model for you?

(3) How are those behaviors and/or attitudes still influencing you?

❖ Read aloud today's focus statement: **We are all born to be in relationship with others, and we need them to be productive. Is there a relationship that can serve as a model for others? John says that being connected to Jesus is essential if we are to be productive in our lives.**

(2) Explore Jesus' Statement That He Is the True Vine

❖ Read John 15:1-17 as if Jesus were speaking to the students.

❖ Distribute paper (preferably unlined) and pencils. Invite the students to sketch a vine, branches, and fruit. Ask them to label the vine "Jesus," the branches using their own name, and the fruit using terms from Galatians 5:22-23: "love, joy, peace, patience, kindness, generosity, faithfulness, gentleness, and self control." Encourage the adults to talk about how the vine, branches, and fruit are interconnected. Consider what happens to the fruit, both physical and spiritual, if it is not securely connected to the vine.

❖ Read or retell "The Necessary Relationship," which includes an anecdote concerning grape-growing.

❖ Look at verses 12-17 and discern what Jesus says here about love. Discuss the relationship between love and bearing fruit. Use information from "Keep on Loving" in Interpreting the Scripture to augment the discussion.

(3) Reflect on the Significance of This Image for the Learners' Faith

❖ Set a live plant on a table before the group. Encourage the students to comment on the health of this plant. Does it appear to be thriving, or has the family dog or a toddler taken chunks out of it? Is it sufficiently watered or looking very dry? If this plant were entered in a county fair, what color ribbon would it win—or would it not win anything?

❖ Ask the students to focus quietly on this plant. Read aloud these reflection questions, pausing after each one.

(1) In what ways does this plant reflect your relationship with Christ?

(2) Imagine yourself as a branch on the vine of Christ. What do you look like? How would you describe your health? Do you, metaphorically speaking, need more water, fertilizer, or sun to become an outstanding specimen? If so, what steps will you take?

(3) What do you need from Christ to nourish you so that you may bear fruit? Ask for whatever you need now.

(4) Pray for a Closer Spiritual Union with Christ

❖ Ask the students to read in unison today's key verse, John 15:5. Encourage the class members to comment on how this verse makes them feel. In the United States, many people prefer to think of themselves as "self-made" and may have real problems imagining that they cannot function apart from God. This verse may be troublesome for some class members. Give them an opportunity to voice their discomfort.

❖ Distribute paper and pencils if you have not already done so. Challenge the students to write a prayer in which they ask to be drawn closer to Christ. Have them consider acknowledging that this intimacy results in healthy spiritual growth. Tell them that they will not be asked to read their prayer aloud, but rather should offer it silently.

(5) Continue the Journey

❖ Break the silence by praying that the adults will remember that Christ offers them secure connections—the branch to the vine—and invite them to do all in their power to keep these connections secure.

❖ Read aloud this preparation for next week's lesson. You may also want to post it on newsprint for the students to copy. **Prepare for next week's session entitled "Love Is Light" by reading 1 John 2:7-17, noting especially verses 7-11, 15-17. With this lesson we begin the spring quarter, "Our Community Now and in God's Future." Keep these ideas in mind as you read: The way individuals treat other people is often a good indication of how they really feel about them. What caution does this raise for us as Christians? John says that we cannot claim to love God and then treat one another shabbily, because love of God and love of neighbor are inseparable. Indeed, we are able to truly love one another because the light of the divine love has made us all children of God.**

❖ Read aloud the following three ideas. Challenge the students to commit themselves to use these activities as a springboard to spiritual growth.

(1) **Research how grapes are grown. What can you learn about the relation between the vine and its fruit? What signs prompt a grower to prune a branch? How is this information helpful as you think about yourself as a branch on the vine of Christ?**

(2) **Think about how you may, through choice or chance, be cut off from a family member or someone else with whom you had a close relationship. What has been lost? What might happen if you reconnect? Try, if possible, to include this person in your life again.**

(3) **Write in your spiritual journal a list of spiritual fruit that you believe you have borne this week. Add a note explaining why a particular action was fruitful.**

❖ Sing or read aloud "I Need Thee Every Hour."

❖ Say this benediction from Jude 24–25 to conclude the session. Include the students by asking them to echo it as you read: **Now to him who is able to keep you from falling, and to make you stand without blemish in the presence of his glory with rejoicing, to the only God our Savior, through Jesus Christ our Lord, be glory, majesty, power, and authority, before all time and now and forever. Amen.**

THIRD QUARTER
Our Community Now and in God's Future

MARCH 4, 2007–MAY 27, 2007

The study for our spring quarter, "Our Community Now and in God's Future," will help us to see ourselves within the context of the community of faith. The purpose of the first unit, which is rooted in 1 John, is to interpret the meaning of God's love for us today. Units 2 and 3 use passages from Revelation to examine the new community that exists in Christ and how that community will live in God's new world.

Unit 1, "Known by Our Love," is four-session unit that explores God's love for us and how it relates to our experiences with one another. The unit begins on March 4 with a session from 1 John 2:7-17, "Love Is Light," which underscores how we live in light when we live in Christ. "Striving for Pure Love," the lesson for March 11 that is based on 1 John 3, helps us understand the importance of love in our relationships with others. On March 18 we turn to 1 John 4:7-21 in a lesson entitled "Showing Divine Love" to recognize God as the source of all love. The unit ends on March 25 with "The Way to Love and Life," a study of 1 John 5:1-12, which helps us understand the connections between love, faith, and eternal life.

The five sessions in Unit 2, "A New Community in Christ," begin on Palm/Passion Sunday, April 1, with a lesson from Revelation 1:1-8 and Luke 19:28-40 entitled "Yielding to Christ's Lordship." The session for April 8, "Discovering Resurrection" delves into both Revelation 1:9-20 and John 20:1-18, 30-31 so that we can hear anew the Easter story. On April 15 we turn to Revelation 4 for a session that teaches us about "Worshiping God Alone," who is worthy of praise. Revelation 5, the focus for the lesson on April 22 entitled "Redeemable," considers the image of Christ our redeemer. We conclude this unit on April 29 with a lesson from Revelation 7, "Source of Security," which focuses on Christ as our protector.

Unit 3, "Living in God's New World," like Unit 2, focuses on the book of Revelation. During these four sessions we will think about what it will mean to live with God in the world that God has prepared for us. The celebration of the marriage feast of the Lamb and his bride is highlighted on May 6 in "Finding Community," a lesson from Revelation 19. On May 13 we delve into Revelation 21:1-8 to envision "The Eternal Home," where we will live free of hunger, thirst, and pain. "Living in Our New Home," the session for May 20 based on Revelation 21:9–22:5, reveals the image of the new city where God is always present. The quarter closes on May 27 with "The Ultimate Happy Ending." In this lesson we will reflect on Christ's return, which will transform everything.

MEET OUR WRITER

DR. DAVID A. deSILVA

David deSilva lives in Ashland, Ohio, where he serves as Trustees' Professor of New Testament and Greek at Ashland Theological Seminary and as music director and organist at Christ United Methodist Church. An ordained elder in the Florida Conference of The United Methodist Church, Dr. deSilva's primary ministries are teaching, writing, sacred music, and raising a family.

DeSilva is the author of eleven books in the area of biblical studies, including *An Introduction to the New Testament: Context, Methods, and Ministry Formation* (Downers Grove: InterVarsity, 2004), *Introducing the Apocrypha* (Grand Rapids: Baker, 2002), *Honor, Patronage, Kinship, and Purity: Unlocking New Testament Culture* (Downers Grove: InterVarsity, 2000), *Perseverance in Gratitude: A Socio-rhetorical Commentary on the Epistle "to the Hebrews"* (Grand Rapids: Eerdmans, 2000), and *New Testament Themes* (St. Louis: Chalice Press, 2001).

He has written several other books for devotional and small group use, including *Praying with John Wesley* (Nashville: Discipleship Resources, 2001), *Paul and the Macedonians* (Nashville: Abingdon Press, 2001), *Afterlife: Finding Hope in the Face of Death* (Nashville: Abingdon Press, 2003), and, together with Emerson Powery of Lee University, a DISCIPLE Short-term Study, *An Invitation to the New Testament* (Nashville: Abingdon Press, 2005). He has contributed more than sixty articles to journals, collections of essays, Bible dictionaries, and Bible commentaries, and wrote the introductions and notes to 1–4 Maccabees and 1–2 Esdras in the *Renovare Spiritual Formation Bible* (San Francisco: HarperSanFrancisco, 2005).

David attended Princeton University, where he earned a Bachelor's degree in English, and then matriculated to Princeton Theological Seminary for the degree of Master of Divinity. In 1995, he was awarded a Ph.D. in Religion from Emory University in Atlanta.

David is married to Donna Jean, his wife of sixteen years. Together they have three marvelous sons: James Adrian, John Austin, and Justin Alexander.

THE BIG PICTURE:
COMMUNITIES IN CRISIS:
THE RECIPIENTS OF 1 JOHN
AND REVELATION

"Community" is increasingly elevated to the status of a core value of corporations, institutions, and, of course, churches. Perhaps you have witnessed occasions where the language of "community" was used to defuse rather than deal directly with difficult disagreements, or to preserve the smooth operations of the status quo rather than risk the kind of conflict that leads to refinement and growth. The New Testament authors had no use for such "community" rhetoric, and least of all the writers of 1 John and Revelation. Here are no white-washed pictures of churches and their members, painted over to look attractive to seekers; rather, here are pictures of congregations in the aftermath of schism, in the grip of competing teachers with incompatible agendas, in the grip of complacent coexistence with Roman imperialism, lacking in love, lacking in life, lacking in courage. If these Christians are going to "have fellowship with one another" and "fellowship with God"—that is, if they are to experience "community"—it will have to be won through careful examination of what holds them together and courageous rededication to living out together their shared mission as the people set apart by God's own choosing to attend to God's witness and purposes in the world.

The First Letter of John is a pastoral letter written to the disciples who remain behind after a significant portion of the congregation left to form a separate church, fracturing the community. The author breathes the same air as the Gospel of John, speaking of the dualities of "light" and "darkness," "truth" and "falsehood," "God" and the "world," and prioritizing "loving" and "abiding." Indeed, 1 John is hardly comprehensible without the larger picture provided by the Fourth Gospel, to which it refers throughout. No doubt the other side in this conversation, the separatists, also drew their inspiration from the Fourth Gospel, which could easily be seen to support their position. (Indeed, it would continue to be used by Gnostics throughout the second century as a primary resource, having to be reclaimed for the orthodox Christian circles with some difficulty on account of its growing association with Gnostic Christianity.) What we witness in 1 John is the end of a long debate about who Jesus is and what it means to follow Jesus, the parting of two divergent streams at the end of the river of first-century Johannine Christianity.

The Elder elevates several major points of disagreement with the separatists, found mainly in the passages that are not featured in our lessons. Several of these focus on the person of Jesus and his relationship to God. The separatists deny "that Jesus is the Christ" (1 John 2:22), more specifically that Jesus was "the Christ having come in the flesh" (1 John 4:2); in so doing, the author asserts, they have lost both the Son and the Father, whom the Son alone reveals (John 1:18). Behind these cryptic references lie the beginnings of Docetic Christianity, a movement that was so intent on preserving the immateriality and impassibility of God (God's freedom from suffering) that they proposed that the "Christ," the divine anointing, came upon Jesus at his baptism and left him just before his death. The man, Jesus, died upon the cross, but not the divine Son, who was above being impacted by events in this material creation. The prologue to John's Gospel, which links the preaching of John the Baptist so closely with the coming of the Word and the Light into the world, could be read to support this alternative biography of Jesus, as could the Baptist's testimony about the Spirit coming upon Jesus only as John's ministry came to its climax (John 1:32-34). Even the most beloved verses of the Fourth Gospel—John 3:16-17—could be read as placing an emphasis on God's *sending* of the Son (that is, as a spirit Being who would enter the human, Jesus, for a brief span of revelation) rather than the *dying* of the Son as that which brings deliverance and life.

The Elder perceived that more was at stake here than "saying the right things" about Jesus. What we say about Jesus has direct implications for how we act as Jesus' followers. It was in the death of the Son—the witness of the blood and the water (1 John 5:6-8)—that God's love for humankind was revealed; *and* it was in the death of the Son that we see the pattern for our own lives, as we are called to lay down our lives for the sake of our sisters and brothers in Christ. True disciples do not follow some spirit being who leads us out from and above the concerns of this material existence, thereby freeing us to ignore the needs of our sisters' and brothers' bodies and circumstances. We follow a dying Christ who empowers us to love one another in and through the pains and challenges of this material existence, to pay special attention to one another's welfare in the here and now. Ultimately, what was at stake was an "embodied" Christ and an "embodied" life of discipleship.

When we turn to Revelation, we cannot forget that we are turning to what is, in effect, another pastoral letter written to specific congregations. Indeed, John the Seer (who is not the same as the author either of the Letters of John or the Fourth Gospel) signals that he is writing a pastoral letter when he writes the typical letter formula: "John to the seven churches that are in Asia: Grace to you and peace . . . " (Revelation 1:4). This grounds Revelation in a specific historical and pastoral setting, and guides us to listen for how it spoke to those Christians living in the cities of the Roman province of Asia Minor as our starting place for interpretation.

It is *how* John chooses to address their congregational challenges that leaves many readers scratching their heads about what this book is supposed to mean. Instead of just laying out his pastoral advice like the author of 1 John, or like Paul in his letters, John the Seer writes in the genre of an apocalypse. Again, this is a signal he clearly gives his readers from the first word in the Greek text: *Apokalypsis Iesou Christou*, "An apocalypse from Jesus Christ" (Revelation 1:1). There are many apocalypses still available from the second century B.C. through the second century A.D. To Daniel and Revelation, we could add 2 *Esdras* (in the Apocrypha), *1 Enoch* (still read as Scripture by the Ethiopic Orthodox churches), the *Shepherd of Hermas* (an immensely popular Christian text from the second century), 2 *Baruch*, the *Apocalypse of Abraham*, and many others. Studying all the available apocalypses helps us understand how our canonical apocalypses were meant to function for their readers.

Apokalypsis means "unveiling." These apocalypses indeed seek to lift the veils that limit their audiences' vision in several ways. First, they lift the veil of the visible sky and allow the hearers to peer into scenes of heavenly worship and other activity; they lift the veil imposed by geographical limitations and allow the hearers to look into infernal regions or the places God has prepared for the reward of the just and punishment of the rebellious. Second, they lift the veil of time that hems human beings in to their "hour upon the stage" so that they can look into the past and into the future. Third, they lift the veil from the realities around the hearers in their everyday world, and allow them to be seen for what they "really are" in the sight of God. In brief, an apocalypse puts the audience's immediate situation in the broader context of a sacred cosmos and a sacred history so as to interpret that immediate situation and identify the "real" needs and challenges of that situation. This is precisely how Revelation works. It allows hearers in each of the seven congregations addressed to "get outside" their situation and the ways in which their society is pressuring them to view their situation long enough to see it all in the light of God's revelation of God's Self, so that they can go back into that situation and respond with faithfulness to God.

The reader of Revelation will notice immediately that this book is full of language taken directly and extensively from Old Testament passages. There is hardly a verse that does not take the reader back into the Old Testament in some way, shape, or form. In this, Revelation is also like other apocalypses. This has led many scholars to view apocalyptic writings as basically an act of interpretation, of reading and re-applying the Scriptures rather than the product of a genuine, ecstatic religious experience (something we scholars rarely experience ourselves). We should never lose sight of the fact that at the heart of Revelation is John's life-long study of his Scriptures, his breathing in and out of their witness to God's character, God's indictment and judgment of domination systems and systemic injustice, and God's liberation of a people from such systems. However, I would also not suggest an either/or approach to the question of how Revelation came to be. First-century Christian religious experience included the awareness of the presence of the Spirit, the gift of inspired utterance, the deliberate seeking of interaction with God in long periods of fasting and prayer (seen most extravagantly in the Jewish apocalypse 2 Esdras 5:13-22; 6:29-37; 9:23-25). We should be wary of imposing our distance from such experiences upon John as he embarked upon his act of "inspired interpretation," the perfect wedding of left-brain and right-brain activity as John applies the witness of Scripture to the social, political, economic, and religious realities of his congregations in the most evocative and imaginative sort of way.

John writes the Revelation toward the end of the first century, near the end of the reign of Domitian (A.D. 81–96). He appears to have exercised the ministry of an itinerant teacher and prophet among the seven congregations he addresses, whose situation he well knows (and which are well spaced for a horseshoe-shaped circuit). At some point, this subversive preacher was removed and exiled to the island of Patmos under the watchful eye of the military garrison there. It is easy to see why, if Revelation is a sample of the kind of message he preached.

We who are so far removed from the situation of the first hearers are often left to speculate wildly about a coming one-world empire under the rule of a deified ruler whose worship is all but mandatory across his domain, but this was the situation for those early Christians since before their births and long after their deaths. This was especially true in Asia Minor, a province that prided itself on fostering the display of honor and loyalty to the emperor in the language and forms of cult and worship. Indeed, Ephesus and Pergamum were locked in a competition for the honor of being named the leading city of the province (the title was *Neokoros*, "temple keeper") in fostering the emperor cult for several decades surrounding the composition of Revelation.

Since Augustus brought unity to the Mediterranean after two devastating civil wars (in which he played no small part), he was hailed as the giver of peace, stability, and the return of prosperity. He was lauded as the instrument of the gods for bestowing their gifts upon humanity. His power and gifts were deemed so great as to merit the forms of gratitude usually reserved for deity, and, indeed, started the trend himself by divinizing his dead adoptive father, Julius Caesar. The emperor cult, which sprang up throughout the eastern Mediterranean at the instigation of local elites rather than at the emperor's request, became an important means by which this religious legitimization of political power was propagated (supported, of course, by festivals, games, well-chosen images on the backs of coins, and the like).

Augustus was also a savvy *imperator* (emperor). Rather than arouse the envy of his fellow senators, as did Julius (ending in Julius's assassination), Augustus wedded his own worship with the worship of the goddess Roma, the personification of the city of Rome and her ruling classes. She, too, was hailed as the city chosen by the gods to bring order, peaceful rule, law, and prosperity to the world through her ever-expanding domination.

Revelation was a direct assault on the political and religious ideology that undergirded Roman imperialism in all its forms, an ideology that had been enjoying a renaissance in the cities of Asia Minor during the reigns of Vespasian (A.D. 69–79) and his sons, Titus (A.D. 79–81) and Domitian (A.D. 81–96) after another series of civil wars devastated the provinces and their resources after the fall of the Julio-Claudian house with the suicide of Nero (68). John refuses to participate in whitewashing Roman rule. Instead, he looks at Roman imperialism from the margins, having seen the voice of Jewish and Christian prophets silenced for their criticism of Rome's self-glorification, having witnessed the economic plunder of the provinces to support the conspicuous consumption of the elites of Rome, and having seen (possibly experienced) the violent and death-dealing ways in which Rome "pacifies" the resistant in the Jewish Revolt of A.D. 66–70.

Revelation lifts the veil from the public image of the goddess Roma, revealing instead a depraved and bloodthirsty whore spreading her contagion across the globe (Revelation 17–18); it lifts the veil from the public image of the emperors, revealing not the agents of peace but the agents of Satan's ongoing campaign against God and God's holy ones (Revelation 12–14). He makes the congregations look up to God's throne and the visions of worshipers surrounding God and the Lamb in ever-widening circles, celebrating God's purposes for humankind in creation (Revelation 4–5), and then confronts them with these visions of subversive rebels offering their worship to idols and to self-proclaimed gods (Revelation 9:20-21; 13:1-18). Weaving together a host of images from Exodus into a new tapestry, he invites the congregations to see that their lives in the midst of that idolatrous society are spent in exile and oppression, and to teach them to witness to God's forthcoming deliverance and God's judgment of all such oppressive structures.

Revelation offers comfort to many Christians in those cities, who experience the rejection of their mother body, the synagogue (Revelation 2:9-10; 3:9), and remember the death of Antipas, who died a martyr's death in Pergamum (Revelation 2:13). But it speaks a word of challenge and rebuke to many other Christians who, reaping the benefits of Rome's exploitative economy, have become far too much at home in Babylon and effectively dead to the Spirit (Revelation 3:1, 16-17). John especially condemns the prophets of compromise, the "Nicolaitans" and "Jezebel" (Revelation 2:14-16, 20-23), who make room for idolatry—and thus support of the legitimization machines of Roman imperialism—so that their followers can claim both Christ and Mammon. John challenges all disciples to find "community" in their identity as God's redeemed and holy ones, in their common witness to God's justice and vision for human society, and in their withdrawal from the tainted prosperity that destroys true community in God.

CLOSE-UP:
EXPLORING REVELATION
THROUGH THE ARTS

The Revelation to John is filled with images that have long fascinated visual artists and musicians. Much is available online that is downloadable and on compact disks to help you make the study of Revelation come alive. Check out the following resources and consider how you might use them. Ideas include:
- ■ playing music as the students enter, meditate, write, or create their own art.
- ■ comparing the art to the portion of Revelation that inspired it, looking at similarities and differences in the details.
- ■ discerning the impact made by the colors, shapes, and placement of objects.
- ■ exploring how images of Revelation have been updated by comparing modern images to those from historical eras

http://myweb.lmu.edu/fjust/Revelation-Art.htm
extensive links to art, music, and other images related to Revelation, compiled by Professor Felix Just, S.J. of Loyola Marymount University

http://camel.conncoll.edu/visual/Durer-prints/index.html
woodcuts by Albrecht Dürer (1471–1528), well known for his "Praying Hands"

http://myweb.lmu.edu/fjust/Dore-Rev.htm
The Doré Bible Gallery, illustrations by Gustave Doré (1832–1883)

http://www.textweek.com/art/revelation.htm
link from "The Text this Week," developed by Professor Felix Just, S.J. of Loyola Marymount University

http://www.catholic-pages.com/bookrack/cd_chant.asp
"1000: A Mass for the End of Time" performed by the Anonymous 4, who revisit the original "millennium madness" with the oldest written Western music known to have survived. This chant from about A.D. 1000 is music written for the Feast of the Ascension, which uses readings from Revelation.

http://www.ambs.edu/LJohns/APJN.htm
resources, including art, that will help you delve into and appreciate Revelation; compiled by Dr. Loren L. Johns

http://www.worshipmusic.com/ptb06.html
"The Bride's Anthem: Adoring Prayers from the Book of Revelation" by Mike Bickle, released in 2000 as part of the Praying the Bible series, which revives the ancient Davidic use of the spoken word set against a background of music

FAITH IN ACTION: CREATING COMMUNITY

Throughout this quarter we will be considering "Our Community Now and in God's Future." We will investigate participation in a loving community life as decribed in 1 John and as envisioned in Revelation. Let's now consider some ways that we can create, nurture, and expand Christian community.

Small Groups

First John focused on God's love and the love that we are to show for one another. Often, that love is best expressed in small groups where "everybody knows your name," and where your joys and sorrows become the joys and sorrows of the group.

Groups serve a variety of functions: education, service, support, fellowship, spiritual formation, prayer. Survey your church to see how many small groups you have and who is included in these groups. How can your Sunday school class serve as a catalyst to create a group for people who are not included in the groups that already exist? Talk about why a particular group is needed, who it would serve, and how it could be created and nurtured. Call on other resource people in the church to help you get the new group(s) publicized, formed, and operating. Much valuable information is available to assist you in developing small group ministries.

Special Events

Does your Sunday school class have any special get-togethers that help the members get to know one another better? Could you have an occasional dinner/cookout/picnic at someone's home? Might you be able to attend a play, concert, or sports event together? Could you go to a park and take a nature walk together? See what kinds of activities would interest your group and then plan fellowship times away from the church. If some members require babysitting service, ask the class to make arrangements for someone to provide childcare at the church and chip in as a group to pay for this care. If the members are not currently getting together outside of class, you may be surprised to see how such times nurture the group and create bonds that go far beyond exchanging pleasantries on Sunday mornings.

Service Projects

Working together for a common cause cements bonds and empowers people to grow in their discipleship as they work to solve problems and enable visions to become realities. How can the adult Sunday school class serve the church? Encourage the students to talk about the needs that they see and how the class might help to meet them. Could the class raise money for something the church needs? Could they paint a room or provide other physical labor to enhance the building and its grounds? Could they do something as ambassadors for the church, perhaps serving as representatives at a neighborhood or ecumenical event? Could they spearhead a church soup kitchen, pantry, or homeless shelter? Could they staff a Parents' Day Out program?

Whatever ways you choose to build community within and beyond your class, the group will be moving more toward the beloved community that joyously experiences God's love and reaches out to others with that love.

UNIT 1: KNOWN BY OUR LOVE
LOVE IS LIGHT

PREVIEWING THE LESSON

Lesson Scripture: 1 John 2:7-11, 15-17
Background Scripture: 1 John 2:7-17
Key Verse: 1 John 2:10

Focus of the Lesson:

The way individuals treat other people is often a good indication of how they really feel about them. What caution does this raise for us as Christians? John says that we cannot claim to love God and then treat one another shabbily, because love of God and love of neighbor are inseparable. Indeed, we are able to truly love one another because the light of the divine love has made us all children of God.

Goals for the Learners:

(1) to summarize John's teachings on love of God and love of others.
(2) to identify how they have experienced God's love through other people.
(3) to name some acts of Christian love and agree to do them.

Pronunciation Guide:

Johannine (joh han' in)
schism (si' zem)

Supplies:

Bibles, newsprint and marker, paper and pencils, hymnals, several pictures from newspapers or magazines illustrating people in need

---

READING THE SCRIPTURE

NRSV

1 John 2:7-11, 15-17

⁷Beloved, I am writing you no new commandment, but an old commandment that you have had from the beginning; the old commandment is the word that you have heard. ⁸Yet I am writing you a new

NIV

1 John 2:7-11, 15-17

⁷Dear friends, I am not writing you a new command but an old one, which you have had since the beginning. This old command is the message you have heard. ⁸Yet I am writing you a new command; its truth is

commandment that is true in him and in you, because the darkness is passing away and the true light is already shining. ⁹Whoever says, "I am in the light," while hating a brother or sister, is still in the darkness. **¹⁰Whoever loves a brother or sister lives in the light, and in such a person there is no cause for stumbling.** ¹¹But whoever hates another believer is in the darkness, walks in the darkness, and does not know the way to go, because the darkness has brought on blindness.

¹⁵Do not love the world or the things in the world. The love of the Father is not in those who love the world; ¹⁶for all that is in the world—the desire of the flesh, the desire of the eyes, the pride in riches—comes not from the Father but from the world. ¹⁷And the world and its desire are passing away, but those who do the will of God live forever.

seen in him and you, because the darkness is passing and the true light is already shining.

⁹Anyone who claims to be in the light but hates his brother is still in the darkness. **¹⁰Whoever loves his brother lives in the light, and there is nothing in him to make him stumble.** ¹¹But whoever hates his brother is in the darkness and walks around in the darkness; he does not know where he is going, because the darkness has blinded him.

¹⁵Do not love the world or anything in the world. If anyone loves the world, the love of the Father is not in him. ¹⁶For everything in the world—the cravings of sinful man, the lust of his eyes and the boasting of what he has and does—comes not from the Father but from the world. ¹⁷The world and its desires pass away, but the man who does the will of God lives forever.

UNDERSTANDING THE SCRIPTURE

1 John 2:7-8. Throughout the first part of this letter, the Elder affirms that his readers remain connected with Jesus, the one who was "from the beginning" (1 John 1:1; 2:13-14; see John 1:1-2), and continue to walk in line with the commandment they received "from the beginning" (2:7), indeed, the commandment they received from Jesus. In the wake of schism, the remaining disciples need to be assured that they remain connected with the authentic gospel and with the bearer of that gospel, and that it was in fact the separatists who strayed from the truth with their innovations. Religious "innovation" was valued negatively in the first century, whereas the renewal of what was "ancient" would be valued quite positively as a message with legitimacy.

Both the Gospel of John and 1 John emphasize the importance of walking in line with Jesus' commandments. First John 2:3-6 has just presented whether or not we

obey Jesus' commandments as the self-check that determines whether or not we "know" Jesus. For the author, Jesus' example is itself the purest expression of these "commandments," the ultimate norm to follow. If we do not walk as Jesus walked, we are not his (2:6).

In Johannine literature, the example of Jesus and the commandments are crystallized in the mandate to "love one another." This is the "old commandment" (compare 1 John 3:11), which stands at the root of the Christian movement, received from Jesus himself (John 13:34-35; 15:12; 2 John 5-6). In *First, Second, and Third John (Interpretation* series), D. Moody Smith suggests that the same command to love one another is also "new" from another point of view. Jesus gave it as the sign and seal of the new age that has dawned with the coming of the light—Christ himself—into the world, relentlessly driving back the darkness.

1 John 2:9-11. At the outset of this letter, the author reminds the congregation that God's character is "light" without any hint of darkness (1:5); similarly God's character is "love" (4:8). The essence of discipleship is to grow into the character of Christ (2:6) and into the character of God (3:3; 4:7). John challenges his readers by stating that the display of lack of love reveals far more about the one who hates than about the one who is hated. Light and darkness is an important antithesis in Johannine literature. Darkness characterizes the age that is passing away; light characterizes the life that Jesus brings (see John 8:12). Whether or not one loves one's fellow Christians as Jesus loves us reveals to which age one belongs. First John 2:11 so closely echoes John 12:35 that the author is probably trying to make a deliberate, interpretive connection: The love of fellow Christians is the ongoing manifestation of the "light" that was with the first disciples in the person of Jesus. Loving one's fellow Christians as Christ loved us produces the same beneficial effects of Christ's presence in the midst of the first disciples—we see clearly where we are going.

1 John 2:12-14. Most translations represent the repeated formula in these verses as "I write to you *because*," as if the author is naming all the motives or reasons he has for writing to them now. But it is equally possible to translate the phrase as "I write to you *that*," as the word is frequently translated after verbs of saying, knowing, believing, perceiving, and other verbs which naturally lead the hearer to expect the "content" associated with the verb to be given.

The pastoral situation addressed by the author might indeed have led its first hearers to interpret these verses in the second way, as the author's words of assurance written to the Christians whose faith in themselves and confidence in their "rightness with God" were shaken by the allegations and departure of their former comrades. He writes to them reminding

them of their spiritual state, a state that remains unchanged by the separatists' rejection of them and breach of the bond of love. (Indeed, it was the spiritual state of the separatists that has shown itself to have changed by their departure; see 1 John 2:18-19.)

The author refers to all the addressees, who are all the Elder's spiritual wards, as "children." The same use of "children" is seen in 2:18; 3:18; 5:21, all addressed to the whole church as those under the spiritual protection and guidance of the author. Within this group, there are the senior members—the "fathers," a gender-specific term for all those who would be mothers and fathers in the faith—and the junior members, the newer generation of Christians who have been given "new birth" through the midwifery of the first generation that connected them to the traditions about Jesus and the new life Jesus brings.

The affirmations are all keyed in closely to the message of the epistle. Forgiveness of sins is underscored early in the epistle (1:8–2:2) as a benefit mediated to disciples by Jesus, and one that is clearly seen as dependent upon our "walk(ing) in the light," that is, in love with one another (1:7). It is not at all difficult to hear behind this also the sayings of Jesus that link the enjoyment of God's forgiveness with our willingness to forgive one another (Matthew 6:12, 14-15), a function of love (see 1 Peter 4:8). The community is connected with the One "who is from the beginning" (1 John 2:13), namely Jesus, and it is the seasoned disciples who guarantee this continuity in the wake of the schism: Their memory reaches back behind the separatists' innovations and questioning of the community's beliefs, anchoring the whole community in the reliable witness of the apostles.

"Conquering" is also an important affirmation (2:13). Many forces are "conquered" in 1 John: the Devil (2:13-14); "them" (4:4), namely the "false prophets" (4:1) who have gone out into the world (the separatists, who have left the congregation and "gone out," 2:18-19); "the world" (5:4-5). The Elder has aligned all of these forces, reassuring the disciples "left behind" by the separatists that they were right to resist them—indeed, that this is a triumph in the face of a hard test.

1 John 2:15-17. The "world" is seen here entirely in its negative aspect, but not as a geographical space or as the population outside the church. In regard to the latter, the author will speak of Jesus as the "Savior of the world" (4:14), just as the evangelist will speak of God's great love for "the world" (John 3:16-17). Rather, he uses the term "world" to name those potent forces at work within and behind our everyday experience, drawing people away from yielding completely to God's love for them and allowing God's love and love for God to direct their whole life. The author uses a simple argument from the consequences to promote his admonition against allowing "love of the world" to drive one's life. Since the inception of the age of light, the world, like the darkness, is passing away and coming to nothing (2:17).

INTERPRETING THE SCRIPTURE

Loving Is Not Optional

The Fourth Gospel and 1 John both balance their emphasis on the aspect of personal decision for Christ (believing in the Son of God, John 20:30-31) with a great deal of attention to the changed life and quality of relationships that must characterize those who believe. For these early Christian leaders, following Jesus is not about private morality, nor about personal creed. It is about the blossoming of the community of disciples through loving relationships. It is about living out the triumph of Jesus as the triumph of love over hatred, light over darkness.

Lest we think this to be optional, Jesus confronts us with it as "commandment" and as a necessary sign that we "love" him (John 14:15, 21; 15:10; 1 John 2:3-8). I cannot "come to the garden alone" and pretend to love Jesus if I do not show love for each fellow-Christian I encounter on the way to that garden. My love for fellow believers is, in the end, the essential proof that I have been born of God and have moved out from the darkness (2:9-11; 4:7-8).

If we turn to the Jesus traditions outside of Johannine texts, the mandate is far more demanding. There, we are summoned to "love our neighbor" and even "love our enemies" indiscriminately (Matthew 5:43-48; 22:39). The Elder sets a more modest beginning before us, a more "manageable" step: Love the sisters and brothers, one's fellow Christians. This was not just a situational need growing out of the pain of schism, a short-term modification of Jesus' commandment to "love the neighbor" and "love the enemies" while the hurt congregation recovered. It is part and parcel of the entire Johannine tradition, commended to us as a place to begin to learn how to love as Jesus loved.

Loving one's fellow Christians is a sign of the dawning of the new age, the triumph of the light over the darkness (2:8). Behind the command to love is the power of God's decisive breaking into our world with God's own love in the Son. Loving another is therefore never impossible: It is fueled by God's own love and assured by God's victory over the darkness, enabling us to love in a more energetic, self-invested, and optimistic way.

Our Relationships Reveal Our Nature

People tend to look for reasons to love someone. We tend to have a series of tests that a person must "pass" or standards that a person must meet in order to be found worthy of our love. I think that we also tend to develop reasons to justify hating someone, excluding them from our love and care based on perceived deficiencies *in them.* The Elder turns this around on us in a most disconcerting way. Our failure to love a fellow believer reveals a deficiency *in us,* that we are still "in the darkness," and deceiving ourselves about being "in the light"—that is, about being genuine followers of Jesus.

What do we see when we look at each particular sister or brother who crosses our path? Do we see someone who potentially advances or hinders our getting what we want? When they displease us, do we respond with resentment and withdrawal of love and care? When this happens, we are to regard it as a warning about our own spiritual state; indeed, as a summons to draw close to the Light, asking God to so fill us with divine love that we can see our Christian sister or brother anew in the light of God's love and walk in love toward him or her.

Making Wise Love Investments

"The world is too much with us"—the poet Wordsworth's complaint was also the Elder's complaint as he considered the ways in which people's lives were driven by their covetous desire for what they saw, their impulses toward self-gratification, and their dead-end quest to establish their value and their "permanence" through the acquisition of goods, power, and respected office. The Greek behind the phrase "the pride of life" uses the word "life" in much the same way as we would in the colloquialism, "get a life!" Get in line with the lifestyle that society promotes as the mark of a person worth our time and attention! The Elder is deeply concerned lest these drives continue to operate within the believers. "Loving the world" in this sense of allowing the values of our addiction-forming, death-dealing society to capture our ambitions and direct our lives pushes out the love of the Father.

The Elder calls us to examine ourselves. What drives you? To what extent is it the love for "the things in the world" (2:15) (acquisitiveness, self-serving indulgence, pride in our position or wealth or status)? To what extent is your daily life shaped by the love you have for God? The Elder speaks of the world and God as forces that can exert tremendous influence upon us. Do your drives and direction come from what you have internalized from the world, or what you have internalized from your experience of God?

We hear much about making wise investments for the future, whether in connection with putting our children through college, with throwing our lives into our careers with a view to advancement, with retirement accounts and mutual funds to build up a secure financial future. The Elder calls us to live out of an entirely different model: discerning and doing the will of God, rather than the will of "the world" whether that confronts us from outside ourselves or wells up from inside our flesh. This means drawing close to God's love, and so internalizing that experience of God's love that it becomes the fire that drives our lives. The Elder doesn't have to give a lot of specific rules about what that will look like. It will show up in an abundance of love and acts of kindness toward our fellow Christians (3:11-24). That will be a great step in the right direction, and enough guidance for now. Disciples have "an anointing from above" (the Holy Spirit, 2:27; see John 14:15-17, 25-26; 16:12-13), and the Elder trusts that Spirit to flesh out the details in the contexts of our own lives.

SHARING THE SCRIPTURE

PREPARING TO TEACH

Preparing Our Hearts

This week's devotional reading is found in 1 Peter 4:1-11. Here we are reminded to live as people who experience the grace of God. In verse 8, Peter writes that the most important action we can take is to "maintain constant love for one another." Love is a noun, signifying a strong, positive emotion; but it is also a verb and, therefore, calls us to act "so that God may be glorified in all things through Jesus Christ" (4:11). As you honestly examine yourself, discern how God's love is being manifested in your life and shared with others. Do you believe that Christ would say you are truly walking in his light? If not, what steps do you need to take?

Pray that you and the adult learners will be open channels through which God's love can flow.

Preparing Our Minds

Study the background Scripture, 1 John 2:7-17 and lesson Scripture, verses 7-11, 15-17. Consider cautions that are raised for us as Christians when we recognize that how we treat others is a good indication of how we feel about them.

Write on newsprint:
❏ information for next week's lesson, found under "Continue the Journey."
❏ activities for further spiritual growth in "Continue the Journey."

Locate at least one picture from a magazine or newspaper showing people in need. Select additional pictures if the class is large.

Plan how you will cover the information suggested under "Summarize John's Teachings on Love of God and Love of Others."

Review the introduction to the quarter; the "Big Picture" article entitled "Communities in Crisis: The Recipients of 1 John and Revelation"; the "Close-up" article, "Exploring Revelation Through the Arts"; and the "Faith in Action" article, "Creating Community," all of which directly precede this lesson. Decide how you will use each of these helps either for this lesson or in subsequent sessions.

LEADING THE CLASS

(1) Gather to Learn

❖ Welcome the class members and introduce any guests.

❖ Pray that all who have gathered will have open hearts and receptive minds as they consider the meaning of this lesson.

❖ Distribute paper and pencils. Read aloud these statements and ask the students to write briefly about how they would respond and/or how they would feel.

■ **You accidentally leave a newly pur-chased book on the sales counter and your friend says, "You certainly are forgetful."**

■ **You have been carefully watching your diet but decide to splurge on a sinful dessert at a restaurant. Your friend says, "If I were as over-weight as you are, I wouldn't dream of eating dessert."**

■ **You invite a friend to a concert, but he begs off, saying he must work. Later you learn that this same friend was attending a party at the home of a mutual friend.**

❖ Invite the students to share their responses with the class. Talk about how other peoples' actions and words reflect how they feel about you.

❖ Read aloud today's focus statement: **The way individuals treat other people is** often a good indication of how they really feel about them. **What caution does this raise for us as Christians?** John says that we cannot claim to love God and then treat one another shabbily, because love of God and love of neighbor are inseparable. Indeed, we are able to truly love one another because the light of the divine love has made us all children of God.

(2) Summarize John's Teachings on Love of God and Love of Others

❖ Begin by giving an overview of this quarter's lessons. The quarterly introduction, found prior to this lesson, will help you do that.

❖ Introduce this quarter's theme by highlighting excerpts from "The Big Picture: Communities in Crisis: The Recipients of 1 John and Revelation" found prior to this session.

❖ Enlist a volunteer to read 1 John 2:7-11.

■ Use Scripture verses found in Understanding the Scripture for verses 7-8 and 9-11, as well as "Loving Is Not Optional" in Interpreting the Scripture, to unpack the meanings of "from the beginning," walking in the light of Jesus, and new commandment/old commandment. You may choose to cover this information in a discussion or a lecture.

■ Ask the class to read in unison today's key verse, 2:10. Provide time for the participants to meditate on how this verse applies to their own lives.

■ Read or retell "Relationships Reveal Our Nature" to help the students further probe what Jesus means when he talks about living "in the light." Hear their comments on this reading.

❖ Choose someone to read 1 John 2:15-17.

■ Encourage the class to give concrete examples of how people "love the world." List ideas on newsprint. Use ideas from "Making Wise Love Investments" in Interpreting the Scripture to augment the discussion.

■ Invite the students to talk with a small group or partner to answer these questions: **What drives you? To what extent is the motivating force in your life the love for "the things in the world" (2:15).**

(3) Give Examples of How the Learners Have Experienced God's Love through Other People

❖ Select one person to begin a class story by telling about a time when someone else showed God's love toward him or her. This should be a brief story that gets to the point quickly. For example, someone might say, *"Last summer when I had a heart attack, members of this church visited me in the hospital, brought food to my house, and helped my spouse with yard chores that I was unable to do then."*

❖ Ask someone else to build on this story by saying, *"That reminds me of the time when . . ."* and then tell his or her story.

❖ Repeat this sequence until everyone who wishes to contribute to the class story has had an opportunity to do so.

❖ Wrap up this segment of the lesson by asking the students to comment on common themes that they heard. Ask if these themes suggest ways that we can help others to experience God's love.

(4) Name Some Acts of Christian Love and Agree to Do Them

❖ Show at least one picture from a magazine or newspaper of people in need. These people may be suffering the effects of a natural disaster, victims of war or violence, or experiencing a personal crisis.

❖ Brainstorm a list of actions that Christians could take to show God's love by helping people in similar circumstances.

❖ **Option:** If the class is so large that it would be difficult for everyone to see one picture, divide into groups, give each group a picture, newsprint, and a marker so that they can brainstorm within the group. Call the groups back together to report on their ideas.

❖ Challenge the students to make a commitment to take one or more actions in love to help those in need. Lead those who are willing to make a commitment to say: **With your help, O God, we will act as ambassadors of your love.**

(5) Continue the Journey

❖ Pray that the students will go forth reflecting the light of God's love to illumine the path for those who walk in darkness.

❖ Read aloud this preparation for next week's lesson. You may also want to post it on newsprint for the students to copy. **Prepare for next week's session entitled "Striving for Pure Love" by reading 1 John 3, and focusing on verses 11-24. Direct your attention to these ideas as you read: Even people who love each other sometimes react angrily or harshly to one another. When we fail to show pure love to one another, what does that say about us as Christians? John acknowledges that we are all prone to such emotional lapses, yet he encourages us to keep striving for purity**

in our love—**because it is by our overall abiding love that God judges us, not by our occasional failures.**

❖ Read aloud the following three ideas. Challenge the students to commit themselves to use these activities as a springboard to spiritual growth.

(1) **Locate a book or article on Howard Thurman, Martin Luther King, Jr., or someone else who has used love as a strategy to work toward peace and justice. How do the methods this person used in order to bring about change reflect the light and love of Christ?**

(2) **Identify someone with whom you have a rocky relationship. What changes can you make to improve this relationship so that you are truly walking in the light?**

(3) **Think seriously about your "pride in riches" (1 John 2:16). How is this attitude hampering your relationship with God? What steps will you take to distance yourself from "the things in the world" (2:15)?**

❖ Sing or read aloud "Let There Be Light."

❖ Say this benediction to conclude the session. You may wish to ask the students to echo it as you read: **Go in peace to love God and your neighbor, both in truth and in action.**

UNIT 1: KNOWN BY OUR LOVE
STRIVING FOR PURE LOVE

PREVIEWING THE LESSON

Lesson Scripture: 1 John 3:11-24
Background Scripture: 1 John 3
Key Verse: 1 John 3:2

Focus of the Lesson:

Even people who love each other sometimes react angrily or harshly to one another. When we fail to show pure love to one another, what does that say about us as Christians? John acknowledges that we are all prone to such emotional lapses, yet he encourages us to keep striving for purity in our love—because it is by our overall abiding love that God judges us, not by our occasional failures.

Goals for the Learners:

(1) to analyze John's teachings on how Christians are to relate to one another.
(2) to discern ways they can express God's love for others.
(3) to identify ways for coping with ill will and hatred and to agree to implement these ways daily.

Supplies:

Bibles, newsprint and marker, paper and pencils, hymnals

READING THE SCRIPTURE

NRSV
1 John 3:2, 11-24

²**Beloved, we are God's children now; what we will be has not yet been revealed.**

¹¹For this is the message you have heard from the beginning, that we should love one another. ¹²We must not be like Cain who was from the evil one and murdered his brother. And why did he murder him? Because his own deeds were evil and his brother's righteous. ¹³Do not be astonished, brothers and sisters, that the world hates

NIV
1 John 3:2, 11-24

²**Dear friends, now we are children of God, and what we will be has not yet been made known.**

¹¹This is the message you heard from the beginning: We should love one another. ¹²Do not be like Cain, who belonged to the evil one and murdered his brother. And why did he murder him? Because his own actions were evil and his brother's were righteous. ¹³Do not be surprised, my brothers,

you. ¹⁴We know that we have passed from death to life because we love one another. Whoever does not love abides in death. ¹⁵All who hate a brother or sister are murderers, and you know that murderers do not have eternal life abiding in them. ¹⁶We know love by this, that he laid down his life for us—and we ought to lay down our lives for one another. ¹⁷How does God's love abide in anyone who has the world's goods and sees a brother or sister in need and yet refuses help?

¹⁸Little children, let us love, not in word or speech, but in truth and action. ¹⁹And by this we will know that we are from the truth and will reassure our hearts before him ²⁰whenever our hearts condemn us; for God is greater than our hearts, and he knows everything. ²¹Beloved, if our hearts do not condemn us, we have boldness before God; ²²and we receive from him whatever we ask, because we obey his commandments and do what pleases him.

²³And this is his commandment, that we should believe in the name of his Son Jesus Christ and love one another, just as he has commanded us. ²⁴All who obey his commandments abide in him, and he abides in them. And by this we know that he abides in us, by the Spirit that he has given us.

if the world hates you. ¹⁴We know that we have passed from death to life, because we love our brothers. Anyone who does not love remains in death. ¹⁵Anyone who hates his brother is a murderer, and you know that no murderer has eternal life in him.

¹⁶This is how we know what love is: Jesus Christ laid down his life for us. And we ought to lay down our lives for our brothers. ¹⁷If anyone has material possessions and sees his brother in need but has no pity on him, how can the love of God be in him? ¹⁸Dear children, let us not love with words or tongue but with actions and in truth. ¹⁹This then is how we know that we belong to the truth, and how we set our hearts at rest in his presence ²⁰whenever our hearts condemn us. For God is greater than our hearts, and he knows everything.

²¹Dear friends, if our hearts do not condemn us, we have confidence before God ²²and receive from him anything we ask, because we obey his commands and do what pleases him. ²³And this is his command: to believe in the name of his Son, Jesus Christ, and to love one another as he commanded us. ²⁴Those who obey his commands live in him, and he in them. And this is how we know that he lives in us: We know it by the Spirit he gave us.

UNDERSTANDING THE SCRIPTURE

1 John 3:1-3. God's love for the disciples is shown in the tremendous gift of adoption into God's own family, an act of love that has changed our natures: We are not just "called" God's children, but "we are." Like most children, we do not now know what we will be when we grow up, but we know it will be good and marvelous, because we are growing into the likeness of the Son (compare Ephesians 4:11-13, where again it is only in the loving community of disciples that the "full stature of Christ" is reached by all, together). When we see Christ as he is,

we will no longer fall short of his mark (see 1 Corinthians 13:12, where Paul expresses a similar hope). In the meanwhile, we are summoned to live in line with our destiny, giving attention to our spiritual formation into Christ-likeness (2:6; 3:3, 16). There is another side to having been made God's family: Our difference from "the world" is also thereby established, and the same hostility against Jesus' witness exists where his witnesses continue Jesus' work (3:1b-2).

1 John 3:4-10. The Elder calls disciples to one essential facet of embodied discipleship: sanctification. Sin, lawlessness, and injustice have no place in the disciple's life, for to make room for these things is to act against Jesus' whole purpose in dying on our behalf. The author knows that disciples will commit sin, and has made provision for that in 1:8–2:2. But he also knows that as the disciples keep drawing closer to God—as the direction of their lives and hearts is God-ward rather than world-ward—God's light will drive back the shadows of sin in our lives more and more, and will drive us to love one another more and more. Continued commitment to make room for sin in all its forms ultimately reveals that our hearts have not been transformed by God, that we have not yielded to God's love and the ways in which that love and light change our very nature.

1 John 3:11-15. The author clarifies here that the message held onto "from the beginning" was Jesus' command to love each other (John 13:34-35; 15:12-13). The antitype of brotherly love is, of course, Cain (Genesis 4:1-10). The situation of Christian brothers and sisters breaking the bond of family love, with the separatists enacting their hatred and rejection of those who remained faithful to the Elder's teaching, makes the conflict between Cain and Abel an appropriate scriptural background. Scripture is silent concerning the reason that God approved Abel's sacrifice while rejecting Cain's, though intertestamental traditions about Cain developed the hint, seen in Genesis 4:7a, that Cain's moral state had something to do with the unacceptability of his offerings. The Elder assumes this interpretation (1 John 3:12b). When confronted with the truth about his own standing in God's sight, Cain allowed envy and resentment against his brother to lead him to one great act: murdering Abel in order to reassert his own value in his own eyes. Rarely do Christians murder each other, but too frequently they imitate Cain's strategy for self-affirmation—harboring resentment and enmity toward a fellow Christian,

affirming oneself by rejecting and tearing down another. This kind of behavior is appropriate for "the world," which has not known the love of God and its transforming power, but not for the community of God's children.

1 John 3:16-18. The author refers to the tradition found in John 15:12-13 that loving one another entails self-sacrificial service as modeled by Jesus in his death on behalf of the community of disciples. New Testament authors consistently teach that the measure of Christ's love for us, and Christ's willingness to pour himself out completely for us, is the model for the disciples in their relationships with one another (Mark 8:34-35; John 15:12-13; Ephesians 5:1-2). A close corollary is that we are to serve one another as Christ humbled himself, set aside his own interests, and took on the role of a servant for us (Mark 10:41-45; John 13:12-17; Philippians 2:1-11).

Jesus taught that genuine love is love in action, seen in the parable of the good Samaritan, where love of the neighbor expresses itself in seeing the very real, pressing, physical and personal needs of another human being and meeting them out of one's own resources. Jesus' half-brother James would remind the churches of this truth as well (see James 1:27; 2:15-17), and in details very close to what we find here. Echoing the teaching of Deuteronomy that a tight fist is a sign of a hard heart (see Deuteronomy 15:7-8, 11), the Elder admonishes the disciples to open up their hands to their needy neighbors within the family of God, by means of which we participate in the breaking forth of God's love into the lives of our sisters and brothers. We lay our lives down for our sisters and brothers one meal, one garment, one hour of showing compassion at a time.

Performing in our actions what we profess with our lips is the means by which to make our profession real in our own lives and credible to others.

1 John 3:19-24. Remembering the

pastoral needs of the audience's situation, we can readily understand why they would question themselves in their hearts about their rightness with God. Brothers and sisters of long-standing have just left their congregation, no doubt because they had come to find continued association with their unenlightened comrades incompatible with their new understanding of the faith. Those who were left, then, would have had ample cause to doubt themselves, especially if the separatists kept sending out missionaries (the "false prophets" of 4:1-6; 2 John 7-11) to draw whomever they could away from the old congregations. There is really no way for them to assure themselves that one's convictions about Jesus are one-hundred percent correct, based as they are on debated interpretations of John's Gospel. But the presence of God's love working through their hearts to become embodied in acts of mutual love and service was hard, physical evidence that God was in their midst and that they remained rooted in God, whatever the separatists claimed.

Confidence before God will enable even more fruitful ministry. The promises about receiving whatever we ask for in prayer have been among the most widely misused verses in Scripture. Despite James's warning that God does not lavish bounty upon us to use for our own self-gratification (James 4:3-4, in terms strikingly reminiscent of the Elder's warning that love for the world and love for God are incompatible), many have preached the opposite. The Elder's assurance is for those who are so committed to allowing God's love to reach through them to the needs of their sisters and brothers, who pray not in line with their own desires, but for the resources and opportunities to "love . . . in truth and in action" (3:18).

INTERPRETING THE SCRIPTURE

Like Parent, Like Child

Classical and Roman period authors speak about children as being like their parents in regard to both their outward appearance and inward character. The Elder shares in this expectation that the disciples, who have been born of God, will come to resemble their Parent more and more in their inward character and their outward actions, particularly as this likeness is reflected in the God-made-Flesh, Jesus (see also Matthew 5:43-48; Luke 6:35-36; Ephesians 4:32–5:1; 1 Peter 1:14-17). He calls us to walk in line with our destiny, seeking to reflect the purity of God's character of light and love as fully as possible (1 John 1:5).

Imagine a light shining in the center of a room. If we move back from it, we are in a dim place and our shadow—our darker part—is quite long. As we move closer and closer to that light, our space becomes brighter and our shadow shrinks. Underneath the light, our shadow is at its smallest. In the light, the shadow would cease to exist. The Elder's vision for the children of God is similar. As we "abide" in Jesus and in the Father (see John 15:1-11; 1 John 3:24; 4:13-17), drawing close to God, God's love keeps filling our lives. As we remain with the Father, we become like what we observe in him (much as we patterned our lives and formed our selves by observing our natural parents, for better and worse). We are made able to love, and thus not to sin, by keeping ourselves firmly fixed in the Father's love.

Give No Ground to Resentment

Cain is the antitype of love because he took his brother's life in an effort to restore, in some bizarre way, his own sense of self-worth. Jesus, as the exemplar of genuine love, laid down his life to give value and life to others. Cain exemplifies the mind-set of the "limited goods" economy, where someone else's gain is my loss and my loss can only be reversed by diminishing someone else. When someone provokes us, making us to feel like we are not receiving our due, or making us feel diminished in some way, we may be tempted to respond like Cain. Of course, we shall be far more subtle than he, but we will still, one way or another, reassert our own sense of value by diminishing the offender. Perhaps we will do this through gossip, diminishing our opponent's standing in other people's eyes. Or we will do it by watching for an opportunity to impede his or her plans down the road. Or we will simply do it by turning him or her into an object for our hate, our contempt, our enmity.

But there is another way to deal with these encounters, one more productive of spiritual maturity. We can receive the chafing as an opportunity from God to examine our own hearts. How does our sense of being provoked provide us with an opportunity to identify a place for growth in spiritual maturity? Does it reveal pride, or a self-serving agenda, a lack of humility on our part? Can we embrace it as such rather than shut our hearts to the indictment that "our works were evil" by shutting our hearts against the sister or brother?

One practical aspect of laying down our lives for our sisters and brothers may involve laying down our desire to hit back, to get back at someone, to fill ourselves up again by diminishing our sister or brother. Instead, we can approach the matter like siblings in a healthy family system, owning any part of the injury that comes from our own self-serving agendas or pride and naming the experience of hurt that came from the encounter, thus opening up a window for mutual confession, forgiveness, and restoration.

True Love

The person who walks down the street of a major city is confronted by the sight of so many people in need that she would never make it more than five blocks in the course of the day if she attempted to attend to each person's or family's need as did the exemplar of love for neighbor in the parable of the good Samaritan. Moreover, she would easily spend more than a day's wages on those needs with nothing left for herself by the end of the day. Perhaps it is the overwhelming awareness of need that has led so many people to block out the sight of the needy altogether, so that they could get through the day and carry on with their "normal" lives. The Elder's more limited designation of the Christian community as a laboratory of love, where we can learn to love as God loves by loving one another well, may be a necessary place to begin.

What would it look like to live out Jesus' command to "love our neighbor as ourselves," to "love one another," within the community of disciples? It would still challenge so much of what we have been led to want for ourselves, and been trained to do in our own interest, by "the world." It is "normal" to put our own accumulation of wealth for tomorrow ahead of the relief of a fellow Christian's need today; to put our enjoyment of the "privacy of our homes" above providing shelter for a fellow Christian who is without a home, or faces domestic violence at her own home; to save our free time for ourselves and our families rather than using it to mentor a brother's or sister's teenager who is making self-destructive life choices; to entrust time-consuming care for the elderly to the paid professionals rather than arrange our lives around the aging family member. But how is such a "normal" life in any way conducive to loving one's neighbor—even limited now to our sisters and brothers in Christ—as oneself?

If we accept that God has made us all

God's own "children," we are challenged to accept the full implications of the corollary: The church universal is one family of sisters and brothers, with all the benefits and duties appertaining thereto. A wider definition of "family," if it is to be a real family in any sense ("in truth and action," 3:18), means accepting a wider circle of mutual responsibility as "normal." Again it comes down to "seeing." If I see another Christian as a member of my family, the family God has brought together, I will naturally love him or her "in truth and in action" to the best of my ability, and the local community of disciples will work together like a family to meet the more daunting needs. We will "lay down our lives"—our time, our money, our desires for ourselves—for one another, to meet one need at a time. The Elder asserts that our own sense of being God's sons and daughters will be proportionately more real to the extent that we respond to the needs of our fellow Christians as we do to the needs of our own family.

SHARING THE SCRIPTURE

PREPARING TO TEACH

Preparing Our Hearts

This week's devotional reading is found in 1 Corinthians 13. In this beloved chapter Paul writes about the gift of love. Even if you know his words from memory, read these thirteen verses as if you have never seen them before. What does this chapter tell you about what love is? What does it tell you about what love is not? If Jesus were to rate you on a scale of one to ten on how you fulfill Paul's mandate to love, what might your rating be? What habits do you need to change to move closer to a "ten"?

Pray that you and the adult learners will strive to love as God loves.

Preparing Our Minds

Study the background Scripture from 1 John 3 and lesson Scripture, verses 11-24. Consider this question as you study: When we fail to show pure love to one another, what does that say about us as Christians?

Write on newsprint:

❑ information for next week's lesson, found under "Continue the Journey."

❑ activities for further spiritual growth in "Continue the Journey."

Plan the lecture suggested under "Analyze John's Teachings on How Christians Are to Relate to One Another."

LEADING THE CLASS

(1) Gather to Learn

❖ Welcome the class members and introduce any guests.

❖ Pray that those who have gathered today will be open to the leading of the Holy Spirit as we study and fellowship together.

❖ Enlist three volunteers to role-play this scenario: **You are adult siblings who generally get along well. Your father has previously died and your mother's funeral was held last week. As you sit in her lawyer's office and hear her will read, you learn that she has left all of her considerable resources to one grandchild who has a disability to cover medical and other expenses for life. One sibling, who is the parent of this child, reacts with overwhelming gratitude. The second sibling is disappointed but accepts the will. The third sibling is outraged, having** already planned to spend what he or she thought would be his or her share of the estate.

❖ Provide time for the class members to comment on what they have seen and heard.

❖ Read aloud today's focus statement: **Even people who love each other sometimes react angrily or harshly to one another. When we fail to show pure love to one another, what does that say about us as Christians? John acknowledges that we are all prone to such emotional lapses, yet he encourages us to keep striving for purity in our love—because it is by our overall abiding love that God judges us, not by our occasional failures.**

(2) Analyze John's Teachings on How Christians Are to Relate to One Another

❖ Invite the class to read in unison today's key verse, 1 John 3:2.

■ Read aloud "Like Parent, Like Child" in Interpreting the Scripture.

■ Prompt the class to talk about (1) how they perceive themselves to be God's children and (2) the kinds of actions and attitudes they expect to be revealed in them as they live as God's children.

❖ Select a volunteer to read 1 John 3:11-17.

■ Present a brief lecture based on verses 11-15 in Understanding the Scripture and the first paragraph of "Give No Ground to Resentment" in Interpreting the Scripture. Use this information to help the students understand why Cain represents the opposite of love.

■ Invite the students to comment on Cain's apparent belief that someone else's gain is my loss and my loss can only be reversed by diminishing someone else. Encourage them to name examples of behaviors that result from this kind of thinking.

❖ Choose someone to read 1 John 3:18-24.

■ Compare verses 18 to James 1:27 and 2:15-17.

■ Talk about how your congregation acts to help those in need. Ask the students to give specific examples.

■ Read aloud the second paragraph of "True Love" in Interpreting the Scripture. Invite the students to respond to the questions in that paragraph.

■ Conclude this portion of the session by asking the students to read silently John 15:1-14, where Jesus himself speaks about abiding in him and loving one another. Discuss how his words relate to the Elder's writings in 1 John 3:18-24.

(3) Discern Ways the Learners Can Express God's Love for Others

❖ Ask the students to name any tragedies that are currently in the news, locally, nationally, or globally.

❖ Brainstorm ways that class members could help those who are coping with these tragedies.

❖ Plan to take action. Perhaps different class members will tackle different situations, individually or in small groups. Or, the class may work together. Whatever the decision, help them to discern what they will do, how they will do it, and when they expect to accomplish this work. Agree on a date to report back on their actions and display a sign reminding the students of this date.

(4) Identify Ways for Coping with Ill Will and Hatred and Agree to Implement These Ways Daily

❖ Remind the students that Cain coped with ill will toward Abel by killing him. Distribute paper and pencils and ask each person to write a paragraph telling about how he or she coped with ill will or hatred in a Christ-like way. Tell the class that some of the stories will be read aloud, though not by the author. Ask them not to sign their names or use the real names of the people involved.

❖ Collect the papers, shuffle them, and redistribute them. Call on several volunteers to read the stories that have been given to them.

❖ Ask the students to comment on any strategies that seemed particularly helpful.

❖ Invite those who are willing to implement any of these strategies to raise their hands as a sign of commitment.

(5) Continue the Journey

❖ Pray that the participants will continue to reflect on what it means to love God and live out that love.

❖ Read aloud this preparation for next week's lesson. You may also want to post it on newsprint for the students to copy. **Prepare for next week's session entitled "Showing Divine Love" by reading 1 John 4:7-21, which is both the background and lesson Scripture. Concentrate on these** ideas as you read: As human beings, we need several kinds of love to become healthy, whole persons. What is the source of our ability to love one another with divine love? John says our love for one another comes from God, who first loved us, and from the Spirit who abides with us.

❖ Read aloud the following three ideas. Challenge the students to commit themselves to use these activities as a springboard to spiritual growth.

(1) **Perform a random act of kindness for a stranger to demonstrate God's love.**

(2) **Collect food and/or clothing from your home and donate it to your church pantry or a local charity that passes on these goods to those who need them.**

(3) **Respond in love when a church member says or does something that causes you to take offense.**

❖ Sing or read aloud "The Gift of Love."

❖ Say this benediction to conclude the session. You may wish to ask the students to echo it as you read: **Go in peace to love God and your neighbor, both in truth and in action.**

UNIT 1: KNOWN BY OUR LOVE
SHOWING DIVINE LOVE

PREVIEWING THE LESSON

Lesson Scripture: 1 John 4:7-21
Background Scripture: 1 John 4:7-21
Key Verse: 1 John 4:19

Focus of the Lesson:
As human beings, we need several kinds of love to become healthy, whole persons. What is the source of our ability to love one another with divine love? John says our love for one another comes from God, who first loved us, and from the Spirit who abides with us.

Goals for the Learners:
(1) to explore John's teaching on God as the source of their love for others.
(2) to reflect on ways this teaching relates to their lives as Christians.
(3) to identify ways to show divine love to others and commit to do so.

Supplies:
Bibles, newsprint and marker, paper and pencils, hymnals

READING THE SCRIPTURE

NRSV
1 John 4:7-21

⁷Beloved, let us love one another, because love is from God; everyone who loves is born of God and knows God. ⁸Whoever does not love does not know God, for God is love. ⁹God's love was revealed among us in this way: God sent his only Son into the world so that we might live through him. ¹⁰In this is love, not that we loved God but that he loved us and sent his Son to be the atoning sacrifice for our sins. ¹¹Beloved, since God loved us so much, we also ought to love one another. ¹²No one has ever seen God; if we love one another, God lives in us, and his love is perfected in us.

NIV
1 John 4:7-21

⁷Dear friends, let us love one another, for love comes from God. Everyone who loves has been born of God and knows God. ⁸Whoever does not love does not know God, because God is love. ⁹This is how God showed his love among us: He sent his one and only Son into the world that we might live through him. ¹⁰This is love: not that we loved God, but that he loved us and sent his Son as an atoning sacrifice for our sins. ¹¹Dear friends, since God so loved us, we also ought to love one another. ¹²No one has ever seen God; but if we love one another,

[13]By this we know that we abide in him and he in us, because he has given us of his Spirit. [14]And we have seen and do testify that the Father has sent his Son as the Savior of the world. [15]God abides in those who confess that Jesus is the Son of God, and they abide in God. [16]So we have known and believe the love that God has for us.

God is love, and those who abide in love abide in God, and God abides in them. [17]Love has been perfected among us in this: that we may have boldness on the day of judgment, because as he is, so are we in this world. [18]There is no fear in love, but perfect love casts out fear; for fear has to do with punishment, and whoever fears has not reached perfection in love. **[19]We love because he first loved us.** [20]Those who say, "I love God," and hate their brothers or sisters, are liars; for those who do not love a brother or sister whom they have seen, cannot love God whom they have not seen. [21]The commandment we have from him is this: those who love God must love their brothers and sisters also.

God lives in us and his love is made complete in us.

[13]We know that we live in him and he in us, because he has given us of his Spirit. [14]And we have seen and testify that the Father has sent his Son to be the Savior of the world. [15]If anyone acknowledges that Jesus is the Son of God, God lives in him and he in God. [16]And so we know and rely on the love God has for us.

God is love. Whoever lives in love lives in God, and God in him. [17]In this way, love is made complete among us so that we will have confidence on the day of judgment, because in this world we are like him. [18]There is no fear in love. But perfect love drives out fear, because fear has to do with punishment. The one who fears is not made perfect in love.

[19]We love because he first loved us. [20]If anyone says, "I love God," yet hates his brother, he is a liar. For anyone who does not love his brother, whom he has seen, cannot love God, whom he has not seen. [21]And he has given us this command: Whoever loves God must also love his brother.

UNDERSTANDING THE SCRIPTURE

1 John 4:7-11. God's initiative in acting redemptively shows the essence of love. The love of God does not wait to respond to another's action, but acts to create a life-giving relationship. It acts with a view to the benefit of the other, even at great cost to God's self, and does not limit that "other" to the smaller circle of those who have loved God or who have treated God as God deserved. Paul articulates a very similar definition of this surprising, essential characteristic of God's love as the love that initiates a relationship independent of the merits (or gross lack of merits) of the "beloved" in Romans 5:6-8.

These definitions of divine love extend back to the Jesus tradition itself, seen especially clearly in Matthew 5:43-48, where God's completeness ("perfection") is manifested in God's ability to give generously in keeping with God's own purposes, unimpeded by the restraints of the character of those who will receive God's gifts. Across the canon, then, we are called to love as God loves—in accordance with God's good purposes for the person before us, not in accordance with his or her worthiness or unworthiness. Those who love in this way show themselves to be "children" of God (Matthew 5:45), or "born of God" (1 John 4:7), since the character of the Parent must take shape in those who are truly "children" of that Parent.

God's love for us, moreover, sets our

value in an absolute sense. We should love one another out of a recognition of this value that God has placed on each one of us, rather than the more relative sense of value produced by our self-centered evaluations of one another (How do you impact me? How do you measure up to my desires for and expectations of you?). The Elder, of course, keeps our focus here on love directed toward "one another" within the church (local and global), which helps us practice the first, critical steps toward reflecting God's character of unlimited love.

1 John 4:12. The Elder sees God as permeating the human sphere though God's love for humankind. God's love is conceived here as a dynamic force that is introduced into human relationships, something that moves toward "perfection" or "completeness." We associate "perfection" with "flawlessness," hence "perfectionism." However, "perfection" language in first-century Greek has more to do with something coming to its appropriate goal, to the final state inherent in itself or in the "divine" plan for it. Hence children are "perfected" when they become adults (we would say, "mature"); the initiate is "perfected" as she completes the rites of initiation and becomes fully what she intended prior to the rite. The Elder says that God's love for us achieves its goal—comes to its mature shape or form—within us when we love one another out of that love we have received and which we recognize that others have received. This is a dynamic conception of God's love that impels us toward relationship rather than remains with us as a commodity.

1 John 4:13-16. The idea of "abiding" (*menein*, sometimes translated "living" or "remaining") is very important in 1 John, and quite appropriate to the Elder's pastoral strategy: He wants those who have "remained" in the house churches supervised by himself and others of like mind to connect their decision to "remain" with the conviction that God "remains" with them

and they in God. The most important witness to this fact is the Holy Spirit, and the disciples' awareness of and engagement with the Spirit of God dwelling in their midst as a community of faith and love. This "Spirit" is also referred to in 1 John 2:20, 27 as "the anointing" that leads them into all truth, teaches them from God's own heart, and allows them to participate in God's own character.

The historical situation is reflected in 4:15-16 insofar as the theological dispute over these very claims ruptured the bonds of love in the Johannine communities. The Elder affirms that an inseparable relationship exists between the confession of Jesus—the man, crucified in the flesh—as the Son of God and the life of love that makes God's love manifest in this world.

1 John 4:17-19. "Perfect" love expresses not a "flawless" love that we manufacture, but the love of God for us and within us maturing fully ("ripening," if you will), "perfected" in the sense of achieving its goal in our lives by transforming us into people who love others with the love of God. By this process God's character is formed in us. When we live in line with God's character, we cannot fear God's judgment any more, for when God inspects us (that is, looks into us as the "one who searches minds and hearts," Revelation 2:23), God will see and approve God's own character within us. Fear enters in proportionately with the distance between our character and God's character. As elsewhere in Scripture (see especially Ephesians 4:32–5:2), God's love for us becomes the norm for our lives as well.

Scribes copying 1 John showed a tendency to "clarify" verse 19 by reading the opening as "we love God" rather than "we love." Perhaps this was due to the social codes of reciprocity that called for a "return" of grace for grace given. Hence, God's initiating love should provoke love for God in our hearts in return. The addition was not intended, however, to introduce a "loophole" into the text by focusing on love for God rather than love for the fellow Christian, since the verses that follow make it clear that "love for God" remains inseparable from love for the sister or brother in Christ.

1 John 4:20-21. Love for God and love for other human beings are strongly linked in the Jesus tradition. In Matthew 22:37-39, Jesus elevates love for God and love for neighbor as the two core commandments of Torah in response to the query of a Jewish sage. When Luke tells the parallel story, however, it is another Jewish teacher who zooms in on these commandments as the heart of the law, with Jesus commending his answer (Luke 10:25-28). As a final variation, Mark has Jesus select the two commandments as the summation of the Torah, with the questioning scribe commending Jesus wholeheartedly (Mark 12:28-34). Luke and Mark show us thereby that Jesus and other Jewish rabbis were united in sharing this focus on love for God and love for neighbor. The Elder limits our attention to how well we love fellow Christians, but also stresses that there is no love for God without loving God's own. The Fourth Gospel had done the same by linking love for Jesus with the keeping of his commandments (John 14:15), which is none other than the command to "love one another" (John 13:35; 15:12).

INTERPRETING THE SCRIPTURE

Wholeness and Genuine Love

The Fourth Gospel states, "from his fullness we have all received, grace upon grace" (John 1:16). It is the fullness of God, or the "perfection" (the "completeness") of God, in Matthew's language (Matthew 5:48), that enables God to love and to extend kindness to friend and enemy alike. It is God's fullness that allows empty human beings, seeking to fill themselves from dry wells in their idolatrous, self-serving lives, ever to be filled at all. God's fullness overflows in acts of love that initiate relationship with human beings. If God waited for human beings to "do right by God" before reaching out in love, God would be shown to be empty and incomplete, just as we are.

The Elder calls disciples to seek that wholeness, that completeness, that God brings into our lives as God's love and God's Spirit "abide" in us, filling our emptiness so that we can, in turn, love as God loves. If we feel that we need specific help to love certain people as God loves, we have God's assurance that God will hear such prayers and give us the wherewithal to love and restore our fellow Christians (3:21-22; 5:14-17). When we recognize in our own lives the economy of God's love described here, then we have the full assurance that we do indeed belong to God.

Knowing That We Know

In the wake of bitter debate and schism, it was vitally important for the Christians who remain in the congregations shepherded by the Elder to be assured that they know that they know the truth of God, and to know how they know what they know. Some number of their formerly dear sisters and brothers have recently abandoned their fellowship, convinced that they knew that the remaining ones did not know the truth of God. This connects with the situation of Christians in the Western world today in several ways. Our society tends to trivialize religion (or at least relativize the claims of each of the variety of world religions), when it is not using religion to fuel political propaganda. North America sees, and Europe has long seen, interest in non-Christian religious traditions or in no religious tradition on the rise, especially among the young to early-middle-aged adult population. The naturalistic, scientific worldview has been firmly in place in higher education for more than a century, purposefully exorcizing the supernaturalistic worldview assumed in historic Jewish and Christian faith, explaining religious experience as a purely psychological, sociological, and cultural phenomenon.

In the wake of such trends, how can we know that we know? How do we know that we have something to offer people seeking to know? This is the pressing question for churches needing to recover a sense of missions and evangelism, or become extinct. The Elder points to two important pillars for this knowledge: (1) the experience of the Divine Other in our midst, the Holy Spirit; (2) the evidence of changed hearts and lives, seen in the sincere love for the family of God exhibited by the sisters and brothers. For the Elder, the former becomes real and convincing only as the love of God leavens the life of the community and becomes manifest in the love of Christians—throughout the whole family of faith, across all human-made boundaries—for one another.

Which Is Easier?

Some of us might think it easier to love the invisible God than the visible, but disagreeable, sister or brother who keeps fighting for a particular worship style in church, or irritates us in some other way. We think it might be easier to love God, but if we do not have the heart to love the person who stands right in front of us as he or she is, how can we presume that we have the heart to love the God who is inaccessible to all our senses, who is thus further removed from our faculties of "knowing"? In other words, if we withhold our love from the sister or brother because he or she does not move as we direct, how can we be sure it is truly "God" that we think we are loving, who surely resists moving according to human expectations more than any human!

The Elder lays significant stress here on "seeing" our sister or brother. We need to train ourselves, however, to "see" the other person—or, better, to see the "other" in another person. Self-centered creatures that we are as we start out on our journey of transformation into Christ-likeness, we need to move away from seeing other people in relation to what they can do for us, how they impede us, how they impact our lives, how they match up to our expectations and desires for them, and move toward seeing them as "other," as they are "in themselves," as they are in God's love for them. As we do this more and more, we are more able truly to love them and not the projections of our own agendas that they represent. And, of course, this opens us up truly to love God as God is, and not as the projection of our own design for a god.

Love and Fear

"The fear of the LORD," in the sense of living with a clear sense of the honor due God and with a commitment to honor God in all that we do, is a very healthy component of discipleship, truly "the beginning of wisdom" (Proverbs 1:7; 9:10). However, many disciples live with a rather unhealthy fear of God, one that suggests to them that the Deity is watching for them to "slip up" in their behavior, their dress, their speech, or their entertainment—and when they do, God help them! Despite Paul's diligent attempts to preserve the "freedom" of the Christian, Christianity is no stranger to the legalism and scrupulous superstition that transform the experience of the Holy into the prison-house of the soul.

The Elder has a word to speak to such disciples. The overwhelming simplicity of the author's "rules" for the Christian life chisels away at the chains of the fearful, fretful mind. More to the point, however, he reveals that God's intention for God's children is not that they "watch their step" at every turn, but rather that they allow God's love to transform their hearts from the inside out, making us more and more like the God who loves and acts in line with that love. The Elder would find a great advocate in Augustine, who wrote in *Homilies on 1 John:* "Love, and do what you will." Perhaps the greatest danger to the soul is that a disciple will "do" all the right things and "say" all the right words, but not be transformed in his or her inmost being by God's love. The Elder brings our attention back to God as the Center, directing us to position ourselves such that God can keep filling us with God's love, and to humble ourselves to let that love affirm and direct us.

SHARING THE SCRIPTURE

PREPARING TO TEACH

Preparing Our Hearts

This week's devotional reading is found in John 21:15-19. As you read this familiar account of one of Jesus' post-resurrection appearances, try to put yourself in Simon Peter's place. Prior to his crucifixion, you denied Jesus three times, and now he asks you three times about your love for him. Each time Peter affirms his love for Jesus, and each time the risen Lord tells him to care for the sheep. What conclusions can you draw concerning the connection between love of Christ and love of his flock? How are you enacting this love? How could you show more love?

Pray that you and the adult learners will be fully aware of the source of love and continually striving to shine forth God's love in your own life.

Preparing Our Minds

Study the background and lesson Scripture, both of which are found in 1 John 4:7-21. As you contemplate this lesson, think about the kinds of love people need in order to be healthy; also think about the source of this love.

Write on newsprint:
❑ information for next week's lesson, found under "Continue the Journey."

❑ activities for further spiritual growth in "Continue the Journey."

Plan the optional lecture suggested under "Explore John's Teaching on God as the Source of the Learners' Love for Others," if you choose to use a lecture.

Caution: In "Explore John's Teaching on God as the Source of the Learners' Love for Others" you are asked to use a different reader for each verse. Do not go around the room and call on each person to read. Some cannot read well, and others are uncomfortable when they are told to read aloud. Expecting everyone to take a turn reading may prompt some people to stay away from the class.

LEADING THE CLASS

(1) Gather to Learn

❖ Welcome the class members and introduce any guests.

❖ Pray that God's love will flow in the heart of each person who is present.

❖ Read each of these statements. Pause after each one and ask the students to describe the kind of love to which it refers. Note that in English the word "love" is often over-used, and the emotion to which it refers in certain contexts may not really be love at all.

◼ I just love your purple hat.

◼ I was so touched when little Sara threw her arms around me and said, "I love you, Aunt Jane."

■ I'm in love with the greatest guy in the world!"

■ My son is a real behavior problem, but I love him too much to give up on him.

❖ Read aloud today's focus statement: **As human beings, we need several kinds of love to become healthy, whole persons. What is the source of our ability to love one another with divine love? John says our love for one another comes from God, who first loved us, and from the Spirit who abides with us.**

(2) Explore John's Teaching on God as the Source of the Learners' Love for Others

❖ Try to enlist enough volunteers so that each one reads only a single verse. If you cannot get enough volunteers, ask those who are willing to keep taking turns reading a single verse until all of the verses have been read.

❖ Draw a circle in the center of a sheet of newsprint. In the center circle write "God's love." Draw lines from that circle, as spokes of a bicycle wheel. Ask the students to look at the passage from 1 John and call out phrases that describe or illuminate God's love, such as *love is from God, God is love, God's love was revealed through Jesus, God's love is perfected in us.* You may wish to draw spokes jutting out from other spokes if two ideas are closely related.

❖ Invite the students to talk about this visual representation of God's love. What new windows does it give them into God's love?

❖ **Option:** Prepare a lecture based on the information in Understanding the Scripture to help the students further understand the background of the Elder's discussion on God's love.

(3) Reflect on Ways This Teaching Relates to the Learners' Lives as Christians

❖ Read aloud "Knowing That We Know" from Interpreting the Scripture.

❖ Point out that, at least in the United States, major differences in reading and interpreting the Scriptures have caused divisions among Christians and others to back away from "organized religion." Discuss these questions.

(1) How can the Elder's teachings concerning God's love reunite people of faith and bring new people into Christ's church?

(2) Two ways of knowing are mentioned: "the experience of the Divine Other in our midst" and "the evidence of changed hearts and lives." What other ways of knowing God do you rely on? Which one(s) are most important to you? Which ways allow others to glimpse God's love for all humanity through you?

(4) Identify Ways to Show Divine Love to Others and Commit to Do So

❖ Encourage the students to recall songs from their childhood Sunday school days that spoke of divine love. Mention (and invite the students to sing if you choose) "Jesus Loves Me," "Jesus Loves the Little Children," and "O How I Love Jesus." Add any other songs that the adults remember on the topic of God's love.

❖ Divide into small groups and ask the students to reminisce about how they learned of God's love and actions they were urged to take to show this love.

❖ Ask the groups to report back on ways that they were taught as children to show God's love for others. (Be mindful of the fact that some students may have had no childhood experiences in the church.) List these ideas on newsprint. Ideas might include: *sharing their toys and other possessions; being kind to parents, siblings, and friends; obeying their parents and others in authority; helping others; loving one's pets.*

❖ Direct attention to this list and challenge the students to suggest ways to make these childhood actions applicable to adults.

What does it mean now, for example, to share their possessions with others?

❖ Go a step beyond face-to-face expressions of love and challenge the adults to identify ways that they can show God's love for all humanity, indeed, all creation. List these ideas on newsprint.

❖ Conclude this portion of the session by asking each person to identify silently at least one loving action that he or she can take this week and either stand or raise a hand to indicate a commitment to take action.

(5) Continue the Journey

❖ Pray that the participants will go forth to show God's love to others.

❖ Read aloud this preparation for next week's lesson. You may also want to post it on newsprint for the students to copy. **Prepare for next week's session entitled "The Way to Love and Life" by reading 1 John 5:1-12, which is both the background and lesson Scripture for this session. Focus on these ideas as you read: People want to believe that life can go on after physical death. What hope of life after death can we find in Jesus Christ? John affirms that our** victorious faith in Jesus Christ will grant us eternal life and empower us to love in the way that God wants.

❖ Read aloud the following three ideas. Challenge the students to commit themselves to use these activities as a springboard to spiritual growth.

(1) **Page through a hymnal or Sunday school songbook. What do the hymns suggest to you about God's love? What do they proclaim that Christians should do in response to God's love?**

(2) **Reconnect with an old friend and do something to affirm your love for this person.**

(3) **Think about how your congregation could show more love for those who already belong and for those who are just visiting or on the fringes.**

❖ Sing or read aloud "Where Charity and Love Prevail."

❖ Say this benediction to conclude the session. You may wish to ask the students to echo it as you read: **Go in peace to love God and your neighbor, both in truth and in action.**

UNIT 1: KNOWN BY OUR LOVE
THE WAY TO LOVE AND LIFE

PREVIEWING THE LESSON

Lesson Scripture: 1 John 5:1-12
Background Scripture: 1 John 5:1-12
Key Verse: 1 John 5:11

Focus of the Lesson:
People want to believe that life can go on after physical death. What hope of life after death can we find in Jesus Christ? John affirms that our victorious faith in Jesus Christ will grant us eternal life and empower us to love in the way that God wants.

Goals for the Learners:
(1) to examine John's teaching regarding the connections between love, faith, and eternal life.
(2) to consider what it means for them to have eternal life now.
(3) to give thanks for the gift of divine love and eternal life in Jesus Christ.

Supplies:
Bibles, newsprint and marker, paper and pencils, hymnals

READING THE SCRIPTURE

NRSV
1 John 5:1-12

[1]Everyone who believes that Jesus is the Christ has been born of God, and everyone who loves the parent loves the child. [2]By this we know that we love the children of God, when we love God and obey his commandments. [3]For the love of God is this, that we obey his commandments. And his commandments are not burdensome, [4]for whatever is born of God conquers the world. And this is the victory that conquers the world, our faith. [5]Who is it that conquers the world but the one who believes that Jesus is the Son of God?

NIV
1 John 5:1-12

[1]Everyone who believes that Jesus is the Christ is born of God, and everyone who loves the father loves his child as well. [2]This is how we know that we love the children of God: by loving God and carrying out his commands. [3]This is love for God: to obey his commands. And his commands are not burdensome, [4]for everyone born of God overcomes the world. This is the victory that has overcome the world, even our faith. [5]Who is it that overcomes the world? Only he who believes that Jesus is the Son of God.

⁶This is the one who came by water and blood, Jesus Christ, not with the water only but with the water and the blood. And the Spirit is the one that testifies, for the Spirit is the truth. ⁷There are three that testify: ⁸the Spirit and the water and the blood, and these three agree. ⁹If we receive human testimony, the testimony of God is greater; for this is the testimony of God that he has testified to his Son. ¹⁰Those who believe in the Son of God have the testimony in their hearts. Those who do not believe in God have made him a liar by not believing in the testimony that God has given concerning his Son. **¹¹And this is the testimony: God gave us eternal life, and this life is in his Son.** ¹²Whoever has the Son has life; whoever does not have the Son of God does not have life.

⁶This is the one who came by water and blood—Jesus Christ. He did not come by water only, but by water and blood. And it is the Spirit who testifies, because the Spirit is the truth. ⁷For there are three that testify: ⁸the Spirit, the water and the blood; and the three are in agreement. ⁹We accept man's testimony, but God's testimony is greater because it is the testimony of God, which he has given about his Son. ¹⁰Anyone who believes in the Son of God has this testimony in his heart. Anyone who does not believe God has made him out to be a liar, because he has not believed the testimony God has given about his Son. **¹¹And this is the testimony: God has given us eternal life, and this life is in his Son.** ¹²He who has the Son has life; he who does not have the Son of God does not have life.

UNDERSTANDING THE SCRIPTURE

1 John 5:1-5. The proper understanding of who Jesus is and how Jesus relates to God emerges as of central importance for the Elder, this time using the language of being "born of God" (5:1) and, a little later, overcoming the world (5:5). The accent in the Greek falls somewhat differently than our English translations tend to represent. The crucial affirmations are that "The Christ is Jesus" and "The Son of God is Jesus." Again the evidence points us to an innovation by the separatists in the Johannine community that had begun to suggest that the "Christ," the divine Spirit or anointing, only rested upon the man, Jesus, and was not personally affected by the death of the man, Jesus. Against the separatists' innovation, the Elder affirms that the "Son of God" or the "Christ" was none other than Jesus himself, the Word truly become flesh (John 1:14), not just co-existing with it and riding above its changing fortunes and suffering. The separatists' innovation was yet one more

attempt to avoid the scandal of a crucified God, to domesticate the radical word of the Gospel. It is easy to see how a disembodied Christology could have led to a disembodied ethic: It is the spirit that matters, not the flesh. Therefore we do not need to care for the bodies of our poorer sisters and brothers all that rigorously, nor fret overmuch about sin in the flesh. The Elder opposes the separatists' teaching on all these fronts. An embodied Christology, however, leads to a proper reverence and love for Jesus (the One begotten from God, 1 John 5:1) and a proper love and care for the sisters and brothers (everyone begotten from God, 1 John 5:1, 2).

The Elder looks to love of God as the basis and guarantee of our ability to love our sisters and brothers, the flip side of knowing that we love God insofar as we love the sisters and brothers (1 John 4:20-21). Again, loving God means keeping God's commandments, which is an echo not only of John 14:15, but also of Wisdom of Solomon 6:18 ("love of [wisdom] is the keeping of her laws"), another sign of how much the wisdom tradition is being reshaped in the Johannine community. Those commandments, in turn, lead us back to love for all the children of God.

Participating in this holy cycle of belief in Jesus as God's Son (and hence the full revelation of God's love and measure of the love we are to have), loving God, and loving one another breaks the cycle of the world's influence upon us (1 John 2:15-17). It begins to move us past the death-dealing rules of this world toward the life-giving economy of the kingdom of God.

1 John 5:6-8. The affirmation that the Son of God came not only "by the water" but also "by the blood" makes sense if we consider the likely "other side" in this argument: The "Son" came upon Jesus at the waters of baptism, but was not personally involved in the suffering of Jesus. On the contrary, asserts the Elder: The Son of God truly suffered in the flesh, in the shedding of the blood of the Passion. The cross was just as much a "witness" to the Son as the testimony of John the Baptist and the testimony of the voice from heaven at the baptism (see John 1:32-34). This verse is sometimes heard to refer to John 19:34, the "blood and water" flowing out from Jesus' side, and hence taken to point exclusively to his death. This reading, however, does not account well for the "not only water" (with which the separatists would have agreed) "and the blood" (the main sticking point of disagreement) in 1 John 5:6. The third witness available on earth is the Spirit, which dwells within and among the believers (see below).

These verses are well known for containing the most theologically advanced textual variants in the New Testament. The early Latin versions (third and fourth centuries A.D.) began to introduce three witnesses "in heaven, the Father, the Word, and the Holy Spirit, and these three are one," only then moving on to the three witnesses "on earth" as we read them here. It is easy to see how the topic of God as witness and the topic of a threefold witness proved irresistible to some early Christian scribes, who formulated a Trinitarian counterpart to the Elder's original three witnesses. Though text critics rightly exclude this from their reconstruction of the original text (no early Greek manuscripts contain it), it bears eloquent witness to the development of the doctrine of the Trinity.

1 John 5:9-10. The Elder urges disciples to place greater value on God's own witness to God's Son than even the testimony of human witnesses, though the latter are clearly important to the Johannine community (see 1 John 1:1-4; John 1:32-34; 19:35; 21:24). It is, then, a matter of discerning Jesus' baptism and death as episodes of God's testimony to the Son, and of discerning the inner testimony of the Holy Spirit, the "anointing" which God has given to disciples as their teacher and guide (1 John 2:20, 27). The Johannine tradition elevates the presence of the Holy Spirit among the community of disciples to a position of great importance. It is the Spirit that brings the new birth (John 3:3-8). The Spirit teaches the believers, reminding them of Jesus' teaching and even extending that body of teaching after his ascension (John 14:25-26; 16:12-14). The Spirit testified to Jesus at his baptism (John 1:32-34), testifies to believers, and empowers their witness (John 15:26-27), as well as testifying to the world abut "sin and righteousness and judgment" (John 16:7-11).

1 John 5:11-12. The Elder writes of this in a condensed way here. In the phrase "having the Son," we are invited to hear the particular emphasis of the Elder's Christology, the manifestation of divine love that the death of the Son enacts, and the cycle of receiving the love of God and allowing God's love to be "perfected" in us as it leavens our love for the sisters and brothers. Furthermore, it is the Spirit, the anointing that God has given us, that bears testimony to us that we have this eternal life. Being in touch with God's eternity—the power of God's love reaching into our mortal lives from beyond mortality, the presence of God's Spirit causing us to live with the immortal God—assures believers of their own eternity.

INTERPRETING THE SCRIPTURE

All My Children

The Elder makes a final plug for the importance of loving one's fellow Christians—those many sons and daughters that have been born of God, having received God's Spirit—as an expression of loving God. He uses something like a proverb or maxim here to undergird his point, one with which most parents would probably resonate: "If you love me, you'll love my children." But the economy of love remains more complex. We can only love God when we love one another, but we can only genuinely love one another when we love God. It is, ultimately, our love relationship with God that fills us with the capacity to love others genuinely; it is only when we love others genuinely that we complete our expression of love for God.

A certain flavor of introversion clings to the Letters of John, a certain inward-focus on love within the little, beleaguered house churches immediately affected by the schism. But the Johannine tradition also reminds us of the scope of God's family, as Jesus died not only for his nation "but to gather into one the dispersed children of God" (John 11:52), all those across the world who would receive Jesus and be born from above. Loving one another needs to begin in the face-to-face interactions of Christians sharing one roof and one church, but it cannot be limited to this, lest we be guilty of "hating"—of failing to care for and show love for in truth and in action—our sisters and brothers beyond the walls of the local church, the denomination, the borders drawn by our nation. Part of "overcoming the world" means loving one another beyond denominational, national, and the other human-made walls that belong not to God, but to the world.

Christology Counts

Despite its emphasis on relationship and love, 1 John also inescapably teaches that Christology—what we believe about Jesus—counts. Why this should be is readily apparent: Our understanding of Jesus directly affects our understanding of discipleship.

Across the New Testament, our discipleship is intentionally patterned after Jesus. Mark challenges disciples to imitate the Messiah who came to serve rather than to be served, who gave away his own life for others rather than trying to make a life for himself (Mark 8:31-37; 9:30-35; 10:32-45). Paul looks to the pre-incarnate Son's choice of humbling and emptying himself in obedience to God and in service to others as the pattern for believers in their relationships with each other (Philippians 2:1-11). Without these affirmations about Christology, the shape of discipleship has no ground. The Elder has taken this a step further. If we fail to see in Jesus, and particularly in the death of Jesus, God's giving of himself in love for us, we will fail to understand the depth of our obligation to love one another—and we will fail to be embraced by the full measure of God's love that makes such love for others a reality.

The answer to Jesus' question, "Who do you say that I am?" very much determines the answer to the question, "Who am I as

Jesus' disciple?" The Jesus Seminar caused quite a stir in the last decade of the twentieth century with its presentation of "another Jesus." The Jesus recovered by the historical methods employed by the Seminar, a partial Jesus at best, was promoted as a more genuine basis for modern Christian faith than the Jesus presented by the Gospels and interpreted by the claims of his first followers. This was Jesus the teacher, the Cynic sage who challenged the injustice of the status quo and incited his followers to counter-cultural witness and life. Jesus was certainly that, but the Elder would retort that he was ever so much more than that. In fact, he would challenge the entire enterprise on the grounds that it did not seek to know Jesus in accordance with the witness of the Holy Spirit given to believers, but excluded "the witness of God" outright. Jesus known by the Jesus Seminar might yield some meaningful challenges to disciples, but only Jesus known by the Spirit yields eternal life.

The Spirit's Witness

First John reminds us of the multidimensionality of our faith. It involves having a full and deep knowledge of what God did in Jesus. It involves relationships of love with the community gathered around that Jesus. But it also involves the cultivation of the knowledge of the Divine Other, a growing in sensitivity to the presence and leading of the Spirit of God. In the final analysis, it is our experience of the Spirit that sets us apart from the "world" in its negative sense, because only the disciples, and not the world, can know and follow the Spirit (John 14:17).

The Elder does not talk about the Spirit's presence in some of the ways familiar from Paul and popular in charismatic Christian circles. That is, the Elder does not stress speaking in tongues or prophesying or any other such manifestations. But, like Paul, the Elder does stress that the Spirit's pres-

ence and guidance are absolutely essential to becoming disciples who are rooted and grounded in God, confident of their identity and future in God.

The dimension of our encounter with God, our learning to open ourselves up to the presence and voice of God, to know God "relationally," is all too easy to pass over in a religious climate where thought and action are primary. For the Elder, it is that relationship with God—knowing God "face-to-face," as it were, thanks to the presence of the Spirit within and among us—that instructs our thoughts and guides and empowers our actions so that we grow to reflect God's character more and more. The disciple, free from the fear of judgment, will encounter the Judge as the friend and guide whom he has known, heard, and responded to throughout his or her life.

You Have Eternal Life

Eternal life is not inherent in our being. It is God's gift. Having eternal life does not free us from experiencing death, but it does free us from living as though death is the end. But what does the Elder mean by "having" eternal life? On the one hand, this means to have the assurance of life beyond the resurrection of the dead (John 5:29). Again the importance of nurturing our experiential relationship with the Spirit of God presses itself upon us: It is this Spirit, and not all the doctrinal affirmations and syllogisms in the world, that gives us real assurance about our life beyond death.

But the Johannine tradition is also very reluctant to put off "eternal life" until the "afterlife." Jesus came to open us up to the experience of "abundant life" in the midst of the here and now (John 10:10). Moreover, the Johannine Jesus claims that knowing "the only true God" and the One whom God sent, Jesus Christ, is eternal life (John 17:3). "Eternal life" invades the present life as our experience of God and of God's Son leavens our moribund existence.

As we experience God, we experience an "Other" in whose presence we are lifted into eternity. We experience a love unlike and beyond any that can be known in mortal relationships and their limitations, which in turn allows us to love beyond the expectations of mortal relationships.

Victory over the world includes transcending our own mortality by virtue of the presence and love of God in our lives. This quality and permanency of life that we begin to experience now becomes the best assurance of the permanent life that we will continue to live beyond death.

SHARING THE SCRIPTURE

PREPARING TO TEACH

Preparing Our Hearts

This week's devotional reading is found in John 17:1-5. Observe that in verse 2 of his prayer, Jesus refers to the authority he has to grant eternal life. In verse 3 he states that the purpose of eternal life is to know God and Jesus, who was sent by God. As explained in a footnote of *The New Interpreter's Study Bible,* eternal life is not to be understood as "a gift of immortality or a future life in heaven, but a life shaped by the knowledge of God as revealed in Jesus." How might this understanding of eternal life challenge or alter your own thinking? What difference does it make as to what you believe about eternal life?

Pray that you and the adult learners will be receptive to the fullest expression of new life.

Preparing Our Minds

Study the background and lesson Scripture, 1 John 5:1-12. As you prepare, think about the hope of life after death that you can find in Jesus Christ.

Write on newsprint:
❑ chart for "Consider What It Means to the Learners to Have Eternal Life Now."
❑ information for next week's lesson, found under "Continue the Journey."

❑ activities for further spiritual growth in "Continue the Journey."

Plan the lecture suggested for "Examine John's Teaching Regarding the Connections between Love, Faith, and Eternal Life."

LEADING THE CLASS

(1) Gather to Learn

❖ Welcome the class members and introduce any guests.

❖ Pray that those who have come to class today will experience the power of God's grace and presence in their midst.

❖ Read aloud these excerpts from an anonymous account of a near-death experience that resulted from a traffic accident: **There was no discontinuity of consciousness. There was no fear or anxiety. . . . I decided to wait for someone or something to make contact with me. I assumed that whoever or whatever entities existed in this new reality knew I had arrived. . . . While I waited I became aware of how good I felt. . . . I was thinking about these feelings when I felt something "move" near me. . . . I recognized the "movement" as being the movement of an entity . . . that had been with me all my life. . . . "Do you want to stay here?" the entity asked. "Yeah, sure! I want to stay." The entity then "reminded" me that I had not fulfilled my purpose yet. . . . I knew that I could stay in this other place without fulfilling the purpose, and it wouldn't be** held against me. However, I felt it was better to go back ("to" Earth), fulfill my purpose, and then return. As I had this thought, I started to have a spinning and falling sensation. . . . When the spinning stopped, I opened my eyes. I was standing next to the car at the bottom of a ravine. . . . I felt the presence of "grace" throughout the aftermath of the accident (and I still do). My injuries required 200 stitches worth of plastic surgery in my face and 40 stitches in my arm. However, I was able to leave the hospital after three days instead of the estimated three weeks. . . . This experience changed my outlook on life and reality in more ways that I can describe.

❖ Talk about how this near-death experience, as well as any that the students wish to report, affects one's view of life after death.

❖ Read aloud today's focus statement: **People want to believe that life can go on after physical death. What hope of life after death can we find in Jesus Christ? John affirms that our victorious faith in Jesus Christ will grant us eternal life and empower us to love in the way that God wants.**

(2) Examine John's Teaching Regarding the Connections between Love, Faith, and Eternal Life

❖ Select a volunteer to read 1 John 5:1-5, which proclaims that faith conquers the world.

■ Distribute paper and pencils. Ask the students to work with a partner to explain these five verses in their own words. Tell them to pay particular attention to the meaning of these phrases: "born of God," "children of God," "obey his commandments," and "conquers the world."

■ Call on volunteers to read their explanations and invite the class to respond. Use information from verses 1-5 in Understanding the Scripture to augment the discussion.

❖ Choose someone to read 1 John 5:6-12, where we learn about the testimony concerning Jesus.

■ Read or plan a brief lecture based on verses 6-8, 9-10, and 11-12 from Understanding the Scripture. Help the students understand the three testimonies regarding Jesus, and how these testimonies relate to eternal life.

■ Encourage the students to discuss any connections they discern between love, faith, and eternal life.

(3) Consider What It Means to the Learners to Have Eternal Life Now

❖ Ask the adults to fill in this chart, which you will prepare on newsprint prior to class. Add as many rows beneath the questions as necessary to include the students' answers.

What Is "Eternal Life"?	Who Is Eligible for Eternal Life?	How Do We Obtain Eternal Life?	When Does Eternal Life Begin?	Where Do We Experience Eternal Life?	Why Do We Receive Eternal Life?

❖ Note similarities and differences among the students' answers.

❖ Consider ways in which Christians experience eternal life now, here on earth.

❖ Read or retell "You Have Eternal Life" in Interpreting the Scripture to add ideas to the discussion.

(4) Give Thanks for the Gift of Divine Love and Eternal Life in Jesus Christ

❖ Ask the learners to stand and strike a pose or remain seated and use a facial expression to convey how the idea of life after death makes them feel.

❖ Invite the adults to look at one another and decide how most people are reacting to the gift of eternal life.

❖ Encourage volunteers to offer sentence prayers to give thanks for God's love that gifts us with eternal life.

(5) Continue the Journey

❖ Conclude the prayer time by praying that today's participants will give thanks for the gift of eternal life that is theirs through Christ Jesus.

❖ Read aloud this preparation for next week's lesson. You may also want to post it on newsprint for the students to copy. **Prepare for next week's session entitled "Yielding to Christ's Lordship" by reading background Scripture from Revelation 1:1-8 and Luke 19:28-40. This lesson for Palm/Passion Sunday will focus on Revelation 1:8 and Luke 19:28-40. Keep these ideas in mind as you read: People will easily rally behind a leader that they trust and love. Who is the ultimate such leader for us? The Revelation passages affirm that Jesus, who encompasses all things, is the ruler of all rulers. Luke's account of the triumphal entry into Jerusalem describes a time when Jesus' kingship was symbolically demonstrated to the world.**

❖ Read aloud the following three ideas. Challenge the students to commit themselves to use these activities as a springboard to spiritual growth.

(1) **Observe within your congregation how love is expressed through obedience to God's commandments.**

(2) **Define what it means to "conquer the world" as the Elder writes in 1 John 5:3-4. How do you participate in the "conquering" that Jesus has already accomplished through his death, by the power of love? What do you still need to "conquer"?**

(3) **Write in your spiritual journal your beliefs about eternal life. What is it? How do you obtain it? When does it begin?**

❖ Sing or read aloud "Because He Lives."

❖ Say this benediction to conclude the session. You may wish to ask the students to echo it as you read: **Go in peace to love God and your neighbor, both in truth and in action.**

UNIT 2: A NEW COMMUNITY IN CHRIST

YIELDING TO CHRIST'S LORDSHIP

PREVIEWING THE LESSON

Lesson Scripture: Luke 19:28-40; Revelation 1:8
Background Scripture: Luke 19:28-40; Revelation 1:1-8
Key Verse: Luke 19:38

Focus of the Lesson:
People will easily rally behind a leader that they trust and love. Who is the ultimate such leader for us? The Revelation passages affirm that Jesus, who encompasses all things, is the ruler of all rulers. Luke's account of the triumphal entry into Jerusalem describes a time when Jesus' kingship was symbolically demonstrated to the world.

Goals for the Learners:
(1) to study the story of Jesus' triumphal entry into Jerusalem and to connect this event with Jesus' kingship as set in the context of the apocalyptic genre of Revelation.
(2) to recognize Jesus' role as their spiritual king.
(3) to make a commitment to Jesus as king of their lives and all creation.

Pronunciation Guide:
Bethphage (beth' fuh jee)   Laodicea (lay od i see' uh)
proleptically (pro lep' ti ke le) [assuming that a future development or action already exists or has been accomplished]

Supplies:
Bibles, newsprint and marker, paper and pencils, hymnals, map of Jerusalem area, art supplies (either green construction paper or palm leaves, scissors, and glue or staples and stapler), optional video or DVD and appropriate player

READING THE SCRIPTURE

NRSV
Luke 19:28-40
   ²⁸After he had said this, he went on ahead, going up to Jerusalem.

NIV
Luke 19:28-40
   ²⁸After Jesus had said this, he went on ahead, going up to Jerusalem. ²⁹As he

29When he had come near Bethphage and Bethany, at the place called the Mount of Olives, he sent two of the disciples, 30saying, "Go into the village ahead of you, and as you enter it you will find tied there a colt that has never been ridden. Untie it and bring it here. 31If anyone asks you, 'Why are you untying it?' just say this, 'The Lord needs it.'" 32So those who were sent departed and found it as he had told them. 33As they were untying the colt, its owners asked them, "Why are you untying the colt?" 34They said, "The Lord needs it." 35Then they brought it to Jesus; and after throwing their cloaks on the colt, they set Jesus on it. 36As he rode along, people kept spreading their cloaks on the road. 37As he was now approaching the path down from the Mount of Olives, the whole multitude of the disciples began to praise God joyfully with a loud voice for all the deeds of power that they had seen, 38saying,

"Blessed is the king
who comes in the name of the Lord!
Peace in heaven,
and glory in the highest heaven!"

39Some of the Pharisees in the crowd said to him, "Teacher, order your disciples to stop." 40He answered, "I tell you, if these were silent, the stones would shout out."

Revelation 1:8
8"I am the Alpha and the Omega," says the Lord God, who is and who was and who is to come, the Almighty.

approached Bethphage and Bethany at the hill called the Mount of Olives, he sent two of his disciples, saying to them, 30"Go to the village ahead of you, and as you enter it, you will find a colt tied there, which no one has ever ridden. Untie it and bring it here. 31If anyone asks you, 'Why are you untying it?' tell him, 'The Lord needs it.'"
32Those who were sent ahead went and found it just as he had told them. 33As they were untying the colt, its owners asked them, "Why are you untying the colt?"
34They replied, "The Lord needs it."
35They brought it to Jesus, threw their cloaks on the colt and put Jesus on it. 36As he went along, people spread their cloaks on the road.
37When he came near the place where the road goes down the Mount of Olives, the whole crowd of disciples began joyfully to praise God in loud voices for all the miracles they had seen:
38"Blessed is the king who comes in the name of the Lord!"
"Peace in heaven and glory in the highest!"
39Some of the Pharisees in the crowd said to Jesus, "Teacher, rebuke your disciples!"
40"I tell you," he replied, "if they keep quiet, the stones will cry out."

Revelation 1:8
8"I am the Alpha and the Omega," says the Lord God, "who is, and who was, and who is to come, the Almighty."

UNDERSTANDING THE SCRIPTURE

Luke 19:28-34. Bethany, just under two miles from Jerusalem, is important in the Gospel story as the home of Mary, Martha, and Lazarus, in whose house Jesus found refreshment and welcome (Luke 10:38-42; John 11:1), and as the town that Jesus frequented during his last week in Jerusalem (see Mark 11:1, 11-12). Situated so close to

Jerusalem, it was also the perfect spot from which to launch his "visitation" to that city.

Are we supposed to understand that Jesus had made previous arrangements with the owners of the donkey, supplying his disciples with information about the "password"? Or does Luke intend for this to be a hint of Jesus' clairvoyance? Similar questions are frequently posed concerning Luke 22:7-13. Jesus' predictions of his own passion, the disciples' desertion, and Judas's betrayal should keep us from dismissing the latter option too quickly.

The detail that the donkey had not previously been ridden might be heard as an echo of the frequent specification that heifers or oxen used for sacred purposes not have previously borne a yoke (see Numbers 19:2; Deuteronomy 21:3; 1 Samuel 6:7). The detail certainly heightens the significance of Jesus' act, suggesting a sacral coronation.

Luke 19:35-36. Neither Luke nor Mark (see Mark 11:1-10) makes explicit the connection between Jesus' riding on a donkey and the prophecy of Zechariah 9:9 that Jerusalem's king would come to her in triumph on such an animal (but see Matthew 21:4-5). The image of a royal procession, however, is clearly indicated here by the action of the disciples, strewing clothes in the path of the coming king (see 2 Kings 9:13 for a similar image).

Luke 19:37-38. Jesus approaches Jerusalem in the midst of the crowd of disciples' celebration of what God had been doing in their midst and expressions of anticipation for what Jesus' installation as "king" would mean. They would be shocked by the events of that week—and by the chief priests' and their entourage's elimination of Jesus—into a transformed understanding of the kingship of Jesus.

In verse 38 the disciples recite an acclamation from Psalm 118, a psalm that enacts a victory procession up to the temple in Jerusalem. Their words, in fact, represent the blessing of the approaching victor by the priests from the house of the Lord. The text of the psalm has been slightly altered from "blessed is the one who comes in the name of the Lord" to "blessed is the coming one, the king in the name of the Lord" (translation mine) to make the regal nature of the procession unmistakable. The same Psalm is quoted by Jesus a little later in Luke (20:17) in context of the parable of the

vineyard, as Jesus refers to himself proleptically as "the stone that the builders rejected," elevated by God to the chief place in the building.

The disciples also are given a clear echo of the song of the angels in Luke 2:14, answering the angels' ascription of glory to God and pronouncement of peace upon earth with a matching acclamation of God and return of the wish of peace. This echo connects the events of Passion Week with the angelic announcement that Jesus would deliver his people, which is coming to fulfillment at last.

Luke 19:39-40. The presence of the Pharisees within this crowd of disciples may be noteworthy. Not all Pharisees opposed Jesus and his teaching, as is clear from the vocal contingent of Pharisees within the Jerusalem church (see Acts 15:5). Their reaction against the disciples' acclamation may be indicative rather of their fear of how such revolutionary claims would be received by the Roman occupation force (a fear that Pilate's execution order would justify).

Jesus' response is quite different from the response related in Matthew 21:15-16. Here, Jesus echoes Habakkuk 2:11, where the stones and timbers used to build the walls of Jerusalem cry out for justice against its ruling elites. For those who detect the allusion, Jesus' words connect his disciples' enthusiasm for his rule with their indictment of the injustice and oppression inflicted by the existing leadership in Jerusalem.

Revelation 1:1-3. These verses make a bold claim for the authority of the Revelation. These are not the words of an edgy prophet, but a message from God's own self, mediated through Jesus, facilitated by an angelic intermediary, and delivered to God's slave, John. Throughout Revelation, John suppresses his own voice beneath those of Jesus, God, and other otherworldly beings whose authority is beyond question. Revelation 1:3 contains the first of seven "beatitudes" (see also 14:13; 16:15;

19:9; 20:6; 22:7, 14): those who are privy to this message enjoy a favored and enviable status, since they are gaining "inside knowledge" about the world in which they live. If they act in line with this knowledge, they will gain eternal advantage.

The proximity of God's intervention ("what must soon take place"; "the time is near") heightens the urgency and therefore the importance of John's message, making it rise to the top of the hearers' list of priorities (and replacing many competing priorities, as the reader of Revelation 2–3 would notice).

Revelation 1:4-6. Several of the seven churches addressed by John are also known from other early Christian letters (Ephesus and Laodicea from the letters of Paul; Ephesus, Smyrna, and Philadelphia from the letters of Ignatius of Antioch, who was executed in A.D. 110). Even though John writes an "apocalypse," he also uses the primary genre of early Christian pastoral communication: the "letter." John's polemic against Greco-Roman religion begins in earnest already in Revelation 1:4. He slightly alters a known epithet of Zeus ("the one who was, is, and will be"), claiming the titles for the One true God: "the one who is" (recalling the wording of Exodus 3:14), "who was," and "the one who is coming." This last alteration introduces a dynamic

that is absent from the static conception of Zeus ("who will be"): This God is coming in visitation and judgment upon the earth. Claiming that crucified Jesus is the "ruler of the kings of the earth" cannot help but be heard also as a polemic against Roman imperialism (the power that crucified Jesus). The seven spirits should not be too quickly identified with the Holy Spirit: The "sevenfold" spirit of God in Isaiah 11:2-3 is not as close a background as the seven archangels who serve God face-to-face (Tobit 12:15; Revelation 8:2).

Revelation 1:7-8. John weaves the words of the Jewish Scriptures throughout Revelation. He sees the world and its future in light of the biblical record of God's interventions in the past, and also introduces the authority of Scripture into his own interpretations of his hearers' situation. Here the audience would clearly hear the words of Daniel 7:13 (already applied to the second coming by Jesus himself; see Matthew 24:30) and Zechariah 12:10-11. The immediacy of John's language ("Look! He comes!" in the Greek) combined with the particulars of these quotations sets the return of Christ as the number one crisis that should occupy the hearers' attention and preparation, lest they find that Day to be a day of wailing and regret.

INTERPRETING THE SCRIPTURE

When the Master Has Need

The Greek wording of Luke 19:33-34 creates a contrast that is not apparent in English translations: "As they were untying the donkey, its masters said to them .... but [the disciples] said, 'Its master has need'." Beyond the claims of "ownership" in the temporary, worldly sense, there is One Owner of creation by virtue of his having made all that is. Such a message runs

counter to our economy, built as it is on capitalism and the notion of private ownership. It also runs counter to the ideas of "property" and "ownership" implanted deep within our own selves, learned from the first time we are able to say "mine!" as we fought with a sibling or playmate over a toy.

Early Christian leaders taught a different theory of economics, in keeping with their Jewish heritage: "The earth is the LORD's, and all that is in it" (Psalm 24:1). God entrusts to us some portion of the creation for our good and the good of all God's people, making us not "property owners" but, rather, "stewards of the manifold grace of God" (1 Peter 4:10). We prove ourselves "noble stewards" as we use these resources as God directs.

If Jesus had not made prior arrangements with the "owners" of the donkey, we should see the surprising power of God at work at two points in the story: Jesus' foreknowledge of what the disciples would encounter, and the donkey's temporal owners' recognition and response to a higher claim of ownership. When the Master calls for what is his—when he "has need" of something in our possession—will we recognize and honor his claim upon those goods or services?

A Different King, a Different Kingdom

Readers of the Passion Story in all four Gospels, as well as readers of Revelation, cannot fail to notice that Jesus is a "king" unlike any other encountered in the history books. He is a ruler who comes in answer to cries for justice from the victims of the world's domination systems, rather than one who commits injustice to secure his regime or serve his own interests. He is a king who ransoms his people with his own blood rather than exploits them to his own advantage, who elevates their dignity by making them "a kingdom, priests serving his God" (Revelation 1:6, recalling the designation of Israel as "a priestly kingdom and a holy nation" in Exodus 19:6). He does not inaugurate his rule by force, though Revelation warns that persistent resistance to his reign will ultimately be swept aside. He unites the hosts of heaven and the throngs of disciples in ascribing honor to God and in peace with one another.

What, then, does it mean for us to follow such a king? On the one hand, the Lucan text points us to worship as the appropriate response to what God has done and what God will bring about. Revelation will also challenge us to make worship the center of our lives, even as God reigns from the center of the cosmos (Revelation 4–5). Recognizing the character of God and the purpose of God for human community—things that become clearer and clearer as we give ourselves to God in worship—will, in turn, have a formative effect on our character and purpose. Jesus' lordship in our lives and our churches becomes evident as we use power as he used power (that is, to redeem others; to bestow dignity on others; to free others from the pangs of injustice). It becomes evident as we withdraw ourselves from participating in and supporting those economic, political, and ideological systems that prevent God's vision for human community from being realized.

The Time of Visitation

The ultimate tragedy of the "triumphal entry" is made clear in the passage that follows our lesson Scripture, as Jesus laments over the fate of Jerusalem (Luke 19:41-44). The leaders and the supporters of the status quo (keeping hold of what privileges could be enjoyed under Roman domination) were not prepared for the time of visitation. They did not recognize that God was bringing God's promises to fulfillment in Jesus as he came to them.

Revelation 1:7 speaks of a new time of visitation, when Jesus returns "on the clouds" as he promised (Matthew 24:30). A great deal of early Christian exhortation was directed toward being prepared to encounter Jesus at this next visitation. Disciples are urged so to live as to be able to greet him as the expected, returning Master rather than as the Judge whose appearing causes us to lament and mourn our failure to use this interim more astutely (see, for example, Matthew 24:42–25:46; Romans 13:11-14; 2 Corinthians 5:9-10; 1 Thessalonians 5:1-11; Hebrews 10:32-39; 1 Peter 1:13-16; 2 Peter 3:8-15a).

John paints a vivid picture of that moment of visitation, reminding his readers who has the last word on our lives and the ultimate claim on our attention and service (Revelation 1:7-8). John wants his readers to consider that Day while it is still "today" (Hebrews 3:7-13), placing their hearts, thoughts, and lives before the view of the returning Christ so that they can discern what is "out of line" with his rule in time to "get in line" before time is no more.

We may be increasingly uncomfortable with the language of an "imminent" return of Christ, and find John's language about what "must soon take place" (1:1) perhaps even embarrassing. But his words and images can still have their necessary impact on our self-diagnosis and on our formation as genuine disciples if we hear his proclamation of "imminence" as a declaration of "priority." John would make closing the distance between how our lives are ordered and the ordering that the rule of Jesus Christ over our lives would bring to pass the top priority of our daily agenda.

Allegiance and Bold Witness

In Luke, Jesus is acclaimed "the king who comes in the name of the Lord" (Luke 19:38); in Revelation, God is acclaimed "the Almighty"—all-powerful One—and Jesus the "ruler of the kings of the earth" (Revelation 1:8, 5). Both are highly charged political claims—claims about who is the legitimate ruler and to whom allegiance is ultimately due where there is conflict with lesser powers. Both are dangerous claims. Some of the Pharisees urge Jesus to rebuke the disciples, silencing this subversive acclamation; John also knows that keeping the commandments of God (foremost among which is withdrawal from idolatrous worship and the acclamation of any other god, like the emperor in the imperial cult of the Eastern Mediterranean) will bring hostility against the disciples. Nevertheless, part of our call as "a kingdom" and "priests" to our God (Revelation 1:6) is to bear witness in our words and in our life choices to the economy and politics of the kingdom of heaven, even where this brings us into disfavor with the political and economic powers of this age.

SHARING THE SCRIPTURE

PREPARING TO TEACH

Preparing Our Hearts

This week's devotional reading is found in Psalm 118:21-28. Note that this psalm, which is cited in Luke 19:38 in today's Scripture lesson, was a hymn of royal entry. Read verses 21-28 as your own prayer of praise and thanksgiving. Ponder each verse and try to relate it to your life. Continue your prayer by naming reasons that you have to be thankful to God this day.

Pray that you and the adult learners will continually bless and praise the God of our salvation.

Preparing Our Minds

Study the background Scripture, Luke 19:28-40 and Revelation 1:1-8. The lesson will focus on Luke 19:28-40 and Revelation 1:8. As you study consider the characteristics of the ultimate leader and who that might be for you.

Write on newsprint:
❑ information for next week's lesson, found under "Continue the Journey."
❑ activities for further spiritual growth in "Continue the Journey."

Plan how you will use "A Different King, A Different Kingdom" from Interpreting the Scripture for "Recognize Jesus' Role as the Learners' Spiritual King."

Option: Locate a video or DVD that includes a depiction of Jesus' entry into Jerusalem. Your local library, Ecufilm, denomination's bookseller, or local conference resource center are likely sources. Be sure to preview the film. When you set up the player in the classroom, cue up the film to the segment you want to show.

LEADING THE CLASS

(1) Gather to Learn

❖ Welcome the class members and introduce any guests.

❖ Pray that all the participants will feel the light and warmth of God's love in the midst of this fellowship of believers.

❖ Invite the students to call out the names of current and historical local, national, or world leaders that people have loved and/or respected. List these names on newsprint.

❖ List on another sheet of newsprint the traits that apparently have made these leaders so beloved that people are/were willing to rally around them.

❖ Read aloud today's focus statement: **People will easily rally behind a leader that they trust and love. Who is the ultimate such leader for us? The Revelation passage affirms that Jesus, who encompasses all things, is the ruler of all rulers. Luke's account of the triumphal entry into Jerusalem describes a time when Jesus' kingship was symbolically demonstrated to the world.**

(2) Study the Story of Jesus' Triumphal Entry into Jerusalem and Connect This Event with Jesus' Kingship

❖ **Option:** Show a segment of a video or DVD that depicts Jesus' entry into Jerusalem. Talk with the class about how this film reflects their understanding of the biblical story. Invite them to add or question details in the film.

❖ Select a volunteer to read Luke 19:28-40.

❖ Locate Bethphage, Bethany, Mount of Olives, and Jerusalem on a map.

❖ Read "When the Master Has Need" in Interpreting the Scripture to help the students delve into this scene.

❖ Study today's key verse, Luke 19:38, by asking the students to turn to Psalm 118 and read it silently. Use information in Understanding the Scripture for Luke 19:37-38 to help the students connect this psalm with Jesus, particularly in his role as king.

(3) Recognize Jesus' Role as the Learners' Spiritual King

❖ Ask someone to read Revelation 1:8. Note that "alpha" and "omega" are the first and last letters of the Greek alphabet, respectively.

❖ Encourage the learners to state how this verse describes their understanding of Jesus as their spiritual king.

❖ Post a sheet of newsprint headed on the left, "Jesus as Ruler" and headed on the right, "Rulers of the World." Encourage the students to suggest ideas for each column. Specifically, you are looking for ideas about how Jesus rules as opposed to how worldly rulers act. You will find many ideas under "A Different King, a Different Kingdom" if you wish to complete this chart yourself using a lecture format.

❖ Discuss how Jesus models a lifestyle for Christian actions and attitudes in a world where power, domination, and economics are stressed. Consider how we as Christians are called to live where the world's values often confront our own?

(4) Make a Commitment to Jesus as King of the Learners' Lives and All Creation

❖ Distribute palm leaves or green construction paper, scissors, and glue or staples. Invite the students to create a cross by cutting or tearing two pieces of palm or paper and attaching them with glue or a staple.

❖ **Option:** If you use construction paper, ask the students to write "Blessed is the king who comes in the name of the Lord" on their cross.

❖ Ask the students wave their palm crosses as you recite together today's key verse, Luke 19:38.

❖ Provide quiet time for the students to reflect on their commitment to Jesus as the king who comes in the name of the Lord. What are they willing to do on this Palm/Passion Sunday to deepen that commitment to Jesus' lordship?

(5) Continue the Journey

❖ Break the silence by praying that the learners will go forth recognizing that Christ is our king and willingly yielding their lives to his Lordship.

❖ Read aloud this preparation for next week's lesson. You may also want to post it on newsprint for the students to copy. **Prepare for next week's session entitled "Discovering Resurrection" by reading background Scripture from John 20:1-18, 30-31 and Revelation 1:9-20. This Easter lesson will spotlight John 20:11-16, 30-31 and Revelation 1:12, 17-18. Think particularly about these ideas as you study: People long to hear good news, especially if it transforms their lives for the better. What transforming good news do we have to celebrate this Easter? John's account of the resurrection tells us that Jesus has conquered sin and death on our behalf, and** the personal witness in Revelation attests to the ongoing presence of the resurrected Lord in the lives of believers.

❖ Read aloud the following three ideas. Challenge the students to commit themselves to use these activities as a springboard to spiritual growth.

(1) **Begin to research candidates for election. If you live in the United States, the candidates for the November, 2008 election are gearing up. What would attract you to or push you away from candidates who are likely to run? What criteria will you use to choose new leaders?**

(2) **Locate information on groups that advocate peace. How do their strategies reflect their peaceful intentions? What words or phrases would you use to describe their leaders?**

(3) **Spend time in prayer and meditation this week recalling the sacrifices that "the king who comes in the name of the Lord" (Luke 19:38) has made on your behalf. What responses will you make to him?**

❖ Sing or read aloud "All Glory, Laud, and Honor."

❖ Say this benediction to conclude the session. You may wish to ask the students to echo it as you read: **Go in peace to love God and your neighbor, both in truth and in action.**

UNIT 2: A NEW COMMUNITY IN CHRIST
DISCOVERING RESURRECTION

PREVIEWING THE LESSON

Lesson Scripture: John 20:11-16, 30-31; Revelation 1:12, 17-18
Background Scripture: John 20:1-18, 30-31; Revelation 1:9-20
Key Verses: Revelation 1:17-18

Focus of the Lesson:
People long to hear good news, especially if it transforms their lives for the better. What transforming good news do we have to celebrate this Easter? John's account of the resurrection tells us that Jesus has conquered sin and death on our behalf, and the personal witness in Revelation attests to the ongoing presence of the resurrected Lord in the lives of believers.

Goals for the Learners:
(1) to hear anew the Easter story.
(2) to experience the ongoing presence of the living Christ.
(3) to celebrate Easter.

Pronunciation Guide:
Domitian (duh mish' uhn)
liminal (li' me nal)
   [barely perceptible with the senses]
Sardis (sahr' dis)

Laodicea (lay od i see' uh)
Nicolaitan (nik uh lay' uh tuhn)
Rabbouni (ra boo' ni)

Supplies:
Bibles, newsprint and marker, paper and pencils, hymnals, newspapers and/or several magazines, CD or tape and appropriate player, votive candles and matches, snacks, paper products

---

READING THE SCRIPTURE

NRSV
John 20:11-16, 30-31

¹¹But Mary stood weeping outside the tomb. As she wept, she bent over to look into the tomb; ¹²and she saw two angels in

NIV
John 20:11-16, 30-31

¹¹But Mary stood outside the tomb crying. As she wept, she bent over to look into the tomb ¹²and saw two angels in white, seated

white, sitting where the body of Jesus had been lying, one at the head and the other at the feet. [13]They said to her, "Woman, why are you weeping?" She said to them, "They have taken away my Lord, and I do not know where they have laid him." [14]When she had said this, she turned around and saw Jesus standing there, but she did not know that it was Jesus. [15]Jesus said to her, "Woman, why are you weeping? Whom are you looking for?" Supposing him to be the gardener, she said to him, "Sir, if you have carried him away, tell me where you have laid him, and I will take him away." [16]Jesus said to her, "Mary!" She turned and said to him in Hebrew, "Rabbouni!" (which means Teacher).

[30]Now Jesus did many other signs in the presence of his disciples, which are not written in this book. [31]But these are written so that you may come to believe that Jesus is the Messiah, the Son of God, and that through believing you may have life in his name.

Revelation 1:12, 17-18
[12]Then I turned to see whose voice it was that spoke to me.
[17]When I saw him, I fell at his feet as though dead. **But he placed his right hand on me, saying, "Do not be afraid; I am the first and the last, [18]and the living one. I was dead, and see, I am alive forever and ever;** and I have the keys of Death and of Hades."

where Jesus' body had been, one at the head and the other at the foot.
[13]They asked her, "Woman, why are you crying?"
"They have taken my Lord away," she said, "and I don't know where they have put him." [14]At this, she turned around and saw Jesus standing there, but she did not realize that it was Jesus.
[15]"Woman," he said, "why are you crying? Who is it you are looking for?"
Thinking he was the gardener, she said, "Sir, if you have carried him away, tell me where you have put him, and I will get him."
[16]Jesus said to her, "Mary."
She turned toward him and cried out in Aramaic, "Rabboni!" (which means Teacher).
[30]Jesus did many other miraculous signs in the presence of his disciples, which are not recorded in this book. [31]But these are written that you may believe that Jesus is the Christ, the Son of God, and that by believing you may have life in his name.

Revelation 1:12, 17-18
[12]I turned around to see the voice that was speaking to me.
[17]When I saw him, I fell at his feet as though dead. **Then he placed his right hand on me and said: "Do not be afraid. I am the First and the Last. [18]I am the Living One; I was dead, and behold I am alive for ever and ever!** And I hold the keys of death and Hades."

UNDERSTANDING THE SCRIPTURE

John 20:1-10. The beloved disciple and Peter are often juxtaposed in the Fourth Gospel, probably not in an attempt to set the two in competition (though the image of the two of them racing to the tomb might suggest this), but to gain a place for the beloved disciple—the disciple whose witness undergirds these communities of readers' faith far more directly than Peter's witness—a place of prominence as a key witness to Jesus and as one to whom Jesus had assigned an important role in the work that would follow Jesus' departure (see John 21:20-24).

The presence of the burial clothes in the tomb functions as a "sign" since, if the body of Jesus had been stolen, the thieves would surely have kept the body wrapped up neatly in the shroud and other linens. The special attention given to the placement of the head coverings, moreover, suggests that the wearer had first sat up straight, then removed the head wrappings, placing them down on the stone slab where his head had been. That the Fourth Evangelist intends for the placement and presence of the linens to be read thus is clear from the climax of this first episode: The beloved disciple saw these things arrayed thus *and believed*—and this without the benefit of being schooled in a reading of the Old Testament that led him to expect this resurrection (as the readers of the Fourth Gospel were). It is important to the evangelist to highlight that they came to faith on the basis of what they experienced, not what they read.

John 20:11-18. This episode began with a focus on Mary, whose love for Jesus brought her to mourn at the tomb before daybreak (20:1), and whose report precipitates the action of John 20:3-10. Mary is once again in the center of our attention. She comes by stages to leave behind the grave clothes and move toward the risen Jesus standing behind her, speaking her name in a beautiful enactment of John 10:3, 14 ("he calls his own sheep by name and leads them out;" "I know my own and my own know me").

The Fourth Evangelist appears to speak about Jesus' ascension differently from what we read in Luke and Acts. In the Fourth Evangelist's understanding, Mary has caught Jesus in a liminal state as he is in the process of glorification, but before its completion after he has ascended to the Father. When Jesus appears to the disciples on that same evening, he bestows the Holy Spirit upon them, signaling that his glorification was now complete (20:22; 7:39), and that he has in fact made the prerequisite return to the Father that would precede the sending of the Holy Spirit (16:4b-18). This would also help account for Jesus' reluc-

tance to be touched at this moment, whereas he will invite the touch of his disciple Thomas a week later, although there is also merit to the traditional view that Jesus was signaling to Mary that the disciples' relationship with him would now be decisively different from the relationship they had when they could, in fact, relate to him via his physical presence.

John 20:30-31. The annals of the books of Kings commonly conclude with a reference to other books that contained the "rest" of the deeds of a particular monarch (see 1 Kings 11:41; 14;19, 29; 15:7, 23, 31; and so on; the literary convention persists in 1 Maccabees 9:22). The Fourth Evangelist is playing on this convention as he calls attention not to where the reader can go for more information, but to the purpose of the information that has been provided: The "signs" should lead to a deeper belief (John 2:11, 23; 4:54). The Fourth Gospel is probably not a missionary document, although that is primarily how the Gospel of John is popularly used, but an invitation to disciples to deepen their understanding of who Jesus is as the Messiah and the Son of God, beyond previous understandings of those titles.

Revelation 1:9-16. The John to whom the Revelation is given presents himself rather modestly as an equal to those whom he addresses. His self-description also invites the addressees to see themselves as those who have a share in the kingdom of God, the trials that faithfulness to God must bring, and the posture of patient endurance by which one arrives at the promised place of rest. This is strategic because several of the congregations he addresses experience *no* trial for their witness (Sardis and Laodicea; see Revelation 3:1-4, 15-18), suggesting that their witness is not all that alive, and some are busily trying to *avoid* trials (for example, those who welcome the Nicolaitans' message that one can make room for a little idolatry and still enjoy the gifts of the One God; see Revelation 2:14-15, 20-23).

The authority of John's message comes from two major sources. The first is the presentation of the "real" speaker as Jesus (as here), or as the Spirit, or God, or angelic beings. The congregations find themselves addressed less by John and more invited into John's religious experience as witnesses alongside him to the messages given by these otherworldly beings. The second is the Hebrew Scriptures, which permeate John's language. John's vision of the glorified Christ resonates with details from Daniel's vision of God, the Son of Man, and a great angel (see Daniel 7:9, 13; 10:5-6). The sounds he hears recall the trumpet blast of God's voice in Exodus 19:16, 19 and the "sound of mighty waters" made by God's throne as it moves in Ezekiel 1:24. This provides continuity between John's vision and earlier experiences of God's presence and representatives, as well as signaling the significance of Jesus now in his glorified existence.

Revelation 1:17-20. The motif of falling down before an otherworldly being, being touched by the being's hand, and hearing the words "Do not fear" are all reminiscent of Daniel 10:9-11, where another seer recounts being overwhelmed by the presence of a superhuman being. Jesus identifies himself with the words spoken by God in Isaiah 44:6, and then in terms more particular to his own experience of dying and rising again to an indestructible life. By virtue of his triumph over death, he now holds power over death and the grave, such that his followers may be assured that death and the grave will not separate them from Jesus and eternal life.

The image of the Son of God holding seven stars in his hand may resonate with another image available to the churches in Asia Minor. After the emperor Domitian's infant son died, the little one was declared a god (and son of the god, Domitian) and portrayed on commemorative coins seated upon the globe with his hands outstretched to seven stars. The glorified Jesus, clothed with the power of the true God, stands in stark contrast with such pretentious imitations from self-glorifying governments.

Just what is meant by the "angels of the churches" is greatly debated. Are these local bishops? Angels responsible for the guidance of churches? Nevertheless, the vision shows us the glorified Christ standing in the midst of his churches, communicating his discernment of their strengths, their weaknesses, and the way to overcome the challenges before them.

INTERPRETING THE SCRIPTURE

When Jesus Calls Your Name

The Fourth Evangelist has been very attentive to the importance of recognizing "signs" and of moving from the "sign" to "belief" in Jesus as the Son of God (see John 2:11, 23; 4:54; 20:30-31). We may not be surprised, then, to see an intensification of interest in "signs" at the climax of Jesus' glorification and the revelation of who Jesus truly is (namely, "the Son of God"). Even though we do not have access to such signs as the disciples did, we are surrounded by signs if we have the eyes to perceive. The sacrament of Holy Communion is one such "visible and outward sign" of an "invisible and inward grace," if we attend to it expectantly. But there are so many other things, events, sights that can become "signs" ushering us into the presence of the divine if the Lord chooses and we are open.

It is perhaps to nurture such an openness that the Fourth Evangelist features Mary—open, loving, seeking—so prominently in his account of Easter morning. In this story, all the necessary preparations for burial were already accomplished before the Sabbath (John 19:40; contrast Luke 24:1), so Mary has no agenda here other than to show her love for Jesus by grieving at his tomb. When the disciples bend down to look into the tomb, they see the linens used to wrap the body (notably, set separately into two places on the slab). When Mary bends down to look into the tomb, she sees not a pair of linen cloths, but a pair of "messengers" of the resurrection. John has structured this story to show how Jesus breaks in upon his disciple, moving her from the physical signs to the real presence of the risen One. These messengers ask, "Woman, why are you weeping," but later we find that these are Jesus' words to her (compare John 20:13 and 20:15). She comes closer to Jesus, but still does not recognize his presence until he calls her by name, at which point she has completed her journey from sign to real presence.

The Jesus of the Fourth Gospel seeks such a relationship with his disciples in every age. The sending of the Holy Spirit is the means by which Jesus remains present with his disciples (John 14:15-18, 25-26; 16:7-15), the means by which Jesus continues to dwell in us and we in him (John 15:1-8; 17:20-23). John thus invites us to become witnesses of the resurrection by loving Jesus and longing to be near him, by seeking him out, by allowing the signs God has placed around us to become avenues by which Jesus can seek us out and meet us, calling us to himself as the signs become messengers, as our imperfect awareness of his presence becomes a complete awareness.

The Living Christ

Revelation presents us with a striking picture of the glorified Jesus, Jesus not as he existed in distant Palestine but as he lives forever in the presence of God on the far side of death. The import of John's weaving of references to Old Testament visions of God and the Son of Man throughout this passage is unmistakable: Beyond the resurrection, Jesus is endowed with the power and glory of God. His oneness with the Father is evident.

Once again, the emphasis on Jesus' resurrected state does not contribute to a sense of our distance from him, but rather his proximity to us. The vision of Jesus standing in the midst of the seven lampstands is an image of Jesus' presence among his churches. The surprise of the book that most dramatically looks ahead to Christ's final coming (already announced in Revelation 1:7) is that he already stands in our midst! The One who will judge the world already inspects his congregations, affirming their faithful discipleship, drawing their attention to the obstacles they must overcome to follow him in complete faithfulness and with complete effectiveness in their witness. (This is the purpose of Revelation 2–3.)

In the opening chapters of Revelation, John orients us to the risen Lord in a very particular way. We are directed to grow in our awareness of his presence, to listen for his word to us (whether communicated through the Spirit, through his "witnesses," or through the sacred texts that continually breathe new life and new insight into our situation), and to respond to both his encouragement and admonition with grateful obedience. The more we thus attend to our relationship with the living Christ, John assures us, the more confident we can be as we look forward to his coming again.

No Dead Ends

As part of his examinations as a student at the university, Oscar Wilde was given a Greek New Testament opened to the Passion Story and told to translate. When his examiners were satisfied that his grasp of Greek was sufficient, they told him to stop. Always irreverent, he is reputed to have said that he would prefer to read on "to see how it ends." John 20 provides a wonderful happy ending to Jesus' story, the fulfillment of all the promises Jesus had made to his disciples about their sorrow turning into joy (John 16:20-22), the triumphant proclamation of the One who "was dead," that "see, I am alive forever and ever" (Revelation 1:18).

But the Easter story is far more personal than that. This same One proclaims: "Because I live, you also will live" (John 14:19). Jesus' resurrection and entry into the presence of God the Father is but the "first fruits" of God's harvest, the "shape of things to come" for all Jesus' followers (see 1 Corinthians 15:20-22; Hebrews 2:9-10; 6:19-20; 12:1-2). It has also given Jesus the power over death and the grave—specifically, the power to "open up" the grave, and "open up" the door to life beyond death, on behalf of his faithful ones.

Easter is significant because we can now live in the assurance that death is not the end of our story, any more than it was the end of Jesus' story. We are emboldened to "die with Christ" to our sinful desires and to our cowardly compacts with the unjust powers around us, to "give away" our lives in Christian service rather than fearfully cling to our lives, knowing that the life we give in service to God we shall receive back again forever.

SHARING THE SCRIPTURE

PREPARING TO TEACH

Preparing Our Hearts

This week's devotional reading is found in Romans 14:7-12. In verse 9 Paul writes, "For to this end Christ died and lived again, so that he might be Lord of both the dead and the living." What difference does Jesus' crucifixion and resurrection make in terms of the way you view life and death? Would you say that the emotion that you most experience when you contemplate your own death is fear, joy, surprise, anxiety about the unknown, or something else? Why do you think this emotion holds sway over you? Write your thoughts in your spiritual journal.

Pray that you and the adult learners will praise God for the life, death, and resurrection of Jesus the Christ.

Preparing Our Minds

Study the background Scripture, John 20:1-18, 30-31 and Revelation 1:9-20; and lesson Scripture, John 20:11-16, 30-31 and Revelation 1:12, 17-18. As you prepare this week's lesson ponder the transforming good news that you are able to celebrate this Easter.

Write on newsprint:
❑ information for next week's lesson, found under "Continue the Journey."
❑ activities for further spiritual growth in "Continue the Journey."

Bring newspapers or relatively current news magazines. (These will not be cut or defaced.)

Select music and an appropriate player for "Experience the Ongoing Presence of the Living Christ." The music you choose might be instrumental meditative pieces, or you may prefer to use Easter hymns.

Set out matches and candles, preferably votive candles, on the class's worship table.

Plan whatever snacks you will bring for "Celebrate Easter." You may want to ask class members to bring some food, too. Be sure to have on hand the paper products and utensils needed to serve these treats.

LEADING THE CLASS

(1) Gather to Learn

❖ Welcome the class members and introduce any guests.

❖ Pray that all who have come together on this special day will celebrate the wonderful news of Easter.

❖ Distribute the newspaper and/or magazines you have brought to class and ask the students to find some good news. (If you don't have any print materials with you, ask the students to report on articles they have read that report good news.) These stories might focus, for example, on rising test scores in the local schools, locating a lost child, or a community escaping the ravages of a natural disaster. Discuss why this good news—whatever it is— would have a positive impact on some people's lives.

❖ Read aloud today's focus statement: **People long to hear good news, especially if it transforms their lives for the better. What transforming good news do we have to celebrate this Easter? John's account of the resurrection tells us that Jesus has conquered sin and death on our behalf, and the personal witness in Revelation attests to the ongoing presence of the resurrected Lord in the lives of believers.**

(2) Hear Anew the Easter Story

❖ Read John 20:11-16 as a drama by selecting readers for the parts of Mary, two angels, Jesus, and a narrator.

■ Call on volunteers to retell this story from Mary's point of view in the first person. Or, if you prefer, read "When Jesus Calls Your Name" in Interpreting the Scripture.

■ Distribute paper and pencils. Invite the students to meditate on this question and write anything that springs to mind. **Jesus is calling your name, too. What does he want you to discover about him and about yourself?**

■ Choose several people who are willing to share with the class what they have discovered.

❖ Select a volunteer to read John 20: 30-31.

■ Use the information for these verses in Understanding the Scripture to help the students recognize:

(a) the literary convention that John is using;

(b) the purpose of this Gospel.

■ Invite the adults to talk about how the Fourth Gospel has helped them to believe "that Jesus is the Messiah, the Son of God" (20:31). Encourage the students to mention specific stories in John that are particularly meaningful to them.

❖ Ask the adults to bow their heads and imagine Christ speaking to them as you read Revelation 1:12, 17-18 aloud.

■ Talk with the class, or in small groups, about words or images that focused sharply in the learners' minds.

■ Read "The Living Christ" from Interpreting the Scripture.

■ Invite the adults to describe how this passage from Revelation enables them to feel closely connected to Christ.

(3) Experience the Ongoing Presence of the Living Christ

❖ Invite volunteers to tell the class, or a small group, about an experience in which they were surprised by God. This could be a life-changing incident, but it need not be.

❖ Play background music. Encourage the students to close their eyes as this music is played and imagine themselves in the presence of the living Christ.

❖ Tell the students, prior to beginning the music, that if they feel led to do so they are invited to come and light a candle as a sign of God's presence in their lives. (If you have fewer candles than students, suggest that the students simply add their lighted match to the candle flame that is already burning.)

❖ **Option:** When the students have responded to the worshipful mood, end this activity by singing "Sweet, Sweet Spirit."

(4) Celebrate Easter

❖ Encourage the students to talk about how your church celebrates Easter. Perhaps some members of long-standing will recall traditions that are no longer observed.

❖ Ask the students to compare and contrast the church's observance of Easter with that of Christmas. Which holiday seems to be more of a "big deal"? Which holiday is more important biblically? (Help the adults understand that although Christmas has become a secular event due to its economic ramifications, Jesus' resurrection, not his birth, was most important to the early church. It should be so for us as well.)

❖ Invite the class to consider ways that Easter could be celebrated so that its importance as the primary holy day of the Christian year can be emphasized. List these ideas on newsprint. Submit these ideas to your pastor, worship committee, or whoever else might be responsible for implementing them.

❖ Close this portion of the lesson by offering snacks, such as Easter candy, eggs, or sweetbread, as a sign of celebration.

(5) Continue the Journey

❖ Pray that Christ's resurrection will take on deeper meaning for all the participants.

❖ Read aloud this preparation for next week's lesson. You may also want to post it on newsprint for the students to copy. **Prepare for next week's session entitled "Worshiping God Alone" by reading Revelation 4, which is both the background and Scripture lesson. Focus on these ideas as you read: Most people want to worship someone or something larger and more powerful than themselves. Who or what is truly worthy of our worship? Revelation 4 describes how God, glorious on the divine throne, is worthy of worship from all beings in heaven and on earth.**

❖ Read aloud the following three ideas. Challenge the students to commit themselves to use these activities as a springboard to spiritual growth.

(1) **Tell someone the good news of the risen Christ, whose resurrection opens the door for those who believe in him to enter into the everlasting presence of God.**

(2) **Be alert to meet God in an unexpected situation this week. Perhaps like Mary you will find the risen Lord in a place you least expect him.**

(3) **Look around your church building and home. Where do you see symbols of Christ's resurrection? What do these symbols represent? Which one(s) is most meaningful to you? Why?**

❖ Sing or read aloud "Cristo Vive (Christ Is Risen)."

❖ Say this benediction to conclude the session. You may wish to ask the students to echo it as you read: **Go in peace to love God and your neighbor, both in truth and in action.**

UNIT 2: A NEW COMMUNITY IN CHRIST
WORSHIPING GOD ALONE

PREVIEWING THE LESSON

Lesson Scripture: Revelation 4
Background Scripture: Revelation 4
Key Verse: Revelation 4:11

Focus of the Lesson:
Most people want to worship someone or something larger and more powerful than themselves. Who or what is truly worthy of our worship? Revelation 4 describes how God, glorious on the divine throne, is worthy of worship from all beings in heaven and on earth.

Goals for the Learners:
(1) to encounter the imagery in Revelation 4 of God as worthy of praise.
(2) to explore the implications of this passage for enriching their own worship.
(3) to praise God.

Pronunciation Guide:
carnelian (kar nel' yen)   Irenaeus (Ir in e' us)
pneumata (pnew' mah tah)   Tobit (toh' bit)

Supplies:
Bibles, newsprint and marker, paper and pencils, hymnals, worship symbols, optional unlined paper and colored pencils, commentaries

---

READING THE SCRIPTURE

NRSV
Revelation 4

¹After this I looked, and there in heaven a door stood open! And the first voice, which I had heard speaking to me like a trumpet, said, "Come up here, and I will show you what must take place after this." ²At once I was in the spirit, and there in heaven stood a throne, with one seated on the throne!

NIV
Revelation 4

¹After this I looked, and there before me was a door standing open in heaven. And the voice I had first heard speaking to me like a trumpet said, "Come up here, and I will show you what must take place after this." ²At once I was in the Spirit, and there before me was a throne in heaven with

[3]And the one seated there looks like jasper and carnelian, and around the throne is a rainbow that looks like an emerald. [4]Around the throne are twenty-four thrones, and seated on the thrones are twenty-four elders, dressed in white robes, with golden crowns on their heads. [5]Coming from the throne are flashes of lightning, and rumblings and peals of thunder, and in front of the throne burn seven flaming torches, which are the seven spirits of God; [6]and in front of the throne there is something like a sea of glass, like crystal.

Around the throne, and on each side of the throne, are four living creatures, full of eyes in front and behind: [7]the first living creature like a lion, the second living creature like an ox, the third living creature with a face like a human face, and the fourth living creature like a flying eagle. [8]And the four living creatures, each of them with six wings, are full of eyes all around and inside. Day and night without ceasing they sing,

"Holy, holy, holy,
the Lord God the Almighty,
who was and is and is to come."

[9]And whenever the living creatures give glory and honor and thanks to the one who is seated on the throne, who lives forever and ever, [10]the twenty-four elders fall before the one who is seated on the throne and worship the one who lives forever and ever; they cast their crowns before the throne, singing,

[11] "You are worthy, our Lord and God,
to receive glory and honor and power,
for you created all things,
and by your will they existed and
were created."

someone sitting on it. [3]And the one who sat there had the appearance of jasper and carnelian. A rainbow, resembling an emerald, encircled the throne. [4]Surrounding the throne were twenty-four other thrones, and seated on them were twenty-four elders. They were dressed in white and had crowns of gold on their heads. [5]From the throne came flashes of lightning, rumblings and peals of thunder. Before the throne, seven lamps were blazing. These are the seven spirits of God. [6]Also before the throne there was what looked like a sea of glass, clear as crystal.

In the center, around the throne, were four living creatures, and they were covered with eyes, in front and in back. [7]The first living creature was like a lion, the second was like an ox, the third had a face like a man, the fourth was like a flying eagle. [8]Each of the four living creatures had six wings and was covered with eyes all around, even under his wings. Day and night they never stop saying:

"Holy, holy, holy
is the Lord God Almighty,
who was, and is, and is to come."

[9]Whenever the living creatures give glory, honor and thanks to him who sits on the throne and who lives for ever and ever, [10]the twenty-four elders fall down before him who sits on the throne, and worship him who lives for ever and ever. They lay their crowns before the throne and say:

[11]"You are worthy, our Lord and God,
to receive glory and honor and power,
for you created all things,
and by your will they were created
and have their being."

UNDERSTANDING THE SCRIPTURE

Revelation 4:1. First-century Jewish and early Christian views of the universe often assume a number of layered heavens, with the realm of God located in a heaven beyond the visible heavens (see, for example, Hebrews 4:14; 9:24; 12:26-28). The "open door" is necessary for John to be able to peer into, and then to enter into by the Spirit, the activity of God's throne room (what the author of Hebrews calls "heaven itself," Hebrews 9:24). This is not an intimation of a "rapture," as if all Christians go where John goes at this point in the drama. The church is still very much present on earth until the end, sealed by God but not exempt from trials (Revelation 7:1-17; 12:17–13:18). The things that "must take place after this" (see Revelation 1:1, 19) refer to the action of Revelation 5 and following, where the Lamb takes the scroll and, with it, the reins of history as he initiates judgment upon the world.

Revelation 4:2-3. The remainder of chapters 4 and 5 consists of a "throne vision" and a narration of the activities in the heavenly court around the throne of God (see Psalm 11:4; 103:19). John draws heavily on the imagery of earlier throne visions, particularly the vision of Ezekiel 1 and Isaiah 6:2-3, to which most of John's imagery can be traced directly. Using traditional language, John depicts God enthroned over the universe.

Revelation 4:4-6a. God is surrounded by various orders of angelic attendants—the cherubim, the seven angels of the presence, the "elders" upon their "thrones," and the undifferentiated masses of angels at the outer circles. Later, we will encounter other angels stationed in the lower heavens, in charge of the winds and the waters of judgment (see Revelation 7:1; 16:5). John's cosmology is almost identical to that of the author of the *Testament of Levi,* a Jewish text from the first-century B.C., suggesting that John is creating a familiar picture in

Revelation 4 rather than a novel and distinctively Christian one (that will come with chapter 5).

An important feature of this heavenly court is that it is also depicted primarily as a heavenly temple (see Revelation 11:19; 14:17; 15:5-6, 8). John builds on a well-established tradition of reading Exodus 25:40 as an indication that Moses was shown not a blueprint for the tabernacle on Sinai, but was shown the heavenly temple in whose holiest place God actually lives, of which the tabernacle would be a copy. This reading of Exodus 25:40 is attested in the early first century A.D. in Wisdom of Solomon 9:8 and is developed most fully later in the first century in Hebrews (see 6:19-20; 8:1-5; 9:11-12, 23-24). Thus it comes as no surprise that John's heaven features angelic priests. Though subject to a wide variety of imaginative readings, the twenty-four elders most likely represent the heavenly counterpart of the twenty-four orders of priests (see 1 Chronicles 24:4; 25:9-31), as they are seen offering incense for the prayers of the holy ones in Revelation 5:8 (a priestly task; see Luke 1:8-10). We would encounter other angelic priests in Revelation 8:2-5 and 15:6 (note especially their dress), as well as the paraphernalia of a temple (an altar of incense in 6:9; 8:3; the ark of the covenant, 11:19).

With the lightning flashes and sounds and thunders of Revelation 4:5, John evokes the appearance of God at Sinai just prior to the giving of the Torah. The same words appear at the strategic junctures of Revelation 8:5, 11:19, and 16:18, reminding us that the God of covenant justice enforces that justice throughout history and at the end of history. The God of the New Covenant is none other than the God of the First Covenant, whose primary goal is that God's people should reflect faithfully God's justice and holiness in the world.

The "seven spirits of God" are often identified with the Holy Spirit on the basis of Isaiah's sevenfold description of the "spirit" that will rest on the heir to David's throne (Isaiah 11:1-3). This is, however, a biased interpretation—all the more as Isaiah never draws attention to the number seven, and as John describes seven *spirits*. Given the tradition of speaking about angels as "spirits" or "winds" (*pneumata,* see Psalm 104:4; Hebrews 1:7) and the tradition of seven angels of the presence (see Tobit 12:15; Revelation 8:2), we are on better ground regarding them as another order of angels (presented using imagery derived from Zechariah 4:2, 10; see Revelation 5:6).

Revelation 4:6b-8. The strange "living creatures" are a development of the cherubim that flanked the mercy seat on the ark (Exodus 37:7-9) and the seraphim that encircle God in Isaiah's vision (Isaiah 6:2-3) and that carry God's throne in Ezekiel 1. Since Irenaeus, the second-century Christian author, these figures have been read as the "four faces" of Christ in the four Gospels (a clever explanation posed more to justify having four Gospels rather than just one in the canon), but they are much more closely and intrinsically connected with this innermost order of angels. That they do not have rest by day and night as they worship God contrasts forcefully with the human beings we will encounter in Revelation 14:9-11, who do not have rest by day or night from their torments because they did *not* worship God, directing their worship toward other gods.

The cherubim's song recalls verbatim the song sung by the cherubim in Isaiah 6:3, the second phrase being artfully reworked to highlight attributes of God especially important for John. That God is "the one who was, and who is, and *is coming*" does not evoke God's eternity (as did a very similar acclamation of Zeus, "who was, is, and will be forever"), but God's forthcoming intervention in history.

Revelation 4:9-11. The scene of worship expands outward to involve every order of angels (completed in Revelation 5:11-12) in the ceaseless adoration of God. The acclamation (very similar to the acclamation found in 1 Chronicles 29:11) makes a very strong political claim on God's behalf that might be missed in the familiar religious language. Taking up "the glory and the honor and the power"—these lists are expanded in 5:12, 14—is illumined by the acclamation of Revelation 11:15-19, which celebrates God taking away the power from human rulers (and their demonic supporter; see Revelation 13:1-4) and ushering in a new empire, the kingdom of God. Who is on these human thrones (Revelation 13:2; 16:10-11)? None other than the Roman emperors and their client kings, whose self-glorifying and self-serving domination, John claims, must come to an end.

The rationale for God's "worthiness" is found in God's creation of all things (a common topic of Jewish texts: Genesis 1:1; Psalm 95:5; 146:6; for example). Because God created all creatures, all creatures are indebted to God, to honor and serve God with all their being. But this is not what John sees as he peers out into the world of the Roman empire and its provinces. The balance of Revelation displays how God vindicates God's honor against a rebellious and ungrateful world.

INTERPRETING THE SCRIPTURE

Finding the Center

The starting point for Revelation, and for the life choices that John urges his seven congregations to make, is the throne of God at the center of the universe. The arrangement of the angelic orders in ever-widening concentric circles around God's throne, and their

God-directed activity, helps us locate the true center of the universe (hint: It's not us). This is a "revelation" for his congregations since, as they look out in their streets, they see many alternative centers of worship around which their neighbors order their lives. Temples and statues to the emperors and to the traditional Greco-Roman gods dominate the public spaces of their cities. Those who worship there consider themselves to be upholding the virtues of piety, justice, and "family values," while looking contemptuously—and suspiciously—at the Christians as a deviant minority who avoid the public centers of worship, gathering in private homes for clandestine rites. As John reveals the bigger picture, however, it is the majority of the Christians' neighbors who actually form the deviant minority, who are out of alignment with the rest of creation that knows its God (see Revelation 9:20-21).

We are also all too often enticed into making idols rather than God the center of our attention and devotion. Idolaters were criticized for worshiping the works of their own hands: We are not far from this in our devotion to consumerism, nationalism, and self-gratification in its many forms. John would have us take stock—with the seven churches that received diagnostic words from the glorified Jesus in chapters 2 and 3—of where the centers of our lives really are. Do we live for what the work of our hands can bring? Do our lives betray the destructive patterns and behaviors that result from that misalignment (see Romans 1:18-32; 1 Peter 4:1-4; Revelation 9:20-21)?

The ceaseless worship of the angelic orders challenges us to never take worship away from God to give our allegiance and obedience and reverence to other gods. It challenges us to find ourselves in our proper place and orientation, always and in everything giving honor to the One who made us.

Encountering God in Worship

Peering through the open door in heaven, we cannot help but be struck by how "real" God is, how unmistakable God's presence there. It is still "mystery," a sight described impressionistically. Nevertheless, God is clearly real and present for the angels and archangels and all the company of heaven as they worship God. The vision of heavenly worship is once again a pattern for our worship. As we join our voices "with angels, archangels, and all the company of heaven," we are not merely talking to ourselves and to one another. The focus of worship is not our edification, however necessary that is. In worship we speak to God, we pay attention to God, we listen to God. We do not only find *ourselves* around God; we find *God* in the acts of adoration, thanksgiving, profession, and petition.

How do we know the presence of God? We know by the experience of God's holiness, just as Isaiah knew he had encountered God when he came to the temple, rather than just performed his religious duties (Isaiah 6:1-8). Our souls recognize the presence of their Maker with the same ecstasy attested by many of the psalmists. John stands in a long tradition of entering into a place where the presence of God is keenly perceived, and invites us to seek this in worship (again, with the psalmists: see Psalm 27:4, 8-9a). For ultimately the center of the universe is not a conviction about God; it is the God who chooses to be available to enter into relationship with each one of God's creatures.

Created, Not Self-Made

I have worked hard throughout my education and my professional life to attain what my family and I enjoy. It would be easy to fall victim to the myth that I am yet another "self-made man," as the expression goes. With this mind-set comes the implications: I owe no one anything; I am self-sufficient; I have earned my right to enjoy what is mine.

If that all seems ugly, it should. If that reminds you of a common Western mind-set, it should. John calls us to remember what the psalmist had declared long ago: "Know that the LORD is God. It is he that made us, and not we ourselves" (Psalm 100:3, following a major variant textual tradition). This alternative view moves gratitude toward God to the center of our being, rather than personal achievement and merit; it calls us to express our gratitude in acts of love, worship, and service. In reminding us of our complete dependence upon God, it also calls us to consider our deep interdependence upon other creatures—our families, our neighbors whose labors are so essential to us, our ecosystem that is too easy to objectify and exploit—so that we learn a new respect for them as essential facets of God's creation.

A Vision for Congregational Worship

The visions of worship in Revelation challenge us in the midst of our contemporary debates about congregational worship, which is moving more and more in a consumer-oriented direction rather than a God-centered one. The focus of worship planning has become worship *style*—what suits my taste, what suits your taste—rather than the declaration of the worthiness and accomplishments of the One seated upon the throne.

the throne. The distance we have strayed can be measured from the fact that the worship of God and the Lamb is meant to unite those from "every tribe and language and people and nation" (Revelation 5:9), whereas our worship often results in division within and between our congregations. In heaven, we will not be divided according to our personal preferences ("Will that be clapping or non-clapping, Ma'am?").

John pushes against our generational, ethnic, and traditional preferences (including the tradition of contemporary Christian services) and pushes us toward designing worship experiences that will represent an expression of devotion and adoration offered to God in the idioms and dialects of *all* present in the worshiping body—from every ethnic background, denominational heritage, age group, cultural and liturgical background. What makes worship "work," for want of a better word, is not the style, but the focus. Ultimately what makes worship "work" is the level of awareness of the Divine Other on the part of each worshiper. Where we are centered on God and not ourselves, and where our worship reflects the diversity of the communion of saints that God has called together and nurtured in worship throughout the centuries, there the eschatological vision for worship begins to be realized.

SHARING THE SCRIPTURE

PREPARING TO TEACH

Preparing Our Hearts

This week's devotional reading is found in Psalm 111. This is truly a hymn of praise. It begins and ends with praise and explains why praise is due to the Lord. Make a list of those reasons. What other reasons can you think of to praise God? Add them to your list. Spend time now in praise. Read several psalms aloud, or sing some hymns or praise choruses. Create an artwork that exudes praise for God.

Pray that you and the adult learners will be mindful of reasons to praise God and take every opportunity to do so.

Preparing Our Minds

Study the background and lesson Scripture, both found in Revelation 4. As you contemplate, think about who or what is truly worthy of your worship.

Write on newsprint:

❑ Psalm 111, if you do not have access to hymnals with a Psalter. Make sure that the students can easily tell where one verse ends and another begins, perhaps by using different colored markers for odd- and even-numbered verses.

❑ information for next week's lesson, found under "Continue the Journey."

❑ activities for further spiritual growth in "Continue the Journey."

Gather some symbols of worship, such as a cross, candle, Bible, chalice, and altar cloth. If you have a worship table, arrange these symbols on the table.

Practice reading Revelation 4 dramatically. Or, during the week contact a student who is an expressive reader and ask him or her to be prepared to present this chapter.

Decide which option you will use to explore the information in the Understanding the Scripture portion for the "Encounter the Imagery in Revelation 4 of God as Worthy of Praise" segment.

LEADING THE CLASS

(1) Gather to Learn

❖ Welcome the class members and introduce any guests.

❖ Pray that everyone who has come will experience the nearness of God and give praise and thanks for that presence.

❖ Encourage the students to tell the class or a small group why they attend worship. What is it that they hope to do or gain or experience or become as a result of worshiping?

❖ Read aloud today's focus statement: **Most people want to worship someone or something larger and more powerful than themselves. Who or what is truly worthy of our worship? Revelation 4 describes how God, glorious on the divine throne, is worthy of worship from all beings in heaven and on earth.**

(2) Encounter the Imagery in Revelation 4 of God as Worthy of Praise

❖ Read, or invite the person you have asked to be prepared to read, Revelation 4. Suggest that the class members close their eyes and imagine themselves in the scene, alert to sensory experiences.

❖ Talk with the class about the scene they envisioned. What could they see, hear, taste, touch, or smell?

❖ **Option:** Distribute (unlined) paper and colored pencils. Ask the students to choose one image from the biblical scene and sketch it, either from memory or by consulting their Bible. Display the sketches, in no particular order, on a wall or bulletin board. Discuss with the class what it might be like to worship in heaven.

❖ Point out the numbers cited in Revelation 4 and allow the adults an opportunity to comment on what they might represent.

❖ Delve into the images with the class by selecting one of these options.

■ **Option 1:** Divide into groups and make these assignments: Revelation 4:1; 4:2-3; 4:4-6a; 4:6b-8; 4:9-11. Distribute copies of *The New International Lesson Annual* (and other commentaries if you do not have enough *Annuals*) and ask the students to research information for their assigned verses. Provide time for them to report back to the class.

■ **Option 2:** Read aloud or use all of the information in Understanding the Scripture to prepare a lecture in which you explain the imagery to the class.

(3) Explore the Implications of This Passage for Enriching the Learners' Worship

❖ Direct the students' attention to the worship table where you have placed symbols of worship. Encourage the students to talk about how these symbols enhance worship for them.

❖ Invite the students to talk about other worship aids that are important to them. Perhaps your sanctuary has stained glass windows, paintings, or sculpture that helps to set the stage for worship. Possibly a choir, praise band, or instrumental ensemble is crucially important for some adults.

❖ Discuss these questions.

(1) How do these accessories help you to worship God?

(2) What would you miss if they were no longer in your worship space?

(3) What would you like to add to your worship service to make it more meaningful to you?

❖ Read aloud "A Vision for Congregational Worship" in Interpreting the Scripture.

❖ Divide the class into groups and ask each one to think of two or three ways that your congregation's worship would be different if you took seriously this vision, which is rooted in Revelation 4. Specifically consider how worship would be more God-centered.

❖ Provide time for the groups to report to the entire class. Record ideas on newsprint so they can be passed on to the pastor and/or worship committee.

(4) Praise God.

❖ Distribute hymnals if your books contain a Psalter and ask the students to read responsively Psalm 111 as an act of praise. If you do not have a Psalter available, write the psalm on newsprint prior to class so that everyone can see it. Read this psalm responsively.

(5) Continue the Journey

❖ Pray that all who have participated today will find new meaning in worship. Also pray for your writer, David, who turns forty today, and for your editor and "Sharing the Scripture" writer, Nan, who is celebrating a birthday on the 19th.

❖ Read aloud this preparation for next week's lesson. You may also want to post it on newsprint for the students to copy. **Prepare for next week's session entitled "Redeemable" by reading Revelation 5, noting particularly verses 1-5, 11-14. Center on these ideas: Most people want to know that there is a possibility for forgiveness when they do something wrong or make a mistake. What guarantee of forgiveness do we have? Revelation 5 reassures us that the Lamb, who is worthy of our praise, has redeemed us.**

❖ Read aloud the following three ideas. Challenge the students to commit themselves to use these activities as a springboard to spiritual growth.

(1) **Attend to all of the aspects of worship as you participate in services this week. What do you see, hear, taste, touch, or smell? What draws you closer to God? How was this service similar to and different from the worship of God in heaven, as described in Revelation 4?**

(2) **Read the entire book of Revelation, noting how the worship of God is presented. (We will continue to study Revelation throughout this quarter.)**

(3) **Write answers to this question in your spiritual journal: In a self-absorbed culture, how do we focus our worship on God?**

❖ Sing or read aloud "Hail, Thou Once Despised Jesus," based on Revelation 4:2-11.

❖ Say this benediction to conclude the session. You may wish to ask the students to echo it as you read: **Go in peace to love God and your neighbor, both in truth and in action.**

UNIT 2: A NEW COMMUNITY IN CHRIST
REDEEMABLE

PREVIEWING THE LESSON

Lesson Scripture: Revelation 5:1-5, 11-14
Background Scripture: Revelation 5
Key Verse: Revelation 5:13

Focus of the Lesson:
Most people want to know that there is a possibility for forgiveness when they do something wrong or make a mistake. What guarantee of forgiveness do we have? Revelation 5 reassures us that the Lamb, who is worthy of our praise, has redeemed us.

Goals for the Learners:
(1) to examine the image in Revelation 5 of Christ, our redeemer, as worthy of praise.
(2) to reflect on their own redemption and its significance for their lives.
(3) to pledge to live as redeemed people.

Pronunciation Guide:
Christology (kris tol' uh jee)   Decalogue (dek' uh log)
Diaspora (di as' puh ruh)   intertestamental (in ter tes te men' tuhl)
Johannine (joh han' in)   Maccabean (mak' uh bee en)
Nicolaitans (nik uh lay' uh taynes)

Supplies:
Bibles, newsprint and marker, paper and pencils, hymnals, picture of heavenly worship, tape or CD of Handel's *Messiah* and appropriate player

---

READING THE SCRIPTURE

NRSV
Revelation 5:1-5, 11-14

[1]Then I saw in the right hand of the one seated on the throne a scroll written on the inside and on the back, sealed with seven seals; [2]and I saw a mighty angel proclaiming with a loud voice, "Who is worthy to open the scroll and break its seals?" [3]And no one in

NIV
Revelation 5:1-5, 11-14

[1]Then I saw in the right hand of him who sat on the throne a scroll with writing on both sides and sealed with seven seals. [2]And I saw a mighty angel proclaiming in a loud voice, "Who is worthy to break the seals and open the scroll?" [3]But no one in heaven or on

heaven or on earth or under the earth was able to open the scroll or to look into it. [4]And I began to weep bitterly because no one was found worthy to open the scroll or to look into it. [5]Then one of the elders said to me, "Do not weep. See, the Lion of the tribe of Judah, the Root of David, has conquered, so that he can open the scroll and its seven seals."

[11]Then I looked, and I heard the voice of many angels surrounding the throne and the living creatures and the elders; they numbered myriads of myriads and thousands of thousands, [12]singing with full voice,

"Worthy is the Lamb that was
    slaughtered
to receive power and wealth and wisdom
    and might
and honor and glory and blessing!"

[13]Then I heard every creature in heaven and on earth and under the earth and in the sea, and all that is in them, singing,

**"To the one seated on the throne and
    to the Lamb
be blessing and honor and glory and
    might
forever and ever!"**

[14]And the four living creatures said, "Amen!" And the elders fell down and worshiped.

earth or under the earth could open the scroll or even look inside it. [4]I wept and wept because no one was found who was worthy to open the scroll or look inside. [5]Then one of the elders said to me, "Do not weep! See, the Lion of the tribe of Judah, the Root of David, has triumphed. He is able to open the scroll and its seven seals."

[11]Then I looked and heard the voice of many angels, numbering thousands upon thousands, and ten thousand times ten thousand. They encircled the throne and the living creatures and the elders. [12]In a loud voice they sang:

"Worthy is the Lamb, who was slain,
to receive power and wealth and wisdom
    and strength
and honor and glory and praise!"

[13]Then I heard every creature in heaven and on earth and under the earth and on the sea, and all that is in them, singing:

**"To him who sits on the throne and to
    the Lamb
be praise and honor and glory and
    power,
      for ever and ever!"**

[14]The four living creatures said, "Amen," and the elders fell down and worshiped.

UNDERSTANDING THE SCRIPTURE

Revelation 5:1-4. The stage has been set in chapter 4 for the action of chapter 5, which involves chiefly the delegation of authority by God to the Lamb, whose entrance is dramatically and purposefully delayed until verse 6. John continues to draw on the imagery of Ezekiel, recalling the scroll, written on both sides, of Ezekiel 2:9-10. This is an ominous resonance, since that scroll was full of words of woe and lamentation. Chapters 6 through 8 of Revelation are framed by the opening of the seals of this scroll, after which we encounter another strong or "mighty angel" (compare

Revelation 5:2 and 10:1) with an opened scroll that John will literally digest (10:9-10) so that he may proclaim the contents. The remainder of the book—the indictments of the Roman system of domination and the punishments of that system and all who are in collusion with its violence, deception, and corruption—presumably contains the oral enactment of this same scroll.

All this to say that the scroll in Revelation 5:1 is unusually important. The being who takes this scroll brings the temporal powers to account before God and sets in motion the reclaiming of the cosmos for God and

God's people. John creates a dramatic scene in which no one is found worthy of such authority. It is no accident that John uses the language of Exodus 20:4 with its prohibition of the making of cult images of anything "in the heaven [above], or in the earth [below], or [in the waters] under the earth" to list all those who are unworthy, declaring the inferiority of all the gods worshiped in the world around his congregations—including the emperor upon his throne. John's tears are actually an indictment of the presumption of all the so-called gods that fill the public spaces of the seven cities, and a dramatic lead-in to his central point: Those whom their neighbors worship are no match for the authority and worthiness of the Lamb!

Revelation 5:5-7. The Lamb is introduced in victorious and Messianic terms as the "Lion of the tribe of Judah," recalling Genesis 49:9-10, in which Judah is described as a lion's offspring. Genesis 49:10 was interpreted as a messianic prophecy in intertestamental Judaism, but the Greek translation used throughout much of the Jewish Diaspora and early Church intensifies this reading: "until the things stored up come to him, and he is the expectation of the nations." John joins this resonance with an image from Isaiah 11:1, identifying Jesus as the promised "shoot" or "root" that David puts forth.

The One named a "Lion" is depicted as a Lamb. We should not imagine a cute, cuddly lamb, but a strong and powerful ram (he is depicted with horns, after all) who—like the Maccabean heroes (also portrayed as horned lambs in the earlier apocalypse 1 Enoch 90:9)—conquers the enemies of God's people. What is distinctive is the manner of conquering, namely through the Lamb's death. Jesus' death as a new Passover sacrifice or as the slaughtered Servant of Isaiah 53:7 is clearly indicated. The Lamb mediates God's presence in this vision: His seven eyes are those same seven angelic ministers that make everything present to God and make God present everywhere (see Zechariah 4:10).

Revelation 5:8-10. The angelic orders (whose priestly role is made evident in 5:8b) offer to the Lamb the same acts of adoration (prostration, the acclamation of worthiness) they offered the One upon the throne, a clear statement about John's Christology.

The acclamation of the Lamb highlights his work of redemption, a word that is at home in the context of buying back hostages or prisoners of war or paying to liberate a person from slavery. To use such language makes a bold statement about the nature of our existence in this world apart from Christ: We are slaves and hostages to hostile powers, the pawns of temporal domination systems (exploitative, self-serving economic and political powers) or of demonic forces. (Paul would use the language of slavery to describe our state of being under sin and death in Romans 6:1-7:6.) Christ conquers our dominators and liberates us by dying on our behalf, a strategy that runs completely counter to the typical battle strategies of worldly leaders—but only thus could Christ have a different effect than those worldly leaders, providing a way out of bondage rather than perpetuating domination.

John uses repetitive language throughout Revelation. This is not due to lack of creativity. On the contrary, it is due to masterful crafting. The phrase "every tribe and language and people and nation" is a case in point. This phrase appears in this or some slightly modified form in Revelation 5:9; 7:9; 10:11; 11:9; 13:7; 17:15. Encountering the phrase in each place makes the hearers connect the dots, as it were, helping them perceive the environment of competition. The Beast and the Harlot rule over "every tribe and people and language and nation" (13:7; see 17:15), but they are not allowed to dominate *all*. The Lamb is at work redeeming people "from every tribe and language and people and nation" (5:9), who stand before God washed and redeemed (7:9), just as the

Lamb's servants bear witness before "many peoples and nations and languages and kings" (10:11; 11:9; 14:6), calling them to decide. Other voices in the seven churches are saying that one can have Christ's benefits and profit from Roman imperialism at the same time; the very rhythms of John's language oppose such conformist Christianity.

The phrase in verse 10, "a kingdom and priests," recalls God's declaration in Exodus 19:6 that his people would be "a priestly kingdom," a people set apart to serve the Holy God, if they would but keep God's commandments. The Lamb gathers such a people for God, and John reminds us throughout of our obligation to keep God's commandments and the witness of Jesus (Revelation 12:17; 14:12), to live out the identity that Jesus bestowed upon us at the cost of his own blood (see also 1 Peter 1:14-19).

Revelation 5:11-14. The circles of adoration expand exponentially in 5:11, 13 in a vision of universal acclamation of God's and the Lamb's right to rule (see note on Revelation 4:9-11 in Understanding the Scripture for April 15). This vision derives ultimately from Isaiah 45:22-23; 66:23; and Psalm 86:9, and was also brought into Christian hope as early as the "Christ Hymn" in Philippians 2:9-11. Of course, John and his congregations do not see "every creature" thus worshiping from day to day. Rather, they continue to see their neighbors participating in the worship of the traditional Greco-Roman gods and in the legitimation of Roman imperial rule via their participation in imperial cult. But John has positioned his congregations to regard their neighbors as the deviant ones, opposing the inevitable rule of God and the Lamb in favor of less worthy "pretenders" to world dominion who temporarily usurp God's praise, honor, and authority.

INTERPRETING THE SCRIPTURE

Jesus' Unique Authority

In the triumphs that celebrated the emperor's victories, he would be acclaimed with the words, "You are indeed worthy," with the honors awarded and the achievements on which these were based proclaimed. Indeed, imperial rule was legitimized in a wide variety of ways. From the images and inscriptions on coins to the regular activity of the cult of "Rome and the Augusti" to civic festivals honoring imperial birthdays to the imperial games, the "worthiness" of the emperor of the power he held and the honors he received were reinforced for subject peoples, especially in the Western empire. Rome and her emperors were presented as the instruments of the gods through whom beneficent rule, peace, order, and prosperity came to the world.

In such a context, John's vision of the Lamb cannot be read as apolitical. Religious allegiances and convictions cannot be relegated safely to the private sphere. "Jezebel" and the "Nicolaitans" might have argued for a separation of religious and socio-political involvement as they sought to make room for idolatry—an inescapable facet of social and economic "public" life in Asia Minor—in the lives of their flocks (see Revelation 2:14-15, 20-25). John, however, calls for complete and uncompromising allegiance to the Lamb who *alone* is worthy of such allegiance. It is to the Lamb, and not the emperor, that the Christians must yield themselves and their resources, thus ascribing to him "power and wealth and . . . honor" (5:12). In their uncompromising avoidance of all forms of idolatry (their commitment to the primary command-ments of the Decalogue), the believers wit-ness to the unique worthiness of Christ to rule and of God and God's Messiah to be acknowledged with divine honors on the basis of our creation and redemption.

Application of this prophetic word is diffi-cult in our context, for it calls us to shake our-selves loose from our wholehearted devotion to a particular nation and a particular "regime," and to examine what these powers look like in the light of God's desires for *all* people and the Lamb's costly efforts to bring together a global people united by allegiance to *him*, and not to any particular domination system. It was no less difficult, however, for John's congregations to look past the public discourse about the glories of Rome and the well-being brought to "all" through her emperors, and to shake themselves loose from the belief that their own security was tied to the stability and strength of the Roman Empire ("Eternal Rome") rather than to the God who sought security and well-being for all the peoples of the world.

Two Approaches to "Kingdom-Building"

The emperors' strategies for building and maintaining empire, pursued by every dom-ination system before and since, are laid bare by John later in Revelation (especially in chapters 12–13, 17–18). They involve mili-tant expansion, violent suppression of per-ceived threats and dissenting voices, the economic exploitation of the colonized peo-ples for the disproportionate consumption of the seat of empire (Rome), and a self-glorifying propaganda system that hides all that is ugly from the "public" view and draws attention only to the most favorable images of empire, those images that will be most strategic in terms of maintaining the assent of the subjects to be governed. What John "reveals" in this apocalypse is precisely the "underside" of empire, the facets of domination that the authorities would rather keep from public view.

In perhaps the most poignant exchange in the Johannine Passion Story, Jesus explains that his "kingdom is not from this world. If my kingdom were from this world, my followers would be fighting" to advance Jesus' interests and prevent his execution (John 18:33-36). We cannot blame Pilate, who has only known the Roman way of domination all his life, for not "getting it." God's ways are not human ways—but human ways, which are all the leaders of the world have ever experienced, are very difficult to let go. Jesus' strategy for kingdom-building takes us here back to the Passion. Jesus conquers by dying, by giving himself to ransom all. He acknowledges no national or ethnic lines in his self-giving; he defends no political or ethnic boundaries, no "in group's" economic interests; he refuses violence and propagandistic "spin" to protect his interests.

We are caught, with John's first audi-ences, in a difficult situation. We are chal-lenged by him to believe and follow the "wisdom" we acclaim to belong to Jesus (5:12), when it runs counter to the "wis-dom" that drives our political and economic machines. We are challenged to ascribe power and wealth and precedence to the One who "finished last" in the world's eyes, the ultimate loser. John's visions of celestial worship, however, and his placing of that dread scroll in the hands of the Lamb, call us urgently to divest ourselves of our inter-ests in human dominations systems and live out an alternative witness to the kingdom of God, lest we find ourselves crying out with the "great ones" of this world: "Hide us from the face of the one seated on the throne and from the wrath of the Lamb" (6:16).

Our God-Given Identity

The effects of Jesus' death are described largely in terms of the new identity he has bestowed upon the people whom he has gathered by means of redemption by his blood.

We are a redeemed people, set free from the power of sin in our lives, the power of the wounds caused by other people's sin, and the power of sick systems. Because we know ourselves to be redeemed already, we can find the courage to explore openly and honestly how deep our enslavement runs, so that we can indeed experience the complete freedom of children of God. Because the cost of our redemption was so great, we owe it to the Lamb to discover this freedom (see 1 Corinthians 6:19-20; Galatians 4:8-9).

We are a multi-ethnic, multi-national, multi-lingual people. This came into being not through some imperial power's expansion, nor through globalization of economy, but because the One God is the God of all peoples. This reality grates against many of our instincts—instincts that, we must admit, come from our participation in fallen systems rather than from our renewal in God. John challenges us to grasp this facet of our identity as God's people as well, learning how to think beyond national self-interest, ethnic prejudices, and linguistic prejudices (it is astounding how many Christians treat the non-nationals in our midst as if God spoke English and they should as well) so that we can embrace the full purpose of Christ in redemption rather than making Christ a symbol of our national and ethnic agendas.

We are a priestly people under God's dominion. As priests, we have been consecrated to God by Christ's sacrifice (see, most fully, Hebrews 9:11–10:25; 13:15-16; 1 Peter 2:4-10). We are called to be "holy"—set apart from the ordinary—for the sake of our close association with the Holy God. "Holiness" in Revelation means non-participation in everything that is stained and corrupted by violence, exploitation, and self-glorification, and results in a powerful and provocative witness to the worldly-minded. Priests are also chiefly "mediators," people who help others connect with God, who bring others into relationship with God. This, too, is a fruit of our witness.

SHARING THE SCRIPTURE

PREPARING TO TEACH

Preparing Our Hearts

This week's devotional reading is found in Psalm 107:1-9. In this song of thanksgiving for deliverance from trouble, the psalmist begins by thanking God for "steadfast love" (107:1) and redemption. In verses 4-9, the writer focuses on God's deliverance of those who have been hungry and thirsty. As you read this excerpt from Psalm 107, think about the ways in which God has delivered you from trouble. Give thanks for the redemption that you enjoy through Christ Jesus.

Pray that you and the adult learners will rely on God for help in time of need. Also pray for those persons who need to know God's redeeming love.

Preparing Our Minds

Study the background Scripture from Revelation 5 and lesson Scripture, verses 1-5, 11-14. As you study, think about forgiveness.

Write on newsprint:
❑ information for next week's lesson, found under "Continue the Journey."
❑ activities for further spiritual growth in "Continue the Journey."

Find a picture of the "Ghent Altarpiece," located at the Cathedral of Saint Bavo in Ghent. Part of the bottom of this early fifteenth-century work by Van Eyck depicts the adoration of the Lamb, inspired by Revelation 5. You may be able to download this picture from the Internet. If you cannot find it, choose a picture of people worshiping God.

Locate a tape or CD of Handel's *Messiah.* You will want to use the chorus, "Worthy Is the Lamb," based on Revelation 5:12, 13.

LEADING THE CLASS

(1) Gather to Learn

❖ Welcome the class members and introduce any guests.

❖ Pray that all who have gathered this day will be aware of the Christ who has come to redeem them.

❖ Invite the students to respond to this quote from R.L. Wheeler: **If I had the wisdom of Solomon, the patience of John, the meekness of Moses, the strength of Samson, the obedience of Abraham, the compassion of Joseph, the tears of Jeremiah, the poetic skill of David, the prophetic voice of Elijah, the courage of Daniel, the greatness of John the Baptist, the endurance and love of Paul, I would still need redemption through Christ's blood, the forgiveness of sin.**

❖ Read aloud today's focus statement: **Most people want to know that there is a possibility for forgiveness when they do something wrong or make a mistake. What guarantee of forgiveness do we have? Revelation 5 reassures us that the Lamb, who is worthy of our praise, has redeemed us.**

(2) Examine the Image of Christ, Our Redeemer, as Worthy of Praise

❖ Choose a volunteer to read Revelation 5:1-5, 11-14.

❖ Display "The Adoration of the Lamb" from the Ghent Altarpiece. Invite the students to comment on this work, or a substitute picture, by answering these questions.

(1) **What details do you note?**

(2) **In what ways does it reflect Revelation 5?**

(3) **Where might you see yourself in this picture?**

❖ Direct the students' attention to Revelation 5:1-5. Encourage the class members to discern what this passage says about who Jesus was and why he is "worthy" to open the scroll. Add ideas from "Jesus' Unique Authority" in Interpreting the Scripture and information for these verses in Understanding the Scripture.

❖ Ask the students to look again at verses 11-14. Talk about today's key verse, 5:13.

■ Look at the Old Testament background for these verses by checking Isaiah 45:22-23; 66:23; and Psalm 86:9. Ask three students to read these passages aloud.

■ Discuss how the adults perceive that people are—or are not—worshiping Jesus in our day. What attitudes and beliefs prompt one to acclaim "blessing and honor and glory and might" to the One seated on the throne?

❖ Read aloud "Two Approaches to 'Kingdom-Building'" in Interpreting the Scripture.

■ On the left side of a sheet of newsprint, ask the students to list the characteristics of the emperor's approach; on the right side, list Jesus' approach.

■ Discuss how Christians may still be ensnared in the emperor's approach.

■ Discuss how Christians can become more aligned with Jesus' approach.

(3) Reflect on the Learners' Redemption and Its Significance for Their Lives

❖ Ask the adults to define "redemption." Be sure to include the ideas of forgiveness and restoration of a relationship, in this case, with God.

❖ Discuss how Jesus' death has given us a new identity as redeemed people.

❖ Read, or have a volunteer read, "Our God-Given Identity" from Interpreting the Scripture.

■ Talk especially about how, as a result of our redemption, we are "multi-ethnic, multi-national, multi-lingual...because the One God is the God of all peoples" (see the third paragraph).

■ Discuss the ways in which we as redeemed people are called to be holy, "a priestly people under God's dominion" (see the fourth paragraph).

(4) Pledge to Live as Redeemed People

❖ Play "Worthy Is the Lamb," the next to last chorus of Handel's *Messiah,* based on Revelation 5:12, 13.

❖ Prompt the students to talk about how Handel's music reflects/affects the meaning of these two verses.

❖ Note that "every creature" sings praise to Christ, according to Revelation 5:13. Clearly, God intended for the entire world to be saved.

❖ Ask the students to contemplate this question: **How, then, do we act as God's redeemed people in relation to other people and in relation to all creation?** Distribute paper and pencils for those who may wish to write their answers.

❖ Invite them to talk with a partner or small group about their ideas, and ask them to affirm that they will live, with God's help, as redeemed people.

(5) Continue the Journey

❖ Pray that the participants will go forth to live as redeemed people who worship and proclaim the worthiness of the Lamb.

❖ Read aloud this preparation for next week's lesson. You may also want to post it on newsprint for the students to copy. **Prepare for next week's session entitled "Source of Security" by reading Revelation 7, paying particular attention to verses 1-3, 9, 13-17. Consider these ideas as you read: Most people long for a sense of security and safety. Where can we look for protection? The vision in Revelation 7 affirms that God's people are protected by the Lamb who redeemed them.**

❖ Read aloud the following three ideas. Challenge the students to commit themselves to use these activities as a springboard to spiritual growth.

(1) **Locate art or music that reflects the majesty of the worship of the Lamb. Focus on this art or music as part of your daily devotions.**

(2) **Forgive someone who has wronged you and do all in your power to restore this relationship.**

(3) **Be aware of the "songs of creation," perhaps the singing of a bird, the barking of a dog, the meowing of a kitten. How do you think God might hear these "songs"?**

❖ Sing or read aloud "This Is the Feast of Victory."

❖ Say this benediction to conclude the session. You may wish to ask the students to echo it as you read: **Go in peace to love God and your neighbor, both in truth and in action.**

UNIT 2: A NEW COMMUNITY IN CHRIST

SOURCE OF SECURITY

PREVIEWING THE LESSON

Lesson Scripture: Revelation 7:1-3, 9, 13-17
Background Scripture: Revelation 7
Key Verse: Revelation 7:14

Focus of the Lesson:
Most people long for a sense of security and safety. Where can we look for protection? The vision in Revelation 7 affirms that God's people are protected by the Lamb who redeemed them.

Goals for the Learners:
(1) to consider the image of Christ as protector as shown in Revelation 7.
(2) to reflect on the ways Christ serves as their protector.
(3) to give thanks for the protection Christ provides.

Pronunciation Guide:
Antiochus (an ti' uh kuhs)   Diocletian (di u klee' shun)
Maccabees (mak' uh beez)   Nicolaitan (nik uh lay' uh tayne)

Supplies:
Bibles, newsprint and marker, paper and pencils, hymnals, pictures of items that protect people, optional meditative background tape or CD and appropriate player

---

READING THE SCRIPTURE

NRSV
Revelation 7:1-3, 9, 13-17

¹After this I saw four angels standing at the four corners of the earth, holding back the four winds of the earth so that no wind could blow on earth or sea or against any tree. ²I saw another angel ascending from the rising of the sun, having the seal of the living God, and he called with a loud voice to the four angels who had been given

NIV
Revelation 7:1-3, 9, 13-17

¹After this I saw four angels standing at the four corners of the earth, holding back the four winds of the earth to prevent any wind from blowing on the land or on the sea or on any tree. ²Then I saw another angel coming up from the east, having the seal of the living God. He called out in a loud voice to the four angels who had been given

power to damage earth and sea, ³saying, "Do not damage the earth or the sea or the trees, until we have marked the servants of our God with a seal on their foreheads."

⁹After this I looked, and there was a great multitude that no one could count, from every nation, from all tribes and peoples and languages, standing before the throne and before the Lamb, robed in white, with palm branches in their hands.

¹³Then one of the elders addressed me, saying, "Who are these, robed in white, and where have they come from?" ¹⁴I said to him, "Sir, you are the one that knows." **Then he said to me, "These are they who have come out of the great ordeal; they have washed their robes and made them white in the blood of the Lamb.**

¹⁵For this reason they are before the
throne of God,
and worship him day and night within
his temple,
and the one who is seated on the throne
will shelter them.
¹⁶They will hunger no more, and thirst no
more;
the sun will not strike them,
nor any scorching heat;
¹⁷For the Lamb at the center of the throne
will be their shepherd,
and he will guide them to springs of the
water of life,
and God will wipe away every tear from
their eyes."

power to harm the land and the sea: ³"Do not harm the land or the sea or the trees until we put a seal on the foreheads of the servants of our God."

⁹After this I looked and there before me was a great multitude that no one could count, from every nation, tribe, people and language, standing before the throne and in front of the Lamb. They were wearing white robes and were holding palm branches in their hands.

¹³Then one of the elders asked me, "These in white robes—who are they, and where did they come from?"

¹⁴I answered, "Sir, you know."

And he said, "These are they who have come out of the great tribulation; they have washed their robes and made them white in the blood of the Lamb. ¹⁵Therefore,
"they are before the throne of God
and serve him day and night in his
temple;
and he who sits on the throne will spread his
tent over them.
¹⁶Never again will they hunger;
never again will they thirst.
The sun will not beat upon them,
nor any scorching heat.
¹⁷For the Lamb at the center of the throne
will be their shepherd;
he will lead them to springs of living
water.
And God will wipe away every tear from
their eyes."

UNDERSTANDING THE SCRIPTURE

Revelation 7:1-3. To the hearer familiar with Ezekiel and Jeremiah, the opening images of this chapter sound an ominous note. The "four winds" are forces of judgment and destruction (Jeremiah 49:36), and the "four corners of the earth" are the object of destructive forces (Ezekiel 7:2-3). The initial impression is confirmed by the triple repetition of the winds "blowing" or "harm-ing" the "land" and the "sea" and "the trees" (Revelation 7:1-3), a refrain that contrasts with the quadruple repetition of the word "seal" or "sealed" (Revelation 7:3-5). John's very language and rhythms force upon the hearers the contrast he seeks to establish: If one does not receive this "seal," one will be subject to the destruction loosed by God's agents of judgment.

Revelation 7:4-8. The sealing of the slaves of God prior to the unleashing of divine plagues recalls the Exodus—a story that Revelation draws upon and reconfigures at every turn through the specific plagues poured out on the oppressor (Revelation 8–9; 16), the song of the redeemed standing by another sea (15:2-4), the bringing of the redeemed into a new land of promise (21:1–22:5). In the Exodus story, the Hebrews are consistently protected from the effects of the plagues experienced by the Egyptians (see Exodus 8:22-24; 9:4-7, 25-26; 10:21-23; 11:4-7). It does not, of course, protect them from the hostility and oppression of Pharaoh (their lot becomes more difficult, in fact). It is clear from the remainder of this chapter that the "seal" is no protection for Christians against persecution and marginalization for their witness to the Lamb. They will indeed endure hardship in the "great ordeal" (Revelation 7:14), and have many tears for God to wipe away.

The image of sealing the faithful, which is not explicit from Exodus, is derived from Ezekiel 9:4-6, in which an angelic figure marks all those who lament with God over the unfaithfulness and idolatry rampant in Jerusalem before six other angelic priestly figures slaughter those idolaters. It is thus an appropriate image to introduce here, as the faithful are sealed before God pours out God's judgments against idolaters (Revelation 9:20-21; 14:9-11; 16:9, 11) on a much broader scale than Ezekiel ever imagined.

John "hears" about those who were sealed, twelve from every tribe of Israel with the exception of Dan. Dan has dropped out from the list due to its association with willful pursuit of idolatrous religion, and the deception and violent force it employed in the service of that religion (see Judges 17–18). Any group that "Babylonish" in character cannot be part of God's people, and so the tribe of Manasseh (a son of Joseph) takes its place in the roster.

The identity of these 144,000, particularly in relation to the innumerable multitude that John "sees" immediately after "hearing" about the sealing of the 144,000, is unclear. One tradition of interpretation reads these as different groups and gives the images a "salvation-historical" reading. The 144,000 represent Jewish Christians, the core of God's new people taken from the masses of God's historic people. They are God's "first fruits" (see Revelation 14:4), in anticipation of God's full harvest from "every nation, from all tribes and peoples and languages" (Revelation 7:9). The renewal of God's beneficent activity for God's historic people leads to God's light and salvation penetrating the nations (as in Isaiah 49:6; Romans 11:1-5, 17-24). The second tradition of interpretation reads the two groups as one and the same, making a statement about the Christians redeemed from *every* nation, Jew and Gentile, being the New Israel (as in Galatians 3:26-29; Philippians 3:3; 1 Peter 2:9-10).

Revelation 7:9-12. The redeemed are presented with palm branches and festal songs in a manner reminiscent of the Feast of Booths (as led by priestly figures also clad in white; see Leviticus 23:40) and the Feast of Dedication (see 2 Maccabees 10:6-7, with the context specifically of remembering and reenacting the Feast of Booths). The parallelism between the Maccabean Revolt (commemorated by the Feast of Dedication) and the "great trial" out of which this multitude comes is worth notice. Antiochus IV, remembered for repressing Judaism in Judea and erecting the "abomination of desolation" in the Jerusalem temple, serves as the prototype for the "beast," its cultic image, and the forthcoming repression of any who do not participate in the imperial cult (the "great trial"; see Daniel 12:1, writing about Antiochus IV's oppression, and Matthew 24:21).

The acclamations of the redeemed in 7:10 and 7:12 anticipate the fuller expressions of God's action in 11:15-19 and 19:10: God's deliverance comes, and God's power and strength manifest themselves, as God topples the domination systems that glorify themselves and harm God's people.

Revelation 7:13-17. The speech pattern in 7:13-14 ("Who are these . . . ?"; "Sir, you are the one that knows") recalls Ezekiel 37:3, linking John once again with the tradition of seers who have been instructed concerning their visions by angelic interpreters. The "great trial" John sees as he interprets the challenges facing authentic disciples in his world and forthcoming future focuses on the cost of refusing to offer divine honors to anyone or anything besides God or the Lamb (see Revelation 12:17–13:18), refusing to acknowledge the absolute claims of the "state." For John, it is not merely a time of suffering, but purposeful suffering in the face of the hostility of a domination system that will not acknowledge the ultimate claims of God on all human beings.

Those who keep themselves pure for God— who have aligned themselves with the angelic hosts who serve God "day and night" (see Revelation 4:8)—will live in God's presence (in the heavenly temple; see note on Revelation 4:4-6a in Understanding the Scripture on April 15) "day and night." In contrast, those who have made room for the worship of the emperor and other state gods will face torment "day and night" for their affronts to God's unique honor (Revelation 14:11). God "will pitch a tent with them," an echo of the promise of Ezekiel 37:27, in line with God's steady desire to make God's home in the midst of God's people (fulfilled fully in Revelation 21:3).

John quotes Isaiah 49:10 almost verbatim in Revelation 7:16, but the whole of Isaiah 49:8-13 is reconfigured in Revelation 7:13-17. Isaiah spoke of a time of oppression, when the people of God were like "prisoners," kept "in darkness." On the "day of salvation," God brings them to an open place where there are no hurtful, threatening forces, gathering together people from across the known world. In the final scene, God comforts and shows compassion for those who have suffered. John believes Isaiah's proclamation of the character of God as comforter and deliverer, knowing that God will yet do for these faithful ones what he had done for them in the past. If the Apocalypse teaches us nothing else, it is that God's character is constant and can be utterly relied on.

John draws on the tradition of God as shepherd (see Ezekiel 34:23; Psalm 23:1), altering it to depict the *Lamb* shepherding the flock. This striking image reminds us that we are being led by one of our own, who has shown complete solidarity with us (see Hebrews 2:10-18). The passage ends with a recitation of Isaiah 25:8 (see also Revelation 21:4), another oracle of deliverance framed with the image of God spreading a feast for God's people, an image that will be brought to the fore in Revelation 19:1-10.

INTERPRETING THE SCRIPTURE

The Seal

Revelation often makes its meaning clear by means of contrastive images. Thus the "seal of the living God" placed upon "the foreheads" of God's slaves has meaning in particular in contrast with the "mark of the beast" placed "on the right hands or the foreheads" of the beast's subjects (Revelation 13:16-17; 14:9-11). The "seal" and the "mark" show to whom one belongs, to whom one gives one's allegiance, worship, and service. We do John's apocalyptic imagination a disservice if we imagine some visible sign or tattoo for either of these: The seal and the mark are more a matter of where you show your face, who people know you to be, whose obedient client you are. There was a great deal of pressure on Christians in Asia Minor to show themselves loyal and grateful clients of the emperor through participating in the imperial cult. If they made room in their lives for a little bit of idolatry, they would be known by their neighbors as good and reliable citizens again, suitable partners in social and economic ventures (hence the "buying and selling" in Revelation 13:16-17). This was the gospel of the Nicolaitans and Jezebel (Revelation 2:14-16, 20-23), who questioned why abstinence from all forms of idolatry needed to be so rigorous when a more "reasonable" approach to discipleship would allow the Church to flourish.

John, however, calls the Christians to wholehearted commitment to the first commandment. By showing themselves to be loyal "slaves of God," the disciples would, moreover, be exempted from the experience of God's punishments upon the idolatrous world (see Revelation 9:4). True, they would still be subjected to the hostility of their non-Christian neighbors and rulers (see Revelation 13:7, 15-17). But by maintaining their separateness from all forms of disloyalty to God, symbolized by their separating themselves from all idolatry, they would also remain distinct and separate when God's wrath was poured out.

Paul spoke of the reception of the Holy Spirit as the "seal" that God had placed on believers, a seal closely linked with baptism (see 2 Corinthians 1:22; Ephesians 1:13; 4:30). John would urge us to lay hold of this "seal," examining ourselves to be sure that we are following the guidance of the Holy Spirit in all that we do, value, and pursue— that we are living as those who belong to God and *not* as those who belong to the domination systems that surround us and vie for our loyalty and acquiescence.

The "Great Trial"

Popular interpretations of Revelation tend to view the "great tribulation" as a future period of satanic apostasy when all Christians will be persecuted. Usually this is combined with some belief about a "rapture," which spares most (Western) Christians from experiencing persecution at all, leaving only post-rapture converts to suffer for Jesus. Against these grossly literalistic readings of Revelation are the facts of history. The global church has suffered "great trial" since its inception. Finding it hard to keep in mind our sisters and brothers throughout the two-thirds of the world that continue to suffer deprivation and death for the sake of their confession, some Western Christians imagine that we must await some future "tribulation" for Revelation to become applicable.

Against this view also is the fact that several voices from the first century also speak of life itself as a "great" or "noble contest" (see 2 Esdras 7:127-129; 4 Maccabees 16:16-23; 2 Timothy 4:7) from which the disciple emerges victorious or defeated. They conquer who remain faithful to who God has called them to be, despite all the enticements, threats, and pressures society can impose. John would affirm this view of life, even though he has a very particular contest in mind (the rising pressures upon his congregations to participate in traditional Greco-Roman religions and thus to affirm the status quo of Roman imperialism).

The army of the redeemed are "robed in white," having washed their robes "in the blood of Lamb" (Revelation 7:9, 14). They have participated actively and intentionally in cleansing themselves from the stains— the dirt—of a world in rebellion against God, and they have labored diligently to keep their white clothes from becoming soiled afresh (see Revelation 3:4-6). They have perceived that the "great contest" of life is not a matter of "getting ahead" or enjoying "the good life," but of being faithful to God and to the testimony that Jesus bore. That fidelity brought them into conflict with their neighbors and with the powers that be, who simply do not operate by God's ways. But they remained undefeated in their single-minded purpose: to live to honor God and God's purposes for all creation, rather than allow the world to mold them into the cogs and consumers it required them to be.

The Cost and the Promise

The vision of being comforted by God as by a Parent drying a loved child's tears, and of being shepherded in safe places by Jesus, has graced countless services on All Saints' Day and provided hope to many grieving believers. The presence of Jesus is the "safe place" that we long for, and the "safe place" that we can experience now in the midst of pain and grief as we learn to seek him in prayer and, as we shape our congregations to become "safe places," in corporate worship and holy friendships. We will find in God the remedy for the grief, sorrow, and pain we experience simply on the basis of being human, but John wants to bring this word of hope specifically to those who experience grief and deprivation resulting from their pursuit of faithfulness to God— to our sisters and brothers suffering perse- cution in Sudan, who die daily from hunger, thirst, and exposure to scorching heat; to our sisters and brothers in India, Indonesia, or several dozen other countries, who lose homes and family members to mob violence, who suffer seeing a family member dragged off to prison for being a Christian, who are separated from their children for teaching them an alien and ille- gal religion.

Considering their contest, we can find in Jesus that "safe place" we require to exam- ine our own values, convictions, and behav- iors more fully (down to the nitty-gritty of spending practices, support for violence, profiting through investments in companies that exploit globalization or ravage the ecosystems of the world), and listen afresh to what the Spirit might be saying to *our* churches. We would find Jesus to be that "safe place" that enables us to begin step- ping out in witness in new ways, if we find that our prosperity and level of ease with our society has seduced us away from faith- fulness to the witness of Jesus more effectively than any persecution.

SHARING THE SCRIPTURE

PREPARING TO TEACH

Preparing Our Hearts

This week's devotional reading is found in Psalm 121. This psalm, which would have been sung as pilgrims made their way to Zion, assures the travelers that God can be trusted to protect them. What evidence of God's protec- tion do you find in this psalm? Do you believe what the psalmist writes? Why or why not?

Pray that you and the adult learners will experience and trust in God's protection.

Preparing Our Minds

Study the background Scripture in Revelation 7, and lesson Scripture, verses 1- 3, 9, 13-17. Think about where you can find protection, a sense of security and safety.

Write on newsprint:
- ❏ options for "Reflect on the Ways Christ Serves as the Learners' Protector."
- ❏ information for next week's lesson, found under "Continue the Journey."
- ❏ activities for further spiritual growth in "Continue the Journey."

Collect pictures from newspapers, maga- zines, or the Internet of things that protect us.

Option: Choose meditative background music for "Reflect on the Ways Christ Serves as the Learners' Protector." Have an appropriate player handy.

LEADING THE CLASS

(1) Gather to Learn

❖ Welcome the class members and introduce any guests.

❖ Pray that the adults who have come today will be enriched as they study and fellowship in this community of faith.

❖ Show magazine or newspaper pictures of things that people often believe will protect them and their possessions, such as guns, Kevlar vests, protection-trained dogs, banks, fences, security systems, insurance, and so on. Talk with the class about how well these things, and others they may name, really protect them.

❖ Read aloud today's focus statement: **Most people long for a sense of security and safety. Where can we look for protection? The vision in Revelation 7 affirms that God's people are protected by the Lamb who redeemed them.**

(2) Consider the Image of Christ as Protector as Shown in Revelation 7

❖ Choose a volunteer to read Revelation 7:1-3, 9, 13-17.

❖ Discuss the image of the seal by following these steps.

■ **Step 1:** Read aloud "The Seal" in Interpreting the Scripture.

■ **Step 2:** Choose some of the Bible passages mentioned in "The Seal" and ask several students to look them up and read them aloud to the class.

■ **Step 3:** Use newsprint to create a contrast between "the seal of the living God" (7:2) and the mark of the beast.

❖ Discuss the image of the "great trial" by following these steps.

■ **Step 1:** Encourage the students to talk about what they think of when they hear the term "great trial" or "great tribulation."

■ **Step 2:** Read aloud "The 'Great Trial'" in Interpreting the Scripture.

■ **Step 3:** Ask volunteers to look up Scripture verses from this reading that you have selected.

■ **Step 4:** Tell this story of Saint Agnes. **In March, 303, the emperor Diocletian issued edicts that brought about bloody persecutions of Christians. Pursued by many noble families as an ideal wife, thirteen year old Agnes consecrated her virginity to Jesus Christ and refused to wed. Spurned suitors accused her before the governor of being a Christian—an accusation that could result in martyrdom. The governor's escalating threats of torment and torture could not dissuade young Agnes. She was sent to a brothel, but no one dared touch her, except one rude young man who was struck blind and fell to the ground, though Agnes prayed and his sight was restored. Enraged, the governor ordered her beheaded, and according to Saint Ambrose, she "went to the place of execution more cheerfully than others go to their wedding."**

■ **Step 5:** Ask these questions.
(1) **What does Agnes' story say to you about the early Christian's trust in God, even under threat of torture?**
(2) **How might Agnes be a role model for you?**
(3) **How are Christians around the globe experiencing persecution right now?**
(4) **How does your own society, perhaps infused with "cultural Christianity" as opposed to "New Testament Christianity," threaten your faith, perhaps even more so than overt persecution?**

(3) Reflect on the Ways Christ Serves as the Learners' Protector

❖ Ask the learners to review silently Revelation 7:13-17.

❖ Note that here we see the image of the Lamb, who acts as the shepherd, protecting his flock.

❖ Distribute paper. Give the students these options, which you may want to write on newsprint. As an option, play meditative background music as the class works.

■ **Option 1:** Sketch an image of the Lamb/Shepherd protecting you.

■ **Option 2:** Fold the paper to make a symbol of the Lamb/Shepherd's protection.

■ **Option 3:** Make a list of the ways that Christ serves as your protector.

■ **Option 4:** Write a short biographical account describing a situation in which Christ protected you.

■ **Option 5:** Write a poem or psalm in which you extol Christ as your protector.

❖ Invite the students to share their work in groups of two or three.

❖ Bring the class together and encourage the students to comment on the ways they have discerned Christ protecting them.

(4) Give Thanks for the Protection Christ Provides

❖ Ask the students to meditate on this statement that reminds us of Christ's protection: **Knowing that the victory belongs to God, we can step out in faith under any circumstances and witness for Christ, both in word and in deed.**

❖ Invite the students to comment on any insights they gleaned as they thought about this statement.

❖ Invite the students to read aloud Psalm 121, which assures us that God will protect us. If your hymnal includes a Psalter, suggest that the adults read responsively.

(5) Continue the Journey

❖ Pray that the participants will claim the assurance of Christ's protection of them.

❖ Read aloud this preparation for next week's lesson. You may also want to post it on newsprint for the students to copy. **Prepare for next week's session entitled "Finding Community" by reading background Scripture from Revelation 19 and lesson Scripture from verses 5-10. Consider these ideas as you study: Most people want to belong to a community that adds meaning to their life. What community can provide this for us? The description of the marriage feast of the Lamb and his bride in Revelation 19 illustrates that the church is a holy community in which we can find the ultimate meaning for our lives.**

❖ Read aloud the following three ideas. Challenge the students to commit themselves to use these activities as a springboard to spiritual growth.

(1) **Research areas of the world where Christians are currently being persecuted. Pray for these people. Check to see if there are additional ways that you can support them.**

(2) **Think seriously about what you depend upon to give you a sense of security. How much safety can this really provide? What shifts in behavior and attitude might you need to make regarding your understanding of security?**

(3) **Offer comfort to someone who is experiencing a crisis. "Dry their tears" by assuring them of Christ's continuing presence and protection in their lives.**

❖ Sing or read aloud "Ye Servants of God."

❖ Say this benediction to conclude the session. You may wish to ask the students to echo it as you read: **Go in peace to love God and your neighbor, both in truth and in action.**

UNIT 3: LIVING IN GOD'S NEW WORLD
FINDING COMMUNITY

PREVIEWING THE LESSON

Lesson Scripture: Revelation 19:5-10
Background Scripture: Revelation 19
Key Verse: Revelation 19:6

Focus of the Lesson:
Most people want to belong to a community that adds meaning to their life. What community can provide this for us? The description of the marriage feast of the Lamb and his bride in Revelation 19 illustrates that the church is a holy community in which we can find the ultimate meaning for our lives.

Goals for the Learners:
(1) to explore the image of the final marriage banquet in Revelation 19.
(2) to consider the implications of this passage for their lives.
(3) to discern steps they can take to help the church become a more meaningful community for themselves and others, and make a commitment to act.

Pronunciation Guide:
eschatological (es kat uh loj′ i kuhl)   *gamos* (gam′ os)
makarism (mak ar is em)   *porneia* (por nia′ ah)

Supplies:
Bibles, newsprint and marker, paper and pencils, hymnals, pictures of brides, tape or CD of wedding music and appropriate player

---

READING THE SCRIPTURE

NRSV
Revelation 19:5-10
⁵And from the throne came a voice saying,
  "Praise our God,
    all you his servants,
  and all who fear him,
    small and great."

NIV
Revelation 19:5-10
⁵Then a voice came from the throne, saying:
  "Praise our God,
    all you his servants,
  you who fear him,
    both small and great!"

---

⁶Then I heard what seemed to be the voice of a great multitude, like the sound of many waters and like the sound of mighty thunderpeals, crying out,

"Hallelujah!
For the Lord our God
the Almighty reigns.
⁷Let us rejoice and exult
and give him the glory,
for the marriage of the Lamb has come,
and his bride has made herself ready;
⁸to her it has been granted to be clothed
with fine linen, bright and pure"—
for the fine linen is the righteous deeds of the saints.

⁹And the angel said to me, "Write this: Blessed are those who are invited to the marriage supper of the Lamb." And he said to me, "These are true words of God." ¹⁰Then I fell down at his feet to worship him, but he said to me, "You must not do that! I am a fellow servant with you and your comrades who hold the testimony of Jesus. Worship God! For the testimony of Jesus is the spirit of prophecy."

⁶Then I heard what sounded like a great multitude, like the roar of rushing waters and like loud peals of thunder, shouting:

"Hallelujah!
For our Lord God Almighty reigns.
⁷Let us rejoice and be glad
and give him glory!
For the wedding of the Lamb has come,
and his bride has made herself ready.
⁸Fine linen, bright and clean,
was given her to wear."
(Fine linen stands for the righteous acts of the saints.)

⁹Then the angel said to me, "Write: 'Blessed are those who are invited to the wedding supper of the Lamb!'" And he added, "These are the true words of God."
¹⁰At this I fell at his feet to worship him. But he said to me, "Do not do it! I am a fellow servant with you and with your brothers who hold to the testimony of Jesus. Worship God! For the testimony of Jesus is the spirit of prophecy."

UNDERSTANDING THE SCRIPTURE

Revelation 19:1-4. We cannot understand the scene of joy and triumph in heaven without considering the great evil that has just been overcome. The allusion in Revelation 19:2 to "the great harlot" encapsulates the exposé of this figure in Revelation 17–18, John's look at Roman imperialism "from the underside." The Christians in first-century Asia Minor would identify "the great city that rules over the kings of the earth" (17:18) as Rome, the center of a multi-ethnic, multi-lingual, global empire (17:15). What John calls the "great harlot" or "great whore" was usually depicted as "Roma Eterna," a goddess frequently seen on coins or as cult statues in imperial cult temples. The goddess Roma would never have gone out in public the way John dresses her!

The "great harlot" is indicted on two counts in Revelation 19:2: destroying or ravaging the earth, and spilling the blood of God's slaves. Rome "ravaged" the earth by seeking to secure the good of the elite few at the expense of the many. Her economy was geared entirely toward the conspicuous consumption by the few (18:3-4, 7, 9, 12-13, 17). Everything Rome does is, in the end, for the good of the Roman elites and, peripherally, the people of Rome.

Such uneven distribution of goods required power and the support of other elites. Hence the second most frequent sin is labeled "fornication," Rome's seduction of strategically targeted parties with the promise of a share in her secure enjoyment of luxury, gaining their support for her program of global domination (Revelation 17:4; 18:3, 23). These enticements are made irresistible by the propaganda that acted like an intoxicant on the minds of the people who did not want to count the true cost of imperialism (see Revelation 18:3, 23). And, of course, every successful domination system relies upon the violent suppression of dissenting or inconvenient persons, those who refuse to give at least lip service to the ideology of empire (17:6; 18:24).

The second heavenly voice uses the language of Isaiah 34:10, an oracle concerning the destruction of Edom, Israel's pre-exilic enemy to the south, to celebrate the inevitable judgment by God of the new enemy of God's people. John can use older prophetic denunciations of self-serving kingdoms in his indictment of Rome because before a God whose judgments are "true and just" (19:2; see also 15:3; 16:7) they must all come to the same end. God will vindicate the blood of devoted servants, spilled to preserve godless empires (see Deuteronomy 32:42; Psalm 79:10; Revelation 6:9-11; 16:5-7). God will vindicate God's own honor, affronted by every empire that serves its own glorification, relies on its own might, and institutionalizes injustice by making greed the driving principle of its economy (see Revelation 18:4-8).

Revelation 19:5-8. The devastation of Babylon is the occasion for crowds of worshipers to praise God. The language of "those who fear him, the small and the great" recalls Psalm 115:13, and reminds us that God seeks the blessing of all with God's favor, the "little people" as well as the "shakers and movers," something that domination systems tend to forget as they exploit the former for the benefit of the latter. It also recalls Revelation 11:15-18, a hymn that is enacted in our passage. God's reign (celebrated in Psalms 93:1; 97:1; 99:1)

comes to expression in the destruction of the domination system that opposes God's kingdom. This again was intimated in the hymn in Revelation 11:17-18, where God's taking "great power" is concurrent with avenging the holy ones and destroying earth's destroyers.

The image of the wedding or the marriage as a metaphor for God's relationship with God's people has a long history in Jewish and Christian literature. Hosea, for example, promised a time when God would marry God's people forever (Hosea 2:19-20). This, then, becomes an image of the eschatological hope, when God and God's people would be perfectly united (see also Matthew 22:1-14; 25:1-13; 2 Corinthians 11:2-3; Ephesians 5:23-32). Here, the bride is adorned with "clean, bright linen," woven from the "righteous acts of the holy ones." John is deeply interested in "works," in doing what is just, what is in keeping with "the commandments of God and the testimony of Jesus" (Revelation 14:13; see also 20:12-13). Deeds matter, because they ultimately show where our loyalties and investments lie.

Revelation 19:9-10. Verse 9 includes one of the *makarisms* of Revelation (see also Revelation 1:3; 14:13; 16:15; 20:6; 22:7, 14)— seven pronouncements of a certain class of people as "blessed, honored, favored." It holds up as an ideal type those who keep themselves unstained by the seductive enticements of Roman imperialism for the sake of remaining pure for union with the Lamb as a member of that New Jerusalem, adorning the bride with one's works of justice and covenant loyalty.

The "testimony of Jesus" recalls John's presentation of Jesus as the "faithful witness" (Revelation 1:5), who revealed the truth about God's values and also revealed the painful truth about how poorly God's values were being enacted in the system in which he lived and moved. John regards "prophecy" to be the continuation of the testimony that Jesus bore in his life, ministry, death, and resurrection, and in the believers' ongoing witness in their own lives, ministries, and even deaths if faithfulness requires it.

Revelation 19:11-21. The rider on the white horse is Jesus (see the description of Jesus' eyes and sword in Revelation 1:14, 16, and the titles of Jesus as "faithful" and "true/genuine" in 1:5; 3:7). John presents him using language taken from Isaiah 63:1-3, where God appears dressed as a warrior returning from taking vengeance upon Edom, a foreign enemy. His title, "King of kings and Lord of lords" (19:16), directly challenges and overturns Rome and her emperors' temporary claim to dominion over the kings of the earth (17:18).

The images of 19:7-9 undergo a dramatic shift in this sequel. The bride clothed in "bright and pure linen" has given way to the Lamb's hosts of supporters, clothed in "white and pure linen," coming to participate, if only as witnesses, to Christ's victory (Revelation 19:14). The marriage supper has given way to "the great supper of God" (19:17), a macabre feast taken from the menu of Ezekiel 39:17-20. This progression of images suggests that Christian witness and acts of justice (the white linen of 19:8) are the means by which disciples participate in Jesus' victory over the domination systems of the world.

The lack of a true battle here and in 20 is highly significant. The military machines of the domination systems of this age may seem like irresistible force—till the awesome power of God is released with the simple pronouncements of judgment from the mouth of the returning Christ, the "Word of God" (compare Hebrews 4:12-13; 2 Esdras 13:33-38; Wisdom 18:15-16).

INTERPRETING THE SCRIPTURE

Finding Community in Babylon

People do, as a rule, seek to find meaning and significance in a community. We need to belong to something larger than ourselves and, despite our modern tendency toward "independence." John's visions remind us, however, that our sin and fallen condition is not merely an individual or private matter. It is also corporate and systemic. We do not just "sin" on our own (though we do this frequently). We also sin in our quest for community, and build for ourselves communities that are nothing short of sinful—indeed, whose sins "are heaped high as heaven" (Revelation 18:5).

In *Making a Just Peace* Bishop Dale C. White put the term "domination system" in my vocabulary. Domination systems could be described as communities formed around the goal of self-interest, securing the good of the protected community at the expense of people outside or "below," whether that expense is measured in terms of the waste of resources and human life (as in militarism), the devastation of ecosystems (a part of so much corporate expansion and the accepted part of "fueling" our economies), the devaluation of segments of the population (as in patriarchy and its relegation of women to "supporting" roles, or in the exploitation of foreign workers to manufacture products for Western corporations), or in terms of the conspicuous consumption of resources by the few (with the concomitant starvation of many). As we will see, at no point does this coincide with God's vision and purposes for community, nor do God's strategies for forming community have anything in common with these Babylonish strategies.

The great danger that John calls to our attention is that those who participate in, support, and profit from these domination systems usually do not sense that they are doing anything sinful. Those who participated in and profited from Roman imperialism from the capital city through the provinces through all the entrepreneurs who connected the two were led astray (Revelation 18:23), inebriated (17:2; 18:3), even "drugged" (sorceries, *pharmakai*, often involved hallucinogenic "pharmaceuticals"). Their minds were so filled with the heady draughts of the community's ideology ("we are bringing law, order, prosperity, growth, freedom") that they would not look at what was actually happening: She "corrupted the earth with her fornication," (19:2).

But our call as Christian disciples is always to "keep awake" and to "be sober" (1 Thessalonians 5:3-8), to let the prophetic voice of the Spirit awaken us to the sins perpetrated for the sake of preserving a Babylonish community, to find the courage to look at the systems to which we belong with the eyes of the God of justice and peace rather than through the clouded intoxicants Babylon holds before our eyes in her cup.

Renouncing the Community of Babylon

Some have questioned whether or not John shows a "Christian" attitude in his delight over the utter, tragic devastation of the city and the concomitant loss of life. It may be, however, that our failure to appreciate that city's evils—how it opposed God's purposes for all people and brought pain, misery, and death to many—prevents us from understanding precisely how "Christian" this response truly is, and therefore how much we, as Christians, need to be on guard against such systemic evils in our world.

No two images could contrast more sharply than a harlot and a bride, no activities more incompatible than "sleeping around" and "marriage" (*porneia*, 19:2; *gamos*, 19:7). The harlot's attire, symbols of an exploitative system designed to gratify the luxury of the few at the cost of the enslavement of the many (18:9, 12-14, 16), contrasts pointedly with the clothing of the bride—acts of justice through which God's purposes for people break through Babylon's stranglehold. Even the "marriage supper" contrasts with the harlot's "open bar"—the cup of the passion of her fornication that she passes around so freely among the nations.

John's presentation of such thoroughly contrasting images carries home the message that one will not find the wholeness of genuine community (well represented by a wedding, an event grounded in family and friends and based on mutual covenant to secure the good of the other, not the good of the self) as long as one clings to life within the paradigm and constraints of domination systems (represented so well by the counterfeit relationships of prostitution). The prophetic word in today's passage challenges us: We will not find ourselves in the joyful community of the marriage supper of the Lamb (Revelation 19:6-9) unless we first "come out" from Babylon (18:4). We are called to renounce our place in, our benefits from, and our continued support of sick and sinful systems that breed death and devastation (19:2) and to "keep" ourselves for the Lamb (19:7-9).

A New Wardrobe

Clothing has been an important image throughout Revelation, as it is elsewhere in the New Testament (see Colossians 3:9-13). In the first half of Revelation, John returns several times to the image of believers having cleansed their robes through their baptism into Christ's death, and to the challenge of keeping one's robes unsullied by participation in the systemic evils of one's society (Revelation 3:4-6; 7:13-14). These "robes" are, of course, symbolic of one's self, one's way of life, one's identification of oneself to others (as clothing still serves as a representation of oneself and, often, one's status to others).

In 19:8 the image shifts to the clothing that adorns the bride of Christ herself, which is stitched together from "the righteous deeds of the saints." As disciples commit themselves to living out God's justice and bringing God's justice and wholeness to those who are both victimized by *and* wantonly profiting from domination systems, they are preparing the bride of Christ. They are also holding onto the "testimony of Jesus" (19:10), continuing to bear witness in the world as Jesus bore witness in the world. By withdrawing our participation in the sins of domination systems (something that will be costly indeed), and by seeking ways to advance God's vision for the wholeness of *all* peoples, we take our place in the bridal chamber, adorning the genuine community of the people of God for her eternal union with Christ in the kingdom of God, a kingdom that comes not through any domination system, but in place of all the domination systems of the world.

SHARING THE SCRIPTURE

PREPARING TO TEACH

Preparing Our Hearts

This week's devotional reading is found in Psalm 148:1-14. This psalm calls upon all creation to praise God. From the heights of the heavens to the depths of the sea all are to acknowledge the glory of the Lord. Read this psalm aloud as an act of praise. Sing a hymn, do a dance, or create a picture in praise to God. Meditate on all the reasons you have to give glory to God.

Pray that you and the adult learners will recognize that praise and worship are important facets of life in the community of faith.

Preparing Our Minds

Study the background Scripture, Revelation 19, and lesson Scripture, Revelation 19:5-10. As you study, think about the kind of community that can add meaning to your life.

Write on newsprint:
❏ information for next week's lesson, found under "Continue the Journey."
❏ activities for further spiritual growth in "Continue the Journey."

Locate pictures of brides on their wedding day, perhaps from one of the many bridal magazines that are on sale at your local newsstand.

Locate a tape or CD of wedding music and an appropriate player.

Prepare the lectures suggested for "Explore the Image of the Final Marriage Banquet in Revelation 19."

LEADING THE CLASS

(1) Gather to Learn

❖ Welcome the class members and introduce any guests.

❖ Pray that those who are participating in today's session will find meaning and fellowship as they study together.

❖ Play the tape or CD of wedding music as background music for this portion of the lesson.

❖ Show pictures you have brought of brides on their wedding day. If you do not have any pictures, ask the class to recall weddings they have attended. Discuss these questions.

(1) What descriptive phrases or words come to mind when you see a bride in her wedding attire?

(2) As you see a bride and hear wedding music, what feelings or

memories come to mind? (Remember that while a wedding itself may be a joyous occasion, some people have had difficult marital experiences and may give negative responses.)

❖ Read aloud today's focus statement: **Most people want to belong to a community that adds meaning to their life. What community can provide this for us? The description of the marriage feast of the Lamb and his bride in Revelation 19 illustrates that the church is a holy community in which we can find the ultimate meaning for our lives.**

(2) Explore the Image of the Final Marriage Banquet in Revelation 19

❖ Use information from verses 1-4 in Understanding the Scripture to set the stage for today's lesson.

❖ Read Revelation 19:5-10 as a drama. Call for volunteers to play the roles of the voice from the throne, John, several people ("great multitude") to offer praise in unison (19:6b-8), an angel, and a narrator.

❖ Use information from verses 5-8, 9-10 in Understanding the Scripture to help the class members unpack the meaning of these verses. You may want to present this as a lecture.

❖ Explore the following images with the class by asking the students to describe how they envision these images and what they might mean.

■ **bride of Christ.** (Think here about the clothing and purity of the bride. Talk about what the church needs to be and do to prepare itself for this role.)

■ **marriage of the Lamb.** (Think about the marriage relationship as an image to illustrate the relationship between God and the people of God. Check out Isaiah 54:5; Jeremiah 3; Hosea 2:19-20; 2 Corinthians 11:2; Ephesians 5:25-32 as examples of this image).

■ **marriage supper of the Lamb.** (Imagine what this feast will be like.)

❖ Consider these theological questions.

(1) What do verses 5-10 say to you about God?

(2) What does this passage say to you about Jesus?

(3) What does this passage suggest about what God expects of those who choose to be part of the community of faith? (Read the last paragraph of "Renouncing the Community of Babylon" in Interpreting the Scripture and ask the students to comment on what it means for twenty-first century Christians to renounce Babylon.)

❖ Provide quiet time for the students to mull over these questions: **What difference does the community of faith make in my life? How is the community enriched because of my presence and participation?**

(3) Consider the Implications of This Passage for the Learners' Lives

❖ Break the silence by inviting the students to gather in groups of three or four and tell stories to illustrate how the church is a meaningful community in their lives.

❖ Invite volunteers to retell quickly any stories they heard that particularly touched them.

❖ Note that the angel told John that he was "a fellow servant" (19:10). Challenge the students to think of a new or ongoing church project where help is needed. Distribute paper and pencils. Ask the students again to work in their groups to write either a job description or a commercial advertising the project and asking for assistance.

❖ Call on each group to read what they have written. See if anyone in the class will respond to the need(s). Perhaps the class as a group would be willing to support one or more of these projects. If so, plan a time to flesh out ideas as to how the class can become involved.

(4) Discern Actions the Learners Can Take to Help the Church Become a More Meaningful Community for Themselves and Others, and Make a Commitment to Act

❖ Discuss the worship service with the class members by asking the following questions. Make a list of their ideas on newsprint to pass on to the worship committee and/or pastor.

(1) **Do you glimpse a vision of heaven on earth as you participate in the weekly service?**

(2) **If so, what elements of worship make the service so special?**

(3) **If not, what changes would make the experience more compelling for you and others?**

❖ Distribute paper and pencils and ask the students to complete this sentence: **To help my church become a more meaningful community as we worship, study, pray, serve, and fellowship together, I will . . . .**

❖ Collect the papers, shuffle them, and read aloud several responses as testimonies to students' commitments.

(5) Continue the Journey

❖ Pray that the students will do what they have committed themselves to do so that their church will be a deeply meaningful community of faith for all who choose to belong.

❖ Read aloud this preparation for next week's lesson. You may also want to post it on newsprint for the students to copy. **Prepare for next week's session entitled "The Eternal Home" by reading** Revelation 21:1-8, which is both the background and lesson Scripture for this lesson. Concentrate on these thoughts as you read: Everyone wants a home in which he or she can be safe from hunger, thirst, and pain. Where does such a home exist? Revelation 21 says that the new heaven and new earth will be a home like this.

❖ Read aloud the following three ideas. Challenge the students to commit themselves to use these activities as a springboard to spiritual growth.

(1) **Do something this week to show yourself as a faithful and true witness for Jesus.**

(2) **Worship God in a congregation that is not your own, preferably one of a different denomination. What effect does this church's worship service have on you? Where do you find a vision of heaven in its service?**

(3) **Ponder this question and write a response in your spiritual journal: How does the purity of heaven lead us to holiness of life on earth with one another?**

❖ Sing or read aloud "Here, O My Lord, I See Thee," which is based on Revelation 19:6-9.

❖ Say this benediction to conclude the session. You may wish to ask the students to echo it as you read: **Go in peace to love God and your neighbor, both in truth and in action.**

UNIT 3: LIVING IN GOD'S NEW WORLD
The Eternal Home

PREVIEWING THE LESSON

Lesson Scripture: Revelation 21:1-8
Background Scripture: Revelation 21:1-8
Key Verse: Revelation 21:3

Focus of the Lesson:
Everyone wants a home in which he or she can be safe from hunger, thirst, and pain. Where does such a home exist? Revelation 21 says that the new heaven and new earth will be a home like this.

Goals for the Learners:
(1) to examine the image of the new Jerusalem as their ultimate home as depicted in Revelation 21.
(2) to appreciate the fullness of life in God's new age.
(3) to develop a plan to fight hunger, thirst, or pain.

Supplies:
Bibles, newsprint and marker, paper and pencils, hymnals, picture(s) of the New Jerusalem, optional commentaries

---

READING THE SCRIPTURE

NRSV
Revelation 21:1-8
   ¹Then I saw a new heaven and a new earth; for the first heaven and the first earth had passed away, and the sea was no more. ²And I saw the holy city, the new Jerusalem, coming down out of heaven from God, prepared as a bride adorned for her husband. ³And I heard a loud voice from the throne saying,

   "See, the home of God is among mortals.
   He will dwell with them;
   they will be his peoples,
   and God himself will be with them;

NIV
Revelation 21:1-8
   ¹Then I saw a new heaven and a new earth, for the first heaven and the first earth had passed away, and there was no longer any sea. ²I saw the Holy City, the new Jerusalem, coming down out of heaven from God, prepared as a bride beautifully dressed for her husband. ³And I heard a loud voice from the throne saying, **"Now the dwelling of God is with men, and he will live with them. They will be his people, and God himself will be with them and be their God.** ⁴He will wipe

⁴he will wipe every tear from their eyes
  Death will be no more;
  mourning and crying and pain will be
    no more,
  for the first things have passed away."
⁵And the one who was seated on the throne said, "See, I am making all things new." Also he said, "Write this, for these words are trustworthy and true." ⁶Then he said to me, "It is done! I am the Alpha and the Omega, the beginning and the end. To the thirsty I will give water as a gift from the spring of the water of life. ⁷Those who conquer will inherit these things, and I will be their God and they will be my children. ⁸But as for the cowardly, the faithless, the polluted, the murderers, the fornicators, the sorcerers, the idolaters, and all liars, their place will be in the lake that burns with fire and sulfur, which is the second death."

every tear from their eyes. There will be no more death or mourning or crying or pain, for the old order of things has passed away."
⁵He who was seated on the throne said, "I am making everything new!" Then he said, "Write this down, for these words are trustworthy and true."
⁶He said to me: "It is done. I am the Alpha and the Omega, the Beginning and the End. To him who is thirsty I will give to drink without cost from the spring of the water of life. ⁷He who overcomes will inherit all this, and I will be his God and he will be my son. ⁸But the cowardly, the unbelieving, the vile, the murderers, the sexually immoral, those who practice magic arts, the idolaters and all liars—their place will be in the fiery lake of burning sulfur. This is the second death."

UNDERSTANDING THE SCRIPTURE

Revelation 21:1-2. The God of creation—of first beginnings—is consistently viewed as the God of new beginnings. A fundamental conviction of the Hebrew prophets, including Isaiah (whose language of "new heavens and a new earth" is most closely echoed here; see Isaiah 65:17; 66:22), was that, no matter how messed up human sinfulness and systemic evil might make this world, God's power of creation and re-creation was always greater. Interpreters debate whether or not God will destroy the present earth and heavens (as in 2 Peter 3:7, 10) and create an utterly new cosmos, or whether John is merely using traditional language to assert God's power to renew God's creation and transform it utterly into what God desired from the beginning (Revelation 21:5 could suggest this). Such debates may miss the point of both expressions of hope (as well as expressions such as found in Hebrews 12:26-28, which anticipates an entirely otherworldly life with God

after the material earth and heavens are "removed"), which is to affirm the conviction that God will create genuine, whole, life-giving community with and among God's people. The absence of a sea—another image that might make us focus too much on the ecology of the new world and too little on the meaning—signifies the removal of danger, chaos, and hostile powers from God's good creation.

That community is envisioned as "the holy city, the new Jerusalem." The image of the city made by God, the place where God's promises to God's people are fulfilled, is common in early Jewish and Christian literature (see Galatians 4:26; Hebrews 11:10, 16; 12:22; 13:14; 2 Esdras 10:44, 53-54). The image connects the future community with its historical heritage, the earthly Jerusalem where God's presence was celebrated in the temple, but where that presence was continually jeopardized by human sinfulness and by foreign domination. In the community of

God's future, no such threats to our communion with God—and our communion with one another in God's presence—will exist.

Revelation 21:3-4. The voice from the throne (God's voice) utters again the promises that God had made with God's people throughout sacred history. Leviticus 26:11-12 spoke of God's placing God's "dwelling in your midst," walking among them with the result that "I will be your God and you shall be my people." This close association was at the heart of the demand for holiness among the Israelites. Ezekiel 37:27 repeated these promises in the context of God's renewal of God's people after exile (and, rather predictably by this point, John's wording is very closely patterned after Ezekiel). Zechariah 8:8 speaks of God gathering the scattered people in Jerusalem and enacting anew the promise to be their God and take them for his people.

All these promises are taken up again by John as reliable indicators of God's intentions for human community. This is the future that God wills to bring about, a future in which mourning, crying out in anguish, and sorrow have no place (borrowing language from Isaiah 65:17, 19), and in which God comforts those who have suffered the ills of a world hostile to God's purpose and witnesses (using Isaiah 25:8 verbatim, as in Revelation 7:17).

Revelation 21:5-6. In a society filled with lies about the divine, the purposes of the gods, and the chosen vehicles for the gods' blessings (for example, Rome and her emperors), God's speaking reliable and true words into the ears of disciples is in itself an act of deliverance. Three times John reminds the hearers that they can and should build their lives around what they are hearing from him (Revelation 19:9; 21:5; 22:6) rather than around the lies and unreliable strategies that drive their neighbors, that this will put them on sure footing before God.

We are transported in this vision to a time when hope is no longer hope, but has become reality: "It has come to pass," or "It is done!" The vivid language John uses, buttressed by the authority of the language of the Hebrew Scriptures, helps the congregations visualize this hope as "reality," catching a glimpse of that for which they are being asked to give up their home and place in Babylon. God is again identified as "the first and the last" (alpha and omega being the first and last letters of the Greek alphabet; see Revelation 1:8), the "origin and the goal" of all things. The domination systems of this world, for all their might, impressiveness, and seeming irresistibility cannot have the last word. They are all mere parentheses in the plan of God.

Isaiah had issued an invitation from God to "everyone who thirsts," urging them to come to God to drink their fill freely (Isaiah 55:1). Conversely, Jeremiah convicted Israel for turning away from God, the true source of living water, in order to try to slake their thirst from the dry, cracked, empty wells that they had made for themselves (Jeremiah 2:13). Domination systems and personal dysfunction arise out of our collective and individual attempts to slake our human thirst for security, for significance, and for a sense of abundance apart from God. Where we turn to God for all these goods, our interpersonal relationships are freed to reflect God's outreaching love and desire for all people rather than our own self-interest and self-preservation at the cost of genuine community.

Revelation 21:7-8. Announcing the inheritance of "those who conquer" takes the listener back to chapters 2 and 3, the seven oracles to the seven churches. Each of these also ended with an announcement of the reward for "those who conquer" (Revelation 2:7, 11, 17, 26; 3:5, 12, 21). "Conquering" is used by John as a synonym for discerning and pursuing the path of faithfulness to God and to the testimony of Jesus in the diverse circumstances of these faith communities. It is an agonistic, competitive verb well-suited to the strenuous challenges to faith that John's audiences encountered (for example, the challenge of remaining loyal to One God in a province where the worship of the traditional gods and the emperor was considered a necessary token of the reliable and loyal citizen).

Those who conquer inherit the community that God provides, as well as the most tender promise of intimacy with God. Originally set in the limited context of God's relationship to the heirs of David's throne (see 2 Samuel 7:14), the words of adoption by God are now applied to all faithful disciples of Jesus (as they are also in 2 Corinthians 6:18; see also Romans 8:15-17; Galatians 3:26-29).

But John also envisions a group excluded from this community where justice and wholeness at last find a home. The list suggests those who have supported the domination systems of the world, participating in its self-glorification (its idolatry), its violence, its pollution (of life, of God's vision for humanity, of the world), its counterfeit unions, and its suppression of the truth—a group that includes disciples who have been conquered by the system, who have proven "faithless" and "cowardly" rather than living out the testimony of Jesus. These ultimately find their community in the lake of fire, sharing the fate of Satan and his pawns throughout history (Revelation 19:20; 20:10, 14-15) who have used domination systems as a major means of opposing God's purposes and involving human beings in their rebellion against God.

INTERPRETING THE SCRIPTURE

Discerning God, Diagnosing Our World

John looks out upon his world and the world of his congregations with profound insight concerning what is from God and what is hostile to God. This insight comes from two primary sources: his openness in prayer to the revelations of the Spirit, and his deep and penetrating knowledge of God's character and purposes as revealed in the Jewish Scriptures. We have encountered this in every lesson; we encounter it again in the rich weaving together of God's promises made in such diverse places as 2 Samuel, Isaiah, and Ezekiel.

By meditating continuously upon the Scriptures, John came to know the character of God as just avenger and as compassionate healer, the heart of God for communion with God's people, the commitments of God to justice and to make a place where God is at home with human beings. Those texts shaped John's knowledge and expectations of God and provided him with the framework by which to evaluate and discern the evils of Roman imperialism. They freed him from being intoxicated himself by the ideology of Rome; they freed him to discern an alternative vision for a community ordered around God and God's purposes rather than the agenda of a few powerful elites; they gave him a voice by which to call others into this alternative vision for a redeemed and redeeming community.

In this way, John provides a model for us as disciples in our engagement with Scripture and with our situation. Revelation opens up for us not merely a particular interpretation of the situation of seven churches against the backdrop of God's place in the cosmos and purposes throughout history, but a mode of interpretation into which we are continually invited. Perhaps the worst interpretive move ever made was to create time charts of "the seven last years," fossilizing Revelation into an end-time calendar of events, rather than allowing this imaginative and provocative book to spur us on in our understanding of God and our ever-new discernment of the paths that enhance or oppose God's vision.

God-Centered Community

The repeated focal point of this passage is the presence of God in the midst of God's people and the intimacy of God with God's people (Revelation 21:3-4, 6-7). At the heart of this vision of community as God intended it and as God provides it is our relationship to God as God's people and our relationship with one another as God's children, an identity shared by all and recognized by all. Community life revolves around this awareness of God's presence and of the common relationship with God that all inhabitants of the city share. This will affect how the community "works" in several ways. Members of the community seek one another's good rather than their own. They fill their emptiness from God's limitless streams rather than from the pursuit of limited, temporal goods that sets people in competition with one another. They seek to honor God and one another in their interactions, and so discover their own dignity as God's children.

This is quite different from the communities we experience in the world. Even our communities of faith fail to embody this model for community. But it is precisely in the global community of faith that we can begin to create this living witness to God-centered community.

No More Grief

Many people long for a place for themselves where they will no longer experience sorrow, suffer pain, or cry out in anguish of spirit, never understanding that it cannot exist for them unless it exists for all. That is, as long as we seek to secure our own pain-free existence by controlling, exploiting, or neglecting others, we will never be free from the ill effects of those who do the

same. John promises us, however, that God has made such a place, a place where *all* experience life in its fullness—as God, not society, defines that fullness.

That place exists in prospect in that safe place that God creates around us when we pray in the midst of any pain or sorrow or grief that we experience. This safe place stands open before us not only for us to find comfort and a respite in the midst of the trials that beset us all as human beings, but also for us to satisfy the thirsts of our souls for security, for significance, and for fullness of life as we faithfully extricate ourselves from Babylon's web. As we renounce those addictive substances and pursuits that mask our pain, we find their genuine counterpart in God. As we renounce those strategies for preserving security and significance that involve the oppression of others, we find new venues for safety and meaning in God's presence. What we discover now in prospect, we shall inherit in all its fullness at the consummation.

Choosing Babylon

The passage ends with the sobering reminder that not everyone will be convinced that they should commit themselves to honoring God and pursuing God's vision for community. Some people will choose to live in Babylon, by the laws of Babylon. They will not give up their conviction that violence is the ultimate answer to preserving their interests, nor their faith in the idolatrous and self-glorifying propaganda that they are fed, nor their coping strategy of "pain-killing" through a variety of intoxicants to deal with the pain that results from living in this life-destroying system. They alienate themselves from the truth of God, and live out the lies that the domination systems of which they are a part require to continue perpetrating their oppression and devastation. Leading the pack in this list are those people who, knowing the truth of God, were too cowardly to continue to bear witness to God's vision, and who thus proved unfaithful to the God who created and redeemed them.

John warns his congregations, within some of which can be found several members who could easily fall into this category, that making peace with Babylon carries a price tag too dreadful for words. The image

of the "lake of fire" begins to capture the endless remorse, grief, and pain—all those things that God wants to eliminate from human community—that belong to those who ultimately decided to oppose God's desires for all people for the sake of their own private good and the good of their limited interest group.

SHARING THE SCRIPTURE

PREPARING TO TEACH

Preparing Our Hearts

This week's devotional reading is found in 2 Peter 3:10-18. Here Peter writes about the dissolution of the earth by fire at the coming of the day of the Lord. At that time, according to Peter, there will be "new heavens and a new earth, where righteousness is at home" (3:13). To prepare for this day and the new life that follows, Peter tells us to be at peace and to "grow in the grace and knowledge of our Lord and Savior Jesus Christ" (3:18). Think about how righteousness is at home in your life. What evidence does your life give of this righteousness? In what ways do you need to grow in grace and knowledge?

Pray that you and the adult learners will prepare carefully for your new home of righteousness.

Preparing Our Minds

Study the background and lesson Scripture, both of which are found in Revelation 21:1-8. As you study, think about what an ideal home would be like, perhaps one where you are safe and no longer experience hunger, thirst, and pain.

Write on newsprint:
❏ information for next week's lesson, found under "Continue the Journey."
❏ activities for further spiritual growth in "Continue the Journey."

Locate an artistic representation of the New Jerusalem by searching books and/or the Internet. Here are a few you might wish to view: "The New Jerusalem" by Gustave Doré; tapestry of "The New Jerusalem," woven by Nicolas Bataille; "The New Jerusalem" from the Bamberg *Apocalypse*, about 1020, AII 42, Bamberg, Staatsbibliothek, all of which can be found on the Internet.

Prepare to present the information from Understanding the Scripture.

Gather several commentaries on Revelation if you choose to use them.

LEADING THE CLASS

(1) Gather to Learn

❖ Welcome the class members and introduce any guests.

❖ Pray that today's participants will be able to imagine a life of peace and security in fellowship with God.

❖ Invite the class members to close their eyes and relax as you lead them in this guided imagery. Tell them that you will pause periodically so that they may think about what you have suggested.

■ **Envision yourself in the home of your dreams. Walk around. What does this home look like? What aromas do you notice? Can you feel stone, wood, plaster, or other textures? What sounds fill this home,** or is there only silence? **Imagine this home.** (Pause)

■ **How do you feel when you are in this home?** (Pause)

❖ Bring the students back together by reading aloud today's focus statement: **Everyone wants a home in which he or she can be safe from hunger, thirst, and pain. Where does such a home exist? Revelation 21 says that the new heaven and new earth will be a home like this.**

(2) Examine the Image of the New Jerusalem as the Learner's Ultimate Home as Depicted in Revelation 21

❖ Choose volunteers to read the parts of John and the voice from the throne. The few words that a narrator would read could be omitted. Ask the two volunteers to read Revelation 21:1-8.

❖ Display the artwork you have brought. Invite the students to comment on how this visual depiction captures the essence of the description in Revelation 21. Had they been the artist, what might they have done differently?

❖ Do a line-by-line study of the text by using one of these methods.

■ **Option 1:** Use information in Understanding the Scripture to unpack the text. Consider writing important points on newsprint as you lecture.

■ **Option 2:** Divide the class into four groups and assign two verses to each group. You may wish to provide the groups with commentaries on Revelation. Encourage the groups to wrestle with the meaning of their assigned verses and then report back to the entire class.

❖ Read the first paragraph of "God-Centered Community."

❖ Encourage the class members to think about how the God-centered community will be like and unlike the faith community they now experience. Use newsprint to create a

chart to show the similarities and differences between the current and future communities.

❖ Conclude this section of the lesson by looking at verses 7 and 8 and discussing the consequences of choosing Babylon (see "Choosing Babylon" in Interpreting the Scripture).

(3) Appreciate the Fullness of Life in God's New Age

❖ Read this quotation by C. S. Lewis (1898-1963): **If you read history, you will find that the Christians who did most for the present world were just those who thought most of the next. The apostles themselves, who set on foot the conversion of the Roman Empire, the great men who built up the Middle Ages, the English evangelicals who abolished the slave trade, all left their mark on earth, precisely because their minds were occupied with heaven. It is since Christians have largely ceased to think of the other world that they have become so ineffective in this.**

❖ Distribute paper and pencils. Invite the adults to list or write about ways in which they believe they are having an impact on this world. Suggest that they consider how their contributions are helping them to prepare for life in God's new age.

❖ Encourage the students to talk with a partner about what they have identified. Perhaps the partner will be able to name additional ways that the other person has a positive impact.

❖ Bring the class back together. Talk in general terms about the ways that we can begin to experience the fullness of life God promises, even as we await the fulfillment here on earth.

(4) Develop a Plan to Fight Hunger, Thirst, or Pain

Work with the adults as a class or in groups to develop a plan to fight hunger, thirst, or pain. Here are possible steps for discerning what the class can do.

■ **Step 1:** Decide which group of people the class would like to serve.

■ **Step 2:** Determine an agency or organization through which you can work. For example, hunger might be addressed through a soup kitchen, food bank, or advocacy group. Thirst might best be addressed by an agency that provides wells and clean water to developing areas. To alleviate pain, class members may want to assist with a hospice, nursing home, or hospital.

■ **Step 3:** Figure out exactly what you can do. Can you provide finances, hands-on assistance, technical help, or something else?

■ **Step 4:** Agree about what you will do, when you will do it, who will be involved, and how you will handle all the details of the project. Assign workers as needed.

■ **Step 5:** Take action.

■ **Step 6:** Evaluate what you have done. How were lives changed because of what the class members did?

❖ Encourage the students to make a commitment to support this project.

(5) Continue the Journey

❖ Pray that the students will go forth to live holy lives as they wait expectantly for the new heaven and earth.

❖ Read aloud this preparation for next week's lesson. You may also want to post it on newsprint for the students to copy. **Prepare for next week's session entitled "Living in Our New Home" by reading** Revelation 21:9–22:5. The lesson will focus on Revelation 21:9-10 and 21:22–22:5. As you study this lesson, keep these ideas in mind: People long for true peace, wholeness, and safety in their lives. Will this ever be possible? Revelation 21 says that those who dwell in God's new Jerusalem will experience these things, because God and the Lamb will be permanently in their midst.

❖ Read aloud the following three ideas. Challenge the students to commit themselves to use these activities as a springboard to spiritual growth.

(1) **Search for artistic depictions or literary descriptions of the new heaven and earth (21:1-4) or hell (21:8). How are the ones that you found similar to and/or different from your own ideas about these places?**

(2) **Use a concordance to find references to "tent" and "tabernacle." Note that Revelation 21:3 as it is written in Greek states that the "tabernacle of God" is with us and that God "will tabernacle" among us. What memories throughout Israelite history does this tabernacle (or tent) metaphor evoke?**

(3) **Do whatever is in your power this week to make your community a better place to live.**

❖ Sing or read aloud "O Holy City, Seen of John," based on Revelation 21:1–22:5.

❖ Say this benediction to conclude the session. You may wish to ask the students to echo it as you read: **Go in peace to love God and your neighbor, both in truth and in action.**

UNIT 3: LIVING IN GOD'S NEW WORLD

LIVING IN OUR NEW HOME

PREVIEWING THE LESSON

Lesson Scripture: Revelation 21:9-10; 21:22–22:5
Background Scripture: Revelation 21:9–22:5
Key Verse: Revelation 22:5

Focus of the Lesson:
People long for true peace, wholeness, and safety in their lives. Will this ever be possible? Revelation 21 says that those who dwell in God's new Jerusalem will experience these things, because God and the Lamb will be permanently in their midst.

Goals for the Learners:
(1) to ponder the image of the new city as a place God is always present as depicted in Revelation 21.
(2) to reflect on the significance of God's continual presence within the community of faith.
(3) to develop a plan to help the church be more of a safe haven for those in the community.

Pronunciation Guide:
apocalyptic (uh pok uh lip' tik)

Supplies:
Bibles, newsprint and marker, paper and pencils, hymnals, optional plain paper and colored pencils, copy of the poem "Chicago" by Carl Sandburg

---

READING THE SCRIPTURE

NRSV
Revelation 21:9-10

⁹Then one of the seven angels who had the seven bowls full of the seven last plagues came and said to me, "Come, I will show you the bride, the wife of the Lamb." ¹⁰And in the spirit he carried me away to a great, high mountain and showed me the holy city

NIV
Revelation 21:9-10

⁹One of the seven angels who had the seven bowls full of the seven last plagues came and said to me, "Come, I will show you the bride, the wife of the Lamb." ¹⁰And he carried me away in the Spirit to a mountain great and high, and showed me the

335

Jerusalem coming down out of heaven from
God.

Holy City, Jerusalem, coming down out of
heaven from God.

Revelation 21:22-27

²²I saw no temple in the city, for its temple
is the Lord God the Almighty and the Lamb.
²³And the city has no need of sun or moon to
shine on it, for the glory of God is its light,
and its lamp is the Lamb. ²⁴The nations will
walk by its light, and the kings of the earth
will bring their glory into it. ²⁵Its gates will
never be shut by day—and there will be no
night there. ²⁶People will bring into it the
glory and the honor of the nations. ²⁷But
nothing unclean will enter it, nor anyone
who practices abomination or falsehood, but
only those who are written in the Lamb's
book of life.

Revelation 21:22-27

²²I did not see a temple in the city,
because the Lord God Almighty and the
Lamb are its temple. ²³The city does not need
the sun or the moon to shine on it, for the
glory of God gives it light, and the Lamb is
its lamp. ²⁴The nations will walk by its light,
and the kings of the earth will bring their
splendor into it. ²⁵On no day will its gates
ever be shut, for there will be no night there.
²⁶The glory and honor of the nations will be
brought into it. ²⁷Nothing impure will ever
enter it, nor will anyone who does what is
shameful or deceitful, but only those whose
names are written in the Lamb's book of life.

Revelation 22:1-5

¹Then the angel showed me the river of
the water of life, bright as crystal, flowing
from the throne of God and of the Lamb
²through the middle of the street of the city.
On either side of the river is the tree of life
with its twelve kinds of fruit, producing its
fruit each month; and the leaves of the tree
are for the healing of the nations. ³Nothing
accursed will be found there any more. But
the throne of God and of the Lamb will be in
it, and his servants will worship him; ⁴they
will see his face, and his name will be on
their foreheads. **⁵And there will be no more
night; they need no light of lamp or sun,
for the Lord God will be their light,** and
they will reign forever and ever.

Revelation 22:1-5

¹Then the angel showed me the river of
the water of life, as clear as crystal, flowing
from the throne of God and of the Lamb
²down the middle of the great street of the
city. On each side of the river stood the tree
of life, bearing twelve crops of fruit, yielding
its fruit every month. And the leaves of the
tree are for the healing of the nations. ³No
longer will there be any curse. The throne of
God and of the Lamb will be in the city, and
his servants will serve him. ⁴They will see
his face, and his name will be on their foreheads. **⁵There will be no more night. They
will not need the light of a lamp or the
light of the sun, for the Lord God will give
them light.** And they will reign for ever and
ever.

UNDERSTANDING THE SCRIPTURE

Revelation 21:9-14. The scene recalls
Ezekiel's encounter, upon a "very high
mountain," with an angelic figure holding a
measuring rod and intending to measure
the city of God and its temple (compare

Ezekiel 40:2-5 particularly with Revelation
21:9-10, 15-17). In both texts, the scene
enacts a promise of hope: in Ezekiel, that the
city and the temple, already destroyed by
the armies of Nebuchadnezzar, would be

restored; in John, that God's vision for that city where God dwells with humanity would be perfected for eternity.

Ezekiel's angel begins with the temple and moves out to measure the city; John's angel, of course, only measures the city, for there is no temple (21:22). Both envision a city with twelve gates, three to a side, one for each of the twelve tribes of Israel (see Ezekiel 48:30-35). John adds the detail that each gate bears the name of one of the twelve tribes inscribed upon it, recalling the breastplate worn by the high priest, which sported twelve stones with the names of the twelve tribes engraved upon them (Exodus 28:21; 39:14). Blending these images, in effect, heightens the sense of the sacredness of this city, which now functions as a whole as Aaron's breastplate did—representing the interface between God and God's whole people. John also modifies Ezekiel's image, which also included foundations, by presenting the names of the twelve apostles engraved upon the city's twelve foundations. John creates an image that emphasizes continuity with God's historic people, Israel, but also brings further specification to who constitutes "Israel"—God's whole people have been gathered together for redemption by the work of the apostles and their successors.

Revelation 21:15-21. Ezekiel's city was also foursquare (48:16), as was his temple area (42:16-19), altar area (43:16), and holy of holies (41:4). The last of these reflects historical reality, since the holy of holies in Solomon's Temple was built as a cube, twenty cubits in length, depth, and height (1 Kings 6:20). John's message is clear: The New Jerusalem *is* the Holy of Holies, now expanded in its dimensions exponentially as a way of proclaiming that the limited access to God enjoyed in the Jerusalem Temple, the shadow of things to come (one man, the high priest, one day per year) has been broadened to all the redeemed (all the Lamb's followers, day without end). God acts to bring all God's people, formerly separated from God's full presence, *into* the Holy of Holies to live with God forever. The

Letter to the Hebrews also shares this perception of God's purposes (see Hebrews 6:19-20; 9:1-14; 10:19-22).

The images of gold, pearls, and gems—that which is most costly and fine in human experience—provide a kind of default language for describing the grandeur of the city that God builds *without* the kind of economic exploitation that Rome practiced to create its counterfeit (Revelation 18:7, 12-13). John describes the twelve foundations of the city's walls as being adorned with various kinds of gemstones, closely reminiscent of the twelve gemstones set in the high priest's breastplate (Exodus 28:17-20). That the names of the apostles were engraved on these foundations (21:14) makes them resemble the high priestly breastplate more and more (Exodus 28:21). Just as the names of the twelve patriarchs on the breastplate represented the whole people of Israel to God when the high priest stood in the Holy of Holies, so now the names of the twelve apostles represent the renewed tribes of Israel, those redeemed through their word (compare Matthew 19:28).

Revelation 21:22-27. The temple provided a means of sensing God's presence in God's city and of interacting with this God. However, it also strictly limited access to God to a few qualified personnel. The breakthrough of the New Jerusalem is the lack of a temple, the removal of all limitations on access to God while losing nothing of the sense of God's presence that the temple conveyed. Here at last the faith of the psalmist that "God is in the midst of the city" (Psalm 46:5) and the hope of the prophet that the city's name would be forever "The LORD is There" (Ezekiel 48:35) are perfected.

John turns his attention now to the visions of restored Jerusalem in Isaiah, particularly the image of God as the light of the city, rendering sun and moon redundant and leaving no place for night (Isaiah 60:19-20). From Isaiah John has also drawn the image of a city whose gates are never shut (Isaiah 60:11), since it will never again be threatened by enemies. Only the allies of God's people will survive; all enemies will perish (for John, the lake of fire will have claimed them all). John has significantly modified Isaiah's vision in regard to what the nations carry into God's city through these open gates: They bring their honor and glory (enhancing New Jerusalem, but also now giving to God what is God's due), but no longer their wealth (contrast Isaiah 60:5-6, 11, 13). New Jerusalem is not just another Babylon, sucking the earth dry of its riches. John's vision is not one born of envy, wanting to see Zion come out on top of Rome, and then enjoying all the goods that Rome sought for itself. In the next paragraph, indeed, we will see that it is quite the contrary.

The open gates cannot be interpreted as a sign that John endorsed universalism, which is the belief that all people will be saved through the universal redemption of Christ (see also Revelation 21:8; 22:15). There is an "outside," and those who have chosen the life and laws of Babylon in this world will not see Jerusalem in the next. The promise of Isaiah 52:1 is tellingly reconfigured here: It is no longer those who are "uncircumcised" that will not enter New Jerusalem, but those who are "uninscribed" in the Lamb's Book of Life (that is, those who have given their allegiance and obedience to the "Beast"; Revelation 13:8).

Revelation 22:1-5. Now, at the end, John's conversation with the Jewish Scriptures reaches back to the very beginning, to the first scene of community in the Garden of Eden. Once again the Tree of Life stands before us, but this time the way to take hold of immortality is no longer blocked by an angel with a flaming sword (Genesis 3:22-24), for the curse pronounced upon all creation due to humankind's rebellion has been lifted (Genesis 3:14-19). Into this scene is woven a "river of the water of life," recalling once again Ezekiel's vision of a river flowing out from beneath the restored temple, giving new life to the earth, causing trees to sprout up on either bank bearing "fresh fruit every month" for food and "leaves for healing" (Ezekiel 47:1, 12). Here, however, John sees one tree, the tree of life, giving the fruit of immortality to the people of God. Moreover, the leaves are for the healing "of the nations," reflecting the early Christian vision of the people of God encompassing those "from every tribe and language and people and nation" (Revelation 5:9). The flow of this river, bringing healing and nourishment out for all to share, stands in stark contrast with the flow of earth's resources *into* Babylon for her own exploitative pleasure and for the good of her elite allies (18:11-20). The longing of the worshipers to see God's face (Psalm 27:8; 42:2) is fulfilled at last, as John returns to the images drawn from Isaiah 60:19 of the light of God's own self—and the Lamb!—beaming forever upon the holy ones who come into their kingdom at last (see Daniel 7:13-14, 18, 27).

INTERPRETING THE SCRIPTURE

Living in the Light of God and the Lamb

Light is a persistent symbol of the invasion of God into our experience, from the first act of God's creation (Genesis 1:3), to the ongoing provision of "light" for human beings in God's wisdom and word (Psalm 119:105), to the coming of Jesus into the world as light to enlighten those who would be God's children (John 1:5, 9), to the consummation where our whole being and our whole living is bathed in God's light and the light of the Lamb (Revelation 21:23; 22:5). The Scriptures consistently present God as

One who wishes to surround us, guide us, and fill us with divine light.

The endpoint of this journey will be reached when God is as real, as present, as palpable to us as the light and warmth of the sun is to us now (21:22-23; 22:5). John's vision of the end of the journey suggests that our growing into maturity as children of God now must involve growing in our awareness of the presence and reality of God in our own lives, the nurturing of a spiritual life in which the light of God shines more and more fully and personally into our hearts and into our lives together in communities of faith, as the forerunner of that greater dawn. Making the spiritual disciplines of prayer and meditation a regular part of each day is one strategy for opening our lives more and more to God's light. Continuing to converse with God, to invite God's light into each situation in which we find ourselves during the day, to ask for God's illumination of those situations and of the path of faithfulness and toward Christ-likeness is a strategy for keeping that light present to us, and ourselves present to God. In this way, God can empower us to live as witnesses here to God's character as light (see 1 John 1:5-7).

Sacred Spaces

Across a wide diversity of cultures and religions, human beings have distinguished sacred spaces, the places where they anticipate interacting with the divine, from ordinary spaces, where they carry on their normal, day-to-day activities. Historic Israel was no different; modern Christianity is also shaped by this basic human impulse. The challenge for us, however, is to appreciate the power of designated sacred spaces while not losing sight of the ways in which God has been pleased to transcend those spaces, making the "ordinary sacred."

Our sanctuaries are physical spaces to which we can physically move: being physical entities ourselves, such physical places and movement assists the intentions and directions of our inward beings. The pouring out of the Holy Spirit upon Jesus' disciples in every age, however, indicates God's desire to move out with us into all the spaces of our lives. For Paul, for example, God is present in the community of believers wherever they are assembled, as well as in the individual bodies of believers (1 Corinthians 3:16-17; 6:19). The author of 1 Peter 2:4-5 also envisions sacred space being created as people are joined to Christ across the world.

Again looking ahead upon the trajectory that John sets us, we are invited to grow in our perception of God's presence—of sacred space—whenever we are in the presence of fellow Christians, attentive to the ways in which God would use those moments to break into our lives. We are also invited to become more attentive to the ways in which we bear God within us, by virtue of the Holy Spirit that he has given us (Romans 8:9-17), sanctifying the entirety of our existence. Far from "cheapening" the holy, such a view of life promises to bring that integrity, that wholeness, that bears the fruit of a consistent walk of faithfulness in the presence of God.

Till We Have Built Jerusalem

John's vision of New Jerusalem offers us a glimpse of God's economy, as it were. Here at last is a kingdom that exists to bless the nations, offering fullness of life and healing from God's ever-renewing abundance rather than hoarding limited goods for its own enjoyment at the expense of any who are not part of its interest group. God's city has no enemies. On the one hand, this state of affairs has been secured by the annihilation of those who drove, and allowed themselves to be driven by, the domination systems of the world. On the other hand, it anticipates a time when all those who have committed to live by God's ways can live safely without fear of division, competition, and hostility—for where the needs (the needs, not the wants) of all are satisfied there is no longer division into warring factions and interest groups.

The tragic element of the apocalyptic vision is that such a place belongs to another time, and lies beyond human capacity to realize. It is, however, precisely here that we find our call to live as a community of witnesses. In the midst of nations that regard one another in terms of allies or enemies in the quest for national security and the acquisition of resources, we are challenged to regard our fellow Christians in every nation as our family: to share our resources and to secure *their* well-being. In the midst of communities of competing interest groups, we are challenged to mobilize our churches not for our own survival, but for the service to others, freely given, that God directs. In the midst of families that employ control, neglect, and abuse as regular strategies, we are challenged not only to eliminate our own contributions to such death-dealing systems but also to make our churches safe havens for those who will only find "family" outside of their homes. In these and many other ways, we are encouraged by John to help the bride of the Lamb live in vibrant witness to her hope of the quality of life beyond the marriage supper, drawing many away from Babylon's addictive enticements with the foretaste of a genuine community.

SHARING THE SCRIPTURE

PREPARING TO TEACH

Preparing Our Hearts

This week's devotional reading is found in Ephesians 1:15-23. Consider each phrase: What does the writer pray for here? Spend time writing a prayer for your own congregation. What would you ask on their behalf? How would you describe Christ as you write your prayer?

Pray that you and the adult learners will give glory to God and our Lord Jesus Christ.

Preparing Our Minds

Study the background Scripture from Revelation 21:9–22:5, and lesson Scripture, 21:9-10; 21:22–22:5. As you delve into this Scripture consider whether or not it will ever be possible to experience peace, wholeness, and safety in your life.

Write on newsprint:
❏ information for next week's lesson, found under "Continue the Journey."
❏ activities for further spiritual growth in "Continue the Journey."

Locate "Chicago," one of the pieces in Carl Sandburg's *Chicago Poems*. You can find this in a book or on the Internet.

Prepare the suggested lecture for "Ponder the Image of the New City as a Place God Is Always Present as Depicted in Revelation 21."

LEADING THE CLASS

(1) Gather to Learn

❖ Welcome the class members and introduce any guests.

❖ Pray that all who have come will feel welcomed and safe in this community of God's people.

❖ **Option 1:** Distribute copies of *The United Methodist Hymnal* and ask the class to read responsively page 734, "Canticle of Hope." Talk with the class about this new home that God has prepared for us. What draws the students to it? What puzzles or surprises them? How would they expect to feel in this new place?

❖ **Option 2:** Read expressively "Chicago," which you can find in Carl Sandburg's *Chicago Poems*. Invite the students to comment on the images of the city that they envisioned. Ask why they would or would not feel safe in such a place.

❖ Read aloud today's focus statement: **People long for true peace, wholeness, and safety in their lives. Will this ever be possible? Revelation 21 says that those who dwell in God's new Jerusalem will experience these things, because God and the Lamb will be permanently in their midst.**

(2) Ponder the Image of the New City as a Place God Is Always Present as Depicted in Revelation 21

❖ Select a volunteer to read Revelation 21:9-10, 22-27.

■ Use information from Understanding the Scripture in a lecture to unpack the meaning of: the very high mountain; the dimensions, construction, and openness of the gates; the people who are in the city.

■ Invite the students to make additional comments and/or raise questions.

❖ Choose someone to read Revelation 22:1-5.

■ Read aloud the information for Revelation 22:1-5 in Understanding the Scripture. Ask the students to look up and read aloud the Old Testament passages that are referred to in this section: Genesis 3:14-19, 22-24; Ezekiel 47:1, 12; Psalm 27:8; 42:2; Isaiah 60:19; Daniel 7:13-14, 18, 27. Discuss how these images enrich their understanding of Revelation.

■ **Option:** Distribute paper and colored pencils. Encourage the students to sketch the New Jerusalem as described in verses 1-5. You may want to reread this passage so it is fresh in their minds as they work.

■ Conclude this section by asking the adults to comment on how this journey through word (and art) refreshes and motivates them to live as Christian disciples.

(3) Reflect on the Significance of God's Continual Presence within the Community of Faith

❖ Read aloud part of the second paragraph in "Living in the Light of God and the Lamb," ending with the words "that greater dawn."

❖ Encourage the students to comment on ways in which they now experience God as real and present.

❖ Invite the students to talk about any actions they might take to grow in their awareness of the presence and reality of God in their lives. (Be sure to suggest prayer and meditation if these disciplines do not come up in the course of the discussion.)

❖ Read the following quotation and ask the students to consider (1) how they are aware of God's presence and continual speaking to them and (2) when and why they ignored God. **God speaks to us unceasingly through the events of our life, through the firmness with which he negates our petty human ordering of it, through the regularity with which he disappoints our plans and our attempts to escape, through his endless defeat of all our calculations by which we hoped to become able to do without him. And little by little he tames us, he draws us into relationship with him. Then one day, when we are helpless on a bed, stopped dead by some reverse, isolated by some misfortune, crushed by a sense of our own powerlessness, one day he brings us to the point of resigning ourselves to listening to his language, to admitting his presence, to recognizing his will. And we realize then that he had always been speaking to us.** (Louis Evely, 1910–   )

(4) Develop a Plan to Help the Church Be More of a Safe Haven for Those in the Community

❖ Invite the students to identify people in the community who need to find a safe haven. Perhaps there are children who need child care. Maybe there is a refugee population in need of acceptance, stability, and assistance. Possibly there are older adults who are only marginally able to remain in their homes. Make a list of these groups on newsprint.

❖ Narrow the list to one or two groups that the class feels it can serve.

❖ Brainstorm ways that your class and/or congregation as a whole can help one of these groups. If you have identified more than one group, divide into teams and let each team do the brainstorming. Invite the teams to report back to the class.

❖ Discuss these questions. Either write the answers on newsprint or distribute paper and pencils to at least one person who will act as a recorder.

(1) **Which ideas sound the most feasible to us, given our time, talent, and resources?**

(2) **What benefit will our ideas/project be to the people we hope to help?**

(3) **What criteria will we use to determine whether or not we did help this group?**

(4) **Who from our class will be involved? What roles will they play?** (You will probably want to form a task force to develop plans for this project.)

(5) **Who else needs to be involved?** (Think here of church boards who may need to give approval, social service agencies, or other government departments that may become involved.)

(6) **How will our participation enable us—and others—to experience God in our midst?**

(5) Continue the Journey

❖ Pray that those who have participated in today's lesson will go forth, aware of God in their midst, and anticipating the new home that is yet to come.

❖ Read aloud this preparation for next week's lesson. You may also want to post it on newsprint for the students to copy. **Prepare for next week's session entitled "The Ultimate Happy Ending" by reading Revelation 22:6-21. The lesson will highlight verses 6-10, 12-13, 16-21. Consider these ideas as you study: Most people would like to live in a world in which happy endings always come to pass, and one can trust that everything will be all right in the end. Given the reality of this world, however, what happy ending can we ever trust to come to pass? Revelation 22 tells us to trust that Jesus Christ will come again and that his coming will transform everything into the ultimate happy ending for us.**

❖ Read aloud the following three ideas. Challenge the students to commit themselves to use these activities as a springboard to spiritual growth.

(1) **Page through a hymnal looking for songs based on Revelation 21 or 22. How do these songs reflect John's writing? In what way do these images speak to you?**

(2) **Read Ezekiel 40. What insight does that book give you into Revelation?**

(3) **Research history in Israel from around A.D. 70 when the temple was destroyed to about A.D. 95 when many scholars feel Revelation was written. Note that Domitian was the emperor from A.D. 81–96. See what you can learn about him and his policies that would shed light on Revelation.**

❖ Sing or read aloud "Shall We Gather at the River."

❖ Say this benediction to conclude the session. You may wish to ask the students to echo it as you read: **Go in peace to love God and your neighbor, both in truth and in action.**

UNIT 3: LIVING IN GOD'S NEW WORLD

THE ULTIMATE HAPPY ENDING

PREVIEWING THE LESSON

Lesson Scripture: Revelation 22:6-10, 12-13, 16-21
Background Scripture: Revelation 22:6-21
Key Verse: Revelation 22:20

Focus of the Lesson:

Most people would like to live in a world in which happy endings always come to pass, and one can trust that everything will be all right in the end. Given the reality of this world, however, what happy ending can we ever trust to come to pass? Revelation 22 tells us to trust that Jesus Christ will come again and that his coming will transform everything into the ultimate happy ending for us.

Goals for the Learners:

(1) to explore the image of Christ's return as depicted in Revelation 22.
(2) to discern their feelings regarding Christ's return.
(3) to make a commitment to prepare for Christ's return.

Pronunciation Guide:

Didache (did' uh kee)   Laodicea (lay od i see' uh)
makarism (mak ar is em)   *marana tha* (mair uh nath' uh)
Nicolaitans (nik uh lay' uh tuhns)   Sardis (sahr' dis)

Supplies:

Bibles, newsprint and marker, paper and pencils, hymnals

READING THE SCRIPTURE

NRSV
Revelation 22:6-10, 12-13, 16-21

⁶And he said to me, "These words are trustworthy and true, for the Lord, the God of the spirits of the prophets, has sent his angel to show his servants what must soon take place."

⁷"See, I am coming soon! Blessed is the

NIV
Revelation 22:6-10, 12-13, 16-21

⁶The angel said to me, "These words are trustworthy and true. The Lord, the God of the spirits of the prophets, sent his angel to show his servants the things that must soon take place."

⁷"Behold, I am coming soon! Blessed is he

one who keeps the words of the prophecy of this book."

⁸I, John, am the one who heard and saw these things. And when I heard and saw them, I fell down to worship at the feet of the angel who showed them to me; ⁹but he said to me, "You must not do that! I am a fellow servant with you and your comrades the prophets, and with those who keep the words of this book. Worship God!"

¹⁰And he said to me, "Do not seal up the words of the prophecy of this book, for the time is near.

¹²"See, I am coming soon; my reward is with me, to repay according to everyone's work. ¹³I am the Alpha and the Omega, the first and the last, the beginning and the end."

¹⁶"It is I, Jesus, who sent my angel to you with this testimony for the churches. I am the root and the descendant of David, the bright morning star."

¹⁷The Spirit and the bride say, "Come."
And let everyone who hears say, "Come."
And let everyone who is thirsty come.
Let anyone who wishes take the water of life as a gift.

¹⁸I warn everyone who hears the words of the prophecy of this book: if anyone adds to them, God will add to that person the plagues described in this book; ¹⁹if anyone takes away from the words of the book of this prophecy, God will take away that person's share in the tree of life and in the holy city, which are described in this book.

²⁰**The one who testifies to these things says, "Surely I am coming soon."**
Amen. Come, Lord Jesus!

²¹The grace of the Lord Jesus be with all the saints. Amen.

who keeps the words of the prophecy in this book."

⁸I, John, am the one who heard and saw these things. And when I had heard and seen them, I fell down to worship at the feet of the angel who had been showing them to me. ⁹But he said to me, "Do not do it! I am a fellow servant with you and with your brothers the prophets and of all who keep the words of this book. Worship God!"

¹⁰Then he told me, "Do not seal up the words of the prophecy of this book, because the time is near.

¹²"Behold, I am coming soon! My reward is with me, and I will give to everyone according to what he has done. ¹³I am the Alpha and the Omega, the First and the Last, the Beginning and the End.

¹⁶"I, Jesus, have sent my angel to give you this testimony for the churches. I am the Root and the Offspring of David, and the bright Morning Star."

¹⁷The Spirit and the bride say, "Come!" And let him who hears say, "Come!" Whoever is thirsty, let him come; and whoever wishes, let him take the free gift of the water of life.

¹⁸I warn everyone who hears the words of the prophecy of this book: If anyone adds anything to them, God will add to him the plagues described in this book. ¹⁹And if anyone takes words away from this book of prophecy, God will take away from him his share in the tree of life and in the holy city, which are described in this book.

²⁰**He who testifies to these things says, "Yes, I am coming soon."**
Amen. Come, Lord Jesus.

²¹The grace of the Lord Jesus be with God's people. Amen.

UNDERSTANDING THE SCRIPTURE

Revelation 22:6-7. The affirmation that "these words are trustworthy and true" greets the hearer a third time (see 19:9; 21:5).

As in both previous contexts, so here, "these words" operate at two levels. First, we have detected the words of the Hebrew prophets and other spokespersons for God woven into John's communication. John has clearly regarded these as trustworthy and true, so much so that he is not reticent to ask his congregations to stake their lives, properties, and sacred honor upon them. Second, the new reconfigurations of those words are affirmed as trustworthy and true—indeed, as the way in which John understands how the old words about God and God's purposes will prove trustworthy and true yet again in the situation of the Christian churches.

The language of these verses recalls the opening three verses of Revelation, both in working through the "chain of revelation" and in pronouncing "blessed," "honored," or "favored" those who "keep" the words of John's proclamation of God—that is, who allow Revelation to re-orient them to their situations and who walk in the path of faithfulness to God that such an orientation unveils. "Keeping" involves obedient action: John will not separate "faith/faithfulness" from "works" (for example, "the righteous deeds of the saints," Revelation 19:8).

Revelation 22:8-9. Although we have paid a great deal of attention to how older traditions, especially the Jewish Scriptures, have shaped John's message, we also have to take seriously his claim to have had significant visionary and auditory experiences. Such were part and parcel of the experience of the Hebrew prophets (Isaiah 6:1-8 remains a stunning example), the early Christian leaders (for example, Paul's experiences of the risen Christ in Acts 9 and his visionary experience of the third heaven in 2 Corinthians 12:1-10, or Peter's dream vision of the clean and unclean animals in Acts 10), and the early Christians themselves (for example, the Spirit-inspired prophecy and revelations that formed a regular part of the worship experience in the Corinthian church; see 1 Corinthians 14:26-33). Because of their vibrant experience of the Holy Spirit, early Christians did not

expect God to communicate only through "rational" means, but were open to a variety of states of consciousness through which God might give guidance to God's people.

Revelation 22:10-11. In Daniel, the seer had been told to "keep the words secret and the book sealed until the time of the end" (Daniel 12:4). Because apocalypses were often written by an anonymous author *in the name of* some famous Old Testament hero of the distant past (for example, Enoch, Abraham, Ezra, Baruch, Daniel), the real author would provide some explanation for why the book received no notice until his time. "Sealing up" or hiding the book explained how the book would remain unknown between the time of the implied author and the actual author and audience, which is always presumed to be "the time of the end" (Daniel 12:4). In other cases, simply having the implied author state that he writes not for his present generation, but for one that will come in the distant future (1 Enoch 1:2) would serve the same end. John subverts this feature of the genre. The real author writes in his own name, and *at* the time of the end. There is no need to "seal up" the words, since they apply immediately.

It is probably in light of the imminence of the end that we should hear verse 11 (which itself speaks in the same idiom as Ezekiel 3:27 and Daniel 12:10). The nearness of the end is such that people might as well just keep on going in the direction they have already chosen. Of course, the rhetorical effect of such a statement is just the reverse: If the end is *that* close, we had better repent and fall in line with God's movement *immediately.*

Revelation 22:12-13. John's conviction that God renders to each according to his or her deeds (Revelation 20:12-13) is shared by Paul (see Romans 2:6-11; 2 Corinthians 5:9-10), the author of 1 Peter (1:17), and Jesus himself (Matthew 25:31-46). This conviction, of course, is deeply rooted in the Hebrew Scriptures as well (see Psalm 28:4, and especially Jeremiah 17:10), going ultimately back to the Torah itself—where to *do* what God wanted brought life, and to neglect what God demanded brought death (Deuteronomy 30:15-20).

Revelation 22:14-17. The final *makarism* or "beatitude" recalls the vision of Revelation 7:13-17, connecting the life choices of the redeemed pictured there with enjoying access to the City of God described in Revelation 21:1–22:5 (entering the city by the gates, 21:24-27; eating from the tree of life, 22:2). Because of the great value attached to being welcomed into God's eternal presence then, the hearers will attach equally great value to the way of life represented by washing one's robes in the blood of the Lamb and keeping their robes unsoiled. That is, they will highly value their attachment to Jesus, prioritize showing fidelity to Jesus in the midst of their situation (however much this exacerbates the tensions they experience with the host society and other groups around them, like the synagogue), examine to what extent they are colluding with, and profiting from, the Roman systems of domination (this will especially hit the Christians in Laodicea and Sardis, and those attracted to the Nicolaitans' compromised Gospel; see Revelation 2:14-15, 20-23; 3:1-6, 14-22), and move away from associations that threaten to "soil" their lives in the sight of God. This second list of those who are "outside" (see 21:8) reinforces the need to dissociate from a lifestyle of compromise with the lies, violence, and economic plunder of Roman imperialism.

Jesus identifies himself as the source of this prophetic admonition (see Revelation 1:1), identifying himself once more as the shoot/root of David (see note on Revelation 5:5-7) and, now, as the "bright morning star," almost certainly playing on messianic readings of Numbers 24:17 and traditions dependent on that text. The poetic invitation of the Spirit, the bride, and "everyone who hears" is most likely to be heard as a prayer that Jesus will "come," but this is matched by an invitation to all who desire that fulfillment that Babylon can never bring to "come" find that fulfillment in God and in what God has promised (echoing Isaiah 55:1 once again; see Revelation 21:6).

Revelation 22:18-21. The curses pronounced upon those who would alter the message John has delivered (for it is the word of *God*, not merely the word of *John*) recall the prohibition against adding to or taking away from the laws God laid down in the Torah (Deuteronomy 4:2). This is indeed appropriate for John's reconfiguring of the testimony of God contained in the Law and the Prophets, the re-embodiment of those texts in a new situation. The book ends with another assurance by Jesus, the ultimate "witness" testifying in Revelation, of his imminent coming, and with an invitation spoken by his faithful disciple longing for his arrival.

INTERPRETING THE SCRIPTURE

How Soon, Exactly?

Throughout this chapter, we are confronted with claims that the events about which we are reading "will happen quickly," indeed, that Jesus "comes soon" or quickly (22:6, 7, 12; 22:10). We are also confronted with the fact that these words were written almost two millennia ago. At this late date, even the consolation that God measures time differently (see 2 Peter 3:8-9) may not fully satisfy. The declarations of imminence clearly served the purpose of empowering disciples in late first-century

Asia Minor to "keep the words of this book," whether that meant continuing in their faithful witness or shaking half-hearted disciples loose from their moorings in Babylon! It seems almost disingenuous to continue to use the topic of imminence to achieve this goal in the sixtieth generation of the church's history.

The creeds of the Christian church that hold all branches of the body together affirm that "Christ will come again in glory to judge the living and the dead." Each disciple must work out how to make this tenet of faith a vital part of their witness and walk. I have come to the place where I regard topics of imminence as topics of ultimacy, or priority. Christ may come very soon; God may see fit to have Christ return in another two millennia. Neither eventuation alters the fact that Christ's return remains God's ultimate act in history, the event that sets the priorities for every believer in every age, the event in relation to which we find reliable bearings in the sea of this world. To make it personal, I pray for Christ's imminent return; I live in this world (or, at least, make it my goal to live) by the ultimacy of Christ's return. What this means, practically, is that all the powers and pursuits of this world that so easily captivate the ear and ensnare the desire are relativized and judged in the light of God's purposes for me and for human community. I am summoned to live for the latter, and discover the possibility of liberation from the former.

A Strange Endorsement

The voice of Jesus, rather than John, dominates the ending of Revelation from 22:12 onwards, and it is in fact Jesus who is presented as uttering the curses upon those who add or subtract from John's message (compare the "I" testifying in 22:16 with the speech of "the one who testifies to these things" in 22:20—it can only be Jesus, the one who will come quickly). Some have read this passage as a warning against adding books to the Bible, but this reading is merely an accident of Revelation's being placed at the close of the canon. To the first readers of Revelation, the passage would clearly apply only to the words of Revelation.

There is a great danger in reading Revelation that we will want it to say more than it does. I fear this is the case with many end-time timetables, which want to turn Revelation into a daily-planner for the "seven last years" and read a "rapture" and other flights of fancy into its pages, claiming John's support for ideas that could not be farther from John's mind (for whom the faithful will suffer and bear witness under threat of death).

There is an equally great danger—perhaps the one that threatens readers from mainline denominations more than the former danger—that we will not want to hear *all* that Revelation has to say. We may not want to wrestle with John's indictment of the world order of his time as "beast" and "harlot," nor with the implications of the same for our often-too-comfortable partnership with contemporary political and economic domination systems. But to hear what is not there in the text and to pass over what is there in the text have the same result: Our discipleship will be malformed, our witness blunted, our robes soiled. And so we are left with this challenge to keep going back through Revelation—through the text in all its entirety and with all its challenges—until we have heard what the Spirit would say to our churches, to affirm and to admonish, in all things to prepare us to meet Christ as deliverer rather than as judge.

Come, Lord Jesus

Marana tha—Aramaic for "Our Lord, come!"—is an ancient Christian prayer, similar in content and form to what we would call a "breath prayer," a short petition that can be said in the space of a single exhalation, centering our hearts and minds on a single focus. Paul offered this prayer in Aramaic (1 Corinthians 16:22); John offers it (in Greek) in response to all that he has seen and heard (Revelation 22:20); the early church continued to offer it regularly, as, for example, in the communion prayers recorded in the *Didache* 10.8 (a late first-century or early second-century Christian manual on ethics and church practice).

The Spirit and the bride say "Come." Do you say, "Come?" We might, perhaps, *not* look forward to Christ's return. All the images of that return in Revelation, as indeed in all of the New Testament, suggest a major disruption in our lives. People who value stability may well not relish the prospect of the radical destabilization of their world. To be blunt, I have found myself wishing for the delay of the second coming! I want to see my sons grow up. I want to achieve my professional goals. I want to live this life in all its fullness.

And it is precisely here that John catches me and admonishes me. He convicts me of my lack of solidarity with my suffering and marginalized sisters and brothers throughout the world, for whom Christ's delay means more grief, more pain, more sorrow. He convicts me of my failure to value what Christ's return will bring to the whole of creation, which is surely greater than the value of my own desires for life. He convicts me of being, ultimately, more in love with this world than with Christ, and, in so doing, calls me to a healthful repentance and a reorienting of my life.

This is, finally, what Revelation seeks to do and has the power to do—to reorient our lives toward Christ by disorienting our lives in this world, helping us to see our engagements (and often our entanglements) in this world in the light of God's character and purposes. As John invites us to join in the breath prayer of the whole Church, he invites us to desire what God will bring to pass, to make those desires our own in all that we do, rather than continuing to pray that God might support our desires and wishes. He invites us to a life of witness and obedience that is indeed summed up in the prayer, "Come, Lord Jesus."

SHARING THE SCRIPTURE

PREPARING TO TEACH

Preparing Our Hearts

This week's devotional reading is found in John 16:17-24. Although the disciples do not truly understand his meaning, Jesus speaks here of his imminent death and how that will cause great pain for his followers. But he assures them that his "going to the Father" (16:17) is not the end of the story for them. He tells the disciples that their "pain will turn into joy" (16:20). When have you faced difficulty or uncertainty only to have the situation end happily? What lessons of faith did you learn from that experience?

Pray that you and the adult learners will recognize that in Christ there is ultimately a happy ending.

Preparing Our Minds

Study the background Scripture, Revelation 22:6-21, and lesson Scripture, verses 6-10, 12-13, 16-21. Contemplate this question as you study: What happy endings do you believe will come to pass in your own life?

Write on newsprint:
- ❏ information for next week's lesson, found under "Continue the Journey."
- ❏ activities for further spiritual growth in "Continue the Journey."

Plan an optional lecture for "Explore the Image of Christ's Return as Depicted in Revelation 22."

LEADING THE CLASS

(1) Gather to Learn

❖ Welcome the class members and introduce any guests.

❖ Pray that those who have gathered will be open to the Spirit's leading as we consider again what it means to live in God's new world.

❖ Say **"Once upon a time"** and ask the adults to talk about what comes to mind when they hear these words. (Likely, they will mention fairy tales, perhaps by Hans Christian Andersen or the Brothers Grimm. These well-known stories, which the class members may refer to by name, are often populated with animals or strange people in most unusual circumstances. By the end of the story, though, all is well and everyone lives happily ever after.)

❖ **Option:** Prompt the students to summarize one or more popular fairy tales and discuss the reversal of fortune that created a happy ending.

❖ Read aloud today's focus statement: **Most people would like to live in a world in which happy endings always come to pass, and one can trust that everything will be all right in the end. Given the reality of this world, however, what happy ending can we ever trust to come to pass? Revelation 22 tells us to trust that Jesus Christ will come again and that his coming will transform everything into the ultimate happy ending for us.**

(2) Explore the Image of Christ's Return as Depicted in Revelation 22

❖ Solicit four volunteers to read Revelation 22:6-10, 12-13, 16-21, each taking the part of John, Jesus, the angel, or the narrator. Since these parts are intertwined, give the

readers a few moments to preview their lines. Tell the class to listen to who is speaking.

❖ Discuss these questions with the group, or answer them yourself in a lecture. Information in Understanding the Scripture will help you to prepare a brief lecture or add to the students' ideas.

(1) **What do we learn about the words that have been spoken about the end time?** (See 22:6.)
(2) **How do you understand Jesus' words, "See, I am coming soon" (22:7, 12, 20) in light of the fact that it has been more than two thousand years since he uttered them?**
(3) **What do you make of John's claim that he "heard and saw these things" (22:8)?** (Talk here about auditory and visionary experiences. The Understanding the Scripture information for Revelation 22:8-9 gives other examples of such experiences that somehow bypass our rational thought processes.)
(4) **What do we learn about Jesus, especially in verse 16?** (See the second paragraph for verses 14-17 in Understanding the Scripture.)

❖ Conclude this portion of the lesson by reading: In writing about the second coming as if it were a play, C. S. Lewis (1898–1963) echoes Jesus' words in verse 12 concerning "reward" when he writes: **"We are led to expect that the Author will have something to say to each of us on the part that each of us has played. The playing it well is what matters infinitely."** Meditate for a few moments on the idea of "reward" and how it currently affects the way you live. Think silently about any lifestyle changes that you want to make.

(3) Discern the Learners' Feelings Regarding Christ's Return

❖ Break the silence by noting that because Christ did not return as quickly as some had imagined he would, Christians throughout history have wondered if he really would return.

❖ Ask the participants to indicate by a show of hands how many believe that Christ will come again. (Accept the results without trying to persuade those who do not agree with your belief. The Scriptures will speak for themselves.)

❖ Read "How Soon, Exactly?" from Interpreting the Scripture and encourage the students to respond by giving their views.

❖ Read the second and third paragraphs of "Come, Lord Jesus" in Interpreting the Scripture. Talk with the class about why some may hope that the second coming will be delayed. Discuss these questions.

(1) **What might Christ say to those who are concerned about disruption and destabilization in our world?**

(2) **Of what value will Christ's return be for all creation?**

(4) Make a Commitment to Prepare for Christ's Return

❖ Distribute paper and pencils. Tell the students to imagine that they can know for certain that Christ will come within forty-eight hours. Ask them to make a list of the things they would do to prepare.

❖ Choose volunteers to read several items on their lists.

❖ Ask the adults to ponder: **If I would take these actions knowing that Christ's return is imminent, what barriers prevent me from taking them now? What do I need to do to prepare myself to meet the Lord upon his return—or my death?**

❖ Encourage the students to talk about the barriers they have identified. See if they can suggest ways around these roadblocks. Remind the students that we have no way of knowing exactly how long we have to make our preparations.

❖ End by reading the key verse, 22:20.

(5) Continue the Journey

❖ Pray that those who have participated today will be prepared for the ultimate happy ending that is to come.

❖ Read aloud this preparation for next week's lesson. You may also want to post it on newsprint for the students to copy. **Prepare for next week's session entitled "Committed to Justice" by reading background Scripture from Amos 5:10-15, 21-24; 8:4-12; 2 Kings 13:23-25. The lesson will concentrate on Amos 5:10-15, 21-24. Focus on these ideas as you study the lesson: Many people experience injustice in today's world. What accounts for this, and what does it have to do with us? Amos says that injustice stems from one part of society ignoring the needs of another, and that, as God's people, we are called to fight such attitudes and behaviors.**

❖ Read aloud the following three ideas. Challenge the students to commit themselves to use these activities as a springboard to spiritual growth.

(1) **Read "The Second Coming," a poem by William Butler Yeats. What does this poem say to you about Yeats' expectations?**

(2) **Read a book concerning Christ's return and evaluate it in light of our study on Revelation.**

(3) **Look for articles in the media related to the second coming. What are some of the ways in which both Christians and non-Christians talk about this event? What speculations about this event can you find?**

❖ Sing or read aloud "Soon and Very Soon."

❖ Say this benediction to conclude the session. You may wish to ask the students to echo it as you read: **Go in peace to love God and your neighbor, both in truth and in action.**

FOURTH QUARTER
Committed to Doing Right

JUNE 3, 2007–AUGUST 26, 2007

The 2006–2007 Sunday school year comes to a close with a thirteen-week study of the prophets, whose messages are set in historical context by exploring texts from 2 Kings or 2 Chronicles. We will be studying Amos, Hosea, Isaiah, Micah, Zephaniah, Habakkuk, Jeremiah, Lamentations (traditionally ascribed to Jeremiah), Ezekiel, Zechariah, and Malachi. Although these prophets proclaimed God's word over several hundred years, their message was consistent: A faithful relationship with God entails specific requirements, one of which is to do right.

Unit 1, "Life as God's People," includes four sessions that examine the need for justice, the people's accountability for wrongdoing, the nature of true worship, and the abundant life God offers. The unit begins on June 3 with "Committed to Justice," based on Amos 5:10-15, 21-24; 8:4-12; and 2 Kings 13:23-25. The prophet Hosea speaks to us on June 10 with "God's Indictment of Israel," rooted in Hosea 4:1-4; 7:1-2; 12:7-9; 14:1-3; and 2 Kings 15:8-10. The prophet calls for "True Worship!" in the session for June 17 that delves into Isaiah 1:10-20 and 2 Kings 15:32-35. The first unit ends on June 24 with a lesson from Isaiah 55:1-11, "Finding Satisfaction," which implores us to "seek the LORD."

In Unit 2, "What Does God Require?," we will spend five weeks studying God's requirements for righteous living, God's justice, God's judgment, the people's disobedience, and the need for trust in God. Micah 2:1-4; 3:1-5, 8-12; 6:6-8 is the basis for the lesson on July 1, "Do the Right Thing." On July 8 we turn to Zephaniah 3:1-13 and 2 Chronicles 34:1-3 to hear Zephaniah's announcement of God's justice in "Getting Ready for Judgment." In "A Reason to Hope," the session for July 15, Habakkuk is willing to wait faithfully for God to act, as recorded in Habakkuk 2:1-20 and 2 Kings 23:35-37. Jeremiah declares the consequences of disobedience in "Your Actions, Your Consequences," the session for July 22, which is based on Jeremiah 7:11-15 and 2 Kings 23:36-37. Unit 2 ends on July 29 as Jeremiah invites the Jewish exiles in Babylon to trust in God. This lesson, "Getting through the Pain," is found in Jeremiah 29:1-14.

Unit 3, "How Shall We Respond?," includes three sessions that emphasize hope, personal responsibility, and repentance as appropriate responses for those who are committed to doing right. The fourth session reassures us that God's judgment is just. As the unit opens on August 5, "Maintaining Hope!" explores the message of 2 Kings 25:1-2, 5-7 and Lamentations 3:25-33, 55-58, where those in crisis are urged to hope in God. In the lesson for August 12, "Personal Consequences of Sin!" we hear the prophet in Ezekiel 18 preach about individual responsibility. "Call for Repentance," the session for August 19, explores the prophet's call for a return to God in Zechariah 1:1-6; 7:8-14; 8:16-17, 20-21, 23. Our Sunday school year ends on August 26 with a description of God's just judgment, found in Malachi 2:17–4:3, in a session entitled "Living Responsibly in the Community of Faith."

MEET OUR WRITER

DR. JOHN INDERMARK

John Indermark is an ordained minister in the United Church of Christ and a freelance writer. His writings focus on resources for Christian education curriculum and spiritual formation books. John lives in southwest Washington state in the town of Naselle. His partner, Judy, works as a 911 dispatcher for Pacific County. John and Judy both enjoy traveling in British Columbia, flyfishing, and beachcombing.

John received a Bachelor of Arts degree in History from St. Louis University in 1972. In 1976, he received a Masters of Divinity degree from Eden Seminary in Webster Groves, Missouri. John was ordained in his home church of Salvator United Church of Christ in St. Louis.

From 1976 until 1992, John served full-time pastorates in the Pacific Northwest Conference of the United Church of Christ (Metaline Falls, Carnation, and Naselle). From 1992 until 2002, he served a variety of interim and supply pastorates in Presbyterian, Methodist, and Lutheran congregations in southwest Washington and northwest Oregon. He also served for two and a half years as an associate chaplain at a state juvenile detention facility in Naselle. John began work as a freelance writer in 1990, which he now does full-time along with occasional preaching.

John's published books include: *Genesis of Grace, Neglected Voices, Setting the Christmas Stage, Traveling the Prayer Paths of Jesus,* and *Turn Toward Promise,* all published by Upper Room Books. A Lenten book based on the parables, tentatively titled *Parables and Passion,* will be published in the fall of 2006. Another book on the theme of hope (tentatively titled *Hope: The Longing for Home*) is scheduled for publication in the fall of 2007. John co-authored with his son, Jeff Indermark, *Seekers, Saints, and Other Hypocrites* and *The Matrix and the Gospel,* young adult study books published by the Presbyterian Church (U.S.A.). The curriculum projects he has worked on include: *The New International Lesson Annual, Seasons of the Spirit, Present Word, Adult Bible Studies,* and *Great Themes of the Bible.*

THE BIG PICTURE: GOD'S COVENANT DEMANDS JUSTICE

This quarter focuses on the core messages of Israel's prophets, who insist covenant relationship with God demands conduct toward neighbor and stranger infused with justice. Three units divide the material covered in this quarter, each of whose themes and emphases we will look at later in this article. For now, however, we will turn to an overview of the period addressed by the prophets.

Prophets of the Northern Kingdom

After the death of Solomon, a period of civil unrest ensued that resulted eventually in the division of the kingdom under Jeroboam I in the north and Rehoboam in the south. The northern kingdom, Israel (sometimes referred to as "Ephraim" from one of the older tribal areas), comprised the largest area, corresponding roughly to what in New Testament times would be known as Galilee and Samaria. The town of Samaria eventually became the capital of the northern kingdom, though Shechem (and nearby Mount Gerizim) remained its chief religious center. The southern kingdom was known as Judah, likewise named for one of the original tribal areas that formed most of its territory. Jerusalem served as both its political and religious capital. Many of the more memorable stories of the era of the divided kingdoms come from the northern kingdom, such as the Elijah and Elisha stories.

Both kingdoms enjoyed relative prosperity in the ninth and into the eight centuries B.C. That prosperity, however, was not shared equally across the board by all. Wealth in particular, and with it power, became increasingly centralized in ruling classes, political and religious. The covenant traditions surrounding the importance of community seemed more and more subservient to the whims of those who exercised extraordinary power and influence. Beyond this, troubling developments loomed on the horizon: In particular, the Assyrian Empire to the north and east entered an aggressive expansionist phase. The response in both kingdoms—though at this point the north was more susceptible simply because of the direction of Assyrian expansion—seemed to rely on a trust that all would be well, regardless, because of God's choosing of Israel. And if practical help were needed, alliances with smaller neighboring countries as well as the power of Egypt to the south would thwart any Assyrian aggression.

In the middle of the eighth century B.C., alternative voices cried out to be heard in Israel and Judah. These individuals came to be called *nabi,* or "prophets." They did not so much fore-tell the future as forth-tell God's word and intents with messages intended to sway and shift present inequities and inconsistencies with covenantal obligations. The two prophets most associated with addressing the northern kingdom were Amos and Hosea. Amos himself came from the southern kingdom. His calling Israel to task during a time when sensitivities were lulled to sleep accounts for the harshness and graphic nature of his language and imagery, designed to catch attention. Hosea, on the other hand, came from the north, and

---

apparently wrote in the midst of the collapse of the northern kingdom under civil war and Assyrian assault.

Micah, like Amos, came from the south. His oracles address both Israel and Judah, particularly the latter. It is from Micah that we have what may be the most concise summary of the whole prophetic tradition: *[God] has told you, O mortal, what is good; and what does the LORD require of you but to do justice, to love kindness, and to walk humbly with your God* (Micah 6:8).

Prophets of the Southern Kingdom: Before the Exile

In 722 B.C., Samaria fell to the invading Assyrian army and the northern kingdom ceased to exist. What happened to its peoples is largely a mystery that sometimes goes named by "the ten lost tribes of Israel" (the southern kingdom consisted basically of only two of the original twelve tribal areas). The great majority of the residents of the northern kingdom were killed and deported. A few either remained or returned among those peoples whom the Assyrians resettled in this region. The faith associated with the Samaritans of Jesus' time (and with a small group that persists to that day in the region around Mount Gerizim) kept alive remnants of a form of Judaism that may well trace to those who may have survived the deportations.

In any event, from 722 B.C. onward, Judaism and the prophetic tradition continues on in the southern kingdom. In what is sometimes a confusing use of terms, this continuing kingdom and land is from this point forward often referred to not as Judah but as Israel—for here the covenant and land and traditions of Jacob's/Israel's descendants continue. Micah and Isaiah prophesy in this period immediately before and then following the northern kingdom's fall, when Judah herself comes under severe threat from an Assyrian takeover. Isaiah in particular had lambasted the leaders of the southern kingdom, King Ahaz in particular, for presuming to think that alliances with Syria and Israel would safeguard the nation (Isaiah 7:1-14). Only trust in God, and renewing the covenant obligations that include justice and righteousness in the land, held out hope. The first 39 chapters of Isaiah, with a few exceptions, have become identified by many scholars as First Isaiah, whose work is attributed to this era at the close of the eighth century.

The decisive moment in this era came with unsuccessful siege laid by the Assyrian king Sennacherib against Jerusalem in 701 B.C. Isaiah 36–37 (and 2 Kings 18–19) narrates the dramatic reversal that results in the Assyrians' defeat. For the time being, all seems well, with Judah's king Hezekiah following Isaiah's counsel. Judah has another century of independence. Even so, another power on the move is hinted in Isaiah 39: Babylon.

In the latter half of the seventh century, and into the sixth century, other prophetic voices take up the prophetic call for Judah's (now usually termed Israel's) renewal. Zephaniah, Jeremiah, and Habakkuk all begin their forth-telling of covenant's obligations during this era. The southern kingdom has shown all the breaches of covenant revealed in the north. Though the times are less prosperous than before, the gaps between rich and poor, powerful and vulnerable, remain no less pronounced. Zephaniah pronounced a coming "day of God" that would be devastating. Israel's leadership, religious and political, came under condemnation for complacency and indifference to good. Jeremiah spoke harsh words of judgment, both on Judah and the surrounding nations.

The one seeming bright spot in this era comes with the reign of King Josiah. In 622 B.C., a scroll is found that details the obligations of covenant. Josiah finds the scroll so antithetical to life as it has come to be in his realm that he tears his clothes and demands someone verify the authenticity of these words. Some scholars argue that the "book of the covenant" was some form of the book of Deuteronomy. Whatever the precise answer may be, Josiah summoned the people to the temple where he ordered the book to be read aloud in a covenant renewal ceremony. The reforms then enacted by Josiah attempted to address the neglect of covenant.

The best of intentions, however, do not always lead to the course intended. In seeking to weaken the allure of the "high places" (sites of worship around the countryside that often seemed drawn toward idolatry), Josiah strengthened the centrality of the Jerusalem temple for worship. Yet by doing so, that played into the hands of powers and theology that rationalized Jerusalem would always be inviolate from judgment. Jeremiah, who valued Josiah and at first supported the reforms, apparently saw it did not go far—or deep—enough. Even the best of covenants written with words did not attain the hoped-for promise of a covenant written on hearts (Jeremiah 31:31-34).

Prophets of the Southern Kingdom: Exile

The expansion of Babylon had now reached a critical stage for Judah/Israel. Some held God would deliver Jerusalem as had happened with Sennacherib. Israel's prophets of this era, and after, spoke otherwise. Habakkuk and Zephaniah wrestled with the implications of the evil about to fall on Judah. Jeremiah announced words that seemed treasonous in their acceptance of Babylonian authority. A rebellion was attempted by Judah, then led by Jehoiakim, around 600 B.C. It proved fatal.

In 597 B.C., the Babylonian armies captured Jerusalem and Jehoiakim's successor. The king and other leading political and religious figures in Jerusalem were deported to Babylon. Among them was a Jew named Ezekiel. A puppet king, Zedekiah, was installed on the throne. In spite of Jeremiah's urgings, Zedekiah eventually decided to pursue independence by forging an alliance with Egypt. Disaster ensued. Jerusalem was besieged, and it fell in 587 B.C. Only now, instead of deporting a few of its leading citizens, the city and temple were razed. A large number of the survivors of the siege were deported, while others (Jeremiah among them) went to Egypt or other places of refuge. Exile had come.

In exile, the prophetic voice continued. Only now, instead of judgment the growing word came to be one of hope. Jeremiah shifted his emphasis in that direction. Ezekiel, after dire warnings and vivid depictions of God's leaving of Jerusalem and the temple, now had other visions. Of a valley of dry bones brought to life. Of the reconstruction of the temple. Of shepherds (king) who would no longer consume the people given to their care, because God would now shepherd God's own flock. Many believe the latter half of Isaiah (chapter 40 onward) actually originated in this time. Words of comfort, visions of restoration—and still, words that emphasized covenant kept in goodness and justice and righteousness.

Later prophets also raised their voices. Of those examined in this quarter's study, Malachi is believed to have written during the time after the return from exile. The return did not exactly match the lofty words spoken in the second half of Isaiah. Difficulties remained. Rebuilding was hard. While the temple had been reconstructed, at least partially, the worship centered there lacked vitality. Malachi urged renewal in worship and its covenantal life. Yet, Malachi understood all those years later that worship alone did not exclusively define covenant or God's call. In Malachi, there is still the concern for the orphan and widow. There is still disdain for those who oppress others economically, or treat strangers without hospitality (Malachi 3:5). The commitment to do right continues to be the prophetic call to Israel—and through Israel, to us.

Closing

These prophetic texts and their call to commitment to do right remain vital in our day. *Commitment* to do right needs encouragement in our time, when the evidence of injustice and the widespread inequities in our time may take the wind out of sails. Commitment requires perseverance over the long haul, which means it requires hope. The prophets did not issue their words lightly. Jeremiah in particular suffered greatly for carrying the weight of his pronouncements. Without commitment, silence and indifference would be the easier choice, then and now.

But the prophetic insistence on doing right does not rely alone upon our ability to shoulder the load. We work, and live, in hope. For the prophets also declared in whose hands history remained, in spite of appearances. The prophets understood that the One who fashioned all of creation, and brought Israel out of the house of bondage and into the light of freedom, was the same One who will bear us through with promises kept and vision fulfilled.

In this unit, you may wish as a leader to pay special attention to prayer—particularly the Lord's Prayer. "Your kingdom come, your will be done." These are not just memorized words. They are intended to energize our commitment and remind us we live as witnesses to and in hopes of God's realm. The prophets understood that, and so they spoke . . . and so their words still have life among us. May you and those with whom you enter these texts find in them such encouragement to live faithfully, such commitment to do right.

FAITH IN ACTION: LIVING RIGHT

During this quarter we are studying the words of prophets whose lives spanned several hundred years but whose message was consistent: People living in covenant relationship with God have requirements placed on them, one of which is to do right. But what does that really mean? The prophets tell us that God requires us to do justice (righteousness), especially on behalf of the most vulnerable members of society; be accountable for our actions; and repent when we fail to live obediently.

Injustice continues to abound as it did in the days of the prophets. Poor people in the United States—even many who work forty hours a week—often lack medical care because they cannot afford health insurance; may not have enough nutritious food to feed their families throughout the month; cannot pay high energy bills; may not have sufficient funds for shelter. The list of inequities goes on and on.

Work with the class to identify instances of injustice in your own community. Determine how the class members, both corporately and individually, can address at least one of these issues. Here are some ideas: (1) *direct service* to those in need (for example, collecting food or clothing, mentoring, hosting guests in a shelter, building or repairing homes); (2) *advocacy* by working to change the policies and systems that perpetuate injustice (for example, supporting legislation that will help the poor, writing letters to newspaper editors, participating in online political action groups); (3) *financial support* (for example, contributing to the church and agencies that offer direct service and/or sponsor advocacy work geared toward righting injustices).

Ezekiel teaches that each person is responsible for his or her own actions and accountable individually to God. We cannot blame anyone else for our shortcomings.

Ask each participant to make a list of recent situations where he or she tried to blame someone else for personal failures or mistakes.

Suggest that the students privately explore their lists to determine under what circumstances they try to "pass the buck." Invite the adults to keep a journal throughout the remainder of the quarter to record similar examples. Challenge them to make a concerted effort to increase their level of accountability in those circumstances where they are likely to shun responsibility.

Repenting or turning around is a major theme in both the Old and New Testaments. When we disobey and stray from God, we need to turn back. Often, this repentance is individual. We have sinned and need forgiveness. Repentance can also be corporate as we repent together of pervasive sins such as discrimination, exclusion, abuse of power and privilege, or abuse of creation.

Work with the class to create a litany that includes corporate sins that the adults can identify. If possible, reproduce this litany and use it at the end of several class sessions instead of the printed prayer suggestions.

CLOSE-UP: TIMELINE OF THE PROPHETS ENCOUNTERED IN "COMMITTED TO DOING RIGHT"

Scholars use clues from the text to arrive at dates, but you will find a wide range of dates for some of the prophets. Often discrepancies are due to scholars' views on whether one or more persons wrote a particular book. For example, most mainline scholars believe that Isaiah was written by two, possibly three, prophets living in different times. Traditionally, however, the book of Isaiah was thought to be the work of one prophet.

Date	Prophet	Meaning of Name of Prophet	King (s) of Judah (fell 587 B.C.)	King(s) of Israel (fell 722/ 721 B.C.)	Prophecy to or about	Concerns and Assurances
760–750	Amos	Burden bearer	Uzziah	Jeroboam II	Israel (ruling classes); Judah; all nations	Oppression of poor; sexual immorality; luxury; corruption
755–725	Hosea	Salvation	Uzziah Jotham Ahaz	Jereoboam II	Israel	Political alliance with Assyria; falling away from God
742–700, or 689	Isaiah of Jerusalem (chapters 1–39)	God's salvation	Jotham Ahaz Hezekiah	Menahme Pekahiah Pekah Hoshea	Judah; Jerusalem	Jerusalem and its king suffer due to sin, but because of God's covenant with David will never fall; political revolts
722–701	Micah	Who is like God?	Ahaz Hezekiah	n/a	Samaria; Jerusalem whole earth	Injustice; oppression of poor and powerless; failure to obey covenant

640–609	Zephaniah	God has protected	Josiah	n/a	Judah; Jerusalem; all peoples	Idolatry; warnings about "Day of the Lord"
626–587	Jeremiah	God will elevate	Josiah Jehoahaz (Shallum) Jehoiakim (Eliakim) Jehoiachin (Jeconiah)	n/a	Judah	Social ills; warnings of disasters caused by people's sin, not God's capriciousness or inability to ward off Babylonians
608–597	Habakkuk	Embrace	Jehoiakim Jehoiachin	n/a	Babylon	Aggression; greed; inhumanity; idolatry; unjust suffering, and evil
593–571	Ezekiel	Strength of God	Zedekiah	n/a	Exiles in Babylon; (Ezekiel is in Babylon); oracles against other nations	God's warnings due to Judah's faithlessness; in exile, words of comfort and assurance of return to land of Israel
540	Second Isaiah (chapters 40–55)	God's salvation	n/a	n/a	Exiles in Babylon	Assurance that despite their exile, God has compassion and will allow the people to return home
520–518	Zechariah	God has remembered	n/a	n/a	Zerubbabel; Joshua; returned remnant	Wickedness; lack of judgment, mercy, and peace; rededication of temple
500–450	Malachi	My messenger	n/a	n/a	Returned exiles	Neglect of covenant obligations; need for right sacrifice

UNIT 1: LIFE AS GOD'S PEOPLE

COMMITTED TO JUSTICE

PREVIEWING THE LESSON

Lesson Scripture: Amos 5:10-15, 21-24
Background Scripture: Amos 5:10-15, 21-24; 8:4-12; 2 Kings 13:23-25
Key Verse: Amos 5:24

Focus of the Lesson:
Many people experience injustice in today's world. What accounts for this, and what does it have to do with us? Amos says that injustice stems from one part of society ignoring the needs of another, and that, as God's people, we are called to fight such attitudes and behaviors.

Goals for the Learners:
(1) to explore the themes of justice and judgment in the book of Amos.
(2) to recall injustices that have affected them.
(3) to identify an injustice and make a commitment to act against it.

Pronunciation Guide:
Amaziah (am uh zi' uh)   *chanan* (khaw nan')
ebyon (eb yone')   *eythan* (ay thawn')
Jeroboam (jer uh boh' uhm)   Joash (joh' ash)
tamim (taw meem')

Supplies:
Bibles, newsprint and marker, paper and pencils, hymnals

READING THE SCRIPTURE

NRSV
Amos 5:10-15, 21-24
¹⁰ They hate the one who reproves in the
    gate,
    and they abhor the one who speaks the
    truth.
¹¹ Therefore because you trample on the
    poor

NIV
Amos 5:10-15, 21-24
¹⁰[Y]ou hate the one who reproves in court
    and despise him who tells the truth.
¹¹You trample on the poor
    and force him to give you grain.
  Therefore, though you have built stone
    mansions,

and take from them levies of grain,
  you have built houses of hewn stone,
    but you shall not live in them;
  you have planted pleasant vineyards,
    but you shall not drink their wine.
¹² For I know how many are your
      transgressions,
    and how great are your sins—
  you who afflict the righteous, who take a
      bribe,
    and push aside the needy in the gate.
¹³ Therefore the prudent will keep silent in
      such a time;
    for it is an evil time.
¹⁴ Seek good and not evil,
    that you may live;
  and so the LORD, the God of hosts, will be
      with you,
    just as you have said.
¹⁵ Hate evil and love good,
    and establish justice in the gate;
  it may be that the LORD, the God of hosts,
    will be gracious to the remnant of
      Joseph.
²¹ I hate, I despise your festivals,
    and I take no delight in your solemn
      assemblies.
²² Even though you offer me your burnt
      offerings and grain offerings,
    I will not accept them;
  and the offerings of well-being of your
      fatted animals
    I will not look upon.
²³ Take away from me the noise of your
      songs;
    I will not listen to the melody of your
      harps.
**²⁴ But let justice roll down like waters,
    and righteousness like an ever-flowing
      stream.**

you will not live in them;
  though you have planted lush vineyards,
    you will not drink their wine.
¹²For I know how many are your offenses
    and how great your sins.
  You oppress the righteous and take bribes
    and you deprive the poor of justice in the
      courts.
¹³Therefore the prudent man keeps quiet in
      such times,
    for the times are evil.
¹⁴Seek good, not evil,
    that you may live.
  Then the LORD God Almighty will be
      with you,
    just as you say he is.
¹⁵Hate evil, love good;
    maintain justice in the courts.
  Perhaps the LORD God Almighty will
      have mercy
    on the remnant of Joseph.
²¹"I hate, I despise your religious feasts;
    I cannot stand your assemblies.
²²Even though you bring me burnt offerings
      and grain offerings,
    I will not accept them.
  Though you bring choice fellowship
      offerings,
    I will have no regard for them.
²³Away with the noise of your songs!
    I will not listen to the music of your
      harps.
**²⁴But let justice roll on like a river,
    righteousness like a never-failing
      stream!**

UNDERSTANDING THE SCRIPTURE

Amos 5:10-11. Amos asserts that judgment falls on a corrupted system of legal justice. The city gates typically served as the location where cases were heard and judgments rendered by elders in the community. Such a public setting only aggravated and made obvious the twisting of justice in favor of individuals of wealth and against not only the poor, but also those who dare speak on their behalf. "Truth" in verse 10 translates the Hebrew word *tamim*, which also carries the meaning of "completeness" or "with integrity." "Hewn stone" signifies hand-cut rock for building. Those who could afford such a luxury instead of using plain field rock for homes had an advantage—but not for long.

Amos 5:12-13. The knowledge of God, seen as cause for wonder in Psalm 139, now comes revealed as cause for judgment. Not one but two words for the errors committed ("transgression," "sins") emphasizes in its repetition the severity of the situation. Verse 12b spells out a three-fold charge. The "needy" (*ebyon*) identifies a group for whom Yahweh—the Deliverer of Israel from Egypt—took great concern. Deuteronomy 15:7-ll employs this same word to assert that covenant relationship with God takes shape in opening one's resources to the poor and needy. The word rendered "prudent" in Amos 5:13 may also mean "prosperous." If the latter meaning is considered, the verse could be taken to say that those who reap the benefits of such injustice will be silenced when judgment descends.

Amos 5:14-15. In verses 4-6 of this same chapter, Amos twice calls on Israel to "seek" God. The setting there sounds more liturgical while here in verse 14 the seeking is of "good," as in just and ethical behavior. As will be developed more at length in the Interpreting the Scripture section, verse 14b presumes that those Amos is addressing have made some prior appeal that God will be with them (regardless?). Amos conditions God's presence upon the practice of justice in the gates. Two key themes conclude verse 15: "gracious" and "remnant of Joseph." Does the latter refer to the people of Israel who left Egypt, or to those about to experience the judgment of exile? While the text does not clarify this, the previous reference to "house of Joseph" in verse 6 would argue for the impending judgment.

Amos 5:21-23. Amos' attack on a corrupt system of justice shifts to a denouncing of Israel's liturgical life. The sacrificial system would fail in its intended purpose of linking the people to God. In a judgment rendered by other prophets as well (see Malachi 1:10 and Jeremiah 14:12), Amos declares God will not accept (literally, "be pleased by") Israel's offerings. The communication of this rejection takes shape in vivid sensory verbs. "I take no delight" (the verb in Hebrew can also be translated as "smell" as it is in the KJV). "I will not look." "I will not listen." It is a devastating image of Israel's injustice closing God's sensitivity to them. Equally ominous is that the verb translated as "listen" also means "answer" or "respond." The crisis is not merely that injustice means God will not hear, but more shockingly, God will not respond.

Amos 5:24. As with verses 14-15, verse 24 inserts a wedge of hope into the oracles of judgment. The imagery is that of a wadi, a streambed dry through much of the year but, in downpours, a torrential stream. God seeks not water, but justice, to wash through Israel. Water, in this arid region, served as a vivid symbol for life. Without water—without justice—the land would dry up. The second half of this verse qualifies that what God seeks is not a momentary burst of equity that will soon disappear. The desired stream of righteousness is modified by the Hebrew word *eythan:* strong, mighty, perennial, everflowing. Justice cannot be a creek that goes dry part or most of the year. It needs to be year-round, all-encompassing.

Amos 8:4-6. Amos returns (see 2:6-8) to a critique of the economic system of Israel. Verse 4 echoes the trampling and ruination of the poor carried out by inequitable judgments in 5:11a. Now, however, Amos makes the crime even more insidious by linking it to false fronts of piety. The problem with the festivals despised in 5:21 is that those who observe them cannot wait for their end so that they can resume profiteering through tampering with measures intended to protect individuals from such greed.

Amos 8:7-10. In most Biblical texts, God's forgetting of the people serves as the image for judgment. Here, God's remembering will be the cause for trouble. The natural disasters of earthquake and flood represent God's dominion over creation soon to be unleashed against those who have flaunted that dominion with injustice. The reference to a solar eclipse may well have in memory just such an event in 763 B.C., shortly before the work of Amos is traditionally dated.

Amos 8:11-12. In spite of the cataclysmic imagery of the previous verses, Amos has reserved his most devastating judgment until last. There will be famine. Israel has known famines in the past, all the way back to the time of Joseph. Then, famine became the means to reunite Joseph with his family. Now, the famine will disorient and

divide ("run to and fro"). What will make this famine more devastating than any other will be the absence of God's word. Genesis 1 asserted the life-giving nature and power of that word. Without that word, just as without water, life will retreat, community will wither. "They shall not find it" asserts one of the biblical witness' most shocking declarations.

2 Kings 14:23-25. This brief excerpt connects with Amos in the person of King Jeroboam, son of Joash, who "did what was evil in the sight of the LORD." Amos 1:1 locates the prophet's ministry in that king's time. In Amos 7:10-13, the court prophet Amaziah takes issue with Amos precisely because Amos allegedly prophesied against Jeroboam. Prophetic words are not written or spoken in a vacuum. They prick persons of power, of whom Jeroboam would have been chief in Amos' time.

INTERPRETING THE SCRIPTURE

Affluence, Poverty, and Sin

Amos has hard words to speak, then and now, to communities that suffer gaps not only between rich and poor—but in how those groups access justice. Like the New Testament letter of James (5:4, 2:6), the prophet clearly points to the seductions of affluence toward amassing greater wealth (Amos 5:11a) and its subsequent use in acquiring favored treatment in the eyes of the law (5:12b).

Amos does not speak here as a student of this or that market theory or judicial structure. Amos brings this perspective from the traditions of God's covenant with Israel. Wherever we place ourselves on the spectrum of economic and legal philosophies, the prophet calls into accountability any and every system with the God-driven demand for justice. God will not look favorably upon any system that routinely disdains the vulnerable.

God declares such enacted disdain "transgression" (a word that can also mean "rebellion") and "sin." Too often in the church's language and liturgy in particular, those two words have been limited exclusively to the failures and foibles of isolated individuals. Certainly, the notion of individual responsibility invites reflection on particular ways I (and you) have sinned. What Amos will not let us forget are the transgressions of whole societies by allowing injustice to be inflicted upon its most vulnerable members. Those "you's" in Amos 5:11-12 reference not individuals but Israel as a community. Judgment is not impending simply because isolated individuals (a few "bad apples") miss the mark. Amos calls Israel—and communities and societies today—to task for breaching the covenant demands of God for the just and equitable treatment of the poor. Deuteronomy 15:7-11 makes God's advocacy on behalf of, and our covenantal responsibilities for, the poor clear. Amos in this passage insists that covenant faithfulness to God, then and now, heed that call.

Where May Grace Be Found?

Amos is not noted for oracles of hope. The few verses in this entire book that clearly envision restoration (9:11-15) are, for that very reason, sometimes considered later additions to the scroll. Yet even in the midst of passages forth-telling judgment, a balancing word of grace occasionally comes. Such a glimpse occurs in Amos 5:15b: "it may be that the LORD, the God of hosts, will be gracious [*chanan*] to the remnant of Joseph."

Where does such hope of *chanan* ("grace," "favor") originate? Once more, Amos speaks from Israel's covenant tradition. In the wake of the golden calf episode, Exodus 33 revealed a land of milk and honey remained in Israel's future—"but I [God] will not go up among you" (33:3b). Moses counters that unless God goes, it would be better if Israel does not go either (33:15). God relents and agrees to go with Israel. But even more important, God reveals that *chanan* remains part of this relationship and God's choosing: "I will be gracious to whom I will be gracious" (33:19).

Amos conditions his declaration of judgment in 5:14-15 with the possibility that God may yet be gracious. As God had been in the wilderness, so God may yet be now.

Where may grace be found? Whenever God's people open themselves to God's presence and leading. Wherever justice goes established, and evil hated, and good loved. Amos understands the fundamental nature of God revealed toward the end of that passage in Exodus 33: "The LORD, the LORD, a God merciful and gracious, slow to anger, and abounding in steadfast love and faithfulness" (Exodus 34:6b).

The grace of God allows the possibility of hope, even in the most difficult of circumstances. Amos does not pull any punches in terms of the transforming changes God seeks in life and community. But Amos knows he stands before One inclined to grace and covenant faithfulness. Do we?

Liturgy as Window-Dressing or God-Invoking

Worship intends to engage individuals and communities with mindfulness of and responsiveness to the holy and living God. Rituals, as with any form of discipline religious or otherwise, have value if they maintain connection with the thing—or the One—they mean to serve.

Amos' condemnation of Israel's liturgical life finds cause in the disconnect between the ritual and ethics. Remember that "liturgy" comes from a word that literally means "work of the people." Amos decries the gap between the works of Israel seen in worship and the works of Israel seen in daily living. Injustice empties religious traditions of meaning and efficacy. God will not accept liturgy that is mere window-dressing.

The prophet's words have peculiar importance for the twenty-first century church. We have rich traditions and creative innovations of worship abroad in our time. Some draw lines, and speak of "worship wars" in congregations struggling to balance conservancy of tradition with seeker styles of non-liturgical worship. The perspective Amos brings us: Those issues are secondary. What remains at stake in the church is the integrity or dichotomy between liturgy (however practiced) and life.

The reason for that has less to do with us and much more to do with God. Styles of worship may come and go. Organs may give way to guitars, or vice-versa. Hymnals may yield to PowerPoint, and back again. Those who preside over worship may resemble preachers or emcees, officiants or aficionados. What Amos demands we dare not forget is that whatever the style, whatever the form, the rituals of faith need to square with how we live our lives as political and economic and social beings. For that is where God puts the emphasis. To ignore that truth risks worship that will go unaccepted, unobserved, and unheard (5:22-23).

Seek Good, Do Justice

Amos cannot be read without noting the centrality of justice to covenant-keeping. Such concern for equity runs the gamut in this work from economic (5:11) to judicial (5:12) to social (6:1).

The dilemma of "translating" Amos into our times comes in the widely divergent ways in which justice is understood among us. Talk to an individual who espouses a staunchly conservative political philosophy and another of a decidedly liberal outlook about what justice means, and you may likely wonder what the two have in common.

One possible response is to throw up our hands and say: The differences are too great. "True" justice is impossible to pin down. That is appealing, but it may lead to disengagement from disputed issues of justice.

Amos writes from a religious tradition, which is part of our tradition, that refuses to cede matters of public and social disputations to those who hold the power cards among us. Amos urges Israel, and the church, on the matter of covenant responsibilities toward individuals and groups made vulnerable for whatever reason. Amos does not counsel us to seek consensus in disputed definitions of justice. Amos counsels us to seek good—yet another covenant term. We do not live in isolation from others. We do not even live as a community in isolation. We live in covenant with God, a covenant that unfailingly calls us into accountability for relationship with one another.

Justice and good define God's intent within covenant community. They form a perennial concern for the people of God, an ever-flowing stream that waters our communities to life . . . or whose absence will wash away hollow artifacts of a once living faith. Amos cannot be any more clear: "Seek good and not evil, that you may live" (5:14).

SHARING THE SCRIPTURE

PREPARING TO TEACH

Preparing Our Hearts

This week's devotional reading is found in Psalm 82. In the midst of the "divine council," God admonishes earthly rulers whose unjust ways oppress the most vulnerable members of society. Where do you perceive actions on the part of today's elected leaders harming the "least, last, and lost" in your own society? What can you do to assist and empower those who are the weakest? What political action can you take?

Pray that you and the adult learners will be alert to instances of systemic injustice and respond in whatever ways you can to create a more just world.

Preparing Our Minds

Study the background Scripture from Amos 5:10-15, 21-24; 8:4-12; and 2 Kings 13:23-25. Our lesson will focus on Amos 5:10-15, 21-24. As you study, think about reasons that injustice exists.

Write on newsprint:
- ❏ information for next week's lesson, found under "Continue the Journey."
- ❏ activities for further spiritual growth in "Continue the Journey."

Review the introduction to the quarter, the "Big Picture" article entitled "God's Covenant Demands Justice"; the "Close-up" article, "Timeline of the Prophets Encountered in 'Committed to Doing Right;'" and the "Faith in Action" article, "Living Right," all of which directly precede this lesson. Decide how you will use each of these helps either for this lesson or in subsequent sessions.

Prepare the suggested lectures for "Explore the Themes of Justice and Judgment in the Book of Amos."

LEADING THE CLASS

(1) Gather to Learn

❖ Welcome the class members and introduce any guests.

❖ Pray that the participants will open their eyes and ears to the words of the prophet.

❖ Ask the students to think about news reports they have heard, seen, or read this week. Suggest that they answer these questions as they describe one or more stories of injustice: **Who was being treated unjustly? Why? What measures are being and/or need to be taken to right this wrong?**

❖ Challenge the class to discuss this question: **What can I do individually or with a group to end this injustice?** List ideas on newsprint.

❖ Read aloud today's focus statement: **Many people experience injustice in today's world. What accounts for this, and what does it have to do with us? Amos says that injustice stems from one part of society ignoring the needs of another, and that, as God's people, we are called to fight such attitudes and behaviors.**

(2) Explore the Themes of Justice and Judgment in the Book of Amos

❖ Begin by giving an overview of this quarter's lessons. The quarterly introduction, found prior to this lesson, will help you do that.

❖ Introduce this quarter's theme by highlighting excerpts from the "Big Picture: God's Covenant Demands Justice," found prior to this session.

❖ Select a volunteer to read Amos 5:10-15.

■ Use the left side of a sheet of newsprint to list the problems that Amos outlines. You may want to do this yourself in a lecture based on entries for these verses in the Understanding the Scripture portion.

■ Encourage the students to name parallel modern examples, and list those on the right side of the newsprint.

■ Talk with the class about how much has *really* changed since Amos' ministry, probably around 750 B.C.

■ Choose someone to read Amos 5:21-24.

■ Read or retell "Liturgy as Window-Dressing or God-Invoking" in Interpreting the Scripture.

■ Divide the students into groups and ask them to discuss these questions.

(1) **In what ways does your congregation "practice what it preaches," especially in the arenas of political, economic, and social justice?**

(2) **What would your community look like if you truly "let justice roll down" (5:24)?**

(3) **What steps could you and your congregation take to enable this justice to abound?**

■ Call on a spokesperson from each group to highlight their discussion.

■ Close by asking the students to report on any surprises or insights they gleaned from the session so far.

(3) Recall Injustices That Have Affected the Learners

❖ Point out that injustice can affect us in at least two ways: (1) We are the victims of injustice; (2) we are the perpetrators of injustice.

❖ Ask the class members to first recall a

time when they were the victims of injustice. Perhaps this injustice was rooted in racism, gender bias, age discrimination, religion, ethnic group, discrimination due to a handicapping condition, or some other form of prejudice, or economic or political oppression. Suggest that the adults think silently about at least one incident.

❖ Talk with the class about how they *felt* as a result of this injustice. (You need not ask them to review the event; just how they responded emotionally to it.)

❖ Challenge the class to remember an incident where they acted unjustly toward an individual or group. (This activity may be more difficult, since people often do not recognize how they have behaved unjustly.)

❖ Talk again about how the students *felt* then and *feel* now as they recall this sinful episode.

❖ Provide quiet time for the students to offer individual prayers of forgiveness for those who have treated them unjustly, even as they ask God to forgive them of the injustices they have wrought upon others.

(4) Identify an Injustice and Make a Commitment to Act Against It

❖ Review the list that the class made in the "Gather to Learn" portion.

❖ Read aloud this quotation from Dr. Martin Luther King, Jr. (1929–1968): **We shall have to repent in this generation, not so much for the evil deeds of the wicked people, but for the appalling silence of the good people.** Provide quiet time for the adults to mull over this statement and then discuss its implications with a small group.

❖ **Option:** If you know someone who is an activist, invite this person to dialogue with the class about how one goes about organizing against economic, political, or social injustice.

❖ Distribute paper and pencils. Ask each student to identify one injustice that he or she would like to address and write that on the paper. Suggest that the students write a

sentence or two about why this issue is important to them and how they hope to address it.

❖ Ask those who are willing to commit themselves to act against the injustice they have identified to read aloud in unison today's key verse, Amos 5:24.

(5) Continue the Journey

❖ Pray that all who have come today will be faithful to God's covenant by upholding justice.

❖ Read aloud this preparation for next week's lesson. You may also want to post it on newsprint for the students to copy. **Prepare for next week's session entitled "God's Indictment of Israel" by reading background Scripture from Hosea 4:1-4; 7:1-2; 12:7-9; 14:1-3; 2 Kings 15:8-10. Our lesson will highlight Hosea 4:1-4; 7:1-2; 12:8-9. As you study, keep this focus before you: People sometimes act callously and selfishly, even when they know better. What is the result when God's people act this way? Hosea says that God holds us accountable for our actions, even though God always works for our redemption.**

❖ Read aloud the following three ideas. Challenge the students to commit themselves to use these activities as a springboard to spiritual growth.

    (1) **Get involved with an Internet "community" that works for biblical justice, such as www.faithful-america.org.**

    (2) **Write a letter to the editor of a newspaper calling for justice on an issue that you care about.**

    (3) **Encourage other Christians to take a stand on an unjust situation.**

❖ Sing or read aloud "For the Healing of the Nations."

❖ Invite the students to say this benediction, based on Micah 6:8, to conclude the session: **The Lord requires me to do justice, and to love kindness, and to walk humbly with my God. Let it be as you have said, Lord.**

UNIT 1: LIFE AS GOD'S PEOPLE
GOD'S INDICTMENT OF ISRAEL

PREVIEWING THE LESSON

Lesson Scripture: Hosea 4:1-4; 7:1-2; 12:8-9
Background Scripture: Hosea 4:1-4; 7:1-2; 12:7-9; 14:1-3; 2 Kings 15:8-10
Key Verse: Hosea 4:1

Focus of the Lesson:
People sometimes act callously and selfishly, even when they know better. What is the result when God's people act this way? Hosea says that God holds us accountable for our actions, even though God always works for our redemption.

Goals for the Learners:
(1) to explore the theme of God's accusations against Israel.
(2) to examine the concepts of faithfulness, loyalty, and knowledge of God in Hosea and their implications for their lives.
(3) to ask God and others whom their actions have hurt for forgiveness.

Pronunciation Guide:
Ephraim (ee fray im)   *hesed* (kheh' sed)
rib (reeb)   Shallum (shal' uhm)
shub (shoob)

Supplies:
Bibles, newsprint and marker, paper and pencils, hymnals

READING THE SCRIPTURE

NRSV
Hosea 4:1-4
¹ Hear the word of the LORD,
    O people of Israel;
  for the LORD has an indictment against
    the inhabitants of the land.
There is no faithfulness or loyalty,
    and no knowledge of God in the land.
² Swearing, lying, and murder,

NIV
Hosea 4:1-4
¹Hear the word of the LORD, you Israelites,
    because the LORD has a charge to bring
    against you who live in the land:
"There is no faithfulness, no love,
    no acknowledgment of God in the land.
²There is only cursing, lying and murder,
    stealing and adultery;

and stealing and adultery break out;
    bloodshed follows bloodshed.
³ Therefore the land mourns,
    and all who live in it languish;
together with the wild animals
    and the birds of the air,
    even the fish of the sea are perishing.
⁴ Yet let no one contend,
    and let none accuse,
for with you is my contention, O priest.

Hosea 7:1-2
¹ [W]hen I would heal Israel,
    the corruption of Ephraim is revealed,
    and the wicked deeds of Samaria;
for they deal falsely,
    the thief breaks in,
    and the bandits raid outside.
² But they do not consider
    that I remember all their wickedness.

Hosea 12:8-9
⁸ Ephraim has said, "Ah, I am rich,
    I have gained wealth for myself;
in all of my gain
    no offense has been found in me
    that would be sin."
⁹ I am the LORD your God
    from the land of Egypt;
I will make you live in tents again,
    as in the days of the appointed festival.

they break all bounds,
    and bloodshed follows bloodshed.
³Because of this the land mourns,
    and all who live in it waste away;
the beasts of the field and the birds of the
    air
    and the fish of the sea are dying.
⁴"But let no man bring a charge,
    let no man accuse another,
for your people are like those
    who bring charges against a priest.

Hosea 7:1-2
¹[W]henever I would heal Israel,
    the sins of Ephraim are exposed
    and the crimes of Samaria revealed.
They practice deceit,
    thieves break into houses,
    bandits rob in the streets;
²but they do not realize
    that I remember all their evil deeds.
Their sins engulf them;
    they are always before me."

Hosea 12:8-9
⁸Ephraim boasts,
    "I am very rich; I have become wealthy.
With all my wealth they will not find in me
    any iniquity or sin."
⁹"I am the LORD your God,
    who brought you out of Egypt;
I will make you live in tents again,
    as in the days of your appointed feasts."

UNDERSTANDING THE SCRIPTURE

Hosea 4:1-3. These verses offer the image of God bringing suit against Israel. In the indictment, qualities essential to covenant are charged to be absent. "Faithfulness" translates a Hebrew word related to "truth" (see 4:1, KJV) "Loyalty" renders the Hebrew *hesed*, a key expression in covenantal language of steadfast loyalty shown by one partner to another. "Knowledge" is not mere "knowing," but conveys a sense of understanding and intimacy of relationship. The absence of these three foundational elements of covenant life reveals the depth of breach brought in this indictment. Likewise, ancient stipulations of covenant life go negated in the list of five "crimes" in verse 2a: Each one of them traces back to the Decalogue given Israel at Sinai (Exodus 20:1-17)."Bloodshed follows bloodshed" likely refers to the tumultuous political times that rocked Hosea's era with one assassination after another (see comments under 2 Kings text).

Lastly, the effects of covenant betrayal spill into the entire created order. It is as if creation goes undone, as the creatures fashioned by God's hand and the land itself suffer the consequences of human folly.

Hosea 4:4. This verse actually introduces a section (4:4-9) that reveals the indictment that falls upon Israel's religious leaders. "Contend" and "contention" in verse 4 translate the same Hebrew word, *rib,* used in verse 1 for "indictment." The implicit nature of this verse finds explicit statement in verse 9: "like people, like priest." The priesthood in Israel functioned as a group "set apart." By birth and by function, they had responsibilities and privileges that set them apart from the whole people. Judgment will break down such barriers. All will share in responsibility for what has become of covenant. In Hebrew, the text of this verse is quite obscure. You will see that reflected in the two very different ways in which the NRSV and the NIV translate this verse.

Hosea 7:1-2. The context of these verses (verse 1 actually begins grammatically in mid-sentence) stretches back to the close of chapter 6. Further charges against the priest are linked to both plottings (6:9) and an allusion to idolatry (6:10). God's desire to restore and heal goes frustrated by actions that make it impossible for God to overlook (7:1). In verse 2, those actions go compounded by a failure to "consider" (the Hebrew verb can also be translated as "say") that God remembers such actions. If the reference to "they" still has in mind the priests singled out in 6:9, the meaning here is a failure to speak and teach ("say") the truth of God's remembrance. Such consideration, however, goes lacking on the part of the whole people— whether by choice or indifference.

Hosea 12:7-8. "Ephraim" is another name for Israel—Israel as the people of the northern kingdom, but Israel also as the new name given to Jacob. That older reference

comes into play here. Verse 7 refers to "false" balances (see also 12:7, KJV, "balances of deceit"). In Genesis 27:35, Isaac confesses to Esau that Jacob "came deceitfully" to steal the father's blessing. Deceit continues to prove troublesome for Jacob/Israel/Ephraim. The earlier significance of God's remembrance in verse 7:2 takes on a powerful variant in verse 8's implication of Ephraim's forgetfulness. As in chapter 7, covenant goes threatened as a result. Hosea has Ephraim assert: "I have gained wealth for myself." Those words mimic the warning spoken at that covenant's beginning in Deuteronomy 8:17. The assertion of one's power apart from God to secure covenant blessings constitutes a forgetfulness that jeopardizes those very blessings.

Hosea 12:9. The first half of this verse sounds almost identical to the beginning of the Decalogue, the commandments that defined Israel's covenant identity (Exodus 20:2). One significant difference arises. Exodus depicts God as the One who "brought you out of the land of Egypt." The clearly ominous tone of Hosea 12:9 depicts God as the One *"from* the land of Egypt." The "appointed festival" has in mind the Feast of Succoth, a harvest festival that involved setting up tents or "booths" as they are sometimes called. The imagery of tents, however, recalled Israel's wilderness sojourn (see Hosea 2:14-15).

Hosea 14:1-3. The Hebrew *shub* ("turn," "return") occurs over sixteen times in Hosea, twice in these verses. The prophet's work as a whole invites change and transformation on Israel's part. Judgment always finds balance in the hope of restoration, far more so in Hosea than, say, Amos. The second half of these verses even graciously provide the words Israel might bring to God in such a turning. The plea for guilt to be removed presumes actions that create guilt. The sacrificial system finds expression here not in what animals are prescribed to be offered, but rather the "fruit of our lips."

Language is restorative, even as it can be creative. Part of the offering involves a laying aside of trust in human measures of power. Formidable military regimes ("Assyria") do not have the power to save, a theme taken up later by Isaiah (30:1-7). Ultimate allegiance does not go owed to material prowess or success ("we will say no more, 'Our God,' to the work of our hands"). Rather, those who are without protector will find a steadfast partner in God.

2 Kings 15:8-10. Hosea 1:1 links the prophet to the time indicated immediately before, but most likely continuing into, the reigns indicated in these verses from 2 Kings 15. The pattern alluded to in verse 9 ("he did what was evil") echoes somewhat the rhythm of the book of Judges, where Israel's sin leads them into disaster. The difference is that there are no intervening moments of victory or justice brought by judges. The narration that begins in 2 Kings 15:8 is a steady descent. The assassination of King Zechariah by Shallum (15:10) likely is but one of the violent upheavals behind Hosea's early indictment against Israel for "bloodshed follows bloodshed" (Hosea 4:2). Shallum reigned all of one month, before himself falling victim to an assassin. Assassinations were common. Of Israel's last six kings, only one did not garner the dubious title of doing what was evil—and the one exception (Shallum) was himself an assassin. In such days did Hosea seek hope and transformation.

INTERPRETING THE SCRIPTURE

The Butterfly Effect

A theory in modern physics holds that something as minute as the flapping of a butterfly's wings may trigger a series of events that result in a tornado halfway across the world. Hosea did not know this theory. Hosea did know, however, that human sin can have grave consequences for the whole of creation.

Hosea, as the other prophets, wrote out of the framework of Israel's covenantal relationship with God. The covenant struck at Sinai codified the behavior and action expected of God's covenant partner. The sorts of things condemned by Hosea (4:2 and 12:8) and other prophets trace directly to those injunctions at Sinai, summed up in what we now refer to as the Ten Commandments. But Israel's covenant tradition did not originate at Sinai. Covenant did not even begin with God's call and promises to Abram. The first covenant identified by the biblical witness comes in the narrative of Noah. Listen to those whom God identifies to be partners of that covenant: "As for me, I am establishing my covenant with you and your descendants after you, and with every living creature that is with you" (Genesis 9:9-10a).

This foundational covenant of the Hebrew Scriptures links those created in the image of God with the whole of creation. Remember, too, that image of God doesn't refer to what we look like. "Image of God" describes human potential to be revealing of God in creation through word and deed and relationship. So why should it be surprising when human sin has negative consequences for that very creation? In the keen perception of Hosea, "victimless sin" is an oxymoron. We have been created in the image of God and called to be God's covenant partner, for our own sake and for the sake of all creation.

Character and Accountability

The commentary on Hosea 4:1 in the previous section identified three key elements of covenant found to be lacking on the part of those addressed by Isaiah: faithfulness, loyalty, and knowledge. Such qualities are not distinguished by the keeping of one command or the avoidance of one sin. Each of them represent a strand intended to weave through the whole of one's relationship with God and neighbor. They are, if you will, part of the "character" covenant seeks to establish. Spirituality and discipleship today can still run aground if we reduce the following of Jesus to this set of rules or that style of liturgy. Covenantal faith intends to infuse the whole of who we are and what we do with qualities like these that filter out into every aspect of our journey with God.

Hosea declares Israel (and us) accountable for such qualities. The NRSV translation of 4:4 suggests that any attempts to counter that accountability are nullified. A common response in the face of criticism or judgment is to point fingers elsewhere: whether in other persons or events beyond our control. God, speaking through Hosea, will have none of that: My contention is with *you*. Encounter with God, in Israel and in church, is not about third parties: It is how it is between God and you, God and me/us. Or as Shakespeare would later phrase that same perspective: "The fault, dear Brutus, is not in our stars, but in ourselves" (*Julius Caesar,* Act I, Scene 2).

Hosea likewise dismisses self-righteous pleas of innocence. The self-deception recounted in 12:8 only seals the certainty of judgment. Individuals and communities who see no culpability will also see no need for change. Repentance opens to grace. Self-congratulation closes on pride. God has formed us with freedom to choose which way we cast our lot.

Covenant Memories

Remembrance—and forgetfulness—loom large in Israel's covenant traditions and in our own. We typically link grace and hope with God's remembrance. God remembered Noah and the ark, and the waters subsided.

God remembered the people of Israel in Egypt, and the exodus resulted. Our life of prayer, in one sense, seeks God's remembering of our situations and those for whom we have concern in ways that bring healing and hope and grace.

The prophets, Hosea among them, see Israel's crisis as one of memory. The people have forgotten that which is good, and just, and faithful. Deuteronomy 8:17 had warned: "Do not say to yourself, 'My power and the might of my own hand have gotten me this wealth.' But remember the LORD your God..." Yet, Hosea charges Israel with saying just that (Hosea 12:8). As a result, God inverts remembrance from a life-giving to a judgment-rendering action: "they do not consider that I remember all their wickedness" (7:2).

The passage summons the church to similar faithful remembrance. Like Israel, God invites us to remember our origins in grace. We have life as individuals and communities of faith, not because we have pulled ourselves up by the bootstraps but because of God's creative power. We have life as individuals and communities of faith, not because survival is up to us but because we may trust God for whatever will be and come.

Discipleship comes in the remembrance and practice of such life-giving and control-yielding ways. For we best remember who we are by remembering Whose we are—and ordering our lives accordingly.

Bad News or Good News?

Perspective always is important when receiving news. One person's good news can be another person's bad news.

If you have any doubt about that, consider news that bears the outcome of an election. If you still have any doubt about that, consider the news that Hosea bears to Israel in 12:9: "I will make you live in tents again."

Those words would not be welcome by folks grown accustomed to settled life in comfortable homes. That news would not be good news to those who recalled the old stories of forty years of wandering in the wilderness. Hosea is the bearer of bad news!

Or is he?

The second chapter of Hosea portrays the wilderness almost as an idyllic time, as if it were the last time Israel kept covenant (2:15b). To return to the wilderness, to dwell in the tents, serves as an image of covenant renewal. Indeed, the covenant to be reconstituted there will restore the harmony with all creation whose undoing goes lamented in 4:3.

So is it good news or bad news? In this passage, it depends upon whether covenant with God is the ultimate good and greatest desire. If so, it is. If the greatest good is keeping things as they are, it is not.

Good news or bad news. The tension remains the same today. Covenant with God, in the teaching of Jesus, involves love of enemy. Is that good news or bad news for you, given the folks you (and I) consider enemies? Covenant with God, in the practice of Jesus, summons forgiveness—not only our being forgiven, but also our forgiving. Is that good news or bad news for you, given the folks it might cause you (and me) to seek out for forgiveness and forgiving? Covenant with God brings news that can often cut both ways: in our favor, against our intransigence; in God's acceptance of us, in God's acceptance of those others who grate on us no end.

Is that good news or bad news? Either way, it is gospel.

SHARING THE SCRIPTURE

PREPARING TO TEACH

Preparing Our Hearts

This week's devotional reading is found in Hosea 14. Here we see the goal of Hosea's prophecy: to persuade people to return to God. The prophet, who proclaimed Samaria's guilt in 13:15-16, says that there is still time for the Israelites to ask God to "Take away all guilt" (14:2). If they turn, God promises to forgive them. Is God speaking to you about "returning"? Do you need to repent and seek God's forgiveness? Spend time now meditating on whatever in your life is displeasing to God and asking God to help you turn around.

Pray that you and the adult learners will be sensitive to words of indictment about your own lives and take action to get right with God.

Preparing Our Minds

Study the background Scripture from Hosea 4:1-4; 7:1-2; 12:7-9; 14:1-3; 2 Kings 15:8-10. This week's lesson will focus on Hosea 4:1-4; 7:1-2; 12:8-9. Keep this question in mind as you read: What is the result when God's people act callously and selfishly?

Write on newsprint:
❑ information for next week's lesson, found under "Continue the Journey."
❑ activities for further spiritual growth in "Continue the Journey."

Plan your approach to the "Explore the Theme of God's Accusations Against Israel" portion. You may wish to prepare an optional lecture.

LEADING THE CLASS

(1) Gather to Learn

❖ Welcome the class members and introduce any guests.

❖ Pray that all who have come will be sensitive to God's voice speaking in their lives.

❖ Read this quotation from James C. Dobson (1936–): **The philosophy of "me first" has the power to blow our world to pieces, whether applied to marriage, business, or international politics.**

❖ Invite the students to give examples to explore the truth of Dobson's statement.

❖ Read aloud today's focus statement: **People sometimes act callously and selfishly, even when they know better. What is the result when God's people act this way? Hosea says that God holds us accountable for our actions, even though God always works for our redemption.**

(2) Explore the Theme of God's Accusations Against Israel

❖ Choose a volunteer to read Hosea 4:1-4.
■ Divide the class into groups and give each one a sheet of newsprint and a marker. Ask the students to determine: (a) God's accusation against Israel, (b) the consequences of their behavior, and (c) modern examples of the kinds of behaviors that God opposes.
■ Provide time for the groups to report back.
■ **Option:** Provide this information by using Hosea 4:1-3, 4 from Understanding the Scripture as the basis for a lecture.
❖ Select someone to read Hosea 7:1-2.
■ Read or retell "Covenant Memories" in Interpreting the Scripture.
■ Summon the class to recall "who we are by remembering Whose we are—and ordering our lives accordingly."
■ Distribute paper and pencils. Ask the students to draw a vertical line and label the top with their birthday and the bottom with today's date. Challenge them to recall their "auto-

biography" with God by marking important dates on this timeline.
■ Allow time for each person to share highlights of the timeline with a partner. Perhaps they will note some common steps on their faith journeys.
❖ Enlist a volunteer to read Hosea 12:8-9.
■ Observe that Ephraim's transgression of claiming that he "did it his way" and "on his own" is held up as an ideal in the United States.
■ Challenge class members to identify situations in which someone's greed and corruption has created problems for others. (You may want to consider some corporate or political scandals.)
■ Assess together God's response to this idea of "gaining wealth for oneself."
■ Suggest that the students think quietly about what God would say to them concerning their view of money.

(3) Examine the Concepts of Faithfulness, Loyalty, and Knowledge of God in Hosea and Their Implications for the Learners' Lives

❖ Ask the students to read in unison today's key verse, Hosea 4:1.
❖ Read the first paragraph of "Character and Accountability."
❖ Discuss these questions. You may want to list answers to the third question on newsprint.
  (1) What would God say to our church in regard to our faithfulness, loyalty, and knowledge of God?
  (2) In which of these areas do we need to make improvements?
  (3) What can we do to live more faithfully and loyally?

(4) Ask God and Others Whom the Learners' Actions Have Hurt for Forgiveness

❖ Point out that Hosea 12:7 refers to the merchant who oppresses people deceitfully.

Oppression and unjust treatment are two ways that we hurt people, but there are many other ways as well. Brainstorm some of these ways and list them on newsprint.

❖ Encourage the students to evaluate their own behaviors in light of this list. Ask them to silently consider this question: **Which of these negative behaviors can I identify in my own life?**

❖ Distribute paper and pencils. Invite the students to make a confidential list of people they have harmed by such behaviors and write a sentence or two stating how they will seek forgiveness.

❖ Ask the students to write individual prayers in which they call upon God for forgiveness and help in returning to actions that reflect faithfulness, loyalty, and a true knowledge of God.

❖ Lead the class in offering their silent prayers with words such as these: **Now, O Lord, we lift up to you the behaviors that we know grieve you and ask your forgiveness as we pray.**

(5) Continue the Journey

❖ Conclude the silent prayers by praying that those who have come today will leave understanding the importance of faithfulness, loyalty, and knowledge of God.

❖ Read aloud this preparation for next week's lesson. You may also want to post it on newsprint for the students to copy. **Prepare for next week's session entitled "True Worship!" by reading background from Isaiah 1:10-20 and 2 Kings 15:32-35. This week's Scripture lesson is found in Isaiah 1:10-11, 14-20. Concentrate on these** ideas as you immerse yourself in the lesson: Most people who seek a worshipful experience want it to be pure and meaningful. How can we have a pure and meaningful experience when we worship God? Isaiah implies that there is a connection between how we live and how we worship.

❖ Read aloud the following three ideas. Challenge the students to commit themselves to use these activities as a springboard to spiritual growth.

(1) **Examine your own life. What indictments might God have against you? Pray that you might return home to God and live faithfully with God.**

(2) **Explore the news media for personal and/or corporate examples of corruption. What would God say about each situation? How does society handle the problem? Do we take action and seek justice, or simply avert our eyes and let the situation go unchecked? What can you do?**

(3) **Read again Hosea 12:8, a verse that flies in the face of the American ideal of being "a self-made man or woman." What impact might this verse have on how you live?**

❖ Sing or read aloud "A Charge to Keep I Have."

❖ Invite the students to say this benediction, based on Micah 6:8, to conclude the session: **The Lord requires me to do justice, and to love kindness, and to walk humbly with my God. Let it be as you have said, Lord.**

UNIT 1: LIFE AS GOD'S PEOPLE
TRUE WORSHIP!

PREVIEWING THE LESSON

Lesson Scripture: Isaiah 1:10-11, 14-20
Background Scripture: Isaiah 1:10-20; 2 Kings 15:32-35
Key Verse: Isaiah 1:17

Focus of the Lesson:

Most people who seek a worshipful experience want it to be pure and meaningful. How can we have a pure and meaningful experience when we worship God? Isaiah implies that there is a connection between how we live and how we worship.

Goals for the Learners:

(1) to examine Isaiah's words regarding true worship.
(2) to make a connection between how they live and how they worship.
(3) to make a commitment to practice a lifestyle of worship.

Pronunciation Guide:

Jotham (joh' thuhm)   *shama* (shaw mah')
torach (to' rakh)   *torah* (to raw')

Supplies:

Bibles, newsprint and marker, paper and pencils, hymnals

READING THE SCRIPTURE

NRSV
Isaiah 1:10-11, 14-20
¹⁰ Hear the word of the LORD,
     you rulers of Sodom!
  Listen to the teaching of our God,
     you people of Gomorrah!
¹¹ What to me is the multitude of your
       sacrifices?
     says the LORD;
  I have had enough of burnt offerings of
       rams

NIV
Isaiah 1:10-11, 14-20
¹⁰Hear the word of the LORD,
     you rulers of Sodom;
  listen to the law of our God,
     you people of Gomorrah!
¹¹"The multitude of your sacrifices—
     what are they to me?" says the LORD.
  "I have more than enough of burnt
      offerings,
     of rams and the fat of fattened animals;

and the fat of fed beasts;
 I do not delight in the blood of bulls,
  or of lambs, or of goats.
¹⁴ Your new moons and your appointed
  festivals
 my soul hates;
they have become a burden to me,
 I am weary of bearing them.
¹⁵ When you stretch out your hands,
 I will hide my eyes from you;
even though you make many prayers,
 I will not listen;
 your hands are full of blood.
¹⁶ Wash yourselves; make yourselves clean;
 remove the evil of your doings
 from before my eyes;
cease to do evil,
¹⁷ learn to do good;
 seek justice,
  rescue the oppressed,
 defend the orphan,
  plead for the widow.
¹⁸ Come now, let us argue it out,
 says the LORD:
though your sins are like scarlet,
 they shall be like snow;
though they are red like crimson,
 they shall become like wool.
¹⁹ If you are willing and obedient,
 you shall eat the good of the land;
²⁰ but if you refuse and rebel,
 you shall be devoured by the sword;
 for the mouth of the LORD has spoken.

I have no pleasure
 in the blood of bulls and lambs and
  goats.
¹⁴Your New Moon festivals and your
  appointed feasts
 my soul hates.
They have become a burden to me;
 I am weary of bearing them.
¹⁵When you spread out your hands in
  prayer,
 I will hide my eyes from you;
even if you offer many prayers,
 I will not listen.
Your hands are full of blood;
¹⁶ wash and make yourselves clean.
Take your evil deeds
 out of my sight!
Stop doing wrong,
¹⁷ learn to do right!
 Seek justice,
  encourage the oppressed.
Defend the cause of the fatherless,
 plead the case of the widow.
¹⁸"Come now, let us reason together,"
 says the LORD.
"Though your sins are like scarlet,
 they shall be as white as snow;
though they are red as crimson,
 they shall be like wool.
¹⁹If you are willing and obedient,
 you will eat the best from the land;
²⁰but if you resist and rebel,
 you will be devoured by the sword."
  For the mouth of the LORD
   has spoken.

UNDERSTANDING THE SCRIPTURE

Isaiah 1:10. The call to "hear" (*shama*) recalls Israel's covenantal history and beginnings. Deuteronomy 6:4 (sometimes called the *Shema*) invites Israel to hear the fundamental confession of the God who is One. Now in Isaiah, as in Amos, the call to hear comes as prelude to judgment. Why? In Hebrew, *shama* means both "to hear" and "to obey." Condemnation comes because of a lack of obedience that will be detailed in ensuing verses. The "word of the LORD" and the "teaching (*torah*) of our God" form the content and potency of Isaiah's call. The identification of the audience as "rulers of

Sodom" and "people of Gomorrah" serves as a devastating indictment of the leaders and people of Judea addressed by the prophet.

Isaiah 1:11-13a. These verses relate God's rejection of Israel's current practice of the sacrificial system. Sacrifices, burnt offerings, and offerings all represented integral components of the priestly system centered in and around the Jerusalem temple. The rhetorical question in verse 12 ("who asked this from your hand?") bears resemblance to the beginning of Micah 6:8 ("what does the LORD require of you"). Micah, too, had indicated even the most extravagant of sacrificial offerings did not fulfill the "good" sought by God (6:6-7). Isaiah 1:13a describes the nature of such efforts and offerings as "futile." That same word appears in Exodus 20:7, where the Decalogue weighs in against anyone who "misuses" God's name, or as the King James version translates it, takes God's name "in vain."

Isaiah 1:13b-14. A slight shift occurs in these verses. From specific rituals, God now takes to task communal gatherings. Sabbath traditions go to the very heart of Judaism. The festival of the New Moon was likewise an important celebration, and not just among Jews. Such observances carried the weight of the *Torah* (first five books) in their institution. Perhaps that underscores a bit of word play in verse 14. There, these gatherings and observances called for by *torah* have become a burden (*torach*) to God. Verse 14 describes how the burden of these empty observances "weary" God. Later, in 7:13, Isaiah uses the same word to describe how the failure of King Ahaz to trust God by asking for a sign "wearies" God.

Isaiah 1:15. God's rejection of Israel's religious practices further deepens. The gestures and words of prayer, perhaps the most intimate form of communion and seeking after God, are declared impotent: "I will hide my eyes . . . I will not listen."

It is a devastating judgment, as severe as any you will find in Amos or other prophets. The reason given: blood on the hands of those who pray. Isaiah does not single out any specific act of violence here. But his emphasis elsewhere on the need for justice and protection for the vulnerable suggests violence done against them by this society, whether by action or indifference. The condemnation brought by blood may bring remembrance of the story of Cain and Abel. There, the blood itself cries out from the ground. How much more clear and vivid would blood show—and cry—on hands and words lifted in prayer!

Isaiah 1:16-17. Nine imperative verbs in these verses reveal what God does ask and seek from Israel. The first two ("wash," "make clean") suggest a preparatory if not ritualistic step of readying oneself for encounter with God (see Isaiah 6:5). The next pair ("remove the evil . . . cease to do evil") insist that breaks must be made. The third pair ("learn to do good . . . seek justice") clarify that covenant faith does not just empty life of the wrong but fills it with that which does good and seeks justice. The final trio of imperatives—"rescue the oppressed, defend the orphan, plead for the widow"—specify what is meant by doing good and seeking justice. The recipients of these actions represent those most vulnerable in that day's society.

Isaiah 1:18. The call to "argue it out" or "reason together" (KJV) returns this passage to the very opening of this book. Isaiah 1:2 describes a summons to trial, where witnesses are gathered and charges are made. Israel then had been summoned to court. In 1:18, Isaiah reveals this procedure to be open-ended. There is opportunity for dialogue, which means there is yet hope. The imagery of scarlet and crimson may hearken back to the stark use of blood in verse 15 that condemns. An opening to that seemingly absolute declaration of hopelessness now appears in verse 18.

Isaiah 1:19-20. Covenantal theology, for Isaiah in particular and the prophets in general, includes the possibility of choice. The tone of verses 19-20 resembles in spirit that of Deuteronomy 30:15-20. There are two ways for Israel to choose. "Obedient" translates *shama,* that same word encountered in the call to "hear" (1:10). Full hearing is not simply listening. Full hearing involves enacting the word. The blessing of such hearing, as it had been for the people of Israel wandering in the wilderness, comes in the gift of land and its life-sustaining bounties. The other choice is couched in the language of refusal and rebellion, language that also has roots in Israel's exodus tradition of covenant. "Refuse" is the word that describes Pharaoh's decision not to let Israel go free (Exodus 4:23). "Rebel" is the word that depicts Israel's balking and murmuring in the wilderness (Numbers 20:10, 24). The two "ifs" of these verses make clear the choice involved. The closing "for the mouth of the LORD has spoken" reveals why those choices are critical.

2 Kings 15:32-35. Isaiah 1:1 mentions King Jotham as one of the Judean kings in whose reigns Isaiah prophesied. The text relates Jotham's reign as a mixed bag, doing right yet allowing the "high places." These sites were associated with worship— perhaps initially of Yahweh, though later tradition (such as Samuel/Kings) holds them suspect of idolatry. The mixed nature of Jotham's kingship may symbolize why Isaiah prophesies both hope and judgment so closely together. Not all is perfect under Jotham, but neither is all lost. There is still hope.

INTERPRETING THE SCRIPTURE

Called to Hear

"I want you to hear me out!" How would you react to such words aimed in your direction? What if the words came prefaced with your first name, or with your first and last name, or with a not-so-pleasant label that called you something you really didn't appreciate?

Scripture, because we look at it as Scripture, sometimes seems flat and unemotional, cut and dried. Do not mistake the words of Isaiah 1:10 (and following) with such unintrusive calm.

These words are a summons. These words are, if you read and listen closely, a slap in the face to the routines we fall into and the insensitivity we develop and the feeling that nothing we do or say really matters anyway.

What energizes this call and summons is a remarkable claim: "the word of the LORD ...the teaching of our God" (1:10). The number of people and institutions making that claim over time, sometimes for preposterous if not pathetically self-serving reasons, may have hardened us to the possibility God might really *have* something to say to us. Something not just new, but something upsetting to who and what we have allowed ourselves to become.

This passage is just such a word. Do not let its setting in ancient Israel deceive you into thinking its message is simply history. This is one of those words every generation needs to wrestle with in its own peculiarities. This is a word that takes our favored views of why God is so fortunate to have such good friends as us, and says: Wait a minute. Are we forgetting something here? Are we forgetting *someone* here?

Hearing, and listening, can be hard work because it poses the possibility—and summons—to transformation.

If you wonder why transformation, if you wonder what transformation, listen anew to Isaiah 1:11-20.

Liturgy, Piety, and Life

Imagine a community of faith devoid of worship or any liturgical practice. Imagine an individual Christian who never prays. Inconceivable.

Or is it?

Isaiah 1:11-15 makes it sound like such things have no use: God has had enough of them. All the things we thought to be pleasing to God and meaningful to spiritual growth have instead become a wearisome burden for God to bear. Enough!

In truth, Isaiah does not lobby here for religion stripped of ritual and devotional practice. Rather, the case is made that even the best of such things, divorced from the conduct of how one lives outside the confines of sanctuaries or prayer closets, get us nowhere and give God no delight.

Keeping that point in mind will save the church a great deal of hand-wringing and unnecessary finger-pointing. We Protestants have especially been all too keen in times past to avoid any sense of ritual. I had folks in a church I once served comment favorably on a predecessor of mine, precisely because the congregation never knew what was going to happen the next week in worship in terms of order or music. Change is fine, but Isaiah 1 is not about the primacy of free-form worship. God can't abide extemporaneous prayer or spontaneous non-order of worship any more than multitudes of sacrifices and printed liturgies, if the worshiping community does not care for the neighbor or watch over the vulnerable.

And for form of worship, you might substitute any number of things that serve as our favored "magnetic north" for the measure of "true" religion. Church polity. Congregational traditions. Scriptural interpretation. Spiritual gifts. Any and all of those may attract the attention—and rejection—communicated by Isaiah 1:10-15. For any and all may weary God, if they are not joined to lives that take seriously the charge of verses 16-17.

What Should We Do?

It can be extremely frustrating to be criticized by someone for what you are (or are

not) doing without any clue as to what is desired. Isaiah 1:11-15 is a devastating critique. To individuals and communities who had been nurtured for generations to sacrifice and pray and gather these words must have been disorienting and jarring. If the text had stopped at verse 15, it would have been an unfair critique.

But there is remedy given, there is direction provided. The direction begins with, of all things, "washing." Washing is about fresh starts and new looks. Washing sets aside what we don't need to carry on (or in) ourselves. The second set of directions is related: a shedding of evil. It's time to stop doing things that do you and others no good. And please note, Isaiah does not mean stop liturgy or prayer. Those are not the problem. The problem is the doing of that which is wrong.

But removing the negative in life is never enough. So how does God through Isaiah go on to speak of what we are positively to do, of what will restore the efficacy to worship and prayer? Seek justice. And the way you go about that, in the eyes of Isaiah 1:17, is not how you punish criminals (as in criminal justice system) but in how you take care of the vulnerable. God's justice is this: "Rescue the oppressed, defend the orphan, plead for the widow" (1:17). Justice cares for those who routinely go uncared for. Justice speaks for those who routinely go unspoken for. Justice gathers up those who routinely go discarded.

Do that, the text implies, and however we form our liturgical and devotional life will no longer weary God. Rather, those practices will do what they were always intended to do: Serve God, and in doing so strengthen us for service of others.

Choices and Consequences

Voter turnouts in the United States, compared to countries new to democracy, are pathetic. It is no longer a matter of surprise to find that less than half of all voters may actually bother casting a ballot to determine who will not only govern us but whose finger will rest on the nuclear button. Explanations abound for the apathy, chief among them the belief that our choices don't really count. It doesn't matter who we elect, they're all the same.

That's not just bad politics. It is bad theology. Our choices in life do matter, and they matter very much. They impact the present. And if Isaiah 1:19-20 is to be believed, they sway the future. Look at the conditions in those two verses. The two "ifs" are present tense—the two "shalls" are future tense. What we choose now impacts what shall be. Isaiah was ahead of his time. In fact, Isaiah remains ahead of a lot of peo-

ple in our time who think we're free to choose whatever we want because the future will take care of itself. Ecologically. Financially. Socially. What those folks don't realize, and what Isaiah does, is that the future *doesn't* just take care of itself. God has invested significant responsibility on those created in God's image to choose wisely. For ourselves. For the sake of others. For the sake of creation.

That is what it means to live, and choose, in covenant with God. We do not live to ourselves alone, we do not *choose* to ourselves alone. Our choices have consequences because God has fashioned us with freedom.

How will you choose? The future, and God, await our choices.

SHARING THE SCRIPTURE

PREPARING TO TEACH

Preparing Our Hearts

This week's devotional reading is found in Isaiah 58:6-12. In the context of an oracle contrasting false and true worship, Isaiah records in verses 6-12 what God expects of us: just actions on behalf of those who are vulnerable and powerless. Healing and restoration will come to those who have set aside the unjust evils that, in part, led to the exile in Babylon. Have you considered how worship can become a way of life, rather than something you "do" for an hour or so each Sunday? What specific actions can you take to lead a life of worship that meets God's expectations? Write your ideas in your spiritual journal.

Pray that you and the adult learners will begin or continue to practice a worship lifestyle that constantly considers the needs of the least, last, and lost.

Preparing Our Minds

Study the background Scripture from Isaiah 1:10-20 and 2 Kings 15:32-35, and les-

son Scripture, found in Isaiah 1:10-11, 14-20. As you prepare, think about how you can have a meaningful worship experience.

Write on newsprint:
- ❏ information for next week's lesson, found under "Continue the Journey."
- ❏ activities for further spiritual growth in "Continue the Journey."

Plan an optional lecture for "Examine Isaiah's Words Regarding True Worship."

LEADING THE CLASS

(1) Gather to Learn

❖ Welcome the class members and introduce any guests.

❖ Pray that today's participants will be open to fresh ideas and new directions from the Spirit.

❖ Distribute paper and pencils. Encourage the adults to work in groups of two or three to create a description of what they consider to be an ideal worship experience. They need not include specifics, such as selecting particular hymns, but should reflect an overall experience. They might consider the atmosphere among the worshipers, art, type of music, level of formality, and type of sermon they find most meaningful.

❖ Provide time for groups to share their ideas. What common ground can the class identify?

❖ Read aloud today's focus statement: **Most people who seek a worshipful experience want it to be pure and meaningful. How can we have a pure and meaningful experience when we worship God? Isaiah implies that there is a connection between how we live and how we worship.**

(2) Examine Isaiah's Words Regarding True Worship

❖ Select a volunteer to read Isaiah 1:10-11, 14-15.

■ Discuss this question with the class: **What does God say to the people about their worship?** Use information for these verses in Understanding the Scripture to augment the discussion, or to create a lecture. Be sure the class understands that the main point is not that God rejects worship, but rather, God rejects worship that tries to coexist with injustice.

❖ Choose someone to read Isaiah 1:16-17.

■ Invite the adults to call out the nine verbs they see in this passage, all of which are in the form of a command, along with the subject to which they refer: *wash (yourselves)*, *make (yourselves) clean*, *remove (the evil)*, *cease (to do evil)*, *learn (to do good)*, *seek (justice)*, *rescue (the oppressed)*, *defend (the orphan)*, *plead (for the widow)*. List this information on newsprint. You may want to read the commentary on these verses found in Understanding the Scripture.

■ Encourage the adults to give concrete examples of how members of

today's church can obey these commands. (For example, what can they do to "rescue the oppressed" or "defend the orphan"?)

■ Consider the relationship between justice and worship by discussing this question: **Can we truly worship God if we treat others or creation unjustly? Why or why not?**

❖ Call for a class member willing to read Isaiah 1:18-20.

■ Read or retell "Choices and Consequences" from the Interpreting the Scripture portion.

■ Note the contrasts in verses 19-20: *willing/refuse* and *obedient/rebel*. Ask the students to consider, perhaps silently, how these words relate to the way we choose to live our lives.

(3) Make a Connection between How the Learners Live and How They Worship

❖ Point out that some Christians believe they have done all they need to do once they attend weekly worship. Read aloud this excerpt from an internet "conversation": **There is no halfway in the Christian life. You are either in or you're out. And being in means giving your life over to God every single day. This was more of a dilemma than anything else I'd encountered in Christianity. . . . I wanted to have it both ways. I wanted to be saved, but I didn't want to be inconvenienced or give up my worldly beliefs and lusts. I didn't want to be uncomfortable, and I didn't want to not quite fit into a world that I'd worked so hard to become a part of. . . . Learning that I had to live the Christian life 24/7 was difficult to accept, but I also knew that it was the only way. No gray area. Once I knew that, I had no choice.**

❖ Distribute paper and pencils if you have not done so. Invite the learners to respond to this individual's ideas by writing about the connections they make between how they live and how they worship.

❖ Divide into pairs or groups and encourage the adults to read or retell what they have written to the group.

❖ Conclude this portion of the session by discussing the role that worship plays in each learner's life.

(1) How do you define worship?

(2) What difference does it make in your daily life as to whether you worship regularly or not?

(3) What are the marks of one who practices a lifestyle of worship? (Make the connection between worship, justice, goodness, truth, and mercy.)

(4) Make a Commitment to Practice a Lifestyle of Worship

❖ Work with the students to write a litany or prayer in which you seek God's help in living a life rooted in worship that seeks justice for all. Record this litany or prayer on newsprint.

❖ Conclude this part of the session by inviting everyone to read aloud whatever they have written.

(5) Continue the Journey

❖ Pray that those who have participated will be mindful that all of their actions are means of worshiping God.

❖ Read aloud this preparation for next week's lesson. You may also want to post it on newsprint for the students to copy. **Prepare for next week's session entitled "Finding Satisfaction" by reading the background Scripture from Isaiah 55:1-11** and focusing on verses 1-3a, 6-11. Give attention to these ideas as you study: Most people want an abundance of good things in their life. What is the source of such abundance for us? Using the image of a great feast to which we are invited, Isaiah says that God is the one who generously provides all good things for us.

❖ Read aloud the following three ideas. Challenge the students to commit themselves to use these activities as a springboard to spiritual growth.

(1) Take some action to help bring about justice for a group or individual that is oppressed, hungry, vulnerable, or in need. How are you affected when you view this action as worship?

(2) Write a prayer in which you ask God to empower you and your congregation to focus on one or more justice issues.

(3) Examine your own life. Can you honestly say that you are obeying God's commands as enumerated in Isaiah 1:16-17? If not, what changes do you need to make? Write notes in your spiritual journal explaining how you will start to make these changes.

❖ Sing or read aloud "The Voice of God Is Calling."

❖ Invite the students to say this benediction, based on Micah 6:8, to conclude the session: **The Lord requires me to do justice, and to love kindness, and to walk humbly with my God. Let it be as you have said, Lord.**

UNIT 1: LIFE AS GOD'S PEOPLE

FINDING SATISFACTION

PREVIEWING THE LESSON

Lesson Scripture: Isaiah 55:1-3a, 6-11
Background Scripture: Isaiah 55:1-11
Key Verse: Isaiah 55:6

Focus of the Lesson:
Most people want an abundance of good things in their life. What is the source of such abundance for us? Using the image of a great feast to which we are invited, Isaiah says that God is the one who generously provides all good things for us.

Goals for the Learners:
(1) to study Isaiah's image of the great feast to which we are invited.
(2) to recognize the abundant goodness of God in their lives.
(3) to give thanks for God's generous good gifts.

Pronunciation Guide:
hesed (kheh' sed)
qara (kaw raw')
qarob (kaw robe')

Supplies:
Bibles, newsprint and marker, paper and pencils, hymnals, magazines, paper, scissors, glue, simple snack food

---

READING THE SCRIPTURE

NRSV
Isaiah 55:1-3a, 6-11
¹ Ho, everyone who thirsts,
   come to the waters;
and you that have no money,
   come, buy and eat!
Come, buy wine and milk
   without money and without price.

NIV
Isaiah 55:1-3a, 6-11
¹"Come, all you who are thirsty,
   come to the waters;
and you who have no money,
   come, buy and eat!
Come, buy wine and milk
   without money and without cost.

² Why do you spend your money for that
    which is not bread,
  and your labor for that which does not
    satisfy?
Listen carefully to me, and eat what is
    good,
  and delight yourselves in rich food.
³ Incline your ear, and come to me;
  listen, so that you may live.
⁶ **Seek the LORD while he may be found,**
  call upon him while he is near;
⁷ let the wicked forsake their way,
  and the unrighteous their thoughts;
let them return to the LORD, that he may
    have mercy on them,
    and to our God, for he will abundantly
    pardon.
⁸ For my thoughts are not your thoughts,
  nor are your ways my ways,
    says the LORD.
⁹ For as the heavens are higher than the
    earth,
  so are my ways higher than your ways
  and my thoughts than your thoughts.
¹⁰For as the rain and the snow come down
    from heaven,
  and do not return there until they have
    watered the earth,
  making it bring forth and sprout,
    giving seed to the sower and bread
    to the eater,
¹¹so shall my word be that goes out from my
    mouth;
  it shall not return to me empty,
  but it shall accomplish that which I
    purpose,
  and succeed in the thing for which I sent
    it.

²Why spend money on what is not bread,
  and your labor on what does not satisfy?
Listen, listen to me, and eat what is good,
  and your soul will delight in the richest of
    fare.
³Give ear and come to me;
  hear me, that your soul may live.
⁶**Seek the LORD while he may be found;**
  call on him while he is near.
⁷Let the wicked forsake his way
  and the evil man his thoughts.
Let him turn to the LORD, and he will have
    mercy on him,
  and to our God, for he will freely pardon.
⁸"For my thoughts are not your thoughts,
  neither are your ways my ways,"
              declares the LORD.
⁹"As the heavens are higher than the earth,
  so are my ways higher than your ways
  and my thoughts than your thoughts.
¹⁰As the rain and the snow
  come down from heaven,
  and do not return to it
  without watering the earth
  and making it bud and flourish,
    so that it yields seed for the sower and
    bread for the eater,
¹¹so is my word that goes out from my
    mouth:
  It will not return to me empty,
  but will accomplish what I desire
    and achieve the purpose for which I sent
    it."

UNDERSTANDING THE SCRIPTURE

Isaiah 55:1. Many scholars believe Isaiah 55 addresses Israel at the end of the exile. A choice awaits the people: remain in Babylon, or join those who return to rebuild. As with earlier texts in Isaiah, ancient themes of exodus and creation are reworked to address present circumstances. The invitation to those who "thirst" employs the same verb used in Exodus 17:3, where the thirsting in the wilderness resulted in God's providing of water from the rock at Horeb. As God provided then (to a murmuring people), God can be trusted to provide now. Likewise, the summons to come to the "waters" echoes the waters of Genesis 1:1, over which the Spirit of God moved to bring life. God's movement will bring, out of exile, new life. "Wine and milk" form two of the promises associated with the land God promised to bring to those who journeyed in the wilderness. The emphasis on "no money" and "without price" stresses the gracious nature of God's imminent activity of new deliverance and re-creation.

Isaiah 55:2-3a. In contrast to its harsh beginnings, exile had become a relatively prosperous and safe place for the people of Israel. If nothing else, it was a "known" quantity, as opposed to the uncertainties of return to a land many had not even seen. Isaiah poses the issue of return by contrasting what they "have" in Babylon with what God will provide in return. That which is not "bread" suggests a feeding or nourishment not limited to physical sustenance. The "bread" of Israel involves relationship with God through covenant, a provisioning by grace that recalls the story of manna and quail in Exodus 16. Eating what is "good" also recalls the story of Daniel 1:5-20, another text set in exile, where the food of the empire comes up lacking in comparison to the "diet" of Daniel and his companions. The imperative verb in verse 3, "listen" (the Hebrew word also means "to obey"), calls the exiles to hear and respond to the "feast" of freedom God prepares.

Isaiah 55:3b-5. In these verses, the old promise of the Davidic covenant now becomes extended in a new way to the whole people of Israel. Using the language of covenant-making that described God's partnering with Abraham (Genesis 15:18), God strikes this new relationship with the people while they are still in exile.

"Steadfast love" (*hesed*) carries the meaning of loyalty to a partner that goes beyond the letter of law. Earlier in Isaiah, the "servant" (whom some identify with the people Israel) receives a commission to be a light for the nations (42:6; 49:6). In these verses now, the consequences of that calling are described by the irony of nations called by and running toward Israel. Covenant with God transforms even those, at the moment, outside it.

Isaiah 55:6. Second Chronicles 15:2 asserts seeking God will result in finding, even as abandoning God will result in abandonment. "While he may be found" in this verse from Isaiah suggests a similar conditionality. The prophets understood exile not so much as God's abandoning Israel as the consequences of Israel rejecting God. Seeking God places the choice back in the hands of the exiles. The grace of God makes provision for the finding; the "while" underscores the importance of human volition. The second half of this verse involves a play on words. Call (*qara*) on God while God is near (*qarob*). Exile struggled with the "farness" of God: from the plight of the exiles, in the distance from a now-destroyed temple. Isaiah tempers that struggle by affirming to the exiles the closeness of God, a nearness that makes the seeking and calling laden with hope.

Isaiah 55:7. While speaking hope, Isaiah does not yield to cheap grace. The key verbs in terms of the people's responses are "forsake" and "turn." Breaks need to be made with actions incompatible with covenant. Breaks may also need to be made with attitudes of contentment and apathy that would insulate the exiles from risking return. What justifies and makes possible such change?

The key verbs for God's actions in this verse are "have mercy" and "pardon." God does not stand poised, ready to pounce on the slightest hint of disobedience. God desires above all else in this to bring renewal and fresh beginnings, even and especially out of past errors and wanderings. Homecoming promises a reception in love, an embrace not at all unlike that later envisioned in a parable of a prodigal son and a loving parent.

Isaiah 55:8-9. "Thoughts" and "ways" cover the totality of how life is both perceived and lived out. The gulf separating human and divine in those perceptions and expressions is imaged in the distance between heaven and earth. In the ancient view of the world, the heavens literally formed a canopy that stretched over the earth. The efforts of Babel had shown the foolhardiness of trying to attain those heights in story form. Isaiah here simply yet profoundly makes that same point in a series of poetic lines rich with parallelism. Notice how the repetition of "thoughts" and "ways" forms the opening and closing structure to this passage, framing its core affirmation of "heavens higher than the earth" in the middle.

Isaiah 55:10-11. The gift of land stood at the heart of God's covenant with Abraham and later on Sinai through Moses. The imagery of Isaiah in these verses draws on the renewal of land. The rain and snow that water the earth call to mind the richness of Psalm 65's depiction of the bounties of God's good creation. But that psalm begins with a declaration of God's deliverance (65:5), whose hope is not just for Israel but the whole of creation. Likewise, these verses in Isaiah intend to summon hope in a new act of deliverance associated with a return to land long thought lost. In spite of the words and power of Babylon to maintain the status quo, Isaiah declares God's powerful word will accomplish its purpose.

INTERPRETING THE SCRIPTURE

The Feast God Provides

This passage opens with a feast, a banquet, freely offered. To hear it more deeply, three other "banquets" come to mind.

Proverbs 9 portrays a feast opened by one who is called Lady Wisdom. An invitation to eat and drink accompanies that banquet, to dine on wisdom rather than folly. For Israel in exile, what was wisdom and what was folly was surely a lively debate. Was it folly, or wisdom, to think a group of exiles could leave the riches of the imperial capital and find an even "richer" life in a land ravaged by war whose buildings and temple were mostly razed and in ruins? Was it wisdom or folly to trust in the promises of One who promised David a line without end, having seen themselves the inglorious end of that line? We do injustice to the tension inherent in Isaiah 55 if we assume the choices, then and now, are all obvious. For what wisdom do we follow in the tables we choose to fill our hopes or seek our securities?

Isaiah speaks of another banquet in chapter 25, beginning at verse 6. That feast, composed of rich foods and fatty meats and well-aged wines, commemorates the death of death. It is a passage that strongly informs narratives of hope in the New Testament, particularly Revelation 21. But consider it now in light of Isaiah 55. Exile had been an experience of death, literally and figuratively, for the people of Israel. The temple destroyed. Homes and lands stripped away. Relationships ended. The exiles in Babylon had, to some degree, been seated at tables that couldn't remove the sight and results of those dyings for years. But now, a new table is announced. People can have hope again—but will they? Will we? We too get used to the ways things are, to the way death holds and takes from us. We get resigned to thinking, and acting, and trusting, that things can never be different:

in our homes, in our churches, in our communities. But then, here comes Isaiah. Come to the waters. Toast the death of death. Do we really have the nerve to join that table? Or do we think those are just words, and death has the final word?

The third banquet evoked by reading Isaiah 55, at least through the eyes of the church, is the table set for us at communion. The grace of this table is, like Isaiah's, just that: grace. Without money. Without price. We find ourselves invited, not because of who we are or what we've done—but thoroughly because of who God is in Jesus Christ. At that table, we receive the wisdom of seeing and experiencing the Holy in the most ordinary of elements. At that table, we face the death of Jesus, of breaking and pouring out, all for the sake of toasting death's death and a table to be tasted anew in God's kingdom. We come seeking God, not because we know we can find God—but trusting God in Christ has already found us and called us to the feast God has always and will always provide.

Seeking God

The key verse for today's passage invites an essential movement of spiritual life: the seeking of God. In my remembrance, the choir in the church I grew up sang these words most every Sunday to preface the confession or pastoral prayer.

Remember the context of these words in Isaiah: They invite seeking and calling from a people likely wondering if God could ever be found again. The search for God is one thing when we do so at ease with our lives and our world. That search is quite another when disease settles into mind or body or society. Why do such things happen? Where can we turn to find God in those circumstances? In those times, the words of Isaiah find a companion in the longing of Psalm 42: "As a deer longs for flowing streams, so my soul longs for you, O God. My soul thirsts for God, for the living God. . . . I say to God, my rock, 'Why have you forgotten me? Why must I

walk about mournfully because the enemy oppresses me?' " (42:1-2a, 9).

When Isaiah counsels Israel in exile—and us—to seek God, ease is not a presumption of the journey. Grace, however, is. Our finding of God likely will come through the awareness that, long before we have a sense of finding of God, God has already found us. Our sense of the farness of God's presence from us at times finds hope through listening and attending to the ways God draws near, unrecognized. Even in the midst of lament, we may seek and call upon the One who may be found and who draws near, the One who is our hope.

Beyond Our Understanding

"My thoughts are not your thoughts, nor are your ways my ways" (Isaiah 55:8).

In exile, the people of Israel had been driven to wonder deep and hard about God's purposes in all of this. "Why" would likely have been the predominant question raised about both the thoughts and ways of God that had left them in Babylon and the Jerusalem temple in ruins. These verses offer a response not unlike that given Job (Job 38 and following). No clear answers explain away everything that has happened, or "fix" what has been lost or hurt. Instead, Isaiah asserts the mystery of God among us, a mystery that is not a matter for human knowledge or intuition to figure out.

Do Isaiah's words comfort you, or confound you? We are not always happy with unanswered questions, particularly those that relate to faith and God's workings. Then again, to presume we could know God's mind fully, or to claim we can understand what will duplicate God's ways completely, oversteps the bounds of human nature. Faith is not the explanation of God. Faith is the trust of God.

Emptiness and Fulfillment

Have you ever been disappointed in something that did not live up to expectations, or meet some need of yours as you hoped? You are not alone.

Societies ancient and modern engage in activities and acquisitions intended to satisfy needs or fulfill hopes. For some folks, acquiring more and more "stuff" (the five dollar word is "materialism") serves as the avenue to make them feel full or satisfied. For others, the acquisition of power, political or social or even religious, forms the motivation that propels life and relationship.

Do such things "satisfy?" Do such things ever bring to fruition the kinds of hopes and needs to spur on their adherents and advocates?

Isaiah closes this passage with an assertion that the word of God does not return empty. Do we believe that? We have been praying for 2000 years and more that the reign of God might come fully on this earth as it is in heaven. Do we still trust that, or do we look at headlines from the nation's capital or any one of a number of world "hot spots" and say, "things will never get better"?

Isaiah invited Israel's exiles to renewed hope. The words of Isaiah still invite modern-day sojourners to renewed hope. Not because we believe in inevitable progress. Not because things couldn't possibly get any worse (they can!). But because we trust our lives to the truth that the promises and sovereign realm of God will have the last and lasting say.

Do you believe that?

SHARING THE SCRIPTURE

PREPARING TO TEACH

Preparing Our Hearts

This week's devotional reading is found in 2 Corinthians 9:10-15, which is part of Paul's writing about the collection for the Christians in Jerusalem. Echoing Isaiah 55:10 and Hosea 10:12 in verse 10, Paul clearly demonstrates that God is the source of great abundance and grace. One who has been blessed has a responsibility to do good works, such as providing generously for others, as an act of justice. In what ways have you been blessed? What good works are you doing to bring about justice for others?

Pray that you and the adult learners will be generous to others as God has poured out blessings upon you.

Preparing Our Minds

Study the background Scripture from Isaiah 55:1-11 and lesson Scripture, verses 1-3a, 6-11. As you read, think about the source of the abundance of good things you have in your life.

Write on newsprint:
❑ information for next week's lesson, found under "Continue the Journey."
❑ activities for further spiritual growth in "Continue the Journey."

Plan the lecture suggested under "Study Isaiah's Image of the Great Feast to Which We Are Invited."

Gather some simple snacks to be used for the lesson. You may wish to contact some class members and ask them to bring something. Also gather art supplies.

LEADING THE CLASS

(1) Gather to Learn

❖ Welcome the class members and introduce any guests.
❖ Pray that all who have gathered will find new life as people of God as they study the Scriptures together.

❖ Provide magazines, paper, scissors, and glue. Ask the students to work in groups to create small collages showing things that they enjoy having or would like to have. They will need to select pictures, cut them out, and glue them to the paper to make the collage. Pictures can overlap.

❖ Invite each group to show their collage to the class, perhaps by passing the papers around.

❖ Discuss reasons why we are so attracted to things. Consider the impact a "consumerist culture" has on our own desires.

❖ Read aloud today's focus statement: **Most people want an abundance of good things in their life. What is the source of such abundance for us? Using the image of a great feast to which we are invited, Isaiah says that God is the one who generously provides all good things for us.**

(2) Study Isaiah's Image of the Great Feast to Which We Are Invited

❖ Ask a volunteer to read Isaiah 55:1-3a (ending with "live" in the NRSV) and verses 6-11.

❖ Present a lecture from Understanding the Scripture to help the students comprehend the background and meaning of Isaiah's words. Include these points:

■ echoes of the first exodus heard in verse 1.

■ God's grace as depicted in verses 1-3a. Note that the Israelites (and us) are invited to an abundant meal that God is hosting at no cost to those who come.

■ contrast in verse 6 between belief that God was far away during exile and God is now close; people may choose to seek God.

■ idea in verse 7 that one must forsake evil thoughts and actions and turn toward God in order for God to forgive.

■ notion in verses 8-9 that "thoughts" and "ways" encompass how life is perceived and how it is lived out.

■ word of hope in verses 10-11.

❖ **Option:** Explore other banquets, described under "The Feast God Provides" in Interpreting the Scripture, and compare these to the one in Isaiah 55.

❖ Note that Isaiah uses the words in verse 1 to invite people into the presence of God, to partake of God's banquet. Consider how your congregation invites people into God's presence by addressing these questions.

(1) **What attracted you to this congregation?**

(2) **What makes this congregation a satisfying place to belong and be with God's people?**

(3) **Does our church regularly attract visitors?**

(4) **If so, what strategies have we used to invite people in and make them feel welcomed?**

(5) **If not, what can we do to ensure that people know they are wanted and welcomed here?**

❖ Ask the class to read Isaiah 55:6-7 in unison. Challenge them to meditate for a few moments on actions and attitudes that they need to turn away from in order to seek the Lord. Break the silence with these words: **You have heard, O God, the cries of our hearts as we choose to turn from the things of this world that do not satisfy and turn to you to receive grace and pardon. Amen.**

❖ Conclude this portion of the session by referring to verses 10 and 11. Encourage volunteers to tell brief stories to demonstrate how God's word has accomplished its purpose in their lives.

(3) Recognize the Abundant Goodness of God in the Learners' Lives

❖ Read aloud the first three paragraphs of "Emptiness and Fulfillment" in

Interpreting the Scripture and discuss the questions in the third paragraph.

❖ Invite the learners to work with a partner or team to identify expressions of God's abundant goodness in their lives. Provide paper or newsprint for each team to list their ideas. If the class enjoys competition, set a time limit and see which team can generate the most responses.

(4) Give Thanks for God's Generous Good Gifts

❖ Distribute paper and pencils. Encourage each student to write a brief grace in which they give thanks for God's good gifts. Some adults may prefer to think about what they want to say rather than write.

❖ Share among the students whatever snack you have brought. Tell them that this snack is to remind them of the banquet alluded to in Isaiah 55.

❖ Invite the students to say or read the grace they have composed as they prepare to eat this snack.

(5) Continue the Journey

❖ Pray that those who have participated today will experience the satisfaction that comes from seeking the Lord.

❖ Read aloud this preparation for next week's lesson. You may also want to post it on newsprint for the students to copy. **Prepare for next week's session entitled "Doing the Right Thing" by reading**

Micah 2:1-4; 3:1-5, 8-12; 6:6-8. Our lesson will highlight Micah 3:1-4; 6:6-8. Focus on these ideas as you study: Most people want to do what is right. How do we know what the right thing is? Micah gives us solid help by highlighting justice, kindness, and the love of God as standards to guide our actions.

❖ Read aloud the following three ideas. Challenge the students to commit themselves to use these activities as a springboard to spiritual growth.

(1) **Offer food in God's name to the victims of a disaster. If you cannot serve as a disaster volunteer, send money to your denomination's relief agency (for example, United Methodist Committee on Relief).**

(2) **Say grace before each meal this week, even when you are eating out. Explain to someone else, perhaps a child, why saying thanks is so important to you.**

(3) **Seek the Lord by forsaking a bad habit or an unjust action or attitude and turning to God for forgiveness.**

❖ Sing or read aloud "Seek the Lord," which is based, in part, on today's key verse, Isaiah 55:6.

❖ Invite the students to say this benediction, based on Micah 6:8, to conclude the session: **The Lord requires me to do justice, and to love kindness, and to walk humbly with my God. Let it be as you have said, Lord.**

UNIT 2: WHAT DOES GOD REQUIRE?

DOING THE RIGHT THING

PREVIEWING THE LESSON

Lesson Scripture: Micah 3:1-4; 6:6-8
Background Scripture: Micah 2:1-4; 3:1-5, 8-12; 6:6-8
Key Verse: Micah 6:8

Focus of the Lesson:
Most people want to do what is right. How do we know what the right thing is? Micah gives us solid help by highlighting justice, kindness, and the love of God as standards to guide our actions.

Goals for the Learners:
(1) to explore Micah's teachings on God's requirements.
(2) to evaluate their actions and attitudes in light of these requirements.
(3) to identify and respond to a situation where justice, kindness, and the love of God are needed.

Pronunciation Guide:
hesed (kheh' sed)   *shalom* (shah lohm')
mishpat (mish pawt')

Supplies:
Bibles, newsprint and marker, paper and pencils, hymnals, map of Palestine and surrounding countries in Old Testament times

---

READING THE SCRIPTURE

NRSV
Micah 3:1-4
¹ And I said:
    Listen, you heads of Jacob
      and rulers of the house of Israel!
    Should you not know justice?—
²   you who hate the good and love the
      evil,
    who tear the skin off my people,

NIV
Micah 3:1-4
¹Then I said,
    "Listen, you leaders of Jacob,
    you rulers of the house of Israel.
    Should you not know justice,
²you who hate good and love evil;
    who tear the skin from my people
    and the flesh from their bones;

and the flesh off their bones;
³ who eat the flesh of my people,
    flay their skin off them,
break their bones in pieces,
    and chop them up like meat in a kettle,
    like flesh in a caldron.
⁴ Then they will cry to the LORD,
    but he will not answer them;
he will hide his face from them at that
        time,
    because they have acted wickedly.

Micah 6:6-8
⁶ "With what shall I come before the LORD,
    and bow myself before God on high?
Shall I come before him with burnt
        offerings,
    with calves a year old?
⁷ Will the LORD be pleased with thousands
        of rams,
    with ten thousands of rivers of oil?
Shall I give my firstborn for my
        transgression,
    the fruit of my body for the sin of my
        soul?"
⁸ **He has told you, O mortal, what is good;**
    and what does the LORD require of you
but to do justice, and to love kindness,
and to walk humbly with your God?

³who eat my people's flesh,
    strip off their skin
    and break their bones in pieces;
who chop them up like meat for the pan,
    like flesh for the pot?"
⁴Then they will cry out to the LORD,
    but he will not answer them.
At that time he will hide his face from them
    because of the evil they have done.

Micah 6:6-8
⁶With what shall I come before the LORD
    and bow down before the exalted God?
Shall I come before him with burnt
        offerings,
    with calves a year old?
⁷Will the LORD be pleased with thousands of
        rams,
    with ten thousand rivers of oil?
Shall I offer my firstborn for my
        transgression,
the fruit of my body for the sin of my soul?
⁸**He has showed you, O man, what is good.**
    And what does the LORD require of
        you?
To act justly and to love mercy
    and to walk humbly with your God.

UNDERSTANDING THE SCRIPTURE

Micah 2:1-4. Like Amos who bewailed those reclining on beds of ease while Israel suffered (Amos 6:4 and following), Micah condemns those who scheme instead of sleep in bed. They have no ethic that restrains their power over others, save that the power to do what they please justifies their deeds. The actions Micah attributes to them in verse 2 (covet, seize, take away, oppress) all rely on violence against the vulnerable. The most damning as well as telling of those actions is the first. "Covet" is the same action prohibited in the Decalogue (Exodus 20:17). Such actions do not simply offend community. They break covenant with God. The consequences of such "devisings" of evil come in God's "devising" (the same verb is used in verse 1 and 3) plans against those who wield power without conscience. The gift of land, at the core of covenant, will be stripped away.

Micah 3:1. This verse identifies the targeted audience of chapter 2: the leaders of Israel. "Heads" and "rulers" initially signify those whose power falls primarily in political and social circles. Within a few verses, Micah will bring in Israel's religious leaders for confrontation. The key issue for such leaders, as the previous text in chapter 2 made clear, is their exercise of power. Micah 3:1 cuts to the core of the primary task and responsibility of power: justice. That Hebrew word, *mishpat*, invokes far more than a sense of bringing someone to a legal reckoning. *Mishpat* entails equity in relationships, and fairness in decisions. The question raised of "should you not know justice" implies privilege and authority bear direct responsibility for maintaining equity, rather than skewing matters to one's own advantage. Implicit also in that charge is that justice *known* requires justice *done*, a covenant theme that will become explicit with 6:8.

Micah 3:2-3. The passage continues by identifying who the prophet has in mind when he refers to those who should know justice. The first identification uses a stunning reversal of the plea of Amos 5:15 (love good and hate evil). For Micah, the leaders have it all backwards by hating good and loving evil. The remaining lines in these verses charge these rulers with a horrific offense: cannibalism. The viciousness of the words and language makes clear the despicable nature of their crimes against people entrusted to their care. Like Ezekiel 34's later condemnation of the "shepherds" (kings), Micah declares that those entrusted in a position to feed and nurture individuals and groups under their care have instead fed on them.

Micah 3:4-5. Such actions will not go unnoticed or unpunished. The judgment imposed will be the withdrawal of God from their presence and side. Their cries without God's answer mirrors the declaration of Isaiah 1:15. There, God's removal of favor and hearing is linked to blood on the hands of those who cry out. The graphic imagery of Micah 3:2-3 reveals the same bloodguilt on those who exercised power irresponsibly and greedily. With verse 5, Micah introduces another party to this folly: self-serving prophets, whose message goes tailored to its reception and reward. The false cry of "peace" will later also be condemned in Jeremiah 6:14. *Shalom* means not simply an absence of conflict, but a wholeness of life dependent upon justice and rest and equity and community well-being. To cry *shalom* only when me and mine prosper, without regard and even with malice for others as is the case in Micah's time, is to speak a lie in the name of God.

Micah 3:8-12. In contrast to those who speak from deceit, Micah reveals his call and mission as empowered by God's Spirit. Before right can be lifted up, wrong must be taken down. Verses 9-11 once more call out the rulers and heads of Israel, in case anyone has forgotten who is being called into account here. Their claims of standing within the tradition of a divine favor never to be withdrawn will suffer a rude awakening. One by one, rulers and priests and prophets are singled out for their crimes. The condemnation is not about the issue of salaries for religious work, but the corruption that comes when money and power tilt vocation toward the strong and away from the vulnerable. A city and society built on such foundations will not stand. One by one, Zion and Jerusalem and temple (3:12) will suffer the consequences of those who have ruined their underpinnings.

Micah 6:6-7. In the previous verses of chapter 6, God brought suit against Israel that opened with a recitation of saving acts in the past. Micah 6:6-7 serve as a type of, "how can we make this right?" The primary appeal concerns what kind of cultic sacrifice would satisfy God. The numbers invoked ("thousands" and "tens of thousands") along with the ultimate consideration of child sacrifice lend a sense of desperation to the situation. Ironically, "firstborn" not only summons memories of Abraham and Isaac, and then the final plague levied upon the Egyptians, but also calls to mind what God had revealed at the very beginning of the exodus narrative: "Then you shall say to Pharaoh . . . 'Israel is my firstborn' " (Exodus 4:22). Through this list of ever-increasing degrees of sacrifice, does God desire Israel's death to make things right?

Micah 6:8. No. What God seeks is for Israel to *live* things right. "Good" in the language of covenant is not only a term for God's blessings, but also for what the people are to seek. What that "good" consists of is nothing new in terms of covenantal obligations. But Micah gives what is "good" a memorable summary here. Do "justice" (*mishpat*). God asked earlier if the leaders should not know *mishpat* (3:1). Here, "knowing" justice invites fulfillment through "doing" justice. Love "kindness" (*hesed*). *Hesed* denotes loyalty and faithfulness in relationships that go beyond duty. Walk "humbly." Humility recognizes we live at the beck and call of God, not the other way around. Proverbs 11:2 captures both the meaning of this command, as well as the pride in the prior charges against Israel's leaders that jeopardizes covenant: "When pride comes, then comes disgrace; but wisdom is with the humble."

INTERPRETING THE SCRIPTURE

Hearing Micah in Context

These are just old words, right? Why bother listening to them today!

Scholars generally consider Micah one of the earliest prophets whose words have come down to us. Micah prophesied such words of judgment and the call to do what is right *before* the crises of Assyria's destruction of the northern kingdom and its threat to Judah. In other words, Micah spoke while folks were still not worried, while these divisions between the haves and have-nots seemed just to be the way things always had been and always would be rather than any decisive cause for concern.

The context of Micah strikes all too close to home in societies grown settled and comfortable in prosperity—or too easily rallied to the threats without while oblivious to or in denial of the threats within. And the threats that elicit Micah's strongest words, and most pressing pleas, involve justice. Justice today sometimes is reduced to a synonym for punishment meted out to criminals. But justice now, like justice then, turns on how society deals with issues of inequities of power and wealth. What is "good" now, like what was "good" then, finds definition not exclusively in what's in it for me and mine, but what gives life and fairness and wholeness to the community.

These are just old words, right?

Shouldn't We Know?

Micah 3:1 raises an interesting question. To folks entrusted with great power and privilege, the question is a rhetorical summons to accountability: *Should you not know justice?*

The question still haunts individuals and communities today. *Should we not know . . .* and we might fill in any number of qualities that covenant, and faith, continually seek of us in our lives. Justice. Mercy. Compassion. *Should we not know?*

The ability to claim ignorance of such things, then and now, offers an excuse for inaction—or wrong action. *I didn't know* forms a familiar response if confronted with inappropriate behavior. Adolescents use it with some frequency, much to the chagrin of parents and teachers. Then again, where do they learn that? Prison abuse scandals in Iraq generated, among other things, those same words. I wasn't taught what I could or couldn't do. I didn't know. So I shouldn't be held accountable.

The problem is, in Micah's time and in our own, we *should* know. Persons and groups who exercise power over others *should* know what abuse of that power can cause. Perhaps Micah's original audience of leaders offered shocked denials. Who, me? I didn't know!

With power, with privilege, goes the responsibility to know. To know not just what you *can* do, but what it can cause. To know not just what it means for you, but what it can mean for others.

Lest we think this is all aimed exclusively at those folks who hold high office or live in another world from you and me: Micah speaks to our world. Micah speaks to the church: *Should you not know justice?* When hard words and news about the injustice that reigns in the world around pummel us into sanctuaried escape, that does not let us off the hook. The church is entrusted with the power of God's grace. The church is entrusted with the privileged hope of God's coming realm. With power, with privilege, goes the responsibility to speak and act with integrity. The church cannot risk resting on the sidelines when the right and the good go trampled, when equity among peoples is a cruel hoax enjoyed by the powerful at the expense of the vulnerable. We know better. At least, through the life and ministry of Jesus Christ, we should.

The Risk of Substitutes

Faced with change, or the invocation *to* change, a common response is to fall back on the familiar, the routine, to get us out of this. Many churches, rural and urban, small and large, have faced decline in the past two or three or more decades. A similar assessment can be made of denominations in general. What do we do in the face of dwindling membership rolls and tightening budgets? Initial responses, sometimes the only responses, have involved just doing *more* of what worked in the 1950's and 1960's. We have brought solutions to the crisis, rather than listened to the crisis for what needs to be done in new days and times.

Micah imagines Israel's response to God's unhappiness with what has come of the covenant taking the same form. What has always worked is sacrifice, so let's just figure out how to do more and more costly

offerings. The problem is, doing more of the same is not what God seeks. Offerings and sacrifices are fine, but they intend to be symbols—not substitutes—for matters of greater consequence. Please note, the offerings and sacrifices that Israel would substitute are all actions called for in the keeping of covenant. They are not, in and of themselves, "bad" things. It's just that they are not the most needful things.

When God seeks change and transformation in our lives, what "substitutes" move us from the heart of that call? In place of the vocations in Micah 6:8, with what do we busy our lives and congregations until we lose sight of what God truly requires and desires from us?

Do the Right Things

It seems every couple of months we read the results of those surveys that indicate some extremely high percentage of people in the United States believe there is a God. Well, hooray for us! What texts like Micah and the teachings of Jesus are far more interested in is: What do you *do* about that? If you know or trust God, how do you act any differently?

Micah gives us a marvelous litany of what those actions ought to involve in the concluding verse. To do the right thing in life, when right is understood as living according to God's purposes, is not just *one* thing. It is the whole of life.

It is, as Micah says, to do justice. All the wishing and hoping that this world's economic and social playing field should be more equitable only goes so far. God seeks, as Micah declares, individuals and communities who roll up sleeves and do what is just. It is also, as Micah says, to love kindness. *Hesed* is a peculiar word in covenant. It is the loyalty one partner has to another. It is the kind of faithfulness that goes the extra mile, that does what it needs to in order to keep faith with the other. To love kindness as Micah speaks of it is to live in ways that not only do all that we can to keep our relationship with God on line. It is also to see to it that we treat our other partners in covenant with the same respect and grace and stick-to-it-tiveness with which God treats us. Finally, to live as God calls us is also to walk humbly with God. Pride goes before a fall, according to Proverbs 16:18. Our walk with God in this

world is not a self-centered preoccupation with what should be done for me, by others and by God. Our walk with God invites the humility of knowing we live by grace, and the humility of offering that same grace toward others.

To do these things in life is to do the right things, by the grace and call of God.

SHARING THE SCRIPTURE

PREPARING TO TEACH

Preparing Our Hearts

This week's devotional reading is found in Hebrews 12:6-12. Why do parents discipline their children? Why does God discipline us? The short answer is probably "so we will do the right thing." Although discipline can cause suffering, the outcome of this suffering is positive. According to Hebrews, divine discipline assures us that we are God's own children. What does such a relationship mean to you as you go about your regular life routines?

Pray that you and the adult learners will be open to God's discipline so that you may be better equipped to reflect the image of our heavenly Father, whose child you are.

Preparing Our Minds

Study the background Scripture from Micah 2:1-4; 3:1-5, 8-12; 6:6-8, and lesson Scripture, found in Micah 3:1-4; 6:6-8. As you read, think about how you know what the right thing to do is.

Write on newsprint:
❑ information for next week's lesson, found under "Continue the Journey."
❑ activities for further spiritual growth in "Continue the Journey."

Locate map(s) for "Explore Micah's Teachings on God's Requirements."

Plan how you will present information on the context for "Explore Micah's Teachings on God's Requirements."

LEADING THE CLASS

(1) Gather to Learn

❖ Welcome the class members and introduce any guests.

❖ Pray that those who are present will affirm their desire to live according to God's requirements.

❖ Read this anonymous quotation: **There is a difference between one who does right because of his own conscience and one who is kept from wrongdoing because of the presence of others.**

❖ Talk with the class about what this quote might mean.
  (1) Why do you believe people do right?
  (2) How much influence do other peoples' opinions have on how you act?

❖ Read aloud today's focus statement: **Most people want to do what is right. How do we know what the right thing is? Micah gives us solid help by highlighting justice, kindness, and the love of God as standards to guide our actions.**

(2) Explore Micah's Teachings on God's Requirements

❖ Set today's session in context by creating a lecture from the information under "Hearing Micah in Context" in the Interpreting the Scripture portion and Micah 2:1-4 in Understanding the Scripture. Use a map to help the class visualize the northern kingdom (also known as Israel), the southern kingdom (also known as Judah), Assyria, and Babylon.

❖ Choose a volunteer to read Micah 3:1-4.
  (1) To whom are the prophet's remarks addressed?
  (2) How are Micah's expectations of these people different from their actual behaviors? (They should know about justice, but they do not act justly. For further discussion see "Shouldn't We Know?" in Interpreting the Scripture.)
  (3) What one word sums up the behavior of these people? (Cannibalism. Talk about any associations the class members make with the idea of people eating other people.)

❖ Select someone to read Micah 6:6-8.
  ■ Note that the focus here is on worship. Refer to verses 6-7 in Understanding the Scripture for additional information.
  ■ Read the key verse, Micah 6:8, aloud several times, asking the class to repeat after you so that they might memorize this crucial verse.

(3) Evaluate the Learners' Actions and Attitudes in Light of These Requirements

❖ Read aloud "The Risk of Substitutes" in Interpreting the Scripture. Discuss with the class their responses to the questions in the last paragraph.

❖ Write on newsprint these three commands: "do justice," "love kindness," and "walk humbly with your God." (Note that

"humbly" may be better translated as "wisely.")
  ■ Divide the class into three groups and give each group a marker and sheet of newsprint. Assign one of the three commands to each group. Encourage the groups to talk about how the church today seems to be fulfilling these commands. Ask for concrete examples to support their statements. The groups may want to think about the church universal or your congregation in particular.
  ■ Ask each group to report back to the class.
  ■ Provide additional time for the students to raise questions about how the church is either sending mixed messages or failing to live up to these high commandments.

❖ Distribute paper and pencils. Challenge the adults to think individually about how they are fulfilling each of the three commands. Suggest that they write brief anecdotes to demonstrate how they are being faithful to these requirements. Tell them that this information will remain confidential. Some adults may prefer not to write.

❖ Bring this section to closure by discussing this question: **If Micah were to speak to our church, what would he say about how we as a body and as individuals are fulfilling God's requirements?**

(4) Identify and Respond to a Situation Where Justice, Kindness, and the Love of God Are Needed

❖ List on newsprint any current events that cry out for justice, kindness, and the love of God.

❖ Narrow the list down to one or two of these situations that the class seems most interested in addressing. Put an asterisk by their selections.

❖ Brainstorm specific ideas as to how the class members could act in the selected situation(s). While prayer is always important and financial contributions may be helpful, encourage the adults to find ways to give of themselves. Such ways might include a hands-on activity (such as staffing a homeless shelter for an evening), an advocacy activity (such as working through the political process to change public policy), or a mentoring/coaching activity (such as working with someone to learn a valuable new skill).

❖ Evaluate how these ideas might impact those who have experienced an injustice.

❖ Seek commitments from the class members to act. Talk about what they are willing to do.

(5) Continue the Journey

❖ Pray that all who have participated in today's class will be mindful of God's requirements of them and continually seek to do the right thing.

❖ Read aloud this preparation for next week's lesson. You may also want to post it on newsprint for the students to copy. **Prepare for next week's session entitled "Getting Ready for Judgment" by reading background Scripture from Zephaniah 3:1-13 and 2 Chronicles 34:1-3. This lesson will focus on Zephaniah 3:1-5, 8-9. Pay particular attention to these ideas as you read: People sometimes act wrongly without** thinking of the consequences to themselves or others. What consequences result when God's people act wrongly? Zephaniah says that God will act justly, bringing both punishment and redemption.

❖ Read aloud the following three ideas. Challenge the students to commit themselves to use these activities as a springboard to spiritual growth.

(1) **Look for opportunities this week to act with love, kindness, and justice. Try to keep a written record of your actions and review it at the end of the week. How would you evaluate your adherence to God's requirements?**

(2) **Identify a particular injustice (for example, racism or sexism) against which you struggle. What concrete actions do you take to overcome this injustice? What else could you do?**

(3) **Research Micah to learn more about his historical context and prophecies. Write in your spiritual journal about how his prophecies still speak to you today.**

❖ Sing or read aloud "What Does the Lord Require," which is based on Micah 6:6-8.

❖ Invite the students to say this benediction, based on Micah 6:8, to conclude the session: **The Lord requires me to do justice, and to love kindness, and to walk humbly with my God. Let it be as you have said, Lord.**

UNIT 2: WHAT DOES GOD REQUIRE?
GETTING READY FOR JUDGMENT

PREVIEWING THE LESSON

Lesson Scripture: Zephaniah 3:1-5, 8-9
Background Scripture: Zephaniah 3:1-13; 2 Chronicles 34:1-3
Key Verse: Zephaniah 3:8

Focus of the Lesson:
People sometimes act wrongly without thinking of the consequences to themselves or others. What consequences result when God's people act wrongly? Zephaniah says that God will act justly, bringing both punishment and redemption.

Goals for the Learners:
(1) to discover Zephaniah's teachings on God's justice.
(2) to reflect on what difference God's justice makes for their faith life.
(3) to be aware of and take responsibility for the consequences of their own actions.

Pronunciation Guide:
mishpat (mish' pat)
qereb (keh' reb)
shama (shaw mah')
Zephaniah (zef uh ni' uh)

Supplies:
Bibles, newsprint and marker, paper and pencils, hymnals, picture of a statue of Lady Justice or Blind Justice

READING THE SCRIPTURE

NRSV
Zephaniah 3:1-5, 8-9
¹ Ah, soiled, defiled,
    oppressing city!
² It has listened to no voice;
    it has accepted no correction.

NIV
Zephaniah 3:1-5, 8-9
¹Woe to the city of oppressors,
    rebellious and defiled!
²She obeys no one,
    she accepts no correction.

It has not trusted in the LORD;
   it has not drawn near to its God.
³ The officials within it
   are roaring lions;
its judges are evening wolves
   that leave nothing until the morning.
⁴ Its prophets are reckless,
   faithless persons;
its priests have profaned what is sacred,
   they have done violence to the law.
⁵ The LORD within it is righteous;
   he does no wrong.
Every morning he renders his judgment,
   each dawn without fail;
but the unjust knows no shame.
⁸ Therefore wait for me, says the LORD,
   for the day when I arise as a witness.
For my decision is to gather nations,
   to assemble kingdoms,
to pour out upon them my indignation,
   all the heat of my anger;
for in the fire of my passion
   all the earth shall be consumed.
⁹ At that time I will change the speech of the
      peoples
   to a pure speech,
that all of them may call on the name of
      the LORD
   and serve him with one accord.

She does not trust in the LORD,
   she does not draw near to her God.
³Her officials are roaring lions,
   her rulers are evening wolves,
   who leave nothing for the morning.
⁴Her prophets are arrogant;
   they are treacherous men.
Her priests profane the sanctuary
   and do violence to the law.
⁵The LORD within her is righteous;
   he does no wrong.
Morning by morning he dispenses his
      justice,
   and every new day he does not fail,
   yet the unrighteous know no shame.
⁸Therefore wait for me," declares the LORD,
   "for the day I will stand up to testify.
I have decided to assemble the nations,
   to gather the kingdoms
and to pour out my wrath on them—
   all my fierce anger.
The whole world will be consumed
   by the fire of my jealous anger.
⁹"Then will I purify the lips of the peoples,
   that all of them may call on the name of
      the LORD
   and serve him shoulder to shoulder."

UNDERSTANDING THE SCRIPTURE

Zephaniah 3:1-2. The opening verse depicts "the city" (Jerusalem) with a triad of accusations: soiled, defiled, oppressing. "Soiled" in Hebrew also carries the sense of "rebellious." "Defiled" suggests the way in which sacredness has been abused. "Oppressing" reflects the state of inequities decried by Zephaniah and other prophets. The second verse continues with a devastating summary of what failings have created those conditions: not listened, not accepted correction, not trusted, not drawn near to God. "Listened" translates *shama*, whose meaning in Hebrew is not only to hear but

to obey. Placing *shama* at the head of this list reflects its centrality to this crisis in particular and to its fundamental role in Judaism (Deuteronomy 6:4). The text attributes these (in)actions to the city, the center of Judah's religious and political and social life. Judgment looms because of these failings at the core.

Zephaniah 3:3-4. As the prophet used a group of four in the previous verses, so now does Zephaniah use the structure of a "quartet" to condemn the leadership of Judah. Officials, judges, prophets, and priests form an umbrella of leadership over all areas of life. Officials and judges deal with the ruling of the nation and the application of its system of justice. As those entrusted with the care and nurture of the people, however, Zephaniah paints them with the image of devouring beasts. "That leave nothing until the morning" suggests the greed and grasping of power that goes unchecked. Prophets ostensibly are those who speak to reform both religious and political powers. The adjectives used to describe them carry the sense of unstable and treacherous, exactly the opposite qualities one would hope for in persons called to stand up and speak truth to power. The priests, whose primary duty is to observe the rituals that honor the sacred, instead profane the holy. Together with the prophets, Zephaniah charges them with the ultimate crime of doing violence to God's Torah.

Zephaniah 3:5. In absolute contrast to the breakdown within the city, Zephaniah lifts up God who is "within it." The Hebrew word *qereb* literally means "in the midst." This word will play a key role in the remainder of this chapter (see verses 11, 12, and 17). The imagery of "morning" and "dawn" is more than a poetic device expressive of the newness God brings. In Israelite society of this time, morning served as the time when persons seeking judgment or rulings would go to the gates (or city center) and plead their cases before the judges. Zephaniah has already made clear the sort of justice available there, by depicting the judges as "evening wolves." Here, God's justice (*mishpat*) is rendered every morning without fail, in marked opposition to the instability and injustice of what threatens to bring Jerusalem and Judah to ruin.

Zephaniah 3:6-7. Israel does not stand alone under God's judgment. Verse 6 graphically describes this judgment of nations. Verse 7 indicates such actions have intended to bring "the city" (once again, Jerusalem and with it Judah) back into covenant. "Correction," a word from the

Hebrew wisdom tradition that involves instruction to a new way, is the same word that occurred in 3:2. As in that verse, however, the result here is negative. Instead of discerning a call to repentance and trust, the nations' judgment has instead for Judah become even greater motivation to drift further from God and covenant.

Zephaniah 3:8. The consequence of this is judgment, in which Judah joins the nations in what Zephaniah refers to as "the day." Zephaniah's constant reference to "the day of the LORD" throughout this book makes clear that the days as they are now will come to an end, and that coming day will be one of reckoning. There is a textual question in this verse. Is the correct wording "when I arise as a *witness*" (as in the NRSV) or when "I rise up to the *prey* [*to plunder*]" (as in the KJV)? Both manuscript traditions bring a valid perspective. "Witness" sounds the note of God's "suit" against Judah, while "prey" offers a stark and troubling image of God's action. In either case, Zephaniah announces God's decision to loose anger. Whereas the covenant with Noah declared waters would never again destroy the earth, Zephaniah indicates fire will consume the earth. Even passing this off to hyperbole does not remove the disturbing nature of this threat.

Zephaniah 3:9-13. The passage abruptly shifts from judgment to hope. Revisiting the imagery of Babel, Zephaniah depicts renewal through a changing of speech. The purpose? "That all of them may call on the name of the LORD." The name of God given to Moses at the burning bush had been a gift and sign of God's deliverance. To call on God becomes the image of hope in Zephaniah for a people who return to their roots in covenant. The mention of Ethiopia in verse 10 raises an interesting issue. The book's first chapter identified the prophet as "Zephaniah son of Cushi." Cush was an ancient term for Africa, leading some scholars to conjecture this prophet was of African descent. Solomon's ties to Sheba and Acts' later story of the Ethiopian eunuch make clear such connections are not at all unlikely. Here, Zephaniah links the return of the remnant from beyond the rivers of Ethiopia. The image may serve not only as a poetic device for "far places," but as a referent from the prophet's own heritage. (See *The New Interpreter's Bible*, volume 7, "Zephaniah," page 699, for further exploration of this theme). The "remnant" will play a key role in how the prophets discern hope in the face of judgment. The closing word that "no one shall make them afraid" mirrors affirmations made in Jeremiah 30:10, Ezekiel 34:28, and Micah 4:4.

2 Chronicles 34:1-3. Did Zephaniah's prophesying have an effect? The beginning of his book associates him with the reign of Josiah. Josiah was one of Judah's last kings, whose efforts at reform after finding a lost scroll (some say Deuteronomy) may have been abetted by the urgings of Zephaniah.

INTERPRETING THE SCRIPTURE

The Coming Day

"The day of the Lord." As noted in the commentary in verse 8, Zephaniah repeatedly asserts this image of impending judgment. We might think that those who carry on about the coming of that day in our time are limited to end-time fanatics or devotees of the "left behind" novels. But every time we offer the Lord's Prayer, we pray for the coming of God's kingdom or realm. We pray for the day of God to come.

"The day is coming." The urgency of such words can be undercut by their delay. When such days do not immediately come, we are tempted to assume they never will. Science has repeatedly warned of global warming related to ozone depletions. But since we do not see it now, today, many people pass it off as alarmism. That is not a new thing. When Ezekiel brought a message similar to Zephaniah's, the people put it off with this: "The vision that he sees is for many years ahead; he prophesies for distant times" (Ezekiel 12:27b).

People who live only in the present have a tendency to dismiss the future. That is particularly true for people, and institutions, who enjoy power and privilege. Why change things? In fact, why not do everything possible to ensure the maintenance of that status quo, no matter the cost to others

or the future? The problem with that thinking is, God is God of the future as much as the present and past. God's day will come.

Is "the day of the Lord" a word of hope or judgment? Clearly, Zephaniah uses its invocation to summon repentance from actions and attitudes that jeopardize covenant. In a society corrupted by abuse of power and disregard for the vulnerable, that coming day cannot help but levy a word of warning. But for those who yearn for God's realm and its justice and compassion, the "day of God" bears the hope of God's future. Faithfulness takes shape in living our lives and reforming our institutions in the light of that coming day and realm.

General System Failure

I have endured my share of computer glitches, ranging from screens momentarily frozen to documents lost. I dread the day experienced by friends whose hard drive crashed because of some general systems failure. For the prophet Zephaniah, Judah's political and religious "systems" verge on crashing. As you listen to those words in verses 2-4, the extent of the "general systems failure" becomes apparent. All authority—civil, religious, judicial, even those whose very purpose is to reform—has been corrupted. The potential correctives to this system—listening, accepting, trusting, drawing near—have been rejected. Zephaniah understands the depth of the problem. Judgment cannot be deterred.

Well, too bad for them, we might think. They should have known better.

But do we? Zephaniah's pronouncements on the failure of Israel's systems intends to invite our own considerations of how such things go in our time. Does political authority seek to serve the common good, or guarantee its own continuity? Does social authority work tirelessly to watch over the vulnerable among us—or to ensure the privilege of the privileged? Is the witness of the church to Micah's timeless formula of doing justice, loving kindness, and walking humbly with God—or do we exhaust ourselves in pointing fingers at who does or doesn't belong in pews or pulpits?

Zephaniah spoke then that we might speak now. His unceasing word about "the day of the LORD" serves as a reminder that all of our days stand under the judgment—and grace—of God. His inclusion of officials and judges along with priests and prophets insists not only that power comes with responsibility, both inside and outside the church. Beyond that, Zephaniah insists that the witness of the faith community can never be limited to life within the sanctuary. Our concern is with the whole of life, for that life and creation are gifts of God entrusted into human hands. To deny the stewardship of that trust misses the truth of our vocation as the people of God.

Getting to the Core

"The LORD *within* it is righteous . . . I will remove *from your midst* your proudly exultant ones . . . I will leave *in the midst* of you a people humble and lowly . . . The LORD, your God, is in your midst" (Zephaniah 3:5, 11, 12, 17, italics added).

In every one of those verses, the Hebrew word *qereb* occurs to point at what forms the core of both judgment and hope.

Zephaniah identifies the core of judgment in those to be removed: "your proudly exultant ones." In the Hebrew Scriptures, in the Gospels and Epistles, in the theological traditions that derive from all those writings, few sins rival that of pride. Indeed, some argue that pride serves as the foundation for all others. Pride here is not the legitimate valuing of self-worth that belongs to every human being and race. If it were, why would Jesus predicate love of neighbor on love of self? No, the pride condemned by prophets and Christ involves that inordinate valuing of self above all others. Religions as much as nations may fall victim to pride's blinders of self-centered importance. And a society anchored in pride, as Zephaniah understood, is on a collision course with humiliation. Or as Proverbs once put it, "Pride goes before destruction, and a haughty spirit before a fall" (Proverbs 16:18)

Zephaniah identifies the core of hope in those who will be left: "a people humble and lowly . . . the remnant of Israel" (3:12, 13). Even though judgment comes, it will not be total. Out of this breakdown of life and community created by the breaking of covenant, a new beginning will arise from a new spirit among God's people: humility and lowliness. Sometimes, church and society have imposed such qualities upon individuals or groups already stripped of power or voice or standing. We can be very good at telling subordinates to be humble, and bypass the CEOs. Humility and lowliness, however, are not burdens to be borne by folks who have nothing else to hope in. They are intended to be qualities of spirit exercised by the whole community. They are the necessary correctives to the pride and haughtiness that values and trusts only self. So where do the lowly and humble find genuine cause for hope and trust?

Zephaniah answers: The God who is in our midst, the Holy One who is righteous. The renewal of our lives and communities awaits centering our lives in the God who is among us. In the church, the meaning of "God among us" (the Hebrew word for that is *Immanuel*) takes shape in Jesus Christ. Which means, among other things, that we find the model for our living God-infused lives in the life and ministry of Jesus. If we would follow Jesus, we will find ourselves among those same ones where Jesus exercised—and received—ministry. The poor, the outcasts, the religious, the not-so-pious, men and women. God is still in our midst—if only our eyes might see, if only our spirits might be opened to "call on the name of the LORD and serve him with one accord" (Zephaniah 3:9).

SHARING THE SCRIPTURE

PREPARING TO TEACH

Preparing Our Hearts

This week's devotional reading is found in Psalm 27:7-14. In this song of confidence ascribed to David, he seeks God's attention and guidance. Read these verses aloud as if you are speaking to God yourself. What do you need from God today? Take time now to offer a silent prayer or to write a prayer in your spiritual journal. Sit quietly and meditate, waiting for a word from God. Once you discern that this is God's word for you, how will you respond?

Pray that you and the adult learners will rely on the God of your salvation.

Preparing Our Minds

Study the background Scripture in Zephaniah 3:1-13 and 2 Chronicles 34:1-3. This week's lesson Scripture is Zephaniah 3:1-5, 8-9. As you ponder this session, think about the consequences that may result when God's people act wrongly.

Write on newsprint:
- ❏ questions for small group discussion under "Discover Zephaniah's Teachings on God's Justice."
- ❏ information for next week's lesson, found under "Continue the Journey."
- ❏ activities for further spiritual growth in "Continue the Journey."

Find a picture of "Lady Justice," also known as "Blind Justice," in a book or on the Internet.

LEADING THE CLASS

(1) Gather to Learn

❖ Welcome the class members and introduce any guests.

❖ Pray that those who have chosen to participate today will make a renewed commitment to live according to God's will and way.

❖ Talk with the class about relatively recent scandals affecting politicians or business leaders. Consider questions such as: **What happened to cause the problem? Who was hurt by the actions? What were the consequences to those who were hurt and to those whose actions created the problem?**

❖ Read aloud today's focus statement: **People sometimes act wrongly without thinking of the consequences to themselves or others. What consequences result when God's people act wrongly? Zephaniah says that God will act justly, bringing both punishment and redemption.**

(2) Discover Zephaniah's Teachings on God's Justice

❖ Enlist a volunteer to read Zephaniah 3:1-5, 8-9.

❖ Discuss these questions, or use them as the basis for a lecture. You will find information in Understanding the Scripture to help you.

(1) **What accusations does Zephaniah level against Jerusalem?** (See verses 1-2.)

(2) **What kind of picture does the writer paint concerning the leadership of the city?** (See verses 3-4.)

(3) **How is this picture in keeping with what you would expect, or is it surprising to you? Why?**

(4) **How does the Lord's presence in Jerusalem contrast with the behavior of the leaders Zephaniah has called to task?** (See verses 5, 8-9.)

(5) **How does God propose to handle the corruption that has been described?** (See verses 8-9.)

(6) **Recalling the image of Babel, verse 9 speaks of a time when God will make it possible for everyone to understand each other's speech. What do you think God's purpose is for taking this action?**

❖ Invite the class to read today's key verse, Zephaniah 3:8, in unison.

❖ Divide the class into small groups to discuss these questions, which you may want to write on newsprint.

(1) **How does the idea of God's judgment fit into your own understanding of the nature of God?**

(2) **How does judgment relate to justice?**

❖ Sum up today's Scripture lesson with this quotation from Thomas à Kempis (about 1380–1471): **You can be certain of this: when the Day of Judgment comes, we shall not be asked what we have read, but what we have done; not how well we have spoken, but how well we have lived.**

❖ Discuss this question: **How does à Kempis' idea about Judgment Day compare to or contrast with Zephaniah's**

understanding of why judgment will occur?

(3) Reflect on What Difference God's Justice Makes for the Learners' Faith Life

❖ Point out that as a prophet Zephaniah was seeing the world as it was and comparing it to how it should and could be if people were faithful to their covenant with God.

❖ Show a picture (or small statue) of "Lady Justice," also known as "Blind Justice," a famous statue depicting justice as a blindfolded woman who holds the scales in balance. Talk about how the students interpret the meaning of this statue. Also consider how this statue might relate to the judgments God makes on behalf of justice.

❖ Ask this question: **What difference does it make to your faith life to believe that God judges and is also just?**

(4) Be Aware of and Take Responsibility for the Consequences of Personal Actions

❖ Point out that part of the problem Zephaniah identifies among the leaders of Jerusalem is that they have failed to take the kind of responsibility for their actions that would bar them from acting unjustly.

❖ Distribute paper and pencils. Encourage the students to write a brief summary of an incident when they acted unjustly, perhaps due to the race, gender, age, or some other artificial divider between themselves and the person who experienced the injustice. Note that for someone to act unjustly he or she need not have a great deal of political power. Consequently, "ordinary" people can act with injustice just as dictators can. Here are a few examples: treating a store clerk in a demeaning manner, treating an older adult as if he or she were incompetent or unimportant, using an unfair of amount of natural resources, or abusing power in the home or workplace. Tell the adults that they will not be asked to share what they have written.

❖ Ask the students to think about the incident they have described and silently listen for a response from God. Suggest these questions for contemplation: **Why is this incident displeasing to God? How did you grow as a result of this incident? What further changes does God expect you to make?**

❖ Invite volunteers to report on any insights they gained through meditative listening that would be of general use to the class.

(5) Continue the Journey

❖ Pray that today's attendees will live so as to be ready for "the day of the LORD."

❖ Read aloud this preparation for next week's lesson. You may also want to post it on newsprint for the students to copy. **Prepare for next week's session entitled "A Reason to Hope" by reading Habakkuk 2:1-20 and 2 Kings 23:35-37. Our class time will focus on Habakkuk 2:6-14. Concentrate on these ideas as you study: When all seems wrong in the world or in their lives, people want a reason to hope. What reasons do we have to hope during such situations? Habakkuk's response is that the God who will not tolerate injustice is the same God who works for our salvation, and this is the source of our hope.**

❖ Read aloud the following three ideas. Challenge the students to commit themselves to use these activities as a springboard to spiritual growth.

(1) **Be aware of your actions this week. Did you act impulsively, cause someone physical or emotional harm, or act unjustly in some other way? How can Zephaniah's words about judgment on "the day of the LORD" help you to control your actions?**

(2) **Examine your behavior this week to see how you would rate yourself on a Justice Scale. Did you, for example, speak up for people who are being oppressed? Did you refrain from purchasing items made or sold by persons who do not receive fair wages? Have you acted with righteousness? If not, what changes will you make?**

(3) **Offer intercessory prayers for those who are victims of injustice and those who perpetrate injustice. Ask God to lead you to help bring about greater justice.**

❖ Sing or read aloud "We Are Called," which is found in *The Faith We Sing*.

❖ Invite the students to say this benediction, based on Micah 6:8, to conclude the session: **The Lord requires me to do justice, and to love kindness, and to walk humbly with my God. Let it be as you have said, Lord.**

UNIT 2: WHAT DOES GOD REQUIRE?
A REASON TO HOPE

PREVIEWING THE LESSON

Lesson Scripture: Habakkuk 2:6-14
Background Scripture: Habakkuk 2:1-20; 2 Kings 23:35-37
Key Verse: Habakkuk 2:14

Focus of the Lesson:
When all seems wrong in the world or in their lives, people want a reason to hope. What reasons do we have to hope during such situations? Habakkuk's response is that the God who will not tolerate injustice is the same God who works for our salvation, and this is the source of our hope.

Goals for the Learners:
(1) to explore Habakkuk's teachings on hope.
(2) to identify situations in which they have put their hope in God.
(3) to renew their hope in God.

Pronunciation Guide:
emunah (em oo naw')   Habakkuk (huh bak' uhk)
Jehoahaz (ji hoh' uh haz)   Jehoiakim (ji hoi' uh kim)
Neco (nee' koh)

Supplies:
Bibles, newsprint and marker, hymnals

READING THE SCRIPTURE

NRSV
Habakkuk 2:6-14

⁶Shall not everyone taunt such people and, with mocking riddles, say about them,
  "Alas for you who heap up what is not
    your own!"
How long will you load yourselves with
  goods taken in pledge?

NIV
Habakkuk 2:6-14

⁶"Will not all of them taunt him with ridicule and scorn, saying,
  " 'Woe to him who piles up stolen goods
    and makes himself wealthy by extortion!
  How long must this go on?'
⁷Will not your debtors suddenly arise?

7 Will not your own creditors suddenly rise,
and those who make you tremble wake
up?
Then you will be booty for them.
8 Because you have plundered many
nations,
all that survive of the peoples shall
plunder you—
because of human bloodshed, and
violence to the earth,
to cities and all who live in them.
9 "Alas for you who get evil gain for your
houses,
setting your nest on high
to be safe from the reach of harm!"
10 You have devised shame for your house
by cutting off many peoples;
you have forfeited your life.
11 The very stones will cry out from the wall,
and the plaster will respond from the
woodwork.
12 "Alas for you who build a town by
bloodshed,
and found a city on iniquity!"
13 Is it not from the LORD of hosts
that peoples labor only to feed the
flames,
and nations weary themselves for
nothing?
14 But the earth will be filled
with the knowledge of the glory of the
LORD,
as the waters cover the sea.

Will they not wake up and make you
tremble?
Then you will become their victim.
8 Because you have plundered many nations,
the peoples who are left will plunder
you.
For you have shed man's blood;
you have destroyed lands and cities and
everyone in them.
9 "Woe to him who builds his realm by
unjust gain
to set his nest on high,
to escape the clutches of ruin!
10 You have plotted the ruin of many peoples,
shaming your own house and forfeiting
your life.
11 The stones of the wall will cry out,
and the beams of the woodwork will
echo it.
12 "Woe to him who builds a city with
bloodshed
and establishes a town by crime!
13 Has not the LORD Almighty determined
that the people's labor is only fuel for the
fire,
that the nations exhaust themselves for
nothing?
14 For the earth will be filled with the
knowledge of the glory of the LORD,
as the waters cover the sea."

UNDERSTANDING THE SCRIPTURE

Habakkuk 2:1-3. The prophet's "complaint" alludes back to two questions raised in chapter 1 regarding the delay in God's response (1:2) and God's seeming indifference in the face of evil (1:13). Some suggest the conditions evoking these questions have to do with Babylon's strong-handed quashing of Judah's rebellion and initial deportation of Jewish leaders in 597 B.C. The meaning of writing the vision plain enough so that a "runner" may read it eludes precise answers. It may have to do with words large enough to be read by those who flee from the invading armies. Or, it may have to do with the ancient practice of sending a runner (or prophet, see Jeremiah 23:21) to bring news. In the case of this text, plainly writing the vision for a runner would be so that God's messenger(s) will make no mistake about the word God brings concerning patience and certainty.

Habakkuk 2:4-5. The first half of verse 4 is muddled by a difficult text in Hebrew. However translated, it intends to contrast the "proud" or "lifted up" with the righteous (or just) who live by faith. Few isolated verses in the Hebrew Scripture play such a vital role as does verse 4 in later Christian theology. Paul quotes this verse in both Romans 1:17 and Galatians 3:11 to build his case that we are justified by faith. The Hebrew word translated here as "faith" (*emunah*) connotes far more than intellectual assent. Rather, it involves a steadiness and loyalty in commitment. The contrast with the proud suggests the righteous are those who stand firm by trusting relationship and covenant with God, rather than an inflated opinion of self-importance.

Habakkuk 2:6-8. Here begins a series of five declarations of "Alas" (*hoy* is a Hebrew interjection used to express warning or sorrow). Such a list has parallels in both the Hebrew Scripture (Isaiah 5:8-23) and the New Testament (Luke 6:24-26). Verse 6 raises the specter that those who practice the ensuing breaches of covenant and community will become object lessons for all to see (the Hebrew here uses words otherwise translated as "parable" and "proverb," see KJV). "Goods taken in pledge" ("stolen goods" in the NIV) translates an unusual word that can mean both "heavy pledges" or "thick clay or mire." The image suggests the very things sought after will become the things that bog them down. "Violence" (2:8) appears with frequency in this book, underscoring the dangerous context of the times.

Habakkuk 2:9-11. The second "alas" identifies those who seek security for themselves while denying it to others. "Evil" and "harm" in verse 9 translate the same Hebrew word, asserting the hypocrisy of profiting from the very kinds of actions they would avoid suffering themselves. "House" and "nest" bring strong images of domestic life. In that era, the association of height with security arose from such places being more defensible. The folly of trying to achieve such immunity by living "above" the clamor becomes clear in verse 11. The very stones crying out from the wall at such injustice parallels Genesis 4:10-11, where the earth cries out at Abel's murder by Cain.

Habakkuk 2:12-13. The third "alas" indicts the building of town and community on violence done to others. Such exercises of power prove deceptive in their staying power. The text infers that such foundations and those who carry them out will come to nothing.

Habakkuk 2:14. The waters covering the sea recall the status of all things at the moment of creation (Genesis 1:1). God's new act of creation will be filling the earth with knowledge of the glory of God. That linkage of filling and God's glory occurs in other key passages. When Moses furnishes the tabernacle with the ark and other elements, Exodus 40:34 declares God's glory filled the tabernacle. When Solomon consecrates the temple, 1 Kings 8:11 reveals God's glory fills the house. The promise of Habakkuk is for God's glory, the sign of God's presence and leading, to fill now the whole earth. It anticipates the vision of Revelation 21:3 (and following), where God's presence will fill and fashion a new heaven and a new earth.

Habakkuk 2:15-17. The fourth "Alas" condemns those who take advantage of neighbors and make them vulnerable. That this judgment has more in mind than simply using intoxicants to take such advantage is made clear by verse 17. Underlying the abuse is violence that has been done. The second half of verse 17 repeats the indictment of verse 8b.

Habakkuk 2:18-19. The fifth and final "alas" ridicules those whose trust (contrast the "righteous" in verse 4) is in human-fashioned idols. The folly of such effort is captured in, "its maker trusts in what has been made." It is a self-enclosed circle that leads nowhere.

Habakkuk 2:20. In contrast to the silence of the idols, the Holy God of Israel summons silence, not only from the faithful, but from the whole earth. It is the silence of awe and respect and authority, not unlike a later "silencing" of the storm in Mark 4:39. The scene may picture the "appointed time" of verse 3, which evokes faithful waiting for the vision that will surely come. In spite of all the turmoil of these times in which Habakkuk writes, in spite of all those who claim thrones of power political and religious: God will stand in the temple, and the whole earth will respond with reverence. The future has been named.

2 Kings 23:35-37. Verse 34 indicated how the Pharaoh Neco had installed Jehoiakim as king of Judah. Egypt and Babylon engaged in a power struggle in the region, and Judah straddled the zone between them. His predecessor Jehoahaz had been pro-Babylonian. As these verses make clear, Jehoiakim toed the line of his Egyptian patron. What remained of Judah's wealth, Jehoiakim paid in a steady stream of protection money to Neco. Verse 37 reveals the pressing issue that would undo Jehoiakim's efforts to obtain security: his covenant unfaithfulness. The next chapter in this book relates Jehoiakim's end in an unsuccessful rebellion against Babylon.

INTERPRETING THE SCRIPTURE

Watching and Hoping for an Answer

The book of Habakkuk begins with questions raised by the prophet to God: how long? (1:2); is this fair? (1:13); where does this end? (1:17). And then Habakkuk stands on the watchtower of the city, in full view of the crisis unfolding, and announces that he watches for God's answer.

Habakkuk is not the only one who has stood there. Parents with a child in an emergency room, stricken with some undeserved illness or accident. Residents of a city, watching towers collapse upon people who just went to work, or who just went to help. How long? Is this fair? Where does this end?

To be fully human is to engage those questions—like Habakkuk, like Job—when things unthinkable and unjust come our way. To raise such complaints is not a denial of faith. Rather, it is an act of trust that we do not speak into an empty void, and that beyond our eyesight and very likely our full understanding is some abiding purpose and unswerving love. In other words, to question and lament is to trade in the risky business of hope.

In reflecting on this text, *The New Interpreter's Bible* quoted a line from Wendell Berry's "Manifesto: The Mad Farmer Liberation Front," which appears in his *Collected Poems:* "Be joyful though you have considered all the facts." Hope can never rest content with the mere "facts" of appearances and passing realities. Habakkuk's perch on the tower may well have offered a view of Babylon's armies converging on the city. Those were the "facts" of the day that would have emptied hope. But hope sees beyond the collection of immediate data, then and now, to perceive greater purposes and deeper ends than what may be apparent at the moment.

That is why the righteous are said to live by "faith," rather than by conventional wisdom or self-congratulating arrogance. Faith trusts, faith waits on, faith works for the vision of God's sovereign realm that is our hope.

Problems at the Core

Scholars debate whether the five statements of "alas" are aimed at Judean breaches of covenant, or Babylonian abuses of power, or whether the former gives opportunity to critique the latter. What is clear, however, is a common theme to these indictments. For in every case, they strip community of life by concentrating power in a privileged few. Greed hoards to self what has been intended for all. "Survival first" grasps to guarantee the safety of me and mine no matter who suffers as a result. Building up one's own place justifies the ruination of other's places. Maintaining control and power over others makes taking advantage of and even exacerbating their vulnerability fair game. Fashioning the god we will serve, rather than serving the God who has fashioned us, attempts to put us at the center of the universe—which is, in truth, what the previous four actions intend to do.

The problems Habakkuk indicts have a long shelf life. Whether in the comparison of CEO compensation packages to those of ordinary wage earners in the same company, or in the distribution of wealth between the richest and poorest, haves continue to have more.

Programs to provide social safety nets suffer from attitudes that neglect how others fare, so long as I am safe and insulated. Political campaigns routinely build foundations for election through a scorched earth policy waged on an opponent's character. Marketing practices regularly transform wants into needs in order to intoxicate consumers. And idolatry? Forget about those antiquated wooden statues. The gods we make these days are the allegiances we demand of ourselves and others that answer to no higher authority than our own reason...or prejudice.

Habakkuk named the problems in his day to ensure hope does not get placed where it does not deserve. The church finds its calling to such truth-telling ministry in order to distinguish hope from wishful thinking and unbridled self-interest.

What Goes Around Comes Around

It is a curious thing in this list of actions indicted: Consequences flow directly from the practices. Those who have hoarded from others will be plundered. Those who have fashioned and fled to supposed sanctuaries will have the very walls of those hiding places shouting out their sin. Those who go to great lengths to make a place for themselves at the expense of others will find that place turn to nothing. Those who abuse the vulnerability of neighbors will experience the terror of vulnerability. Those who would make gods in their own image will be left with a conversation partner devoid of speech and breath. And remember: In the Biblical witness, the speech of God calls creation into being, while the breath of God enlivens us.

But what have these judgments to do with hope?

In the opinion of the writer, they accomplish two things. First, they establish a sense of poetic justice in these texts. To people who cause suffering under the kinds of systems decried by Habakkuk, the word needs to be said: This cannot stand. The mercy of God does not mean God's tolerance of any old thing under the sun. Acts have consequences. And it is not as if God must serve as the executor of such a "will." The consequences described by Habakkuk simply grow out of the lifestyles and attitudes depicted in the "alas" statements.

Second, if this word is heard, it sets up the possibility of repentance and the hope of change. People who do not think something is wrong are not liable to seek an alternative. Does that mean Habakkuk succeeded in such a purpose? The record for his time shades toward, "not greatly." But we do not live in Habakkuk's time. We live in ours. We choose in ours. And the church is still called to speak such words to open the possibility of repentance and the hope of change. For God has neither given up on us nor said "anything goes"; God must still seek renewal and transformation.

God's Glory and Our Hope

"God's glory" provides a fitting image to close this text and these comments on hope. As noted in the commentary on this phrase in Understanding the Scripture the "filling" of God's glory has precedent, first in the wilderness tabernacle and then in the Jerusalem temple. God's presence, which is meaning of God's glory, fills those places. But now, hope takes shape in God's glory filling the whole earth. No longer will the Holy Presence be revealed (or limited!) to a particular sanctuary. The future holds the promise of God's presence manifested throughout creation. It is a rich promise of hope for days to come.

But what of these days? How might that hope find translation into lives and ministries beyond a fond expectation of this verse coming to pass?

When the people traveled through the wilderness, it was the cloud associated with God's glory they followed. God's glory does not only signify the "otherness" of God— God's glory is God's choosing to reveal God's presence and way to those who would follow.

A day when that presence and leading will fill the earth is a vision that intends to spur our following in its way in these days. We need not wait until then to discern God's presence in our midst: leading, guiding, instilling hope that the way we follow this day leads ultimately to the glory of God.

SHARING THE SCRIPTURE

PREPARING TO TEACH

Preparing Our Hearts

This week's devotional reading is found in Psalm 37:27-34. Psalm 37 is an acrostic (letters in Hebrew alphabet used in sequence) designed to instruct readers to be patient and trust in God. As such, it fits into the wisdom tradition. The psalmist, purportedly David, assures that God will "cut off" evildoers but "keep safe forever" those who are righteous and just. What promises does God make to those who are righteous? What reasons does this psalm give you to hope? Write in your spiritual journal about how you feel God is speaking to you through this psalm.

Pray that you and the adult learners will put your hope and trust in God.

Preparing Our Minds

Study the background Scripture from Habakkuk 2:1-20 and 2 Kings 23:35-37. This week's lesson Scripture is Habakkuk 2:6-14. As you read, think about why you have rea-

sons to hope even when all seems wrong in the world or in your own life.

Write on newsprint:
- ❏ these headings, one per sheet: "Political Injustice," "Social/Economic Injustice" for "Gather to Learn."
- ❏ information for next week's lesson, found under "Continue the Journey."
- ❏ activities for further spiritual growth in "Continue the Journey."

Prepare the lecture and readings you will use for "Explore Habakkuk's Teachings on Hope."

LEADING THE CLASS

(1) Gather to Learn

❖ Welcome the class members and introduce any guests.

❖ Pray that those who have come today will find hope even in the midst of challenging circumstances.

❖ Post two sheets of newsprint, one with the heading "Political Injustice," and the other labeled "Social/Economic Injustice." Encourage the students to brainstorm examples apropos each of these headings. These examples may relate to situations anywhere in the world. You may want to divide the class in half and give each group one sheet of newsprint and a marker.

❖ Talk about why the situations the groups/class have identified may cause people to lose hope.

❖ Read aloud today's focus statement: **When all seems wrong in the world or in their lives, people want a reason to hope. What reasons do we have to hope during such situations? Habakkuk's response is that the God who will not tolerate injustice is the same God who works for our salvation, and this is the source of our hope.**

(2) Explore Habakkuk's Teachings on Hope

❖ Choose someone to read Habakkuk 2:6-14.

❖ Use information for verses 6-8, 9-11, 12-13, 14 in Understanding the Scripture to explain the words and images of today's passage in a brief lecture.

❖ Note that our lesson Scripture includes the three "alas" statements found in Habakkuk 2:6, 9, 12. Point out that there are two additional "alas" statements in verses 15 and 19, for a total of five words of "woe."

❖ Read the first paragraph of "What Goes Around Comes Around" in Interpreting the Scripture.

❖ Ask: **How do these judgments relate to today's theme of hope?** (Hear the students' responses and/or use paragraphs three and four of the same section to augment the discussion. Or, if you prefer, use this information in a lecture.)

❖ Invite the students to read in unison today's key verse, 2:14.

■ Read aloud the first, second, and third paragraphs of "God's Glory and Our Hope."

■ Invite the students to imagine what the earth would be like when all people are able to discern God's presence—"the glory of the LORD." Discuss how the world would be different then. Think especially about how the reign of God will set right injustice.

■ Encourage the students to talk about how the images they have envisioned give them hope.

(3) Renew Hope in God

❖ Encourage the students to relax and envision themselves in the situations you will read aloud to them. Be sure to pause to allow them time to think.

■ **Imagine yourself in an unfair situation as a child or teenager when someone powerful was causing you to feel hopeless. Who do you see? A schoolyard bully? An insensitive teacher? An overbearing coach?** (Pause)

■ **Replay in your mind a specific event with this person that was especially difficult for you.** (Pause)

■ **Recall how this situation affected you then. Also explore how this challenge might have affected your growth toward maturity.** (Pause)

■ **Think now of a current or recent situation that also seems unfair. What can your childhood situation teach you about how to handle this?** (Pause)

■ **Renew your hope that God's justice will prevail in this situation by offering a silent prayer for guidance. Open your eyes when you feel ready.** (Pause)

❖ Provide an opportunity for participants to tell a partner any insights that emerged from this activity.

(4) Share with Others That God Is the Source of Hope

❖ Choose one or both of the following situations, which you will need to read aloud, for volunteers to role-play.

■ **Scenario 1: Volunteer 1 was the victim of an armed robbery. He (she) tells Volunteer 2 how hope in God got him (her) through this terrifying ordeal and has enabled him (her) to forgive the attacker. Volunteer 2, who does not have that hope, asks Volunteer 1 about how and why hope is possible in such an unjust and harrowing situation.**

■ **Scenario 2: A strong belief that God is able to bring about justice motivated Volunteer 3 to participate in a nonviolent march to protest against an unjust, oppressive action against the poor. Volunteer 4 wants to know more about the hope Volunteer 3 has that enables him (her) to believe that God will act with justice and to respond courageously on that belief.**

❖ Talk with the class after the role-plays about how hope in God enables people to act in ways that often require risk and a willingness to go against the tide of popular opinion as to the "right" way to act.

❖ Challenge those who will commit themselves to sharing with at least one other person this week their belief in God's ultimate reign of justice to raise their hands.

(5) Continue the Journey

❖ Pray that the participants will live in the hope that God's justice will ultimately prevail.

❖ Read aloud this preparation for next week's lesson. You may also want to post it on newsprint for the students to copy. **Prepare for next week's session entitled "Your Actions, Your Consequences" by reading Jeremiah 7:11-15; 2 Kings 23:36-37, both of which are this week's background and lesson Scriptures. Keep these thoughts in mind as you study: Some people act with impunity, believing they will always be protected from the consequences of their actions. Are Christians to have such a view? Jeremiah states that God holds us accountable, so we will not escape the consequences of what we do.**

❖ Read aloud the following three ideas. Challenge the students to commit themselves to use these activities as a springboard to spiritual growth.

(1) **Write a prayer that demonstrates your sense of hope that God's righteousness will prevail. Pray this prayer each day this week.**

(2) **Offer a word of hope to someone who is struggling.**

(3) **Review the three "alas" statements in Habakkuk 2:6, 9, and 12, which refer to punishments for those who have stolen, extorted, and shed blood. Where do you see examples of such behaviors today? What actions can you take to speak out against these behaviors?**

❖ Sing or read aloud "O God, Our Help in Ages Past."

❖ Invite the students to say this benediction, based on Micah 6:8, to conclude the session: **The Lord requires me to do justice, and to love kindness, and to walk humbly with my God. Let it be as you have said, Lord.**

UNIT 2: WHAT DOES GOD REQUIRE?

YOUR ACTIONS, YOUR CONSEQUENCES

PREVIEWING THE LESSON

Lesson Scripture: Jeremiah 7:11-15; 2 Kings 23:36-37
Background Scripture: Jeremiah 7:11-15; 2 Kings 23:36-37
Key Verses: Jeremiah 7:13, 15

Focus of the Lesson:
Some people act with impunity, believing they will always be protected from the consequences of their actions. Are Christians to have such a view? Jeremiah states that God holds us accountable, so we will not escape the consequences of what we do.

Goals for the Learners:
(1) to explore Jeremiah's teaching on accountability for the consequences of what we do.
(2) to relate the Jeremiah text to examples of hypocrisy in the world and their own lives.
(3) to bring their actions into line with their identity as Christians.

Pronunciation Guide:
asah (aw saw')   *bavith* (bah' yith)
Jehoiakim (ji hoi' uh kim)   *paniym* (paw neem')
Pedaiah (pi day' yuh)   *raah* (raw aw')
Rumah (roo' muh)   *shakan* (shaw kan')
Zebidah (zeb bi' duh)

Supplies:
Bibles, newsprint and marker, paper and pencils, hymnals

READING THE SCRIPTURE

NRSV
Jeremiah 7:11-15

¹¹Has this house, which is called by my name, become a den of robbers in your sight? You know, I too am watching, says

NIV
Jeremiah 7:11-15

¹¹Has this house, which bears my Name, become a den of robbers to you? But I have been watching! declares the LORD.

the LORD. ¹²Go now to my place that was in Shiloh, where I made my name dwell at first, and see what I did to it for the wickedness of my people Israel. ¹³And now, **because you have done all these things,** says the LORD, **and when I spoke to you persistently, you did not listen,** and when I called you, you did not answer, ¹⁴therefore I will do to the house that is called by my name, in which you trust, and to the place that I gave to you and to your ancestors, just what I did to Shiloh. ¹⁵And **I will cast you out of my sight,** just as I cast out all your kinsfolk, all the offspring of Ephraim.

2 Kings 23:36-37

³⁶Jehoiakim was twenty-five years old when he began to reign; he reigned eleven years in Jerusalem. His mother's name was Zebidah daughter of Pedaiah of Rumah. ³⁷He did what was evil in the sight of the LORD, just as all his ancestors had done.

¹²" 'Go now to the place in Shiloh where I first made a dwelling for my Name, and see what I did to it because of the wickedness of my people Israel. ¹³**While you were doing all these things, declares the LORD, I spoke to you again and again, but you did not listen;** I called you, but you did not answer. ¹⁴Therefore, what I did to Shiloh I will now do to the house that bears my Name, the temple you trust in, the place I gave to you and your fathers. ¹⁵**I will thrust you from my presence,** just as I did all your brothers, the people of Ephraim.' "

2 Kings 23:36-37

³⁶Jehoiakim was twenty-five years old when he became king, and he reigned in Jerusalem eleven years. His mother's name was Zebidah daughter of Pedaiah; she was from Rumah. ³⁷And he did evil in the eyes of the LORD, just as his fathers had done.

UNDERSTANDING THE SCRIPTURE

Introduction to Jeremiah 7. The entire seventh chapter of Jeremiah along with the first three verses of chapter 8 form what has been called "the temple sermon." The first two verses provide the setting, which gives this narrative its name. Whether the following verses represent an individual event or a compilation of messages, the unit as a whole declares the need of repentance—and the drastic consequences if that is not forthcoming. Underlying the theology of this section is God's freedom/human responsibility in covenant. Continuing breaches of covenant expectations for justice and fidelity will result in the withdrawal of covenant's central promise: the land. Exodus will be reversed by loss of place and return to slavery.

Jeremiah 7:11. The Gospels narrate this verse's echoing in Jesus' own encounter with a corrupted temple culture. Then as for Jeremiah, sacred space goes profaned and devalued by those who use this place to hide greed behind the veil of piety. The word translated as house, *bavith*, carries a multitude of meanings: house, temple, palace. The indictment Jeremiah brings, while spoken at the gate of the temple, is inclusive of the whole of where Judah's "powers that be" dwell. This is not only a religious crisis; it confronts the whole of society. "Watching" (*raah*) translates a word that also carries several meanings: watch, see, provide, and is closely related to the verb meaning "to feed" or "to shepherd." God's watching suggests not only the act of looking, but those acts that will take into account what has been seen and "provide" what is needed.

Jeremiah 7:12. Shiloh was a city north of Bethel in the tribal region of Ephraim. As noted in the "Precedents" section in Interpreting the Scripture, it was an early center of Jewish worship. In the early monarchy period, it also served as a focal point of Saul's reign. This singling out of Shiloh reflects a tradition of destruction also lifted up in Psalm 78:56-72. To speak of it as the place God's name "dwells" (*shakan*, "to tabernacle or settle down") invokes the tradition of God's presence residing in the ark of the covenant. At the end of this verse, Jeremiah asserts the cause for Shiloh's destruction, that parallels that of Psalm 78. It resulted from "wickedness," a familiar phrase in the prophets for disobedience of God and breach of covenant.

Jeremiah 7:13. The prophet shifts focus from the past misdeeds related to Shiloh's fall to the present actions of Judah. "All these things" hearkens back to the previous charges made in 7:8-10. What stands condemned in that list are not only the blatant disregard of fundamental elements of the covenant and Decalogue, but the hypocrisy of then fleeing to this sanctuary and assuming it will bring safety (7:10). Beyond that, this verse brings to light God's repeated attempts to seek change, only to be rebuffed. "Persistently" is found ten times in the NRSV translation of Jeremiah. God persistently sent prophets in hope of change (7:25). God persistently sought obedience in the gift of this promised land (11:7). All to no avail. Limits do get reached. And by the end of 7:13, the unresponsiveness of Judah reaches its height.

Jeremiah 7:14. "The house that is called by my name" repeats the formula in verse 11 for the temple. Beyond that, it makes a fundamental claim. "Naming" among the Semitic people in general and the Israelites in particular brings a sense of power and authority. When Moses receives the holy name of God at the burning bush, the gift of name brings access to calling upon God directly. In that context, the gift of God's name anticipated the exercise of God's

power in deliverance from Egypt. Notice how Jeremiah brings a subtle yet insightful argument about what is lacking in Israel's faith at this juncture. The people's trust, instead of being rooted in the One by whose name this place is called, is indicated to reside in that place. Dynamic relationship has been replaced with attachment to a static place. More than one person has observed the church's tendency to occasionally suffer from an "edifice complex." That is, we become so locked into institutional survival and the maintenance of the *place* we call church that we neglect the relationship that precedes that place. Jeremiah's critique of misplaced trust still resonates when we make such substitutions in our trust and priorities. Once again, Jeremiah reveals that the end of such false confidence can be seen in the example of Shiloh.

Jeremiah 7:15. Jeremiah in this verse interprets what it will mean for Judah to experience Shiloh's destiny: "I will cast you out of my sight." We are not yet at the point of the hope of a remnant. At this point, in a climactic attempt to stir folks from the placidness and pride that has descended, the prophet speaks of Judah being cast off. "Out of my sight" can be read in one of several ways. Remember that this narrative opened with God's "watching," a word not necessarily judgmental. God's watching is also suggestive of God's keeping, of "seeing to us." Judgment here comes in the form and image of being removed from sight. It is as if someone deeply hurt and aggrieved says to the perpetrator: I do not want to see you again. The Hebrew word translated here as "sight" makes this phrase even more stark. *Paniym* literally means "face." The face of God will be turned away from Israel. Recall the phrase of Aaronic blessing in Numbers 6:25-26: "the LORD make his face to shine upon you, and be gracious to you; the LORD lift up his countenance upon you, and give you peace." The face and countenance (both *paniym*) of God, source of

Israel's blessing, will now be withdrawn, their gifts of grace and peace removed.

2 Kings 23:36-37. The successor to Josiah, Judah's last "good" king, is Jehoiakim, who followed his brother Jehoahaz's three-month reign. Jeremiah's sermon is dated to his time, even as the abuses the prophet identifies readily mirror Jehoiakim's reign. For king as for people, actions have consequences.

INTERPRETING THE SCRIPTURE

I Am Watching

The watchfulness of God. Is that image one of threat, an ominous and intrusive looking over our shoulders? Is that image one of comfort, a watchful eye cast over us as a shepherd keeps watch over those entrusted and enfolded for care? I suppose it depends on where you are and what you're doing.

In this text, "I am watching" invokes warning. Actions thought to be concealed from the public's eye are in fact clearly viewed by God. The hypocrisy of those who would hide their misdeeds in the guise of public piety (see 7:10) is a fool's game. God's watchfulness perceives overt actions and covert motivations. Jeremiah intends in that word to trigger a re-forming of those actions and motivations. But if not, that word reveals that ruses of ethics do not avoid the perception of God, and their eventual consequences.

But for those who are vulnerable, who fall victim to such hypocrisy: "I am watching" summons hope. God does see the truth of these matters. God does see those who would otherwise go unseen in their need. And things will change.

That explains partially why the Christian Scripture most associated with the future's overturning of present suffering and inequities, Revelation, is a book of "visions." It is not just that the prophet who writes "sees" things. In those visions, we are led to trust that God sees (and hears) the cries of this world, and responds by refashioning creation so there will be no tears or crying, where pain and death will be no more. God is watching, and out of that sight comes the vision of transformation that serves as our hope and our calling.

Precedents

"Those who cannot learn from history are doomed to repeat it." While the American philosopher George Santayana is credited with this observation, its underlying truth forms the case Jeremiah makes when he points to the precedent of Shiloh. During the eras of conquest under Joshua and tribal leadership described in Judges, Shiloh had been (with Bethel) a chief shrine of Judaism. Most importantly, it served as the resting place of the ark of the covenant until at least the time of Samuel (1 Samuel 1-3; 4:3-4). The ark represented the very presence of God's dwelling in Israel, underscoring the sacredness of this site.

Yet, when Jeremiah writes, the shrine of Shiloh was no more. Centuries before David had replaced it with Jerusalem as the dwelling place of the ark and the center of Judaism's religious life. Even its continuing but diminished role in the northern kingdom of Israel after the division into two kingdoms came to an end with the destruction of Israel by Assyria in 722 B.C.

Jeremiah lifts up Shiloh as warning to Jerusalem, saying in so many words, so it can be with you. The claims of "God with us" and the presence of the temple (see Jeremiah 7:4) cannot guarantee things as they are will always continue to be. Change is needed. And if change is not forthcoming, look to Shiloh.

Jeremiah's words and message still hold meaning. In what do we vest our assumptions of "life will always be as it is"? Some may presume upon national identity, or Christian affiliation. For Jeremiah, for us, the lesson of Shiloh is clear. To ignore the responsibilities of covenant, with God and with one another, puts everything on the table. There are precedents. God grant us to learn from our history, and the history of others, lest we become another generation's Shiloh.

Doings and Undoings

Do you know the verb that occurs most often in our texts from Jeremiah and 2 Kings? *Asah*, "to do." "See what I *did* . . . because you have *done* . . . I will *do* . . . just what I *did* . . . he *did* what was evil . . . just as all his ancestors had *done*."

If that makes you think these texts are about what we (and God) do, you are absolutely right. To address hypocrisy, you have to peel away the wall of words and gestures and appearances that all is well. You go to what folks *do*. To address transformation, you move from speculation about the nature of God to what it is God *does* or *will do*.

The prophets, of whom Jeremiah is but one, constantly confront Israel with the fundamentals of actions and deeds and doings. But not the prophet only. Recall Jesus' Sermon on the Mount: "Everyone then who hears these words of mine and acts on them will be like a wise man who built his house on rock" (Matthew 7:24). Or the story Jesus tells of a father with two sons. The elder makes a request. One says he will do it, but doesn't. The other says he won't, but then goes ahead and does it. Which one does the will of the Father? The one who does the action, not give it lip service (Matthew 21:28-32).

Ironically, the setting of that story, like Jeremiah, involves warning spiritually arrogant folks who think they have it made.

Religious pedigree is not the point, nor is giving lip service to creeds and ritual. *Doing* the faith counts in the eyes of the prophets and in the assessment of Jesus. When the word goes undone, so do we.

Consequences, Responsibility, and Grace

"Your Actions, Your Consequences" rightly titles this session's text. These are not easy words flowing from the mouth of Jeremiah, either in the time of their original voicing in the temple sermon or in our own time. We may like to talk about consequences and responsibilities when it comes to somebody else, to those *other* people who don't measure up to our standards. But we mostly prefer God to cut us some slack. In that sense, Jeremiah is a hard read for us.

But there is grace in Jeremiah's words as well—perhaps not readily apparent, but there. There is the grace, made perhaps clearer in this chapter's opening verses (especially verses 5-7), that change and repentance remain a viable option, as does a renewed future based on such transformation. In our text Jeremiah is not saying this is how things *must* turn out. Remember in another story how angry Jonah became with Nineveh when they repented, and God then turned from judgment? Grace waits in the wings. Without renewal, however, Jeremiah's warnings will come to pass (and in fact did in a few short years).

But even in the realm of personal responsibility for one's actions, there is grace. Ezekiel will later declare God does not judge folks based on the sins of their parents or predecessors (Ezekiel 18:20). The sins of past generations are not ours to bear. God does not hold us accountable for the acts of another. We are responsible for our actions, our words.

"Your Actions, Your Consequences." It would be misleading to say that title does not carry a sharp edge to it. It does. But as those fashioned in the image of God, with the possibilities for revealing the grace and love of God for others—or for denying those same redemptive qualities—it cannot be otherwise. Grace entrusts us with mar- velous potential, and deep responsibility, to act and speak in covenant with God and one another.

SHARING THE SCRIPTURE

PREPARING TO TEACH

Preparing Our Hearts

This week's devotional reading is found in 2 Chronicles 7:11-16. After Solomon com- pleted "the house of the LORD" and had ded- icated it, God appeared to him again. Verse 14 speaks words of challenge and comfort: "If my people who are called by my name humble themselves, pray, seek my face, and turn from their wicked ways, then I will hear from heaven, and forgive their sin and heal their land." Examine your own heart. In what ways have you disobeyed God? Are you willing to confess your sin and turn away from it? Spend time in prayer, believ- ing that God will respond with forgiveness.

Pray that you and the adult learners will be honest with yourselves about your actions and take responsibility for their con- sequences.

Preparing Our Minds

Study the background and lesson Scripture, both of which are found in Jeremiah 7:11-15 and 2 Kings 23:36-37. As you prepare, think about whether or not Christians are to share the common belief that they can do whatever they please and always be protected from the consequences of their actions.

Write on newsprint:
- ❑ words "Action" and "Consequences" for "Gather to Learn."
- ❑ information for next week's lesson, found under "Continue the Journey."
- ❑ activities for further spiritual growth in "Continue the Journey."

Practice reading expressively Jeremiah's temple sermon, Jeremiah 7:1-15, if you choose that option for "Explore Jeremiah's Teaching on Accountability for the Consequences of What We Do."

Create the optional lecture for "Explore Jeremiah's Teaching on Accountability for the Consequences of What the Learners Do."

LEADING THE CLASS

(1) Gather to Learn

❖ Welcome the class members and introduce any guests.

❖ Pray that those who are participating in today's session will be aware of how Jeremiah's words relate to their lives.

❖ Post newsprint with the word "Action" written on the left, the word "Consequences" on the right. Encourage class members to think of ordinary actions that will likely lead to negative conse- quences. For example, overeating/weight gain; driving recklessly/accident; over- spending/financial problems.

❖ Invite the class to talk about why peo- ple take imprudent action that can cause negative consequences. Also, consider how people respond when the consequences catch up with them. Do they hold them- selves accountable, or blame someone else?

❖ Read aloud today's focus statement: **Some people act with impunity, believing they will always be protected from the consequences of their actions. Are Christians to have such a view? Jeremiah states that God holds us accountable, so we will not escape the consequences of what we do.**

(2) Explore Jeremiah's Teaching on Accountability for the Consequences of What We Do

❖ Set the stage by reading or retelling "Introduction to Jeremiah 7" in Understanding the Scripture.

❖ **Option:** Read aloud Jeremiah's temple sermon in its entirety, 7:1-15.

❖ Study Jeremiah 7:11-15.

■ Distribute paper and pencils. Ask the students to write questions that come to mind as a volunteer reads Jeremiah 7:11-15. Here are some questions they may raise: What does it mean to say that God is "watching" (7:11)? Where is Shiloh and what is its significance (7:12)? What does God plan to do in response to the people's repeated actions (7:13-14)? Who are "the offspring of Ephraim" and what happened to them (7:15)? Use information from Understanding the Scripture and Interpreting the Scripture to help answer the students' questions.

■ **Option:** Write and answer your own questions prior to class. Present them to the class in the form of a lecture. Look at the information in Understanding the Scripture and Interpreting the Scripture to prepare.

❖ Ask someone to read 2 Kings 23:36-37.

■ Point out that Jehoiakim, the second one of Josiah's sons to reign and also a descendant of David, was king (about 609–598 B.C.) when God's judgment began to fall on Judah. Second Kings 24:1 reports that Jehoiakim was Nebuchadnezzar's vassal for three years but then rebelled against him. The Babylonian invasion to punish the rebels is interpreted in 24:3 as God's punishment of Judah and Jerusalem, which the prophets (especially Jeremiah) had warned was coming.

■ Ask: **What lessons can we learn from Jehoiakim about consequences for actions taken by the leaders of God's people?**

(3) Relate the Jeremiah Text to Examples of Hypocrisy in the World and the Learners' Lives

❖ Note that the people in Jeremiah's day pointed to their worship of God in the temple as if it would protect them from punishment for unjust, oppressive, violent actions, and idolatry. Suggest that we may do the same in our day.

❖ Ask the following questions.

(1) **What general examples can you cite of church members assuming that because they attend worship they are free to behave as they choose?** (Do not allow names to be used. Focus on general behaviors that Christians should not engage in, such as evading taxes, treating friends and family shabbily, participating in shady business dealings, or using power inappropriately.)

(2) **What difference could it make in our behavior if we understood that God is watching us?**

(3) **We know that people are often not caught or punished for their unchristian actions. What consequences, if any, do you expect these folks to experience?** (Answers will vary, but recognize that some students may mention God's grace and forgiveness for those who amend their ways. Cite Jeremiah 7:5-7 in support of that understanding. In contrast, verse 15 supports the view that God will severely punish those who disobey.)

(4) Bring Actions into Line with the Learner's Identity as Christians

❖ Invite the students to think silently on this scenario, which you will read slowly and meditatively. Assure them that they will not be asked to share their thoughts with others. **As I mull over this past week, I recall an incident when my actions belied my identity as a Christian. I recognize that my behavior had immediate consequences, but I wonder over the long-term how the person affected by my actions will view Christianity. If I could do over that incident, here's how I would handle it so as to be more accountable for the effect I have on other people and all creation.**

(5) Continue the Journey

❖ Break the silence by praying that this session has made the adults more aware of being accountable to God for all of their actions.

❖ Read aloud this preparation for next week's lesson. You may also want to post it on newsprint for the students to copy. **Prepare for next week's session entitled "Getting through the Pain" by reading Jeremiah 29:1-14, which is both the lesson and background Scripture. Focus on these ideas as you study: In the midst of loss and pain, people will sometimes willingly believe something untrue because it makes them feel better. How can we guard against such a mistake? Jeremiah urges us to hold to our trust in God and to wait patiently for God's healing, which will come in God's own time.**

❖ Read aloud the following three ideas. Challenge the students to commit themselves to use these activities as a springboard to spiritual growth.

(1) **Consider this saying: Right worship can lead to right living. Think back to recent worship experiences. What connections have you made between worship and daily living? Ask God what other steps you need to take to bring your life into line with your worship.**

(2) **Be alert for media stories about individuals and/or groups who acted in ways that somehow hurt others. What consequences do these people now face? How are they responding to being caught? What lessons are in their actions for you?**

(3) **Observe that some people feel today, as in Jeremiah's time, they can do anything as long as they attend worship. Think about what you would say to such a person and, if the opportunity presents itself, talk with that individual.**

❖ Sing or read aloud "Lead Me, Guide Me," found in *The Faith We Sing*.

❖ Invite the students to say this benediction, based on Micah 6:8, to conclude the session: **The Lord requires me to do justice, and to love kindness, and to walk humbly with my God. Let it be as you have said, Lord.**

UNIT 2: WHAT DOES GOD REQUIRE?

GETTING THROUGH THE PAIN

PREVIEWING THE LESSON

Lesson Scripture: Jeremiah 29:1-14
Background Scripture: Jeremiah 29:1-14
Key Verse: Jeremiah 29:11

Focus of the Lesson:
In the midst of loss and pain, people will sometimes willingly believe something untrue because it makes them feel better. How can we guard against such a mistake? Jeremiah urges us to hold to our trust in God and to wait patiently for God's healing, which will come in God's own time.

Goals for the Learners:
(1) to investigate Jeremiah's letter to the exiles in Babylon.
(2) to identify situations requiring them to accept the reality of their circumstances and trust in God.
(3) to pray for complete trust in God.

Pronunciation Guide:
Elasah (el' ush suh)   Gemariah (gem uh ri' uh)
Hananiah (han uh ni'uh)   Hilkiah (hil ki' uh)
Jeconiah (jek uh ni' uh) Jehoiachin (ji hoi' uh kin)
Mattaniah (mat uh ni' uh) Nebuchadnezzar (neb uh kuhd nez' uhr)
shalom (shah lohm')   Shaphan (shay' fuhn)
Zedekiah (zed uh ki' uh)

Supplies:
Bibles, newsprint and marker, paper and pencils, hymnals, optional news articles

---

READING THE SCRIPTURE

NRSV
Jeremiah 29:1-14
¹These are the words of the letter that the prophet Jeremiah sent from Jerusalem to the remaining elders among the exiles, and to

NIV
Jeremiah 29:1-14
¹This is the text of the letter that the prophet Jeremiah sent from Jerusalem to the surviving elders among the exiles and to the

the priests, the prophets, and all the people, whom Nebuchadnezzar had taken into exile from Jerusalem to Babylon. ²This was after King Jeconiah, and the queen mother, the court officials, the leaders of Judah and Jerusalem, the artisans, and the smiths had departed from Jerusalem. ³The letter was sent by the hand of Elasah son of Shaphan and Gemariah son of Hilkiah, whom King Zedekiah of Judah sent to Babylon to King Nebuchadnezzar of Babylon. It said: ⁴Thus says the LORD of hosts, the God of Israel, to all the exiles whom I have sent into exile from Jerusalem to Babylon: ⁵Build houses and live in them; plant gardens and eat what they produce. ⁶Take wives and have sons and daughters; take wives for your sons, and give your daughters in marriage, that they may bear sons and daughters; multiply there, and do not decrease. ⁷But seek the welfare of the city where I have sent you into exile, and pray to the LORD on its behalf, for in its welfare you will find your welfare. ⁸For thus says the LORD of hosts, the God of Israel: Do not let the prophets and the diviners who are among you deceive you, and do not listen to the dreams that they dream, ⁹for it is a lie that they are prophesying to you in my name; I did not send them, says the LORD.

¹⁰For thus says the LORD: Only when Babylon's seventy years are completed will I visit you, and I will fulfill to you my promise and bring you back to this place. **¹¹For surely I know the plans I have for you, says the LORD, plans for your welfare and not for harm, to give you a future with hope.** ¹²Then when you call upon me and come and pray to me, I will hear you. ¹³When you search for me, you will find me; if you seek me with all your heart, ¹⁴I will let you find me, says the LORD, and I will restore your fortunes and gather you from all the nations and all the places where I have driven you, says the LORD, and I will bring you back to the place from which I sent you into exile.

priests, the prophets and all the other people Nebuchadnezzar had carried into exile from Jerusalem to Babylon. ²(This was after King Jehoiachin and the queen mother, the court officials and the leaders of Judah and Jerusalem, the craftsmen and the artisans had gone into exile from Jerusalem.) ³He entrusted the letter to Elasah son of Shaphan and to Gemariah son of Hilkiah, whom Zedekiah king of Judah sent to King Nebuchadnezzar in Babylon. It said:

⁴This is what the LORD Almighty, the God of Israel, says to all those I carried into exile from Jerusalem to Babylon: ⁵"Build houses and settle down; plant gardens and eat what they produce. ⁶Marry and have sons and daughters; find wives for your sons and give your daughters in marriage, so that they too may have sons and daughters. Increase in number there; do not decrease. ⁷Also, seek the peace and prosperity of the city to which I have carried you into exile. Pray to the LORD for it, because if it prospers, you too will prosper." ⁸Yes, this is what the LORD Almighty, the God of Israel, says: "Do not let the prophets and diviners among you deceive you. Do not listen to the dreams you encourage them to have. ⁹They are prophesying lies to you in my name. I have not sent them," declares the LORD.

¹⁰This is what the LORD says: "When seventy years are completed for Babylon, I will come to you and fulfill my gracious promise to bring you back to this place. **¹¹For I know the plans I have for you," declares the LORD, "plans to prosper you and not to harm you, plans to give you hope and a future.** ¹²Then you will call upon me and come and pray to me, and I will listen to you. ¹³You will seek me and find me when you seek me with all your heart. ¹⁴I will be found by you," declares the LORD, "and will bring you back from captivity. I will gather you from all the nations and places where I have banished you," declares the LORD, "and will bring you back to the place from which I carried you into exile."

UNDERSTANDING THE SCRIPTURE

Jeremiah 29:1-3. In 597 B.C., the Babylonian armies commanded by Nebuchadnezzar overran Judah and Jerusalem. Though they did not destroy the city, they took into captivity King Jehoiachin, much of the royal court, and a number of leaders and craftspersons. The captivity of this group was likely intended to guarantee the submission of those left in Judah and Jerusalem. To govern the conquered land, the Babylonians installed Zedekiah (Jehoiachin's uncle, whose given name was Mattaniah according to 2 Kings 24:17) as king. Jeremiah remained in Jerusalem. He would continue to counsel Zedekiah, as he had Jehoiachin, against joining any resistance to Babylonian rule. The dispatching of Jeremiah's letter by a royal messenger from Zedekiah to Nebuchadnezzar suggests Jeremiah had a positive relationship with the new king, at least at this juncture.

Jeremiah 29:4. The letter of Jeremiah begins with a familiar phrase in the prophets: "Thus says the LORD [of hosts]." The word Jeremiah sends is not his own personal interpretation of history or exile. It is the declaring of what God intends at this moment in history. The phrase "of hosts" adds an ironic commentary to this new situation. "Hosts" is a military term, referencing soldiers in general and in this case calling to mind the symbolism of the armies of God's angels. "Lord of hosts" calls to mind God's might typically associated with acts of deliverance, as in the exodus narratives or those of Canaan's conquering. Here, though, the "LORD of hosts" is singled out as the one who has sent the people into exile. It is as if Nebuchadnezzar and his hosts were merely tools for the purposes of God. Exile is not a tragic coincidence, or an unintended outcome. The One with might to deliver has brought Israel to exile!

Jeremiah 29:5-6. If God stands behind exile, so now does God describe Israel's vocation there. The first two imperative verbs, "build" and "plant," suggest exile will not be of short-term duration. Beyond that, they mirror the prophet's own call in 1:10. There, Jeremiah's appointing to announce God's judgment had been followed by the call "to build and to plant." To the exiles in Babylon, Jeremiah now declares the time to be that of building and planting, setting roots that will sustain them during this period. The ensuing admonition to this generation and the next to marry and "multiply" echoes not only Genesis 1:28 but, perhaps more significantly, Exodus 1:20. In that latter verse, the "multiplying" in Egypt sets the stage for God's eventual deliverance of Israel from bondage to a promised land. The allusion hints to where this text in Jeremiah aims.

Jeremiah 29:7. Central to this verse is its threefold repetition of "welfare." That word in Hebrew is *shalom*. "Peace" is another translation, but even that does not do justice to this word. *Shalom* is far more than the absence of war. *Shalom* represents a state of well-being, where peace blends with safety and wholeness of life without need. *Shalom* is God's vision for the future. Jeremiah incredibly links the *shalom* of the exiles with the *shalom* of Babylon. The prophet encourages the exiles not only to seek *shalom* for Babylon, but to pray for the Babylonian's well-being! Perhaps the closest parallel to this vocation comes in the Sermon on the Mount, where Jesus admonishes his followers to love enemies, and pray for those who persecute (Matthew 5:44). In exile, Israel cannot be content to withdraw itself from the life of the wider community, "for in its *shalom* you will find your *shalom*."

Jeremiah 29:8-9. False prophets are an ongoing struggle in the experience and writings of Jeremiah (23:9-40 and 27–28 are warnings and accounts of the difficulties posed). The notions of falsehood, lies, and distortion of truth are undercurrents in the book of Jeremiah. An interesting translation issue occurs at the end of 8b. The NRSV translates that phrase, "do not listen to the dreams that *they* dream." The NIV, however, following a reading also apparent in the KJV, renders that line "do not listen to the dreams *you encourage them to have*." The falsehood belongs not only to the prophets but to those all too willing to accept lies. The "lie," as clarified in 27:16 and in the conflict with Hananiah in chapter 28:10-11, involves the belief that exile will soon end and Judah will be quickly restored.

Jeremiah 29:10-11. Jeremiah contradicts the lie with an assertion of the extended duration of exile: seventy years. Technically, exile lasted from 597 until 538 with the fall of Babylon to Persia and the decree of Cyrus allowing the Jews to resettle Judah and Jerusalem. One suggestion of a symbolic meaning for the number "seventy" is its approximation of human life span (as in Psalm 90:10). The Hebrew word for "visit" as used in Exodus 20:5b and Amos 14a (see KJV) refers to God's punishment. Here, as well as 27:22 (KJV), "visit" serves as a promise of God's restoration. In the face of exile's uncertainties, Jeremiah asserts not only God's sovereignty but God's grace. The plans of God for Israel eventually involve *shalom*, seen in a future with hope. Remember, Jeremiah writes these words to the exiles in Babylon, not those left behind in Judah (for the time being). God's future is through Babylon; God's promises come via the experience of exile.

Jeremiah 29:12-14. Earlier texts in this quarter's lessons (Amos 5:22-23; Isaiah 1:15) asserted the judgment of God's not hearing or seeing because of sin. Now, the vision of Jeremiah connects restoration with the promise of God's revived accessibility. Clearly, the verbs of this text invoke Israel's active seeking of God in the midst of exile: call, come, pray, search, seek. The promise is that, in spite of separation from land and temple, God will be present. Again, listen to the verbs describing God's actions: "I will hear," "I will let you find," "I will restore," "I will gather," "I will bring you back." Jeremiah reiterates God's hand in bringing exile about ("I have driven you," "I sent you into exile"). The difference now is, God begins to point the way forward and out. Exile will not be Israel's end, but the means to its new beginning.

INTERPRETING THE SCRIPTURE

Addressing a Letter

Getting the addresses right on letters is important. A foreign exchange student who lived with us for a year once mailed a postcard from Germany to a friend in a nearby town even smaller than ours. The postmaster returned it, even though he personally knew the recipient. The message didn't get through to the right person.

Jeremiah goes to great lengths to indicate just who he "addresses" this letter to: those who have gone ahead into exile. No less than four times in the opening four verses does Jeremiah explicitly declare he writes to those deported to Babylon.

From our perspective, his words and emphasis might seem redundant. But they are important not only to understanding this text from Jeremiah in particular, but to understanding the Hebrew prophets in general. Namely, audience and context determine the message announced by the prophet. The word Jeremiah brings in this letter is one of authentic hope linked to endurance for those who have been taken away. Jeremiah himself remains in Jerusalem with those who have been left behind. To those folks, Jeremiah continues to insist on the inevitability of judgment. Same prophet, two different emphases. The reason? The "address" of the audience differs. Those who lull themselves into false senses of security need to hear the unsettling word that change is on the way. Those who experience exile need to hear the encouraging word that hope is on the way.

The connection to today involves sensitivity to discerning the "addresses" in which people now live. Not every word the prophets utter is the timely one for any given situation. Speaking judgment to individuals and communities already reeling under pain serves no redeeming purpose. Speaking hope to individuals and communities who wrap themselves in smug satisfaction and seek only their own survival likewise serves no transforming purpose.

Seeking Shalom Here and Now

"Making the best of a bad situation" does not tend to be welcomed advice. We would prefer the situation to be different. We would rather things went our way rather than another. We would wish it could be otherwise.

Jeremiah does not portray exile in misleading terms. He does not say it will not be as bad as everyone thinks. The loss of home and land, the separation from family and friends, is not lightly declared. The anguish of Jeremiah over this message spills through his words at various points in this book and another attributed to him known as Lamentations.

Jeremiah declares the future does not reside in bemoaning the past. Rather, Israel's life and vocation stretches ahead— even in the midst of exile, even in the face of a situation no one would have chosen.

The work of building and planting and creating community does not await when things get better. It begins now. The time of seeking God's *shalom*, not only for one's own but even for those justifiably viewed as conquerors and captors, begins now.

Jeremiah's words challenge persons and communities of faith this day as much as then. Look at the world in which we now live. Violence spirals. Terrorism threatens. Infringements on freedom constrict. Oh, for those good old days! God, however, does not come incarnate in nostalgia. Building and planting, community-making and *shalom*-seeking, are meant to be present-tense verbs in the life and vocation of faith. Today is where faith takes shape. This moment is where hope seeks embodiment.

In truth, Jeremiah is really not saying "make the best of a bad situation." Jeremiah summons the people of Israel, and through them the community of faith today, to make the best of a new situation . . . where "best" means, as it always has meant, living in trust and taking our courage in the good purposes of God for us and for all.

Deceptions

By all appearances, Jeremiah was a traitor. Before Babylon's conquest of Judah and Jerusalem, the prophet counseled King Jehoiachin to have no part in an alliance against Babylon. After the conquest, he maintained the same seemingly pro-Babylon line. He audaciously even buys property from a relative that is currently in enemy hands. His "treason" (another word would be lack of patriotism) eventually lands him in jail (37:11-15). Yet it is this traitor who has it right all along concerning God's purposes and Judah's fate . . . and hope.

Solidly lined up against Jeremiah are those who toe the allegiance to land and temple line. The story of Hananiah (chapter 28) serves as the fitting introduction to why Jeremiah writes a letter of hope to exiles and not to hangers-on in Jerusalem to false hopes. Writing of these opponents, one scholar perceives them as spinners of religious fantasy. They say what folks want to hear, regardless of its ultimate truth. The readiness of folks to believe in what they want to believe is evident in the NIV's translation of the prophet's dreaming what the people encourage. Then as now, we do often get the leaders we deserve—or at least, the ones we prefer and create by settling for image over substance, clichés over truth.

Jeremiah does not cut slack to such deceptions, nor does he give in to despair. Hope is not the immediate escape mechanism of religious fantasy that Hananiah and others immerse themselves and their hearers in to feel better. Hope is seventy years coming—that is to say, a lifetime's work, often longer than our eyes will be blessed to see. But its fulfillment is guaranteed: not because it is what we want to hear, but because of God's sure and promising word.

A Future with Hope

I became reacquainted with the power of Jeremiah 29:11 within the past year. A friend and colleague in her middle years had kidney failure. She was on dialysis, waiting for a transplant. A curriculum conference we participated in set aside a healing service for her. The future was still very much uncertain. Even if a transplant could be done, no guarantees could be made of its success or duration. And what was the verse she chose to frame that service? "Surely I know the plans I have for you, says the LORD, plans for your welfare and not for harm, to give you a future with hope."

It is one thing to recite such verses from the well-being of a secure and healthy and prosperous life. It is quite another to affirm those words in the very real possibility of bad outcomes. Jeremiah first offered these words to folks who had known harm, and had suffered the loss of hope, and who wondered greatly about what the future could possibly hold of peace. To trust these words in that context summons great faith.

They still do. What would it sound like to read these words aloud along the border of Israel and the Palestinian territories, to read them to mothers on both sides who had lost children, to fathers on both sides who had seen too much of war? What do these words sound like in our lives when we know and experience all too well the tug of despair or the stirrings of grief?

You see, those are precisely the places and times where Jeremiah's words come into play. They serve as invitations to radical and deep trust, whose power promises transformation.

SHARING THE SCRIPTURE

PREPARING TO TEACH

Preparing Our Hearts

This week's devotional reading is found in Psalm 145:13b-21. In this hymn of praise, shaped as an acrostic (where each verse begins with a successive letter of the Hebrew alphabet), the psalmist extols God's faithfulness, graciousness, and compassionate care. Read this excerpt as if you were suffering, perhaps feeling hopeless and vulnerable. How would this psalm buoy your spirit? Keep this psalm in mind as you offer intercessory prayer for people and situations on your heart.

Pray that you and the adult learners will find comfort in knowing that God will take care of you.

Preparing Our Minds

Study the background and lesson Scripture, both of which you will find in Jeremiah 29:1-14. As you work on this lesson, think about how people who are suffering can guard against the mistake of believing something untrue because it makes them feel better.

Write on newsprint:
❏ information for next week's lesson, found under "Continue the Journey."

❏ activities for further spiritual growth in "Continue the Journey."

Choose which options you will use.

LEADING THE CLASS

(1) Gather to Learn

❖ Welcome the class members and introduce any guests.

❖ Pray that those who have gathered will be empowered to put their whole trust in God. Read this information: **"Significant Progress in the News," better known as "spin," is a way of manipulating news coverage so that it appears more favorable. "Spin" is often accomplished by selectively using facts or quotations, phrasing information to appear that unproven statements are true, or using euphemistic language to either hide or promote one's agenda. Another technique is to time the release of bad news so that it coincides with more favorable news and is thereby "buried." People who are adept at "spin" are referred to as "spin doctors." They generally work in public relations for politicians or businesses.**

❖ Discuss these questions with the class.

(1) **As you think of recent news, what evidence of "spin" did you observe?**

(2) **We can understand why public relations staff "spin" an unfavorable event. Why, though, does the public accept their version of it?** (You may note that people tend to discount bad news and look for something more positive in the situation.)

❖ **Option:** Locate several specific articles in newspapers or magazines that seem to make bad news sound good. Read or retell these articles and ask the class to respond to them.

❖ Read aloud today's focus statement: **In the midst of loss and pain, people will sometimes willingly believe something untrue because it makes them feel better. How can we guard against such a mistake? Jeremiah urges us to hold to our trust in God and to wait patiently for God's healing, which will come in God's own time.**

(2) Investigate Jeremiah's Letter to the Exiles in Babylon

❖ Read Jeremiah 29:1-3 yourself. Use information for these verses in Understanding the Scripture to help the class comprehend the historical situation.

❖ Select someone to read Jeremiah 29:4-14 as if he or she were reading this letter to the exiles in Babylon and then discuss these questions.

(1) **How would Jeremiah's letter have surprised or shocked you?**

(2) **Would you have believed Jeremiah or the other prophets had painted a far rosier picture of the future? Explain your answer.**

(3) **What effect would this letter have had on your relationship with God?**

(4) **What questions would you like to ask Jeremiah or God about this time in exile?**

❖ Read aloud paragraphs three through six of "Seeking Shalom Here and Now."

■ Encourage the class to think especially about the fifth paragraph by rereading these words: **"Building and planting, community-making and *shalom*-seeking, are meant to be present-tense verbs in the life and vocation of faith. Today is where faith takes shape."**

■ Divide the class into groups and give each group newsprint and a marker or paper and pencils. Challenge the groups to discern places in their neighborhood, nation, or world where "building and planting, community-making and *shalom*-seeking" are critical needs. Ask the groups to brainstorm ways that the class or church could work to fulfill these needs.

■ Call on each group to report back to the class.

(3) Identify Situations Requiring the Learners to Accept the Reality of Their Circumstances and Trust in God

❖ Distribute paper and pencils if you have not already done so. Encourage the adults to take stock of their lives and write responses to these questions.

(1) **Are you where you wanted to be, doing what you wanted to do at this stage in your life, or have unexpected realities disrupted your plans?**

(2) **How can you describe those situations?**

(3) **How might Jeremiah's letter speak to you about dealing with them?**

(4) **Today's key verse, Jeremiah 29:11, affirms that God has plans for our welfare and will give us a future of hope. How can you envision that future?**

❖ **Option**: If the class members are well acquainted, invite them to share what they have written with a partner and receive feedback.

(4) Pray for Complete Trust in God

❖ Invite the students to open their Bibles to Psalm 62, which is a prayer of trust written by one who is facing hard times. Ask someone to read this psalm aloud.

❖ Look at verses 1-7 and ask the students to note the repetition of the phrase "God (he) alone" to discern why the psalmist trusts God.

❖ Check verses 8-10 to discern why people of faith are to trust in God and not in that which is immoral and oppressive.

❖ Talk with the class about how this psalm could have been appropriate for the exiles in Babylon to whom Jeremiah wrote.

❖ Provide quiet time for the class members to reread this psalm silently, ponder situations in their own lives that call them now to trust in God, and pray for that trust.

(5) Continue the Journey

❖ Pray that those who have come will be able to look beyond the current situations in their lives with trust and hope for the future.

❖ Read aloud this preparation for next week's lesson. You may also want to post it on newsprint for the students to copy. **Prepare for next week's session entitled "Maintaining Hope!" by reading background from 2 Kings 25:1-2, 5-7 and Lamentations 3:25-33, 55-58. The lesson will focus on Lamentations 3:25-33, 55-58. Concentrate on these ideas as you study: Painful events occur in everyone's life. How are we to respond when such times come to us? The writer of Lamentations says that we have reason to hope in the midst of despair because of God's unfailing love and care.**

❖ Read aloud the following three ideas. Challenge the students to commit themselves to use these activities as a springboard to spiritual growth.

(1) **Be alert for news that the church "spins," perhaps even inadvertently. How is bad news presented so that it sounds better than it really is?**

(2) **Listen to commentators across the theological and political spectrum. Think about the criteria you use to discern which one(s) seems to be promoting an agenda that is in keeping with your religious, moral, and ethical values. Be aware of "spin" in these messages.**

(3) **Do whatever you can to offer hope to people who are involuntarily living away from their own homes. You may be able to offer material or financial assistance, or simply lend a helping hand or listening ear.**

❖ Sing or read aloud "Stand By Me."

❖ Invite the students to say this benediction, based on Micah 6:8, to conclude the session: **The Lord requires me to do justice, and to love kindness, and to walk humbly with my God. Let it be as you have said, Lord.**

UNIT 3: HOW SHALL WE RESPOND?

MAINTAINING HOPE!

PREVIEWING THE LESSON

Lesson Scripture: Lamentations 3:25-33, 55-58
Background Scripture: 2 Kings 25:1-2, 5-7; Lamentations 3:25-33, 55-58
Key Verse: Lamentations 3:26

Focus of the Lesson:
Painful events occur in everyone's life. How are we to respond when such times come to us? The writer of Lamentations says that we have reason to hope in the midst of despair because of God's unfailing love and care.

Goals for the Learners:
(1) to consider Lamentations' encouragement to hope in God.
(2) to identify ways they maintain hope even under difficult circumstances.
(3) to give thanks for hope in the midst of despair.

Pronunciation Guide:
gaal (gaw al')   *leb* (labe)
hesed (kheh' sed)   *mishpat* (mish pawt')

Supplies:
Bibles, newsprint and marker, paper and pencils, hymnals

READING THE SCRIPTURE

NRSV
Lamentations 3:25-33, 55-58
25 The LORD is good to those who wait for
    him,
     to the soul that seeks him.
**26 It is good that one should wait quietly
    for the salvation of the LORD.**
27 It is good for one to bear
    the yoke in youth,
28 to sit alone in silence

NIV
Lamentations 3:25-33, 55-58
25The LORD is good to those whose hope is in
    him,
     to the one who seeks him;
**26it is good to wait quietly
    for the salvation of the LORD.**
27It is good for a man to bear the yoke
    while he is young.
28Let him sit alone in silence,

when the Lord has imposed it,
²⁹ to put one's mouth to the dust
    (there may yet be hope),
³⁰ to give one's cheek to the smiter,
    and be filled with insults.
³¹ For the Lord will not
    reject forever.
³² Although he causes grief, he will have
        compassion
    according to the abundance of his
        steadfast love;
³³ for he does not willingly afflict
    or grieve anyone.
⁵⁵ I called on your name, O LORD,
    from the depths of the pit;
⁵⁶ you heard my plea, "Do not close your ear
    to my cry for help, but give me relief!"
⁵⁷ You came near when I called on you;
    you said, "Do not fear!"
⁵⁸ You have taken up my cause, O Lord,
    you have redeemed my life.

for the LORD has laid it on him.
²⁹Let him bury his face in the dust—
    there may yet be hope.
³⁰Let him offer his cheek to one who would
        strike him,
    and let him be filled with disgrace.
³¹For men are not cast off
    by the Lord forever.
³²Though he brings grief, he will show
        compassion,
    so great is his unfailing love.
³³For he does not willingly bring affliction
    or grief to the children of men.
⁵⁵I called on your name, O LORD,
    from the depths of the pit.
⁵⁶You heard my plea: "Do not close your
        ears
    to my cry for relief."
⁵⁷You came near when I called you,
    and you said, "Do not fear."
⁵⁸O Lord, you took up my case;
    you redeemed my life.

UNDERSTANDING THE SCRIPTURE

Introduction to Lamentations and Acrostics. The first four chapters of Lamentations consist of acrostic poems of grief or lament (hence, the name). The fifth chapter has the same number of verses as the Hebrew alphabet, twenty-two, but is not a true acrostic. An acrostic poem uses letters of the alphabet to organize the material. Typically, an acrostic employs a different (usually successive) letter of the alphabet to begin each line or poetic unit. The third chapter of Lamentations consists of sixty-six verses. Each letter of the alphabet starts three successive verses. Many scholars view chapter 3 as both the longest and most developed acrostic structure, as well as the central poem among the five, to provide the heart of Lamentations' message. It should not, however, be read out of context of the other four poems. For in those other four,

the overwhelming expression is that of deep grief over what has happened, and the role of God in those events.

Lamentations 3:25-27. "Good" provides not only the acrostic repetition but the thematic concern of these verses. The first expression of "good" refers to God's disposition and action toward those who "wait" and "seek" God. It is a word that stands in stark contrast to images of God in earlier laments. For example, in 3:3 the author says of God: "against me alone he turns his hand, again and again, all day long." The Hebrew word for "wait" used in verse 25 carries with it the sense of expectation and hope. Indeed, it shares the same root for the word translated as "hope" in verse 29. The second and third references to "good" make reference to human response and faithfulness. Remember, the context in which

Lamentations is set and such "good" is considered is the grief surrounding the loss of land and freedom. "Wait" is repeated, only now with the modifier of "quietly." It is not yet the time for loud celebrations. The goodness of "bearing the yoke in youth" may simply be the physical truth that those best able to endure the harsh conditions of defeat and exile are the young and strong.

Lamentations 3:28-30. Three infinitive-based statements ("to sit," "to put," "to give") all modify what it means to wait quietly or bear this yoke. "Silence" in verse 28 is the same Hebrew word translated as "quietly" in verse 26. A thin line separates solitude and loneliness. The author sees God's "imposing" as the motive for quiet solitude in response. The previous (and following) chapters have given voice to loneliness and isolation. The pairing of the image of putting the mouth to the dust while saying there may be hope in verse 29 is unusual and difficult. Does the author mean the bowing down of face to the ground as an act of worship? Is there a suggestion of breath blowing onto the ground in hope of life, as in Genesis 2:7 where God fashions humanity out of dust and breathes life into this new creation? The turning of cheek to smiters echoes an image used in one of the Servant Songs of Isaiah (50:6). Jesus draws on this same imagery (Luke 6:29) to prescribe response in the face of hostile situations and individuals.

Lamentations 3:31-33. Central to the laments of this book is the belief that the grievous situation traces to God's judgment (1:15; 2:5; 3:10-12). Now, however, comes the hope anchored in God's turning. "Forever" of verse 31 carries hints of the Davidic promises, of a kingdom and throne "forever." Only here, hope takes shape in the word that rejection (not promise) does not last forever. The struggle of Lamentations as a whole seeps through the conflicting affirmations of verse 32: God as cause of grief versus God as compassion. "Steadfast love" translates *hesed*, a key

covenant term depicting loyalty and commitment. The verse affirms the abundance of God's *hesed*, a severe act of faith in the midst of exile and ruin. Verse 33 seeks to provide explanation for these seeming contradictions: God does not "willingly" afflict or grieve. The Hebrew word there translated as "willingly" is *leb*: literally, "the heart." The word and hope of this phrase is that what has happened is not God's *heart*. In Hebrew thought, heart is not the seat of emotions—but the place of will and character.

Lamentations 3:55-57. Another triad of verses explores "call and response." The final poem ends with a triplet of verses that certainly sounds as if God's response to the people's call is very much left up in the air (5:20-22). Here, however, the speaker affirms God has not only heard but come near. Note God's response to that cry in verse 57: "Do not fear." This is the only place where Lamentations records any word spoken by God. The "pit" spoken of in verse 55 translates a word that also means "dungeon" or "cistern." If the traditional attribution of Lamentations to Jeremiah is correct, the reference evokes memories of the episode narrated in Jeremiah 38:1-13. Foes of the prophet's urgings for surrender to the Babylonians cast him into a cistern where he sinks into the mud.

Lamentations 3:58. The language of this verse is judicial. God has acted as defense attorney, seeking justice (*mishpat*, "cause") for the client-author. "Redeem" (*gaal*) employs a term usually associated with purchasing the freedom of a slave or hostage. In Exodus 6:6, redemption took the form of the promised deliverance from Egypt. "Redeem" also occurs in Isaiah (43:1; 44:23) as an expression of hope linked to exile's end.

2 Kings 25:1-2, 5-7. The harsh political and social realities brought about by the loss of land and freedom and life as it was known can be heard in this closing narrative to Israel's disappearance as an independent state. Zedekiah's rebellion failed. False hopes died. The last thing the king sees before the brutal infliction of blindness and exile is the sight of his own sons' execution.

The laments of Lamentations dare to voice the sight—and faith—of Israel's loss in an effort to maintain hope that is authentic and not wishful thinking.

INTERPRETING THE SCRIPTURE

Hope Instruct(ur)ed

As noted previously, the third chapter of Lamentations uses acrostic structure to frame its words and message. Scholars have long speculated about the reason for acrostics. Some see it as a device for an author to "show off" the ability to be creative within this structure. But showing off does not come anywhere near the tone of this chapter or book.

Others suggest acrostics are a mnemonic (memory) device. That is, using the letters of the alphabet in the structure enables the words to be remembered and recited with more ease. That might play more of a factor in the constructions of Lamentations than literary skill.

Yet another suggestion comes in the way the structure embodies both the exploration and message. Describing something from "A to Z," so to speak, requires a view from many angles and perspectives. It searches the circumstances to find images and words that truly fit or reflect the reality intended to be set into words.

In the midst of a chapter and book largely taken up with the cry of suffering and God-forsakenness, discerning hope might seem a vain effort. Yet at the core of this carefully structured series of verses is an invitation to hope. Hope for the captives in Babylon or those few left behind in Judah would not have been apparent at all. To be seen, to be experienced, would involve a deep sounding of the experiences and realities that now faced the people of Judah.

Hope emerges in Lamentations, not only in the words themselves but also in this disciplined structure on which they hang. Hope in exile requires discipline. Hope in trying circumstances calls for looking at life from every perspective to catch a glimpse of what makes expectation possible. Hope is not glibness. Hope is deep trust, discovered by those who journey into lament and perceive even there the presence and promise of God.

Where's the Good?

The writer of Lamentations takes risks in verses 26-30. They are, first of all, the risks of speaking contrary to much conventional wisdom, of that time and of our time.

Waiting is not our first choice in life. We prefer to have, to possess, to enjoy—now! Waiting quietly flies in the face of the inclination to demand what we want when we want it. Neither do we seek out bearing yokes, in our youth or in our not so young years. And to "give one's cheeks to the smiters?" Better to do unto others before they do unto you.

On the other hand, these verses take the risks of further weighing down individuals already oppressed and abused. Women who are the victims of domestic violence, children who have been molested, persons made vulnerable by poverty: None of these persons benefit from being told to be silent in the face of such abuse, or to continually turn the other cheek figuratively or literally so that the victimization can continue.

Context can be everything. That is why these words can never be fully understood apart from their setting in the deep laments that form the rest of this book. The "good" in this situation requires holding the contrasting movements of this book in creative tension, and not making platitudes out of powerful struggles to discern faithfulness. Is there good in waiting silently? Absolutely—but not always! Is there good in turning the cheek? At times, yes—but at times, no! And the discernment of which response is called for depends on remaining attentive to God's purposes—purposes that include justice, and compassion, and the dignity of all created in the divine image.

God's Heart

Matters of "heart" loom large in critical junctures in the biblical witness. The assessment of evil in human hearts grieves the heart of God—and precipitates the flood narrative (Genesis 6:6). That same assessment of the human heart follows the flood (Genesis 8:21), but instead of judgment flows God's covenant with Noah and all creation. When Pharaoh's heart hardens (Exodus 7:14)—or is it when God hardens Pharaoh's heart (Exodus 4:21)?—God's deliverance from Egypt through exodus occurs. When Jeremiah envisions a new covenant, it is one written on human hearts (Jeremiah 31:31-33).

The author of Lamentations ventures into matters of the heart when considering God's purposes in judgment and exile. One cannot accuse the author of faintheartedness. The subject of where God is in all of this is daunting. Earlier assertions make clear God's hand in what has fallen upon Israel. Yet what is seen in the "heart" (see verses 31-33 in Understanding the Scripture for the literal meaning of "willingly") is not intent to harm, but desire for relationship marked by compassion and love.

What is it we see in the heart of God, when we look upon the crises afflicting our times, and our communities, and even our lives? What gives clue to the compassion in God's heart when terror or arrogance hold the day? How can one hope in the quality of steadfast love in God's heart when so much unloving action fills our headlines and, too often, our very words and attitudes? Genesis 6 rightly perceives the grief caused to the heart of God by human action. Yet Lamentations here perceives God's heart to be larger than even the grief we cause.

Do you trust that compassion and steadfast love reside in the heart of God? Do you trust that when lament fills your heart, "there may yet be hope"?

Justice and Redemption

Much of Lamentations sounds like a voice (or voices) estranged from hope. The loneliness of the deserted city (1:1) translates into the loneliness of the bereaved who lament (1:16) in isolation. What else can be said when God is perceived as the enemy (2:5)?

Yet, the one who raises such laments also lays hold upon the hope of God as advocate (3:55). Even though the NRSV translates what is at stake as the speaker's "cause" (3:58), the Hebrew makes clear it is "justice." Justice had been the prophets' cry, from Amos to Micah and in most every other voice raised in hopes of stirring Israel and then Judah to covenant. The word then had been that God sides with those denied justice, and God will right those wrongs.

Well, exile has come. Persons of abusive power, as well as innocents, have been swept by the armies of Babylon. And God? God remains the One who will see to justice. When we hear that today, we often limit our hearing to retributive or punitive justice. When the prophets speak "justice," at the forefront of their message is equity. Rightness. A making good of things that have gone out of kilter. God is in the business of redemption—a word sometimes theologized beyond recognition of its original meaning of bringing freedom to hostages and slaves, and with it the hope of new life. Justice and redemption have been this God's way. Exodus reveals that. Prophets remind that. Jesus' preaching of the reign ("kingdom") of God assures that.

Justice and redemption remain the hope of God's people today. And as our hope,

justice and redemption remain central to our callings to ministry. Lamentations rightly lament the gap between those hopes and present circumstances, then and now. But hope anchors the people of God in the trust that God's justice will have the last word in this world and its redemption.

SHARING THE SCRIPTURE

PREPARING TO TEACH

Preparing Our Hearts

This week's devotional reading is found in the beloved Psalm 23. In this psalm attributed to David, we sense the writer's intimacy with God. He feels protected and hopeful, even in "the darkest valley," or as the KJV phrases it, "in the valley of the shadow of death" (23:4). Even in the midst of enemies and evil, the psalmist knows that God will care for him. When problems have assailed you, where do you find hope? What allows you to maintain hope in the throes of a crisis?

Pray that you and the adult learners will be able to face challenging circumstances with the assurance that God, the good shepherd, will care for each of you.

Preparing Our Minds

Study the background from 2 Kings 25: 1-2, 5-7 and Lamentations 3:25-33, 55-58. We will focus on Lamentations 3:25-33, 55-58. As you prepare, consider how we are to respond when painful events occur in our lives.

Write on newsprint:
❏ information for next week's lesson, found under "Continue the Journey."
❏ activities for further spiritual growth in "Continue the Journey."

LEADING THE CLASS

(1) Gather to Learn

❖ Welcome the class members and introduce any guests.

❖ Pray that those who have come will open their hearts and minds to the message that God has for them today.

❖ Read aloud this story submitted to Beliefnet.com in the aftermath of hurricane Katrina: **As help finally began to arrive in New Orleans over the weekend, the weight of the trauma began to set in for many evacuees at the Convention Center. But city resident Anita Roach, instead of joining in the weeping, stood among the others and began to lead them in gospel songs of praise and gratitude.** *The New Orleans Times-Picayune* **described her as "a beacon of beauty and strength against a backdrop of death and despair."**

❖ Ask: **What enables people to find hope in the midst of despair and to help others to experience that hope as well?**

❖ Read aloud today's focus statement: **Painful events occur in everyone's life. How are we to respond when such times come to us? The writer of Lamentations says that we have reason to hope in the midst of despair because of God's unfailing love and care.**

(2) Consider Lamentations' Encouragement to Hope in God

❖ Create the context for today's lesson by presenting information in Understanding the Scripture for 2 Kings 25:1-2, 5-7.

❖ Read or retell "Hope Instruct(ur)ed" to help the students understand the message and form of Lamentations.

❖ Choose a volunteer to read Lamentations 3:25-33 and then discuss these questions.

(1) **What does this passage say to you about God?**

(2) **Suppose you had been one of the people of Judah who had lost everything. What response would you make to the comments in these verses?**

(3) **The writer, traditionally Jeremiah, states in verse 32 that God "causes grief, [but] will have compassion according to the abundance of his steadfast love; for he does not willingly afflict or grieve anyone." Do you believe this statement? If not, which parts are problematic for you? Why?**

❖ Select two or three people to read Lamentations 3:55-58, each using a different translation.

■ Invite the group to call out words to describe the writer's attitude toward God. Record their ideas on newsprint.

■ Distribute paper and pencils. Divide the class into groups of two or three. Challenge the adults to discern the essence of the meaning of verses 55-58 and then rewrite these verses in their own words.

■ Encourage each group to read aloud what they have written.

■ **Option:** Give students an opportunity to state how these verses came alive for them in particular ways.

(3) Identify Ways the Learners Maintain Hope Even Under Difficult Circumstances

❖ Read aloud at least one of the following case studies and encourage the learners

to respond, either as a class or in small groups.

■ **Scenario 1: Your friend Lillian has just learned that her husband Jim has an aggressive cancer. How can you help her to maintain hope even though the odds seem to be against Jim?**

■ **Scenario 2: A traffic accident caused by a reckless driver has killed two children and seriously injured a third of the same family. How can you support the parents and give them hope in this time of crisis and loss?**

■ **Scenario 3: Your company has declared bankruptcy, and you and your co-workers face an uncertain future. How can you maintain hope and help others to do likewise?**

❖ Ask the students to identify symbols of hope that they can visualize when times are difficult. Here are some ideas: *cross, butterfly, ribbon (often yellow, but could be another color), dove, seeds.*

❖ Provide quiet time for each student to select a symbol and visualize it. Suggest that the adults think about situations in their own lives now or in the recent past and connect their symbol to those situations as a reminder that we can always find hope in God.

❖ Break the silence by asking volunteers to name their symbol and explain why it is meaningful to them.

(4) Give Thanks for Hope in the Midst of Despair

❖ Work with the class to write a litany in which they give thanks for hope in the midst of despair.

■ You will need to choose a refrain, such as: *"Even in the darkest hours, we have hope because you are present, O God"* or, *"Lord, hear our prayer."*

■ Encourage the students to brainstorm situations of despair that call for hope. Some of these may be circumstances that the class members have heard of; others may be situations they have encountered personally.

■ Read this litany together.

❖ **Option:** See if the students would be willing to give this litany to the pastor for possible use in a worship service where it is appropriate.

(5) Continue the Journey

❖ Pray that the participants will be able to trust God and remain hopeful, even in dire situations.

❖ Read aloud this preparation for next week's lesson. You may also want to post it on newsprint for the students to copy. **Prepare for next week's session entitled "Personal Consequences of Sin!" by reading Ezekiel 18, noting especially verses 4, 20-23, 30-32. Focus on these ideas as you study: Some people do not take responsibility for their actions; they seek to blame others instead. To what extent are we accountable for what we do? Ezekiel says that we are each responsible for our deeds.**

❖ Read aloud the following three ideas. Challenge the students to commit themselves to use these activities as a springboard to spiritual growth.

(1) Interview someone who has maintained hope while confronting a crisis. Find out what kept this person going. What lessons can you learn from this person's experience?

(2) Review the key verse from Lamentations 3:26. Pour your heart out to God and then spend time waiting quietly for God to direct you.

(3) Learn about a current situation, such as a natural disaster, that could cause people to lose hope. Decide what you can do to offer hope to those who have sustained losses. Take action!

❖ Sing or read aloud "Great Is Thy Faithfulness."

❖ Invite the students to say this benediction, based on Micah 6:8, to conclude the session: **The Lord requires me to do justice, and to love kindness, and to walk humbly with my God. Let it be as you have said, Lord.**

UNIT 3: HOW SHALL WE RESPOND?

PERSONAL CONSEQUENCES OF SIN!

PREVIEWING THE LESSON

Lesson Scripture: Ezekiel 18:4, 20-23, 30-32
Background Scripture: Ezekiel 18
Key Verse: Ezekiel 18:32

Focus of the Lesson:
Some people do not take responsibility for their actions; they seek to blame others instead. To what extent are we accountable for what we do? Ezekiel says that we are each responsible for our deeds.

Goals for the Learners:
(1) to examine Ezekiel's teaching on individual responsibility.
(2) to identify their responsibilities as Christians.
(3) to discern and act on ways to meet those responsibilities as individuals and as a church.

Pronunciation Guide:
chaphets (khaw fates')   *mishpat* (mish pawt')
rasha (raw shaw')   *rishah* (rish aw')
shub (shoob)   *tsaddiyq* (tsad deek')
tsedeq (tseh' dek)

Supplies:
Bibles, newsprint and marker, paper and pencils, hymnals

READING THE SCRIPTURE

NRSV
Ezekiel 18:4, 20-23, 30-32
⁴Know that all lives are mine; the life of the parent as well as the life of the child is mine: it is only the person who sins that shall die.

NIV
Ezekiel 18:4, 20-23, 30-32
⁴"For every living soul belongs to me, the father as well as the son—both alike belong to me. The soul who sins is the one who will die.

²⁰The person who sins shall die. A child shall not suffer for the iniquity of a parent, nor a parent suffer for the iniquity of a child; the righteousness of the righteous shall be his own, and the wickedness of the wicked shall be his own. ²¹But if the wicked turn away from all their sins that they have committed and keep all my statutes and do what is lawful and right, they shall surely live; they shall not die. ²²None of the transgressions that they have committed shall be remembered against them; for the righteousness that they have done they shall live. ²³Have I any pleasure in the death of the wicked, says the Lord GOD, and not rather that they should turn from their ways and live?

³⁰Therefore I will judge you, O house of Israel, all of you according to your ways, says the Lord GOD. Repent and turn from all your transgressions; otherwise iniquity will be your ruin. ³¹Cast away from you all the transgressions that you have committed against me, and get yourselves a new heart and a new spirit! Why will you die, O house of Israel? **³²For I have no pleasure in the death of anyone, says the Lord GOD. Turn, then, and live.**

²⁰"The soul who sins is the one who will die. The son will not share the guilt of the father, nor will the father share the guilt of the son. The righteousness of the righteous man will be credited to him, and the wickedness of the wicked will be charged against him. ²¹"But if a wicked man turns away from all the sins he has committed and keeps all my decrees and does what is just and right, he will surely live; he will not die. ²²None of the offenses he has committed will be remembered against him. Because of the righteous things he has done, he will live. ²³Do I take any pleasure in the death of the wicked? declares the Sovereign LORD. Rather, am I not pleased when they turn from their ways and live?

³⁰"Therefore, O house of Israel, I will judge you, each one according to his ways, declares the Sovereign LORD. Repent! Turn away from all your offenses; then sin will not be your downfall. ³¹Rid yourselves of all the offenses you have committed, and get a new heart and a new spirit. Why will you die, O house of Israel? **³²For I take no pleasure in the death of anyone, declares the Sovereign LORD. Repent and live!"**

UNDERSTANDING THE SCRIPTURE

Ezekiel 18:1-4. "The word of the LORD came to me" serves as a frequent formula in Ezekiel (for example, 6:1, 7:1, 12:1, 13:1, 15:1, 16:1, 17:1). In most cases, it introduces an address to the prophet ("O mortal . . ."). Here, however, there is an abrupt transition from these words to a refutation of a proverb abroad in Israel. Jeremiah 31:29 also quotes this same proverb, an adage apparently invoked by the exiles to attribute their present unfortunate circumstances to the generation(s) preceding them. The abrupt transition noted above conveys a sense of God's irritation at this levying of blame elsewhere. "As I live" is an expres-

sion associated with a vow or oath being taken. That oath invokes the principle of personal accountability. The "right" to make such a vow is rooted in God's sovereignty: "all lives are mine." God is free to determine what constitutes accountability as well as faithfulness in covenant.

Ezekiel 18:5-18. Within the Decalogue (Ten Commandments), Exodus 20:5 suggests there is an intergenerational punishment for sin (though the corresponding intergenerational extension of steadfast love in verse 6 far exceeds it). Ezekiel now makes the case for each generation's responsibility for righteous and unrighteous action through a series of three "cases" in verses 5-18. The first case (18:5-9) is of an individual who demonstrates faithfulness in actions of covenant-keeping (and in avoidance of actions that would break covenant). A list follows of what constitutes such faithfulness, depicting both religious and ethical actions. The second case (18:10-14) is of that individual's child who breaks covenant, doing just the opposite in that same list of actions. The third case (18:15-18) narrates that individual's child, who reverts to the actions of the grandparent and keeps covenant. In each case, a concluding assessment is rendered based on each individual's accountability ("he shall surely live . . . he shall surely die . . . he shall surely live"). The examples of covenant-keeping at beginning and end may serve as emphasis to the exiles that the possibilities for choosing ways that lead to life are truly in their hands. They are not fated to this situation.

Ezekiel 18:19-20. In the first of two "objections" or questions raised (see also 18:25), the community in exile wonders why generations do in fact suffer on account of their predecessors. Again, the intimation seems to be that the community is still in denial regarding their own responsibility for what has come to them (separation from land and home). The remainder of these verses serves as a summary argument for the points Ezekiel has made in the previous section. "Lawful" translates the Hebrew *mishpat*, "justice." It is the same word used in Micah 6:8 ("do justice"). Ezekiel continues the urgings of the earlier prophets, who constantly reminded Israel that covenant involved not simply the observing of religious ritual, but the ethical obligations to live justly in relationship to one another. The second half of verse 20 uses word play to emphasize the central point of accountability: The righteousness (*tsedeq*) of the righteous (*tsaddiyq*), the wickedness (*rishah*) of the wicked (*rasha*), are our own, not another's.

Ezekiel 18:21-24. Having laid out the case for accountability, the prophet shifts in these verses to the possibility of and call to redirect one's life. "Turn away" in verse 21 translates the Hebrew *shub*. This is one of the primary verbs in Hebrew denoting the concept of repentance. It occurs here, and then again in verses 23 ("turn from"), 30 ("repent" *and* "turn from"), and 32 ("turn"). The idea of being fated to some destiny by the actions of previous generations is once again rejected, now on the basis that "turning" to a new way is also one's own responsibility and opportunity. Positively stated in these verses, the wicked may turn and live. Negatively stated in verse 24, the righteous also may "turn" (*shub*) from righteousness. One's actions before and accountability to God are lifelong. Neither good nor evil are imposed givens in our lives. They are ongoing choices and actions.

Ezekiel 18:25-29. The exiled community now raises the second objection or question about the fairness of God. The Hebrew word *takan*, translated here as "unfair," carries the meaning of "weighed" or "pondered." In that sense, the question involves a challenge as to whether God has been fair in terms of thinking this through in an equitable way, or acted frivolously or arbitrarily. The charge is met by a counter-charge: Whose ways are unfair, Israel's or God's? Once again, there is a threefold appeal to turning—to righteousness, to wickedness, and to righteousness—that stresses both the possibility and hope of turning and change for the better. The lawful and right can be done, if chosen. The repetition of the charge and counter-charge serves as a means to emphasize who is thinking this through . . . and who is being unfair.

Ezekiel 18:30-31. The teaching of the possibilities of turning and new life now become imperatives. The language shifts from third-person ("they") to second-person imperative: "Repent . . . turn . . . cast away . . . get yourselves a new heart and a new spirit." This particular line from verse

31 is later echoed in Ezekiel 36:26. In that chapter, largely devoted to promises of restoration, these words form a core element of God's renewal of the people. They are a fitting promise that serves as prelude to the vision of restoration occurring in chapter 37: a valley of dry bones. There, the promised "new spirit" breathes new life into dead bones. Hope, like turning, remains a possibility because of God's power and covenant.

Ezekiel 18:32. God's power alone, however, does not explain Israel's hope. Here, as in verse 23, Ezekiel declares God's pleasure (*chaphets*) resides not in death or punishment, but in life and turning. This chapter on accountability comes to a close, not with an ominous warning but with the disclosure of what pleases God. Micah uses this same word *chaphets* to close his work with a closely related point: "[God] does not retain his anger forever, because he delights [*chaphets*] in showing clemency" (Micah 7:18b). God's pleasure provides the hope of our turning.

INTERPRETING THE SCRIPTURE

Whose We Are

Matters of identity typically find expression in declarations of "who" we are. Often our assertions of identity come in statements about family (I am the child or spouse of ____), vocation (I am a ____), or geography (I am from ___).

Ezekiel 18:4 raises another issue of identity in a declaration of "whose" we are: "know that all lives are mine." We belong to God. In general terms, that serves as a corrective to identities of self-centeredness ("I am beholden to no one") as well as an assertion of our connectedness to others ("I am part of the family of God").

In terms specific to this text, remembering "whose" we are serves critical roles.

In the prophet's ensuing line of argument about personal accountability, "belonging to God" reminds us our lives and in particular our futures are not fated by others. While it is certainly true the actions of others will impact our lives, and perhaps even generations to come, we remain individuals accountable for our actions to the One to whom we belong. The unfaithfulness of others does not strip us of that identity and its calling—nor does the faithfulness of others excuse our inattentiveness to the purposes of God for justice and compassion.

Likewise, remembering "whose" we are underscores the general principle that identity intends to impact behavior. That is, unless we act without integrity to who (and whose) we are, the identity of child of God ought to have some expected outcomes on how we conduct our lives. And as Ezekiel and the other prophets make abundantly clear, "whose" we are as God's people does not unfold only in the rituals we keep and the worship we render. Belonging to God plays out in the way we engage in community with others. Look again at those "lists" of what constitutes right (and wrong) behavior in verses 5-18. The predominant actions involve relationship to neighbor—and in particular, to individuals and groups who are vulnerable. The indebted. The hungry. The naked. The poor. The needy.

To know our lives belong to God is to see our lives connected to all of God's children . . . and to act with the same grace and justice toward them as God acts toward us.

Personal Accountability

Ezekiel has a difficult case to make. As noted in the comments above on verses 5-

18, there is a tradition in the Hebrew Scriptures for understanding the consequences for sin to cross generations. Beyond that tradition, experience asserts this same understanding. Children and future generations do suffer from the consequences of wrong done by parents and ancestors. Talk to a child with a parent who has spent time in prison. Listen to how they have been innocently stigmatized by another's choices. In that sense, we may sympathize with the protest over "fairness" raised in verse 25.

Ezekiel does not deny such rippling effects. What the prophet's message centers on is blame for wrongdoing falling only on the wrongdoer, not on those who happened to be in the "vicinity"—whether by virtue of blood tie or ethnic grouping or national origin. Individuals are responsible for their own actions. Paul has something of this thought in mind when he encourages Christians to live peaceably with others *"so far as it depends on you"* (Romans 12:18, italics added). We are accountable for our relationships, for our actions toward others. We cannot, however, enter into the lives of others and make their decisions for them. That is sometimes a painful lesson for parents to learn when children follow differing paths.

Typically, we think of personal accountability as a weighty responsibility draped on our shoulders. In the context of Ezekiel, however, it intends to serve more of a liberating purpose. The prophet speaks to lift exiles out of despair and resignation. Personal accountability in this context aims to encourage new living and new choices that possess genuine possibilities for change. Fate and destiny are not the driving forces here. God is—a God who waits on individuals and communities to choose covenant and turn from old ways toward new promises. Personal accountability offers that promise, and invites us to live as God has called us into relationship.

Turning: A Life and Death Matter

Turning, however, is the key. Linguistically, the text makes that point by repeatedly using the Hebrew verb throughout this passage to invite human response. The consequences of this turning are significant: They are life and death matters. Look again at the passage, and notice the number of times "life" and "death/die" occur here. The redirecting of conduct and attitude evoked here is not a secondary option, whose consequences will barely be noticed. On the table are the ways that lead to life, and those that lead into even deeper death than exile presents.

"Repentance" is another way of saying the reorientation invited here. That word may carry with it negative associations of brow-beating and guilt-inducing rhetoric. That is not Ezekiel's intent. Again, understand that Ezekiel stresses personal accountability not as a mechanism to induce guilt but to escape despair. Our choices are important. And among those choices is this word to redirect one's life in a God-ward direction.

The signs of repentance as Ezekiel speaks of them echo almost verbatim the signs of righteousness indicated earlier: to "do what is lawful [just] and right" (18:21). The God-ward turn does not mean a turning back on human relationships and social obligations. If anything, it means taking them far more seriously as the primary way in which our covenant with God takes shape and is lived out in community.

Such turning is a life and death matter. So Ezekiel reminds the exiles. So Jesus announces in his very first words at the outset of his ministry: "The kingdom of God has come near; repent" (Mark 1:15b). So the Spirit still invites us to turn God-ward.

The Pleasure of God

Such turning will understand its deepest motive, not in the fear of God's anger, but in the trust of God's love. Twice in this passage, Ezekiel speaks of the *pleasure* of God (18:23, 32). "Pleasure" is not a characteristic we often associate with God. Pleasure seems so, well, pleasurable.

Yet Ezekiel chooses to climax his message of accountability, not with a stern warning of God's approaching (or recently experienced in exile) judgment. No, Ezekiel's final word has to do with God's pleasure, God's desire, God's sheer delight. And it is not death: which means, in the context of his times, not exile, not separation, not despair. God's pleasure involves our life.

Joy and pleasure are closely related terms. Joy is the experience of pleasure ful-filled. What makes God joyful? In the Gospel of Luke, Jesus tells three parables rapid-fire, all having to do with God's joy. The second of them, after spinning the story of a shepherd who leaves behind ninety-nine sheep to go looking for one lost sheep, says this: "There will be more joy in heaven over one sinner who *repents* [there's that word again!] than over ninety-nine righteous persons who need no repentance" (Luke 15:7).

What makes God joyful, what gives God pleasure, is the turning to life. Ezekiel and Jesus see joy, not wrath, in the heart of God toward humanity. May we see, in the possibility of our turning, that joy God opens to us.

SHARING THE SCRIPTURE

PREPARING TO TEACH

Preparing Our Hearts

This week's devotional reading is found in Psalm 18:20-24. This royal psalm of thanksgiving, attributed to David, was said to be written when God saved him from Saul and other enemies. David believes that God has rewarded him because he has acted with righteousness. Could you make the same claims about yourself as David made?

Pray that you and the adult learners will recognize the importance of personal integrity and individual responsibility for your actions.

Preparing Our Minds

Study the background Scripture in Ezekiel 18 and lesson Scripture, verses 4, 20-23, 30-32. As you prepare, think about the extent to which we are accountable for what we do.

Write on newsprint:

❑ chart for "Identify the Learners' Responsibilities as Christians."
❑ information for next week's lesson, found under "Continue the Journey."
❑ activities for further spiritual growth in "Continue the Journey."

As an option, plan the lecture on "repentance" for "Examine Ezekiel's Teaching on Individual Responsibility."

LEADING THE CLASS

(1) Gather to Learn

❖ Welcome the class members and introduce any guests.
❖ Pray that those who have come will be empowered by the Holy Spirit to grow more deeply in their faith.
❖ Challenge the students to brainstorm ways that people try to avoid taking responsibility for their actions. List ideas, such as the following, on newsprint: *it's not my fault; he made me do it; I was angry; my parents always told me not to let people push me around; she deserved it.*

❖ Invite the students to comment on ways that society encourages them to evade responsibility. (For example, if you claim no responsibility in an auto accident, you may avoid higher insurance rates and legal prosecution.)

❖ Read aloud today's focus statement: **Some people do not take responsibility for their actions; they seek to blame others instead. To what extent are we accountable for what we do? Ezekiel says that we are each responsible for our deeds.**

(2) Examine Ezekiel's Teaching on Individual Responsibility

❖ Choose a volunteer to read Ezekiel 18:4.

■ Fill in background by reading aloud information from Ezekiel 18:5-18 in Understanding the Scripture regarding three cases used to demonstrate the prophet's points.

■ Ask someone to continue this section by reading aloud Ezekiel 18:20-23.

■ Encourage the adults to state in a sentence the meaning of these verses. Here is an example: *We are individually accountable for all of our actions.*

■ Compare and contrast these verses in Ezekiel with Exodus 20:5-6, which is part of the Ten Commandments.

■ Use the first two paragraphs in "Personal Accountability" in Interpreting the Scripture to help the class recognize how hard it was for Ezekiel to make his case.

■ Consider why the exiles in Babylon would want to be able to blame their ancestors for their exile. Recall that Ezekiel is part of the exilic community and well aware of their attitudes.

❖ Select someone to read Ezekiel 18:30-32.

■ Note that when we think about personal accountability, often we assume someone wants to be able to "nail" us for our actions. Ask: **What is God's ultimate point in having us bear personal responsibility for our actions?**

■ Discuss "repentance" and its relationship to individual accountability by using information from "Turning: A Life and Death Matter" and "The Pleasure of God," both in Interpreting the Scripture.

(3) Identify the Learners' Responsibilities as Christians

❖ Encourage the students to consider their responsibilities as Christians by completing this chart, which you will have written on newsprint and will leave posted throughout the rest of the session. An example has been supplied as a discussion starter. Don't press for a specific Bible reference, but do try to list as many actions as possible.

Responsibility to Whom	Biblical Teachings and/or Examples	Actions Individual Christians Can Take
Those who hunger	Gleaning/ Ruth (Ruth 2)	Contribute to a food collection

(4) Discern and Act on Ways to Meet Those Responsibilities as Individuals and as a Church

❖ Distribute paper and pencils. Ask the students to look again at the chart they created in the previous section and list all of the actions they are already taking. Then ask them to write one or two actions from the list (or elsewhere) they are not currently taking but could do.

❖ Raise these questions.

(1) Which items have you selected for action?

(2) How can you take action individually? (Invite students who listed a particular action as something they already do to talk about how they do it. Which groups or agencies do they work with? What keeps them motivated to continue?)

(3) How will you hold yourself accountable for taking action? (Again, ask those who are already taking action to state how they hold themselves accountable.)

(4) How might the church take action to address this same issue?

❖ Conclude this section by asking each adult to create one SMART objective for taking each action(s) he or she has selected. (Note that some people use "goal" and "objective" interchangeably, so do not get hung up on the language if some prefer to call this a goal.) A SMART objective is a single sentence that is Specific in detailing the steps that must be taken (what, why, how); Measurable in terms of some quantity; Attainable; Realistic, meaning "do-able"; and Timely in that it sets forth a time-frame in which this is going to be accomplished. Here is an example: *By November 15th I will deliver to the church at least 100 cans and/or boxes of non-perishable food that I have collected from others for use in our congregation's Thanksgiving basket drive.*

❖ Suggest that the students place these papers in their Bible and look at them periodically. On the date that they have stated the work will be completed, ask them to be accountable for the action they have—or have not—taken.

(5) Continue the Journey

❖ Pray that all who have participated will take greater responsibility for their actions.

❖ Read aloud this preparation for next week's lesson. You may also want to post it on newsprint for the students to copy. **Prepare for next week's session entitled "Call for Repentance" by reading background Scripture from Zechariah 1:1-6; 7:8-14; 8:16-17, 20-21, 23. The lesson will delve into Zechariah 1:1-6; 7:8-14. As you study, concentrate on these ideas: People yearn for wholeness and happiness in their lives. Where do we find such fulfillment? Zechariah says that when we return to the Lord, the wholeness and happiness we will have in God's new age becomes available to us now as well.**

❖ Read aloud the following three ideas. Challenge the students to commit themselves to use these activities as a springboard to spiritual growth.

(1) Review your SMART objective. To complete the action you promised to take, you may need to do some research. If so, do the research and make necessary adjustments to your objective. Continue to review and work on your objective.

(2) Help a young person recognize the importance of personal faith in his or her life and take steps to enter into and remain in a right relationship with God through Jesus Christ.

(3) Think about how the actions of your parents or grandparents have had negative effects on you. In keeping with Ezekiel's teaching of personal accountability, write in your spiritual journal about how you have overcome these negatives and taken responsibility for your own life.

❖ Sing or read aloud verses of your choice from "Sinners, Turn: Why Will You Die."

❖ Invite the students to say this benediction, based on Micah 6:8, to conclude the session: **The Lord requires me to do justice, and to love kindness, and to walk humbly with my God. Let it be as you have said, Lord.**

UNIT 3: HOW SHALL WE RESPOND?
CALL FOR REPENTANCE

PREVIEWING THE LESSON

Lesson Scripture: Zechariah 1:1-6; 7:8-14
Background Scripture: Zechariah 1:1-6; 7:8-14; 8:16-17, 20-21, 23
Key Verse: Zechariah 1:3

Focus of the Lesson:
People yearn for wholeness and happiness in their lives. Where do we find such fulfillment? Zechariah says that when we return to the Lord, the wholeness and happiness we will have in God's new age becomes available to us now as well.

Goals for the Learners:
(1) to hear Zechariah's call to return to God.
(2) to consider Zechariah's view of the new age and what it means for them as Christians.
(3) to make a commitment to turn fully to God.

Pronunciation Guide:
Berechiah (NRSV); Berekiah (NIV) (ber uh ki' uh)

Darius (duh ri' uhs)	*derek* (deh' rek)
ger (gare)	*hesed* (kheh' sed)
Iddo (id' oh)	*mishpat* (mish pawt')
shama (shaw mah')	*shub* (shoob)
tsaba (tseb aw aw')	Zechariah (zek uh ri' uh)

Supplies:
Bibles, newsprint and marker, paper and pencils, hymnals

READING THE SCRIPTURE

NRSV

Zechariah 1:1-6

¹In the eighth month, in the second year of Darius, the word of the LORD came to the prophet Zechariah son of Berechiah son of Iddo, saying: ²The LORD was very angry

NIV

Zechariah 1:1-6

¹In the eighth month of the second year of Darius, the word of the LORD came to the prophet Zechariah son of Berekiah, the son of Iddo:

with your ancestors. ³Therefore say to them, Thus says the LORD of hosts: **Return to me, says the LORD of hosts, and I will return to you, says the LORD of hosts.** ⁴Do not be like your ancestors, to whom the former prophets proclaimed, "Thus says the LORD of hosts, Return from your evil ways and from your evil deeds." But they did not hear or heed me, says the LORD. ⁵Your ancestors, where are they? And the prophets, do they live forever? ⁶But my words and my statutes, which I commanded my servants the prophets, did they not overtake your ancestors? So they repented and said, "The LORD of hosts has dealt with us according to our ways and deeds, just as he planned to do."

Zechariah 7:8-14

⁸The word of the LORD came to Zechariah, saying: ⁹Thus says the LORD of hosts: Render true judgments, show kindness and mercy to one another; ¹⁰do not oppress the widow, the orphan, the alien, or the poor; and do not devise evil in your hearts against one another. ¹¹But they refused to listen, and turned a stubborn shoulder, and stopped their ears in order not to hear. ¹²They made their hearts adamant in order not to hear the law and the words that the LORD of hosts had sent by his spirit through the former prophets. Therefore great wrath came from the LORD of hosts. ¹³Just as, when I called, they would not hear, so, when they called, I would not hear, says the LORD of hosts, ¹⁴and I scattered them with a whirlwind among all the nations that they had not known. Thus the land they left was desolate, so that no one went to and fro, and a pleasant land was made desolate.

²"The LORD was very angry with your forefathers. ³Therefore tell the people: This is what the LORD Almighty says: **'Return to me,' declares the LORD Almighty, 'and I will return to you,' says the LORD Almighty**. ⁴Do not be like your forefathers, to whom the earlier prophets proclaimed: This is what the LORD Almighty says: 'Turn from your evil ways and your evil practices.' But they would not listen or pay attention to me, declares the LORD. ⁵Where are your forefathers now? And the prophets, do they live forever? ⁶But did not my words and my decrees, which I commanded my servants the prophets, overtake your forefathers?

"Then they repented and said, 'The LORD Almighty has done to us what our ways and practices deserve, just as he determined to do.'"

Zechariah 7:8-14

⁸And the word of the LORD came again to Zechariah: ⁹"This is what the LORD Almighty says: 'Administer true justice; show mercy and compassion to one another. ¹⁰Do not oppress the widow or the fatherless, the alien or the poor. In your hearts do not think evil of each other.'

¹¹"But they refused to pay attention; stubbornly they turned their backs and stopped up their ears. ¹²They made their hearts as hard as flint and would not listen to the law or to the words that the LORD Almighty had sent by his Spirit through the earlier prophets. So the LORD Almighty was very angry.

¹³" 'When I called, they did not listen; so when they called, I would not listen,' says the LORD Almighty. ¹⁴'I scattered them with a whirlwind among all the nations, where they were strangers. The land was left so desolate behind them that no one could come or go. This is how they made the pleasant land desolate.'"

UNDERSTANDING THE SCRIPTURE

Zechariah 1:1. In 538 B.C., the Persian emperor Cyrus issued an edict that allowed the exiled Jews to return to their land and rebuild the temple. Almost twenty years later, Darius reigned as emperor—and the temple remained unfinished. Zechariah's prophetic ministry began in the second year of Darius' reign (520 B.C.). Zechariah and Haggai were contemporaries, and both urged the completion of the temple, finally accomplished in 515 B.C. Much of the material in Zechariah 1–8 consists of eight visions, an early example of Jewish apocalyptic writing. The texts considered in this session, however, do not come from those vision texts. Rather, they are calls to return with strong connections to the work of Israel's pre-exilic and exilic ("former") prophets. Most scholars suggest that chapters 9–14 come from a century or more later.

Zechariah 1:2-3. Three words of particular importance to Zechariah are introduced in these verses. "Ancestors" appears four times in the opening six verses of this chapter. It keys Zechariah's central message to those who have returned: Don't make the mistakes of the past. The second word modifies the holy name of God first revealed to Moses in the burning bush (*Yhwh*, "Lord"). While Zechariah often uses *Yhwh* alone, he adds to it "of hosts" (*tsaba*) no less than five times in these first six verses. *Tsaba* derives from the language of warfare, referencing armies or soldiers under one's command. In a time of vulnerability, as when Zechariah writes, the term can be heard as reinforcing where and in whom Israel's true security and hope may be found. The third key word is *shub*, translated in these verses as "return" (1:3, 4) or "repent" (1:6). Zechariah has inherited this term and its call from the pre-exilic prophets, and he repeats it to underscore the renewal of covenant in this time of rebuilding.

Zechariah 1:4-6. Note in verses 4 and 6 the pairing of "ways" and "deeds." The word for "ways" (*derek*) also can be translated as "paths." *Derek* seems to be a generalized term for the "way" one goes, while "deeds" are the specific actions that comprise that way. As we have noted in earlier sessions, the breaking of covenant in those "ways" is phrased in the language of not "hearing" (*shama*, 1:4), a Hebrew word that can mean both "hear" and "obey." The thrust of verse 5-6a asserts the

enduring nature of God's words and covenant that remains constant, regardless of how they are kept or broken by the covenant partners. Verse 6b lifts up the possibility of change and returning by once again appealing to the actions of the ancestors.

Zechariah 7:8-10. In ways and words intentionally reminiscent of the earlier prophets, Zechariah briefly sketches what the keeping of covenant will consist of. Like the Ten Commandments, Zechariah states the case first positively with what must be done, and then negatively with what must be avoided. Consistent with those earlier prophets, Zechariah frames the covenant demands in terms of social relationship and obligations, particularly to how one treats the vulnerable. The opening triad of judgment (*mishput*, "justice"), kindness, and compassion (mercy) strongly echoes Micah 6:8. "Alien" translates *ger*, a landless sojourner who dwells in another's region. The reason for extending covenant protection to these outsiders traces back to Deuteronomy 10:19: "You shall also love the stranger [*ger*], for you were strangers in the land of Egypt."

Zechariah 7:11-12. The language of refusal and stubbornness, of closed ears and hardened hearts, sounds an ominous note in this repeated appeal to the past. It is the language of judgment levied upon Pharaoh and Egypt for their refusal to let Israel go (Exodus 7:14). It is also the language used of Israel in the wilderness (Deuteronomy 9:7), and later of Israel before the exile (Jeremiah 5:3). In each case, such refusals had severe consequences, captured here in Zechariah in the phrase of God's "great wrath" (Zechariah 7:12).

Zechariah 7:13-14. Isaiah 1:15 warned against a time when God would not hear, a time created by breach of covenant through violence. Here, Zechariah attributes God's not hearing the call of Israel as an inevitable "reciprocity" generated by Israel's not hearing (*shama*, "obey" as well as "hear") God. Zechariah invokes the image of a whirlwind to describe God's scattering of Israel among the nations. The final half of the verse underscores the transformation of the land. Land stood at the foundation of covenant's promises since the time of Abram. A land once pleasant had become a land desolate.

Zechariah 8:16-17. The injunctions to covenant keeping sound quite similar to those already stated in 7:9-10. Here, however, they are bracketed with statements of "these are the things that you shall do" (8:16a) and "these are things that I hate" (8:17b). The first statement closely parallels Exodus 35:1, the words Moses speaks after coming down off Mount Sinai with the tablets of the covenant. Zechariah repeats them almost verbatim here, in a sense inviting Israel to covenant anew with God at the "mount" of Zion.

Zechariah 8:20-21, 23. The prophetic message has always involved reversal and turn-ing. In this closing image, the reversal has to do with Israel's place among the nations. In the wake of exile and manipulation by foreign powers, Israel's future is seen as one where Israel "leads" the nations. It is not a new vision. Isaiah 2:3 anticipated the "peoples" going to Jerusalem, not to lay siege but to learn of God's ways. Even before that, God's covenanting with Abram included this among its purposes: "in you all the families of the earth shall be blessed" (Genesis 12:3). Zechariah 8:23 portrays such blessing to come in the form of recognizing God's presence in Israel. "God is with you" becomes not only a benediction levied upon Israel, but that which draws all people into its gift. "Ten men from nations of every language" asserts the universality of this blessing and God's worship (ten men being a rabbinic requirement to establish a synagogue ["place of meeting"]).

INTERPRETING THE SCRIPTURE

In a Word: Turn

"Call for Repentance" serves as the topic for this session. "Repentance" is a word that sometimes carries the weight of too narrow an understanding. For reasons quite logical, "repentance" is sometimes heard exclusively as the God-invoked turning from sin. It is that. But it is more.

Why? In Hebrew, the word we often render as "repentance" is sometimes used of God. That is the case in Joshua 7:26. And that is the case here in Zechariah 1:3. The "repentance" ("return") sought of Israel is coupled with the "repentance" ("return") of God. God does not sin, so God cannot in that sense "repent." But God can turn.

To some folks, the notion of God's turning or changing direction can be extraordinarily unsettling. Jonah resisted the trip to Nineveh, but not just because of hatred for the Assyrians. Deep down, Jonah knew God to be capable of turning from judgment to mercy. And when God has a change of mind in Jonah 3:10 (the King James Version says, "God repented"), that is just what Jonah says: "I knew that you were a gracious God . . . ready to *relent*" (4:2; again, the King James Version translates it "repent").

Perhaps what is most unsettling in God's turning, or repenting, or changing, or however else we might want to say it, is the possibility of our turning. For if God can turn, why can't we? Therein lies the rub. We tend to prefer things as they are. Even when things are bad, we hesitate to risk change just in case they might get worse.

Turning, however, is the key. It is, in Zechariah's view, the way of the future for it is no less than the way of God. And in turning to God comes the hope and grace of God's turning to us.

History Lessons

In some religions, ancestor worship is a central element. The Hebrew Scriptures also attest to the respect owed to elders and forbearers. But those Scriptures in general, and Zechariah in particular, also take an honest view of ancestors. The good old days were never so good as we make them out to be. We look at the stories of figures like Abraham and Jacob and David, and we see human beings capable of great faith—and great error.

The times in which Zechariah lived might have enticed the returning exiles to nostalgia. The sight of a temple not yet rebuilt, with ruined walls and buildings surrounding it still likely in sight, might have urged a wistfulness for the way things were. Zechariah, however, urges a different perspective on the past. The task of rebuilding involves more than lifting walls and erecting ruined sanctuaries. The task of rebuilding involves re-forming covenant with God and with one another. And the signs of the former ruins point to the risk of not attending to the cause for their downfall. History and the past are not an object of adoration, but a source of instruction and even warning.

Zechariah's perspective offers a helpful balance when we might think the best times are those that are past. "Do not be like your ancestors" (Zechariah 1:4) is not a disrespecting of how we have come to be who and where we are. Rather, it is an invitation to consider and renew our lives and communities on the living lessons of history. Nostalgia still entices individuals and communities of faith to live in the past. Covenant faithfulness challenges individuals and communities of faith to learn from the past.

What Then Shall We Do?

Critique is merely criticism unless coupled with insight into what can be done to right a situation. Zechariah does not shy away from calling Israel to turning and change. Nor does he leave Israel—or us— empty-handed about what that call involves.

As noted in the commentary on 7:8-10 in the previous section, Zechariah's prescription for what will make for covenant kept has both "thou shalts" and "thou shalt nots." The prophet does not go into excruciating detail. Rather, general principles are offered.

On the positive side, those principles call for community based on a healthy combination of justice and compassion. Such qualities are not simply to sprinkle the language of the new community. They are to be the actions taken on behalf of one another. "Kindness" is at the center of the actions Zechariah lists, and not just in word order. Its word in Hebrew, *hesed*, connotes a sense of loyalty that goes beyond the letter of the law or mere duty. A community formed by God's own *hesed* toward us results in solidarity that "goes the extra mile" on behalf of the other.

On the negative side, the overriding principle has to do with how we treat those in positions of vulnerability. Zechariah's list of those not to be oppressed is a familiar one in the Biblical witness: widows, orphans, strangers, the poor. They are the folks most liable to suffer because of another's power, or even just thoughtlessness. The renewal of covenant, then and now, depends not on ensuring the status quo of those who prosper in it but on caring for those most apt to be left behind or left out.

So God still calls us through Zechariah to return.

Decision Time(s)

Then, it was the second year of the reign of Darius. Exile had been over, or at least the opportunity to return had been open, for almost twenty years. It was a time to rebuild—but the rebuilding had come to a critical juncture. Not only did the temple remain uncompleted: According to the impression left by Zechariah's words, the business of covenant remained incomplete. It was now time for decisions to be made. Finish the temple and then the remaining parts of the city, or give in to despair and fatigue at the enormity of it all. Renew covenant relationship with God through heeding covenantal obligations to community, or fall into the same old routines of taking advantage of others that got Israel into trouble in the first place.

That was then. This is now. We, too, live in an era of decisions to be made about rebuilding and renewing. We, too, face choices as to renewing covenantal relationship with God through heeding covenantal obligations to community, or fall into the same old routines that have gotten us into trouble in our day.

Community, in small and large terms, mattered greatly to Zechariah, for community matters greatly to God. God's vision for community, as glimpsed in the close of the background text, embraces not only

Israel but those "from nations of every language" (8:23). It is a world-embracing vision of community that drives Zechariah's words. It is a world-embracing vision of community that awaits our decisions about justice and kindness and mercy, about widows and orphans and strangers and the poor.

God awaits our decisions in these times given to us. God awaits our "ways and deeds" that will testify to the faith we truly hold. "In the eighth month, in the second year of Darius, the word of the LORD came to the prophet Zechariah" (1:1). In this month, in this year, the word of God comes to us. Render true judgments, show kindness and compassion. As much as things change, some things—some words—stay the same!

SHARING THE SCRIPTURE

PREPARING TO TEACH

Preparing Our Hearts

This week's devotional reading is found in Isaiah 12. While we are accustomed to finding prophecy in Isaiah, this chapter is actually a psalm of thanksgiving for God's salvation. Notice in verse 1 that God was once angry with the writer but now is comforting him. Consider how that might be understood by the exiles who had returned from Babylon. How do you hear these words? What reasons do you have to offer praise and thanks to God? How do you make God's deeds known and proclaim the name of the Lord?

Pray that you and the adult learners will give thanks for God's salvation.

Preparing Our Minds

Study the background Scripture from Zechariah 1:1-6; 7:8-14; 8:16-17, 20-21, 23,

and lesson Scripture, found in Zechariah 1:1-6 and 7:8-14. As you review these passages, think about where you look to find wholeness and happiness in your life.

Write on newsprint:
❏ information for next week's lesson, found under "Continue the Journey."
❏ activities for further spiritual growth in "Continue the Journey."

Plan a lecture to unpack the meaning of Zechariah 7:8-14, as suggested in "Hear Zechariah's Call to Return to God."

LEADING THE CLASS

(1) Gather to Learn

❖ Welcome the class members and introduce any guests.

❖ Pray that all who have gathered will find a new—or renewed—relationship with God this day.

❖ Read this information aloud: **In a 1996 sermon on Zechariah 1:1-6, a pastor quoted a** student's university application: "If I were to write a book, it would most likely be on the value of becoming a Christian. Becoming a Christian is not simply a pledge to read the Bible or to go to church, but it is a change. This change is present spiritually, mentally, and physically. Becoming a Christian means asking Jesus Christ into your life as your personal Savior. This is done not only because you need Him and His forgiveness, but because you wish to fellowship with Him in order to truly live the abundant life that God has given us all.

The acquisition of a strong faith in God, which results from asking Christ to take hold of one's life, will clear away all the unnecessary parts that have been storing themselves deep inside one's inner self. Committing yourself to the Lord is similar to having a million tons of worry, doubt, and guilt lifted from your shoulders. It can only be described as the most beautiful feeling of total freedom ever felt."

The pastor goes on to report that in the last eighteen years this once committed Christian has been in the throes of drug addiction. The pastor wonders: "What would I say to him if he were to ask me for help? Is there hope?"

❖ Ask: **If this man came to you for help, what would you say? Could you offer him hope? Give reasons to support your answers.**

❖ Read aloud today's focus statement: **People yearn for wholeness and happiness in their lives. Where do we find such fulfillment? Zechariah says that when we return to the Lord, the wholeness and happiness we will have in God's new age becomes available to us now as well.**

(2) Hear Zechariah's Call to Return to God

❖ Set the stage for the prophecies we will study today by reading or retelling the information for Zechariah 1:1, found in Interpreting the Scripture.

❖ Solicit a volunteer to read Zechariah 1:1-6.

■ Discuss these questions. Check "In a Word: Turn" in Interpreting the Scripture and comments for Zechariah 1:2-3, 1:4-6 in Understanding the Scripture for help in answering.

(1) **Why was God angry with the ancestors of the people to whom Zechariah spoke?**

(2) **What reason does Zechariah give to encourage the people to return to God?**

(3) **How would you define the words "ways" (1:4, 6) and "deeds" (1:4, 6)?**

(4) **What "ways" and "deeds" today might cause God to be angry?**

(5) **How did the people respond to the prophet?**

❖ Choose someone to read Zechariah 7:8-14.

■ Use information from Understanding the Scripture, 7:8-10, 7:11-12, 7:13-14 to unpack the meaning of these verses in a lecture.

■ Identify with the class:

• what one must do (and not do) to be faithful to the covenant. (Write this information from verse 10 on newsprint now for later use. To get more ideas, use wording from a variety of translations.)

• how people responded to earlier prophets (8:11-12).

• how and why God acted as Zechariah records (8:13-14).

❖ **Option:** To end on a more positive note, explain 8:20-21, 23, which is part of today's background reading, as found in Interpreting the Scripture.

(3) Consider Zechariah's View of the New Age and What It Means for the Learners as Christians

❖ Read aloud paragraphs three and four of "Decision Time(s)" in Interpreting the Scripture.

❖ Look again at the list of "do's" in 7:9 *("render true judgments, show kindness and mercy to one another")* and "don'ts" in 7:10

("*do not oppress the widow, the orphan, the alien, or the poor; and do not devise evil in your hearts against one another*") the class generated in the previous section.

❖ Discuss these questions.

(1) **How do you as individuals and as a church show kindness and mercy to others, especially to those who do not belong to your group?**

(2) **In what ways do you work individually and together through the church to ensure justice for vulnerable members of society, such as widows and orphans?**

(3) **How do you treat aliens? Are distinctions made between those who are legally aliens and those who lack proper documentation? What might God say about how these persons are to be treated?**

(4) **How do you individually and together help the poor to meet their pressing needs? How do you work for justice to eradicate the root causes of poverty?**

(4) Make a Commitment to Turn Fully to God

❖ Provide meditation time for the adults to consider how the world could be different if people obeyed the words of God recorded in Zechariah 7:9-10.

❖ Invite volunteers to share their insights with the group.

❖ Distribute paper and pencils. Ask the students to list for their eyes only any changes they need to make in their lives so as to be fully committed to God and ready for this new era of God's reign to come.

(5) Continue the Journey

❖ Pray that those who have attended will continue to examine their lives and return to God whenever they stumble.

❖ Read aloud this preparation for next week's lesson. You may also want to post it on newsprint for the students to copy. **Prepare for next week's session entitled "Living Responsibly in the Community of Faith" by reading Malachi 2:17–4:3. Our lesson will focus on Malachi 2:17–3:5; 4:1. Pay particular attention to these ideas as you study: Most people feel good when justice and good triumph in the events of daily life. What reason do we have to anticipate such a celebration on a cosmic level? Malachi affirms that God will come one day to judge the world to set all things right.**

❖ Read aloud the following three ideas. Challenge the students to commit themselves to use these activities as a springboard to spiritual growth.

(1) **Research your denomination's understanding of salvation. What can you find about "returning to God"?**

(2) **Investigate the books of Zechariah (especially chapters 1–8) and Haggai. Both of these prophets wrote around the time of the rebuilding of the temple. (Zechariah 9–14 was likely written later.) What similarities and differences do you note in themes and actions?**

(3) **Be keenly aware of your attitudes and actions this week. Write a prayer of repentance that you can use whenever you feel you have strayed and need to return to God.**

❖ Sing or read aloud "Would I Have Answered When You Called," found in *The Faith We Sing.*

❖ Invite the students to say this benediction, based on Micah 6:8, to conclude the session: **The Lord requires me to do justice, and to love kindness, and to walk humbly with my God. Let it be as you have said, Lord.**

UNIT 3: HOW SHALL WE RESPOND?
LIVING RESPONSIBLY IN THE COMMUNITY OF FAITH

PREVIEWING THE LESSON

Lesson Scripture: Malachi 2:17–3:5; 4:1
Background Scripture: Malachi 2:17–3:5; 4:1-3
Key Verses: Malachi 3:1-2

Focus of the Lesson:
Most people feel good when justice and good triumph in the events of daily life. What reason do we have to anticipate such a celebration on a cosmic level? Malachi affirms that God will come one day to judge the world to set all things right.

Goals for the Learners:
(1) to delve into Malachi's words regarding the last days.
(2) to explore the image of God "refining" the Judean people and what that means for the learners as Christians.
(3) to take steps to prepare for the coming of God's realm.

Pronunciation Guide:
malak (mal awk')
mishpat (mish pawt')

Supplies:
Bibles, newsprint and marker, paper and pencils, hymnals, commentary and/or Bible dictionaries, tape or CD of Handel's *Messiah* and appropriate player, matches, bowl (or other vessel in which paper can be burned), container of water

---

READING THE SCRIPTURE

NRSV
Malachi 2:17

¹⁷You have wearied the LORD with your words. Yet you say, "How have we wearied him?" By saying, "All who do evil are good

NIV
Malachi 2:17

¹⁷You have wearied the LORD with your words.
"How have we wearied him?" you ask.

in the sight of the LORD, and he delights in them." Or by asking, "Where is the God of justice?"

Malachi 3:1-5

¹See, I am sending my messenger to prepare the way before me, and the Lord whom you seek will suddenly come to his temple. The messenger of the covenant in whom you delight—indeed, he is coming, says the LORD of hosts. **²But who can endure the day of his coming, and who can stand when he appears?**

For he is like a refiner's fire and like fullers' soap; ³he will sit as a refiner and purifier of silver, and he will purify the descendants of Levi and refine them like gold and silver, until they present offerings to the LORD in righteousness. ⁴Then the offering of Judah and Jerusalem will be pleasing to the LORD as in the days of old and as in former years.

⁵Then I will draw near to you for judgment; I will be swift to bear witness against the sorcerers, against the adulterers, against those who swear falsely, against those who oppress the hired workers in their wages, the widow and the orphan, against those who thrust aside the alien, and do not fear me, says the LORD of hosts.

Malachi 4:1

¹See, the day is coming, burning like an oven, when all the arrogant and all evildoers will be stubble; the day that comes shall burn them up, says the LORD of hosts, so that it will leave them neither root nor branch.

By saying, "All who do evil are good in the eyes of the LORD, and he is pleased with them" or "Where is the God of justice?"

Malachi 3:1-5

¹"See, I will send my messenger, who will prepare the way before me. Then suddenly the Lord you are seeking will come to his temple; the messenger of the covenant, whom you desire, will come," says the LORD Almighty.

²But who can endure the day of his coming? Who can stand when he appears? For he will be like a refiner's fire or a launderer's soap. ³He will sit as a refiner and purifier of silver; he will purify the Levites and refine them like gold and silver. Then the LORD will have men who will bring offerings in righteousness, ⁴and the offerings of Judah and Jerusalem will be acceptable to the LORD, as in days gone by, as in former years.

⁵"So I will come near to you for judgment. I will be quick to testify against sorcerers, adulterers and perjurers, against those who defraud laborers of their wages, who oppress the widows and the fatherless, and deprive aliens of justice, but do not fear me," says the LORD Almighty.

Malachi 4:1

¹"Surely the day is coming; it will burn like a furnace. All the arrogant and every evildoer will be stubble, and that day that is coming will set them on fire," says the LORD Almighty. "Not a root or a branch will be left to them."

UNDERSTANDING THE SCRIPTURE

Malachi 2:17. The idea of "wearying" God is not new to the prophetic tradition (see also Isaiah 7:13 and Isaiah 43:24). In those cases, an unwillingness to trust and Israel's iniquity wearies God. Here, the words of Israel exhaust God. The initial charge of God-wearying words comes in Israel's lament about the way wickedness seems to go unpunished. Most scholars place Malachi in the later Persian period (early to mid-fifth century B.C.), after the temple had been rebuilt but before the reforms of Ezra and Nehemiah. Those times saw significant insecurity in the land, particularly from hostile neighbors but also from natural disasters (the reference to locusts in 3:11 likely has such an outbreak in mind). The return from exile had not brought the grand promises of Second Isaiah into reality, making the question raised by Israel in 2:17 painfully understandable: "Where is the God of justice?" It should also be noted that questions form one of the most distinctive features of the book of Malachi. In only fifty-five verses, twenty-two questions are raised: by Israel of God, and by God of Israel. The work as a whole is very much a dialogue and controversy.

Malachi 3:1-2a. The Hebrew word for messenger is *malak*, a root for the name of the prophet "Malachi." Some scholars suggest the identification of Malachi with this promised messenger. The main argument against that identity comes in the messenger's "eschatological" (end-time) functions that go far beyond the role of this particular prophet. We know little else of this prophet, as the book provides no biographical and precious little historical context. The only clear connection between "Malachi" and the *malak* of God is that Malachi announces his coming. Identifying the messenger's coming to the "temple" underscores this book's central concern for the temple and its priests and their purification.

Malachi 3:2b-3a. "Refiner's fire" and "fuller's soap" invoke images of cleansing, whether in the removing of impurities from precious metals already separated from common ore stock or in the washing of garments. The mention of "descendants of Levi" brings another temple reference. The Levites were the priestly families of Israel, whose sons (and that was a gender-specific case at this point in history) provided the priests for service in the temple. Malachi does not specify how this "refining" will occur: only that it will be the work of the messenger.

Malachi 3:3b-5. "Offerings" come to the forefront in these verses. Offerings were the means by which the temple was supported, both in the materials needed for the sacrifices as well as the support of the priests. While the temple had been rebuilt, its support had apparently fallen on hard times. That may trace to conditions related to the infestation of locusts mentioned already, as well as the more general situation of poverty that gripped an Israel restored to land but not independence from Persian rule and taxes. Even in these hard times, justice (*mishpat* in 3:5) remains at the core of Israel's calling. When Israel had asked where the God of justice was, the answer had come not only in the news of a messenger but in this renewed call to covenant obligations. As with the earlier prophets, Malachi rails against those who mistreat the vulnerable in Israel's midst, including those who are outside the covenant ("alien"). Disregard of those individuals and groups is symptomatic and evidence of a refusal to fear God (3:5).

Malachi 3:6-7. Israel's continued life in spite of such covenantal disregard is now traced to God's grace that does not change. Malachi appeals to covenant's history in general to make that point. Like Zechariah 1:3 in the previous session, Malachi 3:7 offers God's invitation and promise: "Return to me, and I will return to you, says the LORD of hosts." God does not change in seeking out Israel for covenant, nor does Israel's need for turning diminish. Yet, another of Israel's questions turns the matter of turning back on God: "How shall we return?"

Malachi 3:8-12. The answer to this question of "how" comes in a pointed and specific challenge about the lack of generosity in offerings. The issue is not merely Israel's withholding of such gifts: More ominously, Malachi frames the matter by accusing Israel of "robbing" God (3:8). The challenge is to exercise trust in God. Malachi's (and later Ezra's and Nehemiah's) renewal of the temple depended on its ability to function without being impoverished. That context is important to hold in mind, especially today when some ministries make fervent appeals to God "opening the windows of heaven" and pouring down "abundant blessings" so long as you fork over cash to their program. It is not so much the look of impoverishment as the trappings of prosperity that accompanies appeals made in this Scripture's name today.

Malachi 3:13-15. Yet another set of questions of Israel frames a protest against the seeming indifference of God to injustice. In some ways, verse 15 serves as a form of complaint lament. Not only is the unfairness lifted up, but it is phrased in a way as to call God into account. The vanity of serving God sounds a harsh note, echoing the perspective of Ecclesiastes 1:2 and following ("All is vanity. What do people gain from all the toil?")

Malachi 3:16-18. A more reverential attitude on the part of Israel follows in these verses. Israel as God's "special possession" mirrors an affirmation made at the outset of Israel's time in the wilderness (Exodus 19:5). The time of God's revealing does not always come on our own pace, as evidenced by the people's murmuring then as in Malachi's time and the subsequent years of sojourn. But God answers the complaint that the righteous and the wicked will differ, with the strong inference it will be better to be among the former than the latter.

Malachi 4:1-3. Why? God's day is coming. The imagery of refining and purification returns. Arrogance and evil will not survive that day. Those who revere God (see also 3:16) will thrive under a "sun" whose rising will bring healing.

INTERPRETING THE SCRIPTURE

Where Is the God of Justice?

Malachi asserts these words weary God. But before we join the prophet in scorning their speakers, consider when this question may in fact have been on our lips or spirits.

Where is the God of justice when planes glide into skyscrapers? Where is the God of justice when prisoners are tortured? Where is the God of justice, when innocents get caught in cross-fires and the hungry go wanting for food in any number of places at any given time?

Where is the God of justice?

The question is understandable. We empathize, hopefully, with the predicament of those whose cries seem not to be heard. But the question also turns upon those who raise it. For when we demand to know of God, "where were you"—some of us may likely find God echoing it back, "where were you?" Divine presence and redemptive action often take form in the action and witness of faithful individuals and communities willing to risk. For those who suffer the consequences of human evil or natural disaster, "where are you" cries out in hope of being heard. But when we ask the question from the safety of sidelines, the question turns on us: "Where are you" when suffering and injustice run rampant?

The following story is attributed to the German pastor and World War I submarine commander, Martin Niemoller: "First they came for the Communists, but I was not a Communist so I did not speak out. Then they came for the Socialists and Trade Unionists, but I was neither, so I did not speak out. Then they came for the Jews, but I was not a Jew, so I did not speak out. And when they came for me, there was no one left to speak out for me."

Where is the God of justice? All too often, waiting for people of faith to act on God's behalf. Are we not called, after all, to be the body of Christ?

Messengers

"See, I am sending my messenger to prepare the way before me" (3:1). In an age before wireless networking or telegraph lines, messengers served as the primary source of news and information—and royal declarations. Those who were "sent" were invested with the authority of the sender. Treat the messenger of the sovereign in an ill-fashion, and you have mistreated the sovereign. And if the preparations called for by the royal herald were not observed, you risked the wrath of the throne.

Those understandings of messenger, and Malachi's particular word of the messenger God would send, loom significantly in the New Testament. Early on, John the Baptizer became identified with the promised messenger. Even the imagery of purifying fire in Malachi associated with the messenger is mirrored in the Gospels' reports of John's teaching. Jesus' parable of the vineyard (Mark 12:1-9) cannot be fully understood apart from the scandal of treating the messenger with such disdain.

Stifling (or killing) the messenger to suppress the message has a long history. John the Baptizer so suffered. Mark 11:15-18 strongly suggests that the "message" of Jesus' cleansing of the temple (notice the connection of cleansing with Malachi) precipitated the final decision to have Jesus killed.

We still need to be careful with messengers today. Sometimes, we uncritically accept every new word that comes down the pike. Messengers are in no shortage in our day, as in Malachi's. But one of the marks of messengers to whom we ought to pay closest attention is their challenging of conventional wisdoms, political and religious, with radical words of God's grace and our trust. Such words can, in Malachi's phrase, be hard to endure. Yet such words invoking transformation, seeking justice, renewing covenantal obligation with God and neighbor, are neglected at our risk.

Preparation and Transformation

"Refiner's fire" and "fuller's soap" are harsh and stringent images for change. The former involved significant heat in order to remove impurities from metals like silver or copper. The latter used a caustic solution of lye and ash and other alkaline ingredients that were often then trod into the cloth by feet. Neither was pleasant work for the laborers. Yet, both represented final stages of preparation before use. Once refined, precious metals were ready to be worked into the vessels or forms intended. Once washed, the cloth would be allowed to bleach out in the sun in preparation for the final dyeing and cutting into garments or other uses. Either process could be harsh, yet the finished product would be well worth the effort.

Likely Malachi employed these images in hopes of transforming the experienced harshness of that day into the possibilities of what God would bring about through those experiences. Change is never easy to endure, no matter the era.

The message brings both caution and hope to times of change and transformation in our day, as individuals and communities. The caution comes in not advancing these words as a justification or rationale for human suffering. Just because times are bad doesn't mean God is behind the trauma. Indeed, in the face of injustice, as Malachi 3:5 makes clear, God opposes those who inflict suffering on the vulnerable. Sometimes we inflict suffering by sanctioning our opinions about what happens to folks in the guise of religion ("God needed another flower in his garden" to explain away the unexplainable death of an innocent child).

The hope of these words is that good can emerge out of hard and difficult times. Transformation can emerge from times and experiences of difficulty and stress. God's presence and action may be seen and known not so much as "cause" but as "companion."

How did Isaiah put it? "When you pass through the waters, I will be with you; and through the rivers, they shall not overwhelm you; when you walk through fire you shall not be burned, and the flame shall not consume you. For I am the LORD your God" (Isaiah 43:2-3a). Preparation and transformation are not for our punishment or destruction, but that we might better serve the One who calls and bears us up and leads us forward.

Living For the Day

And where does that leading take us? Like other of the prophets, Malachi anticipates a "day"—the coming day of God.

Four times in this brief passage does Malachi announce that day's coming (3:2, 17; and twice in 4:1).

The "day of God's coming" or the "day of the Lord" brings both bad news and good news. God's coming realm will not abide what has weighed down and pained and abused this time and realm in which we live. In Malachi's perception, "that day" will not look kindly on arrogance or evil or oppression.

The day of God's coming also brings good news, however. Malachi sees it as a day where healing and the right hold the upper hand (4:2). Other of the prophets see the good news of this day's coming in the reversal of fortunes it will bring (for example, Isaiah 65:17-25). Jesus speaks of that prophetic tradition when he declares the meek will inherit the earth.

For that day, we live this day. Not in order to escape or deny the realities that remind us we do not yet live in that day, but in order to transform this day in its light and bring its sure and certain hope to our witness.

SHARING THE SCRIPTURE

PREPARING TO TEACH

Preparing Our Hearts

This week's devotional reading is found in Psalm 34:11-22. These verses instruct us in how to live: Fear God, depart from evil, do good, and pursue peace. This passage also assures us that God cares for and rewards the righteous, though the wicked will be punished. What lessons can you glean from the psalmist? How can you act on his teaching? Write ideas in your spiritual journal.

Pray that you and the adult learners will walk in the way of righteousness and justice.

Preparing Our Minds

Study the background Scripture, found in Malachi 2:17–4:3. The lesson Scripture is taken from Malachi 2:17–3:5; 4:1. As you work with these passages, think about reasons that you have to anticipate justice and good triumphing on a cosmic level.

Write on newsprint:
❏ information for next week's lesson, found under "Continue the Journey."
❏ activities for further spiritual growth in "Continue the Journey."

Plan the optional lecture for "Delve into Malachi's Words Regarding the Last Days," or collect reference books if you plan to have the class do that suggested activity.

Locate a tape or CD of Handel's *Messiah* that includes the pieces listed under "Delve into Malachi's Words Regarding the Last Days." Have tape or CD player available.

Find matches and a bowl or other object in which you can burn paper. Have a container of water or a fire extinguisher on hand in case it is needed.

LEADING THE CLASS

(1) Gather to Learn

❖ Welcome the class members and introduce any guests.

❖ Pray that the participants will hear God speaking prophetically to them through today's lesson.

❖ Invite the class members to identify movies where good triumphs over evil, and give a quick synopsis of the plot. *The Star Wars series, Superman, 101 Dalmatians* are well-known examples. Solicit comments as to how moviegoers feel when it becomes clear the good have triumphed.

❖ Read aloud today's focus statement: **Most people feel good when justice and good triumph in the events of daily life. What reason do we have to anticipate such a celebration on a cosmic level? Malachi affirms that God will come one day to judge the world to set all things right.**

(2) Delve into Malachi's Words Regarding the Last Days

❖ Choose a volunteer to read Malachi 2:17–3:5 and 4:1.

❖ Divide the class into groups. Give each group a Bible dictionary, commentary, or other reference that explains the words "refiner" and "fuller's soap" (3:2). Ask each group to report back.

❖ **Option:** Present the information from the previous activity in a lecture.

❖ Observe that Malachi calls the post-exilic community to live responsibly because the day of the Lord is coming when God will judge and separate the righteous from the wicked. Discuss with the class what their expectations are regarding this day of the Lord.

❖ Highlight today's key verses by playing #5 Accompagnato (based on Haggai 2:6-7 and Malachi 3:1), #6 Air (based on Malachi 3:2), and #7 Chorus (based on Malachi 3:3) of Handel's *Messiah*. Discuss with the class how the music helped to interpret the biblical message. Note that as Handel uses these verses Jesus is understood to be the messenger.

(3) Explore the Image of God "Refining" the Judean People and What That Means for the Learners as Christians

❖ Read aloud this story that has circulated on the Internet: **Malachi 3:3 says: "He will sit as a refiner and purifier of silver." This verse puzzled some women in a Bible study and they wondered what this statement meant about the character and nature of God. One of the women offered to find out the process of refining silver and get back to the group at their next Bible Study. That week, the woman called a silversmith and made an appointment to watch him at work. She didn't mention anything about the reason for her interest beyond her curiosity about the process of refining silver. As she watched the silversmith, he held a piece of silver over the fire and let it heat up. He explained that in refining silver, one needed to hold the silver in the middle of the fire where the flames were hottest to burn away all the impurities. The woman thought about God holding us in such a hot spot then she thought again about the verse that says: "He will sit as a refiner and purifier of silver." She asked the silversmith if it was true that he had to sit there in front of the fire the whole time the silver was being refined. The man answered that yes, he not only had to sit there holding the silver, but he had to keep his eyes on the silver the entire time it was in the fire. If the silver was left a moment too long in the flames, it would be destroyed. The woman was silent for a moment. Then she asked the silversmith, "How do you know when the silver is fully refined?" He smiled at her and answered, "Oh, that's easy—when I see my image in it."**

❖ Discuss these questions with the group.

(1) **If you think of the silversmith as God the refiner, what does this story suggest about God's role in the purification?**

(2) **Again if you think of the silversmith as God, what risks do you think God takes in purifying us?**

(3) **What might this story suggest about God's concern for and relationship with you?** (After several adults have responded, you may want to reading the ending of the Internet story: **If today you are feeling the heat of the fire, remember that God has His eye on you and will keep watching you until he sees His image in you.**)

(4) **What clues does this story give concerning how we are made ready to live responsibly in the community of faith?**

(4) Take Steps to Prepare for the Coming of God's Realm

❖ Distribute paper and pencils. If you have used Handel's *Messiah*, you may wish to play the appropriate parts again softly as background music. Invite the students to list areas of their lives where they believe purification is needed. Assure them that this list is confidential.

❖ Invite the students to fold their papers and come forward to deposit them in the bowl you have provided. Place the bowl in a safe place where everyone can see it and light a match to burn the papers. Suggest that the class see this act as a symbol of God's purification of their lives.

(5) Continue the Journey

❖ Pray that all who have come will be willing to undergo purification so as to be able to live now as responsible members of the community of faith and prepare for the coming day of the Lord.

❖ Read aloud this preparation for next week's lesson. You may also want to post it on newsprint for the students to copy. Prepare for next week's session entitled "How Is Creation Possible?" by reading background Scripture from Genesis 1:1-25. During our session we will focus on these selected verses: Genesis 1:1-6, 8, 10, 12-15, 19-20, 22-23, 25. Keep these ideas in mind as you study: Without the earth and its ecosystems, human life would not be possible. How did creation come into being? In the Genesis 1 account, we learn that God chose to create life where none had existed and God provided means of support for that life.

❖ Read aloud the following three ideas. Challenge the students to commit themselves to use these activities as a springboard to spiritual growth.

(1) **View a movie with an end-time theme. Drawing on what we have studied in Malachi (and other prophets), discern how this movie squares with your understanding of biblical expectations for the end times.**

(2) **Pray the Lord's Prayer and then meditate on what you think Jesus means when he says, "Your kingdom come, your will be done on earth as it is in heaven."**

(3) **Ponder Malachi's words. How does his view of God who will judge and separate the good from the wicked square with your idea of who God is and what God will do?**

❖ Sing or read aloud "O Day of God, Draw Nigh."

❖ Invite the students to say this benediction, based on Micah 6:8, to conclude the session: **The Lord requires me to do justice, and to love kindness, and to walk humbly with my God. Let it be as you have said, Lord.**